D1634395

Belfast Studies in Language, Culture and Politics
General Editors: John M. Kirk and Dónall P. Ó Baoill

# Beyond the Anchoring Grounds:
## More Cross-currents in Irish and Scottish Studies

Edited by

Shane Alcobia-Murphy, Johanna Archbold,
John Gibney and Carole Jones

Cló Ollscoil na Banríona
Belfast 2005

First published in 2005
Cló Ollscoil na Banríona
Queen's University Belfast
Belfast, BT7 1NN


Belfast Studies in Language, Culture and Politics
www.bslcp.com

This publication was funded by the Centre for Irish-Scottish Studies, Trinity
College Dublin, the AHRB Research Centre for Irish and Scottish Studies at the
University of Aberdeen, and Queen's University Belfast.


The cover illustration forms only a very small part of 'Cruthni I' by Calum Colvin
and is reproduced with the artist's kind permission.


British Library Cataloguing-in-Publication Data
A catalogue record for this book is available from the British Library.


ISBN 0 85389 885 5


Typeset by Nigel Craig and John Kirk in Granjon
Cover design by Colin Young
Printing by W. & G. Baird, Antrim

# CONTENTS

The papers in this volume were first presented at two conferences entitled *Cross-currents,* each focusing on single-discipline, comparative and interdisciplinary research in the areas of literature, film studies, history and Celtic studies, and held at Trinity College Dublin from 23-25 April 2004 and the University of Aberdeen from 1-3 April 2005.

# CONTRIBUTORS

**Shane Alcobia-Murphy** lectures in the School of Language and Literature, University of Aberdeen. He has completed two monographs, *Governing the Tongue* (Cambridge Scholars Press, 2005) and *Sympathetic Ink* (Liverpool University Press, 2006), and co-edited the first volume of Cross-currents as well as the present proceedings.

**Johanna Archbold** is a native of Dublin who is in the second year of her PhD at Trinity College. Awarded funding from the Higher Education Authority, her research is focusing on the development of the monthly periodical in the North Atlantic Anglophone print cultures of Ireland, Scotland and America, 1770-1830. As well as co-organising the Cross-currents Conference for 2004 hosted by Trinity College Dublin, Johanna is a co-editor of these proceedings.

**Tudor Balinisteanu** is a PhD student at the University of Glasgow. Originally from Romania, he completed his BA (English) at University of Suceava and MA (Irish Studies) at "Babes-Bolyai" University of Cluj. His doctoral thesis is entitled "Worldly Faeries and Otherworldly Women: Reconstructions of Social Myths in the Works of Five Contemporary Scottish and Irish Women Writers". He has published in *Applied Semiotics / Sémiotique appliqué*, online with the Academy for the Study of the Psychoanalytic Arts, and in postgraduate e-journals.

**Sukanya Basu** is completing her PhD at the Research Institute of Irish and Scottish Studies at the University of Aberdeen. Her doctoral research focuses on the concept of the poet-critic, exploring the psychological, aesthetic and commercial imperatives acting on a poet to produce a body of prose. Taking the prose of Seamus Heaney as her prime example, she examines how it communicates the ethical, political and aesthetic assumptions and commitments of his art through his self-reflexive (mis)-reading of four specific poet-critics: Yeats, Eliot, Auden, and Mandelstam.

**Laura Bok** completed her MLitt at the Research Institute of Irish and Scottish Studies at the University of Aberdeen in 2004, her thesis focusing on Ciaran Carson's perception of Belfast. Originally from the Netherlands, she studied Classics at the University of Amsterdam before briefly moving into the field of Scottish and Irish Studies. She is currently doing her doctoral studies in Greek and Latin Literature at the University of Oxford.

**Andreas Boldt**, a native of Northern Germany, has studied at the National University of Ireland, Maynooth, since 1998. As an IRCHSS Government of Ireland postgraduate scholar, he recently completed his PhD thesis in Modern History. He concentrated his studies on the German historian Leopold von Ranke (1795-1886) and his connection to Ireland. Andreas's further interests lie in the area of European history, environmental history, archaeology and historiography.

**David Clark** was born in Edinburgh and has undergraduate degrees from the University of Kent at Canterbury (English and American Literature) and the University of Alicante (Philosophy and Letters). He was awarded a PhD from the University of A Coruña, Galicia, where he now teaches nineteenth- and twentieth-century literature. He is Academic Secretary of the "Amergin" University Institute for Irish Studies at the University of Coruna. David's main interests are in twentieth-century Scottish, Irish and Galician literature, and he is co-editor of *As Nove Ondas*, (The Nine Waves), a volume of essays on Irish, Scottish and Galician studies.

**Anthea Cordner** is a University of Newcastle-Upon-Tyne postgraduate and tutorial assistant and also a visiting lecturer at the University of Sunderland. Her main areas of research are in the prose writing of women from the North of Ireland, trauma theory, and regional and cultural theories, but her areas of interest extend into the contemporary novel and short story, Irish Diaspora and American literature. She has written the entry on Linda Anderson for *Irish Women Writers: An A-to-Z Guide,* edited by Alexander G. Gonzalez (Greenwood Press, 2005).

**Stephen Dornan** completed his doctoral thesis at the Research Institute of Irish and Scottish studies at the University of Aberdeen. His research interests are in eighteenth and nineteenth-century Irish, Scottish and Ulster Scots poetry. He has articles forthcoming in editions of *Scottish Studies Review* and *Irish Studies Review* on the poetry of Thomas Dermody and James Orr respectively.

**Janice M. Fairney** is a PhD student in the Department of Celtic and Scottish Studies at the University of Edinburgh. Her thesis examines émigré Gaels in London and the role which they played in preserving both Gaelic language and culture.

**Gavin Falconer** is a native of Milngavie and studied German and Irish Studies at the University of Liverpool. The former Sub-editor (English and Ulster-Scots) at the Northern Ireland Assembly, he is now a parliamentary reporter in the Houses of the Oireachtas in Dublin. Since 2002 he has been studying at Queen's University Belfast for a PhD on the revival of Scots. He has articles forthcoming in *Scottish Language*, *Scottish Studies Review* and *Études Anglaises*.

**Cassie S. Farrelly** is the administrative director of the Institute of Irish Studies at Fordham University. A 2004 George J. Mitchell Scholar, she completed her M.Phil in Irish Theatre and Film at Trinity College Dublin, where her research focused on representations of refugees and asylum-seekers in contemporary Irish drama. She has dramaturged for professional productions of works by Anne Devlin and Marina Carr in New York and, most recently, the U.S. premiere of Deirdre Hines' *Howling Moons, Silent Sons*.

**Emma Faulkner** completed her undergraduate studies in English Literature and History at the University of Glasgow. She has also concluded an M.Phil Research degree. Her thesis was entitled 'Devising an Offstage: The Dramaturgy of Brian Friel' – an exploration of dramatic devices and stage space. She plans to develop her interest in Irish drama through further research.

**Louise Fuller** is author of *Irish Catholicism since 1950: The Undoing of a Culture* (Dublin: Gill and Macmillan, 2002, 2004), which is based on her doctoral thesis, and several articles on Catholic church history in nineteenth- and twentieth-century Ireland. Her current research work is centred on cultural history and the impact of religion on social and intellectual identity in Ireland in the same periods. She is an IRCHSS Government of Ireland Post-Doctoral Fellow working in the Department of Modern History at the National University of Ireland, Maynooth

**Miriam Gamble** is in the second year of a PhD at Queen's University Belfast. Originally from Belfast, she completed a BA in English Language and Literature at Jesus College, Oxford, before returning to Northern Ireland to study for her MA. Her doctoral thesis is entitled "Form, Genre and Lyric Subjectivity in Contemporary British and Irish Poetry".

**John Gibney** is a PhD student in the Department of Modern History, Trinity College Dublin where he is completing a thesis on "Ireland and the Popish Plot, 1687-81". He is a contributor to the Royal Irish Academy's *Dictionary of Irish Biography* (Cambridge University Press, forthcoming) as well as a co-editor of these proceedings.

**Billy Gunn** is a research postgraduate at the University of Aberdeen. His thesis is on the care and treatment of the insane in Scotland, 1780-1870, with particular emphasis on the career of Dr W.A.F. Browne (1805-1885). Other interests include the variety of roles played by women in the advancement of medical/institutional care during the eighteenth and nineteenth centuries and the history of the parish of Montrose c.1200-1900.

**Ashley Hales** is a PhD candidate in English at the University of Edinburgh aided by an Overseas Research Scholarship. Having completed an MSc at Edinburgh, she now focuses on emigration, early American literature and the new discipline of transatlantic studies. She is editorial and research assistant for the *Edinburgh History of Scottish Literature* (Edinburgh University Press, 2006) and *Transatlantic Literary Studies: A Reader* (also forthcoming from EUP).

**Carole Jones** is a teaching fellow in the School of English, Trinity College Dublin. She recently completed her PhD thesis at Trinity entitled 'Displaced Masculinity: Men, Women and Gender Disorientation in Contemporary Scottish Fiction', and has published papers in *Scottish Studies Review* and *Symbiosis*. Her work focuses on masculinities, and she is currently researching into representations of drag queens in Scottish fictions. Carole is also a co-editor of these proceedings.

**Aoife Kernan** is a graduate of the School of English Studies and the Department of Germanic Studies, Trinity College Dublin. She completed a Master of Research thesis entitled "Escape from Glasgow: The narrative allusions of George Friel's *The Boy Who Wanted Peace* and *Mr. Alfred MA*" at the University of Strathclyde in 2004. Her academic interests include Irish-Scottish literature, specifically Glasgow literature and modernist literature.

**Richard King** holds an Overseas Research Scholarship enabling him to study for a PhD in the School of English at the University of St Andrews. His scholarly interests are with literature of the sea and representations of marine life, particularly cormorants, on which he wrote his master's thesis at Wesleyan University, USA, earning the Rulewater Prize. He has written entries for a literature of the sea encyclopedia and several articles for various maritime publications such as *Sea History*, *Maritime Life and Traditions*, and *The Melville Society Extracts*.

**Aoife Leahy** is a teaching assistant in the Department of Languages and Cultural Studies, University of Limerick. She completed her PhD in the School of English, University College Dublin, in 2003. Her thesis takes an interdisciplinary view of Victorian literature and art and is entitled "The Raphaelesque versus the Pre-Raphaelite in Victorian Fiction: 1850-1900". She has published articles in *Pages*, *New Voices* 4 and *The Wilkie Collins Society Journal*.

**Stefanie Lehner** is a PhD student at the University of Edinburgh. Originally from Berlin, she transferred to Edinburgh to complete her MA and subsequently MSc in English Literature after teaching German in local high schools. Her doctoral thesis has the preliminary title "Subaltern Aesthetics: Mapping Class and Gender in Contemporary Scottish, Irish and Northern Irish Literatures".

**João Lemos** has recently completed his MSc in European Film Studies at the University of Edinburgh. He read French and Portuguese at the University of São Paulo and has a BA in Film Studies from FAAP, São Paulo. He has also directed three short films which have been widely screened in festivals around the world.

**Kirsteen Mackenzie** is a PhD student in the Department of History at the University of Aberdeen. Her research focuses on Presbyterian Church Government and the 'Covenanted Interest' in England, Scotland and Ireland during the Commonwealth and Protectorate.

**Caroline Magennis** is a first year PhD student in the School of English at Queen's University Belfast, where she gained her BA in English and her MA in Irish Writing, and where she is President of the English Society. Her doctoral thesis focuses on representations of masculinity, sexuality and violence in the contemporary Northern Irish novel.

**Emily Mark** is originally from Los Angeles and is currently a doctoral student and Humanities Institute of Ireland Fellow at University College Dublin (Department of History of Art). She completed her BA at the University of Southern California and her MA at Indiana University, and came to Ireland as a George Mitchell Scholar in 2002. Her doctoral dissertation is entitled "Memorials and Monuments to the Irish Famine: Commemorative Art and History".

**Margaret Maxwell** completed her MA in English Literature in 2003 and her MLitt Irish-Scottish Studies in 2004 at the University of Aberdeen. Funded by the Carnegie Trust, she is currently a doctoral student at the Institute. Her thesis explores the function of silence in the dramatic works of Marina Carr, Brian Friel, and Tom Murphy.

**Lisa McGonigle** holds a BA in English Studies from Trinity College Dublin and an MLitt in Irish-Scottish Studies from the University of Aberdeen, where she was supported by an AHRC fees-only award and a maintenance stipend from the College of Arts and Social Sciences.

**Matt McGuire** is currently researching his PhD at the University of Edinburgh, comparing the use of dialect in contemporary Irish and Scottish fiction. Originally from Belfast, he completed both his MA and MSc at Edinburgh. His work has been published in the *Scottish Studies Review*, and he is a contributor to *The Edinburgh Companion to Contemporary Scottish Literature* forthcoming from EUP.

**Tom McInally** is a post-graduate research student in the Department of History at the University of Aberdeen. His research thesis topic is concerned with the cultural influences of the Scots Colleges abroad in the seventeenth and eighteenth centuries.

**Christina Morin** is currently completing a PhD thesis on Charles Robert Maturin and romantic national fiction at Trinity College Dublin. She received a BA in English from Georgetown University in Washington, DC before being awarded an Irish-Scottish Initiative award and settling in Dublin.

**Niall O'Gallagher** is a student in the School of English and Scottish Language and Literature at the University of Glasgow. He graduated from Glasgow in 2003 with First Class Honours in English and Scottish Literature and was the winner of the inaugural Neil Munro medal for excellence in Scottish Literature. His research interests include twentieth and twenty-first century Irish and Scottish writing, and he is currently writing his doctoral thesis on empire in the work of Alasdair Gray.

**Michael O'Sullivan** wrote his doctoral thesis on phenomenological literary criticism at University College Cork and at the University of California, Berkeley. Presently completing a monograph on Joyce and compiling a chapter on narrative for *The Year's Work in Critical and Cultural Theory*, he is also being published on Irish studies, the work of Michel Henry, and ethical criticism. He has taught in Ireland and California.

**Margitta Rouse** is a PhD student at the Freie Universität Berlin, Germany. She has a particular interest in recent poetry in English, and her thesis is focusing on Douglas Dunn's poetry.

**Paul F. Shanks** is currently based at Aberdeen University's Research Institute of Irish and Scottish Studies (RIISS) where he is completing a PhD on James Kelman. His work examines Kelman's fiction in the light of his key literary forebears, especially Beckett, Joyce and Kafka.

**Daniel Smith** is currently writing a PhD at Research Institute of Irish and Scottish Studies at the University of Aberdeen on the representation of violence in Northern Ireland, working primarily with modern film and literature.

**Carol Stewart** completed her PhD at Trinity College Dublin. Her thesis, entitled "'More Instructive Than Any Sermon I Know': The Eighteenth-Century Novel and the Secularisation of Ethics", considers the connection between the decline in authority of the Anglican Church and the rise of the novel in the eighteenth century. An article on Sterne and Anglicanism appears in the *British Journal for Eighteenth-Century Studies* for 2005. She has just taken up a position as an assistant professor of English Literature at Dhofar University in Oman.

**Brendan Sweeney** has recently completed a PhD thesis on Swedish national identity, funded by the Centre for the Study of Human Settlement and Cultural Change, National University of Ireland, Galway. He completed a BA and MA in film and media studies at the University of Copenhagen, and has translated Scandinavian literature. His article on Swedish history will appear in the 2006 edition of *Ethnologia Scandinavica*, and he is also contributing entries on television and media to the *Routledge Encyclopaedia of Scandinavian Culture*. Prior to pursuing an academic career, Brendan worked as a print and radio journalist in Ireland and abroad.

**Liz Thomas** is a PhD student in the Department of Archaeology, Queen's University, Belfast. She is currently researching the archaeologies of government policies and ideologies of relief mechanisms in nineteenth-century Ireland. She is interested in eighteenth, nineteenth and twentieth-century historical archaeology.

**Geraldine Vaughan** is a PhD student and tutor in Late Modern History at the Sorbonne University in Paris. She is currently writing a thesis on Irish immigrants to Scotland, a local perspective (Airdrie, Coatbridge and Greenock), 1851-1921.

**Dan Wall** is working on a doctoral thesis entitled "Countering Cultural Maladies: John Gibson Lockhart and National Literature" at the University of Aberdeen, where he previously completed his MA and MLitt. He has delivered several papers on Romantic literature across Britain.

**Patrick Walsh** is a graduate of Trinity College Dublin, where is currently a PhD candidate in the Department of Modern History. His research is funded by the Irish Research Council for the Humanities and Social Sciences. The title of his doctoral thesis is "The Career of Speaker William Conolly, 1662-1729".

**Jacqui Weeks** is a Mellon Fellow and a twentieth-century scholar at the Univeristy of Notre Dame. Raised in Alaska and New Mexico, she completed her MA at the University of Aberdeen. Her MA dissertation was titled "'Literary Sins' Aesthetic and Cultural Subversions in the Poetry of Robert Service". She has published on John Banville in *Metiér*.

**Andy Wood** is completing his PhD on aspects of contemporarty Asian and black British popular culture at the University of Dundee. He has contributed articles to *Wasafari* and was a contributor and editorial advisor for the *Companion to Contemporary Black British Culture* (Routledge, 2001). He has essays published in the forthcoming books: *A Black British Canon?* (Palgrave, 2006) and *The Edinburgh Companion to Contemporary Scottish Literature* (EUP).

**Jonathan Wright** recently completed his MLitt in Irish and Scottish Studies at the Research Institute of Irish and Scottish Studies, University of Aberdeen. He is currently at Queen's University Belfast,where he is undertaking research for a PhD on the development of Presbyterian politics in post-union Ulster.

# ACKNOWLEDGEMENTS

The Cross-currents conferences, from which the papers in this volume have originated, have resulted from inspired funding applications and the direction of eminent scholars in both disciplines – for their insights and courage, the organizers of these conferences would like to thank the AHRC, the RIISS at the University of Aberdeen, the Centre for Irish-Scottish Studies and the Department of Modern History at Trinity College Dublin, and our publisher, Dr John Kirk, of Cló Ollscoil na Banríona at Queen's University Belfast.

The organizers of the 2004 Cross-currents Conference in Trinity would particularly like to thank Professor Jane Ohlmeyer who opened the conference with great enthusiasm for the field and for postgraduate studies in general; Dr John Bowman for addressing the conference on the topic of his award winning research on the politics of Northern Ireland; Dr Diarmaid Ferriter and Dr Richard Finlay for discussing the past and future histories of small nations like Ireland and Scotland; Professor Murray Pittock for closing the conference with a paper on modern literature; Professor Terence Brown, Professor Brendan Kennelly and Professor Cathal O hÁinle and all of our chairs for giving their time and support to the conference. We would also like to thank Professor David Dickson and Dr Michael Brown for their advice and assistance.

The organizers of the 2005 Aberdeen Cross-currents Conference would like to thank the following people for their guidance, enthusiasm and unflagging support: Sukanya Basu, Laura Bok, Stephen Dornan, Margaret Maxwell, Paul Shanks and Dan Wall. We would also like to thank Dr Enda Delaney for opening the conference with his rousing and intellectually engaging lecture on the theme of "Memory and Commemoration in Irish Studies", Medbh McGuckian and Colette Bryce for their wonderfully rich and inspiring poetry readings, and Professor Tom Devine for his generous support and encouragement.

Finally, the organizers of both these conferences would like to thank all the participants in these conferences, whose openness and academic interest have ensured that the Cross-currents experience was a worthwhile and memorable one.

**Trinity Cross-currents Committee:**
Dr. Crawford Gribben (chair), Johanna Archbold (secretary),
Carole Jones, Heather Jones, Ranke de Vries

**Aberdeen Cross-currents Committee:**
Dr. Shane Alcobia-Murphy (chair), Professor George Watson, Janet Hendry

# Beyond the Anchoring Grounds …

*Shane Alcobia-Murphy, Johanna Archbold, John Gibney and Carole Jones*

> The visible sea at a distance from the shore
> Or beyond the anchoring grounds
> Was called the offing.
>
> The emptier it stood, the more compelled
> The eye that scanned it. (Seamus Heaney, from "Squarings")

Following the publication in 2004 of *To the Other Shore*, the first ever volume of postgraduate essays focusing on Irish and Scottish Studies, held under the auspices of the then Arts and Humanities Research Board (AHRB) Research Centre for Irish and Scottish Studies, it was felt that there were key developments "in the offing" with regards to the discipline, and that has proved to be the case. Five key comparative and interdisciplinary collections of essays have since been published, each breaking new ground in their respective fields: *Unity in Diversity: Studies in Irish and Scottish Gaelic Language, Literature and History* edited by Cathal Ó hÁinle and Donald Meek (Trinity College Dublin, 2004); *These Fissured Isles: Ireland, Scotland and British History, 1798-1848*, edited by Terry Brotherstone, Anna Clark and Kevin Whelan (Edinburgh: John Donald, 2005); *Ireland and Scotland: Culture and Society, 1700-2000*, edited by Ray Ryan and Liam McIlvanney (Dublin: Four Courts, 2005); *Ireland and Scotland: Order and Disorder, 1600-2000*, edited by R.J. Morris and Liam Kennedy (Edinburgh: John Donald, 2005); and *Representing Ireland: Past, Present and Future*, edited by Frank Beardow and Alison O'Malley-Younger (Sunderland: University of Sunderland Press, 2005). In 2005, what had by then become the Arts and Humanities Research Council's (AHRC) Centre for Irish and Scottish Studies, a partnership of three institutions (the University of Aberdeen, Queen's University Belfast and Trinity College Dublin), completed work on fourteen wide-ranging projects, comprising three distinct strands. The historians associated with *The Diaspora Programme* have studied the Scottish diaspora in Scandinavia and Northern Europe (1603-1707), examined aspects of Scottish and Irish medical personnel in the service of the East India Company (1700-1815), explored the role of Scots in the missions of South Africa (1800-1914), and analyzed the experience of the Catholic Irish in the West of Scotland (1846-1922). Scholars collaborating on *The Languages of Scotland and Ireland Programme* organised at Queen's University Belfast a series of symposia from 2001-2004 in the growing area of language and politics. The original motivation for that series lay with the Belfast (Good Friday) Agreement of 1998, which suddenly propelled the development of language policy in Northern Ireland central stage. The organisers, John Kirk and Dónall Ó Baoill, quickly realised that policy for Irish and Scots in Northern Ireland could not be discussed in isolation, without consideration of the Republic of Ireland and Scotland. Thereby evolved the successful formula of critical reflection and discussion on language policy pertaining to the Gaeltacht and the Scotstacht in Northern Ireland, the Republic of Ireland and Scotland. Literary critics working on *The Literatures of Ireland and Scotland Programme* have developed an integrated research strategy that offers a comparative approach to the literature of the two countries in the English language. Finally, two further postgraduate conferences were held in 2004 and 2005 under the auspices of the AHRC Research Centre for Irish and Scottish Studies, each pioneering in their own way and moving beyond the safety of "the anchoring grounds". This collection brings together selected papers from those conferences. In recognition of the seminal nature of all this work, the AHRC granted the Centre £1.25 million Phase II funding "to develop its position as the leader in its field".

The series of postgraduate conferences arising from this initiative were convened under the banner of 'Cross-currents'. In 2004 the Centre for Irish-Scottish Studies at Trinity College Dublin hosted the third Cross-currents Conference. The fourth was hosted in 2005 by the Research Institute for Irish and Scottish Studies at the University of Aberdeen. The aim of these conferences was to facilitate between postgraduates of diverse disciplines communication through participation in formal and informal events. The structure of the conferences aimed to create an atmosphere where postgraduates could gain valuable practical experience through the presentation of papers, or indeed, the organisation of events. The participants of these conferences included those who had attended the previous conferences as well as a significant number of new faces each year. The fact that the organising and editorial committees were also of a similar make-up indicates that the Cross-currents 'brand' has continued to appeal to scholars at all stages of their careers into this interdisciplinary field while also attracting the interest and enthusiasm of new postgraduate students. Both conferences were strengthened by the standard and encouragement of those established academics giving plenary lectures and chairing sessions. Their attendance and openness to discussion added to the sense of shared learning that these conferences sought to facilitate and enhance. Both of these conferences also drew a significant international response which further broadened the contexts within which papers and ideas were discussed. This indicates that the field of Irish and Scottish Studies is growing and engaging more diverse disciplines and opening up comparative possibilities for those more specifically interested in either subject. The fruitful results of these international and interdisciplinary conferences, published here, will hopefully further encourage the practice of publishing the proceedings of postgraduate conferences, as they promote professionalism among aspiring academics and further the dissemination of new research. What follows is intended to provide a documentary précis of these conferences and the postgraduate work that they highlighted.

Though belonging to two separate conferences and delivered in themed sessions, the papers in this collection are arranged alphabetically by author in order to offer the reader the full potential of possible perspectives, contrasts and comparisons that the broad field of Irish and Scottish Studies can cause on any of the featured topics. Indeed, following the precedent set in the first Cross-currents volume, the editors wish to avoid the tendency of strictly separating work done in different areas of study such as history, literature, linguistics, visual arts, for this can undermine the cross-disciplinary ethos of the ongoing series of conferences. As the editors of *To the Other Shore* put it: "Ideally, what will arise from this implementation of the alphabet's arbitrary logic is a play of friction and confluence that is stratified by the constellation of competing factors and alternative groupings, allowing each reader to follow their own connective threads or to leap the sometimes precipitous topic gaps that open up between adjacent essays". Nonetheless, the current editors offer in this introduction one possible thematic path through this expansive collection of papers.

Two papers in this collection focus on the use of space and sound as tools for storytelling and character development by playwrights and writers. From his early theatre successes of the 1960s, Brian Friel has been concerned with stage space, and has given as much attention to action belonging to the world off-stage as on-stage. **Emma Faulkner (2004)** examines examples of such attention from the soundscapes of Friel's plays. Applying the theories of Béla Balázs and Christian Metz, **João Lemos (2005)** sheds new light on the subtle, yet distinctive employment of both sound and silence in Bill Douglas's *Trilogy* (1972-78). Commenting on the uses made of diagetic and non-diagetic sounds, of "non-simultaneous" sound and poignant silences, Lemos relates these filmic techniques to the key aesthetic concept at the heart of the

*Trilogy*: fragmentation.

Arguments of a visual nature are raised by the work of **Liz Thomas (2004)** and **Emily Mark (2005)**. Broadening the traditional boundaries of architectural analysis, Thomas's paper illustrates how the standard plan of workhouses reflected the ideologies of the period, in particular the ideologies that influenced the new poor law policies of Ireland. Using evidence from workhouses in England and Scotland as a basis for comparison, she demonstrates how these plans were adapted to suit varying regional demands, though continuing to be physical manifestations of the poor law policies of centralisation, classification, deterrence, discipline, prudence and uniformity. Mark's paper analyses famine visuality as a series of political and artistic negotiations, a culturally determined phenomenon whose filaments of meaning stretch between 1847 and the present. Taking as her main focus the paintings of the nineteenth-century Scottish artist Erskine Nicol, often critiqued through the lens of sentimentalism and ideologies related to the aestheticization of poverty, Mark demonstrates how his famine imagery sought to convey the emotive dimensions of the disaster, if not its specifics or its scale. Nicol's penchant for comic, tragic, and occasionally crude pictures of the Irish peasantry is revealing, then, of the dominant aesthetic conventions at work in nineteenth-century subject pictures, as well as the shifting, often ambivalent public opinion with regard to the Famine. Examining his work in relation to other Famine images (Daniel MacDonald and graphic work, for example), Mark illuminates the complex currency and rate of dissemination of these images from the nineteenth through to the twenty-first century.

In the past, mythology has been used as a means of explaining our environment and situation. The legacy of Macpherson and his now infamous translations of the mythological Ossianic poetry are re-examined by **Janice Fairney (2004)** in a paper that focuses on the difficulties surrounding the publication of the Gaelic originals of those poems, rather than the more conventional analysis of the translations themselves. This approach highlights the importance of the close circle of trusted friends that Macpherson had who willed those originals into publication long after his death, notably John MacKenzie. MacKenzie was involved in the Highland Society of London, and it was not until 1804 that the society became reassociated with the Gaelic originals of Macpherson's translations and saw to their eventual publication. The paper by **Margitta Rouse (2004)** considers the archipelago of St Kilda which was evacuated in the 1930s. She appraises performative strategies in representation of the island's cultural identity, which has been subject to increased mythologization, against the background of spatial theories, focusing on Douglas Dunn's poem "St Kilda's Parliament: 1879-1979" (1981). Investigating the influence of the Celtic revival on constructions of national identity in Sweden, the paper by **Brendan Sweeney (2005)** provides an intriguing insight into how narrative templates from Scotland and Ireland were redeployed by Northern Europeans to reinterpret their past and construct stable myths of origins. Not only does he trace the development and strategic importance of such foundational myths, based as they were on texts such as Olof Rudbeck's *Atlantica*, Erik Gustaf Geijer's *The Last Scald* and Tegnér's *Svea*, he also shows their relevance in modern-day Sweden, particularly in the wake of that country's accession to the EU and the perceived decline of the welfare state.

Identity was a very common theme at these conferences and one which many of these papers address. The paper by **Laura Bok (2005)** contextualises the poetry of Louis MacNeice in order to investigate his problematic relationship to modern Ireland. While critics have often sought to definitively 'place' MacNeice as either a "Northern Irish poet" or an "English poet of the Auden generation", Bok usefully traces the ways in which displacement is intrinsic to the poet's identity formation. Twentieth-century literature is also the access point used by **Anthea Cordner (2004)** in order to test the boundaries of a multifaceted and fractured Protestantism in Northern Ireland. By highlighting the work of Glenn Patterson and Linda Anderson, Cordner illustrates how they eschew the popular Thriller images of Protestantism, and thus complicates many traditional representations of the group. A variety of interpretations of 'Scottishness' are also suggested in these papers. Complicating the Scottish literary tradition of defining itself in terms of 'Scottishness' the paper by **Aoife Kernan (2004)** concentrates on Geroge Friel's *Mr Alfred MA* (1972) whose author denied the 'Scottish' label, referring to himself as a "Glasgow Irishman". This broader definition of his identity appears to follow through into Friel's work, as the novel negotiates with English, German, Russian and Irish cultural markers. In his paper, **David Clark (2004)** discusses the importance of Ireland – both its political and cultural forms – for the Scottish writer, Neil M. Gunn. Gunn's idealistic vision of Ireland arose from a belief that it exemplified his vision for the future of Scotland – a free state conscious of its Celtic past. And in his paper, which primarily focusses on the debut novels of Jackie Kay, *Trumpet* (1998), and Luke Sutherland, *Jelly Roll* (1998), **Andy Wood (2004)** suggests that modern Scottish literature offers another perspective from which to contemplate the notion of 'Scottishness'. His argument embraces the realm of the historian by utilising these fictional accounts to question the nature of the countries' colonisation and resulting relationships with England. Irish identity is also addressed in the form of the Irish voices that represent the country through their literature. **Sukanya Basu (2004)** examines the interaction between Seamus Heaney's poetic voice and that of his Irish exemplar, W.B. Yeats, to analyse the extent and nature of Yeats's influence on both Heaney's poetry and his aesthetic ideas. Heaney's assorted writings on Yeats along with his poetry reveal points of contiguity between the two Irish writers. Basu's paper crucially highlights the significant Yeatsian echoes that one discovers in Heaney as he struggles with being called "the most important Irish poet since Yeats".

**Michael O'Sullivan (2004)** addresses the recent "turn to theology" in literary criticism, which has called for a rigorous investigation of the religious figure. He highlights how the work of Irish author James Joyce turns from the theological in parodying and interrogating its linguistic structures, playfully pre-empting French phenomenology's and literary criticism's recent tendencies. His parody of religious conceptions of transformation and transubstantiation through his employment of the aesthetic motifs of epiphany and *epiclesis*, recovers for literature a sense that had been reserved for religious discourse. The paper by **Carrie S. Farrelly (2005)** takes as its subject Charlie O'Neill's play *Hurl*, which centres on the experience of a group of asylum-seekers in Ireland who form a hurling team while they await the processing of their applications. *Hurl* is an innovative fusion of athleticism and theatricality, with a plot that questions definitions of Irishness by placing a bastion of Irish identity – national sport – in the capable hands of a team of comprised of people from different races, ethnicities and religions. The paper highlights the timeliness of such a production, placing it in the contemporary context of ongoing political debate in Ireland about immigration.

The interviewer, Peter Wild, has described Eoin McNamee as one of the most politicised Irish writers living today. Recognising his powerful and emotive fictional writing set in the recent violent political past of Northern Ireland, three contributors give their analysis of his work. Drawing on the psychoanalytic theories of Chodorow and Fromm, the paper by **Caroline Magennis (2005)** examines how McNamee's fiction embraces the generic conventions of both literary noir and the post-modern novel to portray the construction and cultivation of a self-consciously militaristic (hyper-) masculinity in a time of violence. Focusing on *Resurrection Man* and *The Ultras*, she explores how McNamee represents the masculine collective in Northern Ireland, the ways in which individualism is sacrificed in these groupings and the impulse to collective violence, and examines the psycho-dynamics involved in this masculine socialisation. **Jacqui Weeks (2005)** delineates the ways in which McNamee's debut novel, *Resurrection Man*, constitutes a meta-fictive preoccupation with form and generic conventions. She argues that, in contrast to the narrative methodologies of both "Troubles

Trash" fiction and historiographic texts, McNamee's novel is "writerly" in the Barthesian sense, bespeaking a representational crisis whereby "[n]eat pre-coded and definitive forms of language and genre are inadequate modes of expression when dealing with incomprehensible murder and horror." In his analysis of McNamee's latest novel, *The Ultras*, **Daniel Smith (2005)** equally pays close attention to the self-reflexive nature of McNamee's narrative style, arguing that the text constitutes not so much an example of *speculative fiction* but rather one of *paranoiac fiction* whereby experience is already predetermined and mediated. McNamee's text, he argues, may well strive at some level to shed light on the life and death of Robert Nairac, but the narrative's insistent foregrounding of its own textual production constantly calls into question the reliability of its findings.

Two more papers discuss language and demonstrate how history can be illuminated by such an analysis. **Niall O'Gallagher (2004)** addresses the Scots linguistic nationalism that accompanied the Scottish cultural debates of the inter-war years and highlights the less considered relationship of the Scots language 'movement' to anti-Irish racism. O'Gallagher contrasts two diverging tendencies in this movement and examines their influence on two of the cultural manifestos of the period, to assess their impact on the Scots language of the early twentieth century. The paper by **Gavin Falconer (2005)** explores why the greatest affinity of core Scots areas in Ulster is with Lowland Scots rather than Hiberno-English and questions whether the application of overarching political or geographic adjectives to linguistic continua is feasible in a territory where nationality and jurisdiction are matters of controversy.

Another set of papers focuses on the broader significance of the fictional work of Irish and Scottish writers in the eighteenth and nineteenth century. **Carol Stewart (2004)** addresses the issue of independence in Smollet's novels illustrating how it had personal, political and perhaps even national dimensions for him. However, though novels offered him independence from patronage which had so dogged his attempts to produce and promote his play, *The Regicide*, the close associations of the novel with the market place resulted in his independence from patronage being replaced by other unwelcome compromises. Charles Robert Maturin was one of several Irish writers abroad that used their work to comment on the contemporary political situation in Ireland, specifically the question of nationhood. **Christina Morin (2004)** focuses on how Maturin continues this commentary by displacing the issues onto other countries with particular reference to his novel *Melmoth the Wanderer* (1820) which uses cannibalism, vampirism and the wandering Jew trope to depict these issues. In a paper that proposes using the treatment of Jews in Walter Scott's *Ivanhoe* and *The Surgeon's Daughter* as an example of how they and other boundary characters contribute to the idea and creation of the nation and indeed the empire, **Ashley Hales (2004)** raises issues of race, religious affiliation and wealth, as well as suggesting a model for how post-colonial nations wrestle with their own identity.

The Subaltern Studies Group is a group of scholars in India interested in the post-colonial and post-imperial societies of India in particular and the developing world in general. Two papers here translate those ideas more broadly as a reading of history from below, with a focus more on what happens among the masses at the base levels of society than among the elite. Drawing on the Subaltern Group's theoretical framework allows for a refutation of the hegemonic status accorded to national discourses by post-colonial criticism and, by foregrounding issues such as race, class and gender, **Stephanie Lehner (2005)** uses this approach to critique the somewhat problematic adoption of post-colonial theory within Irish and Scottish Studies. This allows her to re access post colonial theory's potential as a critical approach for cross-archipelagic studies. Focusing on the fiction of James Kelman and Robert McLiam Wilson, she outlines the ways in which they attempt to "rewrite national paradigms" by foregrounding issues of class disempowerment, voice and representation. Taking Colin Graham's lead, **Lisa McGonigle (2005)** applies ideas of subalternity to the gender subject positions inscribed within Seamus Deane's *Reading in the Dark*. The mother's aphonia within is here "a synecdoche for the authority and self-assertion largely denied to the mother in *Reading in the Dark*". Such a critical focus on the mother's silence is salutary as it highlights a hitherto unrecognised subaltern censuring of the strictures and structures of nationalism at the heart of Deane's novel.

Both **Billy Gunn (2004)** and **Andreas Boldt (2004)** foreground the importance of individual contributions to the making of history. Gunn highlights the contributions of provincial hospitals and institutions to the development of the Scottish mental health system. His paper particularly notes the enthusiasm of the hospital's patron, Susan Carniege, who was responsible for the high level of psychiatric care that was achieved at the Montrose Lunatic Asylum which was unsurpassed in its time. Boldt focuses on Ireland's connection with "the father of modern Irish historiography", German historian Leopold von Ranke. Ranke's Irish wife also had a great influence on his work and this relationship, discussed by Andreas, offers interesting insights into the development of Ranke's views on Irish identity in the mid-nineteenth century.

Interesting occurrences of cross-currents of Irish and Scottish voices are found in two more papers from these conferences. The late eighteenth and early nineteenth-century saw an immense upsurge in millenarian beliefs across Europe. As the New Year had particular resonance for such feeling, **Stephen Dornan (2004)** examines the New Year odes written in Scotland and Ulster during this period. By contextualising these odes in terms of the millenarian culture of the period, Dornan suggests that undertones of this contemporary mood are present in several poems by Robert Burns which are in turn exaggerated in odes from Ulster that appeared in periodicals and newspapers of the period. Another example is found in the modern fiction of James Kelman, as highlighted by **Paul F. Shanks (2004)**. The textual and thematic parallels with Samuel Beckett's post-war texts are constructed in this paper, which also draws a contrast between Samuel Beckett's apolitical and metaphysical stance and Kelman's own motivators of social and political inequality.

Three other papers highlight the importance of understanding the influence of religion when approaching the history of any society in the past. The layered and openly contrasting uses and applications of the 1643 Solemn League and Covenant are traced by **Kirsteen MacKenzie (2004)**. She highlights how it was interpreted differently by Presbyterians in the three kingdoms: by some to justify loyalty to King, or to the Church, or to the original intentions of the Covenant itself. The death of Archbishop Beaton of Glasgow in 1603 marked the end of the Catholic hierarchy in Scotland as well as the beginning of Catholic missionaries to the country. **Tom McInally (2004)** highlights the impact of Gaelic-speaking Irish priests on the numbers of practicing Catholics in the Highlands and islands of Scotland in the late seventeenth century, noting these areas accounted for 90% of Scottish Catholics. The importance and dominance of Catholicism in modern Irish history is difficult to overstate. **Louise Fuller (2004)** delineates how Catholic culture was consolidated by the laws of the Irish state from the early years of independence, and how the actions, words and public appearances of state representatives legitimated the Catholic ethos. Common rituals, discourses and symbols are examined for the powerful part that they played in shaping and reinforcing Irish Catholic identity in the twentieth century.

The impact of migration is addressed by two other papers in this collection. Using a small area east of Scotland's industrial capital Glasgow, **Geraldine Vaughan (2004)** illustrates how Irish migrants, over a fifty year period, developed a sense of belonging in their adopted homeland. This transition is charted through emigrant activity in local politics, which provides a useful tool towards assessing the success of Irish assimilation as well as the desire of Irish migrants to integrate into Scottish society. **Patrick Walsh (2005)** closely examines the key factors behind and effects of increased levels of emigration from Ulster to North America in the early years of the eighteenth century. Drawing on archival material and focusing on the socio-political and religious contexts, he argues that while the agents on the ground stressed the economic consequences of increased migration, the Government were far more concerned with the effects of emigration on the "Protestant Interest".

Being part of a series of conferences which aims to highlight new research from young scholars, it is not surprising that several papers attempt to re-read traditional interpretations. Taking her cue from Richard Kearney's seminal analysis of *Bailegangaire in Transitions* (1988), in which he discerned a key tension at the heart of the play between tradition and modernity, **Margaret Maxwell (2005)** analyses the merging time frames as symptomatic of a search for meaning and self-realization on the characters' part. However, she breaks new ground by reading Mommo's repeated and fragmented narrative as symptomatic of a traumatic neurosis, one which defers closure and expresses guilt only in an occluded form. Drawing on Cathy Caruth's work on trauma and Lacanian psychoanalytical theory, Maxwell successfully accounts for the play's drive to complete Mommo's story. Arguing from the premise that "[l]iterature about an animal is a reflection, a litmus, of our perception of not just that species, but our entire natural environment", **Richard King (2005)** provides an unusual and very interesting eco-critical reading of Liam O'Flaherty's short story, "The Wounded Cormorant". King examines the ornithology of the cormorant, the history of its symbolic use in Anglo-Irish literature, and how the symbol works within O'Flaherty's story. Contrary to its traditional symbolic connotation of gluttony and oppression, the cormorant in O'Flaherty's text, as highlighted by Richard, is "a good shag" ('a good cormorant') and represents nothing evil, just harsh truth in nature. **Dan Wall (2005)** re-reads John Gibson Lockhart's *Life of Robert Burns* in the context of Romantic biography. By foregrounding Lockhart's preoccupation with the creative mind and imagination of his subject, Wall neatly explains the notable absence of many of the material details relating to Burns's life and Lockhart's conception of him. The paper by **Jonathan Wright (2005)** casts new light on the 1981 Maze Hunger Strike, de-emphasizing the parallels that many historians have drawn between the 1918 and 1981 hunger strikes that have resulted in somewhat deterministic readings. Indeed, Wright argues against the tendency to reductively view the strikers as simply "quotations of their forbears"; as he eloquently puts it, the hunger strikers "were not prisoners of their history, destined to follow in the footsteps of earlier generations". Equally contestational, the paper by **Matthew Maguire (2005)** resists the celebratory pronouncement made by Laura Pelschiar that modern Belfast is "a post modern place… the only space where it is possible to build and articulate a (post-) national conscience… [a] multi-voiced and multi-ethnic development of Northern society". His paper suggests that, rather than healing the sectarian fissures of the North, Belfast's developer-led regeneration is merely a reconstitution of this divide. The locus for violence, he contends, has now been shifted from the political to the economic; this new Belfast will house an opportunistic future, but only for those that can afford it.

The curiosities of nineteenth-century laws in Ireland and Scotland were employed by the writer Wilkie Collins to frame some of his novels. **Aoife Leahy (2004)** illustrates how this tendency was due to the author's appreciation for the law as well as a contemporary interest in such regional legal peculiarities. **Miriam Gamble (2005)** dismisses the contention that the poetry of the older generation is somehow well-made, self-contained and indomitable whereas that of the younger generation is experimental and self-interrogating. Comparing the work of Michael Longley with that of Don Paterson, Gamble demonstrates how both adopt an attitude of self-questioning which interrogates poetic capability. While Longley disrupts and interrogates from within the basic parameters of the elegiac genre, Paterson's work exploits traditional lyric structures to question both the status and effectiveness of poetic voice. **Tudor Balinisteanu (2005)** traces the ways in which A. L. Kennedy in *Night Geometry and the Garscadden Trains* (1993) exploits the symbolic value of day-to-day gestures, turns of phrase and routine patterns of behaviour from multiple viewpoints in order to capture a women's reality that is channelled and regulated by various social myths. While concerned with the constituencies women inhabit on the social stage and with the ways in which these construct women's subjective realities, Kennedy's emphasis, he argues, is on how women's subjectivities function; thus, she is able to engage larger discourses whose reified views of women have helped establish as many mythologies about them.

The result of a truly interdisciplinary conference is a shared learning environment where scholars are exposed to different modes of research and methodologies. The interaction between students from different disciplines during the two conferences highlighted just how the historians could benefit from the theoretically informed textual exegesis of the literary paper, and how the student of English could learn from the rigorous archival research undertaken by the historian. Of course, both groups were able to learn much from the sociological and anthropological methodologies adopted by others at these conferences. In conclusion, then, as this generation of postgraduates constitute the next generation of lecturers, it is hoped that the comparative and inter-disciplinary approaches fostered by the Cross-currents series will expand the horizons of future teaching and research methodologies. With future Irish and Scottish Studies postgraduate conferences and publications already in the offing, one can confidently assert that the discipline has shed its often inward-looking, conservative dimension and is now well and truly "beyond the anchoring grounds".

# "Dreaming Brokenly of Deaths by Fire": Deconstructions of Social Myths in A. L. Kennedy's *Night Geometry and the Garscadden Trains*

*Tudor Balinisteanu*

> In Capel Gofeg after sunset, the air would taste of damp smoke and coldness, and the possibilities of fear. The town dreamed brokenly of gunpowder plots and deaths by fire. (Kennedy, 2000: 10)

Kennedy's short stories introduce readers to a range of women's voices that offer alternative views of women within diverse social structures. Her characters voice subjective experiences that point out women's frustrations as regards the ways in which society regulates women's socialization. In her work on the social construction of subjective experience based on women's stories of their everyday memories and experiences, Frigga Haug finds that in these narratives

> The individual's analyses of reality, which we have decoded as her or his way of appropriating the world and which we wish to track down in our everyday stories, move on the terrain of dominant cultural values and counter-cultural, subversive efforts to extract meaning from life. (Haug, 1992: 21)

Kennedy's short stories, through the analyses of everyday experiences of her women characters, make visible the areas of conflict where women struggle to make sense of their lives against the pressures of constraining cultural values. Such efforts may indeed appear subversive when the characters' voices reveal that women's ways of appropriating social reality run counter to the expectations derived from established social meaning structures. These voices offer as many opportunities for women readers to recognize themselves as articulate and capable members in social constituencies thus allowing them to enact modes of socializing that mainstream social discourses have hitherto obscured and marginalized.

## Night Geometry and the Garscadden Trains

The first story sets the tone of this collection. A young woman's life is framed within the time span marked by the deaths of two men: the death of her grandfather marks the girl's entering into adulthood as an autonomous woman, while the foreseeable death of her elderly lover becomes the measure of her own life after he infected her with HIV. The narrator's entire life seems regulated by these men, one the symbol of continued patriarchal linearity, the other a symbol of masculine wisdom. Not only do they stand as references in relation to which beginnings and endings can be defined, bracketing the woman's entire existence, but also the illnesses that afflict them are transferred to her, therefore regulating and timing her life rhythm, measured, as the narrator puts it, in the ticking of her blood pulse.

Douglas Gifford connects this story with the next one in this collection, "Translations", through their reference to Indian mythology, seeing a common ground in the themes of "dreamtime and assuagement of guilt" (Gifford, 1997: 617). Cristie March, however, associates it with betrayal considering that it enacts "physically what occurs emotionally in 'Bix'" (March, 2002: 142). In a broader perspective Michael's (the narrator's lover in "Tea and biscuits") guilt and betrayal integrate into a symbolism encompassing the limitations masculine myths of wisdom place on women's life rhythms. The psychological implications of these limitations are shown through correlatives on the physical level. In "Tea and biscuits" the passage describing the woman's sexual initiation declares it "extremely odd". The oddness is correlated with the contrast between Michael's conventional gestures and conversation and the narrator's finding the experience "a gift and a thing to remember". Offering tea in bed Michael enquires:

"How are you feeling?"
"Very nice."
"You don't hurt?"
"No. I ache a bit." (Kennedy, 1993: 3)

Michael's use of the word "hurt" suggests his rather neutral interest in the physical damage or emotional distress he may have caused. The woman's interpretation of the sexual encounter is more refined, qualifying "hurt" as "ache", i.e. as, psychologically, the beginning of a painful yearning whose physical correlative is a lasting dull pain. Indeed, the passage evinces a cynical note when we realize at the end of the story that the woman's sexual initiation has also been an initiation in death marking her body as irrevocably diseased.

The story also underlines the opposition between creativity and death as forces at work in shaping one's life. The woman's mother gave birth to her laughing:

[…] in a silence, she laughed. She laughed and she found she couldn't stop laughing. Her laughing made her laugh. […] She gave birth weeping and giggling, amazed, and thinking of that first, secret thing that started her laugh. (Kennedy, 1993: 6)

As the narrator, herself nursing dreams of motherhood, records the possibility of women's enjoying their bodies and its perhaps secret magic in a mythology of womanhood that remains unknowable, a discourse that connects women with life is created, reinforced by the narrator's position as a blood donor. Women are pictured as nurturers, withholding an intuitive knowledge about the rhythms of life and literally using their bodies to give and support life. The narrator finds that her blood "was a lovely colour, too. A rich, rich red. I told my mother about it and she laughed" (Kennedy, 1993: 7). It is in her blood, also seen as the bond between daughter and mother, that the secret of creation and joy might be found.

This vision of life as having a secret rhythm whose impulses can be recounted in laughter is contrasted with the masculine wisdom imparted by Michael. The narrator remembers:

that thing […] about the American tribe. Those Indians. They thought that we went through life on a river, all facing the stern of the boat and we only ever looked ahead in dreams. That's what I'll have to do now. I think he told me about that. It sounds like him. (Kennedy, 1993: 8)

The Indian myth implies that reality is either past memory or dreams of the future: a painful yearning. It is never laughter. Laughter requires one to be in the present, living. Also the linearity implied in the Indian story echoes the narrator's own positioning since it refers to her passing into the stages of her life through having always been assisted by men. The mastering of the secrets of life, relationships and death in a patriarchal context seems to be "some kind of start for the conversation" between author and readers in the stories to follow.

In the next story, "Translations", a young man is struggling to make sense of the past through the patriarchal mythologies whose conflicting and overlapping symbolisms define his mind and body as sites of colonisation. The Indian setting echoes the reference in the first story. If in "Tea and biscuits" the emphasis is on the physical colonisation of a woman's body through the initiations in death assisted by male figures, here it is the spirit of the "Dead Man" that infiltrates a young girl's mind. While the girl is asleep beside him the young man tells his story about "how the magic that had killed her daughter first came to him" (Kennedy, 1993: 9). When she woke up "she looked a little frightened" and he reflects: "Perhaps she had heard too much of his voice. But she didn't seem hurt, it seemed she was well" (Kennedy, 1993: 23). The hurt threatening to nestle insidiously in the young girl's mind is perhaps the psychological translation of the bodily hurt nestled in the woman's body in "Tea and biscuits". Like the woman narrator of the first story, although she seems to be well, the young girl may be bearing an ache rooted in a hurt not so immediately visible. The intertextual relationship between the two stories may also be inferred from the mentioning of the girl's dead daughter in "Translations" which reminds us of the narrator of "Tea and biscuits" while the anteriority suggestion creates a temporal framework of generational handing down of death.

In "Translations" the mythological becomes psychological as the young man deals with physical rape by the One Handed Man whose reality is clouded in the liminality of a masculine rite of passage. The One Handed Man's teaching about the magic of love also defines it within the confines of an exclusively masculine relationship. On the other hand the boy is confronted with the cultural rape performed by Christian colonists; "the Fathermacdonalt" teaches him about a Christian love that is diseased with death for it is this "love" that gave birth to a history of violent colonisations where the colonised becomes the coloniser in an infectious spread across continents and peoples: the Scottish priest left his country for Spain only to become a colonizer himself in South America. Thus, it is the translation of physical colonisation into psychological insecurity and ambiguity that Kennedy is concerned with in this story. As Cristie March points out, in terms of technique this narrative involves a blurring between the real and the fantastic with Kennedy "experimenting with [fantastic] themes that become believable embedded within realist narrative" (March, 2002: 153, brackets added).

The story giving the collection's title explores the troublesome incongruence between the landscape of the city and the landscape of the mind. The geometry of the city seen as underlain by a railway network that limits physical movement to "terminating" destinations where life seems to "finish" reflects the narrator's intuitions of inadequacy and closure. Gifford sees this story as typical of Kennedy's narrative method as she has "the teller circling around the deferred central revelation, with hints of unease, insufficiency, betrayal, together with prevailing images of claustrophobia and desired escape" (Gifford, 1997: 617). For Gifford, the trains represent a kind of correlative summing up the issue of pointlessness and ordinariness in the woman's life.

Indeed, the regular, impersonal forms of the city are translated into the dynamic of bodies, with the narrator registering the incongruence between her rich emotional life and the couple's repetitive night geometry:

> It was strange. However we flopped together, however haphazardly we decided to come to rest, the fit would always be the same.
>
> His right arm, cradling my neck.
>
> My head on his shoulder. … (Kennedy, 1993: 26)

In spite of its sameness, the woman initially invests their physical dynamics with a sense of "feeling safe and complete", and when their position reverses with mirror-like precision, offering her the possibility to inhabit her partner's bodily posture, she invests it with a sense of uniqueness that she considers the cornerstone of their love: "I told him I could never do enough, or be enough or give enough back […]. I told him I belonged to him. I think he was asleep" (Kennedy, 1993: 28).

A threatening hint comes with the reference to the Inca's conquest by the Spaniards blending in echoes from the previous story with its themes of psychological colonisation. But in this story it is the geometry of urban life that distils into even the most intimate gestures and has shaped the narrator's mind ways. Eventually she realizes that their bodies' postures signify social roles rather than emotional communication. Kennedy's concern here is with society's colonization of the woman's emotional space with social myths:

Finally, of course, I realised the most original things about us were our fingerprints. Nothing of what we did was ever new. I repeated the roles that Duncan chose to give me in his head – wicked wife, wounded wife, the one he would always come back to, the one he had to leave and I never even noticed. (Kennedy, 1993: 30)

On the one hand, Kennedy points out the constraining effects of social myths about the wife and indirectly about the lover, as we may infer that Duncan's women likewise fulfil roles of mistresses, the psychological awareness of which determines the narrator's sense of bodily discomfort. On the other hand, on a meta-narrative level the story feeds back the vision of the dreariness of Scottish urban life into the larger discourse established by the preceding generation of writers strengthening the mythology of urban realism they have created to replace that of a rural, idyllic Scotland. However, Kennedy's engagement with literary constructions of industrial Scotland lines up with the efforts of the first generation of post-war women's writing which, as Gifford remarks, "refused to throw the ailing baby of community out with the industrial bathwater" (Gifford, 1997: 591). As March observes, the ending of the story, while noting the insignificance of small lives, also suggests a determination that may germinate positive change. Indeed, the urban dweller's sense of identity loss and of society's passivity that reduces her emotions to "incendiary incidents" is counteracted with the narrator's resolute assertion that this will not do. These themes will be taken up again in Kennedy's novels; specifically, the ending of "Night geometry…" seems to nestle the seed of her following book, *Looking for the Possible Dance*:

There is only one thing I want more than proof that I existed and that's some proof, while I'm here, that I exist. (…) We have small lives, easily lost in foreign droughts, or famines; the occasional incendiary incident, or a wall of pale faces, crushed against grillwork, one Saturday afternoon in Spring. This is not enough. (Kennedy, 1993: 34)

The following two stories dwell on concrete aspects relating to the theme of women's silenced minds and derided bodies. After schoolgirl Gracie is sexually abused by her mother's partner he seeks to silence the victim while at the same time attempting to minimize the importance of the event, to reduce it perhaps to the scale of "the occasional incendiary incident": "It's something you do with a friend, Grace, and I'm your friend. I'll be good to you. Don't worry, honey, the next time, it won't hurt" (Kennedy, 1993: 41). The word "hurt" echoes the sexual initiation of the woman in "Tea and biscuits" as well as the themes of colonisations from "Translations".

"Genteel potatoes" is a crucial story in that it registers not only the possibility of taking action against the constraints that social myths effect on the social stage, but also, and more importantly, an awareness of the fact that a discursive struggle exists and can be conducted around the central issues addressed in the collection on the whole. From the very beginning we are told that this is "no more than a story about Grandmother, because it cannot be the truth. If you and I were there to see it now, it might be the truth, but as it is, this is a story" (Kennedy, 1993: 42). As we read it, the story reveals elements of a conventional fable of class resistance, based on which we may associate it with proletarian mythology. However, the ending suggests that although a discourse of resistance based on transcendental social ideals may validate a mythology, it can also provide resources for constructing subjects enabled to act strategically in the meta-narrative world. Grandmother's acts could provide models of empowering social performances. Myths of resistance, once released from the metaphysical space of conceptual abstractions, can help shape the social reality of lived human interactions, and "Genteel potatoes" aptly proves how the here and now is coloured by particular stories positioning subjects in histories that come to embed what counts as truth. The question of how much reality stories contain triggers, in the collection's context, the question of what stories are selected that make possible the account of truth. The diachronic is collapsed into the synchronic as we realise that whether or not the Grandmother's defiance is fact matters less than the possibility of performing the empowered subjectivity the story proposes. As the narrator puts it, the reality that "happens" "before Grandmother and I will even meet and before I can begin this story" (46) cannot be accessed except through the recounting performed by the story-telling voice. In an intertextual relationship with Gracie's story "Genteel potatoes" offers the kind of role that might replace Gracie's subjectivity of denial and silence suggested through the words Gracie keeps saying to herself: "Think of something else to keep it away" (Kennedy, 1993: 35). Stories like that recounting Grandmother's refusal (in a different context) to "think of something else" in order to keep the hurt away could offer a mythology of resistance as a basis for creating empowered subjectivities for women in like situations, or in situations like Gracie's. The subjectivity script offered in "Genteel potatoes" could inspire women's social acts that feed back empowering performances in society.

In a following story, "Sweet memory will die" the narrator is able to discard memories of an abusive childhood as she gives up thoughts of revenge and "no longer cares". As Cristie March suggests, however, "such release can be bittersweet for [Kennedy's] characters". The narrator, in spite of her gaining a long fought for independence, finds that there is "no recompense for the life she had lost" (March, 2002: 135). Kennedy is a writer who never loses sight of a humanity that she finds in excess of words.

"Didacus", following after "Genteel potatoes", is quick to deconstruct a mythologized vision of the working class that the previous story might have been seen to propose, suggesting that Kennedy is a writer keen on preserving the ability to migrate between discourses without allowing the reader fixed stances. Jean, a working class housewife, has given up dreams of setting up a business together with her husband and casually commits adultery. The story suggests her commitment to a memory of freedom as a means to defend herself against the imprisoning habits to which she is confined by her working class status. Unlike in "Genteel potatoes" this woman's voice is silenced against the grillwork of another day in the city:

> The city is going to work, filling up the loans with footsteps and breathing. Maybe the year before there would have been conversation; room for a voice in the mouth. It's too late now for that. (Kennedy, 1993: 50)

"The freedom ahead" she and her husband contemplate is marked by lifelessness and silence. Like the narrator in "Sweet memory will die", Jean no longer cares.

It is precisely the silences of "small people" that make it difficult for the narrator in "The role of notable silences in Scottish history" to tell "the truth". This story is remarkably concerned with how forms of writing create institutional fields that shape identities through discourses. The narrator, a historian, reflects:

> I enjoy my work, it is clean and varied, it pays a good wage. Sadly, it is also a constant temptation. Time and again, it presents the perfect opportunity to lie. It begs you to lie. It also repeatedly proves beyond all shadow of doubt that nothing is less believable than the truth. (Kennedy, 1993: 62-3)

The passage indicts institutionalised forms of discourse for covering up social realities they are not designed to register, for instance the murdering of "insignificant" people. Such murdering is "too recent to become history" and soon becomes "too old to be news" (Kennedy, 1993: 72). The issue of agency is made visible suggesting institutional entrepreneurs concerned with a "historical geography" that, echoing the mechanical geometry of the city in "Night geometry…", fails to map the inner dramas of its inhabitants:

Now while I'm working, I try not to think about the truth and concentrate my full attention on the words instead. Words just say what you want them to; they don't know any better. We get on very well together, even in the dusty mornings when all we have to amuse ourselves are maps and historical geography. (Kennedy, 1993: 63)

This interpretation of the relationship between words and truth is related to past discursive practices of ignoring the real to the purpose of constructing ideologically convenient representations of Scottishness for the present. In these discursive practices the idea of Scottishness has been for a long time either related to notable historical figures or spatialized in landscapes, the narrator comments, invariably containing "a brown and green glen with rocky grey bits and a couple of sheep" (Kennedy, 1993: 64). As such representations do not account for the "insignificant" people, tragic events in their life are attributed to chance and coincidence and therefore social responsibility is erased: the narrator cannot place the random killing of her partner on the social map.

Engaging mythologies of Scottishness, Kennedy shows that in their metaphysical reference they are only able to account for "murders" into which institutional entrepreneurs read a "point", the suggestion being that of nationalism: "there's no point being Scottish if you can't make up your past as you go along" (Kennedy, 1993: 64). These discourses, however, are unable to account for the murders of "small people" whose qualification as chancy and coincidental renders them unsuitable matter for official concern. Kennedy's technique here seems to be a kind of eidetic future in the past, as she points out how past discourses will have already made possible the silences of the present while also showing how the erasures performed in discourses *about* the past are taken up in, and influence, what can be said about the present. She sees, for instance, how the preoccupation with prominent historical figures reflects more of a concern with prominence rather than with those figures' reality. This preoccupation shapes contemporary discourses that allocate far more space to an image of prosperity than to the reality of the poor, as the article on buses ironically suggests. The narrator becomes aware that her partner's death cannot be accounted for without foregrounding the wrongs of an entire tradition of selective constructions of truth, seeing that her partner's murder will be treated as a minor concern and its root cause will not be carefully addressed: he died without a cause. It is precisely the possibilities for the future foretold through the past that remain invisible in official discourses.

On a meta-narrative level the investment of the past with unreality that the concluding passage effects suggests the possibility of a present liberated from the constraints of history where stances can be created for writers with a will to note down the "roaring" "silences" of Scottish mythologies:

Someone else [...] [will] take us out and write us down. My only contribution on the subject is already here: the obituary I wrote him before we first met. It is inaccurate. (Kennedy, 1993: 72)

"The high walk" explores the psychological trauma of betrayal, as Annie's efforts to break with a pattern of familial abuse fail when she discovers her boyfriend's affair with their flatmate Marie. The story engages social myths about the couple offering a liberating role with Anne constructed as an independent, successful woman in spite of the past challenges. According to March "the male narrator cannot understand Anne's choice to see him once but not renew their relationship. She does not conform to 'type', refusing to assume the role of forgiving lover and source of comfort" (March, 2002: 141). The narrator's sense of loss and guilt is illuminated allegorically through the concurrent story of a missing child, echoing the lack of personal fulfilment consequent to his betrayal.

"Star dust" further develops the theme of unfulfilled relationships as the story explores the psychology of women who, unlike Anne, cannot break out from stale emotional spaces. March points out that the narrator's attempt to leave a loveless marriage to join the man she truly loves, given up for the sake of her daughter, is the only memory of happiness she can cling to, investing it with a cinematic quality. But on the other hand we realise that the narrator's involvement with cinematographic discourse references social stereotypes in complex ways. After marrying, the narrator and her husband, Tam, do "the thing that films always want you to do" (Kennedy, 1993: 89). Kennedy points out that the ways in which certain social clichés construct "extraordinary" identities are also insidious ways of making those identities ordinary through the sameness in difference underlying their display. Mythologies of ordinariness are thus created. However the narrator is aware that cinematic constructions can only give a reality effect because ultimately the stories they propose depend on the conceptual arrangements film directors make:

> I look at him [Robert De Niro], and the other ones like him, and they spend so much time and energy on just looking ordinary. There are lights and backgrounds and special effects and music – that's a very important thing – and all of this is there to make them look better than ordinary. (Kennedy, 1993: 86)

Through her narrator Kennedy establishes a dialogue with mythologizing discourses of "ordinariness" in order to expose their constructed nature. Life as experience of the ordinary is contrasted to the conceptual ordinariness of characters in films like *Taxi Driver*:

> I have an idea that the ordinary people should be in the films. They wouldn't have to waste their time forgetting they were stars and they would get their chance to be wonderful. (Kennedy, 1993: 86)

The narrator refuses to mythologize her love affair with Archie: "You have to be very careful when you imagine and you're alone. Some people I've seen have locked themselves up in their heads and swallowed the key" (Kennedy, 1993: 86). Rather than locking herself up in a metaphysical space of ideals, the narrator prefers a kind of discourse that remains open, connected to the reality of experience; a kind of discourse allowing her to participate in the story it tells by performing it rather than by letting herself be performed by it. She controls the "exposure times" and "depths of field", how the reality "happens" and how she can participate in it:

> I love these words. These words are lovely. They are happening now, they are young words and, because I understand them, part of me can still be happening now and young. (Kennedy, 1993: 83)

Thus, it is the storyness of the story, its performative dimension, rather than its conceptual referential field that guarantees its meaning for the woman in "Star dust".

The following two stories deal with the shaping of experience under the pressure of social myths about the lover. In "Bix" the narrator's idealization of his wife prevents him from being able to grapple with her reality as an autonomous woman. According to the image of her he had constructed in his mind she "had carried her joy and love for him like a baby. The nursing of it made her a second Mary [...]" (Kennedy, 1993: 97). He then uses another myth, of the mistress, to get rid of her but cannot control the experience of emptiness and loss this causes. "The poor souls" echoes "Night geometry..." with the female narrator aimlessly travelling by train constructing the city as an alternative realm of ghostly visions as she is unable to control the reality of her husband's betrayal. Like the narrator in "Bix" she must confront the pain of loss of faith in a mythology of family joy and fulfilment. In her imagination she sees her husband in the window of the pizza house, at a table with a woman and a laughing boy. They ate and talked together. It was plain they loved each other: father, mother, only son. [...] If I had just kept faith with him, we could have been that family now. (Kennedy, 1993: 108)

In spite of the fact that struggling to make sense of a reality pervaded by various mythologies makes her characters experience pain and loss, Kennedy suggests that an awareness of the constructed nature of these discourses offers the opportunity to create empowering subjectivities.

"Cap O'Rushes" is written with an awareness of the stories' power to effect social structures. However, the woman in Kennedy's version of the story reinvests, with irony and determination, the roles the traditional folk-tale enshrines. The focus is on the family roles and hierarchies that the folk-tale legitimates: a young woman is rewarded for patience, restraint and for acquiring the skills required for undertaking the home chores; daughter and father are reconciled and the young woman gains a husband. Kennedy's version of Cap O'Rushes' story highlights the suppression performed in the faery-tale's conclusion: what happens after Cap O'Rushes earns her prince? What does "being happy ever after" mean? Perhaps, as Kennedy's version suggests, the young woman continues to perform the home chores, except that this time there is no reward. The folk-tale character of the princely husband is reconstructed within images of greed, self-sufficiency and ego-centeredness. In Kennedy's story, the behaviour of the husband and of the children he controls is likened to that of mythological goblins, traditionally represented as mischievous faery creatures. Prince Charming becomes the Goblin King. We are led to reflect on the mischief performed with the folk-tales' scripting of socialization guidelines for married women. The stifling atmosphere of the social space shared in marriage is represented in imagery specific to caves. Having tidied-up after the family dinner the wife joins the rest of the family in the communal space of the living room:

> She washed up and came through to join them, noticing, when she opened the door, that the room now smelt like a cave as she walked in. A cave where someone had recently spilt gravy.
> The curtains were tight drawn and only the dead blue glow from the television lit the room. (Kennedy, 1993: 113)

In Kennedy's version of "Cap O'Rushes" the social space of the home is forever tainted with the persistent smell of "recently spilt gravy". The married woman remains confined to the scullery. This image of a married woman and of the social space of marriage is contrasted with the image of the independent woman she becomes in the absence of her husband and demanding children. When they are away she is able to reconstruct the social space of the home in positive ways as a space where "she could breathe easily and she felt clean" (Kennedy, 1993: 112). Eventually, rejecting the housewife role by leaving her family the woman is empowered to take active part in the shaping of her social environment. This positive experience is possible, according to March, because she "has shed the cultural baggage that urged her initially to marry the Goblin King" (Kennedy, 1993: 137). The woman's attitude towards her new life is shown in her reflections on the typing job she had taken up to maintain herself:

> She continued with her typing. When she was into the flow of it, the words lined across the paper, as if she was rubbing the whiteness away; not putting a blackness on. She was squeezing the words out from where they were already hiding. This was a comfortable idea. It had nothing to do with the sense of what she wrote, nothing to do with reality at all and it meant that she couldn't be wrong, because she was only finding something, not inventing it. (Kennedy, 1993: 118)

The passage also reflects Kennedy's poetics. Words are used to find experience, not to invent it. The whiteness of the page referred to here suggests the silences that are rubbed off in the discovery process a story presupposes instead of being buried in legitimating tales of myths. Stories 'squeeze' the words out from where they are already hiding. The words that fall into place belong to new found voices rather then to the voices invented (put into place) through a mythology or another. This suggests a call to demythologise authority (i.e. the power, socially invested in authors, to authorise a privileged version of reality). Discourse is a fluid space that gathers a variety of voices, rather than a voice which programmatically interlocks sense and reality. Kennedy's poetic art entails a perspective on discourse that regards it in its eventfulness as dialogue, thus opening discourse up as a participatory social space.

While the first story of the collection shows a woman whose reality obtains between representations of herself in reference to two men, her father and her lover, the journey Kennedy has taken the reader through nears completion with the representation of the autonomous subjectivity of a woman who has taken hold of her inner reality. In "The seaside photographer" the narrator repossesses her relationship with her father with an empowering awareness of both the freedoms and the limitations social myths embed in constructions of the real. The story also suggests that reality is larger than its discursive constructions and registers the impossibility of texts to render that excess: "If, in this world, I could, I would write you whole [...]. All I can do is write you words [...] and feel them between us" (Kennedy, 1993: 126). However, Kennedy seems to point out, in the social relationships that this world is based on, words are all we have.

The final story is also a story of repossessions. Kath repossesses her identity as lover struggling with definitions, wondering which might befit her and becoming aware of the lack of a social category that might register her independence: "You telling me you're not single? You're not married, you're not engaged, you must be single" (Kennedy, 1993: 129). The strictures of social reality are reflected in the woman's perceptions of a constraining physical space. Her husband determines the night geometry of the couple with Kath realising its suffocating pressure and his trespassing into her space:

> You're lying on me. This is my side.
> Which was true, Bobby had always slept on the left hand side. It belonged to him. He was there to be clambered over, or crawled around. For eleven years she had been sandwiched between his back and the wall, his stomach and the wall, his elbows and his knees and the wall. (Kennedy, 1993: 129)

However, this is a story, as March remarks (2002: 137), that offers a character empowered to attain a fulfilling relationship by reclaiming her independence. Leaving her husband, Kath leaves behind the security that the normality of social myths offer but instead learns to see the positive aspects of her independence: "She enjoyed her space now, dreamed expansively, and was glad she hadn't weakened and bought a single bed" (Kennedy, 1993: 129). She learned that while "single" is not a viable definition of herself, accepting it is a starting point for negotiating the limits of her social space. The rejection of rigid, static roles empowers the narrator to repossess her identity as lover in ways that neither restrict her inner life nor impose limits on her physical presence on the social stage. As Kath, looking for the possible dance, finds her own rhythm, she is able to step into the reality of her experiences confident and unafraid:

> Kath felt herself sink into sleep; aware of losing awareness and liking it. Next, she would sleep, while dawn rolled round the world towards tomorrow. Today it was hot. (Kennedy, 1993: 138)

## Conclusion

The short stories collection *Night Geometry and the Garscadden Trains* presents a finely layered account of women's subjectivities as constrained by social myths scripting women's social roles. According to Douglas Gifford, the volume "has a coherence emerging from different perspectives, tones and narratives, so that the reader has a final sense of the author's whole way of looking" (Gifford, 1997: 616). Indeed, the unity of the work is maintained by intertextual cross-references, which also strengthens the sense of fluidity of the discursive space the writer creates, and anchors the reading experience in the present. The texts constitute a discourse with its own ethos making available critical dialogic positions that confront stereotypical socialization patterns. Kennedy exploits the symbolic value of day-to-day gestures, turns of phrase and routine patterns of behaviour from multiple viewpoints in order to capture how women's reality is channelled and regulated by various social myths. She is concerned with the constituencies women inhabit on the social stage and with the ways in which these construct women's subjective realities, exploring how women's subjectivities function in the flux of social life. Kennedy's literary technique relies on fragmentation, shifting perspectives and attention to detail in order to capture how reality is invested subjectively and explore what pressure comes from elements that connect inner life to organized social spaces. Thus, she is able to engage with larger discourses whose reified views of women have helped establish as many mythologies about them. In doing so, she points out how these rigid versions of women have failed to capture the fluidity of their social life.

Engaging social myths of wide significance, Kennedy is sometimes concerned with how these are formed in myths of Scottishness. On the one hand she is concerned with nationalist stories that make official the kind of murder perpetrated through political wars that, official discourses claim, serve a grand historical cause. Kennedy registers the lack of discursive accounts of the murder of "small people" and reveals the need for stories that counteract the prevailing views of national heroes or prestige. The collection on the whole aims to provide accounts of the "ordinariness" of "insignificant" lives that remain side stories to prevailing versions of Scotland and Scottishness: Kennedy neither idealises figures of a glorious past nor is she willing to contribute to the aura of "Scottish working class hero" that some recent writing struggled to create.

The main themes, however, are related to situations of women grappling with the pressures of the social myths of lover, wife and daughter. The stories question the meaning and "reality" of such conceptualizations through strategies that reveal the borderlines between the private and the public creating sites of interaction where the mythological becomes psychological. The conflicts thus revealed are between various geometrical arrangements of society, specifically those of urban Scotland, with women finding it difficult to configure a meaningful identity on their own terms. However, by investing details that often go unnoticed because conceived of as casual in the prevailing social discourses, with symbolic meanings that span entire psychological sites of alternative, fragmentary and discontinuous realities, Kennedy exposes the constructed nature of social myths and shows that their solidity is relative. In changing the symbolic infrastructure of social myths, Kennedy contributes to the strengthening of subject positions for women that are empowering through the new meanings they invest women with, and through the participatory dimension that her strategies uncover.

For all the relativization she performs on social myths, Kennedy's discursive strategies do not create an esoteric subjectivity, thus avoiding traditional dichotomies. Her stories register symptoms of bodily discomfort that complement women's psychological experiences of insufficiency and inadequacy. Psychological discomfort is thus shown as constraining women's ways of socializing their bodies. While the characters' subjectivity is seen as a site of private negotiations of social meanings it is also shown as a space wherein understandings of their bodies are conceived, influencing women's public performance. The reality Kennedy refers to in these stories is neither objective nor confined to transcendental, metaphysical spaces of the mind. Rather, reality is seen as constituted on the interface between the two.

According to Phillips and Hardy, invoking Collins and quoting Boje:

> Microsociologists such as Collins contend that the social world exists neither as an objective entity nor as a set of meanings that people carry in their heads, but in repeated actions of communicating. Collins conceived of these communicating actions as conversations that generate collective action through the *activity* of talking. Narrative theory tells us that action is also generated through the content of talk by "defining characters, sequencing plots, and scripting actions". (Phillips and Hardy, 2002: 56)

Indeed, such theoretical perspectives seem to inform Kennedy's writing and perhaps the author's awareness of such research influenced her stylistic development. Nevertheless, not only does Kennedy show characters striving to establish communication channels but her stories imply the writer's own stance whereby she acts to create dialogic spaces of social negotiation. The short stories of *Night Geometry*… signal a writing style that is attuned to the necessity of communicating women's psychological and social difficulties vis-à-vis social myths that construct them either as symbolic objects referencing their worldliness as wives, lovers and daughters, or within ideal, and therefore unreal, otherworldly spaces. Kennedy's characters definitions, her plot sequencing and the scripting of her scenarios entice women to claim participative membership in the construction of social constituencies. Sketching empowering understandings of women, Kennedy's stories may steer the readers towards positive social action.

## References

Gifford, Douglas. 1997. "Contemporary Fiction II: Seven Writers in Scotland". *A History of Scottish Women's Writing*. Eds. Douglas Gifford and Dorothy McMillan. Edinburgh: Edinburgh University Press. 604-29

Haug Frigga. 1992. *Beyond Female Masochism*. Trans. Rodney Livingstone. London and New York: Verso

Kennedy, A. L. 1993. *Night Geometry and the Garscadden Trains*. London: Phoenix

Kennedy, A. L. 1994. *Looking for the Possible Dance*. London: Minerva

Kennedy, A. L. 2000. *Everything You Need*. London: Vintage

March, Cristie L. 2002. *Rewriting Scotland: Welsh, McLean, Warner, Banks, Galloway and Kennedy*. Manchester and New York: Manchester University Press

Phillips, Nelson and Cynthia Hardy. 2002. *Discourse Analysis. Investigating Processes of Social Construction*. Qualitative Research Methods Series 50. Thousands Oaks, London, New Delhi: Sage Publications

# Inclusive Consciousness: Heaney's Notion of the Exemplary in Yeats[1]

*Sukanya Basu*

Seamus Heaney was born in 1939, significantly in the very same year that W.B.Yeats died. The death of one poet and the birth of the other bring into focus the critical points of continuity and discontinuity that define them as representative Irish poets in their respective eras. While Yeats consciously worked towards and relished the responsibilities of being regarded the leading cultural figure of his time, Heaney has shown a distinct discomfort with being called the "best Irish poet since W.B. Yeats".[2] When asked about his "slipping into the Yeatsian overcoat and so on", Heaney replied that "you cope with it by mocking it and having it mocked for you" (1989a: 5-8). Various critics have made comparisons between the two, from Blake Morrison and Jonathan Allison to Eugene O'Brien who, in his latest book *Seamus Heaney: Searches for Answers* (2003), devotes an entire chapter to discussing the nature and extent of the influence between the two Nobel Prize winning Irish poets.

Austin Clarke (1972: 19) emphasised the nature of the Yeatsian influence on poets on both sides of the border by saying that, "Yeats was rather like an enormous oak-tree, which, of course, kept us in the shade and of course we always hoped that in the end we would reach the sun, but the shadow of that great oak-tree is still there." Writing under that overarching authority, Seamus Heaney too contends with the resulting "anxiety of influence"[3] and he acknowledges Yeats's powerful presence time and again in both his poetry and prose. As Heaney writes in his poem 'Bogland', "Every layer they strip / Seems camped on before" (1998: 41).

As he engages in his own poetic exploration, the reminder of the "great oak-tree" seems to haunt the landscape. There are various ways through which Heaney accommodates and incorporates the spectre of the Yeatsian influence within his own aesthetic system. Heaney's prose-essays and poems need to be analysed closely to dig out the connections between him and his influential literary ancestor. In his foreword to his first prose essay collection *Preoccupations*, Heaney writes, "I had a half-clarified desire to come to poetic terms with myself by considering the example of others" (1980: 13), and his essay 'Yeats as an Example?' in that collection marks a beginning of that course of poetic interaction. Also, Heaney's dialogue with Yeats is an ongoing process that is of vital significance while examining Heaney's own poetic development.

Heaney in his editorial introduction to Yeats's poetry in *The Field Day Anthology of Irish Writing* proclaims Yeats's crucial importance to the history of Irish writing in English: "He has been rightly named a founder, for it was under the aegis of his creative authority that a modern, self-critical and more or less coherent poetic action established itself in Ireland during the last hundred years" (1991: 783). Heaney describes Yeats as both a "national bard" and a "world poet", which extends his influence from the realm of Irish national experience to the more international arena of modern literary practice and reflects on the conjunctions between the two roles. Heaney responds to both of these tendencies in Yeats's work as he charts his

[1] I would like to acknowledge the support of the Research Institute of Irish and Scottish Studies, Aberdeen.
[2] The American poet, Robert Lowell described Heaney's *North* as "a new kind of political poetry by the best Irish poet since W.B.Yeats" (Corcoran 1986: 35).
[3] Harold Bloom's critical term is useful in this context to analyse Irish poets who come after Yeats, like Heaney, who are in no doubt influenced by him. Bloom writes: "Past poets act like the weight of cultural history against whom the strong poet has to struggle to assert himself within the tradition" (1973: 27).

development from a young poet, to a mature and established voice, to finally a renowned public figure of authority.

An important idea that Heaney discovered in Yeats was his drive towards a sense of completeness: "True poetry [...] had to be the speech of the whole man" (Heaney, 1991: 785). He finds reflected in Yeats's life a successful fruition of the idea that the man who sat down to breakfast as a "bundle of accident and incoherence" could be reborn in the poem as something "intended and complete" (Heaney, 1980: 100). In Yeats there is a successful merging of the biographical self with the poetic self to reach a perfect condition of the representative bard who can perfectly emulate and assimilate difference. This willed drive towards wholeness is what Heaney finds vitally exemplary in Yeats's personality and art as he traces Yeats's poetic career:

> He was an artist, devoted to the beautiful; he was a magician, adept among hidden powers; he was a Celt, with a lifeline to the mythological depths; he was a propagandist, with a firm line for journalists. He was all these things, self-consciously and deliberately, yet they did not constitute a dispersal or confusion of his powers or of his personality; on the contrary they concentrated one another, grew from a single root. (1980: 103)

This drive towards unity is also glimpsed in Yeats's Celtic Twilight movement which upheld the Yeatsian idea of the 'Unity of Being', which, though programmatic strove towards an interflow of imaginative energies between the educated and uneducated classes. Heaney quotes Yeats as envisioning a change in the minds of the people through the effects of the imaginative arts:

> We had in Ireland imaginative stories, which the uneducated classes knew and even sang, and might we not make those stories current among the educated classes, rediscovering what I have called 'the applied arts of literature', the association of literature, that is, with music, speech and dance; and at last, it might be so, so deepen the political passion of the nation that all, artist and poet, craftsman and day-labourer would accept a common design? (1989: 240)

This desire for unity and a "common design" did not exclude the notions of variedness and difference in Irish life and Heaney sees Yeats himself as being able to successfully encompass the binaries and oppositions of being Irish within his single entity because of the above mentioned unitary drive of his thought: "Tied by birth to unionism, memorialist of the executed Nationalist rebels of 1916, W.B.Yeats mirrored Ireland's divisions in his self-divisions – yet saw the island as a single cultural entity sprung from common roots in common myths" (Heaney, 1997a: 1).

Heaney himself comments on the essentially complex and diverse nature of Irishness in an interview saying, "I don't think that there is one true bearer of Irishness. There are different versions, different narratives, as we say, and you start out in possession of one of these. Maybe righteously in possession, as one of Yeats's Anglo-Irish, say, – 'no petty people' – or as one of my own 'big-voiced scullions'. But surely you have to grow onto an awareness of the others and attempt to find a way of imagining a whole thing. That really is the challenge, to open the definition and to make the domain of Irishness in Ireland – I hate to use the word *pluralist*, it's so prim and righteous– to make it open and available" (Heaney, 1997b: 117). In his own efforts to open out and make available the various nature of Irish experience, Heaney sees Yeats as an exemplary figure in his ability to take on the strain of both "the major ideologies" of his time. Heaney views poetry as a "working model of inclusive consciousness" (Heaney, 1995: 8) and Eugene O'Brien (2003: 166) rightly identifies the drive towards "complicating the identificatory discourse of Irishness" as an important link between the two poets.

Heaney's prose posits Yeats's art and poetic personality as "dignified, heroic and epoch making" (1991: 783), and expresses admiration towards his "artistic intransigence" because Heaney is aware from his own personal experience of the pressures that impinge on the poet as a public figure. Heaney portrays Yeats as a poet of the sublime who never refrains from emphatically asserting the imaginative power of art. It is this artistic self-belief that Heaney finds exemplary:

> Yeats would never have been 'content to live' merely, because that would have meant throwing words away, throwing gesture away, throwing away possibilities for drama and transcendence. From the beginning of his career he emphasised and realised the otherness of art from life, dream from action, and by the end he moved within his mode of vision as within some invisible ring of influence and defence, some bullet-proof glass of the spirit, exclusive as Caesar in his tent, absorbed as a long-legged fly on the stream. (1980: 99)

Heaney thus identifies in Yeats a kind of "pure, self-possessed energy" that is propelled by his belief that the "artistic process has some kind of absolute validity" (Heaney, 1980: 99). This powerful artistic stance is what illuminates not only his work but is also characteristic of the poetic aura that Yeats created around himself. In spite of later becoming involved with the practicalities of "theatre business, management of men" (Heaney, 1991: 784), Yeats managed to retain his artistic individuality and integrity and that is what Heaney admires. The fact that Yeats's poetic and public selves remained in harmony is what he goes on to highlight. He reiterates that Yeats's wide-ranging interests are unified with the help of his powerful poetic personality: "Yeats bore the implications of his romanticism into action: he propagandized, speechified, fund-raised, administered and politicked in the world of telegrams and anger, all on behalf of the world of vision" (Heaney, 1980: 100).

What he ultimately finds worthy is Yeats's refusal to compromise on his stance as an artist: "I assume that this peremptoriness this apparent arrogance, is exemplary in an artist that it is proper and even necessary for him to insist on his own language, his own vision, his own terms of reference. This will often seem like irresponsibility or affectation, sometimes like callousness, but from the artist's point of view it is an act of integrity, or an act of cunning to protect the integrity" (Heaney, 1980: 101). Heaney seems to approve of the qualities of being secretive and cunning as ways through which poetic integrity can be maintained. Heaney's poems are often characterised by a subtle evasiveness and obliqueness that make it difficult to pin him down to a single position. In *Crediting Poetry* Heaney talks about the ability of poetry to tell the truth at a slant. There is a quality of constant movement in poems such as 'The Frontier of Writing' (1998: 297) where in a car he is able to pass through the roadblocks, the "armour-plated vehicles" and the "posted soldiers", to a space that is "arraigned yet freed". Though the idea of breaking through past the barriers is qualified by the use of the term "arraigned", the idea of the ungoverned tongue is important to Heaney's aesthetics. For Heaney the idea of poetic authority is intimately connected with the notion of poetic integrity and it is towards that he strives in his work. He asserts in his essay 'The Government of the Tongue' that, "The poetic art is credited with an authority of its own. As readers, we submit to the jurisdiction of achieved form, even though that form is achieved not by dint of the moral or ethical exercise of mind but by the self-validating operations of what we call inspiration" (1988: 92). He reaffirms this in 'The Redress of Poetry' and uses a Yeats quote to state his case: "Poetry cannot afford to lose its fundamentally self-delighting inventiveness, its joy in being a process of language as well as a representation of things in the world. To put it in W.B.Yeats's terms, the will must not usurp the work of the imagination" (1995: 5).

For Heaney, this desire for autonomous poetic authority and the assertion of the power of lyric poetry is mixed with a sense of *responsibility* towards the historical suffering and pain of reality. He thus finds as exemplary those moments in Yeats's poems where his "powerful artistic control is vulnerable to the pain or pathos of life itself" (1980: 109). Heaney cites the Yeats poem 'The Man and the Echo' as a case in point: "But hush, for I have lost the theme, / its joy or night seem but a dream; / Up there some hawk or owl has struck / Dropping out of sky or rock, / A stricken rabbit is crying out / And its cry distracts my thought" (Heaney, 2000: 130). Heaney seems to prefer these moments which point to Yeats's "large-minded, whole hearted assent to the natural cycles of living and dying", rather than the more "sinister" and "predatory" appetites suggested by poems such as the 'Lapis Lazuli', or the more consciously theatrical tone of poems such as 'Hound Voice', or the violent undertones of 'The Statues'. The tension between the forces of violence and harmony is also enacted in a poem such as 'Meditations in Time of Civil War' and Heaney, in his reading of the poem, once again highlights the gentler, nurturing aspects to the darker ones, as it is suggestive of his own aesthetic beliefs. In his Nobel Lecture *Crediting Poetry* he reads the image of the honey-bee in the poem as suggestive of "the ideal of an industrious, harmonious nurturing commonwealth" (Heaney, 1998: 463) which counteracts the violent destructiveness of the Civil War underlying the verses. Heaney finds in the lines "Come build in the empty house of the stare" a poetic voice that is able to "touch the base of our sympathetic nature while taking in at the same time the unsympathetic reality of the world to which that nature is constantly exposed" (1998: 467). They become examples of what Heaney calls the "fully realised poem" where "the coordinates of the imagined thing correspond to and allow us to contemplate the complex burden of our own experience" (Heaney, 1995: 10). Heaney thus believes that Yeats's poetry succeeds in effecting "the redress of poetry" by attempting an "act of writing that outstrips the conditions even as it observes them" (1995: 159).

In addition, the figure of the fisherman also binds the two poets together and explores another theme important to both. Heaney notes in the early Yeats a "great desire to attach himself to a tradition and a corpus of belief that was communal" (1980: 106) which later changed by the time he wrote 'The Fisherman', where the fisherman is the solitary artist surrounded by a philistine, cleric-dominated mob. When the real world clashes with the world of art, Yeats constructs his ideal "in scorn of this audience" (Yeats, 1989: 252). The ideal survives in art but is finally merely a dream that does not exist in reality. In Heaney's poem 'Casualty', the real world again collides with that of the artist. The fisherman here, however, is real and is the solitary curfew-breaker who goes against the dictates of his tribe and pays for this disobedience with his life. The poet claims to have tasted freedom in the company of the fisherman friend miles out in the sea, away from the brutal realities of the Troubles. There is the desire to move "well-out, beyond", which is destroyed by the reality of the bomb that kills the fisherman. The individual and the community are set in opposition and the poet uses the figure of his dead friend to question tribal fealties: "Dawn-sniffing revenant, / plodder through midnight rain, / Question me again?" (1998: 154). The opposition of the individual with a larger society or community is crucial in explaining Yeats's later posture as a man who became increasingly alienated from the middle-classes because of his growing disenchantment with the course of Irish history. Heaney explains this shift in tone from an attaching 'we' to a detaching 'I' to his being an "Anglo-Irish Protestant deeply at odds with the mind of Irish Catholic society". Heaney too seeks to move beyond the narrow categories of tribal or communal identities in poems such as 'The First Flight' where he "fends" off the mires of attachment as he masters "new rungs of the air / to survey out of reach"(1998: 273).

In seeking to respond responsibly to the violent realities of the North, Heaney once again turns to Yeats who worked through turbulent periods of Irish history. Heaney talks about how poetry at its greatest moments should attempt, in Yeats's phrase, "to hold in a single thought reality and justice" (Yeats 1962: 25). He mentions this again in *Crediting Poetry* while debating on how to conduct oneself "as a poet in a situation of ongoing political violence and public expectation" (1998: 451). He looks to Yeats in that regard and decides the best way to answer is to be true to the poetic impulse without the binds of factional propaganda. On being asked whether Yeats was a political poet, Heaney replies in an interview that Yeats was essentially a "public poet" like Sophocles:

> Yeats isn't a factional political poet, even if he does represent a definite sector of Irish society and culture and has been castigated by Marxists for having that reactionary, aristocratic prejudice to his imagining. But the whole effort of the imagining is towards inclusiveness. Prefiguring a future. So of course he is a poet of immense political significance, but I think of him as a visionary rather than political. (Heaney, 1997b: 104)

In the same interview, Heaney agonises over the inefficacy of poetic creation in the face of politicised crises and writes that "Auden's remark that poetry makes nothing happen is used too often" to foreclose the question about whether poetry can affect politics. Using Robert Lowell as an example he states that poets can have a political effect, not simply due to the "thematic content" of their work, but because of their established "profile" and "authority" as a poet. He says that like Lowell it is important to exude a visible *gravitas* so that one's intervention in political matters can have a political effect. This aura of influence is what he locates more importantly in the figure of Yeats. The figure of the poet as a public figure becomes iconic, a symbol of resonance in the public world which has a power of statement beyond one's art itself.

In his piece on Yeats in the *Fortnight Supplement* (1989) Heaney writes that Yeats was possessed of that necessary *gravitas* by the age of 50. He goes on to note that in the collections *The Wild Swans at Coole* (1919), *The Tower* (1928) and *The Winding Stair* (1933), Yeats spoke as the voice of greatly representative imagination beyond any party or faction but "utterly from himself and for himself ". This is what Heaney means when he talks about the achievement of a poem as an experience of release: "The fact is that poetry is its own reality and no matter how much a poet may concede to the corrective pressures of social, moral, political and historical reality, the ultimate fidelity should be to the demands and promise of the artistic event" (1998: 101). The poet as a poet is able break free of civic constraints and the bind of one's community to a larger enunciation of identity: "Yeats the poet both endures and embodies the whole field of forces active in Ireland and the world beyond, and is as responsive to the apocalyptic side of himself as to the elegiac" (Heaney, 1989b: II).

What Heaney perceives as laudable is Yeats's nobility, which has nothing to do with birth or rank, but is concerned with the measure of what Wallace Stevens called "our spiritual height and depth" (Stevens, 1984: 36). In his later life and work Yeats "divests himself of his domestic identity to become the voice of a dramatically encompassing imagination, he dons the mantle of the wisdom-speaker and the memory-speaker and becomes the shaman figure who confronts menace with ritual song" (Heaney, 1989b: III). In the figure of Yeats the tower-dweller, Heaney locates a space where the poet was able to immure himself against the world of flux and change. In the later poems the local, historical features of Ireland fall away to reveal the "place of writing" where the poet is able to assume his imagined role as poet-prophet. Thus, in his great poems one feels "the imagination pressing back against the pressure of reality" (Heaney, 1989b: III). Imagination succeeds and self-transformation is achieved.

Heaney's own verse too could be said to chart a movement from the early darkness and the violence of the wells and the Bog-poems to the "shifting brilliancies" of *Seeing Things*: "Me waiting until I was nearly fifty / To credit marvels … / So long for air to brighten, / Time to be dazzled and the heart to lighten" (1998: 347). This recalls Yeats own poem 'Vacillation' which reads. "My fiftieth year had come and gone / … While on the shop and street I gazed / My body of a sudden blazed; / And twenty minutes more or less / it seemed, so great my happiness, / That I was blessed and could bless" (Yeats, 1989: 364). In crediting the marvellous, Heaney, in his later poetry, is able to strike out with confidence towards a newer ways of seeing things.

In his later poem 'Postscript' Heaney engages with Yeats's 'Wild Swans at Coole' and describes poetic inspiration and insight as "A hurry through which known and strange things pass / As big soft buffetings come at the car sideways / and catch the heart off guard and blow it open" (1998: 444). This sudden concentration of power that opens up newer possibilities is what poetry attempts to do, to catch the reader unawares and renew his vision of the world. This is what Heaney takes from Yeats. Eliot is probably correct when he writes that Yeats's real impact was in posture and attitude: "His idiom was too different for there to be any danger of imitation […] the influence of which I speak is due to the figure of the poet himself, to the integrity of his passion for his act and craft which provided such an impulse for its extraordinary development" (1953: 249). Heaney himself seeks to fulfil the social role of "redress" during times of crises when he is "pressed to give voice to much that has hitherto been denied expression in the ethnic, social, sexual and political life" (Heaney, 1995: 5). Yet that public role has with it the burden of public expectation that is "not of poetry as such but of political positions variously approvable by mutually disapproving groups" (1998: 451). Yet learning from Yeats's example he wrestles with those difficult questions and emerges out of them wiser and more confident about the healing sources of poetry:

> For years I was bowed to the desk like some monk bowed over his prie-dieu […Ö] in an attempt to bear his portion of the weight of the world knowing, himself incapable of heroic virtue or redemptive effect, but constrained by his obedience to his rule to repeat the effort and the posture […] Then finally and happily, and not in obedience of dolorous circumstances of my native place but in spite of them, I straightened up. I began a few years ago to try and make space in my reckoning and imagining for the marvellous as well as the murderous. (1998: 458)

Heaney's poetry and prose sound a tentative note of hope which, if only a "momentary stay against confusion" (1995: 194), is a moment of harmony where the oppositions merge in the frontier of writing. With time Heaney's voice has gained the sort of *gravitas* that he had earlier located in Yeats. For him, though, the journey is still on, and as he moves forward the authority that he had sought in his predecessor is slowly granted to his creative voice.

## References

Bloom, Harold. 1973. *The Anxiety of Influence*. Oxford: Oxford University Press

Clarke, Austin. 1972. *Irish Literary Portraits*. Ed. W.R. Rodgers. London: British Broadcasting Corporation

Corcoran, Neil. 1986. *Seamus Heaney*. London: Faber

Eliot, T.S. 1953. *Selected Essays*. London: Faber

Heaney, Seamus. 1980. *Preoccupations: Selected Prose 1968-78*. London: Faber

Heaney, Seamus. 1988. *The Government of the Tongue*. London: Faber

Heaney, Seamus. 1989a. Interview. "Calling the Tune." Interviewer Tom Adair. *The Linehall Review*. Belfast. 5-8

Heaney, Seamus. 1989b. "Yeats' Nobility". *Fortnight Supplement*. 27: March II-III

Heaney, Seamus. 1991. "William Butler Yeats". In ed. Seamus Deane. *The Field Day Anthology of Irish Writing*. Vol. II. Cork: Cork University Press

Heaney, Seamus. 1995. *The Redress of Poetry: Oxford Lectures*. London: Faber

Heaney, Seamus. 1997a. "All Ireland's Bard", *The Atlantic Monthly Online*. November. www.the atlantic.com/issues/97nov/yeats.htm

Heaney, Seamus. 1997b. Interview. "The Art of Poetry". Interviewer H. Cole. *Paris Review* 144: 89-136

Heaney, Seamus. 1998. *Opened Ground: Poems 1966-1996*. London: Faber

Stevens, Wallace. 1984. *The Necessary Angel*. London: Faber

Yeats, W.B. 1989. *Autobiographies: Reveries over Childhood and Youth and the Trembling Veil*. London: Macmillan

Yeats, W.B. 1962. *A Vision*. London: Macmillan

Yeats, W.B. 1989. *Yeats's Poems*. London: Macmillan

Yeats, W.B. 2000. *W.B.Yeats: Poems selected by Seamus Heaney*. London: Faber

# "Indifference and Sentimentality": Louis MacNeice's Ireland

*Laura Bok*

> Who was – and am – dumbfounded to find myself
> In a topographical frame – here, not there –
> The channels of my dreams determined largely
> By random chemistry of soil and air … (MacNeice, 2001: 73)

For Louis MacNeice, born in Belfast to Protestant parents, who themselves were children of Ireland's West, resident in England from the age of ten, his national identity could never be anything but problematic. An exile from his country of birth by choice, MacNeice would remain "too English for the Irish and too Irish for the English" (McDonald, 8) all his life and long after his death. Critics have frequently been unable to "place" MacNeice: for years, he was only grudgingly allowed a place in the canon of Irish literature. One finds critics making widely disparate statements about him, frequently assigning the poet his "proper" place with quite astonishing assurance. Compare Terence Brown's claim that:

> MacNeice did not become, at any stage in his career, fully integrated into English society despite the fact that England was his chosen country of residence and the country that gave him his livelihood. (Brown, 1975: 13)

with Derek Mahon's feeling that "his place was in Oxford, Hampstead or Broadcasting House, among Englishmen who had had the same sort of education as himself" (21). Yet the same Mahon declares that "whoever he is, he is not an Englishman" (29). MacNeice could not escape his split identity if he had wanted to: as Brown points out, "the English tended to think of him as Irish; critics referred to his nationality when they reviewed his books" (13). Viewed as an outsider both in England and in Ireland, MacNeice is "granted at best a resident alien status" (McDonald, 8) in the literary canons of both nations.

"Reading through the *Collected Poems* of Louis MacNeice one notices that, in purely quantitative terms, there is not a great deal specifically about Ireland", says Derek Mahon (21); however, the few poems in which MacNeice does allow Ireland a starring role are all the more fascinating because of what they reveal of their author's feelings towards his motherland at different stages in his life. "In the beginning was the Irish rain" (MacNeice, 1996: 216), is MacNeice's own biblically inspired description of his origins, and this paper shall explore what effect such a background had on the work of the notoriously "displaced" poet.

Rather than indulging in a schizophrenic battle between an irreconcilable "Irish" and "English" self, MacNeice himself never appeared too concerned about being "displaced" in English/Irish terms: at a young age, considering his imminent departure from Ireland to attend boarding school in England, he thought of his Irishness not as something to set him apart from his English schoolfellows, only as an extra asset he could use to good effect:

> And among the other boys I was going to be prominent; remembering school stories I had read I thought I would exploit the fact that I was Irish; the Irish boys or girls in the stories did what they liked and were always popular. (MacNeice, 1996: 63)

MacNeice later remembered being "vastly excited" on first arrival to find England "not just an imitation of Ireland" (1996: 221) – there is no hint of homesickness, then or later. There were many factors that eventually swayed the balance in favour of England as his chosen place of domicile, plain force of habit being just one of them. In fact, MacNeice's inner conflict was not a tortured division of affection between Ireland and England, but an awareness of being torn "between Connemara and Carrickfergus, one way of being 'Irish' and another" (McDonald, 204). MacNeice, who described himself as "an Irishman of Southern blood and Northern upbringing, whose father was a Protestant bishop and also a fervent Home Ruler" (MacNeice, 1990: 189), was devoted to Dublin, disgusted by Irish nationalist navel-gazing, and felt that his true roots lay in the West. He was, however, born in Belfast, and his attitude towards his place of birth shall be examined first.

"I was born in Belfast between the mountain and the gantries" (MacNeice, 2001: 22). Thus, in his poem "Carrickfergus", the poet asserts his claim to Belfast, "that Northern anti-Athens" (MacNeice, 1990: 222), as his own, declaring his right to speak his mind about the city that was his home during the first year of his life. MacNeice rarely had a good word to say about his birthplace, a place that evidently never made him feel like he belonged. Apart from the harsh accent, "not only the ugliest but the least aristocratic of the lot" (1990: 223), the very name of the city seemed hostile to his young ears: "Belfast itself sounded hard and unrelenting", recalls the poet in his memoirs, but he fairly admits that "this may have been due to its associations" (1990: 218). Dublin, on the other hand, "was a glorious name in our family and had pleasurable associations of violence" (1990: 222); clearly, the courtesy extended to the unknown, exotic city MacNeice was only too pleased to appropriate as his own did not apply to the unloved and unlovable city that was his own. We shall examine MacNeice's "tale of two cities" more closely anon.

MacNeice's dislike of Belfast as a physical entity is vividly expressed in the poem of the same name, using images so ugly in sound and colour as to create an impression of almost palpable revulsion:

> Down there at the end of the melancholy lough
> Against the lurid sky over the stained water
> Where hammers clang murderously on the girders
> Like crucifixes the gantries stand. (MacNeice, 2001: 6)

Belfast Lough could naturally not be perceived as anything but "melancholy", while the shipyards and their murderous hammers are sentenced to "down there at the end". The sky is "lurid", the water "stained", but the furious activity of the shipyard carries even more sinister connotations: the words "murderously" and "crucifixes" combine to evoke the religion-based sectarian violence that still blights Belfast today. This is clearly no ordinary industrial town; as Edna Longley says, "In these images Belfast's industry provides the correlatives for some infinitely worse affliction" (1994: 105). This is Belfast at its bleakest. But it is not just the city that is diseased, its people are equally tainted. The poem regards Belfast as unequivocally male, with "the male kind" being responsible for the town's sick condition:

> The sun goes down with a banging of Orange drums
> While the male kind murders each its woman
> To whose prayer for oblivion answers no Madonna. (2001: 6)

The sun goes down on Belfast leaving both sides of the sectarian divide groping in the dark. The menacing soundtrack of the ultra-masculine Orange drums provides an ominous backdrop to the death of all gentler considerations, whereas "the garish Virgin" preserves an unhelpful silence and does not lift a maternal or sisterly finger to help.

MacNeice enjoyed pointing out the differences between Belfast and Dublin, the comparison invariably working out to the disadvantage of the former. While he occasionally conceded Belfast some redeeming features, MacNeice would never make quite as many allowances for his birthplace as for Dublin, his adopted "home from home" (1990: 250). Writing of the two cities in his memoirs, MacNeice tried to even out the balance by giving both their share of good and bad:

> Today I am so at home in Dublin, more than in any other city, that I feel it has always been familiar to me. But, as with Belfast it took me years to penetrate its outer ugliness and dourness, so with Dublin it took me years to see through its soft charm to its bitter prickly kernel – which I quite like too. (1996: 222)

Although Dublin is said to have its darker sides, one is left with the impression that these are really quite attractive and exciting, while ugly and dour Belfast is still dealt a rather poor hand, with none of *its* charm being specified at all.

Yet for all his denunciation of Belfast as a "gloomy" place, and for all the delight he obviously took in contrasting the unfortunate northern city with its superficially friendlier and more glamorous southern counterpart, one cannot help but feel that there is a grudging affection that underlies the relentless stream of abuse hurled at the troubled capital of the North. One senses that MacNeice's flat statement, "This was my mother-city", in "Valediction" (2001: 11-14), a poem that sees MacNeice lashing out with grim pleasure at what is rotten in the state of his motherland, is a reluctant admission of an inescapable but distasteful fact; still, the statement is made with some defiance and is followed by the colloquial and intimate qualification, "these my paps" (2001: 11). MacNeice unintentionally reveals some of his feelings when recording his first impressions of London, the city where he lived for many years. It is thus that he expresses his amazement at the "otherness" of London: "it was not Belfast, it was *foreign*. And foreign it has remained to me" (MacNeice, 1996: 221; emphasis added). London, the foreign city, never home, is contrasted with Belfast: home in spite of all.

As his continual juxtaposing of Belfast and Dublin shows, MacNeice had a particular soft spot for Dublin. But even Dublin does not escape the firing range of his critical eye in "Valediction", the poem in which he swings a poetic demolition ball at most things Irish, being as it is the starting point of the sightseeing tour for the patriotic Irishman:

> Park your car in the city of Dublin, see Sackville Street
> Without the sandbags in the old photos, meet
> The statues of the patriots, history never dies,
> At any rate in Ireland, arson and murder are legacies. (2001: 11)

These same elevated patriots, representatives of Ireland's tumultuous past, whose very presence ensures the continuance of egocentric nationalism, reappear as "Declamatory bronze / On sombre pedestals" in "Dublin" (2001: 47), the first poem in a collection written during a visit to Ireland at the outbreak of the Second World War.[1] The poem, which, as McDonald points out, harkens back to Yeats' "Easter 1916" in metre and imagery (McDonald, 100), appears to be a futile declaration of love to the city of "seedy elegance":

> This was never my town,
> I was not born nor bred
> Nor schooled here and she will not
> Have me alive or dead .... (2001: 47)

---

[1] Originally published as "The Coming of War", it was renamed "The Closing Album".

The four lines neatly emphasize how tenuous the thread is that binds MacNeice to Dublin, and he generously admits: "I like it of course more than it likes me" (1990: 250). He stresses almost gleefully that "She is not an Irish town / And she is not English" (2001: 48); the implication being that both the poet and the town have split identities. As Edna Longley says, "Dublin's mongrel genealogy resembles his own" (1988: 27). However, MacNeice's devotion to the city does not make him forget its less attractive aspects, and Yeats' famous poem, a hallowed symbol of Irish patriotism, is deliberately echoed at a time when nationalism had acquired sour connotations and was causing the Irish State to remain blind to the turmoil on the continent. Still, MacNeice's acknowledgment, "You give me time for thought / And by a juggler's trick / You poise the toppling hour" (2001: 48), indicates that at this crucial moment, Dublin, juggling its conflicting associations, served as the safe retreat the London-based poet required.

MacNeice's childhood was mainly spent in the Rectory at Carrickfergus – abbreviated to Carrick, "which in the local voice sounded like a slap in the face" (MacNeice, 1996: 218) – a house with a large garden which would feature often in his poetry. Ulster at large did not please him any better than its capital. Carrickfergus' depressing surroundings were immortalized in particularly mournful verse in "Carrickfergus":

> The brook ran yellow from the factory stinking of chlorine,
> The yarn-mill called its funeral cry at noon;
> Our lights looked over the lough to the lights of Bangor
> Under the peacock aura of a drowning moon. (2001: 22)

The "stained water" of the "melancholy lough" in "Belfast" has been turned into Carrickfergus' yellow stinking brook, and again the local industry provides associations of death: the "funeral cry", the "drowning moon". The inhabitants were no better: MacNeice would later remember the mill girls, "their voices harsh and embittered and jeering", and the men on corners with their "narrow leering eyes, and sour mouths" (MacNeice, 1996: 49).

The inevitable association of Ulster with the "Troubles" ensured that it would never be let off lightly in MacNeice's imagination. Though part of Northern Ireland's dominant Protestant majority, MacNeice did not adopt the attitudes generally entertained by the more extreme members of this class. Nor did he embrace "the Irish myth of Irishness, with its menacing, but ultimately empty, phantom of national 'identity'" (McDonald, 1). He showed a keen awareness of his separation from the greater part of the Irish population by means of his religion and, consequently, class: "I was the rector's son, born to the anglican order, / Banned for ever from the candles of the Irish poor" (2001: 22). Being neither a Catholic nor underprivileged, factors that he regarded as uniting the "Irish poor", MacNeice felt distanced from his fellow countrymen. However, displays of religious and cultural fervour from the Protestant side, especially Orangism, were equally alien to MacNeice. His childhood memories of seeing Orangemen practising, "their faces set like Crusaders and the whole country rocking with the noise" (1996: 57), reverberate not only in "Belfast", but reappear as the sinister "voodoo of the Orange bands" in "Autumn Journal XVI" (2001: 38).

"Autumn Journal XVI" (2001: 37-41) – written on the eve of World War II – and "Valediction" (2001: 11-14) are the two oft-cited poems in which MacNeice takes an axe to everything that exasperated him about Ireland. "Valediction" is a breathless journey through clichéd Irish tourist spots and explores the darker side of the shamrock, as well as the implications of MacNeice's impotent rage against his motherland for his own position as an Irishman in exile. The uglier consequences of Ireland's obsession with its past have been discussed above with reference to Dublin, where MacNeice deplored the fact that "arson and murder are legacies" of Ireland's living history. His irritation with Irish "storms in a broken teacup"[2] would only increase during the build-up to World War II, in which Ireland, too self-absorbed to care in MacNeice's view, chose to remain neutral. In "Valediction", however, MacNeice struggles with "the trick beauty of a prism", rejecting and loving Ireland in spite of himself:

> I can say Ireland is hooey, Ireland is
> A gallery of fake tapestries,
> But I cannot deny my past to which my self is wed,
> The woven figure cannot undo its thread. (2001: 12)

Like it or not, MacNeice is never able to escape his Irish roots, and to deny them would be tantamount to a self-denial. By calling Ireland "hooey", he is effectively undermining his own position. He is part of Ireland's fabric; if its tapestries are fake, then so is the woven figure that is MacNeice: "Cursèd be he that curses his mother. I cannot be / Anyone else than what this land engendered me" (2001: 12). His answer to this dilemma is a decision to "become as one of your holiday visitors" and he declares: "Farewell, my country, and in perpetuum" (2001: 13). That the farewell can never be "in perpetuum" is made clear not only by the way he "attaches the possessive pronoun to Ireland" (Longley, 1985: 105), but also by the poem's final section. Although seemingly an abdicative blessing – "Therefore I resign, goodbye the chequered and the quiet hills / The gaudily-striped Atlantic" (2001: 13) – the last line looks back in anger to the evils of sectarianism and Ireland's unhealthy reverence of past heroes by saluting "Your drums and your dolled-up Virgins and your ignorant dead" (2001: 14).

"Autumn Journal XVI" (2001: 37-41) resumes MacNeice's love/hate-relationship (summed up in Catullus' famous, if misquoted, dictum, *odi et amo* – a cliché in itself) with Ireland and its politics, now thrown into sharp relief by the greater political turmoil on the continent. As in "Valediction", he sarcastically attacks Ireland's hackneyed and hypocritical self-image:

> The land of scholars and saints:
> Scholars and saints my eye, the land of ambush,
> Purblind manifestoes, never-ending complaints ... (2001: 38)

The first section of the poem is a "pouring of scorn on both Irish houses" (McDonald, 88), though the poet includes himself in the imprecation by using the word "we" for the infighting Irish. He criticizes the inward-looking policies that have isolated Ireland at a time of international crisis: "Let the round tower stand aloof / In a world of bursting mortar!" (2001: 39). His frustration is communicated in the rhetorical question "Why should I want to go back / To you, Ireland, my Ireland?" (2001: 40). With an impending war, Ireland and its internal strife have nothing to offer:

> The blots on the page are so black
> That they cannot be covered with shamrock.
> I hate your grandiose airs,
> Your sob-stuff, your laugh and your swagger,
> Your assumption that everyone cares
> Who is the king of your castle. (2001: 40)

Again, MacNeice confronts Ireland with its own clichés. The Irish character itself is under fire, especially its penchant for self-importance at a time when the world has other matters to

---

[2] From MacNeice's "Prologue" to the never-published essay-collection *The Character of Ireland* (Brown and Reid, 2). The poem was completed in 1959.

consider. Yet, as in "Valediction", Ireland remains "my Ireland" (2001: 40). However, this time MacNeice claims to be ready to say goodbye to the country and his own "useless memories", and he admonishes himself: "Better close the horizon, / Send her no more fantasy, no more longings" (2001: 40).

While Ireland was doing too much on the national and not enough on the international political stage, MacNeice himself made a conscious decision to travel to Ireland when it became clear that war was inevitable. He was in Galway when Germany invaded Poland, in Dublin when Britain declared war on Germany, and subsequently spent some time with his family in Cushendun; all of these places are commemorated in "The Closing Album" (2001: 47-51). Although his poetic acumen cut like a razor through Irish sentimentality, he allowed "the fatalist within" to persuade him, "'War or no war, you have got to go back to the West. If only for a week. Because you may never again'" (1996: 210). For MacNeice, the West of Ireland, where his family's roots lay, had always been a "dream world", especially in contrast to "the puritanism and mud" (1990: 222) of Ulster. His parents, particularly his mother, often spoke of Connemara:

> The very name Connemara seemed too rich for any ordinary place. It appeared to be a country of windswept open spaces and mountains blazing with whins and seas that were never quiet, with drowned palaces beneath them, and seals and eagles and turf smoke and cottagers who were always laughing and who gave you milk when you asked for a glass of water. (1996: 216-217)

MacNeice's sister Elizabeth remembered the effect these stories had on the young children:

> It became for us both a "many-coloured land", a kind of lost Atlantis where we thought that by rights we should be living, and it came to be a point of honour that we did not belong to the North of Ireland. We were in our minds a West of Ireland family exiled from our homeland. (Brown and Reid, 14)

It was his separation, by accident of birth from this west that, more than anything else, made MacNeice feel like a displaced person. However, he was not to set foot in his beloved "home ground" until he was twenty, an experience he described as his "home-coming" (1996: 111). He would later admit: "for many years I lived on a nostalgia for somewhere I had never been" (1996: 217). "Acquisition of the West as his dream world seems fully deliberate", says Dillon Johnston (222): it would serve as a shield against Northern bleakness, the tortuous intricacies of Irish politics and international confusion, and MacNeice would celebrate the "quintessential West" in "Western Landscape" (1979: 255-7), written in 1945, as a timeless place of refuge:

> For the western climate is Lethe,
> The smoky taste of cooking on turf is lotus,
> There are affirmation and abnegation together
> From the broken bog with its veins of amber water…. (1979: 255)

Far from unleashing his critical powers on Ireland, he now humbly asks for permission to celebrate it: "let me honour this country" (1979: 257).

Trying to define MacNeice's attitude towards Ireland, Terence Brown states that

> MacNeice for all his disillusion with his native country could never manage to break with it. He remained to his death an exile rather than an ex-patriot, unable to sever all links with Ireland. (12)

We may ask why MacNeice *should* have to break with Ireland. Living in England enabled him to observe Ireland both as an outsider and as an insider, and his "sense of deracination" (Johnston, 219) made it possible for him to feel both affection and revulsion, to flaunt both his sentimentality and his sarcasm.

As McDonald says, "In terms of 'belonging' to Ireland, MacNeice is relying upon displacement not just for his own independence, but in order to clarify, or read deeply into, the Irish condition" (215-16). MacNeice's final word may be taken from his 1959 poem "Prologue" (quoted in Stallworthy 488-91) in which he effectively "tots up his factors" as he could not quite do in "Valediction". Here, finally, he can regard with equanimity Ireland's "Pros and cons, glitter and filth", and look fondly on as "this island, / Hitched to the sun that sets in the Atlantic, / Lumbers into her misty west".

# References

Brown, Terence, and Alec Reid, eds. 1974. *Time Was Away: The World of Louis MacNeice*. Dublin: The Dolmen Press

Brown, Terence. 1975. *Louis MacNeice: Sceptical Vision*. Dublin: Gill and Macmillan

Johnston, Dillon. 1997. *Irish Poetry after Joyce*. Syracuse: Syracuse University Press

Longley, Edna. 1985. "Louis MacNeice: 'The Walls Are Flowing'". *Across a Roaring Hill: The Protestant Imagination in Modern Ireland*. Eds. Gerald Dawe and Edna Longley. Belfast: Blackstaff Press

Longley, Edna. 1988. *Louis MacNeice: A Critical Study*. London: Faber

Longley, Edna. 1994. *The Living Stream: Literature and Revisionism in Ireland*. Newcastle upon Tyne: Bloodaxe

Longley, Edna. 1996. *Poetry in the Wars*. Newcastle upon Tyne: Bloodaxe

MacNeice, Louis. 1979. *The Collected Poems of Louis MacNeice*. Ed. E.R. Dodds. London: Faber.

MacNeice, Louis. 1990. *Selected Prose of Louis MacNeice*. Ed. Alan Heuser. Oxford: Clarendon Press

MacNeice, Louis. 1996. *The Strings are False: An Unfinished Autobiography*. London: Faber

MacNeice, Louis. 2001. *Louis MacNeice: Poems Selected by Michael Longley*. Ed. Michael Longley. London: Faber

Mahon, Derek. 1996. *Journalism: Selected Prose 1970-1995*. Oldcastle: Gallery Press

McDonald, Peter. 1991. *Louis MacNeice: The Poet in His Contexts*. Oxford: Clarendon Press

Stallworthy, Jon. 1995. *Louis MacNeice*. London: Faber

# Leopold von Ranke and Ireland: The Creation of an Irish Identity in Ranke's *History of England.*

*Andreas Boldt*

This paper will examine the relationship between the German historian Leopold von Ranke (1795-1886) and Ireland and his writing of Irish history in particular. It will concentrate on Ranke's Irish wife, Clarissa Graves, and her family, and explore the manner in which these relationships influenced Ranke's writing of Irish history. After their marriage in England Clarissa Graves went to Berlin to live until her death in 1871. During this time Clarissa von Ranke built up a kind of social circle, better known as the "Salon Ranke", where people of all professions and nationalities met to exchange their ideas and knowledge. Clarissa's brothers Charles, John and Robert Graves had access to Irish manuscripts and they helped Ranke to write his work *History of England* (1859-68). Within his work Ranke stresses the importance of Ireland as an independent nation. As his work does not follow the traditional non-manuscript based polemical works from England, Ranke can be regarded as the father of modern Irish historiography. The paper will give an insight into how far Ranke's work influenced Irish identity and history by not only examining his writing, the manuscripts and books he used, but Ranke's work was influenced by his Irish wife.

Leopold von Ranke was the most influential historian of the nineteenth century. He made important contributions to the emergence of modern history as a discipline and he has been called the father of 'scientific' history. Due to him, methodical principles of archival research and source criticism became commonplace in academic institutions and he is generally credited with the professionalisation of the historian's craft. Ranke was born in Germany in 1795 and taught for seven years in a grammar school (*Gymnasium*) at Frankfurt an der Oder. His first major work, *History of the Latin and Teutonic nations, 1494-1535*, was published late in 1824. This was based on archival research, viewed by Ranke as the foundation of all historical work, and it established his reputation as an historian. Because of the success of his book, Ranke was appointed Professor of History at the University of Berlin. Ranke went abroad late in 1827 and remained away for over three years, searching out documents in Vienna, Florence, Rome and Venice. He had many well-placed connections, which he put to good use, securing access to archives that had not been opened before. The following years were marked with publications mainly on the history of Mediterranean countries and Germany. Particularly noteworthy are *The Conspiracy against Venice* (1831), *History of the Popes* (1836-36) and *History of the Reformation in Germany* (1839 47).

Ranke's marriage to an Irish woman in 1843 changed his whole life. Clarissa Helena Graves, born in Dublin in 1808, came from the well-known Graves family. The Graves family was highly educated and was, in effect, an intellectual dynasty. The roots of the Graves family go back to 1647, when Colonel Graves of Mickleton in Gloucestershire commanded a regiment of horse in the army of the Parliament volunteering for service in Ireland the same year. As a result of the Cromwellian Settlement the Graves family acquired lands and later public office in Limerick.[1] Clarissa's father was John Crosbie Graves (1776-1835) who was Chief Police Magistrate in Dublin. In 1806 he married Helena Perceval from the equally well-known Perceval family who had lived in Ireland for centuries. From 1814 John Crosbie Graves lived at 12 FitzWilliam Square, Dublin.

---

[1] Note of Charles Graves, Royal Irish Academy, Miscellaneous Photostats, Parcel I, No. 14; Cooke, J. 1997. "The Graves family in Ireland". *In Dublin Historical Record*, vol. L, No. 1. 25.

Ranke and Clarissa Graves encountered each other first in Paris around July/August 1843 and they met several times subsequently. A few notes in Ranke's diary indicate that they made a few day trips as well. In September Ranke went to London, followed by Clarissa and her mother. On 1 October they got engaged and on 26 October Clarissa's brother Robert Perceval officiated at the marriage in Bowness, Windermere, Westmoreland. On the same day of their marriage Ranke left England with his wife and headed back to Berlin. Arriving back in Berlin everybody was surprised to learn that Ranke was married. Clarissa was welcomed in Berlin and it was easy for her to make her life in her new home. Soon she became a well-known figure within Berlin society and she built up a kind of socialising circle, better known as "Salon Ranke", where people of all professions and nationalities met to exchange their ideas and knowledge. High ranking people like the brothers Grimm and the philosophic scholar Schelling, the Shakespeare-translator Wilhelm von Schlegel, persons from the ministry like Friedrich Karl von Savigny and Eichhorn, English diplomats Sir Andrew Buchanan and Lord Francis Napier, and especially the Prussian Prince George met at Luisenstrasse, the home of the Rankes, for musical parties, classes in poetry and literature (especially Shakespeare), discussions of policies and history. Clarissa also gave classes in various languages especially French, Italian and English. Even her disease, which afflicted her spinal cord making her unable to move in later years, did not effected the popularity of her salon and Clarissa remained until her death in 1871 the head of a friendship circle of about 400 persons, some of them being close friends of Leopold as well.[2]

Clarissa played a central role in Ranke's private and academic life. She was responsible for finding an appropriate translator to translate his books into English; she asked her brothers Charles, Robert and John for help in getting manuscripts for her husband. All three brothers were not only able to get the contacts to other historians, conferences or archives especially in Ireland, they also sent Ranke copies of manuscripts for his work *History of England*. Research in archives has shown that Charles Graves especially played an important role in Ranke's academic career. For example, it is through his auspices that Ranke became an honorary member of the Royal Irish Academy in 1849[3] and was awarded an honorary degree at Trinity College Dublin in 1865[4], which in some way marked the start of dozens more honorary awards to Ranke in the following years throughout Europe. Charles's admiration of Ranke is noted in a letter of Charles to his sister Clarissa in June 1852, in which he mentions his own historical work but also the hope of an "Irish Ranke":

> While my health was very delicate I took up the study of the Irish language & Ancient History of Ireland as a recreation & alternative … Besides this, my position as Secretary of Council to the Royal Irish Academy obliges me to give attention to matters of Irish Archaeology; & I have felt it to be a duty to use what influence I [have?] for the accomplishment of objects which any Irish literacy men believe to be of the greatest importance. Some day or other, an Irish Ranke will arise to use the materials of history which I am endeavouring to make accessible & then I shall be recognised as a useful though an humble labourer.[5]

With the start of Ranke's work *History of England* he repeatedly asked Charles and Robert about the content of Dublin archives. But it seemed to be difficult to figure out the content of all manuscripts as following note of Clarissa to Robert in 1862 shows:

[2] Bäcker-von Ranke, G. 1976. "Rankes Ehefrau Clarissa, geb. Graves-Perceval". In *Historisch-Politische Hefte der Ranke-Gesellschaft*, No. 21. Göttingen: Historisch-Politische Hefte der Ranke-Gesellschaft. 1-22.
[3] Minutes of the Royal Irish Academy, v
[4] Board Register Book/Minute Book, TCD, MUN/v/5/12.
[5] Ranke-Museum, Wiehe, Englische Briefe, Akte Robert Perceval Graves an Clara Ranke, 1852.

As to the Dublin Archives, Charles introduced to me a clever young Irishman, who told me that Dr Todd, who only knew the contents of the Dublin University Library, and had the keeping of it, was absent in London or Paris at present.[6]

As this has been very unsatisfactory for Ranke, Clarissa wrote to her brother Robert the same year asking for help in figuring out what materials the Dublin archives held. She wrote that Leopold:

[…] bids me ask you if you know to what subject the documents that exist in the Archives in Dublin refer to the times of the restoration and the Revolution – he thinks Charles may be too busy to affort him time to answer to these questions – and that you are still in Dublin. Can you [try?] to get him any information?[7]

Robert answered his sister promptly a few days later:

I did not forget to put to Charles the question you desired as to whether there existed in Dublin documents relating to the era of history in which Ranke is at work. He says there certainly are such documents, but he cannot say whether they are of value. Lord Macaulay was told of them, but did not take the trouble to examine them.[8]

Other letters during this time show that Charles asked historians in Ireland for different details and initial research shows that some sentences seem to recur in Ranke's work. George Petrie, whom Ranke met in 1865, maintained contact with him. One original letter in French was found in his archive, but it does not seem to deal directly with Petrie.[9] Petrie's work about the *Round Towers* and places like Clonmacnoise are given special mention in Ranke's work, which shows that he used the latest knowledge to compose a work about Irish history. The search for materials continued as a letter of Clarissa to Robert shows in 1865: "Ranke wishes if you could tell him, how many families of the old Irish nobility still exist and what the titles are."[10]

In the following months Clarissa thanked her brother Charles for the details about Irish noble families, their history, position and estates. It seems that Charles translated Gaelic manuscripts into English and sent those to Ranke in Berlin. During summer 1865 Ranke went on a trip to England and he was invited to Dublin for an honorary degree from Trinity College Dublin. During his stay he visited the sights, met historians and important politicians and searched in Dublin's archives for sources. In his letters he particularly mentions three names: the historian and archaeologist George Petrie, whom Ranke described with much respect. Sir Thomas Larcom was mentioned as under-secretary for Ireland, and John Wodehouse, Earl of Kimberley was lord lieutenant of Ireland from 1864 to 1866. He was described as an intelligent man with an extensive knowledge of Europe and with whom Ranke had a political discussion (Ranke, 1949: 478-9).

Returning to Berlin Ranke brought several copies of manuscripts with him. In a letter to Charles in November 1865 Ranke conveys his thanks for one of the copies: "My thanks to the Commission's for the Copy of the Brehon Laws I read in this moment."[11] The note is very interesting as the Brehon Laws were published later that year, and Ranke even never

---

[6] Ranke-Museum, Wiehe, Englische Briefe 252.
[7] Ranke-Museum, Wiehe, Englische Briefe, 106.
[8] Ranke-Museum, Wiehe, Englische Briefe, Akte Robert Perceval Graves an Clara Ranke, 28.5.1862.
[9] Petrie Papers, TCD, MS 1931/284.
[10] Ranke-Museum, Wiehe, Clarissa von Ranke, 29.
[11] Ranke-Museum, Wiehe, Englische Briefe, 186.

mentioned the Brehon Laws in his work. This gives only a slight idea of the amount of manuscripts Ranke tried to collect, before he started writing.

In his preface to the *History of England* Ranke wrote that he used 'native' presentations of English history for his work as they had the best insight. He stressed that for the first time he used more sources and documents than ever before. Ranke states that documents recording some historical events, particularly of important parliamentary affairs were missing. In the Public Record Office London and in the British Museum Ranke found unpublished material excluding pamphlets but he gives no details regarding the kind of sources that he found there. Ranke stressed the importance of the documents by foreign ambassadors. Particularly important were the documents of Venice, Rome and Spain. Later on he also used documents from the Netherlands and Germany for his work. As foreign politics influenced English history Ranke tried to use known documents and books as well as unpublished material from London, Dublin and the continent.[12] It is evident that he used several original documents and some of them are reprinted in his fourth volume under the title "History of the war in Ireland". There are reports of the French general Lauzun and extracts from the diary of a Jacobite for the years 1689 and 1690.[13]

In his work, Ranke stresses the importance of characterising Ireland as a 'nation'. In previous works, Ranke suggests that the word does not mean unity of the state but of the people, so that it includes national feelings as well. In the case of Ireland Ranke makes it clear that 'nation' covers not only its population but the unity of the state and the Catholic Church as well. Church and state/people are always one. In the wars against England, the Irish nation fought against English units. For Ranke, it is always the Irish nation that fights, whereas with England or Scotland it is troops that fight. In these cases, England is not seen as a nation or another unity.[14] Probably he realised during his studies of Irish history that the island of Ireland had been recognised as a single political entity throughout most of its history.[15] As already mentioned, Ranke regarded the 'nation' Ireland in a different way than expected. For Ranke, nations could only establish themselves if people shared the same tradition and interests forming some kind of collective identity (Hardtwig: 35; Kemiläinen: 65-7).

Breuning gives a good description of what might be understood as a nation in the nineteenth century. The word *nation* was itself hardly new in the nineteenth century. The Latin term *natio*, meaning 'tribe' or 'race', dates from the era of the Roman Empire. In central Europe, the 'Holy Roman Empire of the German Nation' had been known by that name since the fifteenth century. But these early uses of the word differ significantly from the modern concept of nationhood. In medieval and early modern Europe, the term *nation* connoted at most an amorphous linguistic and cultural community. In the modern era, by contrast, the 'nation' is seen as a political entity consisting of the entire native population living within a contiguous and bounded territory (Breuning and Levinger: 203-4). Ranke utilised this kind of category. For Ireland, Ranke did not share the Hegelian understanding of 'one nation – one land – one language', as Ranke never stressed the importance of language in Ireland. The unity of people, their shared Catholic religion and traditions and the island as a boundary for the nation was for Ranke indication enough for being a nation.

But there are also other indications that Ranke knew very well how to deal with the national question of Ireland. Ranke once mentioned in relation to James I a rewritten genealogy referring to the Milesian kings (Ranke: 507). Even though Ranke did not go into

---

[12] Ranke, L. 1937. *Englische Geschichte, vornehmlich im 17. Jahrhundert. Vol. I* . Meersburg: F.W. Hendel Verlag: 9-11.
[13] Ranke, *Englische Geschichte IV*, pp 271-302.
[14] Ranke, *Englische Geschichte I*, pp 289, 293, 367, 688, 685.
[15] Comerford, R.V. 2003. *Inventing the nation Ireland*. London: Hodder Arnold: 14-5.

further details, it shows his knowledge about Irish origins, well known and publicised in the mid-nineteenth century. Probably due to his wife, Ranke did not check any further the truth behind this myth.[16] Another aspect of Irish identity throughout the centuries, and undoubtedly influenced by his wife Clarissa and her brother Charles Graves, was how the Irish called the English 'Saxons', as in Gaelic sources (Comerford: 56-7), and also in Ranke's work (Ranke: 506). Perhaps, he had also heard of Philip O'Sullivan Beare (c.1590-c.1634), who declared, "all the Catholics of Ireland, irrespective of background, should be called Irish" (Comerford: 59). This is what Ranke did in his work when he wrote about Irish rebellions and revolts in the seventeenth century.

When Ranke wrote his *History of England*, there was no contemporary history of Ireland available to him. Ranke wrote his work before the Public Records Office of Ireland was established in 1870, and he had to make do with a short visit to the archives in the Custom House and at Dublin Castle. He tried to involve everybody in copying manuscripts for him and he probably influenced the decision for the creation of a central archive in Dublin. The contents of the English and Irish Public Records Offices only became fully available to scholars after 1870 with the publication of their contents. Basic narratives such as Bagwell's *Ireland under the Tudors* (3 vols, 1885-90) and Bagwell's *Ireland under the Stuarts* (3 vols, 1909-16) were unavailable to Ranke. He possessed a copy of Thomas Leland's *History of Ireland from the invasion of Henry II* (Dublin, 1773) noted as being more balanced than earlier Protestant histories but its treatment of 1641 remained very polemical (Connolly, 1999: 313). Ranke's only current framework of Irish history was that provided by Macaulay (Macaulay, 1848-55). Ranke was effectively forced to create his own narrative of Irish history, not following the traditional polemical works from England, but trying to explain events in Irish history as well. The two sources published in his appendix relating to Irish history 1688-90 were printed for the first time.

Though Ranke had an impact on Irish historiography he was not quoted by Lecky as a source. Lecky and Bagwell had the opportunity to use mainly primary sources from the Public Records Office, which Ranke had problems in accessing. Bagwell was the first historian who quoted Ranke in relation to reports of Count Lauzun. In his work *Ireland under the Stuarts*, published 1909-10, Ranke had been quoted seven times (Bagwell: 275, 278, 282, 287, 292, 303-4). Bagwell also mentioned Stephens' journal and recalled that the original manuscripts is kept in the British Museum (Bagwell: 218). Murray probably took the hint and published two years later Stephens' journal emphasising the importance of Ranke's work (Murray: xxx-xxxiv). Hay quoted Ranke twice in his work about the Popish plot in footnotes, once Ranke's view is discussed and his book appears in the bibliography (Hay: 73,124, 174-5). It seems that Irish historians may have read Ranke's work but did not take it into account – after all, the Irish and British historical tradition tends to neglect continental works out of a preference for only their own. Nevertheless, Simms when writing about Jacobite Ireland in 1969 rediscovered Ranke, and Ranke's work appears in the bibliography and was quoted a number of times (Simms: 141, 144-5, 155, 159, 171). Simms also listed Ranke's work on an account for eyewitnesses in a later work (Simms: 115). Because of Simms, Ranke was enlisted in the bibliography of *A new history of Ireland* (Moody, Martin and Byrne, 1999: 673). The rediscovery of Ranke within Irish historiography went so far that Ellis just recently quoted him as an important factor in creating the Irish nation:

[…] the organizing principle of this nationalist history, we owe to a nineteenth-century

---

[16] Details about the Milesian myth see: Comerford, *Reinventing Ireland*. 51-65; Murray, D. 2000. *Romanticism, Nationalism and Irish Antiquarian Societies, 1840-80. Maynooth:* The Department of Old and Middle Irish, NUI Maynooth: 27.

German historian who is actually much better remembered for his other, more profitable, dictum about writing history 'wie es eigentlich gewesen ist' – Leopold von Ranke. He thought that history was about the rise of nations – each of which had its own appointed moment of destiny.[17]

## References

Bäcker-von Ranke, G. 1976. "Rankes Ehefrau Clarissa, geb. Graves-Perceval". In *Historisch-Politische Hefte der Ranke-Gesellschaft*, No. 21. Göttingen: Historisch-Politische Hefte der Ranke-Gesellschaft

Bagwell, R. 1963. *Ireland under the Stuarts*, vol. iii. London

Board Register Book/Minute Book, TCD, MUN/v/5/12

Breuning, C. and Levinger, M. 2002. *The Revolutionary Era, 1789-1850*. New York: W.W. Norton and Company

Comerford, R.V. 2003. *Inventing the Nation Ireland*. London: Hodder Arnold

Connolly, S.J. ed. 1999. *The Oxford Companion to Irish History*. Oxford: Oxford University Press

Cooke, J. 1997. "The Graves Family in Ireland". In *Dublin Historical Record*, vol. L, No. 1

Ellis, S. 2002. "The Empire Strikes Back: The Historiographies of Britain and Ireland". In Ellis, S. ed. 2002. *Empires and States in European Perspective*. Pisa: Edizioni Plus

Hardtwig, W. 1986. *Die Geschichtserfahrung der Moderne und die Ästhetisierung der Geschichtsschreibung: Leopold von Ranke*. Berlin

Hay, H.V. 1934, *The Jesuits and the Popish Plot*. London

Kemiläinen, A. 1968. *Die historische Sendung der Deutschen in Leopold von Rankes Geschichtsdenken*. Helsinki: Suomalaisen Tiedeakatemian Toimituksia Annales Academiae Scientirum Afennicae.

Macaulay, T.B. 1848-55. *The History of England from the Accession of James the Second*. London: Longman, Brown, Green, Longmans and Roberts

Minutes of the Royal Irish Academy, vol. III

Moody, T.W., Martin, F.X., and Byrne, F.A. eds. 1999. *A New History of Ireland, Early Modern Ireland 1534-1691*, vol. iii. Oxford: Clarendon Press

Murray, D. 2000. *Romanticism, Nationalism and Irish Antiquarian Societies, 1840-80*. Maynooth: The Department of Old and Middle Irish, NUI Maynooth

Murray, J. 1912. *The Journal of John Stephens*. Oxford: Clarendon Press

Note of Charles Graves, Royal Irish Academy, Miscellaneous Photostats, Parcel I, No. 14

Petrie Papers, TCD, MS 1931/284

Ranke-Museum, Wiehe, Englische Briefe, Akte Robert Perceval Graves an Clara Ranke, 1852

Ranke-Museum, Wiehe, Englische Briefe, Akte Robert Perceval Graves an Clara Ranke, 28.5.1862

Ranke-Museum, Wiehe, Clarissa von Ranke, 29

Ranke-Museum, Wiehe, Englische Briefe, 106

Rankc-Museum, Wiehe, Englische Briefe, 186

Ranke-Museum, Wiehe, Englische Briefe, 252

Ranke, L. 1937. *Englische Geschichte, vornehmlich im 17. Jahrhundert. Vol. I*. Meersburg: F.W. Hendel Verlag

Ranke, L. 1949. *Das Briefwerk*. Hamburg: Hoffmann und Campe Verlag

Simms, J.G. 1986. *War and Politics in Ireland, 1649-1730*. London

Simms, J.G. 2000. *Jacobite Ireland, 1685-91*. Dublin: Four Courts Press

---

[17] Ellis, S. 2002. "The Empire Strikes Back: The Historiographies of Britain and Ireland". In Ellis, S. ed. 2002. *Empires and States in European Perspective*. Pisa: Edizioni Plus: 99.

# The "Hitherandthithering Waters of the Gaelic Soul": Pragmatic Idealism and Idealistic Pragmatism in Neil M. Gunn's Perspectives on Ireland

*David Clark*

While C.M. Grieve ("Hugh MacDiarmid") declared that Scotland required "a Joyce tae prick ilka pluke"(1922: 69), someone who would expose the naked underbelly of Scottish bourgeois complacency, Neil M. Gunn saw Ireland as an ideal, a Scotland-which-might-have-been. The idealisation of Ireland and Irish culture was a standard practice for writers of the "Scottish Renaissance" of the 1920s and 30s, and, in the many essays written by Gunn in this period, Ireland was a constant point of reference. Ireland represented for MacDiarmid a tantalising crucible of modernity and tradition, but for Gunn this mixture was part of a historical process in which Scotland had been wrongfully denied its "true" role as partner and co-possessor of the "Gaelic Soul".

Such a situation, according to Gunn, could only be reversed by looking towards Ireland and using the Irish example as a model for the creation of the future Scottish State. Gunn's idealism is purely pragmatic, in that it serves as a basis for the concrete political proposals that he was to use in his essays. But his pragmatism is also purely idealistic, as it is based on a vision of Ireland – both of the contemporary Free State and of a supposed Celtic unity – more a product of Gunn's imagination than of any close historical analysis. The fact that Gunn had no Gaelic, and as such, in common with many writers of the "Renaissance", had no direct contact with Gaelic culture, is of enormous political importance. The intention behind the usurpation of "another" culture for specific political means was the creation of a vision of Scotland like the vision of Ireland used, in literary terms, by the early Yeats, and politically by Pearse, and which would find its fulfilment in the "creation" of Gaelic Ireland as the approved institutional norm of the De Valera administration from the early 1930s. Gunn's Scotland, and thus the Scotland of the leading "pragmatic idealist" of the Scottish Literary Renaissance, was to be constructed using a distinctively Irish model.

In this paper I intend to use Gunn's non-fiction work of the 1920s and early 1930s, most of which was never edited in book form, as a means of discussing the importance of Ireland for the most politically consistent of the Renaissance writers, for whom the use of Pan-Celtic discourse was typical as a counterpoint to the anti-Irish feeling which existed in certain sectors of Scottish society. MacDiarmid, predictably, saw the need to change the "negative" anti-Irish feeling into "positive" anti-Englishness: "Scottish anti-Irishness is a profound mistake, we ought to be anti-English, and we ought to play our part in a three-to-one policy of Scotland, Ireland and Wales against England to reduce that 'predominant partner' to its proper subordinate role" (MacDiarmid, 1969: 71). Not all of the writers of the Scottish Renaissance were in favour of what was perceived by some as the opportunistic use of Celticism. An attack on the Celtic background of the Scots came from Grassic Gibbon who, in his 1934 essay "The Antique Scene", claims that the Kelts (sic) are "a strain quite alien to the indubitable and original Scot" and "were, and remain, one of the greatest curses of the Scottish scene". Topically comparing the average "Kelt" to "a mere Chicagoan gangster", he states his belief that as a people they were "quick, avaricious, unintelligent, quarrelsome, cultureless and uncivilizable" (1967: 127-129).

Gunn's work constantly echoes the view that tradition is a means by which a community can be linked with its own past. The community which preserves and re-transmits its positive traditions is able to preserve a part of its own past and, it is implied, of its future. Gunn was interested in the vital aspect of tradition, which he described in his essay "President of Eire: The True Value of Tradition" as "a living growth". Ireland, he claims, has been capable of maintaining her own traditions and, as such, has "grown naturally, as a plant grows, out of her own soil and accumulated tradition towards her own flowering" (1938b: 178).

For Gunn, as for Eliot, tradition is, and must be, a vital, living concept which involves the consciousness of "the historical sense", a sense which, as the Anglo-American poet states in his essay "Tradition and the Individual Talent", involves:

> a perception, not only of the pastness of the past, but of its presence; the historical sense compels a man to write not merely with his own generation in his bones, but with a feeling that the whole of the literature of Europe from Homer and within it the whole of the literature of his own country has a simultaneous existence and composes a simultaneous order. (1975: 38)

This "historical sense" is, for Gunn, not simply translatable in literary terms, but is rather a part of the heritage of a community which it has the privilege and the obligation to defend. The community receives a series of traditions – values, customs, rites etc. – and must, according to Gunn, be responsible for the safe-keeping of these traditions and for their eventual transmission to succeeding generations. Tradition is expressed, he claims, through the language and the social customs of a people, which together compose a "spiritual heritage" which "distinguishes them from another people" (1940: 174; 1938: 170). Following Eliot, he emphasises the flexibility of tradition, and its potential adaptability to modernity. Tradition is not a static concept, but is a "living growth" which needs to be constantly re-valued in order that its validity be judged, the sound tree, using Eliot's metaphor, which, on losing it withered leaves, will grow new ones, or the "dry tree" which should be "put to the axe" (Eliot, 1957: 21). Gunn endorses Eliot's deliberately polemical judgement, expressed in "After Strange Gods", that Joyce is the most "ethically orthodox" writer of his time because he is notably a direct product of his own distinctive literary tradition. Joyce who, as Gunn states, is "popularly held to be revolutionary and unorthodox", is in fact a writer who has grown from "the ancient tradition of an isle of saints and scholars" and whose pre-eminence in the field of modern letters asserts the validity of the Irish literary tradition. Thus for Gunn, it is not entirely fortuitous that writers out of that Ireland which has fought so strenuously in recent times for the right to continue its own traditions should hold such a commanding position in letters today (1938b: 179).

Ireland serves as a constant point of reference for Gunn, an example of a sister-nation with a common Celtic inheritance which has transformed its traditions into a dynamic modernity, with the political independence and cultural self-sufficiency he aspired towards for his native Scotland. In his essays written throughout the 1920s and 1930s, Gunn continually evokes the Irish ability to unite tradition with modernity. This union was fundamental to many of the writers who composed the texts of what came to be known as the Scottish Literary Renaissance. On the one hand, it justified their self-proclaimed historical role as heirs to a historically rooted literary tradition. On the other hand, it justified their declared intention of using the stylistic and thematic bases of modernism as a means of shaking Scotland out of her post-Union lethargy and using literature as a means of re-emphasising the particular national identity which, they hoped, would culminate in the recovery of independence from the British state.

Gunn's reading of Eliot, as both Richard Price (1992) and Cairns Craig (1986) have pointed out, was highly selective, and he used only those parts of the poet's criticism which supported his own views on the validity and vitality of tradition. Price shows how Gunn de-complicates "After Strange Gods" by ignoring Eliot's critique of the negative factors involved in his analysis of the concept of tradition. The novelist thus uses Eliot for his own ends, ultimately implying that he himself had "close thematic and intellectual affinities" with outstanding representatives of modernism like Joyce and Eliot (Price, 1991: 49). Craig, on the other hand, suggests that Eliot's views on tradition were exclusive, in that they were used in reference to a limited number of core cultures which were the logical heirs to European tradition. Peripheral cultures, such as Scotland, are incapable of maintaining their own peculiar cultural tradition, and as such can only be admitted as a peripheral part of a larger, greater core culture. In his little-known, short essay, significantly entitled "Was there a Scottish Literature?", Eliot proposes an elitist view of the relationship between core and peripheral cultures, stating that "no literature which fails to sustain a continuous literature can be a great work". The value of a literary work is "dependent on its having a place within a comprehensive tradition", a tradition surging from "one of the five or six great organic formations of history" (1919: 680). Although this essay pre-dates *After Strange Gods* by fifteen years, it appeared in the same year as "Tradition and the Individual Talent" and as such must be taken as seriously as that better-known contemporary work. Eliot's disaffection with the centralising influence of the "great organic formations" had admittedly changed by time of the 1934 publication of *After Strange Gods*, in which he proposes a "spiritual alternative to centralist decadence" (Price 1991: 46), but the distance between this and tacit approval of a separate Scottish literary tradition is still large and can only be bridged by Gunn's highly selective "acquisition" of fragments of Eliot's discourse.

The pragmatic value of linking tradition to modernity was obvious to writers like Gunn and MacDiarmid who were attempting to re-direct the course of Scottish letters in the inter-war period. MacDiarmid considered that modernism constituted "a method of renewing, not replacing tradition" (Bold 1988: 496), while Gunn, as late as 1962, in a letter to F.R. Hart, stated his belief that "what is often called new and revolutionary in our day (like the incantory in Joyce) is just about as old as human time" (Pick 1987: 170). Modernity and tradition were, for the writers of the Scottish Renaissance, complementary rather than conflicting factors.

From his earliest writing Gunn's concern with the concepts of tradition and the community, and their role with regards to the individual, is constantly present. The short stories repeatedly examine the position of the individual within the community, while the non-fiction prose is primarily concerned with the need to maintain a series of positive traditions in order to ensure the survival of that community. The community that does not take into account such traditions is in danger of economic, social and cultural disintegration. Whereas in his fiction Gunn uses the small Highland community as his model, his essays generally apply the same ideas to Scotland as a whole, a Scotland whose unity, that of both Highlands and Lowlands, he based on a belief in a common Celtic cultural past. Events in Ireland, most especially the creation of the Free State in 1921 and the flourishing literary scene, encouraged Gunn, who visited his friend the novelist Maurice Walsh in his Dublin home almost annually throughout the decade. Ireland is a positive reference point in much of his prose. Many of Gunn's articles appeared under the Pseudonym of Dane M' Neil (later the surname was normalised to "McNeil") in JB Salmond's Scots Magazine. The first of these was published in 1928, the year in which Gunn formally joined the young but growing National Party of Scotland. Two of the articles written in that year take a nationalist and pro-Celtic viewpoint in defence of the validity of Scottish culture and its Celtic roots.

In "The Hidden Heart" Gunn reviews Daniel Corkery's *The Hidden Ireland* and tries to place Corkery's arguments within a Scottish context. The Irish writer argues that in Ireland, "the half-clad, bare-foot, starving peasants were the heirs to a culture a thousand years old and they had never forgotten it; nay, more, they practised it, and that in its highest manifestation, in poetry and music, and found therein their only, their last solace" (1928: 333). Gunn argues that Scotland's background is unquestionably Celtic and thus shares the same common cultural heritage with Ireland; he sees "a view of the Celtic background, essentially Scots as well as Irish" (1928: 334), and considers that "this immemorial heritage has become part of our unconscious self" (335). Such a heritage, he believes, is still manifest in modern times, through "the instinctive desire of its people for education, for learning, for those University degrees that, as it were, symbolic possession of the ancient rigorous technique of the bardic schools. Not easily does the leopard change its spots. The Scot is essentially a mental animal" (335). The Scot, Gunn argues, is under the obligation to defend the Celtic traditions to which he is heir, traditions which are at variance with the "world wide gathering of mechanistic forces" (335) represented by modernity. By recovering the "core values" of the Gaelic heritage, Scotland would recuperate the principle of "delight" in "an age wrung pale by materialism" (331) and thus "in saving himself the Scot may assist at saving the world" (335).

The belief in Celtic unity, in the implicit oneness of Irish and Scottish history and culture which Gunn supported unquestioningly throughout the late 1920s and 1930s, is also evident in "Padraic Pearse" and "The Gael will Come Again". The former, published in three short episodes in the *Scots Independent*, journal of the Scots National League, praises Pearse who, for Gunn, "finds everywhere this delight, this native joyousness of the Gael" (1929: 9). Pearse's discovery of past tradition through the literary world of childhood influenced Gunn's thinking at the time of writing *Morning Tide*, Gunn's second novel. "The Gael will Come Again" sees Gunn once again defending distinctively Scottish cultural traditions from attack. The essay was written in reply to an article by A. Urquart, in which the author contrasts Celts and Norsemen in detriment to the former. Gunn's reply defends the Celtic tradition and suggests the potential worth of such tradition in the modern world. The degeneration of Celtic culture comes, he argues, as a result of outside interference, not as something inherently weak within the Celtic people or their social structure. The concerted attacks on the Gaels after Culloden were aimed at breaking a particular way of life. After the defeat of the 1745 Jacobite Rising the distinctive signs of Highland culture – the Gaelic language, the plaid, tartan, whisky, the bagpipes – were prohibited, and the old clan chiefs underwent a process of integration into the English class system and effectively acted as the visible agents of the repression of their own kinsfolk.

Gunn again defends the strength of Gaelic poetry, music and scholarship, and stresses the positive example of the Irishman who is "running his own affairs in a Free state that is financially about the only one in Europe approaching complete solvency" (1931: 327). In two articles published in the first half of 1938 Gunn again returns to the Irish situation as an example of the political future he would like to see in Scotland. In "Eire: How Dublin Received the New Constitution" he congratulates the Irish on the renaming of the Irish Free State for Eire, thus recovering a name which reflects the country's Celtic past, and on the production of the new constitution. He quotes the *Lloyd's Bank Monthly Review* as stating that Ireland's credit is as high as that of any country in the world, and compares the situation with that of Scotland, concluding that "there is one consideration in which the Irish have got us thoroughly beaten: they are alive, consciously and nationally" (1938a: 344).

Similarly in "President of Eire: The True Value of Tradition" Gunn celebrates the appointment of Douglas Hyde as the first President of Éire and stresses the importance of Ireland as a small country which has fought in order to recover a dying tradition, a tradition without which any independent future would be inconceivable: "Ireland fought for her freedom in order that she might grow naturally as a plant grows, out of her own soil and accumulated tradition towards her own flowering. When that tradition is destroyed or inhibited, there is nothing of a similar fructifying nature to take its place" (1938b: 178). Gunn sees the importance of Irish literature as being a part of that tradition, a fact which he claims is confirmed by the apparent unorthodoxy of Joyce's work if regarded within the tradition of English rather than that of Irish letters. Ireland's position leads Gunn to consider the position of Scotland who, he claims, not only denies but publicly ridicules her own tradition, looking towards London for all political, economic and cultural leadership. The success of independent Ireland means that Scotland, or at least "that part of her concerned with the continuance of a living Gaelic spirit" (1938b: 180) should now look instead towards Dublin.

Gunn's literary essays of the 1930s follow a similar line to those of the previous decade. "Literature: Class or National" (1936) attacks an article by Lennox Kerr who had argued the case against the claim that literature is national in origin. Gunn refutes Kerr's thesis by stating that even in Scotland "which has been doing its best with English for some centuries" (1987: 118), the best poetry is that which is written in Scots. He gives the examples of Ireland and Russia as nations which have realised the need to "remould" their own national cultural pattern, and in so doing have given a spectacular impetus to the arts. The case of Ireland is, he suggests, particularly noteworthy on account of the geographical and cultural proximity to Scotland, and "the magnificent outburst of literature in recent years in Ireland synchronised precisely with the national uprising of the people; and it is a fair assumption that had the national spirit not raised its head, the literature would not have appeared" (1987: 120). Gunn's conclusion is again that "a man creates most potently within his own national environment" and therefore "if a man feels Ireland he has no longer a nation of his own, then he will hang on to some other nation" (1987: 121). In Scotland's case, political dependence on England has, he believes, led to Scottish literature's attempts to "hang on" artificially to the English literary tradition. Only in an independent Scotland can great literature be produced, because, "whether we like it or not, the nation is still the basis of all large-scale creative human endeavour, and in that sense, it seems to me, it would be difficult for a Scot to show up impressively before an Irish dramatist or a Russian of the classless state" (1987: 121).

*Whisky and Scotland* (1935) is divided into two distinct parts. The first part restates Gunn's perception of the past and present of the Gaelic people, and reflects the extent to which the writer was involved within the Scottish Nationalist Movement. The first chapter, entitled "Uisgebeatha" (from the Gaelic "water of life") is a whimsical, mythical recreation of the possible origins of the invention of whisky. Using a technique in which he projects his vision of an idealised people – much as he had done with his Picts in his 1933 novel Sun Circle – Gunn tries to invest his mythical proto-Gaels with the characteristics of individualism, democratic principles, cultural richness and peaceful coexistence.

After this mythical introduction, Gunn uses the history of the production of whisky as an excuse by which he can delve into the history of his people. He justifies his method by stating that before approaching the meaning that whisky has for Scotland, it is necessary to "first have some idea of what Scotland means to herself" (44). He insists that the Celtic peoples had a civilisation "long before the Romans freed Barrabas" (17), and defends the pacific nature of the Celts who were by nature civilisers rather than conquerors, but who had been pushed to the fringes of civilisation, towards the sea "until, at last, among many of the Gaels themselves, a shame of their heritage comes over them, and they have been known to deny it with a curious and inverted hate" (65). He praises the virtue and vitality of Celtic traditions. For example:

> [Gaelic poetry] was sun-bred, exuberant and yet vigorous, charged with life or the wild singing of death, positive and challenging. There was a flame at its core. Slowly the flame died down; the red faded to grey; the mind became haunted by dreams; and the inheritors of the ancient rigorous tradition entered, like wraiths, the "Celtic Twilight". (67-68)

Gunn also links the traditions of the Scottish and the Irish Celts. The Irish, he claims, have made better use of their Celtic traditions, and the Irish use of the English language is a modern result of the continuing viability of these traditions. Great modern Irish writers like Joyce and

Synge are seen as presenting a direct line of development from the Irish Bardic tradition. For Gunn, it is relevant to pursue the debate as to whether the Scots or the Irish were the first to produce whisky, given that Irish and Scots constituted no more than two branches of what was intrinsically the same people. "The excursion into Ireland" Gunn believes, "illumines by reflection the Gaelic spirit in Scotland" (70).

Gunn's arguments must be taken, of course, in the political context within which they were written. His argument develops therefore, from a position of solidarity with the Irish Free State to a defence of the national unity of Scotland, before moving on to consider the alleged benefits of nationalism in detriment to what Gunn perceived as the negative aspects of internationalism.

Political pragmatism, perhaps, leads Gunn to disregard the evidence which points to the fact that the first legal and fiscal attacks on whisky were in fact made by successive Edinburgh governments in the seventeenth century before the Act of Union moved the legislature to London. Although Gunn resents the English attempts to relegate Scotland to the role of an English region, he is never openly hostile to England or the English in his articles. In "This English Business" (1942) he does, however, criticise the English tendency to refer to Scots as "English", and to Britain in its entirety as "England". He quotes the editorial of an English magazine, *The Gunner*, which claims that England is the "nucleus" of the United Kingdom around which "various elements have in times past gathered", and he criticises the arrogance with which such a historically false statement can be made. His comments can be seen as a defence of the much-criticised neutrality of Eire in the war:

> This is the sort of potted history that we may all smile at. The idea of Ireland, for example, in times past gathering round England is, as we say, rather rich! How does the editor explain that the greater part of Ireland has not in times present gathered round? […] Any Irishman will answer the question bluntly by saying that throughout history England had tried to wallop the life out of his country and he has not forgotten it. (1942b: 297)

Gunn defends the Scots' right to vindicate their "non-Englishness" on historical terms, arguing that a nation which has fought for over six hundred years in order to defend its own traditions is not willing to relinquish its name, or allow it "to be usurped by the name of what was for so long its enemy" (298). He defends the right of the English to cultivate their own tradition, but asks that they "must try to forgive the Scot for not wanting any share in England's Green and Pleasant Land, or in the tradition covered by the name England" (299).

Gunn's last published articles appeared in the magazine *Anarchy 86* in April 1968. These short pieces, "A Footnote on Co-operation" and "The Wonder Story of the Moray Firth", both strike a characteristic note. The first praises the co-operative fishing policy of the Irish Republic in the 1960s, and restates his continued belief in political independence for the Scottish nation: "if the Irish can do that sort of thing at home, a co-operative association is no dream for Scottish fisheries. I regard self-government for Scotland as co-operation on the national level" (1987: 176).

While Gunn's early short stories are primarily concerned with a thorough, at times critical, examination of the role of the individual within the community, most of the early non-fiction prose stresses the need to maintain a series of positive traditions through which the community, and the individuals of which it is composed, is able to realise its own potential. Although opposed to the sentimental pessimism of the "Twilight", the early Gunn continually reiterated his belief in pan-Celticism, a belief which he used pragmatically, given the envious cultural and political example provided by the Irish Free State in the 1920s.

The pragmatic use of a pro-Gaelic ideal in order to "create" a Scotland based on the Irish example must, however, be questioned in terms of its validity in the highly industrialised Scotland of the twentieth century. Similarly the supposedly "idealistic" usurpation of the perceived cultural heritage of the Gaelic-speaking Scots can justifiably be seen as a type of internal colonialism, in which the dominant Lowland Scotland adopts the superficial trappings of Gaelic Scotland as a pragmatic means of "manufacturing" an all-embracing Scottish identity which, even after hypothetical independence, would reinforce Lowland hegemony while espousing the alleged spiritual values of the Gaels. Gunn's praise of the Irish cultural system, however, combined his respect for separate Irish traditions, and his search for universality through a self-consciously Scottish structure places him, along with other writers of the Scottish Renaissance, in a position to provide a positive model for Scottish literature, a model which is not drawn irresistibly towards the obligatory core. The hypothetically independent Scotland towards which Gunn and other Scottish intellectuals worked in the 1920s and 30s would, therefore, have borne, in terms of culture and historical self-perception, many of the traits of the fledgling Free State. Taking into account the economic, social and – in real terms – cultural differences between the two countries, Ireland and Scotland, in the early twentieth century, it is doubtful, however, whether this would have been an acceptable alternative to the Union for most Lowland Scots.

## References

Bold, Alan. 1988. *MacDiarmid. Christopher Murray Grieve: A Critical Biography*. Glasgow: Collins

Craig, Cairns. 1996. *Out of History: Narrative Paradigms in Scottish and English Culture*. Edinburgh: Polygon

Eliot, T.S. 1919. "Was There a Scottish Literature?" *The Athenaeum* 4657: 680

Eliot, T.S. 1951. *After Strange Gods: Selected Essays*. Ed. F. Kermode. London:

Eliot, T.S. 1975. *"Tradition and the Individual Talent": Selected Prose of T.S. Eliot*. Ed. F. Kermode. London: Faber

Grassic Gibbon, Lewis. 1967. *A Scots Hairst: Essays and Short Stories*. London: Hutchinson

Grieve, C.M. ("Hugh MacDiarmid"). 1922. *Scottish Chapbook* 1.3: 69-73

Gunn, Neil M. 1928. "The Hidden Heart." *Scots Magazine* 9.5: 331-335

Gunn, Neil M. 1929. "Padraic Pearse I: The Man called Pearse". *The Scots Independent* 4.1: 9-10

Gunn, Neil M. 1931. "The Gael Will Come Again". *Scots Magazine* 14.5: 324-327

Gunn, Neil M. 1938a. "Eire: How Dublin Received the New Constitution". *Scots Magazine* 28.5: 340-344

Gunn, Neil M. 1938b. "President of Eire: The True Value of Tradition". *Scots Magazine* 29.3: 177-180

Gunn, Neil M. 1938c. "Nationalism in Writing II: The Theatre Society of Scotland". *Scots Magazine* 30.3: 194-198

Gunn, Neil M. 1940. "On Tradition". *Scots Magazine* 34.2: 131-134

Gunn, Neil M. 1942a. "The Essence of Nationalism". *Scots Magazine* 37.3: 169-172

Gunn, Neil M. 1942b. "This English Business". *Scots Magazine* 37.4: 295-299

Gunn, Neil M. 1968. "A Footnote on Co-Operation". *Anarchy 86* 8.4: 116-117

Gunn, Neil M. 1968 "The Wonder Story of the Moray Firth". *Anarchy 86* 8.4: 122-125

Gunn, Neil M. 1977. *Whisky and Scotland: A Practical and Spiritual Survey*. London: Souvenir Press. First published 1935

Gunn, Neil M. 1987. *Landscape and Light: Essays by Neil M. Gunn*. Ed. Alistair McCleery. Aberdeen: Aberdeen University Press

Hart, F.R. and J.B. Pick. 1981. *Neil M. Gunn: A Highland Life*. Edinburgh. Polygon

MacDiarmid, Hugh. 1969. "The Caledonian Antisyzygy and the Gaelic Idea". *Selected Essays of Hugh MacDiarmid*. Ed. Duncan Glen. London: Jonathan Cape. 56-74

Pick, J.B, ed. 1987. *Neil M. Gunn: Selected Letters*. Edinburgh: Polygon

Price, Richard. 1991. *Neil M. Gunn: The Fabulous Matter of Fact*. Edinburgh: Edinburgh University Press

# Neither Irish Nor British: Exploring The Image of Nation in Northern Irish Protestant Fiction

*Anthea Cordner*

Is there a group that can be placed under the banner of the Northern Irish Protestant and, if so, how does it define itself in fiction, particularly when Protestantism is by its very nature multifarious and fractured? Ireland has a long history of traditions and mythology which can be, and frequently is, reproduced in current literature. In contrast, Northern Ireland has a short history formed from a confusion of sources and competing backgrounds, many of which are based upon the problematic sectarian struggles that are often rejected by the modern Ulster Protestant. An exploration of the literature reveals that beyond the popular blockbuster Thrillers, there is a dearth of material from the Protestant community in current publication. The reasons for, and consequences of this lack of self-representation will necessitate examination on another occasion. What does exist frequently, as for example in the work of writers such as Glenn Patterson and Linda Anderson, engages with the emotional, psychological and cultural influences of the Protestant history, thus enabling a deciphering of how the image of nation is conveyed in contemporary literature.

Two novels that eschew the popular Thriller images of Protestantism are Glenn Patterson's *Fat Lad* (1992), and Linda Anderson's *Cuckoo* (1986). These writers utilise their respective Protestant backgrounds while refuting stereotypical Ulster Protestant labelling. Although neither Anderson nor Patterson specifically set out to write from a Protestant position, it is possible to see how their backgrounds have influenced the style and content of their fiction. As Barry Sloan (2000: 262) notes in *Writers and Protestantism in the North of Ireland*, "While few, if any, Ulster novelists have written specifically as proponents of Catholicism or Protestantism, their fiction commonly foregrounds the community to which the writers themselves belong, however nominally." This holds true for the two main books in this study as they focus on how their protagonists struggle with their Ulster Protestant identification. Anderson's *Cuckoo* employs interesting literary techniques to relate the female protagonist's post-traumatic breakdown and sense of diaspora. It describes her detachment from the available conceptions of national identity; neither British, nor Irish, she has no place to call home. Patterson relates a similar theme of identity crisis in *Fat Lad* when his male character returns to Belfast to find his memory at odds with the reality of his experiences. These fictional depictions reveal an exploration of a Protestant sense of displacement and a necessary revisionism of traditional political and religious inheritance.

The Protestant community in Northern Ireland is multi-stranded, thus a writer's specific denomination will inevitably influence their viewpoint. This creates problems when examining theoretical strands in researching Ulster Protestant literature, and can be influential in the reading of such work. Colin Coulter (1999) in his sociological study of Ulster demonstrates how even the largest denomination, the Presbyterians, have only half of the Catholic Church's membership: "While Ulster Protestants may justifiably be regarded as a majority, it is important to bear in mind that they are in fact a 'majority of minorities'" (14). There is some evidence that this has had an impact on the literature produced by the Protestant writers, although fictional representations have a tendency to lean toward Calvinism as the writer is, more often than not, from a Presbyterian background. Glenn Patterson, for example, writes specifically of Presbyterianism in his latest book *That Which Was* (2004), and in part of his previous book *Number 5* (2003). Janet McNeill captures the education and social systems of the Protestant middle classes in the 1960s by drawing upon her own upbringing as a minister's daughter to include a Presbyterian minister in her novel *As Strangers Here* (1960). Sam Hanna Bell, who has been described as the epitome of an Ulster Protestant writer, produced nostalgic renditions of his diminishing rural Presbyterian community in novels such as *December Bride* (1951) and *The Hollow Ball* (1961), and in particular in his short story collections *Summer Loanen and Other Stories* (1943) and *Erin's Orange Lily: Ulster Customs and Folklore* (1956) which he specifically intended for the purpose of "encouraging Ulster men and women to write for their Region" (King 1999: 7). Contemporary writers cannot merely appropriate these nostalgic depictions or traditional images; their material is overshadowed by the major influence of the Troubles and the controversial political positioning it has created.

In an increasingly secular world, Protestantism in the Ulster region has moved away from its original understanding, as a form of worship and code of beliefs, toward a socio-political label, which is applied to anyone born to Protestant parents, regardless of their attendance or faith in their denomination. It has come to encompass a stereotypical image of unionism as captured by the Ian Paisley's religious-political dogmatism or, as Barry Sloan (2000: 2) describes this image, as "irrationally intolerant, blinkered, contentious, uncultured, dictatorial and lacking in compassion". This impression the majority of Northern Irish Protestants (understandably) refute, and yet must also confront or revise if they are to attempt identification with their cultural traditions. With the onset of the Troubles in 1968 Protestants were supposedly united in unionist opposition to Catholic nationalism, but in essence it is never this simplistic, and writers frequently reject this Ulster Protestant/unionist labelling. A similar point to this is noted by Richard Kearney in *Transitions* (1988) which describes how the generation that grew up in the 1960s and 70s have developed what he terms as "migrant minds". The Ulsterman or woman either physically or mentally detaches him or herself from their 'home' in order to reject traditional concepts of their identity, thus enabling a recreation or renewal of cultural and historical constructions. Both Anderson and Patterson physically and emotionally become detached from their Ulster Protestantism and this rejection of all traditional notions is reflected in their writing.

Linda Anderson, who, like Glenn Patterson, was born into a working-class Protestant family in Belfast, states (2002: 92): "I simply detested Protestantism and Unionism. My identification with the Catholic 'other' was partly a flight from the despised, disowned familiar. I also saw it as a radical, anti-segregationist act." Glenn Patterson believes that the old standards set down in both unionism and nationalism belong to the nineteenth century. He professes his early loss of faith and youthful embracing of nationalist politics as placing him in a political 'middle' ground between republicanism and unionism. In this he embodies the liberal middle-class Protestants represented in Susan McKay's book *Northern Protestants: An Unsettled People* (2000). In an interview with 'Ellen', whom McKay describes as a "middle-of-the-road Protestant", we are given an example of this identity crisis: "'But then I am *not* Irish', said Ellen [...] 'Protestant culture is Orange and I can't identify with that – it is as alien to me as rabid republicanism'" (22-3). Ellen attempts to define identity by a rejection of the stereotypical imagery and religious associations of Presbyterianism and Orangeism; however she finds it similarly problematic to claim an Irish inheritance. It is difficult to decipher what precisely is meant by this "middle-of-the-road" or "middle-ground" Protestantism beyond its rejection of the stoical traditions as previously mentioned. However, there appears to be a certain pre-requisite to embrace the label of Northern Irish, thus accepting a specific regional understanding of 'Irishness', which would appear to point toward a hyphenated Anglo-Irish identity. The specific working through of what this may involve is by no means clear, but the authors considered here display an engagement with certain aspects of this identity issue.

The problems of this dual birthright are explored on several occasions in Patterson's *Fat Lad*, which excavates layers of history by utilising the main protagonist Drew as an embodiment of Northern Ireland's national identity crisis. The title of his book refers to the initial letters of the six counties that make up the region of Northern Ireland and it works to further emphasise how Northern Ireland is set apart from Ireland's traditional feminised imagery, to become instead identified with a specific kind of masculinity as captured in its industrial past. The Protestant Drew, alongside his Catholic friend Hugh, are both the 'fat lad' as they hold important historical associations through their surname, O'Neill, the fabled original possessor of Ulster. This is a difficult amalgamation of traditions and mythology in an attempt to provide a 'common' rather than a 'middle' ground, as Patterson reaches backwards toward an Ulster story embraceable by all communities.

There are several points in the novel when Patterson attempts to revise the Protestant inheritance by scrutinising specific historical issues, and frequently these are also revisions of the birthing trope. For example when Drew and Hugh sing:

> I'm nobody's child, no-ho-body's child,
> I'm like a flower, just growing wild,
> No mammy's kisses, and no daddy's smile,
> Nobody wants me, I'm no-bo-dy's child. (227-8)

This symbolic child is a continuation of Heaney's metaphorical birthing myths where Northern Ireland is violently produced from Ireland and England's 'Act of Union'. In this version it is not Ireland that is the victim of a dominant and violent patriarch, but the child who is rejected by both parents. Being a 'child' of what in essence is neither Irish nor British, leaves both O'Neills devoid of their heritage. The Ulster Protestant, wishing to claim neither unionism nor nationalism is thus dispossessed from the land, the culture, and the history of Ireland and Britain.

Similar revisionism occurs with respect to Belfast, which is traditionally gendered by its association with the Protestant industrial men: Patterson destabilises this with a new image of Belfast personified in a young entrepreneurial woman. There is an indication that the foundations, like the city iconography of the previous piece, must be deconstructed, revisited, or reinterpreted, before a future can be established: "The battle between *de*struction and *con*struction [...] was the oldest battle in Belfast" (204). By exorcising the past, and renewing Belfast's present day representations, Patterson is creating gaps in the national image. At one point he dissects the iconography of male-dominated loyalist Protestantism and juxtapositions it with 'mother' Ireland, thus creating a joint patronage:

> The working-class Protestants' annual burnt offering to the great dead hand of Ulster loyalism which had kept them, as much as their Catholic neighbours, in their slummy places for half a century while erecting the vast, mausoleum pile of Stormount – long home of Unionist Northern Ireland, secured in part, as Drew's father had once said, by the arms brought ashore at Donaghadee, and visible even from this distance, even to myopic Drew, on the rising ground to the Holywood side of the Dundonald gap, almost opposite the cemetery where his mother lay sunk in a green gravelled tomb. (130)

By utilising the common literary trope of mother Ireland, Patterson defamiliarises traditional mythical imagery by replacing the matriarch calling for vengeance with a silent tomb. There is no heraldry, but neither is there any positive image of nation in this passage; neither the unionist "mausoleum", nor the green "tomb" suggest a future for the Northern Irish Protestant trapped in commemorating "the great dead". However, the ending is not wholly negative as suggested in the final scene in *Fat Lad* where Drew discovers the army "making safe" an old World War II bomb buried in the park. This trope exposes the historically hidden dangers and potentially explosive situations in Northern Ireland which still need to be defused. There are no simple solutions, but an acknowledgement that the past lives on in the present, although in time it could be explicated. Patterson's lasting image of nation, therefore, suggests a metamorphosis in progress as the Ulster Protestant exposes the negative cultural iconography of the past, revises historical imagery, and accepts that both Britain and Ireland have an ancestral claim.

Linda Anderson makes similar challenges in *Cuckoo*, her second novel, which explores the protagonist Fran's view of her national identity by utilising the themes of birth, death, sex and love. The novel has an adventurous style that incorporates time-shifts, a diary extract and a funeral scene set out as a play. Fran initially acknowledges her "cuckoo" identity by comparing her sense of displacement and trauma to Lloyd, the 'Black Briton', who cries, "See, Britain not my home! Jamaica not my home! No place my home!" (90). Unlike Patterson, Anderson does not appear to suggest that there is a middle ground in the Northern Irish political question. Nick Fitzpatrick, Fran's boyfriend, has no religious beliefs and stubbornly refuses to acknowledge the political sectarianism all around him, thus his inclusion is representative of the middle-classes as denoted in McKay's interviews. Nick's subsequent death by a rogue bomb however forces Fran to reject middle-ground neutrality, face the reality of the violence, and respond. This pattern of avoidance, grief, and acceptance is a theme that Elmer Kennedy-Andrews (2003) describes as common in realist fiction:

> [T]he world is divided between the public, political realm which is inferior to, and destructive of, a superior private realm of domestic sexuality and personal realisation. The public and the private are held apart, and only by detaching him/herself from community and politics and escaping into an apolitical privacy can the individual find authentic existential fulfilment. Failing this resolution in the private sphere, a tragic closure is inevitable, brought about by bomb, bullet, prison or exile. (17)

Anderson is challenging this traditional literary theme by framing her diary extract within the present day time-scheme of the novel. Her protagonist's story envelops this incident with further juxtaposition of the public/private conflicts, and in each of these she rejects the claustrophobic private realms to make a political statement. In the opening scenes of the novel Fran's passivity leads to a downward spiral into victim-hood, but once she begins to acknowledge her identity and social position she takes back control of her life and future. Anderson would appear to be suggesting that it is naïve, selfish and potentially destructive to try to escape or hide away from the political turmoil.

The central section of the novel unfolds a critical moment for Fran's sense of self. During a discussion with two antagonistic English people in a restaurant, Fran refers to the migrant status she has felt as an Ulster Protestant:

> [I]n the north-east corner of Ireland where I come from, we're British citizens. Some are reluctant and some are enthusiastic about it. I was brought up to exult in being an honorary Brit. It didn't work in my case, and meeting people like you confirms this disenchantment! You see, when I was growing up, it shocked me to realise that some of my compatriots saw me and my kind as oppressors and usurpers and with good reason. I felt I had no right to be there. I didn't belong. And now you're telling me I have no right to be here. Well, you're wrong. I can't be dispossessed any more. (87-8)

Fran's image of her nationality is confused by her classification as British, which she realises is not accepted by her English friends; her specific political epoch, however, would not allow her to be deemed Irish. Thus, she is Irish, in that the place of her birth was the island of Ireland, yet she claims British nationality. In this mutually exclusive dilemma, she finds herself "nobodies child", dispossessed from both the Irish and the British. Fran now feels that she wants to be able to claim both: to be recognised as both Irish and British, a British citizen born in Ireland, a uniquely Northern Irish child. This posits the possibility of embracing multiculturalism within nationalism. To be born the citizen of one country does not exclude the individual from also acknowledging ethnic differences. An Ulster Protestant is Anglo-Irish by birth, and can thus embrace, rather than be rejected by, both the British and Irish cultures.[1]

The above two novels reveal several interesting points concerning Protestantism and the problem of finding a tradition or mythology upon which to base a sense of identity that sees itself as neither Irish nor British. These novels are attempting to find a Northern Irish identity, while acknowledging the negative impact of unionism and religious bigotry on the Ulster Protestant. They reveal a rejection of historical binarism and engage with tentative explorations of an image of nation outside the traditional sectarian politics. The view of nation in Anderson's novels and short stories would suggest that there is a division, not between Protestant and Catholic, but between those who acquiesce with the violence and those who refuse to be in anyway compliant with it. She rejects an apolitical middle ground in favour of a stance against violence and bigotry. Her image of the Northern Ireland Protestant is someone who has the right to choose their future and stake a claim to their Anglo-Irish past. Patterson's novel suggests that, although it is impossible to be free from the traumatic past, it is possible to find a common ground for all who live in Ulster to build a future that is not divisive by religious or political binarism. Like Anderson he points toward the developing global sense of identity that opens, rather than narrows, a sense of self.

This study has been fraught with problematic definitions and explorations of inconclusive political issues represented in regional literature. There are no simple solutions given in the novels studied, nor are all the questions they raise given conclusive or finite answers. However, both novels raise important issues concerning representations of Northern Irish history and its impact on the socio-cultural perceptions and imagery of the contemporary Ulster Protestant.

# References

Anderson, Linda. 1988. *Cuckoo*. Dingle: Brandon
Anderson, Linda. 2002. "Rewriting the North". Unpublished Ph.D. thesis, Open University
Bell, Sam Hanna. 1996. *Erin's Orange Lily and Summer Loanen and Other Stories*. Belfast: Blackstaff
Craig, Patricia. 1992. "Introduction" from: *The Rattle of the North: An Anthology of Ulster Prose*. Ed. P. Craig. Belfast: Blackstaff. 1-12
Coulter, Colin. 1999. *Contemporary Northern Irish Society* London: Pluto
Foster, John Wilson. 1974. *Forces and Themes in Ulster Fiction*. Totowa, NJ: Rowthan and Littlefield
Foster, Roy. 2002. *The Irish Story: Telling Tales and Making it up in Ireland*. London: Penguin

---

[1] This hyphenated additive model of identity can in reverse be compared to many diasporic Irish in America, who alongside other immigrants are able to embrace the possibility of being 'Irish American'. There are, however, in this case several complex issues involved in incorporating all Protestants under the 'British Irish' label, as the political implications would then exclude Catholics who would also wish to be termed 'British Irish' and continue holding a British passport, and it would also not take into account Protestants with nationalist political beliefs who would not wish to have the word 'British' included. In addition, the sensitivity of the Irish toward the term Anglo-Irish due to its association with Ascendancy must also be acknowledged when trying to find a term that is acceptable for this 'middle-ground' group.

Hogg, Clare Dwyer. 2004. "Glenn Patterson: Alternative Ulster". *Independent*. 26 March

Kennedy-Andrews, Elmer. 2003. *Fiction and the Northern Ireland Troubles since 1969: (De-)constructing the North*. Dublin: Four Courts Press

Kearney, Richard. 1988. *Transitions: Narratives in Modern Irish Culture*. Dublin: Wolfhound

King, Sophie Hillian. 1999. "'A Salute from the Banderol': Sam Hanna Bell's Contribution to Ulster Cultural Life". *Writing Ulster No 6: Northern Narrative*. Ed. Bill Lazenbatt. Newtownabbey: University of Ulster. 1-12

Patterson, Glenn. 1992. *Fat Lad*. London: Minerva

Patterson, Glenn. 2003. *Number 5*. London: Penguin-Hamish Hamilton

Sloan, Barry. 2000. *Writers and Protestantism in the North of Ireland: Heirs to Adamnation?* Dublin: Irish Academic Press

Walker, Gail. 2003. "Interview: Oldish Lad, Newish Man – the Writer Without a Label". *Belfast Telegraph*. 28 April

## Acknowledgement

I am grateful to Linda Anderson for permission to quote from her unpublished Ph.D. thesis.

# Ayr, Armagh and Armageddon: Millenarianism in the New Year Odes of Scotland and Ulster, 1786-1806

*Stephen Dornan*

During the late eighteenth and early nineteenth centuries a wave of millennialism and millenarianism swept across Europe and America. This was conspicuous in Ireland, and particularly Ulster, which produced a series of colourful millenarians during this period. One of the most prominent was the Antrim born politician, Francis Dobbs, who had already penned a four book, blank verse epic poem on the impending Millennium, when he addressed the Irish parliament on the subject of a legislative Union with Great Britain on 7 June 1800. In this particular speech he explained his opposition to the proposed Union by arguing that "the Independence of Ireland is written in the immutable records of Heaven" (Dobbs: 45). He went on to "prove" to the house, through a close reading of the apocalyptic texts of Daniel and Revelation, that Christ's Millennium was imminent and, furthermore, that Ireland had been chosen as the scene of the final defeat of Satan. After ingeniously pointing out several symbols in Revelation, including linen and the harp, that have Irish associations, Dobbs concluded with a final clinching piece of evidence:

> But what I rely on more than all is our miraculous exemption from all of the serpent and venomous tribe of reptiles. This appears to me in the highest degree emblematic, that Satan, the Great serpent, is here to receive his first deadly blow. (Dobbs: 46)

Of course many of his contemporaries ridiculed the millenarian bombast of Dobbs, but as studies of popular millenarianism of the period, for instance by JFC Harrison (1979) and Myrtle Hill (2001), have shown, his beliefs were by no means unusual. This is reflected in the fact that Dobbs's speech was widely circulated and attained a significant degree of popularity as well as notoriety. Dobbs, and his contemporary, the United Irish leader, Thomas Russell illustrate that millenarianism, which is sometimes simplistically associated with popular radicalism, existed amongst the educated classes of the Anglican Ascendancy. Indeed, millenarianism transcended the denominational and class differences in Irish and Scottish society during this period. There is plenty of evidence of Presbyterian millenarianism. Robert Burns's Presbyterian Ayrshire, for example, was shaken by the rise of a millenarian sect known as the Buchanites and James Orr, the County Antrim Presbyterian poet and radical, often concludes his poems with apocalyptic or millennial imagery.

This Protestant millenarianism was also replicated in Irish Catholicism. Dobbs, in his famous speech, had naturally seized upon the similarity between the words Armageddon and Armagh as a point of great significance. Three years earlier the travelling Frenchman, the Chevalier de Latocnaye, noted that prophetic dread was part of the stimulus for Catholic migration from that particularly troubled county:

> Although I did not hear, this time, that the Orangemen used the old menace of Connaught or Hell, it was easy to see that their dominating idea was still the expulsion of Catholics, but their manner of action was no longer so terrible [...] they circulated adroitly among the peasants an old prophesy by St. Columba which warned the faithful that 'A time will come when war and famine will destroy in this part of the country all those who have not embraced the new errors,' but, adds the prophesy, 'the massacre will not extend beyond the Shannon, where the faithful shall prosper.' (De Latocnaye: 263)

The apocalyptic dread of the Catholic peasantry of Armagh illustrates the multi-denominational nature of the phenomenon of millenarianism, and Roy Foster notes that this fascination with millennial prophesy continues in strands of Catholicism well into the nineteenth century when they were "focused around the phenomenally popular *Prophesies* of Pastorini, promising a delivery from bondage, and the destruction of Protestantism, in the year 1825" (Foster: 295). This vogue for prophesy was intimately connected with the idea of apocalypse due to the passages of the book of Joel that suggest that a sign of the impending Millenium will be that:

> Your sons and your daughters shall prophesy,
> Your old men shall dream dreams,
> Your young men shall see visions. (Barker:1255)

Furthermore, the word "apocalypse" etymologically connotes a revelation, or the lifting off of a lid; as Paley has suggested, the term involves, like prophesy, "uncovering and disclosure" (Paley: 2). An interest in prophesy was a central characteristic of millenarians and millennialists. The terms "millenarianism" and "millennialism" are used to cover a complex and varied range of beliefs concerning the Millennium, the one thousand year reign of Christ and his saints as prophesied in various passages of the Bible. The distinction between the two terms is that millenarians tended to believe that a cataclysmic apocalypse initiated by divine intervention would herald Christ's return, whereas millennialists envisioned a more gradual progression towards an enlightened utopian age which would be brought about by human endeavour and which would culminate in the return of the Messiah.

This paper will suggest that these common millenarian fears and hopes were particularly potent around, and were exacerbated by, the New Year. This will be illustrated with reference to a series of texts, particularly New Year odes, composed in Scotland and Ulster during the late eighteenth and early nineteenth centuries. The New Year is particularly conducive to millenarian feelings since it tends to foreground the passage of time and promote, in microcosm, an apocalyptic temporal model. The calendar is constructed in such a way that it appears linear throughout the year. But the point at which one year ends and another begins is a fracture, as one unit of time, or epoch, is consigned to the past and another begins. This fracture means that this is the point in the year that the passage of time is most conspicuous and most dramatic and, therefore, it is the moment that our perception of the passage of time is most heightened. People's thoughts, therefore, tend to gravitate towards themes such as transience, mortality and ultimately finality. This is subsequently reflected in their writings.

A passage from John Galt's early nineteenth-century novel, *Annals of the Parish* demonstrates this point. The narrator, a Kirk of Scotland Minister named Micah Balwhidder, has several millenarian traits and is very keen on the year as a unit since his narrative is structured into annals. Balwhidder also has the millenarian's fascination for signs, omens and portents. This is illustrated by a remarkable passage in the chronicle for the year 1793 when he narrates an allegorical dream that he has on the opening night of the year. He writes, "On the opening night of the year I dreamt a very remarkable dream, which, when I now recall to mind, at this distance of time, I cannot but think that there was a cast of prophecy in it" (Galt: 130). The narrator watches from the roof of a church as corpses rise from their graves and fight a battle. In this battle the corpses of the gentry are beaten back into their sculptured and ornate tombs. He then finds himself watching the victorious army celebrating on a plain with a great city in the distance:

> They were going in great pride and might towards the city, but an awful burning rose,
> afar as if it were in the darkness, and the flames stood like a tower of fire that reached

unto the heavens. And I saw a dreadful hand and an arm stretched from out of the cloud, and in its hold was a besom made of the hail and the storm, and it swept the fugitives like dust; and in their place I saw the churchyard, as it were, cleared and spread around, the graves closed, and the ancient tombs, with their coats of arms and their effigies of stone, all as they were in the beginning. (Galt: 130)

The dream obviously refers to the class struggles which were manifesting themselves in Balwhidder's parish through an upsurge in Jacobinism amongst the weavers. But there is certainly an apocalyptic aspect to the imagery of the dream. The passage seems to vindicate the omnipotence of God in the face of the strongest convulsions of human history as the victorious army is nonchalantly swept away. The positioning of this dream on the first night of the year is significant because it illustrates how this heightened awareness of the passage of time could trigger eschatological thoughts, in other words, a consideration of the end of time.

The New Year seems to have had a similar effect on Robert Burns. In a letter to Mrs Dunlop dated 1 January 1789 he mentions that New Year's Day is one of several special moments in the year. He suggests that it causes a heightening of perception and allows the normal routine of life to be challenged:

I own myself to be so little a Presbyterian that I approve of set times & seasons of more than ordinary acts of Devotion; for breaking in that habituated routine of life and thought which is so apt to reduce our existence to a kind of instinct; or even sometimes & with some minds to an state very little superior to mere machinery […] I believe I owe this to that glorious Paper in the Spectator, 'The vision of Mirza'; a piece that struck my young fancy, before I was capable of fixing an idea to a word of three syllables. (De Lancey Ferguson: 293)

The increased awareness of the passage of time evoked by the beginning of the New Year has a defamiliarising effect on life in general and the transience of human existence is emphasised. It is also significant that Burns intertextually refers to a piece which, like Balwhidder's dream, allegorically deals with humanity's relationship to God. The allusion is to Joseph Addison's prose allegory entitled 'The Vision of Mirza'. This is another piece that emphasises the fragility and brevity of human life. The vision includes a consideration of the end of time since it concludes with multitudes of people being swept down a river towards judgement.

A letter to his father, written very early in his literary career, dated 27 December 1781 provides another insight into Burns's thoughts around Hogmanay and pre-echoes some of the themes that arise in the letter of 1789. The letter is framed by references to the impending New Year and it is seems to be this that arouses the series of reflections on transience and the passage of time articulated in this epistle. Furthermore, Burns once again through intertextuality gravitates towards eschatology, this time with a self-explanatory reference to the book of Revelation:

I am quite transported by the thought that ere long, perhaps very soon, I shall bid an eternal adieu to all the pains, & uneasiness & disquietudes of this weary life; for I assure you I am heartily tired of it, and, if I do not very much deceive myself I could contentedly & gladly resign it […] It is for this reason I am more pleased with the 15th, 16th & 17th versus of the 7th Chapter of Revelation than any ten times as many versus in the whole Bible, & would not exchange the noble enthusiasm with which they inspire me, for all that the world has to offer (De Lancey Ferguson: 7).

The verses that Burns alludes to describe God assembling his chosen people from the various tribes of Israel and promising to protect them immediately before the seventh seal is broken.

Once again, therefore, this text composed at the New Year contains a strong eschatological dimension. The extracts from Galt's novel and Burns's letters illustrate how the New Year, and reflection on the New Year, can lead to a heightened perception of the passage of time, and furthermore, they illustrate how this could manifest itself in millenarian undercurrents that suggest the ephemeral nature of the whole of creation and time itself.

These millenarian feelings, which are exacerbated by the onset of a New Year, are evident in the rise of a particular poetic genre during this period. Many poets across the British Isles composed poems on the advent of the New Year. These were often odes, though poems situated on this temporal threshold could also take other forms. These poems often deal with the themes of mortality and transience and often have strong millennial or millenarian overtones. Hugh Tynan, Henry Boyd and James Orr were amongst those Irish poets who used the genre, whilst in Scotland poets such as Robert Burns, Richard Gall and James Hogg wrote pieces situated on this temporal threshold. Many other examples of this type of poem were published anonymously in December or January editions of newspapers and periodicals.

One of the most important examples is Burns's 'Elegy on the Year 1788' which seems to subtly compliment the millenarian undercurrents that seem to populate his thoughts around Hogmanay. In the opening section, the events of 1788 are described as "prodigious" and "dire" (Kinsley: 360). These are words that would have been common in contemporary millenarian language. The word "prodigious" seems to suggest that the events witnessed during this year are out of the ordinary and hints that they are signifiers of something greater, whilst the word "dire" generates a sense of foreboding. The millenarian connotations of Burns's language are illustrated by Harrison who quotes a 1795 millenarian publication entitled *The World's Doom*. The anonymous author argues that "strange prodigies" are "the never failing precursors of dire and calamitous events" and that the abundance of such portentous occurrences in the 1790s suggests that the Millennium is imminent (Harrison: 57).

The millenarian undercurrents of 'Elegy on the Year 1788' are continued with the images of specific prodigious or remarkable events such as the unsettled animals, weeping earth and drying wells in the penultimate stanza:

> Observe the very nowt an' sheep,
> How dowff an' dowie now they creep;
> Nay, even the yirth itsel does cry,
> For Embro' wells are grutten dry. (Kinsley: 61)

These prodigious events, as well as the political tumults referred to in the poem, are essentially what people in the period might have seen as signs of the times; what Hill calls "those contemporary natural and international catastrophes" that often accompany eschatological feelings (Hill: 4). The speaker's descriptions of strange and portentous occurrences exemplify the millenarian interpretation of the world in that "any instance in which the laws of nature appeared to have been set aside, any abnormal or inexplicable happening, any unusual behaviour in man or beast aroused wide-spread interest and speculation" (Harrison: 42). Although Burns was not literally of the opinion that the apocalypse was imminent, he certainly incorporates language and images that were prominent in contemporary millenarianism in this particular New Year poem.

Burns in this instance treats millenarianism in rather a flippant and reductive manner although he displays a familiarity with its imagery. Burns's interest in millenarianism was perhaps nurtured by first hand knowledge of its influence through a sect called the Buchanites who settled in Ayrshire in the 1780s. Elspeth Buchan and her followers became a familiar part of the rural community in Burns's neighbourhood near Dumfries. Burns even acknowledged in a letter to his cousin, which is largely devoted to descriptions of this sect, that he was "personally acquainted" with many of its members (De Lancey Ferguson: 21-22). Although Burns was dismissive of the teachings of their leader, Elspeth Buchan, he does display a familiarity with their tenets. Furthermore, the strong millennial, if not millenarian, elements to several of his songs of the 1790s such as 'The Tree of Liberty' and 'A Man's a Man' illustrate his genuine interest in these concepts. Both of these pieces conclude with similarly optimistic visions of impending utopia and the imagery of penultimate stanza of 'The Tree of Liberty' explicitly evokes the apocalyptic text of Isaiah, chapter 2, which foretells that the nations "shall beat their swords into ploughshares" (Barker: 958).

The millenarian undercurrents in 'Elegy on the Year 1788' have an important function in that they evoke the sense of uncertainty and anxiety which the inhabitants of the country are feeling. Millenarianism, because it entails the expectation of dramatic immanent change, by its very nature emphasises the fragility of the existing status quo. Burns's Britain is a tumultuous and uncertain place in the midst of the Regency Bill Crisis. National figureheads are referred to in unflattering terms and the King, the symbolic head of the body politic, is literally insane. Burns audaciously invokes the mental state of King George III by describing the New Year as "nae hand cuff'd, mizl'd, half shakl'd *Regent*", which alludes to the physical restraints placed on the insane monarch (Noble and Scott Hogg : 427). Meanwhile the leading politicians bicker in an undignified manner like the speaker's "wee birdy cocks" (Kinsley: 360-61). These descriptions could be read as Burns's humorous evocation of the turmoil and tribulations which were supposed to accompany the last days.

Burns's manipulation of genre in 'Elegy on the Year 1788', written in early 1789, is also significant since the poem explicitly engages in a political debate with the traditional New Year odes of the poet Laureate, Thomas Warton. It was an integral part of the Poet Laureate's function during this period to pen these optimistic New Year odes that celebrated the achievements of the nation and Henry James Pye continued this tradition when he took up the office in 1790. Whilst Burns's nation was a tumultuous and uncertain entity, the Laureates often depicted the nation as an eternal entity progressing through time towards an idealised present. In his 'Ode XVI. For the New Year, 1786', for example, Thomas Warton's muse peers into the future and announces that "Albion still shall keep her wonted state" and "still in eternal story shine" (Warton: 97). But the millenarian undercurrents in Burns's poem undermines the Laureates' conception of the nation as eternal and stable, since Millenarianism emphasises the ephemeral nature of all human constructs including the nation.

The genre of the New Year poem, therefore, became a site for political debate and the motif of the millennium was central to this argument. The idea of the millennium, although often associated with radicalism, was still pertinent to several of the Laureate odes as it was to many of the radical answers. The main difference between the treatment of the millennium in Laureate odes and their radical responses is that the Laureate odes seem to hint that the millennium has already begun. Britain is depicted as having emerged through past conflicts and tribulations into a more enlightened age. They contain idealised often almost Utopian depictions of Britain which suggest that they are underpinned by post-millennial paradigms. Post-millennialists believed that the millennium could be brought about by human endeavour, and that a utopian society could be constructed gradually over time. For post-millennialists the second coming of Christ would occur at the conclusion, not the beginning of this regenerative age.

Pre-millenialists, on the other hand, believed that the second coming, and the onset of the millennium would be dramatically inaugurated by the sudden return of the Messiah. This paradigm, tended to be favoured in radical answers to the Laureate odes. The conservative poet Laureates, Warton and Pye, who eulogised the political status quo, could present contemporary Britain as having already attained a perfect almost millennial society, whereas radicals could present it as a corrupt and sinful place ripe for divine intervention, which would bring about a regenerative period. In the poet Laureates' odes the New Year was an auspicious and optimistic moment whilst in radical pieces such as Burns's it was often an ominous moment that presented the prospect of calamity. This reveals the complexity and diversity of beliefs surrounding the millennium and demonstrates how people with very different political aspirations could invoke it to support their ideas. The motif, therefore, and the genre of the New Year poem became a site for political debate.

The ode was the perfect form for this debate to take place in. Both the Poet Laureates and radical poets, paradoxically, found the form a suitable medium in which to express their conflicting messages. For the poet Laureates the ode was an archetypally conservative genre in that it was a Classical form. Its traditional function as a public utterance meant that it was the perfect form to contain the nationalistic, public addresses of the poet Laureates. Ralph Cohen, for example, has recently argued that the odaic form in the eighteenth-century represented a self-conscious attempt to return poetry to its proper channels through emulation of the Classics (Cohen: 205). The conservatively Classical form, therefore, reflected the conservative political message and the bombastic and official overtones of the genre endowed the speaking voice with authority.

The ode, and in particular the Pindaric ode with its dramatic fluctuations in rhyme scheme and metrical construction, proved a potent weapon for radical poets. Odes seem to be structured in such a way as to mimic apocalyptic or millenarian views of time. Coleridge, for instance, recognised that one of the main features of the ode was its "impetuosity of transition" (Mays: 304). It tended to involve sudden shifts in subject matter and to incorporate stanzas of various length and altering rhythm. Therefore, its fractures tended to mirror the temporal fracture which occurs at the New Year and, by implication, the apocalyptic model of time which it promotes. The ode, therefore, was an ideal genre in which to contest this debate. The form substantiated the millenarian themes of the poems since the abrupt structural transitions recalled the temporal transitions that they were evoking in the minds of their readers.

A good example of a radical Ulster New Year ode is the one composed by a poet calling himself Pindaricus. This poem appeared in the *Northern Star*, the newspaper of the United Irish movement, early in 1792. This poem strongly pre-echoes, in terms of theme, if not versification, Coleridge's more famous radical ode of 1796 entitled 'Ode to the Departing Year'. The poem is saturated with references to the political turmoil of 1790s Europe and makes several references to the impending millennium. In Pindaricus's ode, as in Coleridge's, Britain is a corrupt society whose unpleasant leaders are inviting and provoking divine wrath. Referring to Britain's continuing controversial participation in the slave trade Pindaricus writes:

> O God! Forgive this guilty land!
> Blood ill becomes a Christian's hand!
> Let the world at last behold
> Britain, not the Slave of gold.
> First among the nations free,
> Let the rest resemble thee;
> Teach them universal love,
> Copy thus the realms above.
> O give – to save what Heav'n affords,
> Thy King, thy Commons, and thy Lords!
> Lest God should plunge thy Forests in the wave-
> Poor Afric's Peace, and Freedom to her slave. (Pindaricus, 1792)

The poet presents us with a final image of an irate God plunging Britain into the sea unless it mends its ways. This is certainly not the eternal, enlightened and stable isle that the Laureates evoke. This extract also demonstrates the dramatic shifts in rhythm and meter which the form often displayed. The opening couplet is iambic tetrameter, but this gives way to the quicker rhythms of trochaic tetrameter for the following three couplets. The iambic rhythm is restored for the final two couplets, though the last is pentameter rather than tetrameter. These fractures and fluctuations seem to reflect the tempestuous times that the poet is describing.

But the radical odes did not always favour pre-millennial paradigms. A belief in the certainty of divine intervention could potentially engender passivity and encourage submission to the present regime since it was soon to be toppled in any case. Some of these odes seem to oscillate between millenarianism and millennialism. Pindaricus's ode also links the idea of the millennium with the global struggle for freedom that many of the Ulster radicals felt that they were engaging in. He writes that:

> This flame of Freedom must precede
> Thy promis'd reign of grace:
> The age Millenial is decreed,
> But War's alarms must cease.

This seems to suggest that human endeavour must bring about the divinely decreed millennial age. It is people who must kindle this flame of freedom and halt the wars.

Another New Year ode from Ulster written by the Antrim poet James Orr in 1806 also suggests that the millennium will come but must be brought about by human endeavour. It first appeared in the *Belfast Commercial Chronicle*, and interprets the contemporary international conflicts as a sign that the millennial age has not been attained:

> Ah! If the troublers of the times,
> Who mischief perpetrate and plan,
> Reclaim'd from follies, and from crimes,
> Would live as man should live with man,
> Want ne'er would make poor merit wan,
> Nor wealth inflame proud insolence;
> But angel's eyes would gladly scan
> MESSIAH'S reign indeed commence. (Orr, 1806)

Again the suggestion is that it is human failings that are preventing the onset of the millennium. Orr, like Pindaricus and Burns, rejects the optimistic eschatology articulated in the Poet Laureates' odes. It also seems to problematise the notion that the millennium will be inaugurated by divine intervention since it asserts the importance of human action. For Orr, the disappointed radical, the millennium is still a distant prospect as the present represents turbulence and oppression.

The New Year poem, therefore, became an important genre in late eighteenth and early nineteenth-century Britain and Ireland. These poems became, due to their position on a temporal threshold, intimately associated with the millenarian and millennial feelings that were sweeping Britain and Ireland during this tumultuous historical era. Millenarianism and millennialism were complex forces since they transcended denominational and class boundaries and could be found in both pre-millennial and post-millennial forms. This complexity is reflected in the New Year poems of Britain and Ireland which were composed by poets from a diverse range of political, religious and social backgrounds. Consequently, the genre and the motif of the millennium became the site for a lively political debate. New Year odes from Scotland and Ireland, by Robert Burns, James Orr and Pindaricus illustrate the variety of approaches adopted by poets who used the form to subvert the optimistic eschatology articulated annually by the poet Laureates.

## References

Barker, K. ed. 2002. *King James Version, Study Bible*. Grand Rapids: Zondervan

Cohen, R. 2001. "The Return to the Ode". Ed. J. Sitter. *The Cambridge Companion To Eighteenth Century Poetry*. Cambridge: Cambridge University Press

De Lancey Ferguson, J. 1985. *The Letters of Robert Burns*. 2nd edition revised by G. Ross Roy. Volume 1. Oxford: Clarendon Press

De Latocnaye. 1984. *A Frenchman's Walk Through Ireland, 9* Trans. John Stevenson. Belfast: Blackstaff Press. First published 1798

Dobbs, F. 1800. *Memoirs of Francis Dobbs, Esq. Also Genuine reports of his speeches in Parliament, on the subject of an union,...with extracts from his poem on the Millenium*. Dublin: J. Jones

Foster, RF. 1988. *Modern Ireland: 1600-1972*. London: Penguin

Galt, J. 1821. *Annals of the Parish*. Ed. C.E. Brock. 1980. Edinburgh: James Thin

Harrison, JFC. 1979. *The Second Coming: Popular Millenarianism 1780-1850*. London: Routledge

Hill, M. 2001. *The Time of the End: Millenarian Beliefs in Ulster*. Belfast: The Belfast Society

Kinsley, J, ed. 1969. *Burns: Complete Poems and Songs*. Oxford: Clarendon Press

Mays, J.C.C, ed. 2001. *The Collected Works of Samuel Taylor Coleridge: Poetical Works* 1. Princeton: Princeton University Press

Noble, A., and P. Scott Hogg, eds. 2001 *The Canongate Burns: The Poems and Songs of Robert Burns*. Edinburgh: Canongate Classics

Orr, J. 'Ode for the New Year', *Belfast Commercial Chronicle*, 31st December 1806

Paley, M.D. 1999. *Apocalypse and Millennium in English Romantic Poetry*. Oxford: Clarendon Press

Pindaricus. 'An Ode for the New Year, 1792', *Northern Star,* 11th January 1792

Warton, T. 1802. *The Poetical Works of the Late Thomas Warton*. 5th edition, Ed. R. Mant. Volume 2. London

# Macpherson's Legacy: The Publication of the Gaelic Originals by the Highland Society of London

*Janice M. Fairney*

Under the patronage of the Highland Society of London (HSL) the Gaelic originals of James Macpherson's published translations were eventually printed in 1807. These English 'translations' of epic songs or poems allegedly known in Gaelic tradition were published in 1761 and 1763. Macpherson said his translations were the result of collecting the poems of Ossian from both oral tradition and manuscripts. Ossian was reputedly a third-century bard. They offered 'proof' that Gaelic Scotland had an ancient civilisation and provided the Edinburgh *literati* with a truly Scottish epic, which encompassed all their ideals. This led to controversy and debate particularly during the 1760s and 1770s, and on an academic level the debate continues to this day. Dr Samuel Johnson, the English poet, essayist and lexicographer, was the leading antagonist. He believed that Macpherson was a forger and that the poems were fake, and that he did not believe in the existence of ancient manuscripts. He stated that as 'far as we can find, the Erse language was never written till very lately for the purpose of religion. A nation that cannot write, or a language that was never written, has no manuscripts' (Boswell: 1998: 578). Johnson's public attack on Macpherson and the poems of Ossian led to the debate and controversy gaining greater currency. For that reason, the HSL wanted the originals of the poems published, to defend the honour of their country and to prove to Johnson and his supporters that Scotland did have a corpus of ancient Gaelic literature comparable to that of Homer. The events that led to the HSL supporting Macpherson's efforts will be addressed here, rather than the poems themselves.

Macpherson had frequently indicated his intention to publish the originals, and his friends in Edinburgh and London, who believed that this would put an end to the controversy, encouraged this. An early attempt was made by Macpherson to raise the necessary subscriptions for publication of the poems in 1761, but he was not successful. He also had the friendship and acquaintance of some of the future members of the HSL who were to play pivotal roles in the subsequent publication, and these links could plausibly have been formed before the Scotsmen created their society. When the HSL was eventually established in 1778, it was essentially a support group for Highlanders in London, made up for the most part of Scottish nobility, landed gentry and army officers. The members of the society met together, to remember and preserve aspects of the good old days of their youth, in that halcyon time when heroic ballads, tales and songs were constant companions during the long winter nights. Hector Maclean, one of the collectors employed by John Francis Campbell, writing nearly eighty years after the HSL was established, expressed the passion that Highlanders had for these poems:

> A good many of them firmly believe in the extravagance of these stories. They speak of the Ossianic heroes with as much feeling, sympathy, and belief in their existence and reality as the readers of the newspapers do of the exploits of the British army in the Crimea or India. (Campbell, 1890, I: iv-v)

Like those Highlanders that Maclean spoke of, the HSL Committee, entrusted with the task of publishing Macpherson's originals, believed implicitly that the poems were genuine and wanted them in print. Shortly after the HSL's foundation a delegation met with him to discuss and encourage publication. Macpherson informed them "that he was ready to publish the original Gaelic of Ossian, as soon as an adequate fund was provided" (Sinclair, 1813: 16-17).

However, two months later he had changed his mind and asked John Mackenzie to report to the Society that, "he would not publish the Original Gaelic of Ossian if the Fund for that purpose was raised by any mode of Subscription whatever; but that he would publish it at his own private Expence [sic] as soon as his Conveniency [sic] would permit".[1]

However, there was no progress. By 1783, John Murray (later known as Sir John Macgregor Murray), an employee of the East India Company, learnt that there was a need for money if the poems were ever to be published. He appealed to, and aroused the patriotic feelings of, his fellow Highlanders in India; he believed that enough money could be provided for the publication, for they:

> …have Gaelic blood in their veins, and Gaelic sentiments in their hearts:—Men, who know, and feel, that, elegant as Ossian's modern dress is, it is not equal to his native garb; that the Gaelic, barbarous and uncouth as it is represented, has expressions peculiarly nervous and sublime for every noble and exalted idea that can enlarge and elevate the human mind. (Ossian, 1807, I: ccxvii)

Murray succeeded in receiving promises of nearly £1000 for the Ossian cause. As the money was collected, he sent it to Macpherson, but as security he also wrote to John Mackenzie, Secretary of the HSL, asking that the society find someone who would get the poems ready for print "if Mr Macpherson is not up to it".[2] There was a delay. Perhaps the HSL was waiting for some action on Macpherson's part, for it was not until the middle of 1784 that formal correspondence took place requesting a further delegation to discover the cause of delay, as money was no longer an issue.[26] Macpherson responded that a lack of leisure prevented him from "arranging and printing the originals of Ossian, as they have come to my hands".[4]

However, the period of leisure looked for by Macpherson never occurred, as his political career and his work for the Nabob of Arcot took all his time. By the end of 1787, Macpherson had received all the subscription money; and the minutes of the HSL hinted at the unease felt by its members because of Macpherson's lack of progress. A communication was sent expressing concern:

> The Committee being extremely anxious for the honour of their Country, as well as for Mr Macpherson's Credit, that these valuable poems may be preserved are apprehensive that the delay in laying them before the public has made impressions which they are desirous to counteract, and knowing that this may be best and most effectually done by his Ability and zeal they beg that their solicitude on this Subject may be admitted by Mr Macpherson as an apology for repeating their earnest request that he will be pleased to publish with as little further delay as possible the Gaelic works of Ossian. Assuring him that if he is in want of any Aid which the Society can supply, it will be cheerfully and thankfully given.[5]

The same communication was sent three years later. Certainly help did come from individual HSL members who formed a coterie to work from Macpherson's manuscripts. The task of "arranging and printing the originals of the Poems of Ossian, as they have come to my hands" would have been considerable. The originals were for the most part fragments taken down from oral tradition or from old manuscripts, and Macpherson was experimenting with his own

---

[1] NLS, Adv Ms 73.2.24, f. 15.
[2] NLS, DEP MS 268.1, 29 October, 1783.
[3] NLS, MS DEP 268.21, 24-5.
[4] NLS, MS DEP 268.1, 4 July 1784.
[5] NLS, MS DEP 268.21, 79.

simplified Gaelic orthography. John Mackenzie, the secretary, was completely in Macpherson's confidence, and they had planned in detail the necessary steps needed for publication. Robert Macfarlan,[6] who was equally skilled in Gaelic and Latin, began translating Macpherson's Gaelic manuscripts into Latin and fellow member Captain Alexander Morison copied poems from these manuscripts. However, their actions may have been completely independent of the HSL, for there was no further communication between the Society and Macpherson until 1794. In March Macpherson attended a committee meeting of the HSL and presented a specimen of what he called *A Collection of Ancient Poetry*. After examination of the volume the committee resolved:

> that as they do not consider this music ancient, it cannot therefore, on account of the title have the smallest support from the society—but as Mr Macpherson has attended the Committee now formerly. They direct one guinea to be given him for his trouble.[7]

Two years later Macpherson died.

As Literary Executor and close friend, John Mackenzie was given the charge of fulfilling Macpherson's long stated desire. For this he was left £1000 to cover the expense of publication according to the plan they had made between them.[8] Mackenzie was left with a manuscript that was not written according "to the system used at present", and was mixed with Macpherson's own attempt at simplifying the Gaelic orthography. Macpherson expressed a desire for using "the Greek and not the Roman Character in printing the Original: the Greek being better adapted than the Roman to the nature of the Gaelic Tongue, and having been the Character used in writing that Language in ancient times, as appears incontrovertibly from several passages in Caesar".[9] Macpherson had never finally decided which system to use. Thus, Mackenzie was left to decide the question of orthography, and this was the first task he set himself.

As far as Mackenzie was concerned, this was an important and time-consuming conundrum. He consulted the antiquarian George Chalmers who suggested some people Mackenzie should contact. At that time, he contemplated travel to Scotland to speak to them in person.[10] However, his health was not good and he postponed the journey. In 1798, Mackenzie sent a memorandum to Gaelic scholars and other interested parties explaining his task. He outlined his concerns and potential financial difficulties if he were to follow Macpherson's wish to use the Greek alphabet. Later he had printed a sample of Macpherson's simplified Gaelic spelling in Greek characters and sent it to interested Gaelic scholars. There must have been some support for the Greek alphabet for John Mackenzie wrote to Henry Mackenzie, chairman of the Highland Society of Scotland's committee investigating the authenticity of Poems of Ossian, that:

> …there are ideas in agitation for providing the necessary fund for the expense of even an Edition in the Greek character; but they are not sufficiently ripe, nor do I know that they ever shall. That matter depends upon others, not upon me: It is likely however to be decided in the course of the winter or Spring. Of this however be assured, that the original shall be printed in *some* shape: that is a matter of no doubt whatever.[11]

---

[6] He had been employed by the Highland Society in Edinburgh as Gaelic Professor before moving south to London.
[7] NLS, MS DEP 268/22, p. 16.
[8] NLS, Adv MS 73.2.13, f. 37.
[9] NLS, Adv MS 73.2.13, f. 130.
[10] NLS, Adv MS 73.2.13 ff. 134-5.
[11] NLS, Adv MS 73.2.13, f. 126.

Another specimen printed in the Roman alphabet was produced and sent out. It should be noted that both specimens had been printed from proof sheets still in the possession of the printer which Macpherson had printed while he was toying with the prospect of publishing the originals. In the end, both of Macpherson's specimens were given up as unworkable. There were concerns regarding the orthography, especially, that the Gaelic might be expressed poorly by Macpherson's system. The Greek characters were regarded as unworkable, for it would require Highlanders to adapt to a new character once again in order to be able to read and understand their own language. Mackenzie finally decided to use Roman characters with the established orthography, but he decided to await the publication of Rev Alexander Stewart's Gaelic Grammar which would act as a guide to correct the spelling, for Macpherson's manuscripts were "found extremely incorrect and irregular".[12]

During this interval he arranged for Macfarlan to continue translating the manuscripts into Latin, a task begun under the auspices of Macpherson. Mackenzie hoped that, as a Gaelic scholar, Macfarlan would be able "to comprehend the numerous passages which had defied the skill of Mr Macpherson".[13] After the publication of Stewart's Grammar, Rev Thomas Ross of Edinburgh was employed to transcribe the whole work again and standardise the spelling. He used not only Macpherson's own transcription but also another draft manuscript copy,[14] probably written by Captain Morison. Ross also had access to Macfarlan's Latin translation. Macfarlan's translation and Ross' transcription were completed by the summer of 1801. Mackenzie then had to decide on publishing. Macpherson had previously made enquiries regarding the success of such a publication; the London Booksellers he consulted were not very encouraging. Macpherson had also offered ownership of the manuscripts as an inducement to aid publishing, but no one was interested. The quality of edition that Macpherson wanted was not provided by his Legacy, and as early as 1798 Mackenzie had expressed concern that there would not be money available for publication.[15] So at this juncture he looked towards John MacGregor Murray and the Indian Subscription. After seeking legal advice that the £1000 legacy he had been given for publication was, in fact, quite separate from the Indian Subscription, the executors were ready to pay out this money to Murray, which would provide the finances needed for publication. However, Macpherson's heir opposed the action and the matter went to the Law Courts. Mackenzie decided to carry on with the publication on the promise that the Judges would carry in favour of the Subscribers. Mackenzie obtained quotes from printers in Edinburgh and London. Messrs Nicol & Bulmer, London was chosen, and the work went to the press in 1803. Mackenzie, who had been incapacitated by illness for the previous 12 years, died shortly after the first proofs had been received.

On his death, Mackenzie's son George inherited Macpherson's papers. He was entrusted to continue the task begun by Macpherson and continued by his father. In May 1804, he informed the HSL of his immediate intention of publishing the Poems of Ossian in the original Gaelic, with a verbal Latin translation by Robert Macfarlan. He noted that:

> As the Highland Society manifested a great interest and zeal in the publication of these ancient Remains of Celtic Literature, it was his earnest wish, as a tribute justly due to their exertions to introduce the Poems into the world under the Patronage of the Society, in full confidence of their aid to render the Edition of the works of Ossian as complete as possible; and that in order to carry these his intentions into effect, he had given directions to place the original manuscripts of the Poems into the hands of the Secretary.[16]

---

[12] NLS, Adv MS 73.2.24, f. 70.
[13] NLS, Adv MS 73.2.24, f. 70.
[14] NLS, Adv MS 73.2.11, f. 50.
[15] NLS, Adv MS 73.2.13, f. 130.
[16] NLS, MS DEP 268.23, 121.

George Mackenzie did not give up his copyright of the manuscripts when he made his proposal to the HSL. It was for this reason he delivered all the manuscripts to Secretary Alexander Fraser, who had agreed to act as his agent. There was also a threat that Macpherson's heirs were claiming the property of the originals on the death of John Mackenzie. However, Macpherson's heirs decided to leave the manuscripts in the hands of George Mackenzie with the HSL in charge of publication, possibly in the realisation that such an edition would not be financially profitable, for that was Macpherson's own conclusion. Regardless of the issue of copyright, the Society was delighted by the request and immediately appointed a committee consisting of Sir John Sinclair, Sir John Macpherson, Sir John Macgregor Murray and John Macarthur, assisted by the Secretary Alexander Fraser and Deputy Secretary Colin Macrae. Among these six members only three had proficiency in Gaelic. Macrae was a nephew of the late John Mackenzie and was familiar with the progress made by his uncle. The committee wrote to the Highland Society of Scotland (HSS)[17] and other people, including scholars, clergymen and Scottish nobility who might be able to provide assistance in "rendering the said publication of Ossian's Poems in the original Gaelic as perfect as possible".[18] It also asked for assistance in finding the original of the eleven poems in Macpherson's translation, which could not be found among his papers. The HSL also enlarged its field of inquiry to North America, and letters were written to Col. Hamilton in Virginia, Duncan Macrae in South Carolina, and Rev Mr Macdonnel in Canada, for it was felt that some of the missing poems might be known among the Highland emigrants. Sir John Sinclair offered to write an English Dissertation, and John Macarthur was requested to translate some of Cesarotti's writings, which provided evidence on the authenticity of the poems. It was also decided that a new English translation was necessary. The committee believed that a line for line translation with words closer to the Gaelic would provide the English reader with proof of the authenticity of the poems.

A system of correcting proofs was set up, and Rev Alexander Stewart of Moulin agreed to revise and correct the Gaelic orthography. Because of the expense that would be incurred from the numerous parcels being sent between London and Scotland, arrangements were made with the Board of Agriculture for free delivery. Rev Stewart provided copious orthographic information and asked to be considered "as an amicable co-adjutor, not a censorious Castigator". He agreed with the late Mr Mackenzie that 'the Original' ought to be given to the public as near as possible to the manuscripts left by Macpherson, but suggested these exceptions:

> That the Orthography be adapted to the Standard of the Gaelic Scriptures; that manifest corrections and emendations of the Text be adopted, when those can be obtained by collating different copies; and where the Text is evidently corrupted or unintelligible, that a slight conjectural emendation be introduced, when it extends only to a word or a phrase.[19]

There were times when correcting proofs of Ossian's poems had to be set aside while he continued his work on revising the Prophetic Books of the Old Testament for the Gaelic Bible. Nevertheless, the Rev Stewart continued to correct the proofs, even after his move to Dingwall, and would have continued the task to its conclusion. However, the new Minister for the Board of Agriculture, in a cost-cutting measure, decided the Board would no longer cover the expense of free transmission of parcels. The HSL decided the expense would be

---

[17] The Highland Society of Edinburgh changed its name to Highland Society of Scotland and is now known as The Royal Highland and Agricultural Society of Scotland.
[18] NLS, MS DEP 268/23, 122.
[19] NLS, MS DEP 268/1, 2 October 1804.

prohibitive. It decided that Mr Alexander Stewart, Collector of Gaelic Poetry, would continue his namesake's task, following the system that the Rev Stewart "had chalked out".[20]

The death of Robert Macfarlan also necessitated the need to find someone who had the ability to continue the Latin translation. The Rev Stewart of Moulin was the first choice. Because he was busy translating the Old Testament Prophetic Books, he refused, but stated that he would consider revising the Latin. He was certain that the HSL would find a Latin scholar up to the task.[21] Robert Jamieson of Fort William was selected. His task was to finish the remaining arguments of Ossian and to revise any proofs of the Latin translation, which had been printed prior to Macfarlan's death. The committee, as a form of insurance, asked Sir Frederick Eden, a respected Latin scholar to revise the proofs if the task could not be finished. However, once again the young collector, Alexander Stewart, finished the task.

At the suggestion of Charles Stewart, the actual typesetting and proof sheets for the Gaelic sections were done in Edinburgh at the University Press to avoid paper duty, and Rev Thomas Ross superintended the press.[22] By 1805 the Gaelic and Latin versions had been printed, although still going through the process of revisions and corrections. The preface, Sinclair's dissertation and the translation of Cesarotti by Macarthur were still waiting the press. It had been hoped to publish early in 1806. However, the inconclusiveness of the HSS's Report impelled Sinclair to provide irrefutable evidence that the poems were genuine. This insistence delayed the work. He continued writing to different scholars and universities in an attempt to get fresh evidence. Sinclair also sent Rev John Macdonald of Ferintosh as a "Poetical Missionary" to track down evidence in the western parts of Inverness, Sutherland and Ross. Sinclair felt this was a better way than trusting to the mail. Sir John Sinclair found the proof he sought from Bishop Cameron who informed him of a manuscript which had belonged to the Rev Mr John Farquharson, the Prefect of Studies at the Scots College of Douay. Rev James MacGillivray gave evidence that Farquharson had all the poems that were translated by Macpherson and many more.[23] This was what he wanted, and Sinclair now believed he had unquestionable evidence of authenticity. Macpherson was the translator only. Another response which Sinclair regarded as new evidence was a letter from Rev John Anderson who said Macpherson had been employed several winters at his Highland estate "preparing and writing in his own hand, a Gaelic copy of those poems to be printed", and further that he had never heard him say that he was the author.[24] Sinclair was now able to write his dissertation. Macarthur, completed his translation of Cesarotti, and went on to prepare a conclusion for the whole work. He was of the opinion that all the evidence they had provided on the authenticity of Ossian was as strong as "proofs of Holy writ".[25]

The book was published in 1807 containing not only the Gaelic and Latin translation of the Poems of Ossian, but also considerable evidence of their apparent authenticity. To this was added the First Book of Fingal in a new English translation, with additional notes by Rev Thomas Ross. Also, two of the Macpherson's missing poems had been found among his papers, translated into Latin and English by Alexander Stewart. Topographical essays on areas mentioned in Ossian's poems were written by the following eminent Gaelic scholars: Rev Donald Macnicol; Rev William Campbell; Rev John Smith; Rev Ludovick Grant and Rev Norman Macleod. Appendices included a specimen of ancient music, a list of Gaelic books published during the sixteenth, seventeenth and eighteenth centuries and a catalogue of all Gaelic and Irish manuscripts still in existence in Great Britain and Ireland, including a list of the manuscripts that had been collected by Macpherson himself. The final publication was forty years after Macpherson had stated his own desire of publishing the Gaelic originals, and

---

[20] NLS, Adv MS 73.2.11, f. 118.
[21] NLS, MS DEP 268/1, 2 October 1804.
[22] NLS, Adv MS 73.2.24, f. 85.
[23] NLS, Adv MS 73.2.11, ff. 125-9.
[24] NLS, Adv MS 73.2.24, ff. 116-7.
[25] NLS, Adv MS 73.2.11, f. 64.

twenty-eight years since the first official meeting with Macpherson. It had been a long task, but the HSL was satisfied with the finished work. In an advertisement put out by the society prior to publication it was stated that it was:

> The most valuable and most interesting Literary Work that has appeared for many years. The Natives of Scotland in general, and more especially those who are connected with the Northern parts of that Kingdom, must rejoice to learn that the Poems of the immortal Ossian have at length appeared in their native garb, accompanied by Documents which clearly establish their authenticity, independent of the strong internal evidence which is exhibited by the Work itself; from an Examination of which it evidently appears that even in Macpherson's Translation sufficient justice has not been done to the Beauties of the Original.[26]

The Committee believed it had published a very valuable piece of work. It was preserving those ancient Gaelic poems. It had rescued Fingal and his worthies, men who had exhibited "heroic valour , exalted values and the most refined strain of generous and manly sentiments" [27] from oblivion.

The HSL had hoped for financial success but reaped near financial disaster, for the publication raised little interest. By 1813, the Society had still not recovered the £2000 expense of the publication. The HSL appealed to Sir John Macgregor Murray for assistance from the Indian Subscription money. However, Macgregor Murray felt that the HSL had been unwise in making it such an expensive undertaking. He had resigned from the Committee because of this. The subscribers had simply wanted the Gaelic originals published, and any excess should be spent on encouraging the Gaelic language. For them there was no need of evidence, the poems were genuine. The Society received only £700 from those funds, which amounted to almost £3000 at the time of settlement. That was all Macgregor Murray believed the HSL was entitled to for the cost was prohibitive to many who would have wanted a copy of Ossian's poems. For the HSL had, according to Macgregor Murray, "not sent Him to his native hills" but had "entombed Him in your magnificence! You have buried him in Gold".[28] Because there was a lack of sales, the Gaelic Ossian did receive its audience mainly through philanthropic gesture. The books were given out as prizes at Highland Games and copies sent to the General Assembly schools, copies were also sent to many of its branches in the Highland enclaves around the world. It was there that many young emigrant Scots learnt by heart the poems of Ossian from these very books. Rev Macdonnel in Upper Canada wrote that the poems were taught in several schools, and that many youths could repeat many thousand lines of these poems by heart.[29]

The committee felt that the publication of the Gaelic originals was but "one link in the chain of the committee's operations". It wanted a new English translation, and to republish all the collections of Gaelic poetry. It also wanted to "rescue from the grasp of perishable time" other poems in the hope that the society might add:

> To the existing stock some other fugitive Poems & of retrieving, although in an imperfect state, some of the Originals lost or destroyed by Mr Macpherson. Thus a body of materials may be provided for a Gaelic Dictionary, and a Store of interesting Literature furnished to excite Celtic Study, and to transmit unimpaired to future ages the Primitive or at least one of the Primitive Languages of the Universe.[30]

---

[26] NLS, MS DEP 268/24, 122.
[27] NLS, MS DEP 268/24, 122.
[28] NLS, Adv MS 73.2.26, f. 86.
[29] NLS, MS DEP 268/43, 32.
[30] NLS, MS DEP 268/24, 124.

It had begun the task of a new literal English translation. Macpherson had planned a line for line translation of this kind but his version was lost. So from 1804, Rev Thomas Ross was employed to work on a new English translation. He was also instructed to write copious notes, which would prove that Macpherson was only the translator of the poems, and an inferior one at that. Ross eventually translated into English the complete *Poems of Ossian*. Sinclair hoped that Ross's translation would be turned into a prose translation "in easy and floury language which will furnish the reader with the full sense of the original" He was to be helped in this endeavour by Rev Dr Stuart of Luss, Rev Alexander Stewart of Dingwall and Ewen MacLachlan of Aberdeen. Of the three only Ewen MacLachlan became involved, but the plan was never completed. All that was published of Ross's work was the First Book of Fingal, and his notes and dissertation in *The Poems of Ossian in the Original Gaelic*, as already noted. The publication of a complete English translation of Macpherson's Gaelic original by the HSL had to wait until 1841. The translator was Patrick Macgregor, a Scottish born Canadian who was a student at Edinburgh University. He made the HSL an offer that after consideration it did not refuse him. He did not want monetary gain, and in effect his manuscript was a gift, as all he wanted was to be published. With his literal translation of the HSL's "Gaelic Ossian" was a dissertation written by Macgregor which argued strongly in support of the authenticity of Ossian's poems. It included new evidence of the poems' authenticity from Bishop Macdonnel of Ontario. Time had not diminished the impact the poems had among Gaels. Macgregor, like Sinclair before him, believed that Macpherson was a poor translator and that was the only problem. Many may have moved side wards in their belief that Ossian had actually lived, but they still believed implicitly that there was a corpus of ancient poetry traditionally assigned to Ossian. The publication of the new English version was also a financial disaster, and once again philanthropy was used as a means of dealing with the unwanted books.

In the advertisement published at the time of the book launch of Macpherson's Gaelic originals, the HSL stated:

> In the poems now published, some words and passages which are to be found in Mr Macpherson's translation are wanting. These might have been supplied from other transcripts, or oral tradition; but the Committee appointed to superintend the printing of this Work, were scrupulous about making any addition to the manuscripts left by Mr Macpherson. (Ossian, 1807, I: frontispiece)

The society wanted to find those missing poems. Two separate searches had been undertaken, the first by the society's bard Peter Maclean in 1789, the second by Rev John Macdonald of Ferintosh in 1805. The society believed that a further extensive tour was needed to collect all that still remained of ancient Gaelic poetry, heroic tales, the manners and customs of the ancient Caledonians and their historical remains. The HSL sent the young collector Alexander Stewart on a Tour in 1807 to the Highlands and Islands, anxious to find the missing poems but with the foresight to realise that what remained could so easily be lost forever. The HSL budgeted one hundred guineas to cover his expenses. He had proved himself a competent collector, as he and his brother Donald had already collected and compiled an anthology of Gaelic verse entitled *Cochruinneacha taoghta de shaothair nam bard gaëlach*. He was a very good Gaelic scholar who was knowledgeable in several Gaelic dialects. In Stewart the committee saw an able young man capable of fulfilling its desire. Stewart was confident of success in the task he was set. From his previous tour of collecting he believed that "there are scattered rays of ancient Poems still floating in the Highlands, which when carefully collected, in the proper focus will shine with native Lustre sufficient to dazzle those eyes which have hitherto regarded

---

them as a pale moon swimming in the clouds with borrowed light".[31] The HSL was very thorough in its instructions to Stewart, outlining the route he was to take and whom he was to visit, how he was to collect the material whether complete or in fragments, and what he was expected to achieve. The society was very interested in finding any extant versions of Macpherson's translations, particularly the eleven missing poems. He was also to learn by heart the tunes of songs he collected which were to be transcribed into a musical score by Mr Gow,[32] the society's musician. Stewart collected over 7000 lines of ancient poetry from the "oral tradition of old untutored men…the greater part of which bears internal evidence of being the Composition of the immortal Ossian". He also amassed a large collection of "more modern poetry" from the last three centuries, which he believed to be of great merit.

Little did the HSL envisage the impact that their publication of Macpherson's Gaelic originals would have on future generations. By printing them the HSL provided proof to those who doubted the possibility of ancient Gaelic poetry. There was no controversy around this production as there had been with Macpherson's translations. On the whole they were accepted as genuine. The HSL recognised that Macpherson was no saint, but it did not regard the poetry as bogus. Indeed, none of the men who worked to achieve the finished article disbelieved the authenticity of the poems themselves. And this was generally the shared belief among Gaels the world over. The work raised the profile of both the Gaelic language and culture cannot be taken too lightly. It provided legitimacy for Gaelic prose and poetry and the impact that the publication by the HSL of *The Poems of Ossian in the Original Gaelic* had on Gaelic culture. Professor Donald Meek has illustrated the influence of the HSL's "Gaelic Ossian" on later poets such as William Livingston and Neil MacLeod, who used both Ossianic themes and imagery. "Because of its Gaelic garb, the 'Ossian' of 1807 became a literary quarry of great importance for Gaelic composers. For those with a mind to construct large canvases, it provided a model for making epic poems which imitated the style and metre of Gaelic versions" (Meek, 2004: 48). These themes and images were not limited to poetry, as Meek has demonstrated with reference to the prose writings of Dr Norman MacLeod, John Stuart Blackie and John Murdoch. This influence continues to the present day.

The publication of the Gaelic "originals" also provided an impetus for collecting and analysing Gaelic tradition. The HSL had organised three tours of the Highlands and Islands in 1798, 1805 and 1807. Alexander Stewart's tour of 1807 was the most extensive and most productive. The HSL considered sending him on another tour because of his success. It is ironic that Stewart's collection is now missing. It was not published in the nineteenth century due to lack of funds and later due to ignorance of its existence, and languished until a housekeeping exercise discovered the manuscript in the first years of the twentieth century; unfortunately, plans to publish it were not carried out. Stewart's manuscripts would have provided an important contribution to Gaelic scholarship. Stewart's tour was of course followed by other collectors, the greatest among them being John Francis Campbell and Alexander Carmichael.

We cannot underestimate the importance that the publication by the HSL of *The Poems of Ossian in the Original Gaelic* had for Gaelic culture and literature. As Sir John Sinclair said, "If nothing else had been effected by the HSL, but the publication of the Poems of Ossian, in the original Gaelic, the Institution would have proved itself well entitled to the thanks of literature and of its country" (1813: 16). Little did he know that the impact of that publication would still be felt two centuries later.

---

[32] This was John Gow, the second son of Neil Gow. He had moved to London and his band performed at all the HSL General Courts until his death in 1827. With his brother Andrew, he also operated a publishing company in London. 68/25, p. 32.

## References

Anderson, John. Letter to Sir John Sinclair. 13 September 1805. Ossian Committee Correspondence. Adv MS 73.2.24, ff. 116-117

Boswell, J. 1998. *Life of Johnson*. Oxford: Oxford University Press. First published 1791

Campbell, JF. 1890. *Popular Tales of the West Highlands*, 4 vols 2nd ed. London: Hounslow Wildwood House. First published 1860-2

Chalmers, George. Letter to Henry Mackenzie. 9 October 1799. Ossian Committee Correspondence. Adv MS 73.2.13, ff. 134-135

Highland Society of London. *Minute Book 1784-1792*. MS DEP 268/21

Highland Society of London. *Committee Minute Book 1793-1802*. MS DEP 268/22

Highland Society of London. *Minute Book 1793-1805*. MS DEP 268/23

Highland Society of London. *Committee Minute Book 1802-1825*. MS DEP 268/24

Highland Society of London. *Minute Book 1808-1814*. MS DEP 268/25

Highland Society of London. *Extract of Proceedings 1819-1824*. MS DEP 268/43

Highland Society of London. *Minute Extracts*. Ossian Committee Correspondence. Adv MS 73.2.24

MacArthur, John. Letter to Sir John Sinclair, 18 July 1806. *Sinclair's Correspondence*. Adv MS 73.2.11, f. 64

Mackenzie, John. Memorandum. November 1798. Ossian Committee Correspondence. Adv MS 73.2.13, f. 130

Mackenzie, John. Letter to Henry Mackenzie. 22 November 1798. Ossian Committee Correspondence. Adv MS 73.2.13, f. 126

Macpherson, James. Letter to John Mackenzie, HSL. 4 July 1784. Highland Society of London, Correspondence 1781-1820. MS DEP 268/1

Macrae, Colin. Letter to Sir John Sinclair. 15 June 1806. Sinclair Papers. Adv MS 73.2.11, f. 50

Macrae, Colin. Hints for Sir John Sinclair's consideration regarding the conduct of the late Mr Mackenzie relative to Ossian. 1804. Ossian Committee Correspondence. Adv MS 73.2.24, ff. 70-71

Meek, DE. 2004. "The Sublime Gael: The Impact of Macpherson's Ossian on Literary Creativity and Cultural Perception in Gaelic Scotland". In H. Gaskill. Ed. *The Reception of Ossian in Europe*, 40-66. Bristol: Thoemmes Continuum

Murray, John. Letter to John Mackenzie, Sec. to HSL. 29 October 1783. Highland Society of London Correspondence 1781-1820. MS DEP 268/1

Murray, John Macgregor. Letter to Sir John Sinclair. 12 March 1810. Ossian Committee Correspondence. Adv MS 73.2.26, ff. 85-87

Ossian. 1807. *The Poems of Ossian in the Original Gaelic*, 3 vols. London: 'Published under the Sanction of the Highland Society of London'

Prorogative Court of Canterbury. Extract of James Macpherson's will. 1796. Ossian Committee Correspondence. Adv MS 73.2.13, f. 37

Sinclair, Sir John of Ulbster. 1813. *An Account of the Highland Society of London*. London: B MacMillan

Sinclair, Sir John. Copy of letter to Rev Mr Stewart. 1 June 1806. Sinclair Papers. Adv MS 73.2.11, f. 118

Sinclair, Sir John. Original correspondence between Sir John Sinclair and Bishop Cameron regarding the authenticity of Ossian. 1806. Sinclair Papers. Adv MS 73.2.11, ff. 125-129

Stewart, Rev. Alexander. Letter to HSL. 2 October 1804. Highland Society of London Correspondence 1781-1820. MS DEP 268/1

Stewart, Charles. Letter to HSL. 1 August 1804. Ossian Committee Correspondence. Adv MS 73.2.24, f. 85

# "Geer frae lawlin' chiels an' erse": The Scots Language in Ireland

*Gavin Falconer*

A cultural comparison of Northern Ireland with Scotland throws up both similarities and differences. In many aspects, each is marginal to the linguistic patrimony of the other. While a mainstream form of Scots is spoken in the north of Ireland and the sister language of Modern Irish in Scotland, until recently linguistic awareness and links were limited. Part of the reason may lie in the fact that Northern Ireland is marginal also in its Scottishness; the ethnic tag, at least in its unqualified form, is neither accorded by those in Scotland nor aspired to by those in Northern Ireland. Historically, supporters of Irish tended to look South – or, more accurately, west to Donegal – for inspiration, while prior to the 1990s Scots evoked only limited interest in Ulster, even among users, a situation that had obtained since the end of the nineteenth century. Despite this, in many emblematically Scottish cultural fields, such as piping, people from Northern Ireland have proven more than equal to the Scots, regularly winning competitions.

A further element is religion; though Scots influence is everywhere in the North, engagement with Scottish identity, whether in the traditional arts or in language, is generally limited to Protestants. Scotland's ancient tradition of civic nationality may now be the pre-eminent paradigm at home, but in Northern Ireland such questions are generally influenced by confession. One can argue about which of the three main constituent cultures of Northern Ireland – Irish Catholic, Lowland Scots Presbyterian, and English Anglican – predominates, but such arguments are wont to be influenced both by the politics and cultural affiliation of participants in the debate and by contemporary demographic change. A personal observation is that any purely demographic study greatly understates English influence in Northern Ireland, which provides the basis of the legal and educational systems as well as, in the linguistic sphere, that of both high and low language for most people. Of course, if, as the 1996 GRO Scotland study estimated, only 30% of Scots are Scots-speakers, that last point may apply in part to Scotland too.[1]

Figure 1 shows Irish in green (darkest) along the western seaboard of the island, Scots in cobalt (lighter) stretching from the northern and eastern margins of Ulster across the North Channel to Lowland Scotland and the Northern Isles, and Scottish Gaelic in teal (lightest) in the Western Isles and adjacent areas of the Scottish Highlands.[2] The white areas in England represent regions to which English is native, while those in Scotland and Ireland denote regions which were formerly Goidelic-speaking but are now overwhelmingly anglophone; in the case of Scotland, controlled second-language learning has meant that, outside phonology, their inhabitants' Gaelic substratum has had only a limited influence on their speech.

In the 1990s, the glotto-political distance of Northern Ireland to Scotland was sharply reduced by UK Government attempts to co-opt Irish Republicans into constitutional politics and Loyalists into supporting the resulting power-sharing polity. One measure of good faith for both groups has been language, and the UK Government has accepted, and perhaps even encouraged, linkage between Irish and the local dialect of Scots, portrayed as the languages of

---

[1] If "Scots" refers to the traditional dialects, the figure of 30% is of course itself a gross overestimate. Attempts to provide a democratic basis for the promotion of Scots may be undermining attempts to justify support on the basis of furthering linguistic diversity and preventing impending language death, since they reduce the *Abstand* of Scots *vis-à-vis* English and exaggerate the numerical strength of its dwindling speech community.

[2] I am indebted to Dr. John Kirk of Queen's University Belfast for permission to use this map.

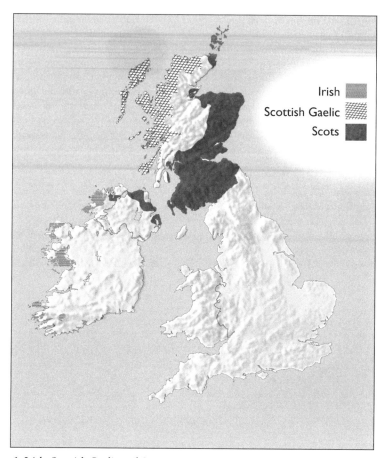

**Figure 1: Irish, Scottish Gaelic and Scots**

Nationalists and Unionists respectively. In a story published in the Irish edition of *The Observer* on 16 January 2005 on a leaked Northern Ireland Office memo entitled 'Iceberg Watch 2004', Henry McDonald reports that "[i]n every concession to republicans, such as more money for the Irish language, the comments section advises that there be a reciprocal amount of largesse for unionist causes."

That anti-Gaelicism and anti-Catholicism are often seen as the same thing can be inferred from the reaction of some participants at the Fourth Symposium on Language and Politics held at Queen's University Belfast in September 2003, who responded to a dispute regarding the etiquette of discussing Scots through the medium of Scottish Gaelic by levelling the charge of sectarianism against the complainant. Whatever the rights and wrongs of the matter, one feels obliged to point out that anti-Gaelic attitudes were commonplace among pre-Reformation Lowlanders and that since the nineteenth century most speakers of Scottish Gaelic have been Presbyterian and most Scottish Catholics English- or Scots-speaking, effectively divorcing anti-Gaelic and anti-Catholic attitudes for ever. The question of whether Irish academia's attitudes towards Scottish language, and towards the variety of Scots spoken in Ireland, can be characterised by the projection of another national experience may be worthy of investigation.

Increased state support for Irish and Scots in Northern Ireland has in some ways rendered centrally important a territory that for many Scottish language campaigners may have been of only peripheral interest. Supporters of the minoritised Goidelic languages of Irish and Scottish Gaelic and of the once and future *Ausbau* language Scots in both Scotland and Ireland have become natural allies. With the principle of state support established, the relevant political comparators for Irish may now lie in Scotland and Wales. It is also worth remembering that the UK Government's first official reference to Scots as a language anywhere was in legislation passed in parallel with the Irish Government to set up the cross-border Ulster-Scots Agency.

The linguistic make-up of Ulster may be more diverse than that of some similarly sized territories owing to the history of Scots and English settlement in a previously Irish-speaking province; its Scots dialects have almost as many different realisations of vowel 7 in the Aitken scheme – most commonly spelt <ui> in literary Scots – as in Scotland itself, owing to staggered colonisation during a period of dynamic change in the seventeenth century. Some important differences from Scotland may be of more recent origin. While in the Lowlands one could draw a class pyramid with regional dialects of Scots at the bottom and RP at the top, in Northern Ireland, the apex would be truncated, since it has hardly any speakers of RP; non-rhotic accents are a rarity even among local newsreaders and politicians.[3] Moreover, the bottom part of the pyramid would have two distinct vertices, South Ulster English and Ulster Scots.[4]

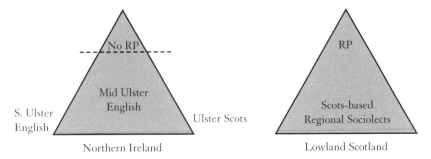

Figure 2: Anglic dialects in Northern Ireland and Lowland Scotland

Though the politicisation of language in Northern Ireland is often problematised, it should not be forgotten that in Scotland such issues can be fraught with questions of class; judging from some contemporary Scots writing, some players may be defining the language as an aggrandised version of what working-class people speak rather than as a rule-governed system

---

[3] Reasons may include the decoupling of Northern Ireland from metropolitan political culture after the passing of the Government of Ireland Act 1920, which set up a devolved administration for six Ulster counties, a change in the balance of power between Anglicans and Presbyterians after Partition, nationalist sentiment among Catholics, the one-way flow of migration, particularly during the troubles, and the fact that Northern Ireland has state-funded grammars instead of independent schools. Seanad Éireann, which includes university representation, has more speakers of RP or a national variant thereof than the Northern Ireland Assembly.

[4] A tripartite division of Anglic in Ireland into Hiberno-English, Anglo-Irish and Ulster Scots as in Todd (1989) is probably no longer appropriate, and some scholars have used the second term to refer to the speech variety identified with the first, for example, Henry (1957). It is a moot point whether Anglicans exist in sufficient numbers to maintain a distinct dialect, except perhaps at the very top of the social scale, where there is access to private education in England. However, such speakers are more common in the Republic, whose total Protestant population, including many border Presbyterians, had fallen to only 3% before the recent economic boom. The existence of South Ulster English as delineated by Harris (1984) is contested, but the general point of a transition to Hiberno-English is not.

in its own right that is well attested in the poetry and dialogue of the great writers of the eighteenth and nineteenth centuries. In Northern Ireland, the fact that working-class people generally speak regional English and that there is no substantial RP-influenced speech community also means that there is no *kudos* in speaking Scots, even, for example, among males in manual trades. For most people, however much it influences their own speech, Ulster Scots is a series of rustic dialects. There is also great ignorance surrounding the provenance, distribution and linguistic status of non-standard features. For example, *Mad Dog*, a recent biography of the UFF leader Johnny Adair by David Lister and Hugh Jordan, contains the following gloss on page 186: "'Hallion' is Northern Irish slang for a lowlife or savage". The descriptor "slang" is typical of uninformed attitudes in the territory.[5]

By far the majority of Northern Ireland people of all classes speak Mid Ulster English, a dialect not unlike Scottish Standard English though with its own distinct character and including some speech forms transitional to South Ulster English, itself a transitional dialect between Mid Ulster English and Southern Hiberno-English.[6] There are no urban forms of Scots in Northern Ireland, although Derry may be slightly more Scots than Belfast owing to early Presbyterian dominance. The speech of the city has Scots enclitic negation but lacks undiphthongised prepositions such as [dun] and [ut] that might have placed it on a par with a Scottish dialect such as Glaswegian. That Ulster speech is a complex confluence is illustrated by the Derry vernacular being not only more Scots but also more Irish than that of Belfast.

Most parts of Northern Ireland, along with Donegal and parts of Monaghan, have a Scots-based non-phonemic rather than English-based phonemic vowel system, something that can be illustrated using the phrase "good food". In Scotland and most of Ulster the environmentally conditioned length of the [u] in the two words is equal, since it precedes a [d] in each case. In the Ulster-Scots areas, the system is a variant of that heard in Scotland, while in working-class Belfast speech, stressed vowels are long. Interestingly, the Ulster accent most "Scottish" to a casual listener is that of the north-west and Donegal, particularly among recently Irish-speaking communities.[7] In most parts of Ulster, the system is sufficiently close to that used in Scotland that, where a degree of "neutrality" or anglicisation is involved, it is often difficult to ascertain a speaker's provenance, more particularly if the observer does not hail from one of the territories in question, something exemplified by the following story, culled from an interview with Mark E. Smith of *The Fall*. In it, Smith recounts a television appearance following the death of the BBC Radio 1 DJ John Peel during which he confused *Newsnight's* Gavin Esler with a member of *The Undertones*.[8]

> "The thing is, I was in a different studio and I couldn't see who I was talking to. I mistook the presenter, Gavin Whatsisname, for the Undertones guy. So when I said to Gavin Thingy, 'Who do you think you are? Are you looking for Peel's job, then?', I thought I was talking to the Undertones bloke." He cackles some more at the memory then adds, quite seriously: "I mean, they've both got the same sort of accent, haven't they?" I find myself nodding in agreement, while at the same time wondering what kind of skewed interior logic could possibly equate broad Bogside with clipped Oxbridge."

---

[5] It could also be argued that the English translation is rather stronger than the actual meaning of the Scots.
[6] While individual elements may appear panlectally, dialect transitions can be relatively abrupt. County Monaghan, for example, has Mid Ulster English, South Ulster English and Southern Hiberno-English within a small area as one moves south.
[7] See Adams (1986).
[8] *The Observer*, 16 January 2005.

The mistake, and journalist Seán O'Hagan's reaction to it, illustrate the nexus of Scottish and Northern accents while underlining the lack of a strongly RP-influenced speech community in Northern Ireland, something known to those better acquainted with the territory.[9]

The most controversial topic in Northern Ireland dialectology is the status of Ulster Scots, which has been claimed as a variety of Scots, a form of Hiberno-English, and an independent language. Attitudes among Irish opinion-formers to the idiom in question may also be relevant with regard to Scots in Scotland. In the political sphere, a belief may be current that Scots was brought to Scotland through forced external colonisation and that Gaelic was spoken in the Lowlands much more recently than is the case. While relations between Highlands and Lowlands have not always been good, it is a matter of historical record that the ancestor of Scots first entered the national territory through the Gaels' conquest of their neighbours rather than the reverse; its decisive spread probably began with the invitation of Norman nobles into the Lowlands during the reign of David I (1124—1153). Despite the obvious inaccuracy of the claim, sometimes heard in Scotland, that Gaelic was never spoken in the Lowlands,[10] the slowness of the language's retreat, along with the stability and dominance of Lowland society, has also meant that many Scots view it as a regional rather than a national language.[11]

In Ireland there may also be an implicit assumption that Scots in general, or Ulster Scots in particular, owes its unique character primarily to contact with a Goidelic substratum. That this is true in neither case has been amply demonstrated by lexical studies. Having analysed 2·5% of entries in *The Dictionary of the Older Scottish Tongue*, Macafee (1997) has calculated the Celtic part of Scots lexis as being 0·8%, the same figure reached by McClure (1995: 68-85) based on 600 words found in *The Scottish National Dictionary*, and while the Gaelic words were largely connected with topography and cultural traditions, therefore being more likely to survive further decline in Scots, they cannot by any stretch of the imagination be claimed as a major constituent of the language. Kirk (1999) has calculated that 61·6% of the non-standard lexis in *The Concise Ulster Dictionary* is either uniquely Scots or shared by Scots and northern English, despite the fact that Scots-speaking areas account for only a small part of the historic province of Ulster. No such study has been carried out of Jim Fenton's *Hamely Tongue* dictionary, which, unlike *The Concise Ulster Dictionary*, is both absolutely contemporary and limited to County Antrim, the only majority-Scotstacht county; it would be surprising if the Scots element were less than 70%. One also suspects that many Irish loanwords in the Scots of Ulster are connected with moribund cultural and economic practices and that continued use would be dependent on the revival of such customs rather than of the idiom as a whole.

This is not in any way intended to belittle the role of Gaelic in the genesis of Scots. Since the latter is, in the main, the product of separate development from English, it follows that it owes a great debt for its existence to the fact that its speakers inherited, or wrested, control of an independent state from its Irish-speaking founders. The modern bundle of isoglosses along the border with England is sometimes cited in support of the argument that Scots is a separate system from English. However, without there having been a Scots state, the clearest dialect

---

[9] Subtle Scottish influence may in any case be more apparent to those not from Scotland or the north of Ireland. Thus the journalist Andrew Marr is sometimes portrayed by impressionists – who of course exaggerate their targets' characteristics – with a pronounced Scottish accent.

[10] A parallel contention is that Highland people sound "too English" in comparison with their Lowland counterparts, despite the fact that the area was never Scots-speaking, with "book English" introduced by the school system from the nineteenth century.

[11] Debates about ineffective "tokenist" promotion of minority languages occur both among genuine activists and as a political front for those who reject linguistic diversity. However, the standing of Scottish Gaelic, and the numbers of those wishing to learn it, might be increased at no cost to the Exchequer by amending current legislation to require the Scottish banks to produce bilingual notes after their next redesign. One would hope that Scots-language campaigners would not attempt to stymie such a move.

border in Anglic dialects would have been along not the Tweed but the Humber. The main reason for there being such an isogloss bundle today is the battle of Carham-on-Tweed fought by the Gaelic-speaking King of Scots Malcolm II in 1018, when what is now south-east Scotland was first absorbed into a Gaelic political entity.[12] Gaelic may have contributed no more than a small part of Scots itself, but the grain of sand around which the pearl of Scots was to grow was the pearl of Gaelic.

Needless to say, the lexical congruity of Scots on the two sides of the Straits of Moyle also poses difficulties for those claiming Ulster Scots as an independent language. Since *The Scottish National Dictionary* and *The Concise Ulster Dictionary* list in the main only vocabulary not shared with contemporary standard English, and since the most common words dominate any text, one wonders whether a database study of a representative sample of Ulster-Scots literature would turn up more than one word in a hundred not shared with Scots, or Scots and English, in actual use.[13] Whatever the exact figure, the sparseness of such vocabulary means that, used unselfconsciously, Ulster Scots presents no difficulties for Scots-speakers from Scotland, something demonstrated in most editions of BBC Radio Ulster's *Kist o' Wurds*.

Classifying Ulster Scots as "Hiberno-English" poses the question of what is understood by the latter term. If it refers simply to Irish varieties of English, one can hardly complain, since functionally, like most varieties of Scots most of the time, Ulster Scots is as a dialect of English. However, one suspects that for many people the term "Hiberno-English" refers to something far less neutral: to dialects derived from midlands English, exhibiting largely seventeenth-century phonology and ample evidence of second-language learning by Irish-speakers in articulation, syntax and lexis, and with internal dialect boundaries defined not so much by retention as by substratal influence and the date and speed of language shift from Irish to English.[14] Many, if not most, studies of Hiberno-English will ignore Ulster entirely.

It is true that there are many overlaps between varieties in Ireland. Scots vocabulary has been attested by Zwickl (2002) throughout Ulster and can be found across the entire northern half of the island.[15] The syntax of Ulster Scots is probably also closer to that of Hiberno-English than that of Scotland.[16] Kallen (1999: 81) argues against "particularistic scholarship" of all kinds but says that Ulster Scots should be studied along with other varieties in Ireland. While it is hard to deny such eminent good sense, the danger of adhering to such an approach too officiously is of ignoring one of the key tasks of the academic linguist: the production of taxonomies.

It is commonplace for forms well-attested in Scots to be claimed as originating through contact with Irish, despite the fact that the population structure of the north of Ireland means that Irish can have played at most a reinforcing role. For example, Todd (1989: 42) claims that the existence of "blended prepositions + pronouns" in Ulster is due to Irish substratal

---

[12] The border was agreed officially by the Treaty of York concluded between Alexander II and Henry III in 1237, but it followed the Tweed-Esk-Solway line determined by the battle.

[13] Wijk (1966: 9) reports that the 1,000 commonest words account for 85% of the words on a given page and the commonest 3,000 for 95%.

[14] Stalmaszczyk (2002: 63) explicitly rejects the term for just this reason.

[15] Not every Irish academic will be in a position to distinguish dialect vocabulary of Irish and Scots origin without recourse to a dictionary, since most will have learnt the former as a second language, concentrating on lexis relevant to contemporary life. By contrast, not all the cultural vocabulary loaned from Irish to Scots will have remained mainstream in the donor system. There may therefore be an assumption that a higher percentage of non-standard vocabulary originates in Irish than is the case.

[16] Even here, however, it is easy to forget that, conventionalised literary representations notwithstanding, the Scots syntax of Scotland also differs from that of Standard English, with the medial object perfect attested in Murray (1873: 222). Moreover, speakers of Ulster Scots and Hiberno-English also dispose over mainstream syntactical structures, and the very stubbornness of syntax to homogenising forces strongly suggests that it is not marked for most people.

influence, failing to consider the possibility that they might simply be phonologically derived and in apparent ignorance of their attestation in Scotland, for example, in Murray (1873: 190).[17] Similar claims are sometimes made regarding singular verb concord. Inflected *be*, used as a consuetudinal present and apparently so Goidelic, is ultimately of Planter origin, however great the role of Irish in its grammaticalisation and vitality. Even cases where a substratal origin is likely or uncontested, such as the *efter* perfect or the non-marking of demonstrative pronouns for number, are not always suitable as demarcators of Ulster Scots and Hiberno-English *vis-à-vis* Scots in Scotland, which has Goidelic contact varieties of its own in the form of Glaswegian and Northern Scots.[18]

Conventionally, Ulster Scots has been classed by Scots-language academics[19] as one of five main dialects of Scots, the others being Central Scots, that of most speakers and literature, Insular Scots, Northern Scots, and Southern Scots.[20] Both Insular and Northern Scots are much more differentiated from the main Central Scots dialect than Ulster Scots in both phonology and vocabulary. In the case of the former, phonological differences are substantial and unpredictable, something seen in the use of the *Umlaut* by many of its writers; they are at least as significant in the case of the latter but diverge regularly from more mainstream varieties, with *fit* for Central Scots *whit* ("what") and *vrocht for wrocht* ("wrought"). Even Southern Scots is arguably less suited to Central Scots orthography because of its diphthongisation of open syllables, being known in common parlance as the "*yow* and *mey*" dialect because of the local realisations of "you" and "me". Its successful representation in such a system would depend on the *a priori* adoption of pan-dialectal principles. By contrast, the only barrier to writing Ulster Scots as Central Scots is vowel 7 mentioned above. As long as that is represented pan-dialectally, something that because of internal diversity would have to be addressed even within Ulster Scots, the dialect can be transcribed using the conventional orthographic principles of literary Scots based on the central variety. The only exceptions are realisations borrowed recently from Hiberno-English such as *houl', oul'* and *boord*, the last of which, despite its immortalisation in the "Ullans" translation of the name of the Ulster-Scots Agency, was pronounced with vowel 7 as recently as when Robert Gregg (1963: 35; 1972) conducted his dialect surveys.[21]

Ultimately, one must conclude that classifying the Scots dialect of Ulster as "Hiberno-English" accords prominence to a relatively minor adstratal element in its make-up while failing to give proper recognition to the main source of its uniqueness, its parent dialects. On such a basis, a Turkish-substrate speaker of Dutch could be said to have stronger linguistic affinities with a Turkish-substrate speaker of German than with a speaker of Dutch without a substrate.[22] It might be claimed with some justification that scholars have become blinded by the sparkle of sunlight on the tiny dialectal disjuncture of the Straits of Moyle while failing to

---

[17] The superficial similarity is evident when one compares Irish *leis* and *dó* with Scots *wi't* and *for't*, etc.

[18] The *efter* or *after* perfect can be heard in Glasgow and the Highlands and islands. In Ulster Scots the plural demonstrative *thir* is sometimes used with singular substantives, while Northern Scots uses singular demonstratives with plural nouns.

[19] See SND introduction, pages 16 to 32.

[20] See also McClure (2002: 55-7).

[21] It will be noted that, in the context of state-sponsored *Ausbau*, the question of whether an idiom can be accommodated within a pan-dialectal orthography is a more important criterion for demarcation than, for example, whether vowel length is shared, since the latter is not represented in conventional Anglic spelling systems. For that reason, the proposal in McCafferty (2001) that Ulster Scots be developed along with Mid Ulster English but separately from Scots in Scotland seems to place too much weight on extralinguistic notions of community. He is, however, probably right in his belief that Ulster Scots is too small to survive alone.

[22] That the *Abstand* between Scots and English is analogous to that between Dutch and German is suggested by Lewis Grassic Gibbon in a note prefacing his novel *Sunset Song*.

recognise that the overlapping Anglic speech forms of Ireland might be much further removed from each other in their most typical forms. On that model, Dutch would be more like German than Afrikaans. However, while such a classification may evidence a dearth of investigation regarding the source dialects, there is no denying that the form of Scots spoken in Ireland is distinctively Irish, or that many of the features that set it apart are shared with the English-based dialects to the south. In that context, it may be appropriate to adapt such terminology rather than dismiss it, referring to "Hiberno-Scots"[23] rather than "Hiberno-English" or "Ulster Scots", the last term being even less neutral owing to state-sponsored politicisation and spurious claims of languageness. Only by acknowledging that the dialect is structurally Scots – and functionally English – yet the property of an Irish speech community which has lent it a unique character can one avoid the particularism feared by Kallen.

Having dealt with the theory, the time may be opportune for a practical comparison. Like

| | |
|---|---|
| **(1a) 'To a Mouse'** | **(1b) 'Lines to a Dying Redbreast'** |
| Thy wee bit housie, too, in ruin! | My wee bit house will then be taen |
| It's silly wa's the winds are strewin'! | That lang has braved the blast alane; |
| And naething now to big a new ane | And scaled, like chaff, alang the plain, |
| O' foggage green! | Though I should lie |
| And bleak December's winds ensuin' | Wi' my auld mither, wife and wean, |
| Baith snell and keen! | Beneath the sky. |
| | |
| **(2a) 'Now Westlin Winds'** | **(2b) 'Summer Time'** |
| The partridge loves the fruitful fells; | The lapwing flutters round about, |
| The plover loves the mountains; | To wile us from her bield— |
| The woodcock haunts the lonely dells; | Lights at our feet, and cries peeweet, |
| The soaring hern the fountains; | Then flies far o'er the field. |
| Through lofty groves the cushat roves, | And gladly from the auld cow's back |
| The path of man to shun it; | The magpie steals the hair, |
| The hazel bush o'erhangs the thrush, | To clothe her nest, where she may rest, |
| The spreading thorn the linnet. | Beyond the school-boy's snare. |
| | |
| **(3a) 'Scots, Wha Hae'** | **(3b) 'O'er green Erin's flowery plains'** |
| Wha will be a traitor knave? | Ere we sink in ruin's wave |
| Wha can fill a coward's grave? | Let us know that we are brave — |
| Wha sae base as be a slave? | Trample on each tyrant knave |
| Let him turn and flee! […] | Brands us with iniquity; |
| | |
| By Oppression's woes and pains! | By the foes we have defied, |
| By your sons in servile chains! | By the death which Emmet died, |
| We will drain our dearest veins, | We will drain life's dearest tide, |
| But they will be free! | But we shall have liberty! |

[23] Such terminology has a long pedigree, having been coined as early as 1830 by the novelist William Carleton in his author's preface to the first edition of his *Traits and Stories of the Irish Peasantry*, albeit in the dismissive phrase "Scoto-Hibernic jargon". The writer is indebted to Dr. Kevin McCafferty for drawing Carleton's usage to his attention. If "Hiberno-English" were reserved for English-based dialects, "Hiberno-Anglic" might provide the most neutral overarching term for it and Hiberno-Scots.

many Ulster poets, David Herbison penned lyrics influenced by, or sharing common ancestors with, works by Robert Burns.[24] How does the language compare? There is no evidence in the three sample texts that Herbison has a spelling philosophy fundamentally different from that of Burns;[25] nor are there any Irish loan words, or any Ulster words at all not also found in Central Scots. The old satirist's trick of swapping name tags could elicit no laughter here, since there is no room for exaggerating the common identity of the language involved. Scholars will no doubt argue about literary merit, but Herbison is obviously a competent poet, and the most obvious linguistic clues to the writers' respective identities are the exclamation marks in "To a Mouse" and the capitalisation of the word *Oppression* in "Scots, Wha Hae", which suggest that the texts are from the eighteenth rather than the nineteenth century. The mention of Robert Emmet, taking the place of William Wallace in "O'er green Erin's flowery plains", shows that it is a call to Irish patriotism; Herbison's Republicanism, though surprising today, was typical of the Ulster-Scots poets and, according to the poet's descendant, Ivan Herbison (1996: 6), one of the reasons behind the decline of their school and, by extension, of the dialect as a whole. The single, but spectacular, Gaelic element is the conventionalised title of the Herbison work, which echoes such poems as Séathrún Céitinn's "Óm sceol ar Ardmhagh Fáil" ('Since my Tidings from Fál's High Plain')[26] and may have been influenced by Anglic versions of Irish folk songs. Though Herbison drops one syllable from some lines of "Now Westlin Winds" and adds two to the final line of "Scots, Wha Hae", his works can still be sung to the same tunes, relatively easily in the case of the former and with more difficulty in the latter case.

The only possible dialect difference that the present writer can identify is the rhyming of *died* and *tide* in the final verse of "O'er green Erin's flowery plains". The words do not rhyme at all in Scots and, while the rhyme is perfect for some contemporary speakers of Scottish Standard English, for most it is not. In the English of Ulster, on the other hand, the two words would usually be pronounced with the same vowel, speakers in the west tending to that in *tide* [əi] and speakers in the east to that in *died* [ai]. However, the difference is very small, and the nebulousness of nascent Scottish Standard English at the time of Burns and the influence of English literary precedents[27] mean that one could not maintain with any certainty based on linguistic evidence alone that the Herbison work was not composed in Scotland.

Of course, though the texts were chosen because the Herbison works allowed easy comparison, it could very plausibly be argued that they are unsuitable for a linguistic study, since the later poet might draw not only from the literary work of the earlier but from his language too. It is true that much of the syntax and vocabulary is repeated. Herbison also follows the functional distribution of Scots and English in the Burns works, using literary Scots in the Habbie "Lines to a Dying Redbreast" and regional or standard English in the other two works. If the entire poem or song were given in each case, the similarities would be even more apparent, since the influence is not always internal to a given verse. The rhyme in the line "To clothe her nest, where she may rest" in "Summer Time" is reminiscent of "I'll grasp thy waist, and, fondly prest," in the final stanza of the Burns song.[28] The dreamy repetition of the excerpt from "Now Westlin Winds" quoted above, which, unlike its other verses and that quoted from the Herbison piece, lacks an internal rhyme in its third line, probably diverges for literary effect.

The charge that the Ulster poets were merely aping their Scottish counterparts has been

---

[24] There are also Ulster versions of Scots folk songs and, in publishing, Ulster editions of the Scots poets. The Belfast edition of Burns was the first published outside Scotland.

[25] One could argue that Burns would have preferred *skailed* to the *scaled* ('spread') of the first Herbison poem to avoid confusion with a homograph.[26] Irish *Fál*, like English *Erin*, is a poetic name for Ireland.

[27] English was itself not immune from admitting such "Shakespearean" rhymes as *love* with *move*.

[28] The imperfect rhyme also provides further evidence that Herbison's pairing of *died* with *tide* does not necessarily set him apart from his literary precursor.

made before, and refuted by the Ulstermen themselves. Thus Thomas Beggs says:

> Should the reader of the following effusions suppose, that in some parts the author has imitated the Scottish Dialect, he would wish to correct the idea by alleging that he has written in his own style – in the language of his native glen – not constrained but spontaneous as the lispings of our first speech. (Cited in Herbison, 1991: 68)

Samuel Thompson makes the same point in verse:

> I love my native land, no doubt,
> Attach'd to her through thick and thin,
> Yet tho' I'm Irish all without,
> I'm every item Scotch within. (Cited in Herbison, 1996: 7)

In fact, the sheer volume of material from Ulster with literally no distinguishing features whatsoever to set it apart from Central Scots calls into question whether the status of Ulster Scots even as one of the main dialect groups of Scots is justified. Based on literary evidence in isolation, it might not be too wide of the mark to refer not to "Hiberno-Scots" but to "Hiberno-Central Scots". Of course, literary canons are not decided by linguistic factors alone, and the distinctiveness of Ulster Scots in articulation and vowel length is not recorded in such writing, while the predominance of verse may not provide the best showcase for its distinctive syntax. Nevertheless, the fact that one might entertain such a thought once again provides compelling evidence against the wisdom of dealing with Ulster Scots as an independent language.[29] Classing the idiom as Hiberno-English is perhaps slightly more understandable when one considers contemporary dialect-levelling and the question of whether the term "Ulster Scots" is taken to refer to core areas only or also includes other Ulster varieties. The vast majority of Scots-language academics, however, would class only areas whose vernacular is strongly influenced by traditional Scots as Scots-speaking; in Ulster, this would mean those core Ulster-Scots areas defined by Robert Gregg (1972).[30] Despite the inherent difficulty of distinguishing between the register and dialect continua alluded to in the discussion of Burns and Herbison, it is unlikely that a taxonomist could include a writer such as W. F. Marshall in the canon of Scots writers, since no suitably Scots pole exists – either in his own writing, outside paraphrase, or in the dialect of his native Tyrone.

An apparent exception to the orthodoxy is Jones (2002: 1), who, having defined Scots as "the principle linguistic medium of face-to-face communication used by the vast majority of speakers who live within the boundaries of Scotland today", which one assumes to be Scottish Standard English, is forced to refer to RP, which may be spoken by as little as 1% of the UK population, as "Standard English" and to traditional Scots as "Working Class Scots", though the most divergent varieties are generally more closely identified with peripheral geography than social class. It could be argued that the variant terminology in the work effectively makes it incompatible with the mainstream of academic literature; that it appears in an introduction to the study of Scots seems especially problematic. The difficulty of redefining what is essentially English acquired from first-language Scots-speakers as Scots itself is seen in the

---

[29] It could also be argued that it greatly reduces the academic validity of specifying writing as being "in Ulster Scots" rather than simply "in Scots", since in many cases the only distinctively Ulster element, the accent, is provided by the reader.

[30] The absence of working-class "urban Scots" in Northern Ireland and the relatively recent history of Plantation mean that it could be argued that the dialect delineation between Ulster Scots and Mid Ulster English is relatively clear.

section on Ulster Scots, which turns out to be a description of the phonology of Belfast English. The potentially divisive nature of the classification can be appreciated in the context of the debate on the cultural identity of Northern Ireland mentioned at the beginning of this paper. Recognising such diluted or submerged varieties as part of the same system runs the risk of understating the English and Irish influences that also characterise the vernacular of the city. If one imagines the *Abstand* between Scots and English as a set of oppositions, primarily phonological and lexical, one sees that in Belfast, unlike the core areas, the vast majority are decided in favour of the latter.[31] One might also ask, if "Scots" is to be defined extralinguistically as what Scots people speak, on what basis it is thought admissible to apply the term to a completely different speech community in Northern Ireland. Though residents may say that they "speak slang" or "use Ulster-Scots words" – both of which are in the vast majority of cases mainstream Scots vocabulary – none thinks that they "speak Scots".[32]

The view that Ulster Scots is a language has perhaps its most influential exposition in the grammar by the cultural geographer Philip Robinson:

> Ulster-Scots is a west Germanic language which is derived from, and has its closest linguistic parallels with, Lowland Scots or Lallans. Indeed, Ulster-Scots has been described as a 'variant' of Scots, and as such has been accommodated within the coverage of the *Scottish National Dictionary* programme. However, many Scots language academics have observed that Ulster-Scots differs from its sister tongue: Ulster-Scots has its own range of dialects, along with its own distinctive literary tradition, vocabulary and grammar; all of which differ in some respects from Lallans. In simple terms, the relationship between Ulster-Scots and Lallans could be compared to the relative positions of Irish and Scottish Gaelic. (1997: 1)

Even the small section above, taken from the first page of the work, contains numerous claims that are demonstrably incorrect. Though Ulster Scots is part of the West Germanic group of languages, that does not legitimise its description as "a west Germanic language". There is to the present writer's knowledge no academic linguist in the world who believes Ulster Scots an independent linguistic system on structural grounds. Nor is he aware of any Scots academic having referred to Ulster Scots as the "sister tongue" of Scots; in conventional discourse, the second term includes the first. Perhaps the most egregious assertion is that Ulster Scots is described as a variant of Scots by *The Scottish National Dictionary*. The exact quote, on page 32 of the introduction, reads as follows: "Ulster Scots is in the main a variant of wm. [west-mid] Scots". In other words, the *SND* is describing Ulster Scots as derived from the West Central sub-dialect of Central Scots (through contact with Ulster Irish and, to a lesser extent, regional English). Since linguists speak on the one hand of languages and on the other of dialects or varieties, generally reserving "variant" for lexical forms, one assumes that the term has been used in the *SND* because of the very specific nature of the source idiom and the remarkably uniform – and therefore predictable – nature of the Ulster dialects' divergence, which, as the

---

[31] Such a statistical approach to linguistic taxonomy, which might be preferable to the current impressionistic and insufficiently informed debate, has also been used to produce super-families of American Indian languages, though in that case for the opposite reason: the very large *Abstand* between individual idioms.

[32] One might also suggest that, since the UK Government's recognition of Scots in its declaration regarding the European Charter for Regional or Minority Languages, it has now become a public policy aspiration to deal with the idiom separately from English. Adumbrating Scots for taxonomic purposes should not be confused with its standardisation and codification, a project which lacks academic relevance given the ongoing lack of state support for transactional Scots, though that is arguably less true in Northern Ireland. It could be argued that suitable criteria for delineation have already been developed in dialect surveys, in particular Gregg (1972) and studies of the southern border of Scotland.

literary corpus suggests, is mainly at the level of articulation.[33] The description of Ulster Scots as a variant of Scots has its origin in a misleading paraphrase.[34]

Robinson's claim that "the relationship between Ulster-Scots and Lallans could be compared to the relative positions of Irish and Scottish Gaelic" is not backed up by reference to the academic literature. Notwithstanding their common roots, Scottish Gaelic and Irish are not generally considered to have a sufficient degree of mutual intelligibility for transactional purposes. The Irish of Donegal and Connemara might provide a better analogy, though even they may differ more than Scots in Scotland and Ulster. One also wonders why Robinson has not adopted parallel terminology by referring to the two dialect groups either as "Ullans and Lallans" or "Ulster-Scots and Scotland-Scots".

Robinson's view on the relative divergence of the Goidelic and Germanic idioms is recalled by Montgomery:

> Just as the Celtic language Gaelic crossed to the Western Isles around AD 500 and developed in Scotland a separate character through the experiences and contacts of its speakers there, so speakers of the Germanic tongue Scots more than a millennium later retraced this route in extending its linguistic territory to the north of Ireland. (2004: 121)

Although one is left free to infer that the *Abstand* of Ulster Scots to its parent speech form is equivalent to that of Scottish Gaelic to Irish, there is no explicit claim on the Robinson model. The mention of the millennium and more between the two migrations may also suggest to thoughtful readers that it is unlikely to be the case. Montgomery (2004: 122) himself states that the largest number of Lowland Scots arrived in Ulster in the 1690s. However, he is under the misapprehension that the European Bureau for Lesser-Used Languages views Ulster Scots as separate from Scots in Scotland (2004: 130). One suspects that an academic with more representative contacts in Ulster would find it impossible to argue, as Montgomery (2004: 131) does, for the recognition of Ulster Scots as a language on apperceptional grounds. In the present writer's experience, the vast majority of ordinary users subscribe to the consensus view that their speech is part of Scots or Scots and English, with the latter faction by far the larger. Moreover, though those groups are geographically, confessionally and politically diverse, the band of those who believe Ulster Scots a separate and independent language is overwhelmingly limited to Northern Ireland and to the Protestant and Unionist communities.[35]

The legislative framework for the promotion of Ulster Scots is vague and apparently contradictory. The Good Friday/Belfast Agreement refers to "the Irish language" but does not accord the same dignity to Ulster Scots. Statutory Instrument 1999 No. 859 The North/South Co-operation (Implementation Bodies) (Northern Ireland) Order 1999 states that:"Ullans [i.e. Ulster Scots] is to be understood as the variety of the Scots language traditionally found in parts of Northern Ireland and Donegal". In the same year, the UK Government agreed to promote

---

[33] Many of the orthographic innovations advocated by Robinson (1997) are borrowed from or inspired by phonetic transcription – one suspects precisely because no conventional orthography could have satisfied the author in its divergence.

[34] In an otherwise exemplary article, Mac Póilin (2001: 3) also refers to Ulster Scots as a "variant" of Scots. It is unfortunate that the passage from Robinson (1997: 1) misrepresenting the scholars of the SND is reproduced on the website of the Ulster-Scots Agency at http://www.ulsterscotsagency.com/01TheUlster-Scotslanguagetoday.asp.

[35] Some observers might even claim that promoters of Ulster Scots as an independent language are not merely Unionist but exhibit a bias – declared or undeclared – towards the "no" camp in their attitude to the Good Friday/Belfast Agreement.

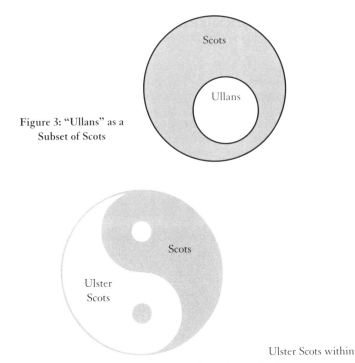

**Figure 3: "Ullans" as a Subset of Scots**

Ulster Scots within

**Figure 4: "Ulster-Scots" and "Scots" as Identifiers of a Single Idiom**

the framework of the European Charter on Regional or Minority Languages in the following terms:

> The United Kingdom declares, in accordance with Article 2, paragraph 1 of the Charter that it recognises that Scots and Ulster Scots meet the Charter's definition of a regional or minority language for the purposes of Part II of the Charter.

The charter declaration seems to overturn the implementation body's definition of Ulster Scots by treating it as an independent language. If "Ullans" is a "variety of the Scots language", after all, why should it be necessary to mention it separately? On the other hand, it is conceivable that the UK Government has simply adopted deviant terminology for its own bureaucratic purposes. None of the other UK declarations regarding the charter dealt with two languages in a single sentence,[36] and the recognition of the Ulster variety was reportedly a direct result of the recognition of Scots in Scotland, though that fact could also be interpreted as indicating a general weakening of the criteria for languageness.

Since Government pronouncements can do nothing to alter the structural unity of Scots on the two sides of the Straits of Moyle without destroying the traditional dialect that they seek to protect, in linguistic terms "Ulster-Scots" and "Scots" refer to a single idiom distinguished on a jurisdictional basis. There are many such cases in the world where a national adjective or regional variant is used to refer to the entirety of a linguistic system. For example, since the

---

[36] In e-mail correspondence addressed to Mr. Andrew Eagle and dated 13 October 2004, Mr. Douglas Ansdell of the Scottish Executive confirmed that the signing of the European Charter was not preceded by consultations with qualified academic linguists.

language known in the Netherlands as *Nederlands* is the equal heritage of Flanders, in the latter territory it is known as *Vlaams*, despite disposing over a single written form as a result of a *taalunie* or language union. The use of the word "Flemish" to describe the Dutch language in Belgium has become so well anchored that casual outside observers may not be aware that a separate language is not meant. In the same way, in southern Ireland, the word *Gaoluinn* is sometimes used to refer to the Irish language as a whole, though the standard word is *Gaeilge*. The difficulty in the case of Ulster is that no suitable stand-alone adjectival form exists pertaining to the historic province. Moreover, Scots is spoken only in parts of four counties, meaning that the application of such an overarching adjective to a peripheral idiom might be rejected by a majority of the area's inhabitants. Using "Ulster-Scots" as an equally valid term is problematic precisely because it is a qualified version of the other word, which suggests, in the parlance discussed above, a variant of Scots as a whole rather than simply another dialect group. Since the term "Ullans", though originating through a contraction of "Ulster Lallans", is opaque, it would make more sense to reverse the nomenclature of the two definitions, stating that in the implementation bodies legislation "Ulster-Scots" is a variety of "Scots" – along with many other geographically qualified regional varieties – and in the charter declaration that "Ullans" and "Scots" meet the definition of a language. It should be noted, however, that native users of the Ulster dialect habitually refer to their idiom as "Scotch" or "Scots" with no qualifier.

There are other legal obstacles to a redefinition of Ulster Scots as an independent language:

1) The charter specifically excludes dialects, leaving any such declaration open to challenge or even ridicule.
2) Unlike the implementation bodies legislation, the European Charter is not legally enforceable.
3) The implementation bodies legislation has the status of a bilateral treaty with the Irish Republic, and a unilateral redefinition of Ulster Scots on the part of the UK Government would thus abrogate a key element of the Good Friday/Belfast Agreement.

Another factor is that the ethnic qualification implied in the advertising of jobs, services and consultations as "Ulster-Scots" excludes Scots-born speakers resident in Northern Ireland, who may number around 5,000, making them just over 14%, or one in seven users.[37] It is hard not to see the present situation as the linguistic equivalent of an apartheid-era park bench marked *slegs vir blankes*. An objection lodged by the present writer with the Equality Commission for Northern Ireland elicited the following response, which could be interpreted as upholding the complaint in principle.

> The Committee was satisfied that the wide range of issues raised by the Complainant concern matters which may be susceptible to analysis as claims of discrimination on grounds such as national origins under the Race Relations Order (Northern Ireland) 1997, as amended.[38]

---

[37] The calculation is based on the c. 30,000 speakers of "Ulster-Scots" identified by the 1999 Northern Ireland Life and Times Survey, the number of Scots-born residents according to the 2001 Northern Ireland census, and the 1996 estimate by the General Register Office for Scotland that 30% of Scots residents (c. 1·5 million) are users of the language.
[38] 'Record of Decision – 16/11/04'.

However, the commission's remit was to rule on the narrow question of whether the Northern Ireland Department of Culture, Arts and Leisure had failed to comply with its approved equality scheme, an issue in which the fact of a discriminatory outcome was apparently irrelevant. The result was a refusal to take the case further.

The Southern Government too could find that it has legal problems with Scots. If the Ulster-Scots Agency were to advertise a post requiring a knowledge of "Ulster-Scots"[39] and, as the Equality Commission conceded possible, the geographical qualifier were deemed unjustifiable on linguistic grounds, the Irish Republic might find itself in breach of the Single European Act, since such geographical qualification excludes 98% of UK Scots-speakers and 100% of those from Great Britain. While the agency's Northern board members are nominated by the province's political parties – in practice, without exception by the Ulster Unionist Party – the Southern members are appointed by the Irish Government directly. Moreover, if a board member resigns, he or she may not be replaced during the suspension of the political institutions. After the recent resignation of the agency chairman Lord Laird, a majority of board members are the direct appointees of the Irish Government; given the current political outlook, without a change in the rules that situation is likely to continue.[40]

Ultimately, the question of whether the UK Government's European Charter declaration rescinds the definition of the implementation bodies legislation may be academic, since the idiom referred to in the latter is not "Ulster Scots" but "Ullans". It is even conceivable that the change in terminology was intended to avoid the charge of breaching a treaty,[41] though such foresight would be unwonted in the Northern Ireland Administration's approach to Scots. However, if there are two Scots languages recognised in Northern Ireland, the Ulster-Scots Agency is on even thinner ground in its mission statement to promote the "use of Ulster Scots as a living language", something fundamentally at odds with its remit as set out in the implementation bodies legislation.

The fact that the agency includes its own interpretation of the European Charter on its website,[42] despite its legal irrelevance to its linguistic work, strongly suggests a belief among staff and board members that its remit has indeed been rewritten unilaterally by the UK Government. As the European Charter has not been signed by the Irish Government or passed by the Oireachtas, its application to the work of the Ulster-Scots Agency, which is also responsible for Scots-speakers in County Donegal, could be interpreted as the first attempt to exercise British sovereign authority over a part of what is now the Irish Republic since 1922. When the Irish Government announced plans to move the offices of the agency's sister organisation, *Foras na Gaeilge*, to Donegal as part of wide-ranging decentralisation plans, they ran into difficulty since, unlike its predecessor organisation, *Bord na Gaeilge*, it is a cross-border body.

Such legal niceties appear not to have been considered in the case of the application of the charter, however. Little could those Republicans and Nationalists, in both parts of the island, who argued so persuasively for the creation of a cross-border language body have guessed that

---

[39] Such an advertisement appeared in *The Belfast Telegraph* on 26 April 2005, referring to "the Ulster-Scots language", though there is no legal basis for the agency's use of the term.

[40] Of course, a legal case brought against the Irish Government would do nothing to challenge the originators of the present discriminatory situation in Northern Ireland, and might even result in its being made permanent, since agreed redefinition would then be in the Irish State's interest.

[41] DCAL itself states the following at http://www.dcalni.gov.uk/allpages.asp?pname=language_faqs#3: "Ulster-Scots is defined in legislation as: 'the variety of the Scots language, which has traditionally been used in parts of Northern Ireland and Donegal'. (The North/South Co-operation (Implementation Bodies) (Northern Ireland) Order 1999)". Apart from the ungrammatical addition of a comma, this is the definition of "Ullans".

[42] Available at http://www.ulsterscotsagency.com/europeancharter.asp.

its practical outworking would be not nascent Irish unity but an embryonic re-enactment of union with Great Britain. It might be argued that their silent acceptance of such apparent infringements of their state's sovereignty is understandable only if they too have accepted the specious equation of "Irish" with "Catholic" and "Scots" with "Protestant".

Needless to say, any redefinition of Ulster Scots is political rather than linguistic in its motivation. The mistake is to believe that a state declaring an idiom a language makes it such for linguists. Such an attitude, exhibiting a strange mixture of cynicism and naïveté in its assertion of a primarily political paradigm, is exemplified by Adrian Langan in his article "Heim Swate Heim"[43] in *Magill* magazine in July 2002, in which the author contends that West Cork English is as divergent from Standard English as Scots.[44] An attempt to argue the ubiquity of politicised redefinition is undermined by the fact that the examples advanced – Serbian, Croatian and Bosnian in former Yugoslavia and Ebonics in the United States – are notorious among linguists and, like Ulster Scots, not believed structurally independent by a majority of speakers. Moreover, attempts to reunify tongues affected by disuse and differential erosion are also branded political. For a linguist, the fundamental difference between unifying the Irish dialects with a common reformed orthography and dividing the Scots is that one makes a positive contribution to linguistic diversity, through improving utility and therefore linguistic survival chances, and the other a negative by effecting the opposite.

Those who argue that Scots as a whole is not a language sometimes forget that the question is primarily not structural but functional.[45] Linguists are agreed that Scots has enough structural *Abstand* to be developed as an independent language. The statement that Scots is "not a language" and therefore "does not deserve" support arguably expresses only the view that it should not become – or return to being – one. An independent Ulster Scots has two further problems. Not only has it never been used in the functional domains of a language historically occupied by Scots in Scotland; structurally, the divergence is so small that in any authentic representation it will always be part of the latter. While it is commonly thought admissible to speak of Scots as an independent idiom because of its history as a language of state and the Government-backed prospect of future development, such arguments cannot be made with regard to the Ulster dialect in isolation. The language of publicly commissioned translations in Northern Ireland strongly suggests that the activist-translators have rejected the notion of an authentic idiom shared with Lowland Scotland in favour of enhancing its identificational value to Ulster Unionists,[46] a practice impossible to divorce from a failure to consult professional linguists in the formulation of policy and the drafting and interpretation of the bureaucratic framework for promotion. By aiming to make Ulster Scots an *Abstand* language, such translations preclude its ever being an *Ausbau* language. Difficult or impossible for native speakers to understand, they are functionally and transactionally bankrupt. The politicised argument that linguists have nothing to say on the question of language status, by allowing activists to make a kirk or a mill of an idiom, creates the conditions for them to make

---

[43] The title, which may have been the work of a sub-editor, does not represent the Ulster-Scots realisation of the vowels in the words, although it may have been adopted as an intentional satire of unjustified respelling.

[44] This may originate in the belief, discussed above, that Scots was produced by substratal influence in the same way as Hiberno-English.

[45] Naturally, this applies only to the traditional language rather than to the heavily dialectalised "urban" varieties of the present day, which exhibit an advanced stage of language death. Indeed, a possible criterion for delineating Scots from English would be whether a speech variety satisfied the *Mindestabstand* or "minimum divergence" required by Kloss (1952: 1978) for it to be developed as an *Ausbau* language.

[46] Given the number of users in Donegal, and Nationalists and Lowland Scots in Northern Ireland, this group could only be about half of Scots-speakers in Ulster, a fact which calls into question the way the idiom is being promoted by the Ulster-Scots Agency, which has even paid for political murals.

a hames of it. Where such *faux*-apperceptional attitudes are allowed to go unchallenged in the context of debate on official recognition, they are akin to a belief that an earthworm can be subdivided into an infinite number of viable new worms.

The case of Scots in Ireland illustrates the inherent problems of any blanket application of adjectives based on notions of origin, political citizenship or national territory to linguistic continua in a case of cultural confluence and ethnic and national controversy. Communities defined theoretically by academics may differ from the "imagined communities" of the objects of their studies; it is commonplace to point out that Catholics and Protestants in Northern Ireland, or Scottish and English citizens in Britain, may in some respects have more in common with those of similar socioeconomic background among the ethnic "other" than those among their own group who are of a different class. Equally, a recourse to the notion of "imagined community" may be a useful heuristic for the linguist in the context of limiting the compass of any study of continua. However, referring to Belfast English as "Scots" goes a step further, since it applies the tag of an imagined community not accepted by users of the speech variety itself and uses it taxonomically.

Rather than circumventing the problems of continua, a failure to decide demarcations based on internal linguistic factors alone may result in a free-for-all where the most skewed ethno-political approaches are accepted as being equally or more valid than those of academics.[47] Basing Government policy for linguistic diversity on the wished-for rather than actual nature of an idiom can waste precious public funds while subjecting the speech form and its users to indignity and ridicule, reducing the size of the speech community and discriminating against those who might otherwise make a positive contribution to its survival; it may even accelerate the process of language death that it is intended to halt.

## References

Adams, G. B. 1986. "Phonological Notes on the English of South Donegal". *The English Dialects of Ulster: An Anthology of Articles on Ulster Speech*. Ed. Michael Barry and Philip Tilling. Cultra: Ulster Folk and Transport Museum

Aitken, A. J. 2002. *The Older Scots Vowels: A History of the Stressed Vowels of Older Scots from the Beginnings to the Eighteenth Century*. Ed. C. I. Macafee Edinburgh: Scottish Text Society

Fenton, J. 2000. *The Hamely Tongue. A Personal Record of Ulster-Scots in County Antrim*. 2nd Edition.. N.p.: Ullans Press

Gregg, R. 1964. "Scotch-Irish Urban Speech in Ulster". in G. B. Adams ed. *Ulster Dialects: An Introductory Symposium*. Ed. G.B. Adams. Cultra: Ulster Folk Museum. 109-39

Gregg, R. 1972. "The Scotch-Irish dialect boundaries in Ulster". *Patterns in the Folk Speech of the British Isles*. Ed. M. Wakelin. London: Athlone

Harris, J. 1984. "English in the North of Ireland". *Language in the British Isles*. Ed. Peter Trudgill. Cambridge: University Press. 115-34

Henry, P. L. 1957. *An Anglo-Irish Dialect of North Roscommon*. Dublin: University College

Herbison, I. 1991. "A Sense of Place: Landscape and Locality in the Work of the Rhyming Weavers". *The Poet's Place: Ulster Literature and Society. Essays in Honour of John Hewitt, 1907-87*. Eds. G. Dawe and J. W. Foster. Belfast: Institute of Irish Studies. 63-75

---

[47] Such attitudes can be seen in the charge that a linguist pointing out that Ulster Scots is a form of Scots called a language for political reasons is also acting politically. This is reminiscent of the accusation, often heard in Northern Ireland, that those who point out that the Orange Order is a sectarian organisation – an uncontroversial view among Scottish Protestants – are themselves somehow sectarian in attacking "Protestant culture".

Herbison, I. 1996. *"The Rest is Silence": Some Remarks on the Disappearance of Ulster-Scots Poetry.* Ballymena: Dunclug Press

Jones, C. 2002. *The English Language in Scotland: An Introduction to Scots.* East Linton: Tuckwell Press

Kallen, J. 1999 "Irish English and the Ulster Scots controversy" *Ulster Folklife* 45: 70-88

Kirk, J. M. 1999. "The Dialect Vocabulary of Ulster". *Cuadernos de Filología Inglesa* 8: 305-34

Kloss, H. 1952, 1978. *Die Entwicklung neuer germanischer Kultursprachen* (erweiterte Auflage). Düsseldorf: Pädagogischer Verlag Schwann

Macafee, C. I. 1997. "Older Scots Lexis". *The Edinburgh History of the Scots Language.* Ed. C. Jones. Edinburgh: University Press

Macafee, C. I. 2002. "The Under-representation of Irish Etymologies in English Dictionaries". *Studia Indogermanica Lódźiensia* (Sigl) Vol. IV: 43-9

McCafferty, K. 2001. "Norway: Consensus and Diversity". *Linguistic Politics.* Eds. J.M. Kirk and D. P. Ó Baoill. Belfast: Cló Ollscoil na Banríona. 89-103

McClure, J. D. 1995. *Scots and its Literature.* Amsterdam: John Benjamin

McClure, J. D. 2002. "The Identity of Scots: A Contemporary Problem". *Studia Indogermanica Lódźiensia* (Sigl) Vol. IV: 51-62

Montgomery, M. 2004. "Ulster-Scots: Lost or Submerged?" *Ulster and Scotland, 1600—2000: History, Language and Identity.* Eds. W. Kelly and J. R. Young. Dublin: Four Courts Press

Murray, J. A. H. 1873. *The Dialect of the Southern Counties of Scotland.* London: Asher and Co. on behalf of the Philological Society

Robinson, P. 1997. *Ulster-Scots: A Grammar of the Traditional Written and Spoken Language.* Belfast: Ullans Press.

Stalmaszczyk, P. 2002. "Issues in Irish English Vocabulary". *Studia Indogermanica Łódêiensia* (Sigl) Vol. IV: 63-71

Todd, L. 1989. *The Language of Irish Literature.* Basingstoke: Macmillan Education

Wijk, A. 1966. *Rules of Pronunciation for the English Language.* Oxford: University Press

Zwickl, S. 2002. *Language Attitudes, Ethnic Identity and Dialect Use across the Northern Ireland Border: Armagh and Monaghan.* Belfast: Cló Ollscoil na Banríona

# Patriotism, National Sport, and Outsiders Playing an Insiders Game

*Cassie S. Farrelly*

Applying the post-nationalist theories of Jurgen Habermas to Northern Ireland, Gerard Delanty argues that post-national identity is constructed in opposition to narrow concepts of nationality founded on "a single identity". Habermas' own discussion of post-nationalism asserts that Western European countries have undergone "processes of globalization, immigration and increased ethnic diversity" among populations that had at one time been homogenous and must now create traditions "based on acceptance of cultural difference" (Delanty, 20-4). Post-nationalism, then, emerges not out of collective identities, but out of superseding limited nationalist definitions. The increased arrival of refugees and asylum-seekers in the Republic of Ireland from varied nations, cultures and religions, is contributing to this process at a time when national debates on immigration, integration and identity are being played out not only in parliamentary chambers, but also in the artistic forum of the theatre.

Successful passage of a recent citizenship referendum in favour of severely restricting citizenship rights to Irish-born children of non-nationals indicates the scope of immigration's influence in the changing Irish political and social landscape. After undergoing a tumultuous and well-documented process to gain political independence and recognition of an Irish national state and culture, the Republic now faces the challenge of moving beyond these definitions into a new post-national state that includes a rapidly changing population. Not surprisingly, this demographic shift has not gone unnoticed by authors and performance artists. As Christopher Murray notes in "The State of Play: Irish Theatre in the 'Nineties'", current Irish theatre is "in pursuit . . . of fresh articulation of who we are as a people . . . and where we are headed as a nation in the age of the Maastrict Treaty" (Murray, 23).

Between 1994 and 2004, seven new productions have confronted the subject of asylum-seekers, featuring plots or main characters whose backgrounds as refugees figure prominently into the plot: *Asylum! Asylum!* (1994), *The Farawayan* (1998), *Native City* (1998), *Guess Who's Coming for the Dinner* (2001), *Limbo* (2001), *Mixing It On the Mountain* (2003) and *Hurl* (2003). Each have plots involving the experiences of refugees in the Republic. In doing so, Irish theatre is acknowledging these refugees as part of the post-national Irish population. In 2003 the St. Patrick's Day Festival Committee commissioned "African Voices in Ireland", a theatre presentation of African oral and dramatic traditions. The 2004 Centenary celebration of Bloomsday included a street re-enactment of the Nelson's Pillar portion of *Ulysses*, using Chinese and West African actors. It is noteworthy that two festivals, honouring world-renowned symbols of Ireland, St. Patrick and James Joyce, have included multi-cultural performers and indicates the extent to which artistic endeavours have adopted immigrant populations into the fabric of Irish national identity. Where efforts are being made on the part of government and social agencies to effect successful integration or deportation of these new arrivals, theatre, as an artistic medium, is in the unique position to integrate them into the stories it tells, to represent them as part of the evolving Irish state.

*Asylum! Asylum!*, produced by the Abbey in 1994, marked the national theatre's first foray into representing this newfound diversity in the country and also challenged the shifting nature of Ireland's identity within the European Union. Subsequent plays have followed suit by placing refugees in the context of other high profile national symbols. Calypso Productions' *Mixing It On the Mountain* rewrote the legend of St. Patrick casting Patrick as a slave from Roman territories in Africa (A Nigerian refugee, Solomon Ijigade, was cast to play Patrick) and Barabbas' 2003 production of *Hurl* by Charlie O'Neill depicted a group of refugees taking on the Irish national sport of hurling.

In analyzing *Hurl*, this paper will discuss the significance of Irish theatre writing refugees and asylum-seekers into national symbols, specifically sport and, by extension, the larger framework of Irish society. *Hurl* premiered at the Galway Arts Festival in July of 2003 before moving to the Dublin Theatre Festival that September. The play follows the attempts of a group of refugees to form an official GAA hurling team—the Freetown Slashers– while waiting to hear if their asylum applications have been rejected or accepted. This attempt meets with opposition from GAA officials who resent this incursion into a sacred Irish national pastime, and the players must overcome everything from physical brutality against them on the pitch, to GAA regulator Rusty Cox calling immigration authorities to deport them. Objecting to the creation this hurling team, Cox snarls, "They're representing the club at our own, native game, hardly a Paddy among them. I mean . . . haven't they enough without taking our game as well?" This line summarizes the root of conflict in O'Neill's play: preservation of a national identity—in part communicated through sport—perceived to be under threat by a changing society increasingly comprised of individuals who fall outside traditional definitions of "Irishness" (O'Neill, 24). For a population excluded by physical characteristics that set them apart and by the legislative process for refugees, what begins in *Hurl* as a method to wait for news of their asylum applications, becomes a microcosm of the struggle to belong in their new country, of the problem-plagued transformation from homogenous culture to multi-ethnic one, of the gradual transition from post-colonial to post-national identity.

Although the team is initiated by recent arrivals to the country, several players who join along the way are Irish-born citizens of non-Irish descent, thus immediately introducing both the idea that immigration to Ireland is not a completely recent phenomenon and also challenging notions of homogenous Irish identity. One of the players, Dong Phuc, is of Vietnamese descent, his parents having arrived in Ireland in a wave of immigration that occurred in the late 1970s and early 80s (O'Neill, 17). An individual who was born and raised in Ireland despite his Asian physical features, his dialogue is written with deliberately crafted Irish dialect and colloquialisms. "Howsitgoin' [sic]?" he asks, wielding his hurling stick. "I'm Irish. Not only that, I'm a culchie. Though inside I know I'm a redneck mucksavage Paddy, part of who I am is Vietnamese" (O'Neill, 17). The Freetown Slashers mobilize a team and forge a sizeable fan-base by the play's conclusion. However, the ending is not entirely rose-tinted. The team organizer, Musa Sesay, is deported before the final match and the play ends on a melancholy note with a scene in which Musa receives news that the Slashers won, while chained as a political prisoner in a Sierra Leone cell.

O'Neill's decision to choose hurling is worth examining. Considered a "home-grown" Irish sport, hurling is a staple of the Gaelic preservation movement of the late nineteenth century that spurred both the creation of the Abbey Theatre and the Gaelic Athletic Association for the Preservation and Cultivation of National Pastimes. Sports considered "foreign"—including football and rugby—are still forbidden from being played in the GAA's signature stadium, Croke Park, reinforcing the nationalistic importance of sports like hurling and camogie as extensions of Irish nationhood and identity.[1] Therefore, in choosing hurling, O'Neill introduces a symbiotic relationship between sport and national identity, foreshadowing that the battle to be played on the hurling field will not be solely be for athletic prowess, but for cultural supremacy as well.

This link between nationalism and sport has been played out on Irish stages before. In analyzing Marie Jones' *A Night in November* and Dermot Bolger's *In High Germany*, both of

---

[1] See http://news.bbc.co.uk/1/hi/northern_ireland/2570305.stm

which centre on the Irish football team's performance in a World Cup competition, Aimee Waha suggests that both plays challenge the concept of a homogenous Irish identity and establish the connection between national athletic teams and the citizens that comprise the nation itself. Fans identify themselves with that team as an extension of their country. Consequently, individuals who would otherwise exist as "Others," on the fringes of this identity, are embraced in the goal to support the national team. In *A Night in November*, Kenneth McCallister, a Northern Irish Protestant, comes to identify himself as Irish (and be accepted as such by other Irish football fans) with neither religious nor border separations intact by the end of the play in which he has followed the Republic's team to the World Cup competition in the United States. Not unlike descendants of new immigrants, residents of Northern Ireland defy tidily packaged definitions of Irishness. Theirs is a fractured version of Irish identity, one which straddles cultural, religious, and economic divides that go beyond the political question of to whom the Northern counties should belong. Faced with a divided sense of belonging, McCallister finds fulfilling identity as an Irish Football Fan, thereby resolving his doubts and leading to his integration via support of a national athletic team (Waha, 63-7). Participation in national sport emerges in Jones' play as a method for the "Other" to achieve belonging.

Moreover, Waha notes that "Sport is thus culturally and socially defined, as it represents and registers the conditions, changes, development, crises and problems of society" (64). O'Neill's concept of a multi-ethnic hurling team foreshadows the ways in which Ireland's growing multi-culturalism will continue to spill over into various social spheres. Political debate in his play about refugees echoes that which has been taking place in Ireland over the last decade. While a Refugee Bill was introduced into the Dáil in 1994, it was not until two years later that the Refugee Act of 1996 was passed. And even as recently as 2002, an EC Eurobarometer survey of Ireland found that 8.6% of Irish saw "loss of independent decision making for [their] country" as the most negative aspect of EU membership. 7.3% stated that "more foreigners, illegal immigrants, asylum seekers and black market workers" was the second most negative aspect.[2] When asked about EU enlargement, 45.9% expressed that there were too many immigrants in the country already, 44% feared unemployment rates would increase and 40.3% expected immigrants to abuse the welfare system.[3]

Differentiating between the notion of "inter-culturalism" and "multi-culturalism" in his program notes for *Hurl*, O'Neill emphasizes that it is not merely enough to have members from different cultures living in Ireland, as multi-culturalism implies. For O'Neill, inter-culturalism asserts that it is equally important for these cultures to mix. The path forward for the emergent diversity in Ireland is in creating a climate wherein cultures actively engage with each other, retaining qualities unique to their backgrounds, while creating a combined culture reflecting this diversity.

As a form that possesses considerable flexibility and hinges on imagination, theatre emerges as a tool for O'Neill's vision. Stage directions dictate that actors should not exit the stage space at any point. Rather, they remain, seated on the sidelines like part of the audience, creating an atmosphere in which audience members are seated at a sporting event and eavesdropping, not watching a play.

O'Neill directly challenges the history behind the belief that hurling is a sacred, Irish-only sport. The Freetown Slashers coach, Lofty McMahon, is a retired priest who spent several

---

[2] See Eurobarometer 56.3-National Report Ireland, 24. Figures reflected here are for First Mentions. Aggregates for the Total Mention, which includes First and Second Mentions, reflect that 12.6% of Irish people are concerned about foreigners and illegal immigrants and 12.4% find loss of independent decision making to be a negative effect. (25). See Appendix C for additional information from this report and from the *Eurobarometer Survey* 60.1.

[3] See *Eurobarometer Survey* 56.3: 45.

years in Sierra Leone before returning home to minister in rural Ireland. He traces the very origins of hurling as being of an immigrant nature. Ireland's national sport, he argues, arrived on the island when the Celts invaded. "As the last ice age was receding on this green land of ours," he tells Rusty, "The Celts caused immigration havoc" (O'Neill, 24). Making an "unannounced social call" in Ireland, they brought elements of their own unique culture, including a game called Camaniocht, which evolved into present-day hurling (O'Neill, 25). The idea that hurling is an inherently and undeniably "Irish" sport is called into question by the number of times Ireland has been invaded, thus challenging designations of "purely Irish.". The notion of hurling as an untainted tenet of Irish culture is, Lofty concludes, a myth.

The Irish pattern of migration to other countries, either as immigrants or as missionaries for the Catholic faith – another bastion of "Irishness" – must also be considered. *Hurl* uses both these traditions of migration to explain how different foreign characters have learned the sport. While in Sierra Leone, Lofty receives a box from his diocese in Ireland meant to hold supplies, which is mistakenly filled with hurling equipment. Surrounded by civil unrest and aware it will be two months before the next shipment can fix the error, Lofty decides to use the hurling equipment and teach the game as an escape from the otherwise dire circumstances. Just as hurling emerged as a tool of anti-colonialism in Ireland, a unifying force to assert Irish identity, Lofty's use of it in Sierra Leone likewise provides escape from oppression.

The profound influence of the Irish Diaspora around the world is represented by another character. Santos from Argentina, already knows how to play the game, having descended from an Irish immigrant enclave that settled there in the late 1800s. He represents this influence of the Diaspora while reflecting the ways in which Irish communities in these foreign countries maintained their culture while assimilating into the existent culture. Neither his name nor his physical features align with traditional definitions of Irishness, but his upbringing has included learning Irish songs and poetry. While Santos is not fleeing dictatorship rule or torture, the collapsing economy in Argentina has prompted him to seek better opportunities elsewhere, not unlike Irish immigrants who arrived in new countries well into the early 1990s as refugees of a struggling economy with high rates of unemployment.

Lighting design and choreography assume a prominent role in simulating the physicality of hurling and conveying unspoken messages. Choreography for the Freetown Slashers team employs fluid, synchronized movements. The point at which the actors begin to portray Rusty Cox's team – a team with a reputation for rough play – their movements lose the grace of the Freetown Slashers and switch to lumbering, ape-like posturing. Here, the myopia that prompts Rusty to object to a multi-cultural hurling team is physically embodied on the stage through the hulking, brutish movements of his team members who lope around the stage like animals. Racism and xenophobia, the choreography suggests, devolves those who perpetuate it. Whipping his team into a violent frenzy, Rusty argues that the Slashers only want to play the game for a "novelty" and should be punished for not giving the sport of hurling the national reverence it deserves. Expression of cultural identity is tied to physical expression of the national sport. Incorporating this activity into the stage choreography reinforces this ideological importance.

Casting choices for the inaugural performance of *Hurl* highlighted the indecipherable line between ethnic traits and cultural identity, visually contributing to O'Neill's message of "inter-culturalism" versus "multi-culturalism". Rusty is played by Irish actor Paul Tylak, who has played non-Irish characters before, including a Kurdish refugee on RTE's Fair City. Actor Anthony Ofoegbu, who played Musa, was raised in London, although his father is from Nigeria and his mother is from Waterford. Castleknock, Dublin-raised Asian actor Alan Wai, in his professional debut, played the Vietnamese player (*Hurl* Performance Program, Actors Bios).

The notion that national identity cannot be defined by participation in or knowledge of nationalist symbols, resonated with at least one theatre critic and, according to that critic, with the audience in attendance at the same performance. Commenting on the scene in which the Freetown Slashers attempt to sing the national anthem in Irish but cannot, *The Guardian* reviewer Helen Meany noted, "As the team members mumble their way through the (Irish language) words before lapsing into an enthusiastic roar, the Galway arts festival audience cheer[ed] in recognition: very few Irish people know the words either." For Meaney, *Hurl's* primary flaws rested in expecting the audience to suspend belief enough to imagine stage choreography as a hurling match and a somewhat overstated social message. *Sunday Tribune* reviewer Rachel Andrews notes that despite these shortcomings, *Hurl* is significant in its decision to mount Ireland's most popular sport against the backdrop of "some of the most profound social changes to ever affect the country." Fintan O'Toole notes that, given Irish theatre's traditional emphasis on staging national mythology, it is surprising that hurling had not been explored by Irish theatre earlier. Comparing *Hurl* to its predecessor and obvious influencer, Paul Mercier's *Studs*, O'Toole points to the strength of emphasizing the tension between athletics enjoyed for its purity, and athletics as an extension of political ideology. Far from seeing the combination of O'Neill's plot with physical presentation as problematic, O'Toole views it as an appropriate reflection of the current state of ethnic transition occurring in the Republic. "If *Hurl* has an uncertain array of modes and moods," he writes, "It is probably because . . . the story of Ireland's encounter with immigration is a narrative with a confused beginning, a murky middle and an unknown end".

In exploring the importance of sport in the Irish national consciousness and, in particular, the role of hurling in this identity, *Hurl* offers a well-formulated critique of where and how passion for athletics can act as a unifying force across ethnic and social divides. For refugees who cannot control a government system where their applications languish in back-logged files, hurling represents an escape and a way to mobilize for a common objective. In doing so, O'Neill's play contextualizes the role hurling played in the formation of Irish national identity under the constraints of post-colonial influence, and updates it, adapting it as a means for integrating non-Irish nationals into society as it transitions to a post-nationalist identity.

## References

Andrews, Rachel. 2003. "Review: *Hurl*". *Sunday Tribune*. 20 July

Delanty, Gerard. 1996. "Habermas and Post-National Identity: Theoretical Perspectives on the Conflict in Northern Ireland". *Irish Political Studies*. 11: 20-32

Meany, Helen. 2003. "Review: *Hurl*". *Guardian*. 28 July

Murray, Christopher. 1996. "The State of Play: Irish Theatre in the 'Nineties". *State of Play: Irish Theatre in the 'Nineties*. Ed. Eberhard Bort. Trier: WVT. Trier. 9-23

O'Neill, Charlie. *Hurl*. Unpublished

O'Toole, Fintan. 2003. "Review: *Hurl*". *Irish Times*. 18 July

Waha, Aimee. 2003. "Football and Identity in Contemporary Irish Drama". *New Voices in Irish Criticism*. Eds. Fionnuala Dillane and Ronan Kelly. Vol. 4. Dublin: Four Courts Press, Dublin. 63-70

# Musical Soundscapes in the Plays of Brian Friel

*Emma Faulkner*

I look on my manuscript as an orchestral score. (Friel, 1972)

Since the 1960s, Brian Friel has been as much concerned with action that takes place offstage as with onstage action. Friel has used a number of devices to demarcate stage space throughout his forty-year career, such as the window in *Translations* (1980) and the baby alarm of *Aristocrats* (1979). However, it is the abstract, invisible sound world of music that Friel employs most often as an instrument to explore the margins of time and space, as Fintan O'Toole (1993: 213-14) argues: "What music and dance do is to take time and mark it." Through the recurrence of music in *Philadelphia, Here I Come!* (1964), *The Loves of Cass McGuire* (1966), *Aristocrats*, *Dancing at Lughnasa* (1990) and *Performances* (2003), Friel gives the audience a double in defining the boundaries between the past and present and on and offstage space. Not only does music demarcate time and space but, in Friel's handling, music can also be viewed as a language more powerful than the spoken word.

Elmer Andrews (1995: 92) claims, "Music fills the silence between [...] past and present, helping to evoke that lost past [...] to dissolve the intractable present, and recreate the world." Not only is Andrews proposing that music actually dissolves the boundary between the present and the past, but in the process the past engulfs the present so that it becomes devoid of its own identity. While it is certainly true to say that music evokes the past, Andrews fails to appreciate that Friel's use of music, as a spatial marker, actually highlights the identity of the present world onstage as well as the offstage past. Therefore, rather than ignoring time and spatial margins, Friel uses simultaneity to establish a two-fold outlook on the offstage past and onstage present in which the boundaries of each are reinforced, rather than broken down.

In Friel's first stage success, *Philadelphia, Here I Come!*, the onstage action takes place on the eve of Gar O'Donnell's departure from his Ballybeg homeland for a new life in Philadelphia. Throughout the play, Public Gar's alter ego, Private Gar, forces him to confront memories of his past involving his late mother; his unrequited love Kate; and also his father, S.B. O'Donnell, whose relationship with his son has suffered a long-term communication breakdown from a mutual embarrassment at exposing emotions. As Public absorbs himself with packing his suitcase, the first movement of Mendelssohn's violin concerto plays onstage from the record player. Private is immediately transported by the music from the present moment onstage – that the theatre audience also occupy – to a nostalgic remembrance of a past that takes place prior to the play's beginning. Accompanied by the concerto, Private's memories of his mother are recalled in a distinctly lyrical tone: "She was small, Madge says, and wild, and young, Madge says, from a place called Bailtefree beyond the mountains; and her eyes were bright, and her hair was loose" (1984a: 37). At this point, Public replaces the Mendelssohn record with a lively ceilidhe number in a desperate effort to pull Private out of his wistful reverie back into his – Public's – present moment onstage. The chaotic ceilidh music may be a far cry from the pristine Mendelssohn concerto, but contrary to Public's plans, it actually reinforces rather than undermines the invisible action of the past. As the record player continues to belt out the throbbing beat, Private is quick to remind Public that the celidhe piece "was Katie's tune" (38), a grim reminder of the girl from his past that he intended to marry until she was discouraged by her parents.

Friel's play with onstage music to convey the past during the present is evident in a later episode involving Gar's father and the invisible alter ego, Private. Private believes that he can alleviate the deadlock in his relationship with his father by communicating a fond childhood memory of them both. At this point, Public plays the second movement of Mendelssohn's violin concerto on the record player while Private approaches S.B. The concerto creates a nostalgic atmosphere as Private exclaims: "Listen! … D'you know what the music says? (To S.B.) It says that once upon a time a boy and his father sat in a blue boat on a lake on an afternoon in May … a beauty that has haunted the boy ever since' (89). Despite Private's efforts to communicate with his father, music falls short of being able to disclose this past memory to S.B. because the latter has no awareness of Private addressing him in the present moment. Moreover, S.B. is also unaware of the Mendelssohn concerto playing so that when his friend, Canon O'Byrne, asks him if he can hear music, S.B. has to presume it must be Gar's record player because he himself cannot hear it. The limitation of the concerto to recreate Gar's past for the other characters means that it is actually the present world, symbolised by communication breakdown, which is indirectly highlighted instead.

Elmer Andrews holds the view that music recreates the world by placing emphasis on the past and dissolving the present, but, as the latter situation involving S.B. would suggest, this is not the case in Friel's theatre. Gar's world is not recreated because the past embodied by the Mendelssohn music is not powerful enough to obliterate the difficulties that plague him in the present – his awkward relationship with his father, his frustration with his homeland and his unrequited love. Instead, Friel toys with onstage music in *Philadelphia, Here I Come!* to simultaneously invoke Private's remembrance of key offstage pasts as well as to highlight the present moment onstage that Public occupies so that rather than bleeding into one another, the margins of both time and space remain intact. While Friel employs onstage music in *Philadelphia* to convey both the past and present and also on and offstage space, in his next play, *The Loves of Cass McGuire*, it is offstage music instead that he devises as an instrument to sound the past.

In The *Loves of Cass McGuire*, Friel utilises the music of Wagner to disclose the key events in the past lives of Cass, Trilbe and Ingram – three residents of the old people's home, Eden House. These people's respective pasts dominate the play's onstage action, even though the events of such are 'offstage', considering they are imagined as having taken place before the play's time and are never witnessed by the audience. In contrast to *Philadelphia, Here I Come!* Wagner's music does not originate from any location onstage but it fades in from the offstage space instead and has such an effect on Cass, Trilbe and Ingram that Friel refers to their individual recollections of their pasts as "rhapsodies", claiming specifically in the 'Author's Note', "I consider this play to be a concerto in which Cass McGuire is the soloist." Each rhapsody is poetic in tone, and the past that is revealed has also been so heavily romanticised that it is obvious such things never happened other than in the rhapsodist's imagination.

Wagner's 'Venusberg' accompanies Trilbe's rhapsody which centres round the life she lived with her husband, Gordon McClelland. She recalls their life in a chateau on the banks of the Loire where they "had servants and music and wine" (1984b: 30), and when Ingram composes his rhapsody to the sound of Wagner's 'Magic Fire', the tone and content is equally musical. Of his honeymoon, Ingram recollects how "there was music in my ears, throbbing, heady, godly music" (46) as he kissed his wife Stella, and danced with her, until suddenly "there was no sound" (ibid.) when tragedy struck and Stella was drowned. Ingram's association of music with his past marriage, and the sudden silence when Stella died, would signify, on a small scale, the use of music to demarcate different time periods. But although Wagner evokes a romantic and tragic version of Ingram's past, it is powerless to cloud over the more grim truth that the audience comes to learn during the present action onstage – rather than drowning, his new wife simply ran off with another man two days after their wedding.

The rhapsody of Cass – the play's central character – is set against the background of Wagner's 'Liebestod'. During her rhapsody, Cass recalls her marriage to Jeff Olsen whom she describes dreamingly as being "manly, with golden hair and kind soft patient eyes" (65), when in reality he was her one-legged drunken employer. Each rhapsody paints a nostalgic picture of the past and covers up the grim actuality of Cass, Trilbe and Ingram's lives, but such is the power of the music that they regard it as 'truth'. In contrast to *Philadelphia, Here I Come!*, where the onstage music reiterates the present moment, the highly lyrical tone of the rhapsodies suggests that music is a language of its own that keeps the offstage action of the past the preoccupation of the onstage space.

In *Aristocrats*, the use of music to demarcate spatial margins and time frames becomes immediately obvious. From the beginning of the play, Claire O'Donnell of Ballybeg Hall plays Chopin music on an offstage piano, so that as much attention is drawn to offstage action as to the action onstage. The association of Chopin with the past is made clear early in Act One as Claire plays the 'Ballade in G minor', and her brother, Casimir, announces, "when I think of Ballybeg Hall it's always like this: the place filled with music" (1984a: 256). Each Chopin piece played holds a particular memory so that as Claire plays Chopin's 'Waltz in A flat major', Casimir goes on to recollect how they used to call it the bedtime waltz "because as soon as Mother'd begin to play it, we'd have to dash upstairs" (268). Later in the play Claire plays Chopin's Sonata No.2 in B flat minor while Casimir recalls further events of the past, such as Yeats's visit to the Hall and also the day his father told him that he would never succeed in life. Here Friel uses offstage music as an instrument firstly to make known the existence of a space beyond the main stage from where the music plays, and secondly, to reveal action from the past that cannot be seen through the playing of the Chopin. But although the music prompts the audience to acknowledge a world offstage, the past that Casimir has constructed is heavily elaborated on in his own mind, much like the rhapsodists' versions of their pasts in *The Loves of Cass McGuire*. Casimir's need in the present moment to reconstruct an imagined past based on the actual past is proof that the present action onstage is not "dissolved", as Andrews's argues, for reasons that also become clear in the second act of the play.

In Act Two, it is the present moment rather than the past that is highlighted as Friel replaces Claire's offstage playing with an onstage tape recording of Chopin. By bringing music onto the main stage, Friel is making a distinction between visible and invisible space, as well as diverting the focus from "remembrance of things past" (289) offstage, to the present moment onstage. But while the Chopin recording plays, Eamon, a local from the village married to Claire's sister Alice, begins to sing a popular verse, 'So Deep is the Night', over the top of the recording. The popular song may be a stark contrast to what Harry White (1999: 6) refers to as the "art music" of Chopin that had been employed to convey the past in Act One; however, it is symbolic because the decline in the standard of the music reflects the present decline of Ballybeg Hall, from being a place of high culture in the past to its present state of decay.

Nowhere in the play is the shift from offstage past to onstage present so marked than when the Chopin tape that has been playing is replaced by another tape recording – a violin lullaby played by Claire's sister, Anna, who is a nun in Africa. As the tape "plays a few bars of the music" (304), Father, who is bed-bound and has remained offstage until this point in the play, enters, hears Anna's music, and screams for his absent daughter so that "the tape's scream and Father's roar overlap for a few seconds" (304). The pristine offstage Chopin music, used in Act One to convey Casimir's fond memories of his mother, has now been exchanged for the unintelligible sound produced as Father's roar is combined with the violin. The resulting sound would imply that music itself has become insane and hysterical in an attempt to reflect the present moment of chaos before Father collapses. Moreover, sound has replaced words as order has succumbed to disorder, and the overlap of Anna's violin and Father's roar is also indicative of an onstage battle in sounds in which neither can conquer. At the end of the play, Friel continues to draw attention to the present with onstage singing of another popular song, 'Sweet Alice', and he instructs in a stage direction that there should be "the impression that this afternoon … may go on indefinitely" (326), very much an indication of a desire to savour the present moment. The play concludes with the rejection of the offstage past symbolised by Chopin and also the rejection of any attempt to look into the future. In *Aristocrats*, Friel uses the performed music of Chopin as a device to distinguish specifically the offstage action of the past, and both popular and recorded music to highlight the present moment onstage. However, not only does Friel use music to demarcate space in *Aristocrats*, but the sound world is asserted as being more powerful than language to convey the past and present.

This latter point is something that Friel pursues in *Dancing at Lughnasa* in his insinuation that music performed or recorded is perhaps now "the way to speak" (1990: 71). Although the lyrical tones of Michael Mundy's opening address would indicate an offstage past – "When I cast my mind back to that summer of 1936 different kinds of memories offer themselves to me" (1) – it is the present action onstage that preoccupies the theatre audience through most of the play, despite Andrews's insistence that the present is dissolved by the past through music. The dominant source of music in the Mundy household is Marconi, the onstage wireless, which delivers "Irish dance music beamed to us all the way from Dublin" (2). The fact that the wireless, an inanimate object, has a name is suggestive that music has become personified as a character in itself. More importantly Marconi is a sign of the present, the new times of the 1930's Industrial Revolution in Donegal which is one of the key periods the play dwells on, and with this token the music that flows from it reflects the action present to the 1930's in the Mundy house.

Michael Mundy, the play's narrator, who occupies the same moment of time as the play's current audience, refers to Marconi's music as "voodoo" (2) because it ignites in his mother and her four sisters an urgency to seize their own immediate moment. This is most evident in Act One when Aunt Maggie remembers a dance competition from her past, and the wireless suddenly bursts in with 'The Mason's Apron', an Irish dance piece. One by one, the sisters leap into raucous frenzied dance, at which Friel explains that "there is a sense of order being consciously subverted" (22), an indication that the order upheld by the past is being undermined by the present moment of dance. This subversion of order provoked by Marconi's musical "voodoo" can be compared to the similar breakdown of order, already discussed, in *Aristocrats* when Anna's violin music overlaps with Father's cry for his daughter.

Music is used to emphasise the present moment later in the play when Michael's father, Gerry, appears after a long absence. Gerry explains to Michael's mother, Chris, what he has been doing in the past, and his future plans, but at this point the song 'Dancing in the Dark' plays from the wireless, plunging Gerry into the present moment with Chris. He dances with her and even proposes to her, a spontaneous reaction to the moment. Chris attempts to hold on to the present by telling Gerry, "Don't talk anymore; no more words. Just dance me down the lane and then you'll leave" (33), a sign as well that Chris recognises the inadequacy of language compared with music when it comes to doing full justice to feeling. This is something that is also evident at the end of Act One as Jack beats out a musical rhythm with two sticks in an attempt to communicate what he cannot say in English, having spoken Swahili for twenty-five years in Africa. Earlier, Jack recalls that on his return to Ireland "there were days when I couldn't remember even the simplest words" (40), so that music can be viewed as a substitute when words fail to suffice.

Although Friel steadily employs onstage music to highlight the present moment onstage during the course of the play, it is really in Michael's final address at the end that offstage music conveys the past. Michael reveals to the audience the conclusion of the Mundy sisters' lives from the perspective of the past such as Jack's death, his mother's loathed employment in a factory for the rest of her days, and his own departure from home when he was grown up, before he nostalgically relates his most persistent memory from his childhood – dancing. As the latter memory becomes more vivid, the thirties song 'It is Time to Say Goodnight' fades in softly from the offstage space. This music is a sign that the offstage past is as important as the action of the present moment conveyed by Marconi. It might also be argued that the play's retreat into the past at the end indicates a fear of looking to the future. But in terms of dramaturgy, the play's conclusion to offstage music is also a reminder by Friel of the diversity and distinction of stage space, and at the same time, Michael's final memories would imply the inadequacy of words over feeling: "Dancing as if language no longer existed because words were no longer necessary" (71).

In *Performances*, on and offstage space is demarcated by the music of Leos Janacek's second String Quartet, 'Intimate Letters'. As with the other plays considered, the perspectives of past and present are juxtaposed by the music coming from different stage space. During the play, a PhD student called Anezka questions Janacek about his second string quartet, which is crucial to the thesis she is writing about his work. In her thesis Anezka wants to argue that Janacek's second String quartet was a declaration of love to Kamila Stosslova, a married woman he was romantically besotted with as he composed the quartet. But Janacek relentlessly denies this, arguing that the work is separate to the private life.

In the beginning, Janacek plays brief excerpts of his string quartet on a piano onstage. As he plays, he attempts to divert Anezka's interest in his past by testing her knowledge of his work to keep her absorbed in the present moment. However, the focus is diverted to Janacek's past when he stops playing the piano onstage and his visiting string quartet plays 'Intimate Letters' offstage. The shift from onstage to offstage music reminds the theatre audience of the double perspective of visible and invisible space being offered by Friel. The music that is played offstage is used to convey Janacek's past because as soon as the quartet start to play Anekza begins to read excerpts of Janacek's love letters in which he tells Kamila, "this quartet, my Intimate Letters to you, my love … was composed in fire out of the furnace that is our great love" (2003: 30). Janacek himself, also confesses that, "I composed from emotions remembered" (30), a sign that music is evocative of the past. However, the past that is conveyed in Janacek's letters does not portray an accurate picture because like the fabricated accounts of the past that Private Gar, the Eden House rhapsodists, and also Casimir present, Janacek's letters from the past would imply that he had embarked on an affair with Kamila – "how our first meeting set my soul ablaze with the most exquisite melodies" (23) – when in reality it only occurred in his head, a fabrication of the truth to inspire him in his musical compositions.

Towards the end of the play, however, the focus is diverted away from Janacek's past and back to the present when the string quartet that have been playing 'Intimate Letters' offstage come onstage and play beside Janacek. The relocation of the quartet from the invisible to the visible space mirrors the similar shift of Chopin from offstage to onstage in Act Two of *Aristocrats*, and it is also telling that the present sound world onstage is now more important than the words of Janacek's letters written in the past. Janacek tells Anezka that Kamila was not the inspiration for 'Intimate Letters', only the desire for the dream sounds of music in his head so that he "came to know no distinction between the dream music and the dream woman!" (34). Anezka leaves horrified that Janacek has undermined Kamila's centrality to his music. Meanwhile, Janacek remains silent onstage listening to the quartet play beside him until the allegro ends the play. As Janacek listens to the music he reads a line or two of the love letters. He then leans back from them and closes his eyes to absorb himself wholly in the music being played in the present moment onstage, a sign that both language and the present moment have succumbed to the sound world of music at the end of the play.

Friel has used music and has manipulated stage space variously throughout his long career. In the works discussed, it would seem that a general trend emerges as Friel employs offstage music to demarcate the offstage past, and also onstage music to highlight the present action and time onstage. At the beginning of this essay, I made reference to Elmer Andrews who proposed the view that music dissolves the boundary between the fictional spaces that are "the present" and "the past". However, it would appear that Friel's drama insists on differentiation in stage times and spaces so that even though the double perspectives of offstage and onstage, past and present, art and popular music, make up the wider soundscape, each continues to retain an identity of its own. Meanwhile, if there is anything that is dissolved by music it might be argued that it is language, as Friel himself said in his 'Notes for a Festival Programme' (Murray, 1999: 177): "What music can provide in the theatre [is] another way of talking, a language without words. And because it is wordless it can hit straight and unmediated into the vein of deep emotion."

## References

Andrews, Elmer. 1995. *The Art of Brian Friel: Neither Dreams nor Reality*. London: MacMillan Press

Friel, Brian. 1972. "Self-Portrait". *Aquarius* 5: 17-22

Friel, Brian. 1984a. *Selected Plays*. Introduced by Seamus Deane. London: Faber

Friel, Brian. 1984b. *The Loves of Cass McGuire*. Loughcrew: The Gallery Press

Friel, Brian. 1990. *Dancing at Lughnasa*. London: Faber and Faber

Friel, Brian. 2003. *Performances*. Loughcrew: The Gallery Press

Brook, Peter. 1968. *The Empty Space*. London: Penguin Books

Burke, P. 1993. "Both Heard and Imagined: Music as Structuring Principle in the plays of Brian Friel". *A Small Nation's Contribution to the World: Essays on Anglo-Irish Literature and Language*. Ed. D. Morse. Gerrards Cross: Colin Smythe

Murray, C, ed. 1999. *Brian Friel: Essays, Diaries, Interviews: 1964-1999*. London: Faber

O'Toole, F. 1993. "Marking Time: From *Making History* to *Dancing at Lughnasa*". *The Achievement of Brian Friel*. Ed. A.J Peacock. Gerrards Cross: Colin Smythe. 202-214

White, H. 1999. "Brian Friel and the Condition of Music". *Irish University Review* Spring-Summer: 6-15

# Irish and Catholic Identity: Ritual, Discourse and the Formation of Consciousness, 1922-1967

*Louise Fuller*

One of the foremost features of Irish society from the time of Independence was the extent to which the state by its laws and by the actions, words and public appearances of its representatives, legitimated the Catholic ethos. This paper examines how Catholic culture was consolidated from the early years of independence with particular reference to some of the rituals, discourse and symbols that played a powerful part in shaping and reinforcing Irish Catholic identity. This moulding of Irish culture was so influential as to result in 'Irish' and 'Catholic' being perceived as synonymous. The key to understanding this lies in developments in the nineteenth century. The struggle for emancipation and later for education rights for Catholics meant that the Catholic Church became increasingly politicized through the century and this was to guarantee it a defining role in any future political shape that the country might take. As Irish language usage declined Catholicism increasingly became the badge of Irish identity – this identification of Irish and Catholic and the profound influence of the Catholic church on Irish society remained intact through the first half of the twentieth century, but began to be undermined from the 1960s.

In the early years of independence an alliance was formed between the Catholic Church authorities and the Free State government, and WT Cosgrave looked to the Church to endorse the authority of his government. The alliance was mutually beneficial – the bishops were prepared to throw their weight behind the new state, which was being contested by anti-Treaty republicans, and the rulers of the new state were happy to accept the authority of the church in matters having to do with education, health or sexual morality, traditionally seen by the church as its areas of competence. Control over the education process was seen by Church authorities as a vital means of transmitting the Catholic cultural heritage.

Cosgrave and de Valera later sought to protect what they saw as the distinctive Irish Catholic tradition by means of legislation and censorship. The coalescence of interests and mutual regard in which the state held the Church and vice versa was clearly evident. On all public occasions – be it the opening of a new school, church or factory – politicians and clerics were present. The discourse engaged in by politicians reflected and reinforced the Catholic ethos. When Fianna Fail was campaigning in the 1932 election, Sean T O'Kelly claimed that "Fianna Fail policy was the policy of Pius XI".[1]

The Eucharistic Congress held in June 1932 gave the Fianna Fáil administration an early opportunity to demonstrate the loyalty of the Irish to their faith and to Rome. But, as Keogh has pointed out, this was not just a religious occasion, "it was a manifestation of Irish Catholic nationalism" (Keogh: 70). This symbiosis of religion and nationalism has to be seen against the background of centuries of Irish history. The Irish Catholic Church had survived discrimination, plantation and persecution and emerged victorious. Against this background, it is perhaps not surprising that a certain triumphalism became the hallmark of Irish Catholicism and an exalted sense of its resilience and merits was echoed time and again in the discourse of statesmen and clergy alike. The concern of politicians like de Valera, Cosgrave and others after them to affirm their Catholicism was understandable also in view of the necessity for the state to establish an identity after the disillusionment and acrimony of the Civil War. As Fanning has pointed out: "Catholicism, always central to so much of Irish nationalist ideology, thus took on an additional significance in the search for national identity" (Fanning: 59).

[1] *Irish Independent*, 11 February 1932.

De Valera's vision in which there was an instinctual association of Catholicism with the Irish language and the Irish way of life, was extolled time and again in his many speeches. In a St Patrick's Day broadcast to the United States in 1935, de Valera saw Catholic Ireland and the Irish nation as synonymous:

> Since the coming of St. Patrick, fifteen hundred years ago, Ireland has been a Christian and a Catholic nation. All the ruthless attempts made through the centuries to force her from this allegiance have not shaken her faith. She remains a Catholic nation.[2]

Through the twenties and thirties the Catholic moral code became enshrined in the law of the land. This process continued uninterrupted and culminated in the drawing up of a new Constitution in 1937. De Valera had always opposed the 1922 constitution, which had made Ireland a dominion of the British crown and he wanted to replace it with a document which would be indigenously Irish, as he saw it. The Constitution drawn up by de Valera, and accepted by the electorate in a referendum on 1 July 1937, reflected how deeply influenced he was by Catholic teaching. In the drafting of the constitution de Valera had consulted closely with Dr. John Charles McQuaid.[3] In Articles 41 to 44 the constitution of 1937 becomes particularly Catholic in its thrust. In Article 44 the State recognised the "special position" of the Catholic Church.[4] In the Dáil de Valera defended the constitution pointing out:

> 93% of the people in this part of Ireland and 75% of the people of Ireland as a whole ... belong to the Catholic Church ... believe in its teachings ...[5]

Their "whole philosophy of life", he went on, "is the philosophy that comes from its teachings". He continued that "it might be said that this does not go, from the Catholic point of view, the distance that would be desired by a number".[6] De Valera was convinced that his constitution would establish Ireland as giving a lead to the world "as a Catholic nation" (Longford & O'Neill: 298, 300) and Seán T O' Kelly proclaimed that "the constitution was worthy of a Catholic nation".[7] Whyte has pointed out the "mood of increasing integralism" (Whyte: 158) in Ireland in the late 1940s noting that "all sorts of forces were at work to make Ireland a more totally committed Catholic state than it had yet become ..." (Whyte: 158-159). When the Inter-Party government replaced the Fianna Fáil administration on February 1948, the Taoiseach John A Costello followed in the footsteps of Cosgrave and de Valera before him, and set the tone of his administration and of the fifties in general when he sent a message of "filial loyalty and of devotion" to Pope Pius XII and promised to "strive for the attainment of a social order in Ireland based on Christian principles".[8]

The close relationship between the Catholic Church and State was highly visible. Archbishop McQuaid was present at the airport to see the Taoiseach off on the Holy Year pilgrimage to Rome on 11 January 1950[9] and he was there to welcome back President O'Kelly on 26 April 1950.[10] The state shared the Catholic Church's definition of reality and publicly

---

[2] *Irish Press*, 18 March 1935, p 2.
[3] It is important to point out that de Valera also consulted representatives of other religious traditions. For an account of the church personnel consulted in the drafting of the Constitution see Keogh: 96-104.
[4] *Bunreacht na hEireann*: 136-46.
[5] *Dail Debates*. 67, Col. 1890. 4 June 1937.
[6] *ibid*., Col. 1891.
[7] *Irish Press*, 24 June 1937.
[8] *Irish Catechetical Directory* (I.C.D.). 1949. 24 February 1948: 705.
[9] I. C.D. 1951. 11 January 1950: 725.
[10] *ibid*. 739.

legitimated its role on many occasions. At that time the anniversary of the Pope's coronation was commemorated by solemn High Mass every year in the Pro-Cathedral. The Taoiseach, Tanaiste, members of the diplomatic corps, representatives of the army, the civic authorities and the Garda Síochána were normally present. On such Church-State occasions public representatives from the President down set the tone and acted as role models. They knelt before the bishop and kissed his ring. The fact that he was addressed as 'My Lord', and that the house he lived in was referred to as the bishop's palace, reinforced in the minds of people his power and that of the Church. John McGahern, reflecting on his own youthful impressions in an *Irish Independent* article in 1993, captured the aura surrounding the bishop: "With his crozier and rich colours and tall hat he was the image of God the Father".[11] The bishops did in fact see themselves as father figures protecting their flocks.

A hymn which evokes the mood of the time was 'Faith of Our Fathers'. It was sung in conjunction with '*Amhrán na bhFiann*', the National Anthem, at All-Ireland football finals, thus reinforcing the dual identity of Irish and Catholic. Another tradition on such occasions was that the Archbishop of Cashel, patron of the Gaelic Athletic Association since its foundation in 1884, threw in the ball at the beginning of the match. These traditions served to express and sustain a way of looking at life in Ireland. Such rituals represent a public ceremonial language which serves to define a community. They take collective sentiments for granted and reinforce them and in so doing serve to define identity and mould consciousness.

In Ireland in the 1950s the Catholic Church exercised a type of cultural hegemony, a concept developed by Gramsci to capture the complex process whereby powerful institutions or groups can disseminate their forms of consciousness through society as a whole (Bates: 360). This moulding of Irish Catholic consciousness had its roots in the nineteenth century when the laity had been socialized into strong religious beliefs, practices and a moral order which provided an all-encompassing definition of reality. The symbolic forms of Catholicism were everywhere to be seen in the home and in public places – holy pictures, in particular the picture of the Sacred Heart with the eternal lamp, the papal marriage blessing, the crucifix, statues of the Blessed Virgin, St. Joseph, the Infant of Prague, St. Martin de Porres and the 'black babies' boxes which were to be found in grocery shops and in public houses alike.

Radio and press also played a key role in legitimating the Catholic ethos. On 15 August 1950 a new daily feature was introduced by Radio Éireann, at the instigation of Archbishop McQuaid, whereby the ringing of the Angelus bell at the Pro-Cathedral was broadcast over the air at six o'clock each evening.[12] *The Irish Independent*, the newspaper with the largest daily circulation, gave extensive coverage to news of Catholic interest well into the 1960s. As well as printing the texts of bishops' Lenten pastorals, often running to two or three pages of newsprint, the lead writer also, on occasion, made reference to them, summarizing the main points and reinforcing them.[13]

Cultural theorists point to the importance of ritual, songs, processions and ceremonies in cultivating an ethos. A potent example of the public expression of Catholicism in Ireland in the 1950s was the procession. Processions were held on *Corpus Christi* and also in May. They normally took a route through the town or village in the countryside, or a route in the vicinity of the church in a city parish. They were followed by benediction, either in the open air or in the church. Householders along the processional route decorated their houses with flags and bunting. Displaying a picture of the Sacred Heart was the practice for the *Corpus Christi* procession while the erection of altars to Our Lady, either in windows or outside houses was

---

[11] John McGahern, *Irish Independent*, 31 July 1993, in Weekender: 1.

[12] *I.C.D. 1951*. 15 August 1950:753.

[13] See *Irish Independent*. 5 February 1951: 4, 6; *Irish Independent*. 1 March 1954: 8, 10; *Irish Independent*, 1956: 8-11.

common for the May celebrations. The Marian Year procession through Dublin was particularly impressive. Tens of thousands thronged the streets of the city centre to watch the procession in which over 25,000 people were estimated to have taken part. The procession which began at the Pro-Cathedral and passed through O'Connell street, was described in the *Irish Independent* as follows:

> ... all traffic was suspended for more than two hours as crowds twenty-deep packed the processional route ... As His Grace gave the benediction, army trumpeteers sounded a royal salute which was carried over the public address system. A hush fell over the streets and the great throng knelt on the roadways. The heart of the city for that brief moment was silent in prayer.[14]

The fact that Ireland in the fifties was a place where such religious events and occasions had the support and co-operation of both the civic authorities and business community speaks volumes about the shared meanings and levels of social solidarity that existed at that time.

A further indication of Ireland's Catholic ethos was the number of crosses erected during the Holy Year, 1950, and statues to the Blessed Virgin during the Marian Year, 1954. Drogheda Corporation erected a cross, forty foot high, on the south bank of the river Boyne on 26 March 1950. It was illuminated at night and could be seen ten miles out to sea.[15] A twenty foot high cross was erected on the summit of Carrantuohill in county Kerry. Mass was celebrated on the summit "attended by 1,500 people who came from all parts of Kerry".[16] The encyclical *Fulgens Corona* (1953) proclaimed 1954 the Marian Year and the Irish Bishops issued a statement at their October 1953 meeting in Maynooth, in which they urged the Irish people to profess their regard for the Blessed Virgin by erecting statues in her honour.[17] Their suggestion was enthusiastically taken up and grottoes and statues were erected in parishes throughout the country. Marian devotion, and in particular devotion to the Rosary, was very popular in Ireland. John Healy's recollection of the ritual in his own household will resonate with many Irish Catholics who grew up in Ireland in the pre-sixties era:

> There was no need for words now. The clock would strike ten. Grandma would put her sewing aside. From a nail on the wall she'd take the big Rosary beads ... we got up from our seats, knelt down with our backs to the fire and one another, leaned our elbows on the seat ... and made the responses. It was so in my mother's day and it would be so in my childhood days. (Healy: 9)

Commitment to the Rosary was reinforced when the Family Rosary crusade was launched by Archbishop Walsh on 25 April, 1954, in Tuam. Thousands of people thronged the GAA stadium for the event and the *Irish Catholic Directory* described how "people were arriving all day and hundreds of motor cars lined the roads approaching the town ... hundreds of men, women and children ... walked in procession ... reciting the rosary".[18] Fr Peyton, the Irish-American 'Rosary Priest' had come to Ireland to appeal for greater devotion to the Rosary and enormous rallies were held all over the country right through the month of May, a traditional month for Marian devotions. A figure "close on 25,000" was reported as having participated in the pilgrimage to Knock on 15 August, the feast of the Assumption in the Marian year, 1954.[19]

---

[14] *Irish Independent*, 17 May 1954: 5.
[15] *I.C.D.* 1951. 26 March 1950: 734.
[16] ibid. 740.
[17] Irish Bishops' statement on the Proclamation of 1954 as Marian Year, *Furrow*, 4.11. November 1953: 666-8.
[18] *I.C.D. 1955*, 25 April 1954: 627.
[19] ibid. 15 August 1954: 641.

Trade union organisations and factory workers were prominently represented in the devotional activities described above. The loyalty of the Irish working classes to Catholicism was noted by the American writer Paul Blanshard in 1954 and by the French writer Jean Blanchard in 1963 (Blanshard: 55, 57; Blanchard: 30). On 29 October 1950 a delegation representing the Workers Union of Ireland went on the Holy Year pilgrimage to Rome.[20] There were many 'industrial tributes' to Our Lady leading up to and during the Marian Year. CIE (State-run national transport company) employees in the Broadstone station in Dublin erected a statue in her honour.[21] Several other 'industrial tributes' were recorded at the time, among them that of the workers of Sunbeam Wolsey, Ltd. of Cork numbering over 2,000 workers.[22] The factory of General Textiles Ltd., Athlone, of more than 700 workers held a tribute on 10 May, 1954.[23] At each of these Mass was celebrated by the local bishop.

Gifts were often sent from Ireland to the Pope. On 10 April 1951, the *Irish Catholic Directory* recorded that a letter was received by the Secretary of the Congress of Irish Unions from Monsignor Montini, Substitute Papal Secretary of State and future Pope Paul VI, acknowledging the address of homage and chasuble presented to Pope Pius XII during the Holy Year in the name of the workers of Ireland. Monsignor Montini wrote that, at a time when so many workers in different countries had 'fallen prey to false theories and ideologies' which were opposed to Christianity,

> it was a source of particular gratification to His Holiness to receive this further proof of the devoted attachment of the workers of Ireland to the Vicar of Christ, and to their fidelity to the Catholic Faith, which is their nation's most precious heritage.[24]

Churchmen visiting from abroad both admired and envied Catholic Ireland. Archbishop P.J.B. McKeefrey of New Zealand visiting in 1950 saw Ireland as:

> a land of faith ... a faith that permeates every phase of personal, social and national life. It could be seen every moment of the day, be it in Church, on a street car ... [25]

He was impressed with the salutations that he and "countless other priests" received continually on O'Connell Street, how eager people were to pay their respects to the priesthood and regarded himself as "privileged to live for a short time in an atmosphere impregnated with the faith".[26]

Catholic culture was *the* popular culture in southern Ireland in the fifties. The question of where, or how other religious traditions fitted into the Irish identity equation was rarely raised. One could be forgiven for deducing that there was at that time no other cultural tradition; however, this was not so as there was in southern Ireland also the Anglo-Irish Protestant tradition. Against the background of the Catholic Church-State consensus and the pursuit of a nationalist Catholic policy by successive governments in the post-Independence era, perhaps for its own pragmatic reasons, this tradition became somewhat muted. In the same way as the *Irish Independent* presented Catholic news, the *Irish Times* was seen as the organ of Irish Protestants in the fifties. Given that Protestants formed approximately 5% of the total population in the Republic, the capacity of Protestantism to be a viable alternative culture to that of Catholicism was negligible and for much of this period there was little overt questioning by Protestants of the prevailing Catholic ethos.

[20] *I.C.D. 1951*, 29 October 1950: 765.
[21] *Irish Independent*. 4 May 1953. 2.
[22] ibid. 10 May 1954: 11.
[23] ibid. 11 May 1954: 5.
[24] *I.C.D.1952*, 1 May 1951: 652-3.
[25] McKeefrey, Archbishop PJB. 'Farewell to Shannon'. *Furrow*, 1.2, March 1950: 5-8.
[26] ibid.

Notwithstanding the hold of Catholicism on the hearts and minds of its followers, the bishops constantly feared what they perceived as threats to the Catholic way of life at that time. Popular songs on the radio, ideas and life styles depicted in the cinema, so-called "evil literature", dancing, alcoholic liquor and "company keeping" were all seen as potentially undermining traditional Catholic values. The bishops were very critical of what was seen as the "endless quest for pleasure" (Fuller: 52-54). The emphasis on subduing the passions, and thus conquering the world the flesh and the devil was an integral part of the Catholic way of life as presented by the bishops in their pastorals. The sexual instinct was viewed in a particularly fearful and suspicious light. The bishops saw dancing, company keeping and the consumption of alcoholic liquor as "occasions of sin", which tempted people away from the true path to salvation. The far-reaching scope of the censorship laws did not alleviate bishops' anxieties in relation to potential corrupting or secularist influences either home-grown or emanating from abroad.

The group most threatened, or certainly most vocal in their criticism of the repressiveness of the Catholic ethos, was the literati. Irish writers were increasingly alienated and bitter about censorship legislation (Adams: 1968; Carlson: 1990), which was understandable given that virtually every leading Irish fiction-writer between 1929 and the mid-1960s suffered under the censorship laws (Fallon: 201). Many of them were deeply resentful of the power of the Catholic Church and argued that censorship had turned Ireland into an intellectual wasteland. For many, self-imposed exile was the only option if they wished to realize their creative and literary identity. In 1940 Sean O'Faolain founded the *Bell*, a literary periodical which he edited until 1946, in which he waged a vigorous campaign against censorship and the detrimental effect it was having on Irish cultural life (Carlson: 147-150). But in an atmosphere where there was little overt questioning or criticism of the Catholic Church, writers were ploughing a lone furrow.

In Ireland there was no tradition of anti-clericalism as experienced in continental Europe. Religious education, such as it was, fostered a culture of dependency, whereby the laity were led to believe that there were black and white answers to moral problems and that the clergy were experts who were not to be challenged. This did not just apply to religious education. In Ireland the Church, as well as exercising structural control over education and legitimating certain forms of knowledge, also influenced how knowledge was approached. The manner in which it did so can be gleaned by examining the papal encyclical *Divini Illius Magistri*, promulgated by Pope Pius XI in 1929. The encyclical provided the inspiration for Irish Catholic education from the 1930s to the 1950s. It did not just confine itself to matters of control in education, but treated of matters of knowledge and related pedagogy and condemned contemporary educational developments having to do with "the child's so-called autonomy and unrestricted liberty". It was feared that this could "belittle or suppress entirely the authority of the teacher".[27] Such fears were in keeping with the Church's censorial approach to knowledge and its fear of any questioning of institutionally sanctioned patterns of thought. The Church's world view was based on Scholastic philosophy which saw knowledge as fixed, unchanging. Knowledge was perceived as existing outside, independent of, and in a sense superior to the person. People were intended to conform to a ready made corpus of knowledge, rather than question it. This philosophy had implications for all aspects of Catholic culture – facets as diverse as schooling, the education and training of priests and religious, catechesis and issues of morality. Rote-learning of received knowledge was the norm which prevailed in the school, seminary and religious houses.

Essentially the tradition which predominated in Irish Catholicism and lasted until the Second Vatican Council was, as Twomey has pointed out, "characterised by a legalistic moral

---

[27] *Divini Illius Magistri* 1942. *Encyclical Letter of His Holiness Pope Pius XI on Christian Education of Youth, 1929*. London.

theology, a highly centralised, authoritarian institution, and a sentimental spirituality" (Twomey: 56). But this kind of Catholic culture began to be challenged from within the Church itself in the fifties. A clerical intelligentsia began to emerge and question the institutionalized Catholic ethos which sought to defend and protect, rather than challenge people to a more thoughtful mature grasp of their faith. Two new Catholic periodicals provided an outlet for more critical thinking. The *Furrow* was founded in 1950 by Dr JG McGarry, professor of Sacred Eloquence and Pastoral Theology at St Patrick's College, Maynooth, and *Doctrine and Life* was founded in 1951 by Fr Anselm Moynihan, OP. In the April 1957 issue of the *Furrow*, Fr Denis Meehan, professor of Divinity and Classics at Maynooth, wrote a provocative article entitled "An Essay in Self-Criticism", in which he posed the question as to whether "the Irish influence in the English-speaking Church [has] been anti-intellectual, or at best unintellectual?" (Meehan: 209-214) Two years later in an article in *Doctrine and Life* Fr John C Kelly SJ, stated his opinion more bluntly, when he opined "too many people in Ireland today are trying to make do with a peasant religion when they are no longer peasants any more" (Kelly: 120).

A significant voice from the mid-fifties was that of Fr Peter Connolly, professor of English at St Patrick's College Maynooth. He focused particularly on the censorship issue, writing critical reviews of films for the *Furrow* as well as contributing several influential articles on the censorship issue to the *Furrow* and other journals. A healthy Catholic culture, as far as Connolly was concerned, did not consist in erecting protective barriers against ideas that might corrupt, but had to concern itself with the all-round moral and intellectual development of Catholics. He pointed to the necessity of training an intellectual Catholic elite "towards a confident balance of freedom and responsibility, of moral theology and artistic judgment, of conscience and sensibility: a body capable of forming its own judgments ..." (Connolly, 1957: 114). He also pointed out that the law must try "to balance the rival claims of various groups in the community" (Connolly, 1959: 156) at a time when there was little overt questioning as to whether the law should reflect the Catholic ethos. In an article in *Hibernia* in 1964 he criticized what he referred to as "a juvenile standard of censorship" (Connolly, 1964: 9), and in 1966 he participated in a seminar on the writing of Edna O'Brien which took place in Limerick (Murphy: 10-13). At this time all four of her novels, which presented a very claustrophobic picture of growing up in Ireland, which many people found decidedly uncomfortable, were banned.

Connolly was, in fact, anticipating the mood of Vatican II (1962-1965), which was to bring about a fundamental reassessment of Catholic culture to meet the challenges of modern secular life – challenges which the Irish church had sought to ward off. Protectionism was no longer a viable option in the era of mass communications that was clearly on the horizon. Socio-cultural, economic and political developments from the early sixties changed Irish society almost beyond recognition. Politicians became more assertive and took initiatives in the area of education from the early sixties. Whereas Radio Éireann had reinforced Catholic culture, the new Irish television station from 1962 provided the means whereby people could air all manner of views and opinions irrespective of whether the Church approved. It demystified with ease the aloofness and mystique which had characterised the episcopal office in the past and deference towards the clergy was gradually eroded. The relaxation of film censorship in 1964 and book censorship in 1967 contributed further to the opening up of Irish society. All of these changes gathered momentum from the sixties and in a changed climate Church teaching was no longer accepted without question. By the 1970s constitutional and legislative support for the Catholic ethos increasingly began to be questioned and was dismantled over the next few decades, spelling the death knell of Catholic culture as experienced and consolidated since independence.

## References

Adams, Michael. 1968. *Censorship: The Irish Experience.* Alabama

Bates, Thomas R. 1975. "Gramsci and the Theory of Hegemony". *Journal of the History of Ideas.* 36

Blanchard, Jean. 1963. *The Church in Contemporary Ireland.* Dublin

Blanshard, Paul. 1954. *The Irish and Catholic Power.* London

*Bunreacht na hÉireann.* Dublin

Carlson, Julia. ed. 1990. *Banned in Ireland: Censorship and the Irish Writer.* London

Connolly, Fr Peter. 1957. "Censorship and Moral Classification of Films". *Furrow.* 8:2. February

Connolly, Fr Peter. 1959. "Censorship". *Christus Rex.* XIII:3. July

Connolly, Fr Peter. 1964. "Turbulent Priests". *Hibernia.* 28:2. February

*Dáil Debates*

*Divini Illius Magistri.* 1942. *Encyclical Letter of His Holiness Pope Pius XI on Christian Education of Youth, 1929.* London

Fallon, Brian. 1998. *An Age of Innocence: Irish Culture 1930-1960.* Dublin

Fanning, Ronan. 1983. *Independent Ireland.* Dublin

Fuller, Louise. 2004. *Irish Catholicism since 1950: The Undoing of a Culture.* Dublin

Healy, John. 1978. *Nineteen Acres.* Galway

"Irish Bishops' statement on the Proclamation of 1954 as Marian Year". *Furrow.* 4:11. November 1953

*Irish Catechetical Directory*

*Irish Independent*

*Irish Press*

Kelly, Fr John C. SJ. 1959. "Solid Virtue in Ireland". *Doctrine and Life.* 9:5 October-November

Keogh, Dermot. 1994. *Twentieth Century Ireland: Nation and State.* Dublin

Longford, The Earl of & O'Neill, Thomas. 1970. *Eamon de Valera.* London *Irish Press.*

McGahern, John. 31 July 1993. *Irish Independent*

McKeefrey, Archbishop PJB. "Farewell to Shannon". *Furrow.* 1:2. March 1950

Meehan, Fr Denis. 1957. "An Essay in Self-Criticism". *Furrow.* 8:4. April

Murphy, James H. ed. 1991. *No Bland Facility: Selected Writings on Literature, Religion and Censorship, Peter Connolly.* Gerrards Cross

Twomey, D. Vincent. 2002. *The End of Irish Catholicism?* Dublin

Whyte, J.H. 1980. *Church and State in Modern Ireland 1923-1979.* Dublin

# Testing Boundaries: Form and Genre in the Poetry of Don Paterson and Michael Longley

*Miriam Gamble*

"One of the finest lyric poets of our century" (John Burnside); "His structures have that ease of utterance which rhyme and rhythm do not injure – the true Yeatsian gift" (Peter Porter). These are two of the accolades which have found their way onto the back covers of recent collections by Michael Longley, and which pay tribute to the delicacy and precision of an oeuvre characterised by the gentlest and yet most incisive of touches (Longley: 2000; 1991). Longley's status as a lyric poet has long been recognised, but whilst such praise as is embodied in these testaments is not, therefore, out of place, it does resonate with troubling connotations; with suggestions that, perhaps, what is often relished (and sometimes disparaged) in Longley involves a certain misinterpretation of the exact nature of his work, and of his achievement as a modern poet.[1] Ever since Yeats' command that Irish poets "learn [their] trade" and "sing whatever is well made" – and, perhaps even more importantly, the reasoning behind this ("That we in coming days may be/ Still the indomitable Irishry)" – there has been a tendency in criticism generally, and specifically in Irish criticism, to divide poetry into two camps: canonical or uncanonical, well-made or experimental, indomitable or self-interrogating, self-contained or responsive (Yeats, 375). Little credence has been given to the idea that there might be any middle ground, or that poetry which seems to display the requisite characteristics of one "side" might have truck with the ideas of the other.[2]

If anything, Longley's position as a member of the "'60s Generation" of Northern Irish poets, and as a prominent elegist, has exacerbated rather than complicated this conviction in relation to his work: whilst critics like Clair Wills see forces of disruption, rebellion and dissonance emerging in the writing of the newer generation of Northern Irish poets, like Paul Muldoon (with whom Don Paterson is frequently identified), the older writers remain firmly contained within narratives of consolation and empowerment, where form and "measure" grant to art the ability to overcome or "mend" the fractures and uncertainties endemic to a fraught society. Longley, along with his contemporaries Seamus Heaney and Derek Mahon, is posited as an exemplar of the paradigm against which the younger poets were reacting, and which is represented at a formal level by the "well-made lyric" drawn attention to by Longley's celebrants (Wills, 15).

However, the use of form by a writer like Paterson, generally recognised as one of the most challenging poets of the "New" generation of the early nineties, and the many similarities between his approach to the issues of formal poetry and that of Michael Longley, draw attention to the problematic nature of such binary divisions, and help to highlight the preoccupations of Longley's work which are often ignored, at the same time suggesting that formal poetry is every bit as capable of being incapable, if not more so, than more explicitly "experimental" work. A brief comparison of the poetry of Longley and Paterson shows that the boundaries, both generational and formal, are not so easily drawn; that lyric "delicacy" is sometimes not that far from lyric fragility; and that both more and less can be done within the bounds of a well-made poem than might initially be recognisable.

---

[1] Wesley MacNair, for example, suggests the healing power of nature as the dominant motif in Longley's seventh collection – "Longley…implies that to ease the heart of war's sorrows, Northern Ireland might consider the ways of love, or the curative message of wild flowers" (272). In fact, the main thrust of *The Weather in Japan* is to question such ideas and, for the most part, to find them ineffective.

[2] See, for example, John Goodby (2000) and Johnston (2001).

A recurrent theme in Longley's collections has been the practice of elegising his father: from "In Memoriam" (1986: 48) to "The Branch" (2000: 50), the products of this never-ending process represent a rigorous engagement with the genre which, far from subscribing to an over-simplified or "consolatory" paradigm, is consistently and variously ruthless in its interrogation of the possibilities or otherwise – even, sometimes, the culpabilities – of elegy. As Ruth Ling suggests, "With many of his lyrics belonging to that category of twentieth-century poetry that, in Edna Longley's recent estimation, especially 'relishes or scrutinizes its own patterns', elegy becomes for him…the ultimate vehicle through which the very validity of his poetics, and more informatively of art itself, might be measured" (2002a: 39). "The Linen Workers" (1986: 149), an early paternal elegy set in the context of the Troubles, and which details the procedures necessary before Longley can "bury his father once again", juxtaposes three separate incidences of death, all of which focus primarily on the absence or presence of teeth in the mouths of the deceased. Setting off a chain of religious imagery which is maintained throughout, it makes the somewhat bizarre assertion that "Christ's teeth ascended with him into heaven":

Through a cavity in one of his molars
The wind whistles: he is fastened for ever
By his exposed canines to a wintry sky.

The reader barely has time to assimilate this before Longley moves on to the memory of his father's false teeth "Brimming in their tumbler" and thence to the dentures and other personal belongings of the linen workers of the title, a group of men murdered at the height of the Troubles for no reason other than denomination. Each separate character, or group of characters, occupies one end-stopped, four line stanza, and it is initially difficult to see any clear connection between them.[1] In the first and third stanzas, there is a linking sense of religious ritual, which both connects the episodes and seems to suggest the possibility of modes of consolation, even transcendence. But in both cases, it is ritual gone wrong – the linen workers are "massacred", and the set of dentures lying on the road are covered with "Blood, food particles, the bread, the wine". Rather than the con- or transubstantiated body and blood of Christ which constitutes the normal substance of Communion, the process is reversed, and Longley presents us with the ideal of bread and wine converted back into the brutally realistic fragments of a last meal, the drops of blood from a damaged mouth. Likewise, Christ's retention of his teeth, which should be emblematic of the unity between spirit and flesh achieved through him, causes only imperfection: not only do they trap him in a half-way position between heaven and earth, as Edna Longley notes (2001: 252), but they themselves are also flawed, characterised more by holes than wholeness, indicative of pain rather than peace.

It is in this context, then, that Longley's efforts to perfect his father's "burial" must be understood. As the first and third stanzas naturally fall together through their use of imagery, so do the second and fourth, which deal solely with the poet's father and, taken independently

---

[1] As Sarah Broom points out, this is a technique frequently employed by Longley, one which reflects "a resistance to narrative, a need to break down the flow of events into static moments" (110). And as Broom also suggests in her reading of "The Camp Fires" (109), such manipulation of syntax is one of the primary means by which Longley challenges the conventions with which he appears to align himself – an approach which may be seen to accentuate the absence of security and standard, rather than the opposite: "Longley's poems invite us to adopt a complex and nuanced perspective on issues like nostalgia and order. They demonstrate, for example, that a high valuing of and a longing for familiarity, continuity, and belonging need not preclude the poetic representation of difference, loss and alienation, but can in fact make it more perceptive and acute" (111). A similar approach can be observed in Paterson's poems about past selves, particularly "19:00: Auchterhouse" (1997, 52), where the younger self, like "the Sunshine Coach", is "stalled/ for ever" in the context that the poem describes.

of the rest of the poem, constitute a fairly simple narrative of fragmentation and reunification. Aided by the rhetorical diction and phrasal inversion of the last two lines, the reader is initially tempted to "make sense" of this less complicated argument on its own terms, and even to figure it as the main thrust of the poem, which falls, in linear terms, into two separate, though interspersed, sections. There is an air of finality and (literally) polish to its self-assertion, which lends itself easily to the idea that the ends have been "tied up":

> Before I can bury my father once again
> I must polish the spectacles, balance them
> Upon his nose, fill his pockets with money
> And into his dead mouth slip the set of teeth.

Aside from the fact that the practice of burial is continuous, however, and the mouth uncompromisingly "dead", we should be wary of any such tendency to rationalise the part above the whole: the bisection of the personal narrative by the public,[4] combined with the recurrent image of the teeth, renders it impossible to read the final stanza in uncomplicated ways. Ironically, being forced to connect, we are forced to fracture; by having to read the entire poem as an entity, we are forced to recognise that its ethos is less one of stitching together and transmogrifying than of breaking down or unravelling into constituent and, moreover, desiccated parts. Longley's effect is achieved by gesturing towards something which he then denies. It need hardly be added that the teeth he proposes to put into his father's mouth cannot finally be figured as those which surface in his memory, but rather, as additional mention of the spectacles makes clear, the other set of dentures which corrupt the poem's slightly off pentameter, which "fell on the road" beside the linen workers.

The two dominant motifs of "The Linen Workers" – the refusal of the power of the image or the poet to transform or unify, and the neat, delicate poem which just misses the mark – are prevalent in one form or another in much of Longley's later output, elegiac or otherwise, and trace, in their expression and development, the movements of a mind continually in combat with its own productions. Indeed, in later collections, this recognition of incapacity is developed further, into a sense of the culpability of art's defining effort, of the violence it enacts upon its subject matter by means both of the over-simplified and selective methods involved in unification, or "making sense", and by the imprecision of language as a mode of representation: poetry, it seems, must always transform, even when it does not want to.

Without ever really developing it, both Broom and Ling suggest this idea when they say, respectively, that, in Longley's oeuvre "Perfection or fulfillment [*sic*] is often imagined as possible only in absence" (106), and that "elegy…becomes a measured enquiry into the appropriateness of elegy as a form" (2002b: 286). Ling, in particular, frequently touches on the sense of guilt expounded by Longley's elegies, but the bias of her essays towards an understanding of his work as always characterised by the *urge* to console prevents her from expanding this beyond a sense of the genre's limitations, and Longley's recognition of them. As her responses to "Wounds" and "The Linen Workers" show, the poems are usually seen to be gesturing towards the "celestial light" of pastoral elegy (2002a: 41) – at most "gently ironising"

---

[4] As Broom suggests when she points out the tendency of Longley's early love poems to accentuate both "the instability of the border between self and other" (105), and "the degree to which physical intimacy is shadowed by or positioned against an awareness of mortality" (103), the practice of interrupting or threatening the space of the personal with wider public issues is an important facet of Longley's poetic response to the Troubles, and a measure of the skill with which he adapts the lyric to meet and represent them. As Edna Longley points out, this technique is in many ways directly representative of the actual manner in which Troubles violence affected its victims: "[In "The Civil Servant"] poetic specificity emphasises the manner of death and…precisely how a domestic interior has been violated" (2001, 248).

elegy's conventions – as opposed to questioning the moral status of that light, or of those conventions, in the context of authorship, and of what Longley describes as the poet's "unforgivable shadow on the sand" (Longley: 2000, 3).

Nowhere does the sense of art as violator come across so forcefully as in one of the many poems in *The Weather in Japan* which takes for its title a simple, concrete image, "The Branch" (2000: 50). Longley has always had a fondness for using such apparently definitive titles, and then refusing them the unifying or explanatory force their prominence would seem to imply. "The Branch", however, is slightly different: taking once more a remnant of the poet's father as its subject matter, it emphasises not so much the image's inability to straighten out or hold through time, as its positive obstruction in the path to such activities; its brutal facility – due, ironically, to the simplicity which makes *it* memorable – to erase more complicated memories. The poem focuses upon an instance of the father's habit of transforming accidents into novelties: in this case, a "Crack across the mirror on [the] bathroom cabinet", which he turns into a branch:

>      that was his way of mending things,
> A streak of brown paint, dabs of green, an accident
> That sprouted leaves

Initially at least, the poem might be read as conveying both a celebration of the lasting result of the father's quirky temperament, and a sense of continuity in which his spirit and legacy are kept alive through his son. The branch *of* the poem is one of those perfect works of art towards the status of which Longley's work is always striving: faced with accident and dissonance it creates homogeneity and new growth. Recollection of the branch sets off a chain of memories in Longley's mind, which take on an immediate presence in the poem's second "section":

>      awakening the child in me
> To the funny faces he pulls when he is shaving.
> He wears a vest, white buttons at his collarbone.

The branch appears to have the capacity to take the poet back in time, to bring before him images so lucid that they almost take on the character of embodiments. Crisp sibilants and light, firm vowels create the sense of a visual and physical moment cut neatly from the temporal flow.

However, the last two lines of the poem destroy this illusion, in sound quality as well as sense: consonants soften and vowels become blurry, as Longley begins to lose his father's "soapy nostrils" among the branch's leaves. It is not that the branch has "failed" in its bid to unify, to cover up the evidence of time's deleterious effects and thus to carry something through. Rather, it has done its job *too* well: by patching up the cracks it escorts though time an image of the father which is devoid of individuality, of all the faults and eccentricities which render someone human. The actual branch itself could not have caused the two sides of his father's face to "join up": clearly, it would have divided them. But symbolically, it eradicates fine differences – between the two sides of a face which are never symmetrical; between his father's face in the one moment which the branch has managed to preserve and all the other millions upon millions of moments it chooses to neglect because, taken together, they highlight mutability. By unifying, it dismembers; by creating new and permanent growth, it "shuts up the peacock fan", in Larkin's phrase, that is the living past (Larkin, 54). Faced with a choice between this and a more representative, if fallible, imperfection, Longley sides, finally, with the original crack, dividing his poem into two almost connecting and almost symmetrical sections, which stress, in their formal appearance as in their use of tenses, not only the non-homogeneity of organic material, but also the unsurpassable difference between moments of time. The past tense of the first "stanza" can never quite be connected to the present tense of the second's vision.[5]

Longley's view (and practice) of art, then, consistently refuses notions of perfectibility and lyric or elegiac control. Reaching for the ceremony of traditional forms of elegy in "The Linen Workers", he finds himself unable to concede to the premises behind those forms; aiming for the purity of the delicate lyric, he refuses to grant the precision of his language or the presence of his imagery definitive status.[6] In his later poetry, Longley does not tend to use specific forms, or even rhyme, regarding these, as his short poem "Form" indicates, merely as impedimenta (1995: 1). And comparing Longley's poem to Don Paterson's of the same name, the reader encounters central similarities which might lead him or her to expect a similar eschewal in Paterson's poetry. A short lyric poem in Scots Gallic, "Form" describes an idyllic morning on which the speaker, having literally "jumped the gate" out of his normal existence, finds the roots of a dead willow tree encased in ice and, stripping away the "burnin case", discovers its essentials, "a pure sang" cleansed of dirt or any other externalities. The first thirteen of the poem's twenty-six lines deal in wholly ecstatic terms with the discovery of something so exactly made, so uncontaminated. This, it seems to imply, is what poetic form is all about.

But in the fourteenth line, the tone changes from one of celebration to a poignant wistfulness: addressing the willow roots, the speaker gets down to the real issue at hand – the problems linked to the ease of this procedure:

> I mind I thocht
> if this wis aa
> there wis til it:
> dook the thing
> in the winterburn
> then pu' the sark
> o broad daylicht
> fae its back
> and raise it
> to the cauld sun (2003, 33)

Poetry is not, it seems, a simple matter of washing off the unnecessary parts and holding the result up to the light. As only dead willow roots can be so tightly held in a case of ice – or is it the ice that kills them? – so no living object can be pared down so successfully, uncovered and explained.

We might well be surprised, then, by the wealth of traditional forms in Paterson's first collection. Foul-mouthed, often sordid, writing about sex, drink and football teams, Paterson exploded onto the poetic scene with *Nil Nil* in 1993. As Edna Longley remarks, he does have a penchant for abysmal book titles (2004: 87), but in this case, the very unrepresentative nature of the title may well be part of the point: combined with Paterson's self-created image of boozy musician, autodidact and general lad-about-town,[7] the cover illustration of a broken goal post must have done as much to send readers in completely the wrong direction as it did to prepare

---

[5] Ling makes a similar point in relation to the layout of "Bjorn Olinder's Pictures" (2002b: 294).

[6] For a general overview of the distinctions drawn between "traditional", or "consolatory", and "modern", or "melancholic", mourning, see Ramazani, 1-31.

[7] See, for example, Paterson's interview with Matt Seaton: "Don Paterson confesses to feeling a little fragile. Clearly a good time was had…we meet in the somewhat fleeting time available between his hangover and the next train to Edinburgh. The pink-rimmed eyes would be a temporary aberration, but the grey crew-cut and short-cropped beard give him the look of a younger John Peel."

them for the contents of this extraordinary debut. The images may be endemic to Paterson's subject matter, but they in no way represent his method of approaching it.

In tightly wrought, formally adept poems, Paterson takes his often commonplace and deceptively simple foci in the least predictable directions, turning a pool game against himself into a disturbing meditation on the problems of defining the self, comparing serendipitous meetings with an ex-lover to one-off planetary collisions. Obsessively investigating the habitual, he raises endless questions about memory and time, selfhood and non-entity, control and helplessness – questions which aim to challenge the kind of complacencies normally associated with formal poetry, and whose focus is as much *upon* that poetry, its structure and its voice, as upon what is or is not conveyed by it. Form and subject matter interact closely as the poems push at the boundaries of the known, and of the knowing entity which talks about it.

In "An Elliptical Stylus" (1993: 20-1), Paterson's attempt at paternal elegy, he refuses the kind of "resonance" and "cauterization" we expect from formal poetry, and particularly formal poetry which nestles within the apparently safe area of "articulacy and inheritance". Taking as its focal point a memorable but frustrating incident from his childhood, in which his father attempts, unsuccessfully, to meet the demands of the ideal of inheritance,[8] Paterson's narrative not only hones in upon the failure to obtain the object necessary to seal this sense of unity (and thus upon its own failure, as narrative, to provide "something axiomatic"), it pursues the logical consequences of that failure by delving into the now uncertain area of Paterson's, and by extension poetry's, origins.

Poetry is clearly identified with the elliptical stylus as described in both the first and third stanzas: its ability to make music billow out "into three dimensions/ as if we could have walked between the players" strikes clear consonances with the aim to "body forth" the thing that is described, to capture absent things and even to give dimension, through the medium of language, to the intangible, the bodiless. And the emphasis on skill, balance and precision in the third stanza recalls the self-conscious drawing of analogies elsewhere in the collection, such as the "immaculate clearance" of a pool table, or the perfectly timed release of a hand brake (1, 6). The stylus brings to mind not only a writer's pen, but the very action, or supposed action, of the art itself: the idea of the "sharp nip" lowered gently, perfectly honed to pick up and record, unaltered, the mysterious beats of whatever heart or song it is currently in harmony with, is an irresistible one for poets, as is the notion of language balanced between the precision of the hit target and the mystique of slight ellipsis – the aura of the unsayable, which raises the poet over and above the capabilities of ordinary mortals. Paterson's reader, however, is not met by the presence of such comforting assurance: his father is silenced, and not roused, by the events of the poem, and far from speaking for him in the manner promised by the third stanza, the voice exempts itself from any such capacity, merely asserting that "he can well afford to make his *own*/ excuses", the reader their own "interpretation".

As a paternal elegy, the poem sets out to fail by focusing upon, rather than obviating faults; as a forum for the examination of selfhood, it stresses open-endedness rather than clarity; and as a lyric poem, it refuses to present itself, or any argument contained within it, as having a definitive status – even the argument involving the credentials of its author. The third stanza is in fact an extract from a separate poem, which Paterson might have written had he been the shop attendant's rather than his father's son. But it cannot thus be viewed as mere pastiche: referred to as "'Fidelities', the poem I'm writing now", it has to be accepted as a poem that

---

[8] The poem centres on an incident in a shop, to which the speaker and his father have gone in order to purchase an elliptical stylus. The shop assistant mocks them because they do not own, and cannot afford, a record player advanced enough to support the new equipment. During the drive home the father is silent, whilst the son meditates angrily on what has happened – "which is where the story sticks".

Paterson actually is writing "now" (where "now" relates to the time of writing, not the time of reading). And although it may be true that Paterson finally sets "his own" poem at a remove from this, the questions raised by its presence in the larger framework remain unanswered. If Paterson has inherited, or learnt anything from the figure of his father, it is a studied imperfection, a stress on failure and uncertainty which sits oddly with the poem's overly aggressive tone. At the last, "An Elliptical Stylus" turns full circle on itself, challenging even the possibility that Paterson might not be his father's son, and raising the idea that it might have captured something of his father after all. It refuses to close even these two doors, the opening of which onto other possibilities was the catalyst to all the problems in the first place.

The modulation of the voice at the close of "An Elliptical Stylus" – the threat it issues to the reader of physical violence, and the way in which it takes upon itself the ability to make generalised assumptions about that reader's character – is indicative of a further question in Paterson's mind about the status of the written word, its powers of conveyance and containment. The closing lines in fact do more to accentuate the impossibility of their threat than to maintain the mask of authorial control: the conditional nature of "I'd swing for him, and every other cunt/ happy to let my father know his station,/ which probably includes yourself" points not only to the pastness of the subject in relation to the writing, but also to the distance between writing and writer, the physical absence of the poet from the page, and the facts of what the poem cannot do, rather than what it can. While it travels on through time, meeting new readers and interpretations, it leaves Paterson and the moment of writing far behind. "An Elliptical Stylus" not only fails to explain Paterson, but also to contain him in any realistic and lasting sense.

Paterson's poetry about poetry, then, is pessimistic, or at least sceptical, about its own ability to carry out the designated functions of poetry: to contain within formal strictures and evocative words the living (or dead) contours of its subject matter. Yet there is one way in which he finds it possible to take a wholly positive view. Hand in hand with the bitter denunciation of the art's incapacities in one sphere, is, in Paterson's work, the often celebratory appraisal of its virtuosity in another: as a work of fiction, something which sets out intentionally to misrepresent and simplify, to propose a toast "not to love, or life, or real feeling,/ but to their sentimental residue" (Paterson, 1997: 18). If there is any confidence in Paterson's mind as to poetry's ability to "do something" it rests here, suggesting less an idyllic unconsciousness of the difficulties faced by contemporary writing, than a full engagement with their implications. As Longley's more recent collections are home to a number of poems like "The Branch" which, accepting life and art as imperfectible half measures, take pleasure in the very quirkiness and oddity of the individual, so Paterson often revels in the very artificiality of the "well-made poem", the "favourite hour" during which one may idealise, and so replace "the vast/ infinitesimal letdown" of reality (Paterson, 2004: 39). Set against the backdrop of bodies of work which test and find wanting ideas of perfectability, of the closure and containment supposed to be endemic to a kind of poetry which does not engage with superficial rupture, or the obliteration of voice, these poems are both expressions of temporary relief and indications of a differing agenda. They suggest not only that we may have mistaken the attitude behind lyric poetry, but also that we may have overlooked its true abilities.

Both of these poets, then, do find it possible to celebrate art for what it is, but their celebration should not be confused with over-simplified notions of the capacity of language or of form, with Romantic attitudes which have no place in the complex atmosphere of post-modernity, and which indicate an outmoded confidence in the power of lyric personality. These are celebrations fatally tinged by the knowledge of themselves as compromise measures, as texts which will never arrive at the heights for which they reach, but which perhaps do more to accentuate the impossibility of reaching those heights by dallying with the vehicles through which they are supposed to be attained. Form and genre, in the hands of Longley and

Paterson, are less the tools of an ideal which sits in comfortable opposition to the fragments of "experimental" poetry, than the means of exploding this illusion from within; of accentuating fracture by the invocation of its opposite, and of showing things sliding just beyond their reach. That, one might say, is the *true* Yeatsian gift.

# References

Broom, Sarah, 2002. "Learning about Dying: Mutability and the Classics in the Poetry of Michael Longley". *New Hibernia Review*. 6.1: 94-112

Goodby, John. *Irish Poetry since 1950: From Stillness into History*. Manchester: Manchester University Press

Johnston, Dillon. 2001. *The Poetic Economies of England and Ireland, 1912-2000*. Basingstoke: Palgrave

Larkin, Philip. 1990. *Collected Poems*. Ed. Anthony Thwaite. London: Faber

Ling, Ruth. 2002a. "The Double Design of Michael Longley's Recent Elegies: *The Ghost Orchid and Broken Dishes*". *Irish Studies Review* 10.1: 39-50

Ling, Ruth. 2002b. "*The Weather in Japan:* Tact and Tension in Michael Longley's New Elegies". Irish University Review 32.2: 286-302

Longley, Edna. 2001. "Northern Ireland: Commemoration, Elegy, Forgetting". *History and Memory in Modern Ireland*. Ed. Ian McBride. Cambridge: Cambridge University Press 223-253

Longley, Edna. 2004. "Samples of Air". *Metre*. 16: 82-9

Longley, Michael. 1995. *The Ghost Orchid*. London: Cape

Longley, Michael. 1991. *Gorse Fires*. London: Secker and Warburg

Longley, Michael. 1986. *Poems 1963-1983*. Harmondsworth: Penguin

Longley, Michael. 2000. *The Weather in Japan*. London: Cape

McNair, Wesley. 2003. "Michael Longley's Journey into the Real World in *The Weather in Japan*". *Colby Quarterly*. 39.3: 270-5

Paterson, Don. 1997. *God's Gift to Women*. London: Faber

Paterson, Don. 2003. *Landing Light*. London: Faber

Paterson, Don. 1993. *Nil Nil*. London: Faber

Ramazani, Jahan. 1994. *Poetry of Mourning: The Modern Elegy from Hardy to Heaney*. Chicago: Chicago University Press

Seaton, Mat. 2004. Interview with Don Paterson. Guardian. 21 January: http://books.guardian.co.uk/poetry/features/0,12887,1127482,00.html

Wills, Clair. 1993. *Improprieties: Politics and Sexuality in Northern Irish Poetry*. Oxford: Oxford University Press

Yeats, W. B. 1992. *The Poems*. Ed. Daniel Albright. London: Random House

# A Pioneering Institution in Scottish Mental Health Care: The Montrose Lunatic Asylum, 1782-1822

*Billy Gunn*

In June 1882 Dr James Howden, the incumbent Medical Superintendent of Sunnyside Royal Hospital, wrote in his annual report, "The Montrose Asylum . . . was the first public hospital in Scotland devoted to the treatment of the insane. Now, every district in Scotland possesses an institution of this nature, but it is not a little remarkable that the idea, or at least the practical application of it should have originated in a small provincial town" (15). One hundred and fourteen years later a modern critic of the asylum system, the historian Professor Andrew Scull, was to describe it rather disdainfully as "the obscure provincial asylum of Montrose", in his co-authored book *Masters of Bedlam* (93). Both men expressed, though from different perspectives, their surprise that Montrose should have any place of distinction in the evolution of Scottish psychiatry because of its provinciality, inferring that in being provincial a barrier existed that hindered the development of both the intellectual and humanitarian capacities of the inhabitants. They have done so without taking due consideration of the history and geographical situation of the town.

During the eighteenth century, Montrose was a busy seaport heavily involved in international trade by sea and had had good overseas connections for at least two centuries. The prosperity of the town came from both its rich hinterland and its trade with England and with Europe, particularly the Baltic countries. The town also had trading links with the East and West Indies. A number of Montrose merchants had established themselves in cities such as London, Rotterdam, and Gothenburg and they acted as one of the most productive avenues through which information flowed (Jackson and Lythe: 132-142). Not only did the town and its inhabitants have access to wealth through those international connections they also had access to the current thinking and new ideas permeating those societies abroad. In addition to these international connections information arrived into the town through the newspapers and periodicals of the day and through visitors from abroad and those foreign nationals who settled in and around the town. Merchants were leading men in local government in the eighteenth century and in Montrose's case evidence of influences from far beyond the town being brought to fruition can be seen in the Flemish design of the Town House, for example. Montrose then, despite its provinciality was not cut off from the prevailing influences of the day and could and did act upon those influences if they thought it would bring benefits to the town. Another significant way in which this response manifested itself was in the humanitarian decision to erect a hospital for the mentally ill an enlightened decision, which was in line with the thinking of the day more associated with bigger cities such as Edinburgh.

The names of Philippe Pinel (1745-1826), who has been described as "the founder of psychiatry in France" (Weiner: 725) because of his pioneering work with the mentally ill in the Bicêtre and the Salpêtrière, and Samuel Tuke (1784-1857), founder of a mental hospital called The Retreat, near York in England, have long been synonymous with the system of treatment designated as moral management. With that synonymity comes the inference that this particular regime in the care and treatment of the insane somehow arrived suddenly with them. It did not. The term 'moral management' was derived from Pinel's 'traitement moral', which he first used publicly in his *Memoir on madness*, a paper that he read before the Society for Natural History in Paris on the 11th of December 1794.[1] Neither Pinel nor Tuke invented

---

[1] Weiner, D.B. 1992. "Philippe Pinel's "Memoir on madness" of December 11, 1794: A fundamental text of modern psychiatry". *American Journal of Psychiatry*. 149:6. 725, 727, hereafter cited as Weiner, Pinel's Memoir.

the system of moral management. They took what already existed of the more humane methods being employed by others in the treatment of mental illness a stage further by placing a much greater emphasis on the use of psychology while minimising the perceived need for physical restraint. At the Montrose Royal Lunatic Asylum, a system of treatment was employed from its opening in 1782 which incorporated much of what came to be known as moral management. This paper will demonstrate that the system of treatment employed at Montrose pre-dated both Pinel's work with the insane at the Salpêtrière, Paris, by eighteen years, and Tuke's at the Retreat near York by fourteen, and thus show that both Pinel and Tuke were building on principles and practices already known and used.

## The Foundation of the Hospital

Prior to March 1779 Mrs Susan Carnegie,[2] a wealthy gentlewoman with much local influence, and the Provost of Montrose, Alexander Christie discussed the plight of the mentally ill whose illness was being compounded because of their confinement in the local jail (Sinclair: 547). The result of their deliberations was a decision to establish a hospital specifically to house those suffering from mental illness. It was not, as some have mistakenly stated, 1769 that the campaign to build the Montrose Lunatic Hospital was begun, but ten years later (Rice: 45). A thorough search of the Carnegie papers undertaken by AA Cormack, while writing his biography of Susan Carnegie in the 1960s, and by the present author who also searched the Burgh of Montrose Town Council Minutes 1771-1794, give no indication of any movement to establish a lunatic asylum in the town before 1779.[3] In March of 1779 Carnegie and Christie launched a subscription for the erection of the hospital and despite much "envy, malice, avarice and pettiness",[4] they had within six months raised sufficient funds to get the project underway. In the personal papers of Susan Carnegie, there are many examples of her charitable work prior to the asylum undertaking, as well as details of her social connections, and it was she who took the principal role in bringing the enterprise to fruition as Christie revealed in a letter to one of his colleagues.[5] Her letters are also a testament of her compassion, and inner strength, and with these qualities, allied to her "masculine understanding",[6] she had the ability to convince many others of both the economic and social viability of her proposed asylum. Funds were to come from the landed gentry, merchants, tradesmen, business women, the Kirk Session and individuals from Sweden to Jamaica, and London to India indicating the extent of both the local and international network of kith and kin that had spread from a small provincial seaport.[7] A tender of £420 to build what was later described as a "house and garden in the links" (Presley: 3) was accepted on the 3rd January 1780, and due to the surplus of funds it was decided to add a dispensary and sick ward as well[8] (Table 1). Three months prior to its opening Mr James Booth was appointed the first "Keeper", and on 6th of May 1782 the first lunatic patient entered this historic institution (Cormack: 279; Poole: 12).

---

[2] The papers of Alexander A. Cormack (1891-1976), historian include the papers of Susan Carnegie (1744-1821), Charleton, Montrose Angus are housed in the Special Archives and Collections, University of Aberdeen.

[3] Cormack: 270-290; Susan Carnegie had the wisdom to establish the practicality of her project before embarking upon it and my research of her papers indicates that her project was begun, allowing for discussion, at the start of 1779. M1/1/9 Town Council Minutes 1771-1794.

[4] Susan Carnegie to Elizabeth Brown, 21st July 1792.

[5] MS43/9/3/21: Provost Alexander Christie to Mr Robert Speid, December 24th 1779. In it he refers to "Mrs Carnegie's hospital".

[6] George Dempster to William Henderson, 20th January 1804; *Montrose Chronicle*, Obituary, 25th April 1821 original letter of MC found in Susan Carnegie's "Memorabilia"; Cormack: 362.

[7] Poole: 1841. Appendices 2-10.

[8] Montrose Lunatic Hospital: 2; Poole: 3; Cormack: 276-278.

Table 1: Brief Chronology of Montrose Royal Lunatic Asylum 1779-1840

| Brief Chronology of Montrose Royal Lunatic Asylum 1779-1840 | | |
|---|---|---|
| **Date** | **Significant Landmarks** | **Patients** |
| March 1779 | Susan Carnegie and Provost Christie open subscription list | |
| August 1779 | £632 1shilling & 9pennies to date. Invitations for tender sent out | |
| January 1780 | Tender for £420 accepted. Construction gets underway | |
| June 1781 | Construction complete, keys handed over, fitting out begins | |
| April 1782 | Fitting out complete. James Booth appointed Keeper with his wife as 'matron' | |
| May 1782 | Fist patient admitted | |
| 1791 | Number of patients | 37 |
| 1794 | Dr Paterson suggests appointment of full time physician for mental patients | |
| 1799 | Full time physician needed *'particularly for attending the lunatics'* who would *'have leisure and time to study this particular branch of physic, which for the good of mankind, it is much to be wished were farther advanced, and would have encouragement from the expectation of gaining a reputation in it.'* Susan Carnegie | |
| 1803 | Susan Carnegie suggests managers apply for a Royal Charter | |
| October 1810 | Royal Charter granted by King George III, ironically sometimes referred to as the 'Mad Monarch' | |
| 1815 | Sheriffs given power to inspect Asylums | |
| 1823 | Number of patients | 56 |
| 1824 | James Ingram succeeds James Booth who retired after 42 years service | |
| 1834 | Dr W. A. F. Browne appointed first full time Medical Superintendent. Gas lighting introduced; proposal to pay patients for their labour; first official matron appointed; dismemberment of tripartite institution proposed and accepted. | |
| 1837 | Browne delivers a set of lectures to the Managers of the Asylum. They are published later in the year and became what one critic has described as *'the single most influential portrait by a medical writer of the horrors of the traditional madhouse system'* which turned out to be *'an extraordinarily effective piece of propaganda'* furthering the cause of the Asylum as the most appropriate place to treat mental illness | |
| 1838 | Dr Richard Poole succeeds Browne who moves to take up the reins at the new state-of-the-art Crichton Royal Institution, Dumfries | |
| 1839 | New Royal Infirmary with Dispensary completed | |
| 1840 | Asylum becomes a single purpose institution; number of patients. | 75 |

As Dr Howden indicated above, the idea of an institution for the accommodation of the insane did not originate in Montrose. There were other institutions housing lunatics in Scotland before the completion of Susan Carnegie's Asylum. In Glasgow, for example, there were four known private places of confinement for lunatics plus the Town Hospital (Rice: 44). The accommodation for the insane in the Glasgow Hospital was wretched, consisting of cells which were no more than "horrible dens, cold and damp and dreary, simply places of restraint since devoid of all positive function whether of treatment or even humane guardianship" (Ferguson: 275). In the county of Edinburgh there were somewhere between sixteen and thirty-three private places of confinement containing around one hundred patients. While the vast majority of them housed single patients, the others housed between eight and twenty-six. Besides these, there were two public institutions, St Cuthbert's housing about thirty patients, and a rather handsome Bedlam, which had existed from 1703 containing an unknown number of inmates.[9] However, from the poetic account of one woman confined there the method of treatment employed was one that sought to control and contain mental illness by physical violence and fear rather than a more subtle psychological approach:

> In the bonny cells of Bedlam
> Ere I was ane and twenty
> I had hempen bracelets strong
> And merry whips ding-dong
> And prayer and fasting plenty. (Birnie: 40)

Further evidence of Bedlam's ineffectiveness is seen in the incorporation of "a small number of cells" (Turner: 97) for the accommodation of lunatics in the new Royal Infirmary of Edinburgh founded in 1738. This first Bedlam was subsequently replaced by a new one and was ironically turned into an "infirmary for the sick and a hospice for the children" (Birnie: 40) in 1746. Having failed to provide treatment for the mentally ill it was at least enabled to provide some for the physically ill. The second Bedlam, erected in 1748 alongside the Charity Workhouse, which was opened in 1743, came under the authority of the Workhouse managers. It contained twenty-one cells for both paying and pauper lunatics and included an apartment, which was used as a house of correction (Birnie: 40, 45-46). However, it fared little better than the old one although, as Professor Rab Houston has shown, there were those who left the institution "recovered" ".[10] In the estimation of an anonymous reporter, "it is scarcely possible to conceive a situation less adapted, either to promote recovery, or to confer that comfort which even the incurably insane are capable of enjoying".[11] What was, and probably still remains, the most celebrated event revealing the conditions within the new Bedlam was the death there in 1774 of the poet Robert Ferguson (Risse: 107; Cormack: 271). That conditions had not improved thirty years after that tragic event is revealed by Sir Andrew Halliday, a determined campaigner on behalf of the mentally ill, when he declared, "that the swine in Germany are better cared for" (Halliday: 8-9) than the inmates of Bedlam. Elsewhere, the new Infirmary at Dumfries opened its doors in 1778 to patients suffering from both physical and mental illness. Only four mentally ill patients could be accommodated in its early years and the treatment they received amounted to little more than "seclusion and restraint according to the old mad-house system".[12]

The Montrose Lunatic Asylum was erected in "the hope that by providing a quiet and convenient asylum for them, by good treatment and medical aid some of these unfortunate persons might be restored to society."[13] Within the perception of it as a curative establishment for all sections of society lies the most significant factor in defining and designating the Montrose Lunatic Hospital as being the first true public mental hospital in Scotland in the modern sense. Not only did it provide a curative environment for those afflicted with mental illness, it also became a place where pauper incurables received a higher level of care and nourishment than they would have receive at home.[14] In essence, the Asylum actually functioned both as a hospital and hospice, a dual role which would cause problems in later

---

[9] Sheriff Clerk of Edinburgh: 1825.; Keddie: 202; Rice: 44.

[10] Houston, R.A. 2003: 14.

[11] Baird, Dr. 1807.

[12] Irving: 22; *Report of a committee of the county of Dumfries appointed 5th October, 1830, to consider the necessity of a lunatic asylum for the counties of Dumfries, Kirkcudbright, and Wigtown*. 1, 3.

[13] Montrose Royal Lunatic Asylum. 1807. *Minute Book 1797-1807*. Volume 1. Susan Carnegie to the Managers of the Lunatic Asylum, 1st of August 1815.

[14] Great Britain. Scottish Lunacy Commission. 1969. *Report of the Royal Commissioners on Lunatic asylums and the laws relating to them in Scotland, 1857*. Volume 5. Shannon. Irish University Press. 81.

years. Nor was it to be an exclusive institution but one that would embrace all of the community's mentally afflicted, regardless of social class.[15] There was also an economic motive behind this in that the higher rates of board paid by the wealthier patients would be used to subsidise the care and treatment of the poorer patients. It was because of the unexpected success of the fundraising that it was decided other services could be provided alongside that of treating the mentally ill. The Dispensary became operational at the same time as the lunatic wards and although a sick ward was also included it was to be several years before it was fully operational.[16] With the exception of Edinburgh's Bedlam, those other institutions described above only provided very basic accommodation for the mentally ill as an afterthought.

## Inside the walls of the asylum

The earliest surviving record giving a brief but telling snapshot of what happened within the walls of the Asylum was published five years after its opening in 1787.[17] Over the four and a half year period the report covers, forty-four lunatic patients had been admitted, of whom ten had been discharged, cured or relieved and fourteen had died. Twenty remained in the Asylum. There are several occupations and amusements mentioned with a clear indication that other pursuits were also followed. During their lucid intervals patients were engaged in such activities as spinning yarn from which others amongst them made a form of coarse sheeting that was used in-house thus helping to offset the costs of running the institution. Other activities engaged in by some patients were knitting stockings, needlework, reading, and painting. Given that the hospital has been described as a house and garden in the links it is reasonable to surmise, that gardening was one of those unlisted employments. This use of occupational therapy demonstrates an early awareness of the principle of keeping the mind of the lunatic busy, as a means of distracting them from their delusions. More significantly, what is seen to be in operation is a system of treatment that came to be known as moral treatment after the publication of Philippe Pinel's works on insanity in France, most especially his *Treatise on Insanity* in 1806.[18] The regime in operation at Montrose pre-dated by fourteen years the opening of the Tukes' Quaker Retreat at York in 1796, and by eighteen years Pinel's pioneering work in the Salpêtrière, which began in 1800 (Weiner: 725).

As stated earlier, moral management came into the language of early psychiatry because of a mistranslation of Pinel's *traitement moral*, which more precisely translated should read as psychological treatment (Weiner: 727). Like madness, it was a term which had no one definition or description. Writing in 1813 Samuel Tuke, for example, divided moral treatment at the Retreat into three parts:

a) by what means the power of the patient to control the disorder is strengthened or assisted
b) what modes of coercion are employed, when restraint is absolutely necessary
c) by what means the general comfort of the insane is promoted.(Tuke: 138)

After twenty-two years of practising what he preached, and five years of striving to encourage others to do likewise in his role as a Scottish Lunacy Commissioner, Dr W.A.F. Browne gave this succinct definition, "Moral treatment may be defined – every mode by which the mind is influenced through the mind itself; in contradistinction to medical treatment, in which the

---

[15] Susan Carnegie to Miss Brown, 21st July 1792.
[16] *State of the Lunatic Hospital*: 1-2; Cormack: 278.
[17] *State of the Lunatic Hospital and Dispensary at Montrose, from the 26th May 1782 to the 1st of January 1787.* (Note the absence of Infirmary from the title).
[18] Pinel: 1962; Weiner, 1979: 1128-1134; Weiner: 725-732.

mind is acted upon remotely by material agents, and *through* the body" (Browne: 313). This form of psychological treatment is what was attempted at the Montrose Asylum from the beginning.

The report, unfortunately, does not contain details of any other treatments that patients may have received during their confinement. There were no case records kept until 1818 and for the first seven years after that date they are more notable for what they do not contain rather than what they do. Between 1825 and 1834 there was a significant improvement of the details being recorded by the attending physicians but again they contain a minimum of information. What could be termed as proper case notes only began to be recorded for each patient when Dr W. A. F. Browne took up his appointment as the Asylum's first Medical Superintendent in 1834.[19] What is deducible from the scant patient records available is that some patients did receive medical treatment for those physical symptoms, which were at that time thought to be connected to the cause of the mental illness. Cupping, purging, vomiting, evacuation of the bowels, bleeding, etc., were the medical means of the day employed in the treatment of insanity, but there is also reason to believe that electro-therapy similar to that pioneered by John Wesley may also have been employed as early as 1786.[20] Were this fact to be substantiated it would have made the Montrose Asylum a world leader in the pioneering of treatments for mental illness. It is interesting to note, too, that there is a basic understanding of the need for classification. The Managers, in seeking to extend the benefits of the Hospital, resolved to build several new cells separate from the main house, into which they could place those lunatics who were the most furious and loathsome. By doing so, not only would the capacity to receive a greater number of patients be increased, but also by rendering the house more cleanly and quiet, there would be a better chance of cure for those less severe cases admitted. This reveals some knowledge of the most current thinking in the treatment of lunatics at a time when it was still very much standard practice to accommodate all those designated as insane in the same place. Of more local concern, it would, at least in part, help to allay the fears of those who were not keen to see the Hospital expanded without due consideration for the comfort and healing of all the patients it was to contain.[21] Each of the local doctors gave of their service free to both the lunatic inmates and the outpatients of the dispensary – 580 benefited from their services over the first four-and-a-half years of the institutions existence. Twenty-two others were detained for treatment with more serious complaints, some of which required surgical operations in the unfinished sick ward. By 1818, not only were patients arriving from major centres such as Edinburgh, Glasgow, Dundee, and Aberdeen, but also Perth and Inverness, an indication that, at best, the services provided in these locations were inadequate or at worst non-existent.

Also contained within the report is the first set of Regulations of the Lunatic Hospital, seven in all, a modest number by later standards. No admission was permitted merely on the word of a relative; there was the added safeguard of the necessity of a certificate of lunacy requiring the signature of two physicians or surgeons. The insane inhabitants of the parish of Montrose were given priority over others when it came to admission to the hospital and when poor lunatics belonging to the parish applied for admission they were always to be admitted without charge. The number of gratis patients was restricted to ten and, as the records show, there was rarely a time that this provision was not used to the full. Others in difficult financial circumstances benefited by receiving admission at reduced rates of board which could range

---

[19] Dr W.A.F. Browne began his career as a psychologist when he took up the post of Medical Superintendent, the first person to hold that office, at the Montrose Asylum in June 1834. After four successful years there, he went to the brand new Crichton Royal Institution at Dumfries and brought it international fame by his innovative approach in dealing with the insane.

[20] *State of the Lunatic Hospital*, 2. On electrotherapy see, for example, Gadsby: 1996; Rowbottom: 1984.

[21] Sir Alexander Ramsay to Susan Carnegie 7th December 1775 quoted in Cormack: 279.

from £5-£8 per annum. Their distance from the town and the level of contribution made by a particular parish towards the maintenance of the Asylum would determine the rate of board for those beyond the parish of Montrose. No maximum rate of board was laid down, but a minimum of £10 sterling was set for those pauper lunatics who came from parishes that did not contribute towards the erection or ongoing maintenance of the asylum. Patients' friends had to provide for their clothing needs, and should a patient die while in the Asylum those friends also had to pay any funeral expenses. Those who could were expected to "pay such board . . . so as to become a benefit to the Hospital"; in other words, the better off were to subsidise the less well off. Those deemed to have recovered sufficiently were to be discharged to the care of either their family, friends, or as was often the case, to the home of a reputable member of the community with their place being kept op[en for them]in case of relapse. What we see in effect is an early form of care in the community being practised as early as the late eighteenth century. It also reveals that although the finances of the institution seem to be in good order they were not yet considered sufficient to allow an infirmary to be fully established. Thus, the production of the *State of the Lunatic Hospital* was not merely to disseminate information it was also designed to solicit further support to permit expansion, and secure the long-term future of the Hospital.

From the *Register of Lunatics* come the first indications of the treatment received. The Register at first gives a brief history of those patients in the asylum on the 1st of June 1818, some of whom had been more than thirty years confined, and it confirms that a minority of patients received the standard medical means of the time in attempts to cure mental illness. On few occasions were these remedies considered efficacious and it is sometimes pointedly stated that they were without effect. Thus, the principal means of cure was the use of an early form of "occupational therapy"allied to the psychological skills of James Booth, which in some cases led to patients aiding their fellow patients in the recovery process. After the opening of the Quaker Retreat near York in 1796 many medical prescriptions "which had been highly recommended by writers on insanity, received an ample trial [there] but they appeared too inefficacious to deserve the appellation of remedies" (Tuke: 111-112). Like James Booth, and the attending physicians at Montrose before them, the asylum attendants at the York Retreat largely ignored such remedies. The Register also reveals the methods of restraint used to control the more furious and violent patients. Sometimes an unruly patient would simply be locked in their cell, on other occasions a violent or destructive patient would be subject to the straitjacket, leather muffs or straps to prevent the infliction of self-injury, the tearing of clothes or the ruination of bedding. Those presenting a real physical danger to the staff and their fellow patients were subject to "extraordinary restraint" but what that constituted is not made clear. However, two cases give an indication of what that may have been. One case is recorded where a patient admitted in 1805 was considered to be so dangerous that he was sometimes obliged to be chained in his cell, and another case where the feet and hands of a former soldier were at times necessary to be bound by leather straps. The mechanical restraint record of the Montrose Asylum between 1782 and 1818, as near as can be ascertained from the existing records, is as follows: out of fifty patients, six (three men and three women) were subject to the rare application of mechanical restraint comprising of leather muffs or the "straitwaistcoat", one was subject to more frequent instances of restraint, and another, on occasion, to be chained. None were subject to the use of mechanical restraint on a continuous basis. It is worthy of note at this point that both the Tukes at the Retreat and Philippe Pinel at the Salpêtrière in Paris, also resorted to the use of mechanical restraint in their supposedly model asylums (Tuke: 138, 143, 163, 164, 166).

While the medical services of the asylum were undertaken gratis by the town's physicians on a monthly rota, the day-to-day care of the inmates was in the hands of James Booth and his wife. Their position required them to live in, and for twenty-five years they lived and worked in the asylum. Their efforts received the highest praise from the Managers as well as the writer of the Montrose section in Sir John Sinclair's *Statistical Account of Scotland* c.1793, "The order and cleanliness of the house, and the humanity and frugality of the Master and Mistress merit the highest encomiums" (Sinclair: 548). James Booth did not, and would not allow any mental patient to be physically struck or verbally abused, and it was a principle, which his successors were to maintain.[22] Given that the physicians attended twice a week, unless otherwise called in to administer medical attention, the cure of the lunatic patients was very much down to the Booths. Not only were they responsible for the cleanliness of the hospital, they also prepared the food, saw to the laundry, comforted the patients day and night if necessary, and kept control of the day-to-day running of the institution. Alongside these responsibilities, James Booth was also a competent apothecary who both prepared and administered medical remedies to mentally and physically ill patients alike. Although the signatures of two medical men were required on the certificate of lunacy for the admission of a patient, what the role of the Booths at Montrose indicates is that the part played by the medical profession at that time was in many respects secondary to that of the non-medically-qualified Keeper and Matron.

## Conclusion

As a busy seaport, which traded extensively with northern Europe, as well as far flung parts of the British Empire, the inhabitants of Montrose were exposed to the influences of different cultures over many centuries, and as such were less parochial or provincial than may be at first supposed. With its well-educated, well-travelled landed gentry, merchant, and military classes besides those local adventurers who uprooted themselves in search of riches, the wherewithal both intellectually and financially to consider and build a hospital for the care and cure of insanity was well within the capability of the parish of Montrose. The greater surprise must surely be the failure of Edinburgh to be the first to found such an institution (Poole: 6-7fn). By the later eighteenth century, Edinburgh was well established as the leading centre for medical education in Europe and there were a number of treatises on insanity produced by Edinburgh University scholars. Where Edinburgh failed Susan Carnegie and the Montrose Lunatic Hospital succeeded. The existing records clearly show that operating in the Hospital was a system of treatment in which there was a deliberate policy of attempted cure. It was a humane system, which incorporated "occupational therapy", classification, and good diet (*Minute Books*, Vol. 1-4). While mechanical restraint was not totally abolished, it was severely restricted, which in itself was no insignificant achievement in an age when brutal restraint was still very much a part of the treatment of the insane. Permeating the system was a basic psychology, which sought to address the problem of mental illness more effectively, and what Philippe Pinel did through his empirical approach was give the system a name, moral treatment, and a language, which manifested it. Samuel Tuke, and Pinel certainly improved upon the type of system in operation at Montrose but they did not invent it. James Booth and Jean-Baptiste Pussin, Pinel's unsung mentor, were equals in their philosophy of treatment for the mentally ill, a philosophy that gave others something to build on. Pussin's work was taken forward with the appointment of Pinel as "physician of the infirmaries"[23] in 1793. The Managers at Montrose failed to appoint a full-time physician to their Hospital for the mentally ill until 1834, and so Booth's work continued along in the same humane way that it began. That does not mean, however, that it was unknown. Although more research needs to be done it seems evident that the asylum at Montrose was known of in several parts of Britain, not least

---

[22] Montrose Royal Lunatic Asylum. 1822. *Minute Book* vol. iii. 3rd December 1822 ; Weiner: 731; Weiner, 1979: 1133
[23] Weiner, "Pinel's Memoir", 726

because of the fundraising for it that brought in donations from London and other places in England. Together Susan Carnegie and the Montrose Lunatic Hospital showed that there was a better way to treat insanity in Scotland, and it is a contribution to the history of Scottish psychiatry that should not be ignored.

## References

Baird, Dr. 1807. *Address to the public respecting the establishment of a Lunatic asylum at Edinburgh*. Edinburgh: James Ballantyne & Co. 4.

Birnie, A. 1938. "The Edinburgh Charity Workhouse, 1740-1845". *The Book of the Old Edinburgh Club*. 22

Browne, WAF. 1864. "The Moral Treatment of the Insane; a Lecture by WAF Browne, Commissioner in Lunacy for Scotland". *The Journal of Mental Science*. 10: 51 October 1864

Cormack, A.A. 1966. *Susan Carnegie 1744-1821: her life of service*. Aberdeen: Aberdeen University Press

Ferguson, T. 1948. *The Dawn of Scottish Social Welfare: A Survey from Medieval Times to 1863*. London: T Nelson and Sons

Gadsby, J.G. 1996. *Rev. John Wesley MA: Holistic Healing, Electrotherapy, and Complementary Medicine*. Leicester: Teamprint

Halliday, A. 1816. *A Letter to Lord Binning containing some remarks on the state of lunatic asylums, and on the number and condition of the insane poor in Scotland*. Edinburgh: Pillans

Houston, R.A. 2003. "Care of the mentally disabled in and around Edinburgh c. 1680-1820". *Journal of the Royal College of Physicians of Edinburgh*. 33 (supplement 12): 14

Howden, J.C. 1882. *Montrose Royal Lunatic Asylum Annual Report*. Montrose: George Walker

Irving, G. 1975. *Dumfries and Galloway Royal Infirmary: The First Two Hundred Years, 1776-1975*. Dumfries. Dinwiddie

Jackson, G., and Lythe, S.G.E. eds. 1993.*The Port of Montrose: A History of Its Harbour, Trade and Shipping/ initiated by David G. Adams*. Tayport: Hutton Press

Keddie, KMG. 1982. "Straitjackets and Seclusion: Montrose Asylum, 1781-1834". *Medical History*. Wellcome Institute for the History of Medicine. 26

Montrose Royal Lunatic Asylum. 1807. *Minute Book 1797-1807*. Volume 1.

Montrose Royal Lunatic Asylum. 1822. *Minute Book*. Volume 3.

Pinel, Philippe. 1806. *A Treatise on Insanity*, translated from the French by D.D. Davis, (Facsimile of the London edition 1806) New York. Hafner Publishing Company.1962

Poole, R. 1841. *Memoranda regarding the Royal Lunatic Asylum, Infirmary, and Dispensary, of Montrose*. Montrose: J & D Nichol

Presly, A.S. 1981. *A Sunnyside chronicle: a history of Sunnyside Royal Hospital*. Dundee: Tayside Health Board

*Report of a committee of the county of Dumfries appointed 5th October, 1830, to consider the necessity of a lunatic asylum for the counties of Dumfries, Kirkcudbright, and Wigtown*. Dumfries: Dinwiddie

Rice, F.J. 1985. "The origins of an organisation of insanity in Scotland". *Scottish Economic and Social History* 5

Risse, G.B. 1986. *Hospital life in Enlightenment Scotland*. Cambridge. Cambridge University Press

Rowbottom, M. 1984. *Electricity and Medicine: A history of their interaction*. London. Macmillan

Scottish Lunacy Commission. 1969. *Report of the Royal Commissioners on Lunatic Asylums and the Laws Relating to Them in Scotland, 1857*. Volume 5. Shannon. Irish University Press

Scull, A., MacKenzie, C., Hervey, N. 1996. *Masters of Bedlam: The Transformation of the Mad-doctoring Trade*. Princeton: Princeton University Press

Sheriff Clerk of Edinburgh. 1825. *Report of the Sheriff Clerk of Edinburgh 7th February* 1825

Sinclair, Sir John. 1976. *The Statistical Account of Scotland, 1791-1799*. Vol. 13. Wakefield: EP Publishing.

Tuke, S, 1813. *Description of the Retreat an Institution near York for insane persons of the Society of Friends*. York

Turner, A.L. 1937. *Story of a great hospital; the Royal Infirmary of Edinburgh, 1729-1929*. Edinburgh:

Weiner, D.B. 1992. "Philippe Pinel's "Memoir on madness" of December 11, 1794: A fundamental text of modern psychiatry". *American Journal of Psychiatry*. 149:6.

Weiner, D.B. 1992. "Observations of Citizen Pussin on the Insane". *American Journal of Psychiatry*. 136:9

# Walter Scott's Jews and how they Shaped the Nation

*Ashley Hales*

As Irish and Scottish authors negotiate Self and Other in particularly fraught national contexts at the beginning of the nineteenth century, the questions on which they reflect have a wider resonance than the immediate circumstances in which they were writing. Although this paper limits itself to close readings of two of Walter Scott's novels and to this particular historical and literary period, the questions raised by these texts are of ongoing significance in the contemporary debates around nationalism, cultural geography and post-colonialism.

The term 'nationalism' is a recent invention and usually revolves around definitions of the nation-state. Of course there are several other understandings of 'nation' without such a political definition: Ernest Renan imagined the nation as a soul, a spiritual principle; Joseph Stalin emphasised the cohesion of several factors to define the nation, specifically, as Anthony Smith (1994: 15) places it, within the categories of "economic life, language, and territory"; and Max Weber called attention to a "myth of common descent" (ibid) unifying ethnic groups into nations. Weber (1994: 25) states: "The significance of the 'nation' is usually anchored in the superiority, or at least the irreplaceability, of the culture values that are to be preserved and developed only through the cultivation of the peculiarity of the group". To similar effect, Walker Connor (1994: 45) comments, "a group of people must know ethnically what they are not before they know what they are." This ethnic peculiarity necessitates a cultural homogeneity which produces cohesion, resulting in a polarised view of *us* (the particular nation in question) versus *them* (the Other, a one-sided pejorative term such as in the Occident's characterisation of the Orient). Weber's view is dangerous if we allow concretised types to be translated uncritically onto both historical and literary works. By defining the nation against an Other, whether that Other is without or within, a particular nation may gain a sense of nationality in reference to what it is *not*. The Other in these novels by Scott is the Jews; they are excluded from the centre of political composition in *Ivanhoe* (1820) and *The Surgeon's Daughter* (1827). They function similarly to the multifarious definitions of the nation and cannot be absolutely categorised into places the majority would have them fit. Thus they make nation-formation more complex and discursive rather than a typological totalising narrative.

The Jews in these works emblematise the discourse of Orientalism, which Edward Said (1995: 12) writes as existing "in an uneven exchange with various kinds of power, shaped to a degree by the exchange with power political […] power intellectual […] power cultural […and] power moral". As the Jews in these two works are situated at the periphery, they can acutely comment on impending modernity – even heralding it – while maintaining a critical distance and questioning the political, intellectual, cultural and moral foundations of the nation. These characters require we understand national emergence in spatial terms, through the way in which ideologies are mapped onto physical space. The Jews, as peripheral outsiders from the processes of nation-formation and the nation's imperialist extension, question the foundations of the nation as singularly exclusive, hierarchical, monolingual and male.

Isaac and Rebecca in Scott's *Ivanhoe* operate in significant ways throughout the novel: they represent the final phase of commerce (one of the mainstays of modernity) in comparison to a rural, feudal and agrarian understanding of history, and they have no homeland of their own and therefore exist on the periphery. From such a vantage point, they comment on and critique established mores. Although Isaac seems to fit the norms of a subservient, rich Jew, Rebecca resists definition by such terms and thereby complicates any possible cohesion within the outsider position of being Jewish in Britain. As we contemplate the ways in which the Jews help to form the nation, our terms again grow increasingly complex: on one hand, we may analyse how they shaped a particularly 'English' nation if we view the narrative as commenting upon its setting of twelfth-century Saxons and Normans; on the other hand, we may also view the narrative from its publication date in 1820 and observe Scott negotiating what it means to be British, more than 110 years after the Act of Union (1707) that joined Scotland and England, through the historicising filter of the twelfth century. Scott's literary output during the period of *Ivanhoe* and after seems to illustrate that he had abandoned his ideas of unlimited progress ensconced within the stadialist view of history. Instead, he was more interested in negotiating a space for the peripheral individual who must "take part in myths that represent the struggle that the individual has to define himself in relation to his community", as Graham McMaster (1981: 45-6) has put it. McMaster (1981: 150), noting the change in Scott's works; observes, "the mode of the novels retreats to pseudo-realism; fantasy and allegory are abandoned; social change and civil violence are examined in a largely discursive mode". By setting *Ivanhoe* amidst the Crusades and *The Surgeon's Daughter* during the British colonial rule of India, Scott enlarges the sphere of what constitutes 'the nation' and, by doing so, causes, as Ian Duncan (1996: xix) puts it, "subjects [to be] strangers in relation to their place and origins, all are disinherited, all occupy a colonial subjectivity". Although central figures do not feel the alienation of which Duncan suggests they are a part, the Jews obviously call our attention to the alienated political figure that nevertheless participates in national formation through critique and challenge to the centre.

In *Ivanhoe*, the reader is first introduced to Isaac seeking shelter in Cedric's castle; the Saxons shudder at the "apprehended contamination of his nearer approach" (64), "while Isaac thus stood an outcast in the present society, like his people among the nations, looking in vain for welcome or resting place" (65). Although Isaac plays the part of the subservient Jew, this is not rewarded because he is still considered a disease and representative of his peoples' disinheritance. As such he cannot be welcomed into the intimacy of the dining table, disrupting the Saxons' homogeneity. Isaac, later clothed in the richest furs and gabardine at the tournament, presents an irreconcilable image; he cannot be simply the downtrodden and outcast who is therefore pitied, categorised as 'untouchable', ignored, and then cast aside. Additionally, his daughter Rebecca is striking and "might indeed have compared with the proudest beauties of England" (93), as she is dressed in brightly coloured silks and a turban adorned with an ostrich feather. Rebecca's luxurious beauty gives flesh to foreignness, and both bar her from and allows her access into central society. The social theoretician Zygmunt Bauman (1998: 144) explains the characteristic apprehension towards the Jews:

> [T]he apprehension and vexation related not to something or someone disquieting through otherness and unfamiliarity, but to something or someone that does not fit the structure or the orderly world, does not fall easily into any of the established categories, emits therefore contradictory signals as to the proper conduct – and in the result blurs the borderlines which ought to be kept watertight and undermines the reassuringly monotonous, repetitive and predictable nature of the life-world.

The Jews' wealth and beauty calls them into the social centre that values these commodities. But because they are Jewish – different and uncompromising about their faith, way of life and history – they are ultimately banned from central roles within the nation (although they occupy the centre of the novel). On the borderlines of the nation, their very presence questions the nation's legitimacy, because in the Jews' presence, its unity wavers, trembles and loses clarity.

Their foreignness ostracises the Jews from homogeneity, but their commerce brings them into increasing contact with ruling groups, as their money filters back into their capital. Their wealth is a partial ticket into society allowing them access to the power centre through investments, loans and bribes. Isaac wants to reduce the Jews' relationship with the emerging nation to commercial interaction, but Rebecca sees that such a paring down of relations requires her to give up a broader social conference. That is, if she were to see the situation as her father does, personal interactions between boundary figures and those in the centre would only revolve around monetary and purely functional definitions, rather than in any exchange of advice or criticism.

A significant component of the Jews' commercial success is their multilingualism. The narrator comments in an aside, "his [Isaac's] traffic had rendered every tongue spoken in Britain familiar to him" (127). Rebecca likewise responds later in the novel to her pursuer, Brian De Bois-Guilbert, in Saxon and in French. Such multilingual capabilities come as a result of the Jews' nomadic life, interaction with many people groups, and acclimatising to cultural differences as they enter into discourse with strangers. Speaking many languages continues to place the Jews at the boundary, as their fluency renders their experience, comfort and knowledge base larger than those in positions of political authority, and such a peripheral position excites fear in those with power to lose. Multilingualism gives the Jews access to wider codes of meaning and renders truth more complex and multi-dimensional. Commerce allows them to physically cross national borders and, in doing so, they metaphorically traverse boundaries making them cross-cultural at a time when such hybridity was rejected and feared. Zygmunt Bauman (1998: 144) remarks, "The Jews were the low moving up, and thus instilled in the high the fear of going down; they epitomized the world not just *turned*, but keeping on *turning* upside down – the world in which nothing stands still and can be relied upon." Although the Jews represent modernity's growth through their close ties with commercialisation, they also challenge modernity as they continually cross boundaries – hierarchical power structures, traditional gender roles, medical practices, to name a few – and, in doing so, continually require those in the centre to remain in flux rather than to continue comfortably static in their self-ordered, categorised world.

By physically and metaphorically inhabiting a space on the fringes of society, Isaac and Rebecca engage with the social hierarchy but are not consumed by it; Rebecca may accurately comment, therefore, on absurdities to which those in the centre are blind. Because Isaac sees his relationship with those in the centre of British nation-formation as purely commercial, he does not emerge from such a self-defined role and, thus, he lacks the ability to effectively critique the centre. Rebecca's viewpoint of the Black Knight's siege of Front-de-Bœuf's castle illustrates her ability to both aid the centre (in this case by explaining the battle to Ivanhoe) and to question the basis for its actions:

> [A]vailing herself of the protection of the large ancient shield, which she placed against the lower part of the window, Rebecca, with tolerable security to herself, could witness part of what was passing without the castle [...]. Indeed the situation which she thus obtained was peculiarly favourable for this purpose, because, being placed on an angle of the main building, Rebecca could not only see what passed beyond the precincts of the castle, but also commanded a view of the outwork likely to be the first object of the meditated assault. (309-310)

It is no accident that Rebecca fills such a mediating role between the battle and Ivanhoe; on the boundary she cannot take part in any action but, from one remove, she is able to "command a view" of both the attack and the counter-attack, just as she resides on the boundary of the nation and may thus widen the perspective of those in the centre. It is helpful to note she hides behind an ancient shield, just as her ancient ethnic and religious community defines and protects her character. Such a vantage point requires her to be vulnerable and thus puts her in danger from the attack. It also places such a vociferous boundary figure in danger by heralding a non-conformist attitude. As she relays the battle's events to Ivanhoe, she questions their foundation: "'Glory? […] alas, is the rusted mail which hangs a hatchment over the champions dim and mouldering tomb'" (316). Rebecca brings the conversation from the immediate quest for glory to its lasting detrimental effects. By promulgating a larger worldview, Rebecca questions the very foundations upon which the historically emerging English nation is built. Although she is partially safe residing outside the centre, it is also the case that she cannot engage equally in social discourse and is not recognised as having the authority to critique; she therefore leaves altogether. Isaac and Rebecca have become too marginal and must travel to another space where their commerce, but ultimately their lives, will prosper. Rebecca and her father, because they are not heirs to British developmental imperialism, must carve out for themselves a new history in another landscape. Ian Duncan (1996: xx) writes in his introduction to *Ivanhoe*, "Jews and women inhabit a different history from the official imperial one of expansion and synthesis." Their marginal history resists expansion and synthesis because they are not granted access to the society at large; they are not grafted into a wider understanding of the nation and thus must live and tell an Other narrative as an undercurrent to the official story of the dominant history.

In *The Surgeon's Daughter*, Zilia de Monçada, the Portuguese Jew and mother of the illegitimate Richard Middlemas, functions somewhat similarly to Isaac and Rebecca, although her part is less influential in the novel. The reader hears the entire story of Richard Tresham's wooing of her late in the novel. Their flight to Scotland from London and the subsequent birth of their child is important spatially. This progression north deviates from the *Waverley* (1814) model, which, as Katie Trumpener (1997: 72) notes, "transform[s] spatial difference into developmental time"; instead this journey is a purposeful travelling away from the political, commercial and powerful centre of London. It is a peripheral and increasingly marginalised travel away from the centre, rather than a developmentally regressive journey. The space Zilia and Tresham inhabit must be increasingly peripheral and Other (they move from London to Scotland to India) if they are to be successful in making a religiously mixed love and marriage flourish. We first hear of Zilia when Mrs Grey tells her husband, "'She cannot speak a word like a Christian being'" (163), perpetuating a denigrated image of Zilia, and automatically placing her on the margin as she cannot be situated centrally within Christianised Britain. However, Zilia does know Spanish, Portuguese, and a little French. Such multilingualism emphasises her foreignness in rural Scotland, allies her with Isaac and Rebecca and substantiates her place on the fringes of social homogeneity.

In this novel emphasis is again placed on the Jews as modern commercial agents. Zilia's father "had come to London, in prosecution of his commerce" (238) and he is often pictured as counting money with "mercantile deliberation" (173). Seignior Monçada fits a stereotypical mould, while his daughter breaks out of it and is punished by failing to please everybody and subsequently falling out of her father's, husband's and son's good graces. On the other hand, it is Richard and Zilia's financial success (built upon her father's London banking business and Tresham's profits in imperial India) that allows them to move more freely across boundaries; their wealth allows them liberty of movement where they may live where they please, set up home as they wish in what Scott describes as a "luxury which was then a novelty in Europe" (229), and enter more fully into society than if they were poor. However, for all the 'freedom' wealth promises, Zilia cannot be simultaneously reconciled to all the men in her life. She becomes consumed and dies in a frenzy of music, interestingly playing the harpsichord (a symbol of European culture, privilege and refinery) which Scott later refers to as a harp. The symbolic undertones of the harp bring to mind Trumpener's comments about the instrument that, as a "bardic instrument, the cherished vehicle of Irish, Welsh, and Scottish nationalism, and [as it was known later] as the emblem of nationalist republicanism, the harp stands for an art that honors the organic relationship between a people, their land and their culture" (1997: 19). Her death amidst ancient music performed on a harpsichord models, on the one hand, her refractory embodiment of both European modernism and luxury and, on the other hand, ancient cultural and religious tradition. Richard's boyhood friend, Hartley, relates Richard's parents' troubled history, Zilia's death and her gift of 2,000 pounds to Richard, and "yet [Richard] counted over the money with mercantile accuracy" (242). The motif of commerce is here imaged another way in their son's quest for fortune and prestige. The phrase harkens back to Seignior Monçada and is evidence of how far we have moved from Isaac and Rebecca's commercial ties as something valued as it increases the religious treasury; here, personal wealth is the only concern as financial gain parallels the nation's political acquisition of territory.

Whereas Rebecca's peripheral position enabled her to criticise the homogenous centre, Zilia's peripheral identity creates internal fragmentation because she functions as suffering mother and is obedient to the wishes of both her father and husband, until she cannot properly enter any independent space and dies. That is, she cannot command any portion of her own autonomy – she is separated from her father, her husband and her firstborn son at various points in the story – and, in such a liminal place, becomes internally isolated. Such a space may be what Homi Bhabha (1994: 309) speaks of in *Nation and Narration*:

> The marginal or 'minority' is not the space of a celebratory, or utopian, self-marginalization. It is a much more substantial intervention into those justifications of modernity – progress, homogeneity, cultural organicism, the tendencies within cultures in the name of the national interest or the ethnic prerogative.

Zilia, estranged from her father and his commercialism, cannot typify progress. Also as a Jew she cannot take part in the homogeneity of the nation, although she profits from its imperial presence, and as an isolated individual her existence challenges any notion of "cultural organicism". She cannot remove herself from her context and seek another frontier as do Isaac and Rebecca, and thus it seems her death is the only removal she may take. Zilia's presence challenges central ideas of cultural and national uniformity, but she cannot take action or critique her context because she has consented to its racial, religious and imperial rhetoric by falling in love with and marrying Tresham, a British Christian military officer with a Jacobite background.

Returning to Weber's understanding of the nation as one where the cohesion of disparate elements into a homogenous whole is what institutes feelings of nationalism, this nationalistic imprint only arises from first recognising what the nation is not, rather than what it is. The historical English nation emerging in *Ivanhoe* defines itself against the Jews; it is Christian rather than Jewish, feudal rather than commercial, monolingual rather than multilingual. As a Scot, Walter Scott negotiates Britishness through the critical distance this novel allows him, and perhaps he tries to understand, through the use of peripheral figures like the Jews, how the Scottish fit into the larger politically constituted entity of Britain. In *The Surgeon's Daughter*, Zilia and her father are seen as Other, but take differing tracks. Seignior Monçada assimilates into a wealthy Jewish Londoner while Zilia seeks acceptance from the centre by falling in love with a Christian, which leads to her destruction.

Scott uses boundary figures to complicate simplistic and neatly categorised understandings of nation-formation, and exposes the inherent problems with overtly controllable worldviews. The twentieth-century architectural philosopher Gaston Bachelard notes the ramifications of living on such a boundary. He writes in *The Poetics of Space,* "If there exists a border-line surface between such an inside and outside, this surface is painful on both sides" (1958: 215). He also observes, regarding the dialectic between outside and inside, how such a position excites fear and confusion: "we absorb a mixture of being and nothingness [...] The center of 'being-there' [that is, being central] wavers and trembles. Intimate space loses its clarity, while exterior space loses its void" (ibid.). Such a painful space Bachelard articulates epitomises the space Jews occupy here in Scott's works, and that which colonised peoples later inhabit. Katie Trumpener in her influential work, *Bardic Nationalism*, notes the connection between Irish and Scottish national and historical fiction. She writes (1997: 11-2): "These genres are transported out of British peripheries into the colonies of the new British Empire, where they form the primary models for early colonial fiction." It is not only the ideas and characters in these novels that question hierarchical relationships embodied within the establishments of power, race, religion, language and gender, which are all performed within the sphere of national and imperial contexts. Their transmission as texts also raises the same questions. As Scott's historical novels became the "paradigmatic novel of empire" to use Trumpener's phrase (1997: xiii), they necessarily participate in the imperialism of print capitalism. Notable characters within the texts, such as Rebecca and Zilia, call hegemonic discourses into question. But the novels' textual presence and dissemination seem to validate imperial power (at least in cultural and capitalist transmission of symbolic goods) while the individual texts simultaneously call into question such unbending hierarchies of class, race, religion and gender, through their Jewish voices.

## References

Bachelard, Gaston. 1994. *The Poetics of Space*. Trans. Maria Jolas. Boston: Beacon Press. First published 1958

Bauman, Zygmunt. 1998. "Allosemitism: Premodern, Modern, Postmodern". *Modernity, Culture, and 'the Jew'*. Eds. Bryan Cheyette and Laura Marcus. Cambridge: Polity Press

Bhabha, Homi. 1994. "Introduction" *Nation and Narration*. Rpt. in *Nationalism*. Eds. John Hutchinson and Anthony D. Smith,Oxford: Oxford University Press. First published 1990

Connor, Walker. 1994. "A Nation is a Nation, is a State, is an Ethnic group, is a …". In John Hutchinson and Anthony D. Smith. *Nationalism*. Oxford: Oxford University Press. First published 1978

Duncan, Ian. 1996. "Introduction". *Ivanhoe*. Oxford: Oxford University Press

McMaster, Graham. 1981. *Scott and Society*. Cambridge: Cambridge University Press

Said, Edward W. 1995. *Orientalism: Western Conceptions of the Orient*. Second ed. London and New York: Penguin Books

Scott, Walter. 1996. *Ivanhoe*. Oxford: Oxford University Press. First published 1820

Scott, Walter. 2000. *The Surgeon's Daughter in Chronicles of the Canongate*. Edinburgh: Edinburgh University Press. First published 1827

Trumpener, Katie. 1997. *Bardic Nationalism: The Romantic Novel and the British Empire*. Princeton: Princeton University Press

Weber, Max. 1994. "The Nation". *Nationalism*. Eds. John Hutchinson and Anthony D. Smith. Oxford: Oxford University Press. First published in 1948

# Eliot, Joyce and George Friel's *Mr Alfred MA*

*Aoife Kernan*

This paper focuses on the narrative structures in George Friel's novel *Mr Alfred MA* (1972) and its engagement with non-Scottish modernist texts. I will begin by discussing the novel's engagement with T.S. Eliot's poetry, in particular 'The Love Song of J Alfred Prufrock', and then offer a more in-depth commentary on the novel's echoes of James Joyce's *Ulysses* (1921) narrative, specifically focusing on the 'Circe' episode.

Published in 1972 and set wholly in Glasgow, *Mr Alfred MA* is George Friel's most critically acclaimed and successful novel. The story presents "a bitter and sharp-edged satire on life in the modern urban wasteland" (Burns 1988: 37) as Mr Alfred, a middle-aged schoolteacher, social outsider and failed poet, is progressively anaesthetised by boredom, sexual frustration and alcoholism. Mr Alfred is challenged and eventually destroyed by the values of a progressively uncivilised Glasgow. His insolent students, with their spiteful gang violence and disregard for his lessons, reflect the urban Glasgow world outside the school. Unable to cope, Alfred's career collapses. He is gradually demoted from teaching boys to teaching girls and, following an attempted affair with Rose, a young schoolgirl, he is finally transferred to a new school. The youth culture of graffiti and gang violence increasingly confounds and fascinates Alfred until his final confrontation with Tod, a figure who according to John Burns (1988: 36) "personifies all the evil which is out to destroy him". This encounter with Tod results in Alfred's arrest and final commitment to a mental asylum, at which point the novel closes.

The language, imagery and narrative structure of *Mr Alfred MA* deny an exclusively Scottish reading. Although written and set wholly in Glasgow, the novel's narrative voice and the character of Mr Alfred engage with the voices of Evelyn Waugh's *A Handful of Dust* (1934), James Joyce's *Ulysses* and *The Portrait of the Artist as a Young Man* (1916/17), Goethe's *Faust* (1808), Mikhail Bulgakov's *The Master and the Margarita* (1966), and Eliot's 'The Love Song of Alfred J. Prufrock' (1917) and *The Waste Land* (1922) among others. The narrative voices of *Mr Alfred MA* are slippery and elude definition, while such English, German, Russian, and Irish cultural markers reach beyond Scotland's borders and demonstrate an engagement with the international modernist tradition.

## The Allusions to T.S. Eliot

James Gillespie, a lifelong friend, and old college classmate of Friel, documents his admiration and reading of T.S. Eliot, writing that he "had a great attachment to Eliot as a poet, and what little I knew or understand of Eliot goes back to what George used to expound to me in free moments in the Union" (1985: 50). Mr. Alfred's character closely resembles Eliot's J. Alfred Prufrock. Both characters share an elusive forename and the name Alfred. Like Prufrock, Mr Alfred is also "full of high sentence, but a bit obtuse" (Eliot 1998: 4, l.21). The daily existence of Friel's Alfred, as 'a veteran pub crawler' (390) through the streets of Glasgow, mirrors Prufrock's crab-like crawl. Alfred also goes at "dusk through narrow streets" (Eliot 1998: 3, l.72) dressed in disguise. Alcohol is his "anaesthetic between the week's drudgery behind and the week's drudgery ahead" (391), echoing Prufrock's numb condition as a "patient etherised upon a table" (Eliot 1998: 1, l.3).

Introduced to the reader supping beer in a busy bar, Alfred is "anxious to be sociable" (390) echoing Prufrock's repeated question, "do I dare?" (Eliot 1998: 2, l.39 & 46). Prufrock declares, "And I have known the arms already, known them all – / Arms that are braceleted and white and bare" (3, l.64/65), and wonders, "how should I begin?" (3, l.71). Sharing Prufrock's frustrated lust, Alfred fails to engage in meaningful conversation with Stella, a barmaid. He wonders how he would get on with Stella if "he tried to make love to her" and concludes that "even if she ever gave him the chance he would muck it up somehow" (391). Just as Prufrock fears humiliation and retreats from the party to "descend the stair" (2, l.40), Alfred also descends stairs to escape from a woman. In Alfred's case this is one of Glasgow's prostitutes. The narrator writes, "He descended, leaving her loitering at the top of the stairs" (393), and Alfred surmises, "when he was young he even hoped to love a woman" (390). Keyless and alone, Alfred suffers the same isolation as Prufrock. Friel's narrator comments, "Now every door seemed locked, and without a key he was afraid to knock" (390).

This sense of keylessness continues the narrator's allusions to Eliot's poetry. For example, the speaker in 'What the Thunder Said' of the *The Waste Land* also describes an isolated personal keyless prison declaring, "We think of the Key, each in his prison / Thinking of the Key, each confirms his prison" (Eliot 1998: 42, l. 414-415). The critic Harriet Davidson (1994:129) suggests that Eliot's keyless imagery underpins "an inhuman landscape where repetition suggests pointless circularity". The same can be said for Alfred's experience of Glasgow. Similarly trapped in an endless pursuit of women, alcohol and recognition, Alfred's continuous search for the key to his troubles reconfirms and compounds his loneliness.

## Allusions to Joyce

This sense of keylessness brings me to the narrative allusions in *Mr. Alfred MA* to Joyce's writing. James Gillespie (1985: 50) further acknowledges Friel's admiration and loyalty to Joyce recalling, "But supreme in all his interests was Joyce. Joyce seemed to be his model in so many ways". A sense of keylessness is prevalent in the *Ulysses* narrative. Both Stephen Dedalus and Leopold Bloom are outsiders and just as Alfred wanders Glasgow keyless, both Joyce's characters also wander Dublin without keys. As the first episode of *Ulysses* ends, Buck Mulligan asks Stephen for the key to the tower, which he reluctantly surrenders, forcing him to wander the city (1986: 3-19). Bloom, like Stephen and Alfred, is also doomed to wander Dublin as he has left his key in the pair of trousers he wore the previous day. The allusions to a state of keylessness in Ulysses are numerous. For example, Bloom seeks to secure an advertisement for Keyes, a Dublin tea merchant in Episode Seven. In addition, he wanders Dublin in the 'Circe' episode carrying a "gent's sterling silver Waterbury keyless watch" (358). Also similar to Prufrock and Alfred, Bloom is too afraid to risk disturbing a woman by ascending the stairs to retrieve the key from Molly, his wife. Friel's narrative informs the reader that "without a key" Alfred "was afraid to knock" (390). The *Ulysses* narrative likewise plays on the notion of knocking on doors without a key: "what were then the alternatives before the, premeditatedly (respectively) and inadvertently, keyless couple. To enter or not to enter. To knock or not to knock" (546).

Friel's narrative makes further allusions to *Ulysses*. Mr. Alfred resembles the young Stephen. Like Stephen, he begins the novel working as a teacher for boys. He shares Stephen's similar artistic aspirations and explicitly identifies himself further with both Dedalus and Joyce declaring, "the tawse of the Scotch dominie is never wielded like the Jesuit's pandybat that distressed the young Stephen Dedalus. Not that the pandybat did Joyce any harm. It gave him material. It showed him what life is like" (427). In addition, Mr. Alfred associates his poetic failure, creative frustration and loneliness as proof of his deficiency regarding Stephen's

---

[1] Ariel declares, 'Hell is empty, / And all the devils are here' (Act 1.2: 214/215).
[2] Caliban declares, 'You taught me language, and my profit on't / Is, I know how to curse' (Act 1.2: 363/364).

characteristics in *Portrait of An Artist as a Young Man*. Dedalus asserts his creative mission statement in *The Portrait* by declaring that he will achieve his artistic goals by allowing himself to use "silence, exile, and cunning" (269). Considering these qualities Alfred judges himself a failure. Depressed and defeated, and directly echoing Stephen's words, he attributes his artistic failure to the fact that "he had silence and exile but no cunning" (455).

Alfred's hallucinatory encounter with Tod, the nightmarish figure, also continues the novel's allusions to Joyce's *Ulysses*. Alfred's "nightly tour of dark streets and dingy pubs" (555) around Glasgow echoes the 'Circe' episode in which Bloom wanders around Nighttown, the frenetic seedy red-light district of Dublin seeking Stephan. Although the first fourteen episodes of *Ulysses* convince the reader that he/she is privy to Bloom's private thoughts, his hallucinations in the 'Circe' episode reveal his innermost thoughts, his secret sexual indiscretions and social pretensions in a Kafkaesque show-trial. Similarly, Tod reveals Alfred's personal desperation, loneliness and hopelessness, vocalising Alfred's secret anarchic desire for a Glaswegian Cultural Revolution. Bloom's hallucinations in the 'Circe' episode are the unconscious nightmare of *Ulysses*, while during his encounter with Tod, Alfred "waited in a dream to be rescued from a nightmare" (561). Much like Friel's Alfred / Tod scene, Bloom's visions draw on puns, musical terminology, Shakespeare and the Bible. For example, quoting Shakespeare's *The Tempest*, Bloom declares, "Hell is empty, and all the devils are here" (421).[1] Also citing *The Tempest*, Alfred declares in his nightmarish state of confusion, "Taught them language. And the profit on it is. Caliban shall be his own master" (580).[2] Furthermore, just as Alfred's Tod is a devil figure alter-ego, Bloom is also identified with a devil figure in his show trial, "the man called Bloom is from the roots of hell" (401).

Both Alfred and Bloom allude to multiple identities in their respective episodes. Alfred's mind "seemed someone else's" (562) while Bloom's identity constantly shifts and changes during his trial. Alfred's inappropriate behaviour with and lust for the schoolgirl Rose recalls Bloom's charge of lechery during his trial. Alfred identifies with "the devil seeking whom he may deflower" (571) while several young girls recount stories of Bloom as a voyeur. The Artane Orphans chant, "You hig, you hog, you dirty dog! / You think the ladies love you!" (405) Ultimately, Alfred's phantasmagorical hallucinations depict his vision of a necessary but anarchic cultural hell – a vision that culminates in his penultimate psychological breakdown. Similarly Bloom's Circe nightmare ends in the most personal and disturbing images as he imagines the figure of his infant son as a dead eleven year old corpse and his voice is reduced to a mere whisper:

> *Against the dark wall a figure appears slowly, a fairy boy of eleven, a changeling, kidnapped, dressed in an Eton suit with glass shoes and a little bronze helmet, holding a book in his hand. He reads from right to left inaudibly, smiling, kissing the page.* Bloom (*wonderstruck, calls inaudibly*) Rudy! (497)

The Alfred/Tod Cultural Revolution attacks the universal literati and strives to speak a universal language. The attack echoes Stephen's claims in the 'Circe' episode that "gesture, not music not odours, would be a universal language" (353). Tod's "gesture" will be a universal human conflict reduced "to its simplest terms. My boys from the north get killed fighting my boys from the south?" (566).

The final appearance of two policemen, who apprehend Alfred at the end of the Alfred/Tod scene, further mirror the final scene of the 'Circe' episode. As Private Compton declares, "Here's the Cops" (Joyce 1986: 491). Just as Joyce's policemen seek to identify the crowd by taking names, Friel's policemen likewise attempt to identify and define Mr. Alfred. The two officers do not recognise either Mr Alfred or indeed the words he writes on the wall. They identify him thus: "'A foreign bugger,' said Quinn. 'What lingo's that?' 'No idea,' said

King. 'He's not Paki, is he?' 'Doesn't look like one,' said Quinn" (578). Unsure of who or what he is, the two policemen arrest Alfred anyway. This misidentification echoes Bloom's address to the jury during his hallucinations in 'Circe'. Bloom explains, "I am a man misunderstood. I am being made a scapegoat of" (373). Alfred too becomes a scapegoat for all that is wrong in Glasgow's society and this becomes evident during his interviews with two psychiatrists. There are no labels to brand or confine him and in a list that further echoes Bloom's extensive lists in 'Circe' the doctors believe:

> The mans got pedophobia, homichlophobia, dromophobia, xenophobia, ochlophobia, haphephobia, planomania, kleptophobia, thanatophobia, he's an onychophagist, he's got gerontophobia, but notice he has no dysphagia, he's got zoophobia, gataphobia, arachnophobia, kainophobia, climacophobia, acrophobia, hodophobia, he suffers from intermittent tachylogia, he's got agoraphobia, and kenophobia, thermophobia and melissophobia. (586/587)

Having staked all on the precision of language, Alfred becomes ironically victimised by its over-precision. Labelled beyond recognition, distraught and frustrated, Alfred is a shadow of his former articulate self. The acceleration of fragmented multiple allusions in the Alfred/Tod scene continue the narrative's analogies with the modernist poetry of T.S. Eliot. Alfred and Tod, as two fragmented voices of one psyche, both offer disjointed and seemingly random allusions. Together, their voices recall the tormented voice of 'What the Thunder Said' in *The Waste Land*, which laments the "fragments I have shored against my ruins" (Eliot 1998: 42, l.431). Mr Alfred's search for order and meaning mirrors Eliot's speaker who asks, "Shall I at least set my lands in order?" (42, l.426). Eliot's "speaker is answered by a series of allusions which are neither properly my lands" or in any discernible order (Davidson 1994: 131). The final section echoes the voices of Dante, Hesse et al. The mutation, degradation, and fragmentation of *The Waste Land's* final section are further reflected in Alfred's final confusion, his personal exile, the almost frantic allusions of Tod and Alfred, and ultimately in Alfred's final submission to Tod's Cultural Revolution. Alfred's literary fragments cannot stave off his ruinous fate.

## Modernism and Mr. Alfred

The *Mr Alfred MA* narrative is clearly not constructed in simply Scottish terms. By this I mean that the narrative does not confine itself within the boundaries of issues that reflect, engage with, or symbolise the Scottish literary tradition. The allusions to both Eliot and Joyce illustrate a narrative move way from a literary tradition in Scotland, which, according to Berthold Schoene (1995: 144), focuses on the "construction and maintenance of Scottish national identity as a fixed value and closed system of typical characteristics mistaken for archetypal, natural givens".

The isolation of *Mr Alfred MA* within the Scottish critical tradition is reinforced by the narrow perception the tradition has of its own modernist movement. Cairns Craig (1987: 6) describes Scottish modernism as "unlike the modernism of Joyce or Eliot" arguing that Scotland did not need to engage with international works, having its own past to fall back on. Craig writes:

> In Joyce's *Ulysses*, for instance, the presentation of Leopold Bloom, advertising salesman, as a new version of the epic hero is a juxtaposition made possible by the art itself. In Scotland there seemed to remain the possibility of a real continuity between

present and Scottish past, so that such artistically forced continuities were unnecessary. (1987: 6)

Craig is not the only critic to read Scotland's modernism introspectively. Alan Bold attributes a similar narrowness to Scottish twentieth-century literary writing:

> Scottish literature in the twentieth century has been stylistically conservative and thematically consistent. It has limits rather than limitations and has observed various literary rules; there has been no Ulysses and no general dissatisfaction with the traditional pattern of the novel as a story fleshed out with characters who struggle heroically toward a clearly defined conclusion. (1994: 101)

Such comments reinforce the limited and circumscribed terms in which modern Scottish literature reads itself. Persistent reading in terms of the past limits the reception of Scottish literature with regard to cultures beyond Scotland. Craig identifies the destructive consequences of thinking solely in terms of 'Scottishnesss' and asserts that Scotland's literature requires "a sense of tradition which is essentialist neither in its historical mode (identifying the 'real' nation with one portion of its past) nor in its denial that the nation exists in a continual series of interchanges with other nations and with ideas and forms of life which can be traced to an origin outside the nation itself" (1999: 30). Douglas Gifford (1985: 6) argues that modern Scottish literature must be read within the framework established by the writers of the Scottish Renaissance. Alan Bold (1989: 101-2) also focuses on the past, claiming that Sir Walter Scott "first invented, then perfected the historical novel" providing the Scottish writer with a method of searching the past to discover "perennially relevant Scottish topics" in order to define the present. Even the most recent survey of Scottish literature seeks to classify *Mr. Alfred MA* as entirely Scottish, claiming:

> Friel's ending is surreal and apocalyptic, in his scenes of Alfred's final descent into madness, and his meeting, real or imaginary, with a familiar demonic figure in Scottish fiction, in this case in the nightmare embodiment of all Glasgow's evils, the demonic Tod, the archetypal monster product of debased streets and bad living. The novel presents a final picture of the decline of Glasgow into surreal wasteland. (Dunnigan et al, 2002: 871)

## Conclusion

The engagement of *Mr Alfred MA* with Eliot and Joyce, among other Russian, German and English texts, marks a move away from traditional perceptions of Scottish modernism. The narrative attempts a universal intertextuality that eludes reductive categorisation. As Douglas Gifford writes of *Mr Alfred MA* in the introduction to the 1987 edition, "It is in the end not to be read simply within a Scottish cultural context, but as a major European statement about the breakdown of traditional values, of community, and most important of all, breakdown of communication" (Friel 1984: v). The singular "principal of Scottishness" as Horst Prillinger (2000: 17) describes it, is inappropriate as Alfred's "transcending literary sensibility" (Walker 1996: 325), and echoes of international modernism spill into the novel's narrative voice, generating an infinite number of perspectives, that reach far beyond the borders of Glasgow and Scotland.

## References

Bold, Alan. 1983. *Modern Scottish Literature Vol. 4*. London: Longman

Bold, Alan. 1994. *Herald*, Weekender Section. 5 February

Bulgakov, Mikhail. 1983. *The Master and Margarita*. Trans. by Michael Glennon. Glasgow: Fontana. First published 1966

Burns, John. 1988. "Parables for our Time". *Cencrastus* 29: 36-37

Craig, Cairns ed. 1987. *The History of Scottish Literature*. Aberdeen: Aberdeen University Press

Craig, Cairns. 1996. *Out of History: Narrative Paradigms in Scottish and British Culture*. Edinburgh: Polygon

Craig, Cairns. 1999. *The Modern Scottish Novel: Narrative and National Imagination*. Edinburgh: Edinburgh University Press

Davidson, Harriet. 1994. "Improper Desire: Reading the Waste Land". Ed. David Moody. *The Cambridge Companion to T.S. Eliot*. Cambridge: Cambridge University Press. 121-131

Dunnigan, Sarah, Douglas Gifford, Alan MacGillivray, eds. 2002. *Scottish Literature In English and Scots*. Edinburgh: Edinburgh University Press

Eliot, T.S. 1949. *Selected Essays*. 2nd rev. enl edn. London: Faber

Eliot, T.S. 1962. *Notes Towards the Definition of Culture*. London: Faber & Faber. First published 1949

Eliot, T.S. 1998. *The Wasteland, Prufrock And Other Poems*. New York: Dover

Friel, George. 1987. *Mr. Alfred MA* Edinburgh: Canongate

Friel, George. 1999. *George Friel: A Glasgow Trilogy*. Edinburgh: Canongate

Gifford, Douglas. 1985. *The Dear Green Place?: The Novel in the West of Scotland* Glasgow: Third Eye Centre

Gillespie, James. 1985. "Friel in the Thirties". *Edinburgh Review* 71: 50

Goethe, Johann Wolfgang, 1949. "Faust". *Goethe's Werke III*. Hamburg: Christian Wegner Verlag. First published 1808

Joyce, James. 1986. *Ulysses*. London: The Bodley Head. First published 1921

Joyce, James. 1992. *A Portrait of the Artist as a Young Man*. London: Penguin Classics. First published 1916/17

Prillinger, Horst. 2000. *Family and The Scottish Working Class Novel 1984-1994*. Frankfurt Am Main: Peter Lang

Schöne, Berthold. 1995. "A Passage to Scotland: Scotland Literature and the British Post-colonial Tradition". *Scotlands* 2.1: 107-122

Shakespeare, William. 1996. *The Tempest*. London: Penguin

Walker, Marshall. 1996. *Scottish Literature Since 1707*. London: Longman

Waugh, Evelyn. 1951. *A Handful of Dust*. London: Penguin. First published 1934

# Liam O'Flaherty's "The Wounded Cormorant"

*Richard J. King*

Liam O'Flaherty (1896-1984) was a prolific Irish author of novels, short stories, autobiographies, essays, and articles. He is known for his novels *The Assassin* (1928), *Famine* (1937), and *The Informer* (1925), which was made into a Hollywood film. His most respected literary achievements, however, are his short stories, which focus on animals and Irish peasant life. In 1925 O'Flaherty published "The Wounded Cormorant".[1] It is one of his most famous and anthologized tales. In the story a goat kicks a stone off a cliff edge. The stone falls onto a rock and splinters, sending a shard that breaks the leg of one of the cormorants roosting on the rock. The cormorant suffers from the pain. In struggling to rejoin the flock, it is rejected, then maimed further by the others, who finally shove it off a ledge to its death. "The Wounded Cormorant" is like many of O'Flaherty's animal stories: it is less than two thousand words, has a simple plot and includes no human characters, uses a small amount of anthropomorphism, and is narrated like a fable in direct third person.

For an eco-critical reading of "The Wounded Cormorant", I here collect relevant zoological information then trace the tradition of how this seabird is depicted in Irish and British literature before O'Flaherty. I check to see if his story aligns with tradition, then examine the tale for its zoological accuracy, scientific understanding, and "green" morals. Lastly, I examine how the author's social views might have influenced O'Flaherty's perception of his natural world and his presentation of this seabird.

## What is a cormorant?

Cormorants are seabirds. They eat fish and other small animals. They do not eat dead material. For nabbing prey, cormorants have a long neck and hook on the end of their beak. They have wide feet with webbed toes. Invisible to the distant viewer, cormorants have brightly coloured eyes and brightly coloured skin around their beak and face, particularly when breeding.

Cormorants live near almost any major body of water around the world. Depending on the chosen taxonomy, there are between twenty-seven and thirty-seven species of cormorants (Harrison, 293; Johnsgard, 10-11). There are two cormorant species in the British Isles: the Great Cormorant (*Phalacrocorax carbo*) and the European Shag (*Phalacrocorax aristotelis*). The Great Cormorant is a larger seabird, with bright black feathers, white around its face, and a white patch on the thigh when breeding. The European Shag is more common. It is a smaller bird with feathers that are tinted more brown and green. When breeding the European Shag has a lifted tuft of feathers on its head, the likely derivation for the name.

In "The Wounded Cormorant" O'Flaherty does not clarify which species he intends. Either species could arguably fit the descriptions used in the story. "The Wounded Cormorant" is set on Inishmore (Árainn).[2] The habitat of the steep cliffs of Clogher Mor (An Clochar Mór), where O'Flaherty places the incident, is more likely for the European Shag, but it would not be out of range or impossible for the Great Cormorant.[3]

---

[1] "The Wounded Cormorant" first appeared in *The Nation and the Athenaeum*, a journal often renamed, in Vol. 38, 28 Nov. 1925, 317-8 (Kelly, 149, and British Library).
[2] See Cahalan, 53-4.
[3] See Johnsgard, 73, 305, and Merne.

Cormorants have long been considered more voracious than other seabirds though this is scientifically dubious. This perception is long rooted in Irish and British literature, which likely both caused and reflected negative public opinion.

## How did Irish and British authors see cormorants before O'Flaherty?

Irish and British writers have long connected cormorants with two negative themes: greed and evil. Most scholars believe the word "cormorant" comes from the Latin, *corvus marinus*, meaning "sea-raven" (*OED*, III, 936). The genus name, *Phalacrocorax*, translated literally from Greek, means "bald crow" or "bald raven" (Borror, 29, 73).

In English, the *OED* explains the word cormorant has meant a greedy and rapacious individual, and could be qualified by referring to someone as a "money-cormorant". "Cormorancy" has meant a "greedy oppressive class". The adjective "cormorous" is defined as "insatiable" (III, 936). A flock of cormorants can be called a "gulp" (Bird, 280).[4] Fowler found that cormorants have long symbolized "greedy exploitation of the weak," and an outlet for people's distaste for the clergy (228).

Many authors in Irish and British literature describe the bird as gluttonous or used the word cormorant to signify greed, including Geoffrey Chaucer, Sir Philip Sidney, Joshua Sylvester, Michael Drayton, William Congreve, Alexander Pope, and Samuel Taylor Coleridge.[5] Shakespeare used "cormorant" in four plays. In *Love's Labour's Lost*, King Ferdinand says, "When, spite of cormorant devouring time" (Act. I, Sc.1, 281).

Andrew Marvell used cormorants in his "The Unfortunate Lover" (1648-9). Here the birds are pilferers and greedy. Interpretations vary on the meaning of this poem, but some scholars believe the cormorants symbolize religious figures or the Scots and Parliamentarians that put Charles I in custody.[6] Marvell writes:

A num'rous fleet of corm'rants black,
That sailed insulting o'er the wrack,
Received into their cruel care
Th'unfortunate and abject heir;
Guardians most fit to entertain
The orphan of the hurricane.

They fed him up with hopes and air,
Which soon digested to despair;
And as one corm'rant fed him, still
Another on his heart did bill.
Thus while they famish him, and feast,
He both consumèd and increased. (90)

In "Balaustion's Adventure" (1871), Browning uses the cormorant as a metaphor for a gluttonous carrion eater, a vulture, and a pirate, eager to capitalize on another's death. In this poem a ship must alter course to face human pirates and certain death. Browning's narrator claims:

---

[4] I am unsure of how widespread this term is in Britain or Ireland. The *OED* does not list this definition.
[5] Chaucer, Geoffrey ("The Parliament of Fowls": 14th C.); Sidney, Sir Philip ("The Last Eclogues": 1590); Sylvester, Joshua ("The Fifth Day of the First Week": late sixteenth-early seventeenth C.); Drayton, Michael ("The Twenty-fifth Song": 1622); Congreve, William (*The Old Batchelour*: 1693); Coleridge, Samuel Taylor (1796 quotation in *The Road to Xanadu*). For all but last two references see Munsterberg.
[6] See Smith in *The Poems of Andrew Marvell*, 88-90. Smith dates the poem at 1648-9.

> And we were just about
> To turn and face the foe, as some tired bird
> Barbarians pelt at, drive with shouts away
> From shelter in what rocks, however rude,
> She makes for, to escape the kindled eye,
> Split beak, crook'd claw o' the creature, cormorant
> Or ossifrage, that, hardly baffled, hangs
> Afloat i' the foam, to take her if she turn.
> So were we at destruction's very edge. (13)

In Scottish folklore, the female Cailleach, a gruesome hag that eats men's bodies, usually appears as a raven or crow, but can also appear as a cormorant. The Cailleach, according to Armstrong, has its roots in Celtic legends, such as the war-goddess Badb Catha, or the "Raven of Battle" (83).

As in Browning and in Scottish legend, authors have used cormorants not just to symbolize greed and gluttony, but in a second way: to symbolize dark and evil. This has roots in the cormorant's dark colour, its nearly silent voice, and its snake-like neck. Cormorants are infamous for the way they spread their wings, holding them open and nearly still when standing on a rock or the piling of a wharf.

Cormorant appears four times in the Bible. The bird is listed among animals not to be eaten because they are not clean. Cormorants are one of the few animals that are named to inhabit a land that the Lord has destroyed to punish its people, connecting the bird with death.[7] In *The Faerie Queene* (1596) Spenser ties cormorants with a dark and evil place, and in *Paradise Lost* (1667) Milton likens the devil to a cormorant. He describes Satan:

> Thence up he flew, and on the tree of life,
> The middle tree and highest there that grew,
> Sat like a cormorant. (227-8)

Coleridge uses Milton's image in his "The Devil's Thoughts" (1799). P.B. Shelley uses the cormorant to add to a dark, stormy mood in his "The Witch of Atlas" (1820), as does Yeats in his "The Madness of King Goll" (1887). Sir Walter Scott does the same in his *The Antiquary* (1816). He uses a Scots word for cormorant or shag: *skart*.

Irish words for cormorant and shag vary. The cormorant and shag is sgarbh with some making the distinction for the European Shag as *sgarbh-an-sgumain*. The cormorant is also *geocaire*, meaning "glutton" and a "debauchee". Shag is also *Cailleach-bheag-an-dhubh*, meaning literally "small black hag".[8]

In *Riders to the Sea*, set on the Aran islands and published two decades before "The Wounded Cormorant", J.M. Synge alludes to the Irish word for "shag". A grieving character cries out, "Isn't it a bitter thing to think of him floating that way to the far north, and no one to keen [mourn for] him but the black hags that do be flying on the sea?" (7-8). Synge, like O'Flaherty, surely knew that Irish folklore, as with so many other cultures, connects the color black with bad luck, the ancient, and evil (Synge, 188).

## O'Flaherty's cormorants

It is likely that O'Flaherty knew of at least some of the negative cormorant symbolism in literature, in folktales, and perhaps even in his readings of the Bible when training for the

---

[7] See Deuteronomy, Leviticus, Isaiah, and Zephaniah.
[8] See Bateman; Murphy; O'Reilly; and Hull, 96.

priesthood. In "The Wounded Cormorant" O'Flaherty seems, at first, to follow in step with this tradition. He tells of two species of birds, "rock-birds"[9] and gulls, then describes cormorants, in juxtaposition, as the only species that is still eating, with "their swollen gullets" (141), thus reinforcing the cormorant's image as greedy. After a shard injures the individual and the flock flees into the water, O'Flaherty brings in the darker, evil image of the cormorants by describing the birds' colour and alluding to a serpent: the cormorants "like upright snakes" (141). O'Flaherty completes the story by having the cormorants destroy the struggling bird, one of its own: "They fell upon it fiercely, tearing at its body with their beaks, plucking out its black feathers and rooting it about with their feet" (145). O'Flaherty shows the cormorant as greedy and evil in the same way as did his predecessors. However, O'Flaherty goes further.

No Irish or British writer, yet discovered, has written more than a few lines about a cormorant, let alone focused an entire story or poem on the bird. The creation of a cormorant protagonist is a first. O'Flaherty creates an isolated, injured, and doomed creature, inevitably sympathetic, that is killed by chance and the will of its fellows. As an example to show its effect, consider that scholar Washburn writes in 1989, "The bird's noble attempt, the attack of the flock, the futility of effort and, finally, the bird's death evoke all sorts of visceral and rational responses" (122). Washburn reads the cormorant as "noble". Finally a good cormorant. Or at least one with which a reader can empathize.

O'Flaherty also excuses the flock for killing its injured member. It is a requirement to their survival. When the stone first lands on the rock, the cormorants immediately fly into the water, scanning for enemies. The cormorants are constantly wary of predators. They are "slightly terrified" about another stone falling. O'Flaherty writes of the injured protagonist later in the story: "At all costs it must reach them or perish. Cast out from the flock, death was certain. Sea-gulls would devour it" (144). The cormorant protagonist and the others of its species are victims—they are prey—while their predator is a tall *white* bird high on the cliffs. O'Flaherty suggests their group cruelty is due to necessity. The world is greedy and dark, not the cormorants.

## Does the story have an environmental message?

Helene O'Connor describes Liam O'Flaherty as a literary ecologist. She writes: "Since the 1920s O'Flaherty has written simple, almost clinically objective stories about the peasants and animals he has observed so carefully on his native Aran Islands" (47). O'Connor states that he had an intimate understanding of the natural world, arguing that "[t]he authenticity conveyed [in his short stories] could have been achieved only through long and painstaking vigil" (54).

O'Connor is not alone in her praise for O'Flaherty's keen eye for the natural world. Saul writes how the physical behaviours of his animals "seem based on sensitive and minute observation" (109). Biographers and his personal letters describe how he often sat for hours to observe the traits of animals. O'Flaherty grew up near Clogher Mor and observed the coast and its creatures since he was a child, and as carefully, some say, as a marine biologist. Cahalan describes the descriptions in O'Flaherty's "An Charraid Dhubh" (The Black Rock, 1953) as so full of specific detail about the geology and the marine flora and fauna that it is "like something out of a *National Geographic* article or a Jacques Cousteau film" (58).

---

[9] Johns (1909: 317) writes that rock-birds are the auk, the puffin, and the guillemot. The Guillemot (*Uria aalge*) is the only white-bellied seabird that fits in the range of the Aran Islands based on Sharrock's findings, but the Guillemot's behaviour in the water does not reflect O'Flaherty's description. Swann (1913: 200) records that Rock Dove can be the Irish name for the Black Guillemot (*Cepphus grylle*), but its underparts are only white in winter. Liam's older brother Tom O'Flaherty describes rock-birds as guillemots in his *Cliffmen of the West* (1935) excerpted in Ó hEithir and Ó hEithir, 183.

With cormorants, however, a few of O'Flaherty's zoological details are questionable. For example, adult cormorants and shags are nearly mute, except in the nesting colony where they can give pig-like grunts, little barks, and clicking, creaking sounds. Yet O'Flaherty gives these birds improbable, perhaps impossible sounds in "The Wounded Cormorant". Both the injured and healthy cormorants "scream", "shriek", and "cackle" several times. At one point the flock "began to make curious screaming noises", but this is the only hint that these sounds might be abnormal behaviour (143).

O'Flaherty does not specify which cormorant species he means, whether they are cormorants or shags. To be fair, cormorant is the more general term.[10] Shag had rarely been used in Irish and British literature before him. Marryat uses the word in an expression in *Jacob Faithful* (1834), but the next significant literary usage of "shag" does not occur until Hugh MacDiarmid's "Shags' Nests", a decade after "The Wounded Cormorant". Irish ornithologist Oscar Merne began seabird nest censuses of the Aran Islands in the 1970s, finding only European Shags (10 May 2005).[11] A list of birds of the Aran Islands appears in the *Gaelic Journal* in 1899, listing both cormorant and shag, in both English and Irish (Feehan, 63). Merne believes O'Flaherty's descriptions fit those of the European Shag and not the Great Cormorant (12 May 2005). Did O'Flaherty know the difference?

Cormorants do not, as O'Flaherty describes, dive from the air "headlong into the sea" (142). Cormorant species on the coast of Ireland will land on the water, then dive under the surface (Johnsgard, 57-60). Cormorants and shags do not have "long, thin wings" (144). Their wings are wide and wedge-shaped. Merne and Coghlan question how much a cormorant would actually be affected by an injury to a leg. It also would be quite rare behaviour for a flock of cormorants to attack and kill an injured member in this way, though this mobbing of a same-species individual has been recorded in crows, gulls, and other birds.[12] Either O'Flaherty is making up this behaviour for the sake of the story or he is recording a rare incident that few if any naturalists and scientists have observed.

With other details, O'Flaherty is unquestionably accurate. When agitated, cormorants do "shiver" their heads. Among other correct behaviours, he describes their swooping and close-to-the surface flight. Gulls would threaten an injured cormorant. The most aggressive would be the Greater Black-backed Gull (*Larus marinus*), present on the Aran Islands.[13]

Since some of O'Flaherty's descriptions of nature in "The Wounded Cormorant" are questionable is he still ecologically-minded? Is there still an environmental message? (The answer, of course, is "yes"). Perfect ornithology is not critical to the story, and the author makes no claim of accuracy. "The Wounded Cormorant" is significant for literary ecology because he bends traditional cormorant symbolism. He shows the cormorant as any another creature, no worse or better. The story focuses on this animal, showing empathy for an individual of a species never before depicted as a protagonist and one that is normally degraded. O'Flaherty shows a narrator who has taken the time to observe the cormorant, regardless if it is accurate. In Irish and British literature the gull is more commonly a subject, usually as a symbol for

[10] Liam's older brother Tom does not specify a species in his 1934 *Aranmen All*. Here he recalls low-flying cormorants that he and his friends shot at from the rocks (excerpted in Ó hEithir and Ó hEithir, 177). In Liam O'Flaherty's story "Trapped" (1926), he describes a cliff similar to Clogher Mor with a place on a ledge called the "Cormorants' Bed." Black birds fly off when a man approaches. L. O'Flaherty also uses "cormorant" several times in *The Black Soul* (1924) set on islands modeled after the Arans.

[11] Cramp, Bourne and Saunders (1974) found that only Shags nested on the Aran Islands but Sharrock (1977) recorded Great Cormorants there as does D'Arcy in Feehan, et. al. (1994). Merne is probably the most accurate for the Aran islands.

[12] Graves and Merne have doubts and have not witnessed anything like this in cormorants, but neither said it would be impossible. Goethe records the behaviour in other birds.

[13] Sharrock, 208-9 and Armstrong, 1957: 208. Also Graves who writes how quickly Black-backed Gulls on the Isle of May (Scotland) will eat an injured bird.

freedom, adventure, or even a man in love.[14] O'Flaherty flips the normal metaphors and has a gull as the predator and the threat.

One gets the sense that O'Flaherty could have treated this story the same if it was the gull or the rock bird, choosing only different predators, emphasizing that all life is feeding and being fed upon. He pursues this theme in greater detail in other works. Ecologists teach that all species are equally important to an ecosystem, common or rare, aesthetically beautiful to humans or not. In this way, "The Wounded Cormorant" does have an environmental message.

In addition, "The Wounded Cormorant" shows a recognition of chance events in nature. As O'Connor states, O'Flaherty is "absorbed by the inexorable ecology of the universe which changes everything in a matter of moments". One random kick by a goat causes the death of a cormorant. O'Flaherty emphasizes this by framing the story with a paragraph at the beginning and end that describes the sea heaving and pulling at the seaweed where the injury and final death occur. The sea washes the dead cormorant off the rock in the final sentence, nodding to the age and indefatigability of the ocean, thus the smallness of individual life. O'Flaherty writes of this concept extensively in his semi-autobiographical novel *The Black Soul*, published only one year before "The Wounded Cormorant". Note the colour, of course, of the disturbed soul in this title. O'Flaherty's narrator, a disillusioned veteran of WWI, says:

> "I am a part of nature." Before, he had considered himself superior to nature. Now it struck him that he was merely a component part of the universe, just an atom, with less power than the smallest fleck of foam that was snatched by the wind from the nostrils of an advancing wave. Ha! … He watched the tens of millions of people in cities striving for wealth, power and fame, sacrificing everything to gain honour and property … He saw others, lean-faced men, with anger in their eyes and hunger in their stomachs, shouting at the fat-bellied men, agitating for revolution and liberty, shouting about ideals and principles, honour, self-sacrifice, brotherly love! They were still more ridiculous. Did the sea have principles? … Nothing was assured but the air, the earth and the sea. He fancied that he could see the cormorants sitting stupidly on the Jagged Rock, bobbing their heads lazily. "We have lived here five hundred years," they croaked sardonically. "And we have heard it all, all before now! but tell us what does it end in? In ashes and oblivion?" (89-93)

As in *The Black Soul*, O'Flaherty does not bring in religion, destiny, or any higher force into "The Wounded Cormorant". Events just happen.

### How does O'Flaherty's politics affect the story?

In "The Wounded Cormorant" O'Flaherty shows this seabird as equal to other creatures and exemplary of a life within a cruel, random system. By the time he wrote this story, O'Flaherty had been an active member of the Communist Party, wrote for socialist newspapers and journals, fought for the Irish Republicans, and been a member of the Industrial Workers of the World. He grew up in poverty. Like so many of his stories and novels, "The Wounded Cormorant" asks for comparisons between animals and humans. O'Connor writes that O'Flaherty's respect for peasants and their "historical and ecological significance" appears in every story (49).

Does he intend cormorants to be a symbol for the working class? If so, what better animal to represent the downtrodden Irish labourer? The cormorant is a common bird accused of being greedy because it is hungry. It is a dark, unornamented animal, whose physical beauty is

---

[14] See Munsterberg.

rarely noticed or acknowledged. It had never been sympathetically depicted in literature. It is nearly always quiet, without a strong public voice. Perhaps O'Flaherty even knew of their silence, but intentionally wanted the reader to hear their screams, their voice, which society never does. He refers to the flock as the injured cormorant's "comrades". And is it too extreme or radical to push the metaphor and call the gull a symbol for the English, who loomed on a cliff while the Irish tore apart each other? This story was written seventy-five years after the Potato Famine and just two years after the Irish Civil War.

Like the American Jack London, O'Flaherty responded to theories of Social Darwinism, the concept of loosely, though incorrectly, converting Darwin's theories of natural selection into notions of survival of the fittest to explain the behaviour of man. O'Flaherty was also influenced by theories of Naturalism, describing humans in animal-like terms. "The Wounded Cormorant" alludes to humans acting in animal-like ways by describing the behaviour of these birds who attack their weaker fellow, injured only by being in the wrong place at the wrong time within a harsh, indifferent system.

Literary scholars have pointed to O'Flaherty's Naturalism. O'Connor explains that one of O'Flaherty's major interests was showing how man and animals act on their basic drive for survival. She writes, "[O'Flaherty] captures men and animals at the loneliest moments of their lives—the moments of crisis…when his [sic] leg is broken, the wounded cormorant is killed by his own flock" (48). The injured cormorant immediately becomes simply a lonely, unfortunate creature like any other animal or person. Forkner writes, "O'Flaherty has often been described as the most 'naturalistic' of the Irish realists" (Cahalan, 53). Kelly writes of "The Wounded Cormorant":

> The cormorant is more of a symbol than a separate entity. The story is an illustration of 'Nature red in tooth and claw', with no mercy for the weak, and the long strands of seaweed in the opening paragraph point forward to the cormorant's torn and bloody body at the end, lynched and rejected by its fellows. (6)

O'Flaherty writes in a period when biological and environmental ideas are cramming into social and political theories, often displacing traditional religion and faiths.

## Conclusion

O'Flaherty was not what we would call an environmentalist by today's terms, supporting conservation or lecturing about protecting animals. It would be absurd to suggest he had a career goal to alter public opinion about cormorants. In one sense he did have a soft spot for the bird, indicated by his choice of subject in "The Wounded Cormorant" and as evidenced by a letter written two years after publishing the story, after a visit to the Aran islands: "The people are sadly inferior to the land itself. But the sea birds are almost worthy of it. The great cormorants thrilled me" (Cahalan, 54-55).[15] In another sense, however, his messages about cormorants are mixed in *The Black Soul*. He shows them as a mirror for humility against the larger forces of nature, but not intelligent ones. He also shows these seabirds as both greedy and evil just as his British and Irish literary predecessors. The narrator hears a cormorant "dismally" flying past the house after remembering being hit by a shell in the war. In a morose moment later in the story, the narrator has a premonition of his death, reminiscent of Prometheus:

> The wind would sing a cunning hissing song, trying to calm his fears so that the sea

---

[15] 'Great' is probably just an adjective here, not a declaration of species.

would crawl up unawares and devour him. Then all those black cormorants that he had seen on the Jagged Reef would strain out their twisted long necks and tear pieces from his carcass. They would swallow the pieces without chewing them and tear again. Then he discovered himself counting the number of cormorants that were tearing at his body and he tried to shout. But he was too agitated to shout. He crept down under the blankets and commenced to cry. (85-6)

Perhaps O'Connor and others have overemphasized O'Flaherty's keen eye for the natural world, at least with cormorants. On the other hand, O'Flaherty might have observed rare seabird behaviour on the Aran islands or altered zoological details for the sake of his story. Regardless, O'Connor is correct in calling him a literary ecologist, at least in regards to "The Wounded Cormorant", because of his creation of an empathetic protagonist and his representation of an ungoverned natural world.

It matters how the cormorant or any individual species is portrayed in literature over time. Literature about an animal is a reflection, a litmus, of our perception of not just that species, but our entire natural environment, seen through one author's imaginative writing with his or her zoological knowledge and understanding of ecology. Furthermore, a writer's perception and product is connected with his or her social and political views, thus reflective of his or her generation in this way, too. In "Some Principles of Ecocriticism", Howarth writes, "Ecocriticism seeks to examine how metaphors of nature and land are used and abused" (81). Liam O'Flaherty's "The Wounded Cormorant" and the literary history of the depiction of this seabird before him, shows how one species has been used and abused.

## References

Armstrong, Edward. A. 1957. "Birds of the Aran Islands." *Irish Naturalist's Journal*.12.8: 207-8

Armstrong, Edward A. 1958. *The Folklore of Birds*. London: Collins

Bateman, Meg. Literary Scholar. 13 January 2005. Personal communication by email: Collection of the author

Bird, David M. 1999. *The Bird Almanac*. Buffalo: Firefly Books

Borror, Donald J. 1971. *Dictionary of Word Roots and Combining Forms*. Palo Alto: National Press Books

Browning, Robert. 1999. *The Complete Works of Robert Browning*, Vol. X. Allan C. Eds. Dooley and Susan E. Dooley. Athens: Ohio University Press

Cahalan, James M. 1991. *Liam O'Flaherty: A Study of Short Fiction*. Boston: Twayne Publishers

Coghlan, Stephanie. Naturalist. 24, 26 January, 9 February 2005. Personal communication by email, letter: Collection of the author

Cramp, Stanley, W.E.P. Bourne and David Saunders. 1974. *The Seabirds of Britain and Ireland*. London: Collins

Goethe, F. 1940. "Ueber 'Anstoss-Nehmen' bei Vögeln." *Zeitshrift fur Tierpsychologie*, 3: 371-374

Graves, Jeffrey. Ornithologist. 10 February, 10 March 2005. Personal communication by interview and email: Collection of the author

Feehan, John, et al. 1994. *The Book of Aran: The Aran Islands, Co. Galway*. Eds. John Waddell et al. Newtownlynch: Tír Eolas

Harrison, Peter. 1985. *Seabirds*. Boston: Houghton Mifflin

Howarth, William. 1996. "Some Principles of Ecocriticism." *The Ecocriticism Reader*. Eds. Cheryll Glotfelty and Harold Fromm. London: University of Georgia Press. 69-91

Hull, Robin. 2001. *Scottish Birds: Culture and Tradition*. Edinburgh: Mercat Press

Johnsgard, Paul A. 1993. *Cormorants, Darters, and Pelicans of the World*. London: Smithsonian Institution Press

Kelly, Angeline A. 1970. *Liam O'Flaherty the Storyteller*. New York: Harper and Row Publishers

Marvell, Andrew. 2003. *The Poems of Andrew Marvell*. Nigel Smith, ed. London: Longman

Merne, Oscar. Ornithologist. 10, 12, 16 May 2005. Personal communication by email: Collection of the author

Milton, John. 1998. *Paradise Lost*. Ed. Alastair Fowler. 2nd Edition. London: Longman

Munsterberg, Peggy, ed. 1984. *Penguin Book of Bird Poetry*. Harmondsworth: Penguin

Murphy, Andrew. Literary Scholar. 25 March 2005. Personal communication by email: Collection of the author

O'Connor, Helene. 1972. "Liam O'Flaherty: Literary Ecologist." *Éire-Ireland*. 5.2: 2, 47-54

O'Flaherty, Liam. 1924. *The Black Soul*. London: Jonathan Cape

O'Flaherty, Liam. 1926. "The Wounded Cormorant." *The Tent*. London: Jonathan Cape

Ó hEithir, Breandán and Ruairí Ó hEithir, eds. 1991. *An Aran Reader*. Dublin: The Lilliput Press

O'Reilly, Edward. 1864. *An Irish-English Dictionary*. Dublin: James Duffy and Co.

Saul, George Brandon. 1963. "A Wild Sowing: The Short Stories of Liam O'Flaherty." *A Review of English Literature*. Ed. A. Norman Jeffares. 4.3. (July): 108-13

Shakespeare, William. 1998. *The Complete Works*. Eds. Stanley Wells and Gary Taylor. Oxford: Clarendon Press

Sharrock, J.T.R. 1977. *The Atlas of Breeding Birds in Britain and Ireland*. Berkhamsted: T. & A.D. Poyser

Simpson, J.A. and E.S.C. Weiner. 1989. *The Oxford English Dictionary, Second Edition*. Vols. III, XIV, XV. Oxford: Clarendon Press

Synge, J.M. 1995. "Riders to the Sea." *The Playboy of the Western World and Other Plays*. Ed. Ann Saddlemyer. Oxford: Clarendon Press

Washburn, Judith. 1989. "Objective Narration in Liam O'Flaherty's Short Stories." *Éire-Ireland*. 120-5

Wright, William Aldis, ed. 1909. *The Authorized Version of the English Bible 1611*. Cambridge: Cambridge University Press

# Vile Verdicts: The Art of Scottish and Irish Law in the Novels of Wilkie Collins

*Aoife Leahy*

In this paper I will examine two novels by Wilkie Collins that address interesting Scottish and Irish variations (or deviations, according to characters in the texts) in nineteenth-century British law. The first novel, *Man and Wife* (1870), deals with two generations of intertwined families and the effects of complex regional laws on the marriages of a mother and daughter, each named Anne Silvester. The second, *The Law and the Lady* (1875), follows on from some of the issues of marital law raised in *Man and Wife*, but focuses mainly on the notorious middle verdict of Not Proven in Scottish criminal cases.

In the Prologue of *Man and Wife*, the marriage of Anne and John Vanborough is proved to be invalid, although they have been married for thirteen years and have a daughter who was previously considered to be legitimate. Since Anne was a Catholic, her husband converted to Catholicism so that she would marry him and, although neither was Irish, they happened to marry in Ireland. Now that Vanborough wants to discard his wife to marry more advantageously, he investigates the marriage to find a loophole to set him free. His solicitor, Delamayn, finds exactly what is needed: no convert to Catholicism can be married by a Catholic priest in Ireland, unless a year has first elapsed. Delamayn explains that not only is such a marriage invalid, but the priest has committed a criminal act:

> By the Irish Statute of George the Second [...] every marriage celebrated by a Popish priest, between two Protestants, or between a Papist and any person who has been a Protestant within twelve months of the marriage, is declared null and void [...] Mr Vanborough is a single man; Mrs Vanborough is a single woman; their child is illegitimate, and the priest, Ambrose Redman, is liable to be tried, and punished, as a felon, for marrying them. (27-8)

Although other novels by Collins such as *The Haunted Hotel* (1878) and *Blind Love* (1890) are set partially in Ireland, this is not the case in *Man and Wife*. The Vanborough marriage ceremony is spoken of retrospectively, and John's betrayal of his wife takes place in Hampstead, reflecting the fact that two Englishmen – Vanborough and Delamayn – are ultimately responsible. Although Collins uses Ireland as an idyllic retreat for Agnes Lockwood in *The Haunted Hotel*, he does not always idealise the location, since *Blind Love* interrogates terrorism against landowners in a rural town. In *Man and Wife*, however, the setting of the marriage is simply absent, because in a sense, it is irrelevant.

Although Delamayn refers to what he calls the "Irish marriage-law" (27), the omniscient narrator sets the responsibility firmly on the English legislature and on Delamayn himself as part of a flawed legal system. The narrator tells us that, "Mr Delamayn stated the law, as that law still stands [in 1870], to the disgrace of the English Legislature, and the English Nation" (27). Ireland is not the site of responsibility for the marriage law, since the act was an imposition by George II on Ireland, and was intended to limit the rights of Catholics. It is, thus, a disgrace of the English legislature. Furthermore, as a typical English solicitor, Delamayn fails by interpreting the law in terms of cold facts or statements and does not exert his moral responsibility to suggest that Vanborough should remarry his wife and make provision for their daughter, although this could certainly now be done. As Collins had shown in *No Name* (1862), a couple could marry and nevertheless will their assets to their illegitimate child, particularly if there were no subsequent heirs born within the marriage. Although Delamayn is deficient in human emotions and accepts the mistreatment of Anne because "the law justified it" (38), he also lacks the imagination to see how the law may be moulded creatively until it fits the lives of real people. Later in the text, Sir Patrick Lundie shows how a more imaginative and more humane use of the law is possible.

The deserted Anne reverts to her maiden name, Silvester, and starts a new life under the protection of her friend Blanche. The shock of the invalidity of her marriage causes her early death, however, and in her last moments she is haunted by the fear that her daughter – another Anne Silvester, since the girl now has no legal claim to her father's name without his consent – will suffer a similar fate. This plot device allows Collins to link the Irish and Scottish marriage laws together, since the daughter will suffer due to Scottish law, just as the mother has suffered due to Irish law. Given that the only real similarity between the two sets of laws was the uncertainty that each could bring to a marriage, Collins needed to find such a fictional link.

In the second generation of *Man and Wife*, Delamayn's son Geoffrey seduces the younger Anne Silvester who has grown up to be a respectable governess. Anne becomes pregnant while she is in Scotland with her employers and decides that her only options are suicide or a private marriage, since Geoffrey will not marry her publicly. She persuades him to deliberately enter into a Scottish irregular marriage to ensure that their child is legitimate. By presenting themselves at an inn, and declaring to the landlady that they are married, Geoffrey and Anne will be man and wife under Scottish law. Anne explains, "You know that we are in Scotland. You know that there are neither forms, ceremonies, nor delays in marriage, here […] A man and a woman who wish to be married [in Scotland] have only to declare themselves married? and the thing is done" (86). Although this sounds more like a weekend away than a wedding ceremony, the agreement of both parties to take this pretence at an inn as the beginning of their marriage would be legally binding. No minister or witnesses (aside from the unwitting landlady) would be required in Anne's plan, thus preventing the exposure that might cut Geoffrey out of his father's will. Geoffrey is called to England urgently hours before the plan is to be executed, however, and sends his friend Arthur to take a letter to Anne at the inn. Asking for Anne as his wife, to prevent shocking the landlady, it is thus Arthur who apparently enters into the planned irregular marriage. Geoffrey, mirroring his father in his mistreatment of women, takes advantage of the mistake and never returns to keep his promise to Anne.

Collins highlights the potentially disastrous consequences of irregular marriages by involving the fates of a chain of characters in the event at the inn. Arthur has already proposed marriage to Blanche, Anne's pupil and the daughter of her mother's friend. Understandably, he is unaware that he may have accidentally married someone else, without his knowledge or consent. Geoffrey's family plan to marry him to a wealthy widow, so it is in his interests to disown Anne and claim in public that she is married to Arthur. This would free him of the dangers posed if Anne sued him for breach of promise, a common concern after failed engagements in the nineteenth century. While Geoffrey decides what to do in the background, Anne suffers a stillbirth amongst strangers, remaining unconscious and under medical care for weeks. Upon her recovery, Blanche has married Arthur, but Geoffrey is already claiming that this marriage is invalid. Blanche's marriage to Arthur, in front of a congregation, with a minister and a licence, is in sharp contrast to the irregular marriage. Nevertheless, the marriage that comes first takes precedent, if it can be legally established. Until the matter is resolved, Blanche and Arthur cannot have children, since they could be declared illegitimate at a later date, and Anne cannot marry any genuine suitor.

After disagreements between solicitors as to whether Anne and Arthur can really be considered Man and Wife, the matter is finally settled by the letter that Geoffrey sent to the inn with Arthur. In his haste, Geoffrey had written his message on the back of a letter from Anne, which she had signed "Your loving wife" (154). His addition promises to marry her, and is signed "Your loving husband" (154). This written declaration is enough to establish that Anne and Geoffrey are married under Scottish law: "A written promise of marriage exchanged between a man and a woman, in Scotland, marries that man and woman under Scotch law" (523). Because the date and the time of day are both written on the postscript, it can be established that Anne was not a single woman when Arthur visited her at the inn. What was intended as a note becomes, effectively, a marriage licence, a chilling warning to Collins' readers to be wary of what they sign when visiting Scotland. Unfortunately for Anne, she is forced to claim Geoffrey as her husband to validate Blanche's marriage to Arthur, although she no longer has any wish to marry him after the loss of their child. There are no grounds for divorce, so only the death of either husband or wife can dissolve this irregular marriage. In a Wilkie Collins novel, however, such a marriage will come to its dramatic conclusion. Geoffrey begins a plot to murder Anne, only to be killed himself by his insane landlady Hester Dethridge. This leaves Anne free to remarry and reinforces Collins' tongue-in-cheek exposure of the dangerous nature of landladies, women who may murder their tenants or who may simply bear witness to the indiscretions that establish irregular marriages.

Wilkie Collins is a highly ironical writer, who is often distanced from his characters and even his narrators, but he makes his own viewpoint clear on this occasion in an appendix to the main text. In a rather Swiftian comment, he declares: "A legal enactment providing for the sale of your wife, when you have done with her, or of your husband, when you really can't put up with him any longer, appears to be all that is wanting to render this North British estimate of the estate of Matrimony practically complete" (Appendix Note B, 646). Collins leaves the reader with no doubt that he disapproves of Scottish law in relation to irregular marriages. Unlike the Prologue, in which Ireland as a location is noticeably absent, the Scottish marriage section of the story is set firmly in Scotland. The inn where the disputed marriage between Anne and Arthur takes place is inhabited by a comically stereotypical Scottish waiter, Bishopriggs, who makes lewd jokes about young married couples. Bishopriggs' comments go on for several chapters and are absurdly over the top: "Eh, my leddy! here he is in flesh and blood. Mercy presairve us! do you lock the door of the nuptial chamber in your husband's face? [...] I'm away before she falls into your arms! Rely on it, I'll no' come in again, without knocking first!" (125). Bishopriggs steals Geoffrey's letter at one point and adds to the confusion over which man is married to Anne for some time. His inappropriate behaviour and lack of respect for the institution of marriage, punctuated by his colloquial expletives, seems to reinforce the idea that Scotland is to blame for its own irregular marriages. In this case, the bad law is not an imposition from outside, but an archaic tradition that Collins feels should be abandoned. *Man and Wife* also provides the reader with Sir Patrick Lundie, however, an upper-class character who declares himself to be Scottish and wanders about "humming an old Scotch air" (90). Trained in the niceties of Scottish law, Sir Patrick has a highly creative and imaginative approach to solving legal problems that may be linked to his Celtic outlook, in contrast to the dry approach of English solicitors. It seems regrettable that Collins does not make Sir Patrick more overtly Scottish, since unlike Bishopriggs, his speech and manners are quite anglicised. Yet his first name could link Ireland and Scotland together in a positive sense if Collins intends his reader to recall Saint Patrick, the Scottish-born patron saint of Ireland.

Also balancing the attack on the Scottish marriage laws is Collins' attention to Hester Dethridge at the end of the novel. Married in England, she is persecuted by a drunken and abusive husband. English law does not give her the right to separate her life and property from his, until she is driven to murder him. Her subsequent attack on Geoffrey frees Anne in the only way possible, by the ultimate dissolution of marriage with the death of one party. Collins declares in the preface to Man and Wife that his fiction "is founded on facts, and aspires to afford what help it may towards hastening the reform of certain abuses which have been too long suffered to exist amongst us" (Preface, 5). He goes on to argue for the reformation of marriage laws throughout Great Britain and Ireland, making particular reference in the preface to cases similar to Hester Dethridge's situation. Collins does not state what is always implied in his fiction, that the careful studying of his characters' predicaments will instruct his readers in what not to do in their own legal crises, as if his novels were handbooks full of case studies. The claim that his novels are manifestos for reform may be partially true, but Collins also demonstrates how to manipulate the law as it now exists, whether his reader finds himself – or, as is more likely, herself – in Ireland, Scotland or England. Collins' assertion that he is attempting "to convince the reader that I am not leading him astray" (5) by providing factual information in his preface and appendix, only thinly veils the fact that many of his novels answer legal questions that trouble women in particular.

What should a lady do if she fears her marriage is invalid? Linking Collins' 1875 novel *The Law and the Lady* back to the earlier *Man and Wife* (1870) is the teaser on the first page as Valeria marries her husband Eustace Macallan. She asks the reader: "Was it really possible, in spite of his mother's objections to our marriage, that we were Man and Wife?" (7). The intertextual hint that the marriage may not be valid is explained by the fact that Eustace has married under a false surname, Woodville, to conceal his past. When Valeria discovers this, her investigations are set in motion, as she fears that she is still a single woman. There is a danger that Eustace could simply discard her in the future without any legal consequences to him, just as Vanborough disposes of his spouse in *Man and Wife*. This strand of the storyline is resolved early in the narrative, however, for marriages under false names were legally valid as long as one party was unaware of the deception. In a sense, the Collins' self-referential clue sets the reader on a false trail, but the novel does follow on from Man and Wife in that another aspect of Scottish law is dealt with.

In *The Law and the Lady*, a peculiarity of Scottish law means that Eustace has been found neither guilty nor innocent of murdering his first wife. Instead, the verdict is Not Proven, a middle option that allows the jury to admit that they lack the evidence to convict the accused without asserting a belief that he is innocent. Eustace's friend Major Fitz-David argues that such a verdict must be unjust:

> There is a verdict allowed by the Scotch law, which (so far as I know) is not permitted by the laws of any other civilised country on the face of the earth. When the jury are in doubt whether to condemn or acquit the prisoner brought before them, they are permitted in Scotland, to express that doubt by a form of compromise. (101)

The main action of the novel concerns the quest of Valeria, as Eustace's second wife, to clear her husband's name and finally prove his innocence. She goes through the published Report of the Trial[1] to learn about Eustace's case and, following it with her, the reader gains a better understanding of the reasons for the verdict. The jury compromises on a Not Proven verdict because of compelling arguments for and against finding Eustace guilty of murder. Eustace's first wife Sara died of an arsenic overdose, arsenic that Eustace himself had purchased. He asserts that his wife asked him to buy it for household use. The prosecution argues that he deliberately poisoned her, while the defence argues that Sara secretly took small quantities of the poison to improve her blotchy complexion and went too far. Small amounts of arsenic can be used as an effective beauty product, albeit with an obvious risk to the user. The real truth is that Sara committed suicide because Eustace did not love her, something that is only

---

[1] For an account of court reports, see Anthea Trodd, 1989.

discovered when her suicide note is retrieved years later thanks to Valeria's investigations.

Valeria's anger at the use of the Scottish verdict rather than a so-called English one is clearly expressed in a letter to Eustace: "I told you that the first thought that came to me, when I heard what the Scotch jury had done, was the thought of setting their Vile Verdict right [...] to change that underhand Scotch verdict of Not Proven, into an honest English verdict of Not Guilty" (116). Yet the working out of the plot seems to indicate the verdict was the fairest one at the time, in the face of conflicting evidence. It made it less likely that an innocent man like Eustace would be found Guilty and executed. As Jenny Bourne Taylor (Collins, 1999: 423n) has pointed out, real life murder suspects like John Lovie and Madeleine Smith were acquitted on the Not Proven verdict in the nineteenth century and this spared their lives. Valeria and Eustace now have the means to begin proceedings that could lead to a Not Guilty verdict, as their solicitor explains:

> [Eustace Macallan] cannot be tried again on what we call the criminal charge [...] But, if the facts which were involved at the criminal trial can also be shown to be involved in a civil case (and in this case they can), the entire matter may be made the subject of a new legal inquiry; and the verdict of a second jury, completely vindicating your husband, may thus be obtained. (385-6)

They decide, however, to wait in honour of Sara's memory, but the letter will allow their son to clear the Macallan name in the future. Only biased characters in *The Law and the Lady* argue that the Scottish verdict is a trap for the unfortunate English person who is unlucky enough to be tried in Scotland. Collins is ultimately open about the Not Proven verdict, and does not insert a footnote or appendix to condemn it in his own voice. Intriguingly, the Not Proven verdict is still possible in Scotland today and continues to provide an extra twist in the plots of more recent murder mysteries. This includes a 1993 episode of *Taggart* entitled "Fatal Inheritance", in which Hannah Gordon plays Dr Janet Napier, a woman whose case has been deemed Not Proven by her jury as the story begins.

The characters discussed in both novels are victims of the law, but the converse is always possible in Wilkie Collins' stories. Collins exposes potentially bad laws in his novels, laws that punish those who have done no wrong. Yet he also hints that even unsound laws could have positive outcomes, liberating those who learned to manipulate them correctly. The reader can see, for instance, how the elder Anne Silvester in *Man and Wife* could have found a way to separate herself from her unworthy husband had it been her wish instead of his, avoiding Hester Dethridge's extreme solution of murder. Under different circumstances, the 'Irish' statute intended to discriminate against Catholics could, ironically, have freed a Catholic woman into a new and independent life. For Collins, the law is an art to be mastered and the author always implies that a more creative understanding of the law could lead to progress of the sort that mere reforms alone could not accomplish. Coming from a family of artists, Collins studied the law as a young man[2] and these two elements often seem married together in his novels. It is clear that *The Law and the Lady's* Valeria has discovered an important witness when Miserrimus Dexter is interviewed by her in chapters entitled 'First View' (201) and 'Second View' (208), newspaper headlines normally reserved for important exhibitions of art. Typically, the first view was the private exhibition and the second the public, just as Valeria sees Dexter in his private and then publicly acceptable aspects in rapid succession. The court case fails to uncover the truth because only the public Dexter appeared as a witness; Valeria succeeds because she is imaginative enough to find fresh perspectives on the facts.

Many of Collins' characters fall into peril not because their fate is inevitable, but because

---

[2] For a description of Collins' legal training, see Catherine Peters, 1991: 68-9.

they are unaware of the gaps or loopholes in the law that could have saved them. In *No Name*, Mr and Mrs Vanstone accidentally disinherit their own children by marrying, but drawing up the correct legal documents at the right moment would have prevented this. Happily, Collins' readers can use his novels as guides to avoid making the same mistakes. Even better, the younger Anne Silvester is guaranteed a happy ending in the closing pages of *Man and Wife* because she finally marries Sir Patrick, a gentleman who is not only wealthy and kind but who is also an expert in the law. Sir Patrick understands the law as a delicate art that is to be practised compassionately, and this is what sets him aside from merely factual practitioners like Delamayn. He uses artistic language to explain points of law to his friends and "would put the view in quite a new light" (198), being imaginative enough to see possibilities that others miss. He declares early in the case that Anne and Arthur are not married, but could be married if one decided to claim the other, while other solicitors will not accept this accurate but necessarily inconclusive interpretation. Sir Patrick is the ideal solicitor, creatively and compassionately moulding the law to suit the needs of those around him. He does not allow his niece Blanche to marry before drafting the correct marriage settlements for her, anticipating any problems that could emerge from a breakdown of the marriage long before they arise. If every woman had an imaginative legal expert permanently at her disposal, as Collins seems to infer, the quality of women's lives would improve dramatically.

Collins' other novels prove that 'standard' or English laws could be just as convoluted and confusing as anything presented in *Man and Wife* and *The Law and the Lady*. Some of his most famous novels, including The Woman in White (1860), depend on marriage laws and illegitimacy to give their villains their motives for crime. *No Name* is even more complicated than *Man and Wife* in its depiction of a legally disastrous marriage. Why then, are Scottish and Irish laws picked out for special attention? Perhaps even this can be explained in terms of art. In Collins' day, exhibitions of Scottish and Irish paintings were extremely popular events, not because they were better or worse than English exhibitions, but for their own particular flavour. *Man and Wife* and *The Law and the Lady* demonstrate, like all of Collins' novels, an artistic appreciation for the law. They expand the reader's horizons, however, by providing a separate display of regional laws that are interesting enough to be exhibited for attention in their own right.

## References

Chandler, Glenn. 1993. "Fatal Inheritance". *Taggart*. Directed by Mary Murray. ITV Broadcast 1 Jan

Collins, Wilkie. 1999. *The Law and the Lady*. Ed. Jenny Bourne Taylor. Oxford: Oxford University Press. First published 1875

Collins, Wilkie. 1999. *Man and Wife*. With preface and appendix by the author. Ed. Norman Page. Oxford: Oxford University Press. First published 1870

Peters, Catherine. 1991. *The King of Inventors: A Life of Wilkie Collins*. London: Secker & Warburg

Trodd, Anthea. 1989. *Domestic Crime in the Victorian Novel*. London: Palgrave Macmillan

# Reassessing Post-colonial Criticism for (Northern) Ireland and Scotland: Rewriting National Paradigms

*Stefanie Lehner*

This paper examines the contentious use of post-colonial theory in Irish and Scottish Studies in order to illuminate the problematics inherent in a post-colonialism which centres its analysis around the monolithic terminology of the colonial divide and maintains the teleological discourse of the nation as the main and only level at which the post-colonial seems to be of any relevance. The first part of my analysis aims to re-access its potential as an enabling *ethical* criticism for cross-archipelagic Studies through the insights of subaltern concerns, and this provides the basis for the second part of the paper which looks closely at the work of the Scottish writer James Kelman and the Northern Irish writer Robert McLiam Wilson.

## The Contentions of Post-colonialism's National Telos

To begin with, it is important to emphasise that the emergence of a resurgent nationalism plays an important role in the anti-colonial struggle for liberation. One of post-colonialism's foundational texts, Frantz Fanon's *The Wretched of the Earth* (1965), privileges nationalism "as the principal remedial means whereby the colonised culture overcomes the psychological damage of colonial racism" (Gandhi, 111). As post-colonialism has tended to postulate the post-colonial nation as "the only legitimate end of decolonisation" (Gandhi, 111), such a conception of 'post'-colonial seems in regard to its implicit temporal dimension – as often marked by the use of a hyphen – to imply a linear logic of progress which shows the potential to obscure the unchanged power-relations within national formations. While Fanon already warned of the "empty shell" (119) of its ensuing bourgeois ideology, a more succinct critique of the nationalist project has come from the Subaltern Studies Group in India. Its name, deriving from the terminology of the Italian Marxist Antonio Gramsci, connotes its alignment with oppressed social groups that have been subjugated, excluded and oppressed by the hegemonic classes. By foregrounding how class issues intersect with other marginalised identity formations related to gender, sexuality and ethnicity, the Subaltern Studies method ruptures the notion that a resurgent national culture can somehow resolve the vexed issues of identity and belonging.

While Subaltern Studies actually facilitates a post-colonial understanding across the national divide, many academics have, however, proven reluctant to abandon the comforting paradigms of national cultures and literatures. Furthermore, the claim for a post-colonial reading of Ireland and Scotland is, in regard to their relation to Britishness and the British Empire, contentious. One of the key texts of post-colonialsm, *The Empire Writes Back* (1989), asserts that "[w]hile it is possible to argue that these societies were the first victims of English expansion, their subsequent complicity in the British imperial enterprise makes it difficult for colonized peoples outside Britain to accept their identity as post-colonial" (2003, 31-2). Consequently, their inclusion under *their* definition of 'post-colonial' is denied. The historical, political and economic relations of Ireland and Scotland in the imperial project complicate the easy allocation post-colonialism seems to make in terms of coloniser-colonised. Thus, while post-colonialism's major strength lies in its role as an ethical criticism which morally evaluates colonial relationships in their fundamental inequality and continuing political outcomes, the uneasy fit Ireland and Scotland present to this crucial ethical examination illuminates a major problematic of post-colonial theory.

## Post-colonial Approaches in Irish and Scottish Studies: A Critique

Post-colonial theories have become increasingly applied to readings of Irish literature. As Colin Graham remarks, in order to justify Ireland's post-colonial status Irish post-colonialism has made its claims through boasting its originality (Ireland was the *first* to be colonised and to decolonise), or its complete exceptionality (Ireland is the *last* to be decolonised) (Graham 2003: 246). This sort of privileging emphasis on Ireland's "anomalous" status has created what Bart Moore-Gilbert calls a "distasteful [...] beauty parade [of] the most oppressed colonial [...] or the most 'truly' post-colonial subjects" (12). In this "'compare and contrast' attitude to imperial suffering" (Graham 2003: 245), Ireland, in contrast to Scotland, has argued its case for an acknowledged place on the post-colonial agenda. In this regard, Declan Kiberd's *Inventing Ireland* (1995) asserts Ireland's leadership to "the developing world" as "the first people to decolonise in the twentieth century" (5). Yet, while post-colonial comparisons such as Kiberd's have sought to get away from British or European contexts, their post-colonial readings of Ireland seem to get entangled in what Joep Leerssen calls "auto-exoticism": the attempts to present Ireland's unique "Otherness" to direct attention towards a wider-world-view remain organised around a putatively English "core".[1]

Accordingly, as Irish post-colonial readings have often focused on the constituting influence English colonialism had on anti-colonial Irish nationalism, they have tended to fall back on what Edward Said has termed the "rhetoric of blame".[2] Field Day's critique of the "ultimate failure" of Irish cultural nationalism" (Deane 1990: 3) seems at first an astounding echo of the Subaltern Studies Group. However, its endeavour to establish a 'counter-hegemony' in opposition to British cultural imperialism seeks, in Seamus Deane's words, to retrieve "a meta-narrative which is [...] hospitable to all the micro-narratives" (1991: xix). This establishment of a national canon preserves not only the ideological necessity of the nation as the essential and even liberating unit of culture, but also replicates the same excluding structures as colonialism. Thus, Deane's stance towards Irish nationalism is inconsistent: he is reluctant to leave behind the concept of the nation; instead, he embraces the ethics of the colonial divide by simply blaming the British for its failure (Graham 2001: 87-89). While the predominance of the 'nation'-narrative for post-colonial identitarian politics has subsumed other issues such as class and gender, it presents in the Irish context further problematics in terms of its political implications in the polarized debate between Revisionism and Nationalism.

Thus, as Richard Kirkland suggests in his recent *Identity Parades* (2002), instead of fitting Ireland within a pre-existing paradigm it should be used as a force to rethink the post-colonial. This is what Graham seeks to propagate in his salient approach to Irish post-colonialism. By invoking the Subaltern critique on nationalism, Graham recognises how the "critical turn" in post-colonial studies enabled liberation from unilateral power dynamics. He recognises how the renowned work of Homi Bhabha complicates the colonial discourse by disclosing its inherent ambivalence which breaks the ultimate opposition of the colonial divide through mimicry, irony and subversion. Adopting Bhabha's concepts, Graham's advocacy of the "liminal spaces" of the colonial encounter enables a post-colonial reading of Ireland as well as

---

[1] Leerssen describes this as "a mode of seeing, presenting and representing oneself in one's otherness (in this case: one's non-Englishness)", which leads to "a paradoxical dissociation of the Irish author from his/her Irish subject matter. The destinatory vector towards an English audience is so strong that the author no longer identifies with the country which is represented, but becomes an intermediary, an exteriorized, detached observer" (Leerssen, 35-7).

[2] Said regards the post-colonial "rhetoric of blame" as responsible for the violence and misunderstanding which spring from the growing nationalistic hostilities between the Western and the non-Western world. This oppositional mutual blaming is, as Gandhi states, often "manipulated by what we might call the post-colonial right" (129). See Said, 19.

Scotland, which instead of treating them as homogeneous entities comprised entirely of oppressors or victims acknowledges their inner differences and specificities.

However, Bhabha's poststructuralist "hybridity" has been severely criticised for its apolitical stance; in short, as Aijaz Ahmad points out, there is a neglect of any "material coordinates" (287). Ahmad's attack on a post-colonial theory which is "remarkably free of gender, class [and] identifiable political location" (287) foregrounds how these issues, which are often in conflict with nationalist discourses, mark important sites of resistance against (neo-)colonialism. The radical potential inherent in a post-colonial criticism which combines the material focus of a Gramscian-influenced Subaltern method with Bhabha's post-structuralist notion of cultural difference is able to undercut the unitary fabric of post-colonial readings which maintain the teleological necessity of the nation. Thus, by resuscitating the dissidences subalterneity noisily brings into the post-colonial debate, such an approach is able to expose affiliate disempowerments across and within national boundaries.

Furthermore, the problematic position of Ulster "in-between" its surrounding nationalisms challenges the neat demarcations between national identities. However, while Northern Ireland has repeatedly attained a post-colonial relevance in regard to its "anomalous state", it is ironic, then, that David Lloyd complains in *Bullán* about the lacking attention to "larger tendencies" (87) and propagates a comparative context beyond "the insular scholarship within Ireland" (92). But as comparisons with non-European countries tend to cause such aforementioned "exoticism and orientalism", Graham and Willy Maley suggest that it should be far more constructive to seek comparisons with "nations closer to home – Scotland springs to mind – from which much could be learned" (151). Yet, whereas Scotland's similar historic position within the Empire should grant it, in Maley's term, "a post-colonial passport", post-colonial readings have been opposed or overlooked in Scotland.

Nevertheless, Craig Beveridge and Ronald Turnbull's *The Eclipse of Scottish Culture* (1989) uses Fanon's concept of "inferiorisation" to explain how an internalised parochial status has lead to "a profound self-hatred" (Craig, 1996: 12). Recuperating the idea that a reinvigorated national culture resolves the identity crisis, they show the tendency to subsume other issues under the privileged aspect of the "national". This is apparent in Craig's argument that "it is by the colour of our vowels: the rigidity of class speech in Britain" (1996: 12) upon which Scotland's inferiorisation is based on. There is a risk here of conflating racial discriminations (colour) with issues of class and nationality. This analysis also ignores class distinctions within Scotland – as his concern seems to revolve solely around working-class speech. Berthold Schoene, who argues for the appliance of Fanon's "evolutionary" stages to the history of Scottish Literature, is, as he states, however "doubtful […] that a post-colonial analysis of contemporary Scottish literature would be at all appropriate" (116-17). Asserting that "over the last few decades [Scottish literature] has ceased to be preoccupied with its post-colonial status" (117), he addresses the notion that the increasing devolution can liberate Scotland from issues of inequality and disempowerment. While Michael Gardiner seems justifiably worried about "the promiscuous use" (24) of post-colonial theory, he denies Scotland a post-colonial status as he considers its use to be "always […] undermined by other types of subjective structuring such as class, ethnicity [and] sexual difference" (39). However, as I have argued above, he ignores that post-colonial criticism has in recent years gone a considerable way to refine and redefine its terms by moving away from crude categorisations in dichotomies of national relevance.

Refuting the hegemony of national discourses found in "conventional" post-colonial criticism, the Subaltern method offers the potential to trace affiliate concerns within the socio-cultural archipelago of my survey. By foregrounding such issues as class, race and gender, it permits the establishment of affiliations between writers that circumvent the naïve equation of nations as already agreed concepts. As such, it provides an enabling critical approach for the work of contemporary Scottish and Northern Irish writers, as Kelman and McLiam Wilson, which is able to illustrate their political commitment to uncover the iniquitous power relations that exist within national or metropolitan constellations.

## James Kelman and Robert McLiam Wilson: Rewriting National Paradigms

Concerned with questions of identity, in particular class and representation, which affect the everyday experiences of ordinary people, both writers explore in their novels the "liminal spaces" of their native Glasgow and Belfast – both former imperial cities whose increasing poverty has been screened off in their official representation, as apparent in their respective 'City of Culture' campaigns. I will now briefly look at their linguistic and stylistic interventions as a means to resist the still prevailing cultural imperialism, which Kelman addressed in his Booker Prize speech wherein he connects his work to an outspoken "post-colonial" agenda "towards decolonisation and self-determination" (Kelman cited in Chadwick, n.p.). Their working-class background offers them a critical distance to the language of power and authority in their differing yet complimentary strategies, which are not reducible to some national predisposition, but inflected by issues of class.

Similar to Ngugi Wa Thiong'O, who states that "[l]anguage carries culture, and culture carries, particularly through orature and literature, the entire body of values by which we come to perceive ourselves and our place in the world" (118), Kelman's "politics of voice" is alive to the power-nexus of languages, literatures and the norm-setting authority of British culture. As he asserts in an interview:

[L]anguage is the culture – if you lose your language you've lost your culture [...]. That's what happens with all these stupid fucking books by bad average writers because they've lost their culture, they've given it away. Not only that, what they're saying is it's inferior, because they make anybody who comes from that culture speak in a hybrid language, whereas they speak standard English. And their language is the superior one. (McLean, 72)

Rejecting the inscribed value-system of this linguistic hegemony, Kelman aims to create what he terms a "value-free prose" (Kelman cited in Jaggi, n.p.). By transforming the English language, as he states, "as something that could be mine", his transcription of "the Scottish working-class way of speaking a language" (Kelman cited in Jaggi, n.p.) intermingles English with the demotic speech of his local dialect. Including, through his use of as many "fuck's" and "cunt's" as you hear on Glasgow's streets, the previously excluded speech of the majority of people in the written language of his fiction, he exposes the distorting gap that exists between "official" literary representations and reality. Abolishing the hegemonic implications of any authorial positioning by "getting rid of that standard third party narrative voice" (McNeill, 4), the narration is freed from any hierarchical demarcation. Emphasised by the lack of any speech-markers, the narrative voice resides on an equal level to the characters.

While Kelman's "politics of voice" are able to realise an authentic rendition of his oral culture, McLiam Wilson's language use is overshadowed by what Maley calls the Irish "politics of pronunciation" (2002: 21) as determined by colonial legacies and class boundaries. Thus, McLiam Wilson's choice seeks rather to follow the Joycean example of parodying and satirising the English language. This becomes apparent in the opening paragraph of his debut novel, *Ripley Bogle*, entitled "It Begins":

*(Enter man with money. He waits. Enter woman, misclothed and passionate. They rut. Exeunt.)*

'Aaaaaaaaeeeeeeiiiiccchhhh!'

> The world's disquiet gets underway. Birth scene. The calm cry of parturition. For the one. The incandescent infant. Mrs Bogle screaming her way through the unwilling production of Master Ripley Bogle, the famed. Splayed knees and bucking loins. Dirty, heavyheaded, eponymous bastard shoving his angry way out. (1)

Displaying an inventive creativity through the creation of new words such as "misclothed", the articulate expressions of "parturition" and "incandescent" rub rather uneasily against the colloquial "rut" and "bastard", and the adjective-noun combination of "calm cry" or "incandescent infant" seem incongruous. Through this discrepancy between different registers of speech and the unexpected combinations of words, Wilson challenges accepted linguistic norms of English.

This is also underlined by the way the eponymous hero's destitution as a tramp in London from Belfast's Catholic working-class is put into stark contrast with his stylised use of English. Kelman also uses this contrast of linguistic registers connoting class and power in a scene in *How Late It Was, How Late*. The Doctor's patronising attitude towards Sammy marks him as the powerless "other": "I find your language offensive" (225). While it is actually the doctor whose treatment and language is offensive, Kelman exposes the gap that exists between their unequal power relations. In contrast to Bogle's mimicry which, in Bhabha's conception, menaces the authority position that the mastery of English signifies, Sammy angrily refuses to accommodate his language use to any authority: "Ah well fuck ye then" (225). Whereas Kelman's refusal to take part in 'their' "language-power-game" enables his close "facticity" to the actualities of working-class speech, McLiam Wilson, by contrast, creates a satiric displacement. This produces a Brechtian *Verfremdungseffekt*, which aims, as Brecht states, "to make the spectator adopt an attitude of inquiry and criticism in his approach to the incident" (136). This is also achieved through McLiam Wilson's use of shifting narrative positions (between first-person and third-person narration) which functions – similar to Kelman's internalised polyphony (through his use of a free indirect discourse) – to multiply the viewpoints, and defies any stable positioning or singular vision of the world. These created double perspectives allow subversions of the unitary discourses of both colonialism and nationalism.

Bogle's defiant claim for a hybrid identity – dubbing himself "Ripley Irish British Bogle" (16) in opposition to the North's two opposing camps – allows him an ironic mimicry of both Irish and British positions. This becomes apparent in his solidarity-seeking comment on the continuing colonial politics of the British in Northern Ireland:

> I always felt rather sorry for the British in Ireland. They didn't want to be there. […] Let's face it. Most European countries had their empire at some time or another. Eventually, they crumble and another one comes along. […] The British got it wrong. They grew all philanthropic and noble. They were the only imperial power trying to give their empire back. That was their mistake. We wogs, us wogs, we didn't like that. Not at all. (111)

By adopting a sympathetic understanding towards the British in his voice, he modulates this perspective with his own Irishness by combining the imperialistic offence of "wogs" with the communal pronoun "we". Bogle's schizophrenic ambiguity between Irish and British positions moves, as he states, always "[f]rom one extreme to the other" (184). "Before fleeing [his] beastly birthplace" (190) he rebels against what Eve Patten calls "the pretension and trappings of home" (138):

> We Irish, we're all fucking idiots. No other place can rival us for the senseless
> sentimentality in which we wallow. Us and Ulster. The God-beloved fucking Irish, as
> they'd like to think. As a people we're a shambles; as a nation – a disgrace; as a culture
> we're a bore ... individually we're often repellent. But we love it, us Irish fellows. [...]
> All that old Irishness crap promoted by Americans and professors of English
> Literature. menace and cupidity. All balls. (190)

Yet in Cambridge it is from this adopted perspective of the "stamp of downing Celticism" (204)
that Bogle savagely mocks the dissolved identity of the former imperial power:

> In one of my epic, universal moments, I conclude with rare intelligence that an
> Englishman's lack of interest in himself naturally precludes any interest in others
> Remote, impersonal, disengaged. Easy pickings for the dark, concocted vitality of the
> Celt (i.e. me). (202)

Such a carnivalesque inversion of the established power-hierarchy turns from the mimicry of
English colonial authority, in Bhabha's understanding, "a difference that is almost nothing but
not quite – to *menace* – a difference that is almost total but not quite" (91). Thus, the seemingly
innocent "pet of the smart set" (204) who proves so susceptible to the assimilation of English
cultural (pre)conceptions soon exceeds "the leeway people gave [him] on account of [his]
Irishness and hard-boy image": "I persisted on going to far. I picked fights, skipped lectures,
told lies, got pissed, taunted dons and made fewer friends. I fucked everyone off in a big way"
(246). Through Bogle's satiric imitation of the colonial inscription of the barbaric "other",
Wilson exposes this Irishness simply as the copy of a copy, which undermines any notion of an
"authentic" identity.

Bogle's marginal status in society as well as his liminal position in-between the oppositional
identitarian politics of both colonialism and nationalism signifies his subaltern, ghostlike
presence, which is inherent in his name. As Jennifer Jeffers observes, "bogle" is a dialect word
from Ulster Scots connoting a spirit or poltergeist (132). Relatable to Bhabha's notion of the
"uncanny", Bogle's ambiguous hybridity has become "incommensurable"; located "*beyond
control*" it cannot be "fixed" nor made "knowledg*able*" (12). By always "trying to appear other
than what you are" (65-6), this mischievous spirit haunts not only the totalising constructions
which seek to determine his identity, but also constantly disrupts his own narrative
consciousness:

> All of my clarifying intentions are being undermined and I feel that old, familiarly
> Bogleian sensation of life slipping away from me. Gamely, I struggle to exert some
> kind of control. (272)

However, having lost all control of his own narrative through his assuming mimicry of
changing masks, the Bogleian changeling has also lost the control over a coherent self.

Both writers parody the conventional paradigms of their respective narrative traditions.
Ripley Bogle's autobiographical anecdotes of Belfast play in a deliberate *adulteration* on the
dominant themes of the Northern Irish thriller (as the motifs of "love-across-the-barricades",
exile romance and betrayal of best friend), which he exposes in the end as fabricated versions
of his stage-Irish masquerade. Kelman's A *Disaffection* similarly parodies romantic
nationalism, as apparent in Patrick Doyle's search for "totality" through the pipes. Seeking to
escape his fragmented and isolated existence as a school-teacher, Doyle's withdrawal into
romantic solitude, as well as his musings on the redemptive qualities of a mystified
Scottishness, aims, as with Bogle's *auto-exotic* versions of Irishness, to expose the characters'

complicity in escapist constructions which are products of a dominant ideology they seek to oppose. The Romantic "dream of totality" is – as well as the notion of authenticity – produced, as Lee Spinks reveals, "by the fragmentation of cultural and political life in the era of late capitalism" (98). Chiming with Fredric Jameson's characterisations of postmodernism's 'schizophrenic mood', Doyle who is "caught between the poles" (57) of his insuperable dualism has, as with Bogle, become detached from any interaction with "the real" or the world of politics.

Doyle's retreat into solipsism – "Everywhere you looked always this fucking I. I I I. I got really sick of it" (145) – conflicts with his demand for political engagement – "We're responsible for it, the present polity!" (149). He has become incapable of transcribing this command into action: "What he sought was the doing, the act!" (10). As he withdraws from the political sphere into "intellectual" contemplation, Doyle adopts what John Macmurray sees as "the attitude of spectators, not of participants", which substitutes "for real activity an activity of the imagination" (16). This is apparent in his incessant reflections which continually defer and delay his intention to play the pipes: "But get rid of the distancing. Stop trying to widen the gulf between yourself and the playing" (67). Yet such a "distancing", which would actually allow him to transgress from his limited spectator-perspective to establish a critical distance to his own ideological entrapment in his allotted social position, is for Doyle, for whom "Irony was death"(86), inaccessible. Not so for Kelman, however, who describes Doyle's futile endeavour to "get beyond the outer reaches of greater Glasgow" in a detached voice with sarcastic irony: "He'll never do it" (69). In his recurrent attempts "to get away, out of things fast" (188), this "MacDoyle" (299), who adopts an Irish tag to convey the mythical magic of his pipes to some youngsters, muses on the possibilities of a redemptive Scottishness:

> Unless! The fates were trying to tell him something! Could his destiny lie in such a direction! West to the Highland and to the Islands. A Scotsman of the old school. Maybe he was put here to decide the fate of a nation! (104)

Kelman's irony is underlined as this national representative has lost any moral value assessment:

> He did not know what to do. Not any longer, he just didni know. He didni know what was right and what was not right, what was wrong and what was not wrong that being not wrong, that being right. (303)

In Doyle's confused indeterminacy, his imagination is haunted by "a poltergeist for fuck sake or a Scottish leprechaun" (188). By relating this disturbing presence to Scottish national imaginations, Kelman, similar to McLiam Wilson, aims to expose the falsifying constructions of national visions whose focus on the mystical 'beyond' overlooks the prevailing concerns of city life. Yet as the concerns of class, gender and race, which Doyle tries to stand up for, will never stop their haunting presence in the 'real world', neither will the haunting presence of the false "polis" stop to control the modern city-state[5]: "Funny how come so many officers-of-the-law crop up these days. Patrick seems surrounded by them. Everywhere he looks" (209). Doyle's ambiguous mimicry of the dominant social logic certainly makes him in the fixing gaze of the "polis" "a suspicious being", who is not only "dangerous" to the authority of the state apparatus, but in his disaffection from society also "dangerous to himself"(337). Exposed to this 'panopticum'-like surveillance, given his loss of agency, Doyle can merely run away.

---

[5] As Cairns Craig observes, the state controlled by the "polis", as expressed in dialect Scots, stands in stark contrast to the "polis" of the Greek city state (1999: 106).

Both novels investigate the destructive and politically debilitating consequences the ideological systems of colonialism, nationalism, and capitalism have on the individual. Both characters have, to use Leerssen's words, reached the position of "detached observers". Caught between conflicting social positions, Doyle and Bogle have, in R.D. Laing's terms, become "divided selves".[4] However, in contrast to previous national imaginings – like the state-sponsored *re-imagining* that Glasgow and Belfast have seen through their respective redevelopments as part of their "City of Culture" crusades – both writers are engaged in establishing a new urban dialectic between the "Real" and the "Imaginary". Kelman and McLiam Wilson's effort to offer their characters possibilities to interpret their city space by creating their own "mental maps" of subjective orientation points to its urban totality and can thus be related to Jameson's concept of "cognitive mapping":

> [T]he mental map of the city space [...] can be extrapolated to that mental map of the social and global totality we all carry around in our heads [...] urban alienation is directly proportional to the mental unmapability of local city spaces [...] the dialectic between the here and now of immediate perception and the imaginative or imaginary sense of the city as an absent totality [...] presents something like a spatial analogue of Althusser's great formulation of ideology itself [...] this positive conception of ideology as a necessary function in any form of social life has the great merit of stressing the gap between the local positioning of the individual subject and the totality of class structures in which he or she is situated. (353)

Their characters, as Benjaminian observing "flâneurs", signify the attempts to circumvent the sense of individual alienation, entrapment and displacement from the city's "absent totality" by trying to understand its network of power-structures. "Cognitive mapping" thus proffers a political possibility to re-negotiate the empty hybridity of post-colonialism, and enables to forge new political connections and solidarities.

## References

Ahmad, Aijaz. 1996. "The Politics of Literary Post-coloniality". In *Contemporary Post-colonial Theory: A Reader*. Ed. Padmiri Mongia. London: Arnold. 276-93

Ashcroft, Bill, G. Griffith, and H. Tiffin. 2003. *The Empire Writes Back*. London: Routledge

Bhabha, Homi K. 1994. *The Location of Culture*. London: Routledge

Brecht, Berthold. 1964. "Short Description of a New Technique of Acting which Produces an Alienation Effect". In *Brecht on Theatre*. Ed. and Trans. John Willett. London: Methuen. 136-47

Chadwick, Alan. "Colourful Language". *The Sunday Times Scotland*. 23 July 1995: N.p.

Craig, Cairns. 1999. *The Modern Scottish Novel*. Edinburgh: Edinburgh University Press

Craig, Cairns. 1996. *Out of History*. Edinburgh: Polygon

Deane, Seamus. 1991. "General Introduction". *Field Day Anthology of Irish Writing*. Vol. I. Gen. Ed. S. Deane. Derry: Field Day

Deane, Seamus.1990."Introduction". In *Nationalism, Colonialism and Literature: Terry Eagleton, Fredric Jameson and Edward W Said*. Minneapolis: University of Minnesota. 3-19

Fanon, Frantz. 2001. *The Wretched of the Earth*. London: Penguin

Gandhi, Leela. 1998. *Post-colonial Theory: A Critical Introduction*. Edinburgh: Edinburgh

---

[4] See R.D. Laing's study of schizophrenia, *The Divided Self*.

University Press

Gardiner, Michael. 1996. "Democracy and Scottish Post-coloniality". *Scotlands* 3.2. 24-41

Graham, Colin and Willy Maley. 1999. "Introduction: Irish Studies and Post-colonial Theory". *Irish Studies Review* 7.2: 149-151

Graham, Colin. 2003. "Ireland (Post-colonialism) Scotland". In *Ireland (Ulster) Scotland: Concepts, Contexts, Comparisons*. Eds. Edna Longley, Eamonn Hughes and Des O'Rourke. Belfast: Queens University. 244-50

Graham, Colin. 2001. *Deconstructing Ireland: Identity, Theory, Culture*. Edinburgh: Edinburgh University Press

Jaggi, M. 1998. "Speaking in Tongues". *Guardian*, 18 July

Jameson, Fredric. 1988. "Cognitive Mapping". In *Marxism and the Interpretation of Culture*. Eds. Cary Nelson and Lawrence Greenberg. Chicago: University of Illinois Press. 347-360

Jeffers, Jennifer. 2002. *The Irish Novel at the End of the Twentieth Century: Gender, Bodies, Power*. Houndmills: Palgrave

Kelman, James. 1998. *How Late It Was, How Late*. London: Vintage

Kelman, James.1989. *A Disaffection*. London: Vintage. 1999

Kiberd, Declan. 1995. *Inventing Ireland: The Literature of the Modern Nation*. London: Jonathan Cape

Laing, R.D. 1965. *The Divided Self: An Existential Study in Sanity and Madness*. London: Penguin.

Leerssen, Joep. 1996. *Remembrance and Imagination: Patterns in the Historical and Literary Representations of Ireland in the Nineteenth Century*. Cork: Cork University Press

Lloyd, David. 1997. "Cultural Theory and Ireland". *Bullán* 3.1: 87- 92

Macmurray, John. 1970. *The Self as Agent*. Vol. I of *The Form of the Personal*. London: Faber

Maley, Willy. 2002. "Ireland, versus, Scotland: crossing the (English) language barrier". In *Across the margins*. Eds. G. Norquay and G. Smith. Manchester: Manchester University Press. 13-30.

McLean Duncan. 1989. "James Kelman Interviewed". *Edinburgh Review* 71: 64-80

McLiamWilson, Robert. 1989. *Ripley Bogle*. London: Vintage. 1998

McNeill, Kirsty. 1989. "Interview with James Kelman". *Chapman* 57: 1-9

Moore-Gilbert, Bart. 1997. *Post-colonial Theory: Contexts, Practices, Politics*. London: Verso

Ngugi Wa Thiong'O. 1985. "The Language of African Literature". *New Left Review* 150: 109-27

Patten, Eve. 1995. "Fiction in Conflict: Northern Ireland's Prodigal Novelists". In *Peripheral Visions: Images of Nationhood in Contemporary British Fiction*. Ed. I. Bell. Cardiff: University of Wales Press. 128-48

Reizbaum, Marilyn. 1992. "Canonical Double Cross: Scottish and Irish Women's Writing". In *Decolonizing Tradition: New Views of Twentieth-Century 'British' Literary Canons*. Ed. Karen Lawrence. Chicago: University of Illinois Press. 165-9

Said, Edward. 1993. *Culture and Imperialism*. London: Chatto & Windus

Schoene, Berthold. 1995. "A Passage to Scotland: Scottish Literature and the British Post-colonial Condition". *Scotlands* 2.1: 107- 21

Spinks, Lee. 2001. "In Juxtaposition to Which: Narrative, System and Subjectivity in the Fiction of James Kelman". *Edinburgh Review* 108: 85- 105

# The Silent Scot: The Use of Sound in Bill Douglas's *Trilogy*

*João Lemos*

> *Le cinéma sonore a inventé le silence.* (Bresson, 47)

Over the last decades there has been an increased interest in the role of sound in film. However, it would be fair to say that its multiple possibilities have not yet been investigated in depth, a deficiency that could be attributed to the fact that the sound track generally tends to be dwarfed by the image track in a film. This is especially the case in studies of directors who are not usually known as 'sound stylists': despite their interesting use of sound, this feature is usually obliterated by other more recognisable directorial traits. Such is the case of the Scottish director Bill Douglas. His *Trilogy* – *My Childhood* (1972), *My Ain Folk* (1973) and *My Way Home* (1978) – is undoubtedly a unique achievement in the history of Scottish and British cinema. With his *magnum opus* he not only created a genuine and personal work, but also distinguished himself with a very particular cinematic approach. Among his choices as a director, his use of sound is clearly one of the most important tools to his aesthetic conception. Douglas articulated in his trilogy the subject matter of memories of his childhood and adolescence, and the effectiveness and poignancy of his approach were undoubtedly achieved not only through his use of image but also through his distinctive employment of few but significant sounds. This paper aims to explore the role of the sound track in his films, leading to a discussion of his use of "silence" as essential to the creation of a distinctive atmosphere in the trilogy. The focus of the analyses will ultimately be on the use of sound as a means of conveying his memories and as an essential feature of his social realist style.

Bill Douglas's use of sound in his *Trilogy* could almost be seen as a practical application of Hungarian theorist Béla Balázs's view that "sound is justified only when it has artistic significance; that is, when it has some dramaturgical part to play or if it is required to establish an atmosphere" (Balázs , 240). The French film theorist Christian Metz defined cinema's "matter of expression" as "five tracks": "image", "speech", "noise", "music" and "written materials" (Stam, 212). Despite the natural tendency to think of film as essentially an image dominated medium, we must point out that three out of five tracks identified by Metz are sound devices. Metz's definition is useful to our appreciation of Douglas's use of sound. To begin with, we can identify a sparse employment of the "speech" track throughout the trilogy. Since Douglas's characters remain most of the time silent, his dialogues tend to be sharp and poignant, with only a few straightforward lines. John Caughie observes these circumstances commenting that:

> For Douglas, speech is as gestural as the image, telling us little, alluding to a lot. Meaning comes after the image, is never simply given in it. It is this which makes the films 'difficult', resistant to instant psychology. (Caughie, 1993: 202-3)

The narrative of the *Trilogy* develops predominantly from a "first person" perspective. This becomes obvious in the beginning of *My Ain Folk* when Douglas uses a written text on the screen emphatically in the first person. It is interesting to notice that by choosing to use a written piece in a moment where one would usually expect a voice-off, the director emphasises the silence of the main character Jamie, played by Stephen Archibald in the three films and functioning as Douglas's alter ego.

"Music" is never used in a non-diegetic way throughout the trilogy. In fact, it is employed diegetically in only a few (but significant) moments – such as the polyphonic spree in the beginning of *My Way Home*, when the children get mouth organs for Christmas. Finally, and in accordance with his economical style, Douglas developed a well-crafted use of "noise". Working with distinct and, more importantly, recognisable noises, Douglas transforms the sound track of his films. In his minimalist manner, the scarce and effective sounds of doors opening and closing, the wind, sirens, mechanical noises, steps, animal sounds, the fireplace, the train and the airplane prove essential in creating a unique atmosphere of anguish and bleakness.

A fine illustration of Douglas's sound style is the conclusion of each instalment of the trilogy. *My Childhood* is a film which resembles in many ways both Roberto Rossellini's *Germania Anno Zero* (1948) and Robert Bresson's *Mouchette* (1967). Just before the end of *My Childhood*, probably the most poignant of the trilogy, Jamie seems to reach an emotional nadir after all the bitterness he has been through, culminating in the death of his grandmother. He runs to the railway line and puts his ears in the tracks. There is a cut suggesting a passage of time – an ellipsis – after which we can hear the noise of the train far away. Following a shot of the train itself, Jamie runs to a passage over the line and jumps inside a coal wagon. We see him now inside the wagon, the train then disappearing in the distance. Along the tracks the wind blows through the grass but we can only hear the sound of the train fading away. Soon after the image fades to black and the film ends. Like in the other films of the *Trilogy*, the credits run in total silence. Through the minimalist use of sound, Jamie's desolation is materialized and underscored.

The last sequence of *My Ain Folk* is highly symbolic and its use of sound is also highly distinctive. The narrative once again closes with death, this time of Jamie's grandfather, and as a consequence he ends up being sent to a children's home. As the van which is taking him goes up a steep street – the Mound in Edinburgh – it crosses a pipe band playing, significantly, "Scotland the Brave."[1] The van and the band gradually disappear in opposite ways and, as Douglas puts it in his screenplay, "the music dies away on the empty street" (1993: 82). Douglas uses here an obvious symbol of Scottish identity in an ironic way – through the diegetic use of music that fades into silence – amalgamating a felling of misplacement and the mood of despair and desolation.

Concluding the *Trilogy*, the very last sequence of *My Way Home* is particularly noteworthy for its use of "nonsimultaneous" sound, combining diegetic and non-diegetic noises. Describing the film's conclusion, Douglas states:

> Then the sounds of things drift away and it is as if Jamie is deep inside himself. Deep inside his mind's eye he is seeing the place of his childhood. It comes to him first as a small abstraction of things, then a gradual opening out to something all-embracing. And there is a sound that comes with it, growing, a gathering up like a long sigh. The sound extends itself towards the window, becomes that of a plane taking off. Beyond the window there is an orchard in full bloom. And the sun is a promising thing. In flight the sound remains constant for a while before dying to nothing, save for the hint of a homely dog, alive with it, barking. (Douglas, 1993: 116)

The result, given that this is a stratagem not present in the other films, is both unexpected and impressive. When the protagonist is finally leaving Egypt and returning home, we hear an

---

[1] According to the screenplay included in the book *Bill Douglas: A Lanternist's Account* the pipe band is playing the song "Scotland Forever." See Douglas, 1993: 82. O'Hagan has argued that the pipe band is playing "Scotland the Brave" (212). Noble states that the pipe band first plays the song "The Rowan Tree" and then plays "Scotland the Brave" (1990: 144).

airplane sound without ever seeing one. This sound overflows the final images of the film, first of an empty house, and finally of an orchard. The airplane sound fades away, replaced by the tweeting of birds followed by complete silence. This "orchard in full bloom" (Douglas, 1993: 116) is the very last image of the trilogy.

As a result of Douglas's scarce use of the speech, noise and music tracks, "silence" acquires a heightened dimension in the *Trilogy*. Explored in different and meaningful ways, "silence" envelops the films which in turn require a greater effort of concentration from the spectator. What emerges from this aesthetic choice is that every single sound and noise – mostly from everyday life – is underlined and magnified. Douglas has skilfully explored the lesson that, in film, few images are as powerful as a human being staring in silence. Béla Balázs pointed out in his *Theory of the Film*: "The act of keeping silent is often an intentional, dramatically expressive act, and always an indication of some quite definite state of mind" (226). It is crucial to stress here the weight of a recurrent image in Douglas' *Trilogy*: when the characters, especially Stephen Archibald's Jamie, are absorbed in silence in numerous moments during the films, much of their intensity stems from the spellbound shots of their eyes. Jamie's look, for instance, is simultaneously that of a young boy and the glance of someone contemplating the world in a very particular way. Balázs also remarks that:

> Silence, too, is an acoustic effect, but only where sounds can be heard. The presentation of silence is one of the most specific dramatic effects of the sound film. No other art can reproduce silence, neither painting nor sculpture, neither literature nor the silent film could do so. (117)

In his "silent" manner, and perhaps mostly because of it, Douglas achieves an intensity in terms of cinematic aesthetic that is far from the ordinary. And it is also through silence that he tackles a foremost aspect of British national cinema: "Social Realism". John Caughie pointed out that:

> The silence – the absence of a connected discourse which might give you an easier access to the experience of the characters – is not simply formal. Within it, there seems to me to lie an unstated anger and grief at the hardness of poverty: an anger about the deprivation of memory and the past which is absent from the gentler nostalgias that are now being constructed. (203)

Silence is also a chief element in the construction of the Scottish identity of the *Trilogy's* protagonist, Jamie. Andrew Noble suggests that most of the characters of the *Trilogy* – especially here in regard to *My Childhood* – are "depressed" and "culturally deprived," but above all "beyond speech" (1990: 139). It is important to highlight the multifaceted and ambivalent composition of Jamie's identity, which is by no means clichéd. The choice of title for the last episode – *My Way Home* – is to some extent an ironic comment, for Jamie only really 'blossoms' in Egypt, and not in his home Scottish soil. Andrew O'Hagan observes these circumstances commenting that:

> Only when Jamie escapes from Scotland, once conscripted and sent to Egypt in *My Way Home*, does he move towards a sense of hope and burgeoning creativity. An awakening to a world beyond the successive "homes" he has encountered as a child – befriending a genteel Englishman and seeing Arabs in conditions and states he can identify with – brings him to a more pluralistic conception of the world and his place in it. (213)

Significantly, the Scottish Film Foundation rejected Douglas's application for funding for the *Trilogy*, allegedly claiming that it did not present a "forward-looking" image of Scotland. The project ended up being completely backed by the London based British Film Institute (Noble: 1990, 148). This is especially ironic if we consider that Douglas's *Trilogy* is widely considered one of the greatest cinematic and aesthetic achievements in the history of Scottish and British cinema. However, we must point out that despite being an essentially Scottish work, the *Trilogy* has equally a universal dimension. By dealing with complex social issues, Douglas avoids the commonplace paternalistic perspective and eschews didacticism, thus preserving the complexities of the situation presented, with its major contradictions and with no self-pity.

Having noted how Douglas's economical use of sound interacts with the overpowering presence of "silence" to create not only an atmosphere of isolation and bleakness, but also to touch on issues of national identity, one can go further and suggest that his achievements in sound are a direct result of the key aesthetic concept in the *Trilogy*: fragmentation. The three films adopt a fragmented approach on several levels: firstly, there is a literal segmentation in the use of sound – simultaneously in speech, noise and music – intercalated with silence (there is no use of an omniscient voice-over); secondly, there is a fragmentation in the framing composition; and thirdly, the narrative itself is fragmented. Life, in Douglas's *Trilogy*, is not presented as a continuous narrative; rather, it is presented as full of ambiguity, gaps, uncertainty and self-reflection. Thus, the *Trilogy* does not follow a conventional narrative form; on the contrary, it creates an extraordinary and seductive sensorial experience, making use of cinematic procedures to reproduce the doings and undoings of memory. Douglas brings together his sweeping creative élan and oft-noted interest in the cinematic representation of memory. The main consequence of this choice is that the onus is put on the spectator to piece together an individual response, thus underlining how we might consider this and every other aspect of the film as a kind of subjective construction, to glide seamlessly between 'truth' and fantasy, or zip between past, present and future, as if such freedoms had always been part of cinema's established grammar. In Douglas's own words:

> It is a deliberate attempt to contract the length of the feature film as it is accepted in the commercial cinema. I have pared down to reach for the essentials. The autobiographical factor is the main component. The childhood of the title is literally my childhood and the incidents I recount are, with few variations, things that actually happened to me. This is not a dreamlike film composed of languid memories. It is a hard film made up of elementary contrasts: a few big events that have a great importance and the silence and the sounds that surround them. (Douglas cited in Noble, 1990: 139)

These films also bring a crucial historical moment to the screen, the immediate post-war years, seen and heard in the course of a magnificent reconstruction of one's life through memory. Elisabeth Weis and John Belton here summarize some ideas of the theorist Béla Balázs:

> The potential of the sound film lies in its ability to recover certain "lost" sensations for us, such as the sounds of objects of nature, the sounds of certain spaces, or the sound of silence, which can only be heard in the context of other sounds. (80)

According to Robert Stam, "the 'lateness' of the study of sound in the cinema [...] has to do, perhaps, with the conventional view of sound as a mere addendum or supplement to the image" (213). David Bordwell and Kristin Thompson expand upon this idea, reminding us that "sound is perhaps the hardest technique to study" (347) since it can convey very strong feelings in an effective way without ever being noticed. Douglas, despite not being immediately recognized as a "sound stylist", has proved that an intelligent use of sound in cinema can be achieved with simplicity: it does not always require blending several layers, nor breaking the notions of synchronicity and continuity. Sometimes the most effective device is simplicity, and in Douglas's case it always reaches an elevated and distinctive style.

By dealing with the theme of childhood, Douglas's choices also proved to be appropriate for bringing back a "lost" time of one's life. Douglas explores these possibilities with elegance and ability, recreating in a unique cinematic work one's misplaced identity. In his essay "Palace of Dreams: The making of a film-maker" Douglas mentions that his chief concept for the making of the trilogy can be summarized in a quotation from Chekhov: "I can write only from memory, I never write directly from life. The subject must pass through the sieve of my memory, so that alone what is important or typical remains there as on a filter" (Chekhov cited in Douglas, 1978: n.p.). It is interesting that Douglas has extracted this gem precisely from Chekhov, an artist like himself from a modest background and who also had a very difficult childhood. This fragmented construction of the films, which derives directly from this approach through memory, is reflected undoubtedly in his use of sound. Only what is important and essential remains, immersed in an eloquent silence.

## References

Balázs, Béla. 1952. *Theory of the Film*. London: Dennis Dobson

Bordwell, David and Kirstin Thompson. 2004. *Film Art: An Introduction*. 7th ed. New York: McGraw-Hill

Bresson, Robert. 1975. *Notes sur le Cinématographe*. Paris: Gallimard

Burch, Noël. 1981. *Theory of Film Practice*. Princeton: Princeton University Press

Dick, Eddie, Andrew Noble, and Duncan Petrie, eds. 1993. *Bill Douglas: A Lanternist's Account*. London: British Film Institute

Douglas, Bill. 1978. "Palace of Dreams: The Making of a Film-maker". *Bill Douglas Centre* web page. http://info.ex.ac.uk/bill.douglas/palace.html

Ezra, Elizabeth, ed. 2004. *European Cinema*. Oxford: Oxford University Press

Graham, Rhys. 2000. "The Glimpse Given Life: An Elegy for Bill Douglas". *Senses Of Cinema*. http://www.sensesofcinema.com/contents/00/10/douglas.html

Martin, Marcel. 1985. *Le langage cinématographique*. 4th ed. Paris: Cerf

Noble, Andrew. 1990. "Bill Douglas' *Trilogy*". *From Limelight to Satellite: A Scottish Film Book*. Ed. Eddie Dick. London: British Film Institute and Scottish Film Council

Stam, Robert. 2000. *Film Theory: An Introduction*. Oxford: Blackwell Street, Sarah. 1997. British National Cinema. London: Routledge

Weis, Elisabeth and John Belton, eds. 1985. *Film Sound: Theory and Practice*. New York: Columbia University Press

# Loyalty to King or Covenant Retained: Presbyterians in the Three Nations and the English Commonwealth, 1649-1653

*Kirsteen Mackenzie*

Between the defeat of Charles II's army at Worcester on 3 September 1651 and the dissolution of the "Rump" Parliament in April 1653, the Stuart kingdoms of England, Scotland and Ireland, and their colonies, were finally incorporated into the English Commonwealth.[1] The defeat of Charles II's army at Worcester destroyed the last major military threat to the existence of the English Commonwealth and allowed the regime to conquer the remaining royalist strongholds throughout the three kingdoms and overseas (Gardiner: 41-151).[2] The regime consolidated these conquests by imposing the Engagement, an oath to be taken by the male inhabitants of England and Ireland, to acknowledge the sovereignty of the Commonwealth over both nations and the colonies. In Scotland the Commonwealth imposed the Tender of Incorporation, an oath to be taken by the burghs and shires of Scotland (Adair: 200), which required them to accept the assimilation of Scotland into the English Commonwealth.[3] This paper will discuss how the Presbyterian clergy and laity in the three kingdoms reacted to attempts by the Commonwealth government to incorporate them into the political community, by imposing the Engagement or the Tender of Incorporation upon them.

## I

In 1650 the inhabitants of Ulster were required to take the Engagement but due to their refusal to take the oath, Presbyterian ministers were imprisoned (Seymour: 77). During 1650 and 1651 many Irish Presbyterians either fled their parishes to avoid capture and imprisonment by the English Commonwealth, or were sent to Scotland by the English whereupon they took charges in the Scottish Church, leaving only about six or seven Presbyterian ministers in Ireland by 1652 (Reid: 214-215, 248).

 In response to the arrest of ministers preaching the Scottish covenanting interest in August of 1652 (Dunlop: I, 256), the Irish Presbyterian clergy submitted papers stating their objections to the Engagement. A meeting with the English commissioners took place in October 1652 (Adair: 192-193) to resolve any obstacles for the taking the Engagement. However, the Irish

[1] For a detailed narrative of events throughout the three kingdoms and the colonies between 1651and 1653 see Gardiner: 8-340.
[2] Garrisons which held out for Charles II of Britain after Worcester in the three kingdoms and the colonies: Isle of Man and Jersey, surrendered to Commonwealth forces 31October and 12 December 1651, respectively. Castle Cornet in Guernsey surrendered 17 December 1651. Major garrisons in Ireland: Limerick surrenders to parliamentary forces 27 October 1651. Roscommon surrendered 3 April and Jamestown 7April 1652. Galway surrendered 12 May 1652. Innisboffin and the garrison on the Isle of Lough Oughter did not surrender until 14 February and 27 April 1653, respectively. Garrisons in the colonies: Barbados surrendered 11 January 1652, submission of Virginia 12 March 1652 Maryland with the Bermudas 29 March 1652. For major garrisons in Scotland (except Isle of Man) see Dow: 14-71. Aberdeen submitted 7 September 1651, Dumbarton Castle 29 December 1651, Brodrick Castle 6 April 1652, Bass Rock concluded articles of surrender 3 March 1652, Dunnottar Castle surrendered 24 May 1652.
[3] Gardiner: 391. Engagement to be taken by all men of the age of eighteen "I do declare and promise, that I will be true and faithful to the Commonwealth of England, as it is now established, without a King or House of Lords". See Dunlop: 283, 303, 314, 327; Terry: 64. The oath to be taken by burghs and shires who had accepted the Tender of Incorporation "you shall sweare yt yo shall bee true and faithfull to the Comon Wealth of England as It is now Established without a King or House of Lords, you shall well and truly execute the office of within the towne and Burgh of and the Liberties thereof according to the best of yor skill, knowledge, and power, soe helpe you God".

Presbyterians could not decide whether to take the oath and subsequently debated its merits for six hours. They were not debating the legitimacy of the English Parliament's authority in Ireland, since they could not recognise a government that had displaced the monarch and had its power residing solely in the House of Commons in England. They were debating whether they could live in peace under the English government (ibid.).

The parliamentary commissioners were willing to accept an alternative "negative oath" which would allow the clergy to declare their intentions to live at peace under the Commonwealth, without pledging to recognise the government in the form it took. But the clergy refused this oath – not because of outright objection, but because of continuing confusion as to whether to take the Engagement or not (Adair: 193). They were given six weeks to compile their case and put their final decision before the commissioners (Adair: 194). To enable them to put a case forward and stop any confusion, they consulted their Irish brethren in Scotland and proposed to their fellow compatriots that:

> They did not purpose to raise people in arms, but to live as a godly people, and to inform and prepare the people for suffering in the maintenance of the Gospel, if God called them to it. (ibid.)

Thus, the Presbyterians in Ireland promised the Commonwealth government that they would live in peace under the regime, but under their covenanting principles. However, an answer was not given due to their representative being grounded in Scotland before their next meeting with the commissioners (Adair: 194). Therefore, the commissioners recommended that two of the Presbyterian clergy should meet Charles Fleetwood to see if they could satisfy him with their proposals. They explained to Fleetwood and the Council of Officers that they could live in peace under the regime, but could not promise loyalty and support for its cause because of their loyalty to the monarchy (Adair: 195).

In the spring of 1653 commissioners were sent out into the counties of Ireland to press the Engagement throughout the country (Adair: 197-198). According to Patrick Adair, minister of Cairncastle,[4] members of Presbyterian parishes, with their ministers, in Carrickfergus refused to take the Engagement. In response, the government refused the ministers' liberty to go out of the town and threatened them with transportation to England. Despite this the ministers remained resolute in refusing to take the Engagement (Adair: 198).

The Commonwealth government reported a slightly different response from the Presbyterian laity in Ireland towards the Engagement. They stated in their letters from Dublin that some signed the Engagement and those who did, did not sign on conscientious grounds. Others signed the negative oath whereby they did not pledge loyalty to the government and the form it took, but only to live peacefully under the Commonwealth (Seymour: 79). The former retaining their loyalty to the Covenant and the Stuart monarchy through conscience only, and the latter by visibly taking an alternative oath.

But by May of that year the commissioners began to accept the ministers' refusal to take the Engagement. In April 1653 Oliver Cromwell dissolved the Rump Parliament and therefore the need to pledge loyalty to the Engagement was over (Adair: 198-200). In response to the commissioners' decision not to press the Engagement, the Presbyterian ministers went to their parishes and kept the next Sunday as a day of thanksgiving (Seymour: 80).

## II

Between 1649 and 1653 English Presbyterians became divided in their attitudes towards the Engagement. Both Sarah Barber and Edward Vallance, in the most recent analyses of the

---

[4] Presbyterian Church in Ireland: 261.

Engagement controversy,[5] show why Presbyterians had a problem with the Engagement. Presbyterians debated the Engagement on conscientious grounds, having already signed the Solemn League and Covenant, and could not reconcile themselves with a regime that had executed the King (Barber: 182; Vallance, 2001: 60). Two different responses to this "crisis of conscience" can be seen in the pamphlets of Presbyterians, Edward Gee and Francis Rous.

Francis Rous, a Cornish MP and Presbyterian, was a prominent promoter of the ideas of a group known to historians as the "de factoists", who accepted the Engagement.[6] They argued that the Engagement could be taken because the manner in which the government was established could be ignored. They put forward the case based on Romans 13, that government, any government, whether its motives were for good or ill, was ordained by God and therefore should be obeyed (Barber, 1990: 55). Francis Rous argued further in his pamphlet, *The Lawfulness of Obeying the Present Government*, that the "legality" of a government, or the right of succession by direct bloodline, were not the reasons why a given authority should be obeyed. He argued this by proving that although Nero's regime was illegal, God gave him power and people obeyed. He further argued that the English and/or British monarchy itself was a power which throughout its history had established its presence over the English people by force, not the people's will. The authority, whether legal or illegal must be obeyed, otherwise chaos will rule (Rous: 11). Rous also attacked the Presbyterian anti-Engagement argument that they could not forswear the Solemn League and Covenant. He stated that the Covenant did not forbid an individual to pledge loyalty to a government, especially when the alternative was anarchy (Rous: 11).

Edward Gee, a Presbyterian minister from Lancashire, made a contrasting argument (Smart: 115) on behalf of Presbyterian ministers in the north-west of England in a pamphlet entitled *A Plea for Non-Subscribers* (Smart, 1976: 126). Ian Smart is right to comment that the two major objections of the ministers in the north-west of England to the Engagement were the suspect legal grounds of the English Commonwealth's possession of power, and the requirement to forswear the Solemn League and Covenant in taking the Engagement (Smart: 122). Gee argued that the possession of power by the Commonwealth was on unsafe legal foundations because of the way power was seized, therefore making the Commonwealth "unjust", "unwarranted" and "oppressive" (Gee: 11-12). The manner and form in which the government was set up was illegal and Gee stated that there is a legal government for the kingdoms: the government of the King rather than the Commonwealth. This was because legal government could only be formed from three estates: King, Lords and Commons. The Commonwealth was illegal because not only does it consist of one estate, the Commons, but also the army had set it up (Gee: 20). Therefore the new form of government called a "Commonwealth" is an invention of the army; it is not the ancient government of King, Lords, and Commons (Gee: 27-8). This, of course, was against the Covenant pledge to protect the ancient form of government for the King and his posterity (Gee: 30-1). Furthermore, Gee argued that people are still bound to the Covenant and therefore cannot swear to the Engagement. It was only God who could end the obligations of the Covenant, not man (Gee: 41-3).

## III

The Kirk as a whole disliked the Tender of Incorporation pressed upon Scottish shires and burghs in 1652. The Kirk was split into two groups known as the Protesters and Resolutioners. The Protesters believed that only those fully committed to the Kirk and its Solemn League and

---

[5] Barber: 174-201. "Chapter 7 – the Engagement of Loyalty"; Vallance, 2001: 59-77; Vallance, 2002: 408-424
[6] For examples of work on the de factoists see Skinner: 79-98; Burgess: 515-536; Barber, 1990: 44-57.

Covenant should involve themselves with politics and the Kirk. The less extreme Resolutioners believed that Royalists and others who had been excommunicated by the Kirk could once again co-exist alongside the godly in affairs of church and state in order to defeat the English Commonwealth (Stevenson: 193-5). Indeed, Robert Baillie, a Resolutioner, was a leading spokesman for the Presbyterian ministry against the Tender of Incorporation.[7] To Baillie, the Tender tempted the Scottish nation to:

> lay aside the King, and to make the third article of our Covenant stand well enough with a freedome to change Monarchie with a Scottish Republic, this to me is a high-enough crime.[8]

Robert Blair, another Resolutioner, did not like the Tender because he thought Scotland would lose its own identity and therefore, "will be as when the poor bird is embodied into the hawk that hath eaten it up" (McCrie: 291-2).

The Resolutioners responded to the Tender by organising a meeting at St Andrews on the first Tuesday of April 1652 which resolved to send letters to all parts of the kingdom, advising against taking the Tender (McCrie: 294-5). During the previous month, ministers in Fife had made efforts by refusing the summons of the English commissioners to be read (Whitlock: 394). Ministers in Edinburgh also tried to effect the burgh's response to the Tender by preaching against the burgh's deliberations over the Tender and encouraged the laity to avoid compliance with the English.[9]

The Protesters in their *Declaration as to English Actings* believed that those parliamentary commissioners who came to negotiate the Tender had taken the Covenant and therefore, by their work, were disregarding the Covenant (Stephen: 33). The Protesters believed God would pour his wrath on the English because:

> He is a jealous God, a great and terrible God, that keepeth the Covenant; and his desire and command is that we should also keep the Covenant. And how dreadfull are these things which He threatened and brought upon His owne people Israell because they did not keep covenant, but dealt falslie therein! (Stephen: 33)

There was a small but significant minority which consisted of Sir James Hope's group of friends who were looking forward to union because it offered fulfilment of their apocalyptic vision of a state based on consent, but the majority of the Presbyterian laity did not greet the Tender with enthusiasm (Williamson: 309).

According to Blair, most of the laity in the country accepted the Tender with only a few refusing (McCrie: 294) 30 shires and 58 burghs were called upon by the English parliament to accept the Tender and were to send deputies to discuss the settlement of Scotland at Dalkeith (Terry: 12-14). They were requested to give their assent to the Tender, which consisted of three proposals. Firstly, that Scotland should be incorporated into and made one with the Commonwealth of England, thereby acknowledging a government established in England without a King and a House of Lords and that the benefits of this free state may be given to the people of Scotland. Secondly, that they promise to live peaceably under the Commonwealth and give due obedience to the authority of the Parliament of the Commonwealth of England. Thirdly, that "concise desires" are offered for bringing to the effect the said union and settlement with speed and best satisfaction for Scotland. Answers

---

[7] Laing: 175. Answer to Mr Blair April 1 1652 "I have declared myselfe against it more than any other have".
[8] ibid.175-176. Answer to Mr Blair April 1 1652.
[9] *Weekly Intelligencer*. 1652, March 23-March 30: 399. *A Perfect Diurnall*. 1651, March 15-March 22: 1745. *Several Proceedings in Parliament*. 1651, February 19-Febuary 26: 1961

were to be given by the 18 March 1652. From the English point of view they were to be an acceptance of Parliament's *Declaration of the Parliament of the Commonwealth of England Concerning the Settlement of Scotland*, which included an acceptance of toleration (Terry: xxi-xxii, xxv, 15; Dow: 3).

Frances Dow is correct in stating that the majority of constituencies who were asked to reply and accept the Tender did so.[10] John Young estimates out of 30 shires and 58 burghs, 18 shires and 24 burghs sent representatives to Dalkeith, and 29 shires and 44 burghs accepted the Tender, the majority of those that were requested to accept (Young: 297). This was because the commissioners who were sent to Dalkeith had no time to consult with their contemporaries, leaving no time for them to debate and object to the Tender (Dow: 37). Plus, many consented because of the English military pressure and the non-existence of real military and political challenge from those who supported the King (Young: 297).

Many constituencies accepted the Tender for material reasons, because they had much to lose by not accepting the Tender, whereas the ministry had the chance of gaining much by their high moral stance (Dow: 39). Dow is also correct that this acceptance of the Tender did not mean that the laity were lukewarm towards the Kirk. This final section in the paper, attempts to expand on Dow's comment and argues that far from deserting their covenanting principles when signing the tender, the majority of the shires and burghs were defiantly standing by those principles.[11]

## IV

73 constituencies assented to the first and second parts of the Tender which may indicate a rejection of covenanting principles. In assenting to the first and second parts of the Tender, the shires and burghs rejected the third clause in the Covenant, to protect the King. To promise to live in peace under this regime was to reject the call in the third clause in the Covenant to "endeavour with our estates and our lives to defend the King's Majesty's person and authority". But positive replies show that those who assented still adhered to covenanting principles and therefore the Tender was arguably more than a series of complaints about English rule in Scotland (Dow: 43). They were underhanded rejections and quiet protests against the overturning of the Solemn League and Covenant, which the Tender indirectly advocated.

Many of the answers desired that the Protestant religion in Scotland should remain unaltered, as laid down by the Church of Scotland. This included Dumfriesshire, Whigtonshire, Nairnshire, Invernesshire and Bute (Terry: 19, 37-44, 70, 81, 96, 100-1, 107, 148-9, 157-160, 170-1). Interestingly, Argyllshire requested that the form of worship as prescribed by the Kirk should remain unaltered for fear of incurring God's wrath (Terry: 170-1). Therefore, many shires and burghs still recognised the spiritual and moral authority of the Kirk over the people of Scotland, disagreeing with English toleration that would subordinate the Kirk to the civil sphere. But also, by still recognising the moral and spiritual authority of the Kirk over the people, they also still recognise the superiority of its laws and Covenants in Scotland.

Desires from Edinburgh and other burghs, including Aberdeen and Dundee, showed their loyalty to the Covenant more clearly in their desire:

> that the Protestant Religion may be established in uniformitie the whole Island by advise of the most godlie and learned men of both Nations Conforme to the Word of God.[12]

[10] Dow: 37. 73 out of 89 constituencies accepted the Tender.
[11] *Mercurius Politicus*. 1652, March 18 to March 25: 1476
[12] Terry: 37-8, 53-5, 70, 60-1, 107, 162-3, 128-9, 159-60.

This statement reaffirms the original aims of the Kirk and English Parliament as laid out in the Solemn League and Covenant of 1643. They wanted the Reformed Protestant religion, particularly Presbyterian Church Government, to be established uniformly throughout England and Scotland. They also wanted a situation to be created so "godly men" of both nations could achieve this. Thus they resurrected the ideal of the Westminster Assembly, a forum for the establishment of Presbyterianism as the state religion in Scotland and England in the 1640s (Dow: 4). Also, many of the assents and desires looked forward to making the union satisfactory for both kingdoms.[13] Therefore, shires and burghs rejected full incorporation into the Commonwealth and still hoped for a confederation between the two kingdoms, as outlined in the Covenant (Macinnes: 207).

Others, like Dumfriesshire, wanted the Church of Scotland to be established throughout Scotland and asked for a forum so that the ministry in Scotland could debate with the ministry of England on the issue of toleration, and in particular, the "lawful and unlawfullness" of its establishment.[14] Also, many shires and burghs asked to be "protected" in practising their religion and one constituency asks that many "godly consciences" could be quietened so they could do so.[15] It is evident by these proposals that they were not keen on religious toleration, which was contrary to the Covenant aimed at establishing Presbyterianism throughout the three kingdoms (Gardiner: 268).

There were constitutional demands too, for example, Stirling,[16] Dumfriesshire, Aberdeenshire and many others[17] wanted Scotland to use its own established laws, therefore upholding the clause in the Solemn League Covenant to preserve separate law making bodies of both kingdoms (Gardiner: 269). In particular, Stirling remained loyal to the Covenant and to the Stuart monarchy. Stirling suggested that the Commonwealth should have a name comprehending both nations, Great Britain, and thus the island should keep the identity given to it by its Stuart sovereigns (Terry: 53-5). St Andrews, in its petition to the Commissioners, referred to itself as a Royal Burgh (Terry: 110).

Some constituencies welcomed the union such as Dumbarton and Lanarkshire who "cheerfully" assented to the union.[18] Perhaps these constituencies misunderstood the nature of the union tendered, believing that by accepting it they were upholding the Covenant (Terry: 34-5).[19] Contrary to these answers were the replies from Glasgow and Morayshire. Glasgow dissented because Scotland would lose the right to govern itself, which was against the Covenant and therefore was against their consciences The English government would also allow the toleration of sects, which was contrary to the Covenant. Furthermore, there were not enough guidelines to show what else would happen to Scotland under the regime. Therefore, under these circumstances Glasgow did not sign the Tender (Terry: 34-5).

Morayshire objected to the Tender because of the toleration of religious sects they felt would be introduced into Scotland. They did not agree with the confiscation of estates because they had not invaded England to cause injury to that nation, but to enact a Covenant which both England and Scotland had signed up to in order to protect common religion and liberties Another dissent was that of Kirkcudbright (Terry: 112-115, 120). Kirkcudbright objected to the Tender because it revoked the solemn promise that England made before God that they would protect Scotland's laws, estates and government. For Kirkcudbright, in particular, the

---

[13] Terry: 31, 48, 45, 73.

[14] Terry: 39-41, 70, 148-9.

[15] ibid 148-9, 42-4, 96, 100-1.

[16] Terry: 78-80, 34-35, 42-43, 78-80.

[17] Terry: 43-44, 53-55, 70, 77-78, 60-61, 73, 96, 100-101, 107, 162-163, 123-126, 128-129, 148-9, 157-160, 170-171.

[18] Terry: 161, 50, 56, 49, 52, 58.

[19] Terry: 34-35. See Glasgow's complaint about the vagueness of the settlement of Scotland as outlined in the Tender.

Tender revoked the third article of the Covenant that aimed to protect the person of the King and liberties, which the kingdoms derived from his person.

It also contradicted the second and first articles of the Solemn League and Covenant, since toleration leaves the door open to heresy and superstition and does not aim to preserve the doctrine and worship of the Church of Scotland. Kirkcudbright also argued that the Commonwealth of England could not confiscate estates of Covenanters on the grounds of paying for the wars, since Covenanters had been paying for the wars through their estates on behalf of the Parliament in England. Finally, they declared that they were bound by the sixth article of the Covenant which was not to desert the Covenant whatsoever (Terry: 118-9, 120).

There were those who were forced into assent, or forced to change their dissents to assents. There were those who used equivocations and delaying tactics to avoid any real compliance with the regime. These took two different forms, firstly no answer whatsoever and secondly an answer, but without offering the English advice on union. Dumbarton wanted to change its mind about assenting to the union but was forbidden to do so by the English Commonwealth (Williamson: 312-3). Edinburgh refused to assent to the Tender and as a result the army removed Sir James Stewart, the leader of the opposition to the Tender in the burgh, and replaced him and his supporters with a more compliant elite (Dow: 54). Glasgow, Morayshire and Kirkcudbright were all forced to change their rejections to the Tender to assents.[20]

There were also constituencies that used delaying tactics or equivocations to avoid any real compliance with the regime, thus remaining loyal to Kirk, Covenant or Royal authority. Some constituencies such as Haddington, North Berwick and Dunbar did not offer any advice to the English on union.[21] Some did not give an answer at all. Absence can perhaps also be seen as a delaying tactic, hoping that the authorities would not pursue them for an answer, thus allowing people to avoid oaths they did not wish to take for fear of forswearing themselves. It is very interesting to note that out of all the assents to the Tender, Orkney and Shetland's assent is the only one that pledged to encourage the recognition of the English Parliament's authority in their community (Terry: 123-6; Dow: 44).

## Conclusion

In conclusion it can be said that the Presbyterians in the three kingdoms resisted and others, a minority, accepted attempts by the English Commonwealth to incorporate them into the political community by means of the Engagement and the Tender of Incorporation. The Irish Presbyterians promised to live in peace under the regime but could not give their loyalty to the Commonwealth due to their support for the monarchy or the Covenant. By May 1653 they were no longer pressed by the government to take the Engagement due to the downfall of the regime and therefore, the Irish Presbyterians retained their loyalty to the monarchy.

The English Presbyterians debated subscribing to the Engagement. In the case of Edward Gee he saw that it conflicted with the vow they took regarding the Covenant to uphold monarchy. Francis Rous believed that he was faithful to the Covenant because it did not advocate that the country should slip into anarchy. The Scottish ministry tried to discourage the burghs and shires from taking the Tender, due to the temptation it put in the way of the laity to break the Covenant. The ministers felt that the majority of the laity were disregarding the Covenant by accepting the Tender. But in reality, there was only a very small minority that looked forward to the Tender of Incorporation. Those who signed the Tender, and those who dissented from it, were still loyal to the Covenant, Kirk or the monarchy.

---

[20] Terry: 34-5, 112-115, 118-120.
[21] Terry: 185, 20-2, 34, 86-8, 93-4, 135, 138-9, 145-9, 166.

## References

Adair, P. 1866. *A True Narrative of the Rise and Progress of the Presbyterian Church in Ireland 1623-1670*. Belfast: C Aitchison

Barber, S. 1990. "The Engagement for the Council of State and the Establishment of The Commonwealth Government". *Historical Research*. Vol. LXIII: 44-57

Barber, S. 1998. *Regicide and Republicanism: Politics and Ethics in the English Revolution 1646-1659*. Edinburgh: Edinburgh University Press

Burgess, G. 1986. "Usurpation, Obligation and Obedience in the Thought of the Engagement Controversy". *Historical Journal*. Vol. XXIX: 515-536

Dow, F.D. 1979. *Cromwellian Scotland*. Edinburgh: John Donald

Dunlop, R. ed. 1913. *Ireland under the Commonwealth: being a selection of Documents relating to the government of Ireland from 1651 to 1659*. 2 Vols. Manchester: University of Manchester

Gardiner, S.R. ed. 1968. *Constitutional Documents of the Puritan Revolution 1625-1660*. Oxford: Oxford University Press

Gardiner, S.R. 1988. *History of the Commonwealth and Protectorate*. Vol. 2 1651-53. Adlestrop, Gloucestershire: The Windrush Press

Gee, E. 1650. *A Plea for Non-Subscribers or The Grounds and Reasons of many Ministers in Cheshire, Lancashire and the Parts adjoining for their refusal of The late ENGAGEMENT*. London: n.p

Laing, D. ed. 1842. *The Letters and Journals of Robert Baillie A.M. Principal of the University of Glasgow M.DC.XXXVII.-M.DC.LXII. in three volumes. Volume third* Edinburgh: R. Ogle

McCrie, T. ed. 1848. *The Life of Mr Robert Blair, Minister of St Andrews, containing his autobiography, From 1593 to 1636, with supplement to his life, and continuation of the history of the times by his son in law, Mr William Row, Minister of Ceres*. Edinburgh: Wodrow Society

Macinnes, A.I. 2000. "Covenanting Ideology in Seventeenth-century Scotland". In ed J.H. Ohlmeyer, *Political Thought in Seventeenth Century Ireland: Kingdom or Colony*. Cambridge: Cambridge University Press. 191-220

*Mercurius Politicus*. 1652. March 18 to March 25

Presbyterian Church in Ireland. 1982. *A History of Congregations in the Presbyterian Church in Ireland, 1610-1982*. Belfast: Presbyterian Historical Society of Ireland

Reid, J.S. 1837. *History of the Presbyterian Church in Ireland*. London: Whittaker

Rous, F. 1649. *The Lawfulnes of obeying the Present Government Proposed By one That loves all Presbyterian lovers of Truth and Peace, and is of their Communion*. London: J Wright

Seymour, St J.D. 1921. *Puritans in Ireland 1647-1661*. Oxford: Oxford University Press

Skinner, Q. 1972. "Conquest and consent: Thomas Hobbes and the Engagement controversy". In ed. G.E. Aylmer. *The Interregnum: The Quest for a Settlement 1646-1660*. London: Macmillian. 79-98

Smart, I.M. 1976. "Edward Gee and the Matter of Authority". *Journal of Ecclesiastical History* Vol. 27.2: 115-127

Stephen, W. ed. 1921. *Register of the consultations of the ministers of Edinburgh and some other brethren of the ministry*. Volume I. Edinburgh: Scottish History Society

Stevenson, D. 1977. *Revolution and Counter-revolution in Scotland, 1644-1651*. London: Royal Historical Society

Terry, C.S. ed. 1902. *The Cromwellian union: papers relating to the negotiations for An incorporating union between England and Scotland 1651-1652, with an appendix relating to negotiations in 1670*. Edinburgh: Scottish History Society

Vallance, E. 2001. "Oaths, Casuistry, and Equivocation: Anglican Responses to the Engagement Controversy". *Historical Journal*. Vol. 44.1: 59-77

Vallance, E. 2002. "Protestation, Vow, Covenant and Engagement: Swearing Allegiance in the English Civil War". *Historical Research*. Vol. LXXV. No. 190: 408-424

*Weekly Intelligencer*. 1652. March 23-March 30, 399

Whitlock, B. 1853. *Memorials of English affairs from the beginning of the reign of Charles the First to the happy restoration of King Charles the Second*. Volume Third. Oxford: Oxford University Press

Williamson, A. H. 1995. "Union with England Traditional, Union with England Radical: Sir James Hope and the Mid-seventeenth-century British State". *English Historical Review*. Vol. CX: 316. 303-322

Young, J.R. 1996. *The Scottish Parliament 1639-1661: A Political and Constitutional Analysis*. Edinburgh: John Donald

# "The Unrelenting Protagonist": Masculinity and the Anti-Hero in the Novels of Eoin McNamee

*Caroline Magennis*

The Northern Irish novelist Eoin McNamee specialises in the fictionalisation of recent Northern Irish history and in *Resurrection Man* and *The Ultras* he chooses to represent two of the most controversial figures of the Troubles. Victor Kelly is a fictional manifestation of Lenny Murphy, leader of the Shankill Butchers and Captain Robert Nairac was an ambitious young army officer whose death remains shrouded in mystery. McNamee's protagonists follow tropes more often used for traditional crime fiction and literary noir and this reflects the conflict between genre and the subject matter of his work. There is a tension between his noir-soaked vision of contemporary Northern Ireland and the sociological realities of the situation. In his novels McNamee employs the techniques of the postmodern novel, using narratives laden with references to modern media, and this, combined with his use of the conventions of literary noir, provides a unique way of looking at masculinity in contemporary Northern Ireland.

In literary criticism, gendered readings of texts tend to focus exclusively on the feminine, with masculinity seen as the standard by which other forms of identity are measured. Only recently has masculinity been seriously focused on by literary critics, and even then the discussion can be limited to discussion of homoerotics in renaissance drama or the austere masculine forms of modernist prose and poetry. That is not to say, of course, that many texts have not a great deal to reveal to us about the machinations of masculinity. As Peter Middleton has commented in *The Inward Gaze: Masculinity and Subjectivity in Modern Culture*: "Modern writers have revelled in masculinity without ever quite naming it" (3). It is with this in mind that I approach the novels of Eoin McNamee, replete as they are with comment on and representation of the myriad forms in which masculinity manifests itself in the recent history of Northern Ireland. The themes McNamee explores in his fiction are not entirely new to Ulster prose. As far back as 1974, John Wilson Foster recognised these themes in Northern Irish fiction: "Any fiction writer who wants to illuminate Ulster society has to press realism and psychology into service in the exploration of three things: sex, violence and sectarianism" (254). In the Northern Ireland McNamee creates and the men he chooses to fill it with he explores the way in which masculine identity can be created and maintained in a society under siege from within and from without.

In *The Noir Thriller* Lee Horsley sets out the tropes and narrative devices used in this genre, and these can be readily applied to McNamee's work. Horsley emphasises the importance of the protagonist in the development of literary noir. She notes that the central character can take on a number of guises: "In noir; victim, criminal and investigator can all act as protagonist" (10). McNamee uses a number of narrative techniques in his novels to portray the lives of his protagonists. Although he employs the omniscient narrator he also uses secondary characters, who are often implicated in some way in the plot, to gradually illuminate the central figures. We receive our information about events surrounding the protagonist often at the same time they do, allowing the text to gently unfold and intrigue. In *The Ultras* this role is taken by the obsessed and tragic ex-policeman Blair Agnew, and in *Resurrection Man* we have the cynical alcoholic journalist Ryan. This narrative technique is common in the noir thriller, adding to a sense of suspense. Horsley notes that:

As reader, our own sense of disorientation may be reinforced by the fact that we only gradually, by means of a non-linear narrative, discover causes and consequences. Our piecemeal discovery of information corresponds to the protagonist's difficulties in arriving at any secure knowledge by means of orderly enquiry. (12)

The history of both Kelly and Nairac is shown to us in flashback throughout the text, indeed we know both men are marked for death from the outset. It is important to note how the roles of the protagonists fluctuate dramatically in both *Resurrection Man* and *The Ultras* as Victor Kelly and Robert Nairac eventually progress from hunter to hunted, their hyper-masculine identities secured by violent death at a young age. Horsley notes that "treacherous confusions of his role and the movement of the protagonist from one role to another constitute key structural elements in the noir narrative" (10).

When Dorcas Kelly visits her son Victor in prison she muses that he looks like an "unrelenting protagonist" (McNamee, 1994: 71), an idea that will affect one's reading of *Resurrection Man*. Although the Resurrection Men, as they are dubbed by the media, are a gang, Victor Kelly is the focus of this text and McNamee takes us through his home life, his schooling and his violent career leading ultimately to his death. In the first chapter of the novel we are shown Victor's upbringing and his relationship with his family, centring in particular on his mother. We see Victor's first brush with sectarianism through the preachers that gather in the Cornmarket, a meeting point in the middle of Belfast city centre. Victor's first glimpse of ineffectual masculinity, of the domestic man emasculated, was provided by his home life. His father, James, is meek, timid, and self-conscious when he shouts at local football matches. His silence and absence had an effect on the young Victor Kelly, leaving him with no strong male role model. Ervin Staub, in *The Roots of Evil*, notes that hostility between fathers and sons contributes to boys' aggression (72). One could suggest that Victor's lack of a strong male role model contributes towards his lack of respect for authority and hierarchy; even in a paramilitary organisation he is a maverick outsider. In the absence of a male role model at home, Victor finds it in the bullies and paramilitaries that occupy his streets, befriending those who once bullied him and, with them, extorts money from younger boys.

Similarly, in *The Ultras*, we gain information about Robert Nairac's upbringing and early encounters with the forms of masculinity he would come to exemplify. He learns order, self-discipline and self-sufficiency in his Catholic public school. A romantic view of military culture was ingrained in the young Robert, who keeps war comics and built models of wartime aircraft. His ophthalmic surgeon father provides him with access to a language that is scientific, ordered and masculine in tone. This language of etymology gives the young Robert a vocabulary of rationality, of the subduing of emotions. Ironically, he recalls his father's lexicon when he is facing death. Nairac is a man of relatively few words and in the text he is the subject of much speculation yet retains a relative silence. Blair Agnew even needs to collate a dossier to try to understand this enigma. There is a certain power in Nairac's withholding of information, and this controlling of data will come to play a large part in the lives of many characters in the text. Peter Middleton notes in *The Inward Gaze: Masculinity and Subjectivity in Modern Culture* that '[m]en have a vested interest in silence' (3). This is a society in which knowledge and secrecy are key. In the military, the managing of information is paramount, and this is seen as a most masculine virtue, diametrically opposed to qualities such as communication and empathy which are generally considered to be more feminine.

Nairac engages in the activities of masculine socialisation to such an extent that he almost descends into parody. Like the young Victor Kelly, he receives beatings from older boys at school and this hierarchy will perpetuate itself, as the beaten boy becomes the fearless Army Captain. His father advises him that fear was a glandular emotion and Nairac comes to realise that "You did not show fear" (McNamee, 2004: 57). His favourite sport, uncommon for someone of his class, is boxing. His boxing coach is surprised at his level of proficiency for a college boy. He thrives on physical combat of all kinds, and the boxing ring is one place where violence is accepted and encouraged. In these types of conflict one must continually prove oneself; you are only as good as your last fight. This is an integral element in the construction of masculinity, that it must continually be reasserted to be considered valid. The performance must not end, the mask must not slip. In his essay "Subject Honor, Object Shame" Roger Lancaster contends that "[a]s a gestural system, machismo has a steep temporal dimension, and yesterday's victories count for little tomorrow" (42). Even as a young army captain, Nairac arm-wrestles with a fellow officer, Ball, at the bar. There is a certain level of schoolboy humour and camaraderie that persists in accounts of Nairac. He is described variously as a "bit of a boy's own type", "a boy soldier" (McNamee, 2004: 230) and we are told that he had "a tendency towards undergraduate drinking games" (McNamee, 2004: 173).

It is often useful to employ psychoanalytic theory when interpreting a figures such as Kelly and Nairac who commit acts of extreme violence. Lee Horsley notes that there are two concepts important to the development of the protagonist in the Noir thriller and one can apply these to McNamee's central characters:

> The first is the representation of the protagonist's subjectivity- his perceptions (both accurate and deluded), his state of mind, his desires, obsessions and anxieties; the second is the extent to which he functions as a victim, transgressor or investigator. (8)

Nancy Chodorow's analysis of masculinity and extreme violence becomes helpful in interpreting characters who engage in such activities:

> If we try to analyse those individuals engaged in ethnic violence, we might well find that their individual unconscious fantasises involved not threats to self-hood, but, for instance, reparative wishes towards a parent, survivor guilt, separation fears, depressive anxiety, homosexual panic, defensive masculinity, identification with a soldier father, manic denial of survival, triumphant elation at survival, mourning a loss, or any number of other fantasies. (249)

In his work *The Anatomy of Human Destructiveness* Erich Fromm looks at the psychology of sadists. He notes that sadism "is the transformation of impotence into the experience of omnipotence, it is the religion of psychical cripples" (386). He also claims that violent sadism often manifests itself in the human relationships of the perpetrator, that "for the sadistic character everything living is to be controllable; living beings become things" (388). This is certainly true of the ways in which Victor Kelly seeks control over his on-off girlfriend Heather, his friends, and other members of the loyalist paramilitary group with which he is aligned, the UVF. The obvious question must be raised as to whether men such as these merely used the violent situation in Northern Ireland to legitimise their psychotic behaviour. The manner by which the Resurrection Men tortured and murdered their victims certainly alludes to a more than political motive for these killings, suggesting something altogether more sinister. Elmer Kennedy-Andrews argues in *Fiction and the Northern Ireland Troubles since 1969: (de-) constructing the North* that "McNamee explores the possibility of existential fulfilment through violence" (128). In reading his letters from prison, Victor's mother Dorcas is worried about the vocabulary of mental illness her son has acquired, in particular, agonising over the term "psycho-pathology".

Kennedy-Andrews also aligns Victor Kelly with what the psychiatrist Robert Lifton termed the "Protean Man". For Lifton, this type of man was characterised by an interminable series of experiments and explorations, each of which can be readily abandoned for new quests.[1] Kennedy-Andrews interprets Victor's violence as being a result of "uncertainty about his own identity" (123) and that he looks to images of masculinity in popular culture in order to provide him with a defined sense of self and masculine identity. One could interpret Victor as conceiving a form of masculinity which combines a keen eye for the aesthetic conventions of the 1970s, a sensibility inherited from classic gangster films, an understanding of forms of masculine notoriety and an awareness of the political consequences his actions had for the Belfast in which he lives.

*Resurrection Man* explores the way in which Victor Kelly's masculine identity was shaped and constructed by the media. In his essay "Violence and Vision: The Prosthetics and Aesthetics of Terror" Allen Feldman notes the "cinematic aesthetic" in the story told to him by a loyalist paramilitary and states that "The violent imagination in Northern Ireland is a visual imagination" (49-50). In using these techniques McNamee places himself within a genre, but his subject matter ensures that he is never too typical of it. One could also assert that McNamee as an author has also been influenced by these images, particularly in terms of the stylistic elements of film noir and gangster thrillers. The text's constant references to forms of media, from cinematic narrative to the presence of Ryan the journalist throughout the novel, establish the post-modern narrative of the text. Kennedy Andrews notes that "the stylish depthlessness of postmodern culture characterises the whole of the novel" (124).

In *Plotting Terror: Novelists and Terrorists in Contemporary Fiction*, Margaret Scanlan argues that *Resurrection Man* has a "strong postmodern bent" and this, coupled with its preoccupation with modern media, forces the reader to look at the conflict in Northern Ireland in a new, often disturbing way (37). In using the different narrative perspectives of various media agencies, from television news to Ryan's paper, and allowing his characters to use cinematic motifs, McNamee is employing the multi-faceted narrative that is crucial to the postmodern novel. This multiple viewpoint allows him to create multiple representations of multiple masculinities.

Victor Kelly's first brush with violent masculinity was from the films at the Apollo cinema in Belfast where he watches ultra-masculine tough guys settle their differences and assert their authority and identity through violence. This undoubtedly influences Victor as he adopts the pose and language of these films and applies their codes of behaviour to his everyday life, with varied consequences. When he encounters two older boys who wish to fight him he muses on how one of his movie heroes, Edward G. Robinson, would cope with the situation. His mother delights in the gangster rhetoric he uses when joking about his father. Victor comes to see the effectiveness of such a masculine façade and uses it during his criminal career to intimidate and insert himself into a similar mythology. In the police line up he gives "a Cagney smile, elegant and derisive" (McNamee, 1994: 53). When Victor has to ask Darkie if he can punish the latter's men we see an alpha-male clash of egos played out as the two men battle for supremacy, the old guard and the new. Victor imagines it like the great Western battles that he has seen in countless films: "The choreographed movements leading towards a duel" (McNamee, 1994: 41). Victor Kelly is always keenly aware of the significance of his actions, and the consequence they have for his masculine persona. Even at the apex of his power, he loves to watch cartoons on television, delighting in their unreal violence.

Victor's weapon of choice ensures his notoriety and his status as a malevolent outsider in the paramilitary world. In his work *The Shankill Butchers*, a history of the murders on which *Resurrection Man* is based, Martin Dillon argues that:

> The knife has been used by those on the fringes of paramilitary organizations: people out of control and therefore not subject to the kinds of discipline imposed by the majority of terrorists groupings. (111)

---

[1] See Kennedy-Andrews, 114-115. For more on the 'Protean Man' see Lifton, 13-27.

When the killings begin to strike fear into the population Victor Kelly adores the recognition he gets in the sectarian graffiti in Belfast.

Like Victor Kelly, Captain Robert Nairac in *The Ultras* is a figure who casts a long shadow over the world he inhabits but always retains an element of enigmatic mystery. Nairac was an ambitious young Army Officer who was stationed in Northern Ireland, and often conducted operations in the border counties. He fascinates many of the characters in the text and Blair Agnew devotes his life to an ultimately futile pursuit for the truth regarding his demise. In the final chapter, the suicide note of Blair's anorexic daughter Lorna, we discover that she very much identified with the secrecy that defined and shaped Nairac's existence. McNamee ensures that Nairac embodies almost unrealistic hyper-masculine qualities, reflecting the shifting nature of the historical appraisals of both this man and other military figures. The book opens with his death at the hands of shadowy assailants, so we get a sense of a doomed and fatalistic man throughout the text. We are told that this high-ranking army officer "looked like a drifter, a man sought after by police forces" (McNamee, 2004: 235).

This idea of secrecy also surrounds Victor Kelly as he starts to get paranoid towards the end of *Resurrection Man*, imagining himself "surrounded by rumour and speculation" (McNamee, 1994: 145). McNamee presents Victor as having almost superhuman qualities, as Victor draws an olfactory map of households and indiscretions around the Ormeau Road in Belfast. In the sectarian knife murders, the other participants torture the victim but it is Victor that cuts his throat. He understands the importance of fashionable dress and accessories in cultivating a masculine persona. He often observes how well-dressed he is compared to the nationalist paramilitary members. Nairac's masculinity is also often demonstrated through his physicality. Even his walk is described as predatory. We are told that he has a very firm handshake that conveys authority, strength and manliness. McNamee constructs Nairac as an almost legendary figure: he notes "Nairac's affinity for striking poses of unconscious heroism" (McNamee, 2004: 43). He is acutely aware of the construction of a persona with his "facile self-dramatising" (McNamee, 2004: 45). When Nairac visits the brothel we see him cultivate this enigmatic personality as the women fawn over him yet he retains power by being separate and withholding himself.

The pose of military violence also attracts Victor Kelly as he "saw himself as a general conducting pre-dawn briefings with a roomful of men with drawn faces, targets circled on the map" (McNamee, 1994: 46). He appreciates how the media can provide a sense of immortality. Before he gets his photograph taken in Castlereagh interrogation centre he grooms himself: "He knew that these photographs were important, that in the future they would be released to the press" (McNamee, 1994: 52). While dealing with Kelly and Nairac's individual psychological issues, McNamee also alerts us to the social conditions which legitimise such forms of behaviour. In an interview I conducted with McNamee in September 2004, he comments, regarding Kelly and Nairac, that:

I don't believe that they could have been psychotic without the system or systems which surrounded them, which is not to say that damaged psyches were not present in both cases.

If the novel is set in the mid-to-late 1970s, which textual clues and the chronology of the Shankill Butcher murders would indicate, we see a portrayal of a society which was very much polarised in terms of both sectarianism and class. The situation at this time can be seen as legitimising forms of masculinity and behaviours which would not be deemed acceptable in other situations, the ultra-violent "hard-man" is seen as firmly part of the community at this time, rather than a maverick outsider or social scourge. In *The Shankill Butchers* Martin Dillon explores how these men succeeded for so long because they were part of a community that accepted and protected them. This is a time when murder can be interpreted as political no matter how sadistic and brutal. Victor Kelly personifies this hyper-aggressive hyper-masculinity. Nairac also embodies a masculinity that is self-consciously militaristic and specialises in controlled aggression and calculated gestures. He deals in the covert and the "evocation of masculine virtue" (McNamee, 2004: 4). This is a masculinity that is synonymous with military, particularly colonial, conflict. This attitude is not place-specific; one cannot help thinking that any other society in which Nairac was stationed would have been treated with the same cool, detached authority. He has the status of a maverick, someone perceived to be on the edge of the conflict yet whose role cannot be construed as peripheral. David Erskine, who works in military intelligence, notes after a meeting with Nairac that "There was always the temptation to mythologize the moment as far as Robert was concerned" (McNamee, 2004: 113). Knox, a higher ranking army officer specialising in military intelligence, notices this quality in Nairac as he had detected a "potential for larger themes in Robert, something classical, the stark fatalist outlines of a blood narrative" (McNamee, 2004: 89).

Like Victor Kelly, he is acutely aware of how to perform a highly potent form of masculinity. Nairac understands universal practices of masculinity when he implores other officers to go into the bars of the Catholic Ardoyne area in North Belfast and smoke cigarettes with the locals in order to gain their respect. He also notes subtle shifts in accents around the country and uses this to his advantage. He prefers going out on exercises before dawn in order to intimidate the local people; he understands the need for a psychological side to warfare. He often went out without any backup and wanted it to be like that: he wanted to cultivate this mystery. He has intense respect for General Sir Frank Kitson's work on counter-insurgency, having seen him lecture, and regards his book as the "bloody bible" (McNamee, 2004: 114). We see the creation of Nairac as the archetypal army officer, accustomed to violence and more comfortable with conflict than social interaction. He learns military history at Sandhurst, he becomes absorbed into the canon of violence which is almost exclusively male. He becomes acquainted with "the amassed knowledge of violent death afflicted…You gather death. You subvert. You infiltrate. War as subtext" (McNamee, 2004: 149).

Through McNamee's protagonists in these novels we are afforded an alternative view of the conflict in Northern Ireland. His use of narrative techniques adopted from both the postmodern novel and the noir aesthetic give us a fuller understanding of how masculinity is constructed and understood today. Given that the conflict in Northern Ireland occurred in an age where forms of modern media began to come to prominence in everyday life, McNamee's style of narrative and forms of masculinity appear wholly appropriate and revelatory.

## References

Chodorow, Nancy J. 2002. "The Enemy Outside: Thoughts on the Psychodynamics of Extreme Violence with Special Attention to Men and Masculinity". In *Masculinity Studies & Feminist Theory: New Directions*. Ed. Judith Kegan Gardiner. New York: Columbia University Press

Dillon, Martin. 1989. *The Shankill Butchers: A Case Study of Mass Murder*. London Hutchinson

Feldman, Allen. 2000. "Violence and Vision: The Prosthetics and Aesthetics of Terror". In *Violence and Subjectivity*. Ed. Veena Das et al. Berkeley: University of California Press

Foster, John Wilson. 1974. *Forces and Themes in Ulster Fiction*. Dublin: Gill and Macmillan

Fromm, Erich. 1997. *The Anatomy of Human Destructiveness*. London: Pimlico

Horsley, Lee. 2001. *The Noir Thriller*. Basingstoke: Palgrave

Kennedy-Andrews, Elmer. 2002. *Fiction and the Northern Ireland Troubles since 1969: (De-) constructing the North*. Dublin: Four Courts

Lifton, Robert Jay. 1968. "Protean Man." *Partisan Review*. 35: 13-27

McNamee, Eoin. 1994. *Resurrection Man*. London: Picador

McNamee, Eoin. 2004. *The Ultras*. London: Faber

Middleton, Peter. 1992. *The Inward Gaze: Masculinity and Subjectivity in Modern Culture*. London: Routledge

Scanlan, Margaret. 2001. *Plotting Terror: Novelists and Terrorists in Contemporary Fiction*. Charlottesville: University Press of Virginia

Staub, Ervin. 1989. *The Roots of Evil: The Origins of Genocide and Other Group Violence*. Cambridge: Cambridge University Press

# Pathos and Paddywhackery: Erskine Nicol and the Painting of the Irish Famine

*Emily D. Mark*

In the mid-1990s Ireland and Irish diasporic communities worldwide marked the 150th anniversary of the Irish Famine.[1] The occasion of the anniversary sparked a surge of interest in Famine history and memory, and was accompanied by a new wave of scholarly and popular publications, commemorative music and theatre pieces, local history projects – even a commemorative rock concert featuring the Corrs and Van Morrison bearing the cringe-worthy tag "a celebration over disaster". The Irish government's Famine Commemoration Committee, led by TD Avril Doyle, disbursed over half a million Irish pounds to commemorative projects between 1995 and 1997.[2] Prominent amongst all the Famine projects, from the terribly mawkish to the indisputably moving, has been the construction of over 50 permanent Famine monuments and memorials throughout the diaspora.[3] Found in Ireland, Northern Ireland, England, Scotland, Wales, Canada, the U.S., and Australia, these contemporary commemorations represent a remarkable outpouring of visual responses to Famine memory. While many of these monuments are relatively small, local affairs, others – such as Brian Tolle's *Irish Hunger Memorial* in New York (2002) and Glenna Goodacre's *Irish Memorial* in Philadelphia (2003) – are offered as major public artworks, particularly those located in North America.

There is no little irony that the most durable of the 150th commemoration's productions are works of visual art. The Famine has long had the reputation as an "unrepresentable" event, one that did not excite the imagination of nineteenth-century artists, and found little visual expression. However, even a cursory examination of contemporary commemorations – such as Goodacre's *Irish Memorial* and the *An Gorta Mór* memorial in Roscommon – illustrates how heavily many of them have relied upon nineteenth-century models and representational tropes. Such borrowings suggest that a long genealogy of Famine visuality is already in place, though its specific branches have only recently attracted critical attention as a subject of inquiry. The visual expression of "famine" (conceptually and historically) is attendant to the constraints of artistic convention, market forces, and shifting ideological contexts that have shaped how we "see" the Famine from 1840 through to today.

Given the current intense interest in material projections of Irish historical memory, a critical analysis of the development of Famine visuality should appropriately begin with representations that emerge from first-hand experiences of Famine. Despite visual similarities, these original nineteenth-century works should be distinguished from the retrospective distillations of "memory" and "remembering" that define later commemorative works of art. Appropriately for a conference emphasizing the "cross-currents" between Scotland and Ireland, this brief paper takes as its focus the most prolific painter of the Irish during the late nineteenth century: the Scottish painter Erskine Nicol. Nicol is a painter relatively unknown today, his biography only partially complete. Yet he resided on the upper tiers of his profession as an Associate of the Royal Academy, and his small, cabinet-sized paintings were heavily engraved and widely consumed by popular audiences.

---

[1] Two excellent overviews of the Famine commemorative period can be found in Gray (2004) and Kelleher (2002).
[2] For details of recipient projects see Famine Commemoration Committee (not dated); Mullan, ed. (1995).
[3] This paper represents part of a larger dissertation project, which involves the cataloguing and analysis of twentieth century worldwide Famine memorials.

Creator of dozens of canvases of the Irish poor in the late nineteenth century, Nicol is largely absent from discussions of Famine representation. This exclusion is likely based on three principles. First is Nicol's penchant for images of Irish Paddywhackery—comic and often derogatory scenes of Irish "character" that have rendered much of his work distasteful for modern viewers. Such imagery does not easily conform to our expectation of thoughtful artistic engagements with the defining crisis of Ireland in the nineteenth century. Second is the undeniable fact that Nicol rarely painted famine directly, although this is neither remarkable nor unexpected in the prevailing colonial and artistic context, as Catherine Marshall has pointed out (1996).[4] If anything, however, the sublimation of stark representations of Famine suffering surely renders Nicol's canvases more, not less, interesting. The third basis for Nicol's marginalization has deeper roots, related to more general assumptions that have impeded the development of a Famine art history and visuality to date.

Before turning to Nicol's work specifically, a detour should be taken to address a few of these consonant issues related to Famine visuality. Media presents the first obstacle: when one examines the Famine-related output of the nineteenth century, it is immediately obvious that graphic work dominates the visual record. Undoubtedly the most famous of all famine images are those engravings which featured in the *Illustrated London News*, including iconic representations like *Bridget O'Donnell and Her Children*, and *Searching for Potatoes in a stubble field,* whose impact on contemporary Famine visuality has already been noted (Figs. 1-2). Unfortunately usage of graphic images in modern histories has mostly been confined to illustration of academic and popular books on the Famine; only rarely have these engravings themselves been interrogated with respect to their adherence (or rejection) of aesthetic conventions, as well as to their credibility as mimetic representations within the highly mediated, nascent form of illustrated journalism.[5] Although engraving work will not be discussed in detail here, it should be noted that many artists employed by the *Illustrated London News*, like the artist James Mahony who is most likely responsible for these images, worked also as painters within the academic or "fine" art tradition. Conventions employed more simplistically (at least from an aesthetic standpoint) in graphic illustration feature in full-flower in fine art. Thus painted treatments of the Famine (which will constitute the bulk of the examples in this paper) offer an ideal, if neglected, starting point for a consideration of nineteenth century Famine visuality.

Another obstacle in the development of a Famine art history relates to two problems of chronology: first, the difficulty of ascribing a beginning and ending to the experience of Famine, and second the development of social realism as a genre in Britain and Ireland. Ireland had of course for centuries experienced intermittent periods of famine before the intense and devastating crop failure and subsequent crisis that occurred in the 1840s.[6] Our present day concept of the "Great" Famine is itself clearly a historical construct; it may help us to make sense of the past, but to ascribe such narrow boundaries onto the experience of poverty and famine is to confuse our sensibilities with those of the nineteenth century. This point has been made by several commentators, including Cormac Ó Gráda, who criticized the Irish Government's ending of commemorative activities in 1997, sidestepping the fact that some of the worst was yet to come in 1849 and 1850 (1994, 1996).[7] The equivocal boundaries of Famine

---

[4] Marshall notes Irish history painting's relative unpopularity during this period (owing to its political potentialities); this was compounded by the often stifling conservatism of influential organs of commentary and critique like the Royal Academy and the Art Journal. See also Barlow and Trodd, eds. (2000).

[5] Notable exceptions include Crawford (1994), and Sinnema (1998).

[6] Ireland experienced a particularly devastating (though today little-known) famine in 1741, known in Irish as *bliadhain an áir* (year of the slaughter), with proportional mortality rates similar to those of the Great Famine. See Dickson (1997).

[7] For a contemporary perspective on this issue see also Curry (1992).

chronology have also been addressed by others concerned with Famine literary representation, most cogently by Christopher Morash who refers to 'the fundamental indeterminacy of the Famine... as an exemplary instance of the epistemological elusiveness of the past itself, exacerbated in this instance by the nature of the event' (1995: 3).

However, this recognition of Famine's blurred temporal boundaries has not percolated to art history, which usually limits discussion to the only Irish painting actually produced during the Famine years of 1845-50 with the Famine explicitly indicated in its title: Daniel MacDonald's *The Discovery of the Potato Blight in Ireland* (1847) (Fig. 3). While this painting has special significance given its direct engagement with Famine, it is a mistake to call off the search for Famine representation so prematurely, or to assume that provenances should strictly dictate relevance. This is particularly the case since British and Irish social realist painting and graphic work is far more common in the 1850s/60s than between 1840-1850, and the height of its popularity reached in the 1880s/90s.

The omission of relevant painted work from a Famine art history is exacerbated by the difficulty of what constitutes a "Famine subject", whether painted or engraved. This demarcation is far from straightforward, yet it accurately mirrors the complex and diffuse social reality of Famine. A surfeit of categories arise when all possibilities of famine-related subjects are considered: depictions of starvation and impoverished/emaciated human figures; representations of graveyards, death, and funerals; depictions of relief efforts (soup kitchens, workhouses, etc.); scenes of evictions, emigration, and social/political unrest; political humour and satire; landscapes and genre scenes depicting the generalised poverty of the Irish peasants; and even botanical/scientific illustrations (of potato fungus, for example). A recognition of the inspecificity of the Famine "subject" forces us to confront a range of competing images that offer interpretations of how the Irish poor lived and looked in the 1840s.

Given that the idea of the "Great" Famine of 1845-1850 is a retrospective categorization, not to mention a phenomenon understood wildly differently by those who experienced it at the time, it must be acknowledged that a working definition of "Famine imagery" should incorporate imagery concerned with the plight of Irish poverty and agrarian distress generally, as opposed to seeking a particular visual response to a singular historical event. In other words, from the perspective of both nineteenth and twentieth century viewers, images of the Irish Famine are part of a larger genealogy of Irish genre and landscape depictions; what "counts" as an interpretive image of the Famine proves quite flexible. While there is considerable truth in the observation that direct acknowledgments of the Famine in painted work are rare, depictions of its context and effects are not, and candidates for a revived history of Famine visuality come to the fore.

The work of Erskine Nicol embodies many of the contradictions just set out, yet his approach and training are typical of a genre painter working under the standard artistic rubrics regulated by institutions like the Royal Academy. Born in Leith, Scotland in 1825, Nicol trained at the Trustees' Academy in Edinburgh before moving to Ireland in 1845, where he remained until 1850 teaching art at the Department of Science and Art in Dublin. In 1850 he returned to Edinburgh and was elected an associate of the Royal Scottish Academy in 1855 and an academician in 1859; he became an Associate of the Royal Academy in 1869, and died in London in 1904.

Time spent in Ireland provided Nicol with an abundance of source material he was to draw upon for the rest of his career: scenes of peasant country life, usually Irish in derivation (though sometimes his Scottish and Irish scenes are indistinguishable). Nicol's pictures run the gamut of provincial tragedy and comedy: festivals, eviction, emigration, and miscellaneous genre scenes tending towards the humorous. Though his contemporaries criticized his attention to "low" subject matter he was generally acknowledged by them as a capable and accomplished painter (Dafforne: 1870), and despite his reliance on a relatively narrow field of subject matter, his range of expression within the provincial vignette is quite varied. Notwithstanding the observation that Nicol, despite his residence in Ireland during the worst years of the Famine, never directly painted the subject (as previously noted, no academic tradition existed that would have permitted exhibition of truly realistic representations, and Nicol was no mould-breaker), it is his sentimental version of Famine-era Ireland that was to prove one of the more prosperous and long-lived veins of representation.

The abundance of stereotyped depictions of the Irish "Paddy" in his work likely contributes to his low profile today: titles like *Spake, darlin* (1868) and *Waitin' for the praties* (1852) ring harshly on modern ears. The canvas *Bright Prospects* (1850s), used as an illustration for a 1910 Irish travelogue,[8] is a typical rendering of the inebriated, caricatured Paddy figure. Nicol's painting clearly aimed at a middle-class audience; he eschews complicated philosophical overtones comprehensible only to the classically educated, and restricts his canvases to mostly smaller, easily digestible, and more affordable cabinet-sized paintings. Often contrasted with the accomplishments of the Scottish painter David Wilkie, Nicol's work was sometimes viewed as derivative and lacking in the qualities which elevated Wilkie's painting: "the capacity of expressing his ideas and his insight in beautiful and appropriate pictorial terms" (Caw, 1908: 163). While Caw located Nicol's deficiencies in execution as opposed to selection of subject, he too criticized Nicol for being 'over-fond of the Irishman of farce' (164). The suggestion in *The Art Journal* that Nicol should attempt 'more elevated phases of Irish life and character' (Dafforne, 65) indicates the opinion of his contemporaries that his brand of humour, however popular, might also aspire to do more than entertain.

In contrast to his crude stereotypes of Irish "character", Nicol frequently created sympathetic and evocative depictions of the plight of the poor; his inconsistency in representation is problematic for anyone wishing to ascribe a definitive mindset or dismiss Nicol as a relic of pejorative Victorian attitudes toward the Irish. Nicol's painting *An Ejected Family* (1853) (Fig. 4) is one example of his more serious Famine-related treatments. Nicol dealt often with themes of land ownership, tenant/landlord relationships, and the tragedy of eviction, including works entitled *Notice to Quit, The Renewal of the Lease Refused, The Deputation, Paying the Rent,* and *Signing the New Lease*. Like his comic works, however, these paintings present a tableau enacted by recognizable types, neutering his work of any outright political sentiments. The universalising aspects of *An Ejected Family's* composition (agreeable, attractive family, sensitive landscape, absence of agents of the eviction) elides with George Eliot's comment in *Middlemarch* on "the softening influence of the fine arts which makes other people's hardships picturesque".[9] Although more precise in their detailing of social situations, Nicol's paintings cautiously toe what Julian Treuherz has described as "a fine dividing line": "… though they [the viewer] wanted to be touched, they did not want to be pained" (1987: 10).

Nicol shares much in common with Thomas Faed (1826-1900), his Scottish contemporary who also specialized in sentimental genre scenes of the poor. Faed's great Academy success *The Mitherless Bairn* (1855) utilizes many of the same tropes: the phonetic title, identifiably racial character, stage-like setting, and syrupy subject of an orphaned, homeless boy about to burst into tears. Like Nicol, Faed's painting is probably "more social than realist" (Treuherz, 41); like Nicol his views of poverty are carefully constructed and highly theatrical. Since the work of Hogarth in the eighteenth century, the lives of the lower classes had moved increasingly to the foreground of British painting, no longer confined to the periphery of landscape as staffage decoration in a Claudean schema.

Yet before representations of the poor were to acquire the tint of reformist zeal that imbued later nineteenth century social realism with serious purpose, the satirical and/or moral

---

[8] Although published in 1910, this travelogue bears striking resemblance to the author Mrs. S.C. Hall's earlier multi-volume account published 70 years earlier, with 16 reproductions of Nicol's works used as illustrations: Hall (1841-3). See also McConkey (1990: 24-26).
[9] Eliot, *Middlemarch* (1870-1), Ch. 39, cited in Treuherz, (1987: 10).

overtones of mid-century genre scene began to give way to the sentimental, and the sharper delineations of character and psychology found in David Wilkie's brand of realism softened. Faed and Nicol belong to this strand of idealised and melodramatic poverty, which might also be interpreted as an extension of the ideological process John Barrell describes as operative in eighteenth century landscape painting (1980). Harsh realities of lower class existence are muted, and depictions of the poor aestheticized or romanticized so as to appear an organic extension of a "natural" social order, which was in fact patently constructed and fiercely enforced. In the case of Ireland, scenes of picturesque poverty, and English viewers' approbation of their morally uplifting and edifying qualities, had a potent ideological dimension, related to the Malthusian doctrine of laissez-faire economics, colonial expectations of self-sufficiency and the perceived moral failure of the Irish to prevent or deal with the ravages of the Famine.[10] A comfortable distance is created between the subject in paint and the reality in the fields, a mechanism of reassurance when in actuality this narrowing gap between opposite ends of the social stratum alarmed the aristocracy, and later, the middle classes.

Thus the comic, the picturesque and the sentimental function as dialectics of distance: the aestheticization of poverty compels little viewer identification with subject; humour and pity act equally to create a benign image of the poor. Nicol's paintings of evictions and other tragic subjects, while lacking his characteristic comic punch in favour of enhanced sensitivity and emotional evocation, are nevertheless artificial performances of sentimentality. In recent years some have argued for the rehabilitation of the sentimental aesthetic,[11] usually on the basis of its connection to ethical or philanthropic action. Painting dismissed in the modern period as mawkish or emotionally indulgent is redeemed as a worthy expression of charitable sentiment and moral idealism that in principle, if not always in practice, was well-intended. On this basis sentimentality is celebrated for the positive qualities it emphasizes (generosity, sincerity, moral steadfastness) rather than those elements it chooses to exclude. Viewed ideologically, however, sentimentalism begins to fracture into those discourses based on structures of power: exoticism, imperialism, feminism, etc. We can begin to discern that one of the primary characteristics of sentimentalism, even when viewed positively, is its closed structure. As the psychologist Ciarán Benson has remarked:

> Sentimentality is repetition, a closed loop of feeling. It involves an attitude to art as the occasion for activating emotion already familiar to the person and desired by them for that very reason. The work of art, and it need not be a good one, functions as a trigger for feelings tied to other purposes. It is the repetition of the experience in a near reflex way that is the purpose of the music or poem or whatever. (2001: 219)

In this sense sentimentality seems antithetical to the practice of art; its narrow system of emotional reciprocity guarantees it will function to limit representational possibilities. Such limitations would eventually be rejected by the Aesthetics and later movements leading to Modernism; however, the value of sentimentalism as an aesthetic of power underlines its popularity for representations of the nineteenth century poor, and especially the colonised Irish.

The extent to which picturesque and sentimental tropes dominate typologies of painted Famine scenes is evident when *An Ejected Family* is compared to Daniel MacDonald's *The Discovery of the Potato Blight* of 1847. (MacDonald was a minor painter from Cork.) Like Nicol, MacDonald utilizes the multi-generational family group as subject; the figures are

---

[10] The subject of providentialism during the Famine years, and its vocal proponent Charles Trevelyan, has been examined at length by Famine historians. See Gray (1995); Foley and Ryder, eds. (1998); Bourke (1993); Donnelly Jr. (1996).
[11] See Solomon (2004).

similarly grouped centrally in an evocative landscape, and illuminated against a dark, tumultuous sky. His figures are again beautifully composed and dressed, and the colour red is infused into clothing details to picturesque effect. The ubiquitous 'innocent' is embodied in the small child (again on the left side of the composition) who gazes uncomprehendingly at her family. Differences between the two pictures point to Nicol's particular talent and fondness for capturing "character": "His brush seldom portrayed beauty… but his adroit touch is singularly happy in its application to the suntanned faces of pronounced physiognomy and dilapidated costume" (McKay cited in McEwan, 436). Similar scenes of eviction are prevalent enough in the later nineteenth century to have been dubbed a "sub-genre" by one critic (Curtis Jr.: 2003, 87); other examples include Robert Kelly's *An Ejectment in Ireland* (1848), Frederick Goodall's *An Irish Eviction* (1850), and Lady Elizabeth Butler's *Evicted* (1890). These eviction compositions are formulaic and reflect very closely elements utilized by Nicol; the repetition of type exhibits the circularity common to "sentimental" representations noted by Benson. Nicol's presentation of 'an emotional stage Irish scene' certainly rendered them apolitical and acceptable to the establishment (Kennedy: 1993, 20); Bourke and Breathnach-Lynch: 1999, 116), but it also demonstrates Famine-subject painting's conscription within sentimentalism that would prove very difficult to escape.

Beyond eviction, scenes of emigration feature as more numerous and varied than any other type of Famine-related subject pictures. The subject of estrangement, of leaving loved ones behind, and the drama attendant with a loved one's departure appealed to a wide artistic community, as attested by the range of artworks from Ford Madox Brown's well-known *The Last of England* (1855) to Hubert von Herkomer's *Pressing to the West: A Scene in Castle Garden, New York* (1884). The divergent interests of painters who attempted such subjects makes generalization difficult; romantic and realist treatments may be found of English, Scottish, and Irish scenes (occasionally, but not always distinct). More realistic views of emigrant experience, particularly when attempted on epic scale, continued to draw criticism for their "artlessness" in depicting ugliness and misery, as John Ruskin's stinging comment on Herkomer's work demonstrates:

> Some artists are apt to become satirists and reformers instead of painters; to use the indignant passion of their freedom no less vainly than if they had sold themselves into slavery. Thus Mr. Herkomer… spends his best strength in painting a heap of promiscuous emigrants in the agonies of starvation. (Ruskin cited in Treuherz, 96)

Despite the efforts of artists like Herkomer who sought a more objective and complex view of social reality, the experience of emigrants usually met the same visual fate as the victim of eviction: emotive, poignant despair, located in the figures of a multi-generational family symbolizing departure, death, loss, and (more rarely) arrival and hope. Erskine Nicol's *Irish Emigrants Waiting for the Train* (1864) (Fig. 5)[12] was exhibited at the Royal Academy in 1864; other works of his on the emigration theme include *Outward Bound* and its mid-nineteenth century companion *Homeward Bound* (Fig. 7), and *Irish Emigrant Arriving at Liverpool* (1871). Again, the politics are rendered ambiguous; there is no indication of why the individuals depicted are emigrating, although the sorrow of the scene is once more personified by a central female figure in distinctive, colourful dress. Such a representation stretches the boundaries of the category "Famine-related subject", as neither main character appears too worse for wear, nor is there any direct reference to Famine-wrought hardship. As we have seen thus far, however, pictorial accuracy is no prerequisite for images of the Irish poor during the 1840s; Nicol's work is evidence of the manner in which types are sustained through time without

---

[12] Two nearly identical versions of this work exist in the Tate Gallery and Sheffield Art Museum.

regard to factuality. The painting might be interpreted as a study of character contrasts: the female figure sits in melancholic reverie, a wistful expression momentarily crossing her pretty features. Her companion, a rough country labourer, seems poised in mid-exclamation, and his posture and facial expression portray him as a coarse but non-threatening bumpkin.

The figures' juxtaposed mental states are one of the dichotomous representational tropes utilized frequently to frame the emigration subject: home and away, poverty versus success, the backward heavy-hearted glance versus the confident and/or fearful gaze into the future. The *Punch* cartoon 'Here and There: or, Emigration, A Remedy' from 1848 (Fig. 6) shows this model applied more sharply. Yet most emigration paintings focus on the moment of departure, not arrival; the future remains a mythologized unknown. The pictures capture less the reality of emigration than a construct simplifying the emotions involved, a model of nostalgic fantasy feeding into the sensibilities of the viewer. The emigration narrative in paintings like Nicol's is homogenized and sanitised; it reflects a gentle, passive acceptance of what undoubtedly constituted a painful and bitter inevitability. The easy malleability of the emigration subject to existing modes of representation (be they picturesque, sentimental, or realist) may explain its pervasiveness as a category within Irish genre painting.

## Conclusion

In conclusion, I wish to make a few comments on the durability of some of the Famine iconography present in the work of Erskine Nicol, even in the wake of modernism and the rejection of Victorian aesthetics in the contemporary period. The potency of theatrical sentimentality as a directive for viewer response has been retained in some contemporary Famine commemorations, and the deployment of Irish stereotypes revived as a means of evoking a new mythology of patrimony and pathos. A Famine memorial from 1999 in an Irish American community centre just outside Chicago attempts to pull all heartstrings, simultaneously and forcefully, with its encyclopaedia of Irish symbology: the impoverished family and exposed skeletal children, the high cross, the harp, the thatched cottage, the phantasmagorial spectre of death- everything but the wolfhound.[13] Likewise, the construct of emigration still presents a linear historical moralizing: compare Nicol's "here and there" lithographs *Outward Bound* and *Homeward Bound* (mid nineteenth century) (Fig. 7), and Robert Shure's Boston Famine Memorial (1998) (Fig. 8). Both present a simplified narrative of conquest and success that sidesteps a messier humanity in favour of transforming poverty into as a vehicle for moral contemplation which implies a "natural" progression towards modernity. While such works may move one to sympathy, they stop short of eliciting an empathetic response and evade any true confrontation between viewer and subject. Though in both cases there may be more history than art to these examples, they offer a compelling argument for the initiation of a diachronic visual study of the Famine that can help explain the persistence of the artificial tragic spectacle in Famine imagery, and account for the ideological impulses that underlie this choice of representation across disparate temporal and spatial frontiers.

---

[13] Chicago Gaelic Park Memorial Project, http://www.cgp-chicago.org

Figure 1

'Bridget O'Donnell and her children',
Illustrated London News, 22 December 1849
Image coutsey of 'Views of the Famine', Vassar University
(http://vassun.vassar.edu/~sttaylor/FAMINE)

An Gorta Mór Memorial, Roscommon,
Co. Roscommon (1999)
Photograph: E. Mark

Figure 2

'Searching for Potatoes in a stubble field',
Illustrated London News, 22 December 1849
Image coutsey of 'Views of the Famine', Vassar University
(http://vassun.vassar.edu/~sttaylor/FAMINE)

Glenna Goodacre, Irish Memorial,
Philadelphia, Pennsylvania (2003)
Photograph: E. Mark

Figure 3
Daniel MacDonald
*The Discovery of the Potato Blight in Ireland* (1847)
Reproduced by kind permission of the UCD Delargy Centre for Irish Folklore
and the National Folklore Collection

Figure 4
Erskine Nicol,
An Ejected Family (1853)
Courtesy of the National Gallery of Ireland

Figure 5
Erskine Nicol
*Irish Emigrants Waiting for the Train* (1864)
(c) Tate, London 2005

Figure 6
'Here and There: or, Emigration, A Remedy', Punch, 15 July 1848
Image coutsey of 'Views of the Famine', Vassar University
(http://vassun.vassar.edu/~sttaylor/FAMINE)

Figure 7
Erskine Nicol
*Outward Bound / Homeward Bound* (1850s)
Coutsey of National Library of Ireland

Figure 8
Robert Shure
*Boston Irish Famine Memorial* (1998)
Photograph: E. Mark

## References

Barlow, Paul, and Colin Trodd, eds. 2000. *Governing Cultures: Art Institutions in Victorian London*. Aldershot: Ashgate Press

Barrell, John. 1980. *The Dark Side of the Landscape: The Rural Poor in English Painting, 1730 1840*. Cambridge: Cambridge University Press

Benson, Ciarán. 2001. *The Cultural Psychology of Self*. London: Routledge

Bourke, Austin. 1993."*The Visitation of God"?: The Potato and the Great Irish Famine*. Dublin: Lilliput Press

Bourke, Marie, and Síghle Breathnach-Lynch. 1999. *Discover Irish Art at the National Gallery of Ireland*. Dublin: National Gallery of Ireland

Caw, James L. 1908. *Scottish Painting, Past and Present*. Edinburgh: T.C. and E.C. Jack

Crawford, Margaret. 1994. "The Great Irish Famine 1845-9: Image versus Reality". In *Ireland: Art into History*. Ed. Raymond Gillespie and Brian P. Kennedy. Dublin: Town House. 75-88

Curry, B. 1992. "Is Famine a Discrete Event?" *Disasters*. 16

Curtis Jr., L. Perry. 2003. "The Land for the People: Post-Famine Images of Evictions". In *Éire – Land*, ed. Vera Kreilkamp. Chestnut Hill: Chicago University Press. 85-92.

Dafforne, James. 1870. "British Artists: Their Style and Character. Erskine Nicol, R.S.A., A.R.A." *Art Journal (London)*. 1 March: 65-7

Dickson, David. 1997. *Arctic Ireland: The Extraordinary Story of the Great Frost and Forgotten Famine of 1740-41*. Belfast: White Row Press

Donnelly Jr., James S. 1996. "'Irish Property Must Pay for Irish poverty': British Public Opinion and the Great Irish Famine". In *"Fearful Realities": New Perspectives on the Famine*. Eds. Chris Morash and Richard Hayes. Dublin: Irish Academic Press. 60-76

Famine Commemoration Committee. N.d. *Ireland's Famine: Commemoration and Awareness*. Dublin: N.p.

Foley, Tadhg, and Sean Ryder, eds. 1998. *Ideology and Ireland in the Nineteenth Century*. Dublin: Four Courts Press

Gray, Peter. 1995. "Ideology and the Famine". In *Famine Echoes*. Ed. Cathal Póirtéir. Dublin: Gill and Macmillan. 86-103

Gray, Peter. 2004. "Memory and Commemoration of the Great Irish Famine". In *The Memory of Catastrophe*. Eds. Peter Gray and Kendrick Oliver. Manchester: Manchester University Press.

Hall, Mr & Mrs S.C. 1841-3. *Ireland: Its Scenery, and Character*. 3 vols. London: How and Parsons

Kelleher, Margaret. 2002. "Hunger and History: Monuments to the Great Irish Famine." *Textual Practice* 16.2: 249-76.

Kennedy, Brian P. 1993. *Irish Painting*. Dublin: Town House and Country House

Marshall, Catherine. 1996. "Painting Irish History: The Famine." *History Ireland*. 4.3: 46-50

McConkey, Kenneth. 1990. *A Free Spirit: Irish Art 1860-1960*. Woodbridge: Antique Collectors' Club in association with Pyms Gallery, London

McEwan, Peter J.M. 1994. *Dictionary of Scottish Art and Architecture*. Woodbridge: Antique Collectors' Club

Morash, Christopher. 1995. *Writing the Irish Famine*. Oxford: Clarendon Press

Mullan, Don, ed. 1995. *A Glimmer of Light: An Overview of Great Hunger Commemorative Events in Ireland and throughout the World*. Dublin: CONCERN Worldwide

Ó Gráda, Cormac. 1994. "Satisfying a Great Hunger for Guilt and Self-pity." *Sunday Tribune*. May 15: N.p.

Ó Gráda, Cormac. 1996. "Making Irish Famine history in 1995." *History Workshop Journal* 42 (Fall): 195-214

Sinnema, Peter W. 1998. *Dynamics of the Pictured Page: Representing the Nation in the Illustrated London News*. Aldershot: Ashgate

Solomon, Robert C. 2004. *In Defense of Sentimentality*. Oxford: Oxford University Press

Treuherz, Julian. 1987. *Hard Times: Social Realism in Victorian Art*. London: Lund Humphries in association with Manchester City Art Gallery

Valone, David A., and Christine Kinealy, eds. 2002. *Ireland's Great Hunger: Silence, Memory, and Commemoration*. Lanham, MD: University Press of America

# "What Time Is It?": The Juxtaposition of Tradition and Postmodernity in Tom Murphy's *Bailegangaire*.[1]

*Margaret Maxwell*[2]

In his introduction to *Transitions: Narratives of Irish Culture*, Richard Kearney poses the question: "Is it possible to make the transition between past and future, between that which is familiar to us and that which is foreign?" (9). This is an issue that is explored by Tom Murphy in *Bailegangaire*. The theatrical space of this play inhabits two time-frames simultaneously: the pre-Lamass economic-expansion period of the 1950s, juxtaposed to the mass-production and economic instability of the 1980s. The play's narratives embody a "crisis of culture", as outlined by Kearney, that place in direct conflict the claims of tradition and modernity. These (seemingly) diametrically opposed concepts are enshrined in the contemporary movements of *revivalism* and *modernism*: the former seeking to "revive the past", the latter choosing to "rewrite or repudiate it altogether". Each cultural narrative, as Kearney states, amounts to "a reinterpretation of its own history, an attempt to retell the story of the past as it relates to the present". It is, in short, the space "where the text of imagination interweaves with the context of history": "a point of transit between past and future" (10).

This point of transit is the space that Murphy sets out to explore in *Bailegangaire*. In a paper published in the *Canadian Journal of Irish Studies* entitled "Refiguring Lost Narratives – Prefiguring New Ones", Shaun Richards argues that Murphy "mobilizes both past and present in the service of the future" (91). He posits the play's dramatic intent as being to "hold the impoverished rural Irish actuality against the pastoral Irish ideal as articulated by successive nationalist ideologies and, simultaneously, to expose the vacuousness of a fragile economic progress" (95). Neither world is delineated favourably in the play. Mommo's narrative attests to the desperate poverty that De Valera's rural idyll had imposed, whilst the contemporary moment is epitomized by failed inward-investment (as evinced by the impending Japanese plant closure), and by Dolly's hi-tech "new liquorice-all-sorts-coloured house" (150). By juxtaposing these two vastly different worlds through the medium of the kitchen-sink drama that he once categorically dismissed, Murphy foregrounds the fact that such a prodigious change had occurred within only a generation.[3] In *The Postmodern Condition*, Jean-François Lyotard identifies the circumstances that allow for this phenomenon; there is, he says, a "temporal disjunction" in relation to "the postmodern age", a phenomenon recognizable since the mid- to late 1950s (3). Accordingly, "regional/temporal disparities" in development result in the realization of such a condition at a pace commensurate with the rate of industrialization attendant upon that society (Richards, 81-2). The somewhat problematic term, "postmodernity", is said to denote:

> a culture of fragmentary sensations, eclectic nostalgia, disposable simulacra, and
> promiscuous superficiality, in which the traditionally valued qualities of depth,

---

[1] In interview, Tom Murphy voiced reservations about the utilization of words like "post-modern and post-post-modern and post-colonial" (Ni Anluain, 185). This paper uses the term "postmodern", however, to foreground the *"transitional crisis"* (Kearney, 14) of the peculiarly Irish phenomenon, as identified by Fintan O'Toole, of being "a post-modern society without ever fully becoming a modern one" (O'Toole, 35).
[2] I should like to acknowledge the support of the Carnegie Trust for the Universities of Scotland, through the Caledonian Research Foundation.
[3] Murphy recollects that, when writing his first play, *On The Outside* – a collaboration with Noel O'Donoghue – it was decided that, 'one thing is sure, it's not going to be set in a kitchen': thus defiantly setting themselves against this tradition (Roche, 131).

coherence, meaning, originality and authenticity are evacuated or dissolved amid the random swirl of empty signals. (Baldick, 201)

By realizing these conditions within the traditional setting of the play, Murphy effectively bears witness to the validity of O'Toole's claim (as instanced above).

This is dramatically literalized in the fragmentary nature of Mommo's "endlessly incomplete story", the limiting consequence of which, says Richards, is to "freeze-frame past and present without admitting an end which will liberate both into future" (95). However, the process of intercutting an historical account with the events of the present day, thereby realizing the end of the narrative, allows Murphy to "project [...] a unified past and present into a potential future" (92). Before this can be achieved, however, the theatre audience/reader must struggle to make some sort of linear sense of these conflicting mono-/dialogues; Mommo's rambling narrative impinges on, and serves to frustrate, the concurrent contemporary dialogues of Dolly and Mary. Hers is the oral story-telling tradition of the seanachie, and Mary draws emphasis to this quality when she reminisces that, "People used to come miles to hear you tell stories" (116). Her reiterative story, as Nicholas Grene notes, is delivered in "a rich mix of language, the Irish and the Irishisms blending with an orotund vocabulary of Latinate English"; as a result, an audience will be "borne along on its rhythms, scarcely attending to its content" (1991: 221-2).

By contrast, Dolly and Mary's dialogues are illustrative of a more post-modern form of fragmentation: a random swirl of empty *signifiers*. Where Mommo's tale is tuned in and out, like the radio programme that is switched on and off throughout the play, their conversation acts as "interference" to this tale; thus, frustrating the telling/hearing of the story. Moreover, they impede the relating of each other's narratives: Dolly claims to "talk straight", but she hides her pregnancy, and skirts around her "plan" without coming to the point; Mary avoids the issue, obliquely voicing her suspicions with the question "Why don't you take off your coat?" (101, 106, 112, 131). Indeed, throughout the play, communication is frustrated by the characters, each of whom engage in equivocating, contractual language games, the function of which is to eschew clarification. Consequently, they talk simultaneously, cut each other off, ask oblique questions, avoid giving answers, and trail into ellipsis.

Due to Mommo's persistent recitation, the very fabric of Mary and Dolly's dialogue becomes intricately interwoven with moments from the past. When Mommo does recognize the present it is, like her narrative, at one remove; Mary is reduced in status to yet another "stranger" – one who is attendant upon her – because Mommo refuses to recognise in her the now grown-up granddaughter of the story, who was expected to be "well able to look after" the others (124), yet wasn't. Her transition between worlds is seamlessly, if provisionally, executed; when she does make this transition, it is invariably to ask: "What time is it?" This repetend encapsulates the plight of all three characters, who, whilst enslaved to the past, are unable to reconcile it with the present, or, resultantly, to project a future. As Jochem Achilles notes, for instance, Mary's compulsion to care, as attested to by her chosen profession, is recognizably a result of the accident, and her failure to look after Tom's fatal burns. Similarly, Dolly's life has been prescribed by her childish role of being "like a filmstar" (161): the stage directions emphasise this, describing her as "[l]ike her name, dolled up, gaudy rural fashion" (99).[4]

Towards the end of Act Two, the sisters form a tableau in which they are described as being *"two figures frozen in time"* (161). Time is always a variable commodity: "What time is it? [...] Seven. Eight" (95). However, Dolly does make one attempt to ground them unambiguously in time: "Ten to ten, 1984" (141). The *mise en scène* is described as *"a country kitchen in the old style"*, with *"some modern conveniences"* (91); here, the archaic and the modern struggle for supremacy in a set which alternates between electric and candle lighting. This

[4] See Achilles 83.

inability to firmly establish time is reflected in their confused identities: Mommo refers to herself as the stranger's wife; for her, Mary is "Miss", a servant, whilst for Mary, her own previous life as a nurse is rejected because "that wasn't me at all" (159); and Dolly answers Mommo's, *"Who are you?"* uncertainly with, "Dolly, I think" (109). The merging of time-frames in the above manner is indicative of the "search for meaning and self realization in the modern present" (Richards, 94). In this present, cars pass by and Dolly arrives on the trusty Honda that "goes like a bomb" (107); Mommo's tale, however, harks back to an age of measured travel by horse and cart: one pulled by the aptly named Pedlar. Dolly may be disillusioned with her new-found state of affluence and mod-cons, yet at Mommo's there is no inside convenience. At the point outlined above, when they are "frozen in time", Mary has made the decision to leave home, and not take Dolly's child. It is the "sound of speed" (146, 161), in the form of the (ironically dubbed) "funeral cortege" from the factory, that first breaks this frozen image and, arguably, the spell of the past. Dolly laughingly encapsulates their predicament through Mommo's idiomatic, "Jesus, misfortunes!" Then, as stage directions identify, *'the unexpected*. MOMMO's *voice'*:

> **MOMMO.** What time is it?
> *Silence.*
> **MARY.** Seven. (*In a whisper, waiting, frozen*). (161)

This is the point at which, seemingly triggered by their laughter, Mommo moves on to complete her narrative.

This monologue is, of course, the catalyst for change. In "Discourse in the Novel", Mikhail Bakhtin asserts that language is "never unitary". Rather, it is "dialogic", "ly[ing] on the borderline between oneself and the other"; moreover, it is "stratified and heteroglot", and "represents the co-existence of socio-ideological contradictions between the present and the past":

> It becomes "one's own" only when the speaker populates it with his own intention, his own accent, when he appropriates the word, adopting it to his own semantic and expressive intention. [...T]he word does not exist in a neutral and impersonal language [...] but rather it exists in other people's mouths, in other people's contexts, serving other people's intentions: it is from there that one must take the word, and make it one's own. (293-4)

Prompted by an idle remark of Dolly's, Mary comes to intuit the necessity to "live out the – story – finish it, move on to a place where, perhaps, we could make some kind of a new start" (153). She progressively comes to adopt Mommo's idiom: at first in sardonic parody, expressive of her own frustrated search for "home"; then, as the stage directions specify, *"speaking simultaneously/silently with* MOMMO" (136); subsequently, as a means of coaxing from her the 'last piece that you never tell' (157); and finally, appropriating her words as a conscious choice, to incorporate a past narrative-style into an enabling present narrative. This conscious choice is silently foregrounded in her pause before the idiomatic "-fambly" (170). In so doing, she recognizes the truth of George Steiner's statement that "a language contains within itself the boundless potential of discovery, of re-compositions of reality, of articulate dreams" (xiv).

The critical consensus, to date, recognizes this need for, and realization of, narrative closure in Mommo's story, that will allow her to "face the trauma which lies behind its obsessive re-telling", and thus "free the family from its tragic inheritance" (Grene, 227). The essence of Mommo's obsessive "unfinished symphony" invites a Freudian interpretation of trauma; this recognizes a "response to an unexpected or overwhelming violent event or events that are not fully grasped as they occur, but |which| return later in repeated flashbacks, nightmares, and other repetitive phenomena" (Caruth, 91). Dolly highlights this response in Mommo when she talks of "the day we buried Grandad': 'Not a tear [...] Not a tear – And – *And!* – Tom buried in that same hole in the ground a couple of days before. Not a tear, then or since" (143). In *Unclaimed Experience*, Cathy Caruth explores Freud's "passionate fascination" with traumatic experiences, and highlights the "crucial link" between literature and Freud's theory. She discusses the ways in which texts "speak about and speak through the profound story of traumatic experience", and considers trauma, thematically, in relation to "accident", "history" and "the voice of the other" (3-4). Such a tri-part framework can be applied to Mommo's condition, which is born out of a tragic accident, the consequences of which create a "traumatising shock", is symptomatic of the ongoing struggle of a survived trauma, and which responds to the appeal of the "voice of another", eventually recognized through their dual-monologue.

These themes work reciprocally, for, not only does Mommo respond to Mary's adoption of her own tale as a means of teasing out the undisclosed conclusion, but, in so doing, Mary comes to a realization of her own narrative voice through her utilization of Mommo's rhetoric. The narratives that Mary must reconcile are juxtaposed in her outburst at the end of Act One:

> **MARY.** (*Pulling away from* DOLLY *to shout at* MOMMO). Finish it, finish it, that much at least – [...]
> (*To* DOLLY *who is following her*) Why don't you take off your coat! (To MOMMO) What was waiting for them at dawn when they got home in the morning? (131)

These issues cannot be resolved until Mommo's narrative reaches its natural end and Mary can "conclude" with an open-ended narrative of promise: "a brand new baby to gladden their home" (170). Mommo's compulsive repetition can be seen to be a "traumatic neurosis" which "emerges as the unwitting re-enactment of an event that one simply cannot leave behind" (Caruth, 2). Mommo is so trapped in reiterating her narrative that Dolly can prompt her with a casual "Good man Josie!" (105, 112, 130) and she will pick up the threads of the tale and continue. Similarly, both Mary and Dolly's intricate knowledge of the story stand as testimony to its perpetuation, as do the state of Mary's nerves in the first act. Stage directions, for instance, identify her as *"seated beside the fire, looking at nothing"*, and *"possibly near breaking point"* (91). Moreover, her demeanour throughout the first act attests to the fact that Mommo's monomaniacal narrative is indicative of a soul-destroying state of normalcy. The girls are, therefore, also able to take up the commentary at any given point. Mary, for instance, interjects: "Not a gansey" into Mommo's narrative, but then corrects herself as Mommo continues, relentlessly, "*Nor* a gansey": thus illustrating her near word-perfect status (113).

The tragic deaths that result from the night of the laughing competition – wistfully referred to as "the nicest night ever" (131, 156, 164, 165) – have triggered the trauma that keeps Mommo trapped in time within a narrative, the conclusion of which she cannot articulate. To hang the play upon Caruth's Freudian framework, Mommo's story becomes "a kind of double telling, the oscillation between a *crisis of death* and the correlative *crisis of life*: between the story of the unbearable nature of an event and the story of the unbearable nature of its survival" (7). In light of this reading, Mommo's narrative is symptomatic of a traumatic neurosis: it manifests as "the unwitting re-enactment of an event that one simply cannot leave behind" (2). According to Freud, trauma resists simple comprehension; moreover, traumatic experience is followed by a period of *latency* in which the subject appears unaffected by the trauma (witness Mommo's tearless state at the graveside). What returns to haunt the victim at a later date "is not only the reality of the violent event but also the reality of the way that its violence has not yet been fully known" (6). Thus, Mommo's narrative defers closure, eschewing the *consequences* of the laughing competition, which remain latent, and indulging in denial: "I don't remember any more of it" (159); consequently, the trauma repeats itself "exactly and unremittingly, through the unknowing acts of the survivor [Mommo] and against [her] very will" (Caruth, 2). By projecting the laughterless fate onto the Bochtáns, and punctuating her own narrative with the parodic laughter of the protagonists, Mommo again negates reality. Hers is a laughter that *"has defiance, hatred in the sound"* (93); yet the genuine laughter of Dolly and Mary, in Act Two, serves as catalyst to the final part of the story, in which Mommo's repressed tears find expression in the *"hih-hih-hih which punctuates her story"*; these come to *"sound more like tears – ingrown sobs – […] than laughter"* as she recounts the "misfortunes" of a lifetime (164). Increasingly, laughter moves from being a destructive, or sinister, force, as demonstrated in the fateful "laughing competition", to one of release and healing. In the second act, for instance, stage directions specify that Mary and Dolly *"forget themselves"*, and start *"laughing their own laughter"* at Mommo's dramatization, the exchange ending with *"the three of them laughing"* together. This transformation is encapsulated in Mary's tears at the end of the play: in this instance, her crying is *"infused with a sound like the laughter of relief"* (170).

The incomprehensibility of the trauma, as manifest by the repetitive nature of the story, parallels the Freudian theory of dreams insofar that it is a form of "repetitive seeing". It works as a delay that "reveals the eradicable gap between the reality of a death and the desire that cannot overcome it except in the fiction" (Caruth, 95). To this end, the dénouement is never articulated, the protagonists are never personalized (their true identities remain hidden behind the protective distancing device of the third-person narrative), and Tom is perpetually and allusively "in Galway" (98, 107, 125, 165). Mommo's guilt is articulated, somewhat obliquely, in the refrain "the cursed paraffin" (93, 122, 168), in her admission that "sure, they *could* have got home" (140, 149; emphasis added), and in her obsession with the loss of "the sweets" (precious gifts for the children). Moreover, the last part of Mommo's tale reveals that "the stranger's wife" felt "no heed on her now to be gettin' on home", but was "offerin' to herself congratulations at hearin' herself laughin'" (161-3). This guilt emerges as a Freudian wish-fulfilment that allows for the potential encapsulated in the statement "Tom is in Galway". Mommo's story is, as Grene recognizes, a "penitential retelling" of events (1991: 223). It can be no coincidence, therefore, that the word that Mommo subconsciously uses as a stalling device, when Mary tries to coax the end of the story from her, is "pardon". Dolly draws attention to this fact when she calls Mommo's tale her "confession" (141).

The baldness of Dolly's assertion that "Tom is dead […] Now do ye know?" elicits only a blank "I do", followed instantly by the non-sequitur, "I'm waiting for someone". This "someone" is her father for whom she is perpetually waiting. Mommo has become infantilized by the (n)ever present corrective authority wielded by "me father". Her narrative is punctuated with the refrain: "I want to see me father", "he has a big stick". This patriarchal authority is immortalized in Mommo's narrative; his words serve to check its flow, frustrating its conclusion. This is the Lacanian Law-of-the-Father under the symbolic order: the laws and restrictions that control desire as embodied in language. For Lacan, language is empty, and all communication constitutes a futile attempt to impose order on desire. Mommo's cyclical narrative can be seen as a potentially endless search to articulate loss under this restrictive medium. Before she can be granted the absolution she seeks, she must defy this image of authority by completing her "unfinished symphony" (122), and admitting to the tragic events.

Caruth discusses this in her exploration of Lacan's reading of traumatic awakenings:

> The dream thus becomes, in Lacan's analysis, no longer a function of sleep, but rather a function of awakening. If Freud asks, *What does it mean to sleep?* Lacan discovers at the heart of the question another one, perhaps even more urgent: *What does it mean to awaken?* (99)

"Repetition", says Lacan, "demands the new"; "[t]his newness is enacted in the fact that the words are no longer mastered or possessed by the one who says them" (107). Previously, Mary's main concern was to stop Mommo's story; however, prompted by an idle remark of Dolly's – "Why doesn't she finish it? And have done with it" (102) – she suddenly becomes aware of the need to "Live out the – story – finish it, move on to a place where, perhaps, we can make some kind of a new start" (153).

This is realized at the close of the play, which achieves, as Richards states, a "totalizing harmony' (96). Mommo finally calls Mary by her name, allowing her "to conclude", after she has added "[her] bit" to the narrative, thus arriving at Kearney's "point of transit between past and future" (10). Moreover, she has decided to help Dolly after all, by taking the baby. This promise is first articulated with the words, "you're going to be alright, Dolly" (167). Whilst this echoes the *un*fulfilled promised blessing (160) once conferred upon Mary herself, that she had hung on to, vainly, for "oh, twenty years", hers differs in that it is *not* an empty promise: she will be there to help her sister. Thus, the past is reinvented "as a living transmission of meaning", rather than entrenched in "a deposit of unchangeable truth" (Kearney, 17):

> To conclude. It's a strange old place, alright, in whatever wisdom He has to have made it this way. But in whatever wisdom there is, in the year of 1984, it was decided to give that – fambly … of strangers another chance, and a brand new baby to gladden their home. (170)

It is no coincidence that the final word of the play is "home". Mommo's journey has finally been completed, and with her homecoming, Mary makes peace with her own familial *omphalos*. Mommo's narrative achieves closure proper when she is able to recognize herself and her husband, Seamus, as "the strangers, that decent man an' his decent wife the same", in the story (96, 119), instead of taking refuge behind the façade of the third person narrative. By utilizing Mommo's diglossic narrative to enable her own, Mary can suggest, through fiction, a future of possibilities. She has discovered, by "circularity", "another means home" (99); this is suggestive of a future narrative that *accommodates* the past, without being enslaved to it.

### References

Achilles, Jochem. 1996. "The Change of Paradigms and the Return of the Repressed in Tom Murphy's Drama". In *The Classical World and the Mediterranean*. Eds. Giuseppe Serpillo and Donatella Badin. Tema: Università di Sassari. 79-86
Bakhtin, Mikhail. 1981. "Discourse in the Novel". In *The Dialogic Imagination: Four Essays by M.M Bakhtin*. Ed. Michael Holquist. Trans. Caryl Emerson and Michael Holquist. Austin: University of Texas Press
Baldick, Chris. Ed. 2001, 2004. *Oxford Concise Dictionary of Literary Terms*. Oxford: OUP
Caruth, Cathy. 1996. *Unclaimed Experience*. Baltimore: John Hopkins University Press
Grene, Nicholas. 1991. "Talking, Singling, Storytelling: Tom Murphy's After Tragedy". *Colby Quarterly*. 27.4: 210-24
Grene, Nicholas. 1999. *The Politics of Irish Drama*. Cambridge: CUP
Hawthorn, Jeremy. 2000. *A Glossary of Contemporary Literary Theory*. London: Arnold
Kearney, Richard. 1988. *Transitions: Narratives in Modern Irish Culture*. Dublin: Wolfhound
Llewellyn-Jones, Margaret. 2002. *Contemporary Irish Drama and Cultural Identity* Bristol, Portland: Intellect
Lyotard, Jean-François. 1979, 1984. *The Postmodern Condition: A Report on Knowledge*. Trans. Geoff Bennington and Brian Massumi. Manchester: Manchester University Press

Murphy, Tom. 1993. *Bailegangaire. Plays: 2.* London: Methuen

Ni Anluain, Cliodhna. Ed. 2000. *Reading The Future: Irish Writers in Conversation with Mike Murphy.* Dublin: Lilliput

O'Toole, Fintan. 1994. *Black Hole, Green Card.* Dublin: New Island Books

Richards, Shaun. 1989. "'Refiguring Lost Narratives – Prefiguring New Ones': The Theatre of Tom Murphy". *Canadian Journal of Irish Studies.* 15.1: 80-100

Roche, Anthony. 1994. *Contemporary Irish Drama.* Dublin: Gill & Macmillan

Steiner, George. 1975, 1992, 1998. *After Babel: Aspects of Language and Translation.* Oxford: OUP

# Silencing the (M)other in Seamus Deane's *Reading in the Dark*

*Lisa McGonigle*

In *(Un)like subjects: Women, Theory, Fiction*, Geraldine Meaney cites Elaine Showalter's definition of "gynesis", a strand of feminist criticism which seeks "[t]o understand the space granted to the feminine in the symbolic contract…to repossess as a field of inquiry all the space of the Other, the gaps, the silences and absences of discourse and representation, to which the feminine has traditionally been relegated" (1993: 4). Within the Irish literary tradition, the space assigned to the feminine is limited indeed and, as Meaney notes elsewhere, "it may be a shocking thought that the Irish woman reading Irish fiction finds in it only a profound silence, her own silence" (1994: 199). This essay investigates Seamus Deane's *Reading in the Dark* (1996) in the light of Meaney's contention and focuses upon the "clear, plain silence" (5)[1] which pervades the text from its opening line, with a "thin membrane of silence" (27) restricting the mother in particular from start to end.

In exploring the silence which reverberates so deafeningly throughout the text, Colin Graham's lead in "focusing on how ideas of subalternity can be applied to gender issues in an Irish context" is of immense use (2003: 151). Originally a military term indicating those in lower ranks, "the subaltern" gained widespread currency in critical thinking via Marxist theorist Antonio Gramsci, who used it to refer to oppressed societal groups. It was later co-opted by a collective of Indian scholars known as the Subaltern Studies group and thus gained its current specificity in post-colonial thought. Concentrating on the experience of those traditionally occluded and silenced by the dominant discourses of the nation, Subaltern Studies, in Graham's words, "aligns itself with groups inside society which it sees as excluded, dominated, elided and oppressed by the State (effectively, women, peasants, the working classes and other minority and marginalised ethnic and social groups)" (1994: 31). In her celebrated essay "Can the Subaltern Speak?", Gayatri Chakravotry Spivak introduced a specifically gendered dimension to the project by contending that "if, in the context of colonial production, the subaltern has no history and cannot speak, the subaltern as female is even more deeply in shadow" (Spivak, 83). Given the persistent overshadowing and silencing of women within Irish culture, Graham describes Spivak's work as a "vital reference point" for the interrogation of Irish gender constructs, and because of the "silence everywhere" (Deane, 1996: 43) in *Reading in the Dark*, the subaltern is particularly appropriate for an analysis of the mother's positioning within the text (Graham, 2003; 157).

Not all critics, it must be stated, are amenable to approaching gender issues in this manner. Jennifer Jeffers, in *The Irish Novel at the end of Twentieth Century: Gender, Bodies, Power*, counters that:

> By focusing on the particularities of gender, the body, and the power matrix of the given situation instead of resorting to overgeneralisations ("subalternity"), we can begin to reformulate the Irish identity as a complex and indeterminable entity. (Jeffers, 7)

As Jeffers's stated aim for the study is "to analyse and pull apart the power matrix that has constructed the Irish woman", her haste in dismissing subalternity is regrettable, particularly since her reading of Deane's novel fails to take cognisance of the mother's position (Jeffers, 7). Subalternity is not a "one-size-fits-all" generalisation, as Edna Longley likewise snubbed post-

---

[1] All page numbers refer to Seamus Deane's *Reading in the Dark* (London: Jonathan Cape, 1996).

colonialism, but is instead a concept enabling the exploration of texts in a manner attentive to suppressed and occluded voices, particularly those of women (Longley, 30).

When Liam Harte, on the other hand, does draw upon the subaltern in his analysis of *Reading in the Dark*, he fails to realise the relevance of this to the mother's situation. Harte observes that "in the novel ... speech and subjectivity are fundamentally and inextricably linked" and contends:

> His [the narrator's] positioning corresponds in some ways to that of the subaltern within colonial discourse theory in that his desire for interpretiv agency signifies his struggle for post-colonial subjectivity, since without understanding and enunciation there can be no self-realisation for the colonised subject. (Harte, 157)

Harte notes that, in contrast to the narrator, the mother "remains shrouded in silence" but he does not explore the implications and consequences of this, thus failing to develop the full potential of subalternity in an otherwise strong reading of the text (Harte, 162). He instead prioritises Eddie, the father's brother who was wrongly executed as a police informer; Harte argues that "because he is believed to have committed a double transgression, there is no cultural space in which Eddie's story can be told" (Harte, 155). The mother is also marginalised in Eoin Flannery's "Reading in the Light of *Reading in the Dark*" which similarly places Eddie's "phantasmal" presence at the centre of the text. Flannery uses the exact same wording as Harte – "no cultural space" – to describe Eddie's posthumous plight, claiming:

> The boy's paternal uncle, Eddie, is implicit in the "clear, plain silence" on the stairwell, as he is central to the silences at the heart of the family. He is a figure who asserts his presence in the phantasmal shape of this "silence" ... his phantasmal or nomadic presence is accentuated by his inability to be represented or integrated within either of the "accepted" narratives, and thus, Eddie's is an occluded memory...there is no cultural space in which Eddie' story can be told. (Flannery, 216)

Yet if Eddie is a spectral presence then it is the mother who, from the first episode of the text to the last, is "haunted" (6) by the past, "haunted, haunted" (229), lacking even more the "cultural space" in which to tell *her* story, the importance of which is demonstrated in the text's epigraph: "the people were saying no two were e'er wed/but one had a sorrow that never was said".[2] The mother is crucially aware of Eddie's innocence and knows McIlhenny, with whom she was once romantically involved, to be the true informer. However, by warning McIlhenny that he had been observed informing to the police, she enabled him to escape to Chicago and evade the retribution which would otherwise have awaited him. Such actions, from the viewpoint of the nationalist community which the family inhabit, would be considered even more abhorrent than those which Eddie is believed to have committed, and the subsequent discovery that it was her own father who ordered the erroneous execution of Eddie compounds the mother's sense of shame. When combined, these factors leave the mother unable to exorcise the ghost of Eddie by revealing the truth and she remains instead in the "shadow" (6) of the past, silent and obscured.

"Haunted forever" (229) by her awareness of and collusion in these events, the mother's unspeakable and self-destructive knowledge has significant import. "Their marriage mutated slowly around the secrets that she kept in a nucleus within herself" (228) the narrator says of his parents, and the family is paralysed by:

> Silence everywhere. My father knowing something about Eddie, not saying it, not talking but sometimes nearly talking, signalling. I felt we lived in an empty space with a long cry

---

[2] See Peach, 45-54.

from him ramifying through it. At other times, it appeared to be as cunning and articulate as a labyrinth, closely designed, with someone sobbing at the heart of it. (43) This is indeed a labyrinth of secrecy and lies with the mother, ensnared in the deceptions and thus unable to assert her voice, "wailing and sobbing" (105) at its centre. Her first appearance in the text is as "an old mother with her nerves…crying quietly at the fireside" (6) and her sorrow is not assuaged; she later emits a "long wail of agony" (18), and later still "she cried and cried, the whole top half of her body shuddering" (119). When she suffers a breakdown, she is initially numbed with grief and pain but "then, at last, the real crying began, a lethal sobbing that ran its fright through us like an epidemic" (142). "She cried for weeks, then months" (143) the narrator reports, and describes how: "I wanted to run into the maw of this sobbing, to throw my arms wide to receive it, to shout into it, to make it come at me in words, words, words and no more of this ceaseless noise, its animality, its broken inflection of my mother" (143). Denied the narrative structures through which to tell her story, Liam's quip "better to have loved and not be able to talk than never to have loved at all" (162) is a grim, if unknowing, comment on the mother's plight.

Imprisoned as she is in this silence, the mother is unable to confess to the family "something she wanted to be forgiven for" (135), namely withholding knowledge of Eddie's innocence and colluding instead with McIlhenny. She attempts, however, to make known her grief by alluding to Liadán, the subject of an Irish poem in which "the woman lamented that she had done a terrible thing, she had forsaken the man she loved" (194). Deane explains that: "There was the previous generation, uneducated, who derived their stories from folklore, from legend, and these stories are very subtly coded ways of dealing with trauma and difficulty. He [the narrator] doesn't recognise at first how these stories actually deal with the very thing that he was trying to pursue" (Deane, 1997: 30). Within this particular socio-political formation, in which "discretion is the better part of candour" (86) because of the layers of duplicity and deceit, storytelling is a powerful tool enabling themes too painful or hazardous to confront directly to be explored instead obliquely.[3] Alongside the mother's self-identification with Liadán, the family's persistent refusal to speak about the past is coded in the form of silenced folkloric figures, as the stories told by the older generation are largely populated by characters rendered mute by a profound shock. Brigid McLaughlin "stopped talking. Until the day she died she never spoke again" (70) after her supernatural encounter with the ghostly children. Larry McLaughlin likewise "never speaks" (84), ostensibly because he "had sex with the devil" (186), more probably as a result of being involved with Eddie's execution. Katie, the narrator's aunt, explains that "some families … are devil-haunted … . It's a curse a family can never shake off. Maybe it's something terrible in the family's history, some terrible deed that was done in the past, and it just spreads and spreads down the generations" (66). Such folktales subtly explain the gaps and absences in their own family history as without addressing the matter directly, the existence of past trauma can nonetheless be acknowledged.

Indeed, from a psychological perspective, "silence is recognised as one of the most immediate reactions to severe trauma" (Moane, 114). For the older generation, who lack the narrator's temporal and emotional distance from the past, silence presents itself as a strategic coping mechanism and is the manner in which they attempt to deal with the family's psychic scars.[4] Deane remarked that:

There's an element in the novel where the older generation is looking at this young child growing up and trying to dig it all up again, and saying "Oh for Christ's sake, stop, let's get rid of that history, let's find some way of leaving it behind". The only way out is by keeping a secret, keeping things secret. It's very un-American in that sense.

---

[3] See Harte, 159
[4] See Peach, 45-54; Kennedy-Andrews, 222-3.

There's no talking cure, no implication that by revealing everything you will somehow overcome it. (Deane, 1997: 30)

"So broken was my father's family", the narrator reflects, "that it felt to me like a catastrophe you could live with only if you kept it quiet, let it die down of its own accord like a dangerous fire" (43). He comes to appreciate that his mother cannot reveal the truth about Eddie and McIlhenny because "saying it out loud would destroy everything, make their marriage impossible" (224). "Was it her way of loving him, not telling him?" (187), he wonders about his parents' relationship. He even describes the permanent silence induced by his mother's stroke as "almost a mercy" (230), feeling that it is only when she is "sealed in her silence" (230) that "we could love each other at last" (230). Such is the family's fragility, fractured as it is by silence and shame, that the shrillness of speech could shatter it entirely.

Nonetheless, if the family's past contains what Linden Peach describes as "a pain that arguably is too terrible to bear and perhaps should not be passed on … yet should not be eschewed", this deadlock has borne down heavily on the mother, since it is she who possesses full knowledge of the tragedies and trauma (Peach, 47). Even if a simple "talking cure" would not remedy the family's pain, this does not lessen the stressful intensity of maintaining a silence borne of remorse and regret. The mother strains "as though there were pounds of pressure bearing down on her" (139), struggling under an immense and incommunicable burden. Her inability to speak results in her degeneration into madness and this is depicted in the text as a form of expression and relief. In contrast to the many characters who have been "silenced in one way or the other" (206), for example, Crazy Joe Johnson is incessantly "talking to everyone he met" (81), recounting "a garbled mess of things – stories, questions, conundrums" (83) and enacting a "multi-voiced drama" (212). The mother likewise acquires a "new voice" (145) in her psychosis and the narrator comprehends that "she was telling herself a story that only appeared now and then in her speech" (145). This "telling, and not telling" (146) occurs elliptically and fragmentally, "connected remarks separated by days, weeks, months" (145). The narrator grasps that "she had been in love with someone else, not quite my father" (146) and furthermore, because he has come to share his mother's secrets:

> It wasn't just that she was trapped by what had happened. She was trapped by my knowing it. It must be shame, I decided. She's paralysed by shame. She was ashamed of what she had done to my father. She was ashamed, I knew it. Every time she saw me, she felt exposed. (223)

When asked what she would like for her birthday, the mother replies "just for that one day, the seventeenth of May, to forget everything" (224). Being constantly aware of the torn family history in this manner is a tortuous punishment which the mother, silenced and subaltern, must endure. As Crazy Joe remarks, "that's what punishment does; makes you remember everything" (193), which echoes the sentiment expressed in Brian Friel's *Translations* that "to remember everything is a form of madness" (Friel, 81).

Trapped as she is by the multiple deceptions, voice is a synecdoche for the authority and self-assertion largely denied to the mother in *Reading in the Dark*. When Sergeant Burke – a member of the local police force – pays an unwelcome visit to the house, for example, "her immediate impulse was to shout at him to leave but she had no voice…she was left looking for the voice" (204). Elmer Kennedy-Andrews argues that:

> In this novel where the personal and political are so closely intertwined, the mother's grief, says Deane, "is, in some ways, aligned to Irish history". Conditioned to let the coloniser speak for her, the mother has no language for her guilt and grief: "the mother is, in her grief, taking the shock, the trauma of a history into herself, but she can find no escape from it". (220)

However, it is important to separate Deane's own comments from the nationalist gloss which Kennedy-Andrews puts on them. If, for Deane, the mother in some ways symbolises the Irish cultural condition, it is not a simplistic dichotomy between coloniser and colonised which has rendered her subaltern, but instead her exposure to the double-crossings, distortions and cruel violence inflicted by the nationalist community upon itself. "From the context of the notion of the "subaltern" in contemporary cultural criticism", Colin Graham notes, "it is clear that the term brings with it a particular type of post-colonial thinking – one which is aware of the failure of nationalism in the post-colonial world"; in other words it is a mode of reading which enacts a critical self-appraisal of nationalism rather than an "ethically-loaded" condemnation of imperial rule (Graham, 2003: 153).[5] As subalternity involves freeing up the voices repressed by the strictures and structures of nationalism, focusing on the mother's silence in *Reading in the Dark* therefore entails censuring the community in which she lives, correctly described by Kennedy-Andrews as a "culture of treachery and lies". (Kennedy-Andrews, 221) Indeed, rather than being the brutal agent of a harsh colonial regime, Sergeant Burke urges the mother to put an end to the "poison" (201) spreading through the family, to effect "a separation from all that grief, a walking away from it, a settling" (202) by breaking the silence which stifles her. Furthermore, rather than simply passing over the mother's voicelessness unawares, thereby occluding her even further, an awareness of and sympathy of her disempowerment is displayed, with the narrator recognising that "Christ in heaven knew what she could do, for what power had she" (203). This serves to make apparent the disparities of agency and voice which have resulted in her silence or, in Spivak's words, "to question the unquestioned muting of the subaltern woman" (Spivak, 91). The use of silence as a key textual leitmotif in *Reading in the Dark* thus subverts the "traditional construction of "Woman" as "mute spectacle, silent cipher" within Irish literary culture" and contains an implicit critique of the women's silencing by the nationalist tradition (Mahoney, 146, quoting Smyth). Although the mother may be mute and silent, she is reduced to neither spectacle nor cipher but is instead a complex and discrete character in her own right, central to the silence which informs and defines the text. As "contemporary post-coloniality has the potential to shatter the self-image of nationalism rather than to radicalise it", recognising the mother as subaltern is a powerful aid in both exploring the text's intricacies of secrecy and speechlessness and acknowledging the wider political significance of her plight (Graham, 1994: 35).

## References

Deane, Seamus. 1996. *Reading in the Dark*. London: Jonathan Cape

Deane, Seamus. 1997. Interview with Carol Rumens. *Fortnight*. July-August 1997: 30

Flannery, Eoin. 2004. "Reading in the Light of *Reading in the Dark*". Irish Studies Review. 12.1: 70-80

Friel, Brian. 1981. *Translations*. London: Faber

Graham, Colin. 1994. "Liminal Spaces: Post-colonial Theories and Irish Culture". *Irish Review*. 16. Autumn-Winter: 29-43

Graham, Colin. 2003. "Subalternity and Gender: problems of post-colonial Irishness". *Theorizing Ireland*. Ed. Claire Connolly. Basingstoke: Palgrave

Gramsci, Antonio. 2000. *The Gramsci Reader: Selected Writings 1916-1935*. Ed. David Forgasc. New York: New York University Press, 2000)

Harte, Liam. 2000. "History Lessons: Post-colonialism and Seamus Deane's *Reading in the Dark*". *Irish University Review*. 30.1. Spring-Summer: 149-162

---

[5] See also Graham (1994) and Harte (2000) for a discussion of how Deane treats nationalism in his critical writings.

Jeffers, Jennifer. 2002. *The Irish Novel at the End of the Twentieth Century: Gender, Bodies and Power*. Basingstoke: Palgrave

Kennedy-Andrews, Elmer. 2002. *Fiction and the Northern Irish Troubles since 1969: (De-)constructing the North*. Dublin: Four Courts Press

Longley, Edna. 1994. *The Living Stream: Literature and Revisionism in Ireland*. Newcastle-upon-Tyne: Bloodaxe Books

Mahoney, Elizabeth. 1999. "Citizens of its Hiding Place: Gender and Urban Space in Irish Women's Poetry". In *Ireland in Proximity: History, Gender, Space*. Eds. Scott Brewster, Virginia Crossman, Fiona Becket and David Alderson. London: Routledge. 145-157

Meaney, Geraldine. 1993. *(Un)like Subjects: Women, Theory, Fiction*. London: Routledge

Meaney, Geraldine. 1994. "Sex and Nation: Women in Irish Culture and Politics". In *A Dozen LIPs*. Dublin: Attic Press. 188-205

Moane, Geraldine. 2002. "Colonialism and the Celtic Tiger: Legacies of History and the Quest for Vision". In *Reinventing Ireland: Culture, Society and the Global Economy*. Eds. Peadar Kirby, Luke Gibbons and Michael Cronin. London: Pluto Press. 109-124

Peach, Linden. 2004. *The Contemporary Irish Novel: Critical Readings*. Basingstoke: Palgrave

Smyth, Ailbhe. 1989. "The Floozie in the Jacuzzi". *Irish Review*. 6. Spring: 7-24

Spivak, Gayatri Chakravotry. 1993. "Can the Subaltern Speak?" In *Colonial Discourse and Post-colonial Theory*. Eds Laura Chrismas and Patrick Williams. Harlow: Prentice Hall. 66-111

# Glasgow and Belfast: Capitals of Culture?

*Matthew McGuire*

This paper seeks to examine the changes to the Belfast cityscape that followed in the wake of the *Belfast (Good Friday) Agreement* (1998), aiming to locate these developments within their wider cultural context and to contest claims that the Peace Process marks a significant turning point in the direction of Northern Irish history. By comparing Belfast's transformation with the regeneration of Glasgow during the 1990s, the following paper will look to redress a critical imbalance which would regard Northern Ireland as a uniquely anomalous political space. It will argue that whilst the overt political violence of the Troubles has diminished with the developments of the Peace Process, a different type of violence has become enshrined within the fabric of Northern Irish life; namely, that which arises from the historical moment of late capitalism and the expanding influence of global economic culture. Whilst it would be misleading to equate this economic violence with that of the Troubles, the following argument seeks to question the type of society and the essentially limited set of horizons that it is currently on offer to the people of Northern Ireland.

In 1998 at the signing of the *Belfast (Good Friday) Agreement*, the British Prime Minister Tony Blair remarked: "I believe today courage has triumphed. I said when I arrived here on Wednesday night that I felt the hand of history upon us. Today I hope that the burden of history can be lifted from our shoulders" (cited in O'Neil, 3). In the age of ubiquitous political sound bite, such rhetorical prophecy has become all too familiar. For the Prime Minister history is something which must be escaped, a burden to be lifted from our shoulders. Similarly, throughout the Peace Process the people of Northern Ireland have continually been implored to find new historical narratives, to re-negotiate the co-ordinates of the past and look beyond the narrow confines of sectarian identity politics. The Prime Minister's statement resonates with Seamus Heaney's famous description of the North as a place of "anachronistic passions" (Heaney, 757). Left behind by the modernizing forces of improvement, Northern Ireland has fallen from the linear path of historical progress and finds itself trapped in an eternal return, endlessly repeating the same violent sectarian narratives. For the Belfast poet Ciaran Carson the Troubles have conspired in this sense of arrested historical development, with the same images appearing on the news night after night: the exploding building, the masked paramilitary, the grieving mother.

> There's a lot of recurrent images, like recurrent dreams. This is like real life, or life in Belfast. Assassinations, bombs, they keep happening in the same patterns; the same images on TV, the ritual condemnations. (Carson, 86)

The Peace Process is a deliberate attempt to break this cycle of violence and as such can only be welcomed. However, it is the subsequent re-inscription of the North within the grand narrative of historical development that must ultimately be questioned. Rather than suture the scars of the past, the changes to the Belfast cityscape evince merely the reconfiguration of old wounds; sectarian violence has been replaced by an economic violence, the advance of which has been relatively uncontested as it slowly weaves itself into the fabric of Northern Irish life.

Whilst political aspects of the Peace Process have stuttered and at times ground to a complete halt, other changes have followed a much less interrupted path. Formerly a desolate wasteland scarred by years of bombing, Belfast now boasts state of the art concert venues, the Odyssey ice hockey arena and "The Titanic Quarter", a multi-million pound waterside property development. In analyzing these changes to Belfast my argument draws on the work of Walter Benjamin from the 1930s, in particular his study of cities such as Berlin, Moscow and most famously Paris during the time of Baudelaire. For Benjamin the process of physiognomy involves reading the city as a text. Through scrutinizing the physical landscape one can reveal and ultimately interrogate its underlying social and economic structures. Hence, analysis of the Belfast cityscape provides a unique barometer with which to measure the political and cultural developments that have accompanied the Peace Process and the signing of the Good Friday Agreement.

As cities, Glasgow and Belfast share similar DNA – a heady mix of industry, religion and mass immigration – and the cross-pollination that has shaped both topographies remains clearly visible today. One only has to look at the weekly ferry crossings from Belfast by Celtic and Rangers fans to observe a sectarian meta-narrative that is a feature of both topographies. However, there are important, marked differences in the effects that this tribalism has had on the social, cultural and political landscape of each city. Glasgow has had nothing like the paramilitary violence that has afflicted Belfast since 1969, nor are its democratic politics divided along overtly sectarian lines. The dominant party in Glasgow has been the Labour Party, with the Scottish Socialist Party recently making some inroads. In contrast, politics within the North have traditionally formed along lines of sectarian division, with the Unionist DUP and UUP on one side and the Nationalist SDLP and Sinn Fein on the other. Leaving these obvious differences aside, it is the cities' parallel experience of economic decline and post-industrial regeneration that the following paper will foreground. In its 1913 heyday, shipbuilding in Glasgow directly employed 60,000 men with another 40,000 in related industries. Similarly in Belfast, Harland and Wolff, the yard that famously built the Titanic, at one time had 35,000 men on its books. Today both the Clyde and Queen's Island have all but ceased to exist as fully functioning shipyards and in the late twentieth century both Glasgow and Belfast have been forced to renegotiate the rapidly changing post-industrial economic landscape.

The key moment in Glasgow's regeneration was its year as European Capital of Culture in 1990. Belfast recently attempted to emulate this experience by bidding for the same award in 2008, a competition eventually won by Liverpool. The title of the award is worth pausing over. The year as European Capital of Culture in 1990 allowed Glasgow to rebrand itself and as a result dramatically increase its annual revenue from tourism. This coincidental financial injection has become so significant that we are compelled to re-examine the award and ask whether the Capital of Culture isn't actually a manifestation of the Culture of Capital.

So, what exactly was Glasgow's experience in 1990 as the European Capital of Culture? The council invested £35 million in an extensive arts program with the dual purpose of celebrating local talent and attracting acclaimed international acts to the city. Notable events included performances by Luciano Pavarotti, Frank Sinatra and the Bolshoi Ballet. The year-long festival, which included over 3,000 musical events, helped to attract a record number of tourists to the city with bed space occupancy increasing by 39% on the year before. Furthermore, this upsurge in cultural tourism was no isolated trend, concluding when Glasgow passed the mantle to Dublin the following year. From 1991 to 1998 UK tourist trips to the city increased by 88%, whilst overseas visitors went up 25%. These numbers have had a profound impact upon the landscape of the city and the opportunities for the people that live there. Whereas heavy industry had formerly been the major source of employment, Glasgow has transformed itself into a service driven economy. Currently this type of work accounts for 84% of the city's overall employment. The council also used the Year of Culture as a catalyst in their gentrification of Glasgow focused primarily on the Merchant City, a disused warehouse district in the city centre. By 1988 some 2000 luxury flats had been created with another 2000 proposed as part of a concerted attempt to attract private investment back to the city centre.[1]

---

[1] The data concerning the transformation of the Glasgow economy is taken from Peter Booth and Robin Boyle (22-40).

From media coverage at the time it would seem that the city did succeed in dramatically re-inventing itself. Indeed, the further one traveled from Glasgow itself the more spectacular this transformation was perceived to be; the *Wall Street Journal* announced "Glasgow's No Mean City Anymore" whilst the *LA Examiner* rather lyrically reported, "the ugly duckling of Europe has turned into a swan" (cited in Hamilton, 4-5).

At first glance it would seem that Glasgow 1990 was an unquestionable success. However, the year of culture was not without its detractors. In planning the 1990 festival Glasgow council employed advertising agency Saatchi and Saatchi to mastermind the process of rebranding of their city. This becomes controversial when we recall that it was the same agency that previously helped the Conservative Party to repeated election success during the 1980s, installing more than a decade of Thatcher government. It was Thatcher's deliberate disbanding of heavy industry, the destruction of the trade unions and the de-regulation of labour markets which radically transformed Britain, expanding monetarism and consolidating a late capitalist consumer culture within the UK. For Michael Donnelly, the one-time assistant curator of Glasgow's People's Palace museum, "1990 was a year when an intellectually bankrupt and brutally undemocratic administration projected its mediocre image onto the city and ordered us to adore it" (cited in Kemp, 19). Local artists, including the author James Kelman, formed a protest movement under the banner 'Workers City' attempting to challenge the elliptical repackaging of Glasgow's history, which redefined it as a Merchant City, built on the wealth of British imperial trade. This narrative would ignore the thousands of working-class people who had been employed in Glasgow's heavy industries and upon whose toil the city was also undoubtedly built. Several individual events from the Year of Culture program foregrounded this process of marginalisation. An architecture exhibition celebrated the beauty of Glasgow's Victorian heritage whilst ignoring the failed social experiment of its high-rise tower blocks, what the author William McIlvanney has poignantly referred to as Glasgow's "penal architecture" (cited in Spring, 46). When the city's working-class tradition was addressed, it was often nothing more than a simple exercise in nostalgia. "The Ship" was a nightly show on the Clyde where a mock-up boat was built and dramatically launched. *Scotland on Sunday* reported that "The Ship" was "reeking with easy options and intellectual laziness … exploiting that appetite for the past by twanging easily on the heart strings and the memory cells" (cited in Kemp, 26). The Year of Culture was replete with the commodification of history. The past was repackaged and the importance of historical authenticity was summarily supplanted by an overriding concern for economic and commercial interest.

Turning to the social impact of the Year of Culture, one could argue that the ends justified the means. The dramatic rebirth and structural transformation of the Glasgow economy could make such historical and cultural objections seem slightly precious. After all, is there anything wrong with appropriating the past in order to increase employment opportunities in the present? It is important to recognize that Glasgow's new service based economy is far from a utopian paradise, created from the ashes of industrial holocaust. It is significant that service industry jobs earn substantially lower hourly wages than manufacturing ones. Most service work is deregulated, leading to an undermining of the coherence and strength of the labour movement and an erosion of corporatist bargaining. As a result, many service workers operate on short term or temporary contracts, inevitably eroding job security and exacerbating financial uncertainties. Far from entering a new chapter in its history, twenty-first century Glasgow can be seen to be repeat patterns of social inequality that characterized the industrial era and were so conspicuously elided in the celebrations during the Year of Culture.

In turning to examine Belfast, the following argument will focus on three distinct aspects of the city's recent regeneration: the unsuccessful bid to become European Capital of Culture 2008, the development of the Titanic Quarter and the Belfast Giants, and the city's newly arrived ice hockey team.

It is unsurprising that the British government would cite the Glasgow experience in its address to those cities bidding for the 2008 Capital of Culture award. Chris Smith, the Secretary of State for Culture, Media and Sport wrote:

> Glasgow 1990 delivered a tremendous boost to the city, and fostered major developments in cultural events and attractions. Glasgow experienced substantial economic and social benefits and made excellent use of arts and culture to strengthen and communicate its regeneration. (Smith, 2)

What we witness here is the appropriation of culture as a tool for the communication of the city's social and economic regeneration. Glasgow's success is not measured by the quality or quantity of cultural events, or their representation of the people who actually live there. Culture has ceased to serve a critical function and instead merely evinces the socio-economic changes that have transformed the landscape of the city.

In response to the Government's encouragement, a local group called "Imagine Belfast" was formed in order to bid for the 2008 City of Culture award.[2] A project entitled "Through the Eyes of a Child" proposed the creation of a fantasy land modeled on the Narnia chronicles of C. S. Lewis, who was born in Belfast in 1898. This theme drew on one of the underlying and familiar motifs of the Peace Process, the need to find alternative narratives beyond the well-trodden pathways of sectarian identity politics. The rather patronising idea was that the people of Northern Ireland would benefit dramatically from learning how to look through the unprejudiced eyes of a child. However, it is deeply ironic that a society seeking a reprieve from religious bigotry would choose a renowned Christian allegorist to figurehead a cultural festival. Even more problematic is the tenuous nature of the author's connection with the city of his birth. Although born in the Belfast, Lewis lived most of his life outside of Northern Ireland. He went to boarding school in England and studied at Oxford where he became a University professor and is buried today. Coincidentally, none of Lewis's major works make any detailed or sustained reference to the city of Belfast. This highlights the problem that confronts Northern Ireland as it has attempted to renegotiate the co-ordinates of the past throughout the Peace Process. Memory plays a vital role in how people both experience and interpret the present (Connerton, 2). As such, the choice of Lewis can be read as a courageous attempt to redefine a narrow sectarian reading of the past by offering a cultural symbol that cuts across traditional tribal loyalties. However, we must also be aware of the difficulty inherent in this kind of attempt at historical appropriation. Lewis's life and work could also be read as a symptom of a more familiar narrative, one governed by privileged access to education, emigration and the ability to create an art that thematically eschews the cultural specificity of Belfast.

When the bid adjudicators arrived in Belfast their first stop was the Odyssey arena, the city's newest concert venue and home to the Belfast Giants, an ice hockey franchise founded in 2000. The dramatic success of this new sport within Northern Ireland owes a lot to the clever marketing on the behalf of the Belfast Giants who, riding on the wave of the Peace Process, deliberately molded themselves as the team for the "whole community". Ice hockey is after all a game free from the sectarian baggage of other sports in the North such as football, rugby and GAA. The spectacle of the Belfast Giants undoubtedly belongs to what Laura Pelaschiar describes as "the new metropolitan atmosphere" of Belfast's "harmonious postmodern reality" (125). They are a team with no discernible history, coinciding with the postmodern tendency to eschew any authoritative or definitive version of the past. The Giants are surely an example of the rich multi-culturalism that has long been absent from the insular reality of Northern Ireland since the dark days of the Troubles, when people from outside simply stopped visiting

---

[2] The full proposal for the Imagine Belfast bid can be found on http://www.artscouncil-ni.org/news/2002/new20032002.htm

the province. Even more significant is the fact that the Giants are a winning team. In their inaugural season in 2002 they were crowned British Superleague Champions, a sporting symbol of the new, prosperous and successful Northern Ireland. However, there are certain aspects of the Giants phenomenon that are worth reconsidering. Before hailing them as a homegrown success story, it is worth remembering that none of the players on the Giants team are actually from the city itself: they are all Canadian imports. Furthermore, Belfast is supposedly a city hung-over from years of violence. It is puzzling then that people should be flocking to watch ice hockey, a sport where fighting is a regular and much applauded feature of the game. Indeed the Giants website even features snapshots from the season's juiciest brawls.[3] It is Fredric Jameson that identifies the cultural dominant of postmodernism as a byproduct of a particular historical moment; namely, the rise of multi-national capitalism and the consolidation of post-industrial consumer society. The Belfast Giants would certainly cohere with this particular definition. One would like to imagine that their sponsorship from Belfast City Council is part of a brand new anti-sectarian initiative within the corridors of power. However, the real reason the City Council loves the Giants is the 5,000 "bednights" and the £600,000 spent by visiting fans each season (Graham, 2-3). The Giants undoubtedly echo Lyotard's celebration of postmodernism as an embodiment of contemporary multiculturalism.

> One listens to reggae, watches a Western, eats McDonalds food for lunch… wears Paris perfume in Tokyo and 'retro' clothes in Hong Kong…. (Lyotard, 76)

We could easily add, "…watches ice hockey in Belfast". But as Alex Callinicos rightly points out, this all depends upon exactly who "one" is (162). Such luxury of choice exists only for those who can afford it. So, we must ask exactly who the Belfast Giants are for, after all, they are supposedly the team for the whole community. At a cost of around £40 for a family ticket the Giants would seem to be a team only for those who can afford the price of entry. Whilst renegotiating the sectarian landscape of Northern Ireland's sporting life, the Giants have succeeded in highlighting a new divide which is increasingly defining the landscape in the wake of the Peace Process; namely, that which exists between the rich and the poor.

Another theme of the Capital of Culture bid emerged under the banner "Made in Belfast" and sought to celebrate the city's industrial history and its recent renaissance as a centre for artistic and cultural production. Arguably Belfast's most significant heritage project concerns the Titanic Quarter, a multi-million pound redevelopment of the disused Harland and Wolff shipyard, which famously built the Titanic almost a century ago. The website states:

> Titanic Quarter is a new brand emerging on the horizon in the east of Belfast City. Harnessing the rich maritime and industrial history of Belfast, the potential of Titanic Quarter is as extraordinary as the many ships built by the world famous shipyard on the site.[4]

The developers plan to build 450 modern apartments along with office buildings and other employment space. This will be "the most attractive waterfront residential location ever to come on the market in Belfast and we expect a lot of interest in this site". So what is wrong with giving Belfast this long overdue facelift? Let us pause to reconsider some of the so-called "extraordinary" aspects of the Titanic myth.

At the time of its launch in 1912, the Titanic was a grandiose celebration of the industrial age. It was the largest man-made, moveable object on the planet; the last word in luxury, and the first liner to have its own on-deck swimming pool (Wade, 4-15). As is well known, during its maiden voyage disaster struck when the Titanic hit an iceberg, causing its eventual sinking and the death of over 1500 passengers and crew. During this fateful night several myths were born, infusing the tragedy of the Titanic with a sense of stoic heroism. When the ship first

---

[3] See http://www.belfastgiants.com   [4] See http://www.titanic-quarter.com

began to sink the wealthy American industrialist, Benjamin Guggenheim, supposedly returned to his cabin to dress for dinner, declaring, "If we are to die tonight, then we will die like gentlemen" (cited in Wade, 11). This myth of masculine chivalry is further compounded by the famous lifeboat edict: "women and children and first". But as with most myths, the facts tell a rather different story. Whereas 97% of first class female passengers survived the sinking, only 46% of those in third class were saved. A similar fate affected the children of the Titanic: of the 29 children in first and second class accommodation only 1 was lost, whereas in third class, 50 out of a total 73 children died.[5] The disaster of the Titanic was by no means a loss shared equally amongst every class of passenger. As these figures demonstrate, the wealthy first class travelers fared much better than the poor in the scramble for the lifeboats.

The "Titanic Quarter" has little interest in the unwritten narratives of the historic ship or the people who built it. It will undoubtedly make little mention of the 5 men who died during its construction. Nor will it address the effects of asbestosis and the other health hazards that affect thousands of former shipyard workers. It is doubtful if it will acknowledge the shipyard's role as arguably Northern Ireland's largest single example of sectarianism discrimination in the workplace. The modern rejuvenation of the dockyards draws on a deliberately elliptical version of the past, turning history into a commodity in order that it might be sold back to the people. But perhaps this is in keeping with the original spirit of Harland and Wolff who were after all, two foreign investors out to make a profit through founding a Belfast shipyard. Again the question remains, exactly who is the Titanic Quarter for? As this particular ship sets sail for the future it would seem to only have room for the small minority of people who can afford to buy and live in "luxury waterside apartments".

In conclusion, it is worth remembering that these economic changes have developed within a political vacuum, as the Peace Process falters and the Northern Ireland Assembly has been temporarily suspended. This signals a wider political phenomenon, as governments and individual nation states become increasingly impotent against the forces of the global economics. The aim of my argument has not been to draw a simplistic and crude equivalence between the economic violence that is inherent in late capitalist society and the sectarian conflict during the Troubles. Rather, my intention has been to highlight the as yet unexamined socio-economic changes which have accompanied the Peace Process and the limited possibilities that they offer for the people of Belfast. Despite the *Belfast (Good Friday) Agreement* promising a new democratic future for the people of the North, it would seem that the agenda for transformation is to be predominantly set by market forces, a process that necessarily demands further and continued scrutiny.

## References

Booth, Peter and Robin Boyle. 1993. "See Glasgow, See Culture". In *Cultural Policy and Urban Regeneration: the West European Experience*. Eds. Franco Bianchini and Michael Parkinson. Manchester: Manchester University Press. 22-40.

Callinicos, Alex. 1989. *Against Postmodernism*. Cambridge, Polity Press

Carson, Ciaran. 1990. Interview by Rand Brandes. *Irish Review*. 8: 77-90

Connerton, Paul. 1989. *How Societies Remember*. Cambridge: Cambridge University Press

Gilloch, Graeme. 1996. *Myths and Metroplois: Walter Benjamin and the City*. Cambridge: Polity Press

Graham, Colin. 2003. "Belfast Giants". *The Vacuum*. 5: 2-3.

Hamilton, Christine. 2002. "Press Content Analysis". *Media Pack: Glasgow 1990 European Capital of Culture*. Glasgow: centre for Cultural Research. 4-5

Heaney, Seamus. 1969. "Delerium of the Brave". *The Listener*. 27 November: 757

Hobsbawm, Eric and Ranger, Terence. 1983. *The Invention of Tradition*. Cambridge: Cambridge University Press

Jameson, Fredric. 1991. *Postmodernism or The Cultural Logic of Late Capitalism*. London: Verso

Kemp, David. 1990. *Glasgow 1990: The True Story Behind the Hype*. Scotland: Framedram

Lyotard, Jean Francois. 1984. *The Postmodern Condition: A Report on Knowledge* Manchester: Manchester University Press

O'Neil, Brendan. 1998. "Good Friday Agreement: A Peace of Nothing". *Living Marxism*, 110.3: 3

Pelaschiar, Laura. 2000. "Transforming Belfast: The Evolving Role of the City in Northern Irish Fiction". *Irish University Review*. 30.1: 117-31.

Smith, Chris. 2000. *European Capital of Culture 2008: Criteria and Information for Applicants*. London: Department for Culture, Media and Sport; Local, Regional and International Division.

Spring, Ian. 1990. *Phantom Village: The Myth of the New Glasgow*. Edinburgh: Polygon

Wade, Wyn Craig. 1980. *The Titanic: End of a Dream*. London: Weidenfield and Nicolson

# The Impact of Irish Catholic Priests in Seventeenth-century, Gaelic-speaking Scotland

*Tom McInally*

## Introduction

The missionary work of Irish Catholic priests in seventeenth century Gaelic-speaking Scotland had significant effects in fostering and retaining Catholicism in the western highlands and islands; the letters of the missionaries themselves to their superiors amply demonstrate this fact. Their reports are supported by the findings of two surveys of the Catholic population of Scotland carried out by the Catholic Church and the Kirk in the late seventeenth and early eighteenth centuries. However, before examining the impact of their work it is worth examining how Irish priests came to be involved in Scottish affairs at this time.

The Scottish Catholic hierarchy ended in 1603 with the death in Paris of the last pre-Reformation primate, James Beaton, Archbishop of Glasgow. The Church in Rome did not appoint a replacement and without a hierarchy Scotland formally became a missionary country (Bellesheim: 327). Prior to Beaton's death it had been recognised that if the Catholic faith were to continue in Scotland a significant number of priests would have to be trained abroad, and to this end Scots colleges were set up in Douai, Rome and Paris. Later other colleges in Madrid, Regensberg and Wurtzburg were established to educate priests for the Scottish mission (Gordon: v). The first students who entered the new seminaries came primarily from the Lowlands and North-east of Scotland and were almost exclusively English speaking. Enrolment of native Gaelic speakers did not happen within the first half century of the colleges' existence; the first who can be vouched for, Robert Munro from Ross, being, enrolled in Douai in 1663 and Rome in 1668.[1] The reasons why Scots Gaelic speakers did not enter the seminaries until this relatively late stage are difficult to identify fully but the high costs of travel and education together with low levels of literacy in the western highlands and islands were undoubtedly factors.

The lack of Gaelic speaking trainees for the priesthood was noted in a report from the Scottish Mission to Rome in 1623 which said that there were no priests in the country at that time who could speak Gaelic.[2] The importance of this deficiency can be gauged by the fact that Gaelic speakers occupied large parts of Scotland at the beginning of the seventeenth century. Although use of the language had been in retreat for many years great tracts of the country were still largely or exclusively Gaelic speaking, though the full extent of the Gaidhealtachd is difficult to determine. When the Scottish Mission was divided into a Highland and a Lowland District in 1727[3] the area allocated to the Highland District included Ross, Cromarty, Sutherland, Caithness, large parts of Inverness-shire, Badenoch, Lochaber, Argyll, Breadalbane, Menteith, Strathearn, Glenrannoch, Glengarry and the mountainous parts of Dunbarton, Marr and Moray. As well as these, the islands of the Inner and Outer Hebrides and Orkney and Shetland and the towns of Inverness, Forfar, Perth and Stirling were added (Macdonald: 56-74). Many living in these towns would have been bi-lingual or spoke only

---

[1] New Spalding Club. 1906. *Records of the Scots Colleges* vol1 45 "Douai Diary" entry no.356 and 118 "Rome Register" entry no.195

[2] Vatican library. Barb. Lat., vol 8628 f. 83v *"ex Scotis hucusque catholicis non fuerit sacerdos qui dicto idiomate utatur"*.

[3] A. Bellesheim. 1890. *History of the Catholic Church in Scotland* vol. 3 Edinburgh.187

English. The inhabitants of the Orkneys and Shetlands, indeed, had never been Gaelic speakers, but the great majority living in the Highland District of the Mission spoke only Gaelic. The superior of the Irish Franciscan College at Louvain writing to Rome in 1618 explained to his correspondents that "it is very true that the greater part of the Scottish nation uses the Irish (sic) language".[4] Clearly, the Scottish Catholic mission could not ignore such a large part of its community in its missionary endeavours.

The absence of suitable Scottish priests resulted in appeals being made to the Irish church for missionaries able to converse in English and Gaelic (Giblin, 1964: xii). Scottish and Irish Gaelic had not diverged enough by the seventeenth century to be mutually unintelligible.[5] The Classical Gaelic of bardic tradition was also used in the poetry of both countries. This proved helpful to one of the Ulster missionaries, Fr Cornelius Ward, who posing as an itinerant bard was able to gain access to Sir John Campbell of Calder and obtain his conversion (Giblin, 1964: 53-54).

The approach to the Irish for help in Scotland was motivated by the need to find Gaelic speaking priests but there were other reasons why the Irish were eminently suited for this missionary work. From the second half of the sixteenth century in many parts of Catholic Europe communities of Irish (O'Scea: 27-48) had been established together with colleges (O'Connell: 49-64) for the education of Irish youth. France in particular was attractive to many Irish students. By 1650 it was claimed that Paris had more Irish students than any other part of the world (Chambers: 158). Eminent Irish scholars such as David Rothe, bishop of Ossary, had based themselves in Paris and published theological works there (Chambers: 160-63). In Louvain, John Colgan, the Franciscan friar and intellectual, built networks of contacts particularly with Rome (Chambers: 157). By the early seventeenth century Irish intellectual life represented a significant part of the European counter-reformation. Many Irish students on completion of their studies remained in France and sought employment within the diocesan structures of the French church or relied on the ex-patriate Irish communities for support. There were more priests available in France than could be easily supported. The request for help in the Scottish missions was directed to the Irish community in Europe because of their pre-eminence in numbers of priests available and commitment to counter-reformation work as well as their linguistic suitability for the mission in Gaelic speaking Scotland.

## The Scottish Mission

Before dealing with the Irish missionary efforts in Scotland it is worth looking briefly at the activities of indigenous Scots Catholics. From 1580 only the Jesuits were carrying out co-ordinated missionary work in Scotland, although Minim friars and other individual priests were working independently. The Jesuit practice based on the principle of *cuius regio, eius religio* concentrated their efforts on members of the nobility and gentry who had retained the old faith or were sympathetic to it. The priest lived as a member of the household often in the guise of a tutor or doctor to divert suspicion. In this way they were able to carry out their ministry, support noble families and their tenantry and attempt conversions (Bellesheim, 4: 58-9). The most notable individual success using this approach was achieved at the court of King James VI, which contained a number of prominent Catholics such as the Chancellor, Lord Dunfermline. In 1598 the Jesuit, Father Abercromby, achieved the conversion of James' consort, Anne of Denmark (Bellesheim, 3: 347).

---

[4] Vatican Archives Borghese, II. Vol. 104 f. 140r *"E molte ben vero che la detta nazione Scozzese per la maggiore parte usa della lingua irlandese"*.
[5] On his first arrival in the Hebrides, Fr Edmund McCann one of the early missionaries, was recognised as a stranger from his dress and accent but had no difficulty in conversing with the islanders. Archivum de Sacra Congregatione De Propaganda Fide, *Scritt. rif. nelle cong. gen.*, vol. 312, ff 66r-71r as reported in Giblin, 1964: 4-5.

Jesuit efforts in the North East of Scotland were also successful among a number of important families (Bellesheim, 4· 61). Lodging in their households, sometimes for many years, they were able to ensure that a large part of the population of Moray and Aberdeenshire had access to the sacraments.[6] Even though many of them later converted to Protestantism they remained sympathetic to Catholicism, giving refuge to priests and refusing to enforce the penal laws against their Catholic tenants. In the highland areas of the North East most of the tenantry were Gaelic speakers. The Jesuit priests who came to work among them had to learn Gaelic while in post. This was noted in Strathglass where the priests were given shelter and support by Thomas Chisholm, Laird of Strathglass.[7]

The missionary efforts in the North East of Scotland and Eastern Highlands enabled those regions in the seventeenth century to retain the largest population of Catholics in Scotland outside the extreme Western Highlands and Islands. But the number of priests available was too small to devote the effort required for the huge geographical area of the Gaidhealtachd and consequently the greater part had been largely neglected before the arrival of Irish missionaries in the first half of the seventeenth century.

## The Irish Missions

### The First Irish Franciscan Mission

By 1611 a number of appeals had been made by Scottish Catholics to Pope Paul V to send Irish Franciscans to the Highlands and Islands of Scotland – referred to as Montana Scotia (Giblin, 1952: 9). These requests were passed onto Lucio Morra, the papal nuncio in the Spanish Netherlands, to discuss with the superiors of the Irish Franciscan College of St Anthony at Louvain. Initial reaction from the Franciscans was not favourable, given the additional burden that such a commitment represented. But in 1612 they sent John Ogilvie, a Scottish Franciscan residing at the college, to Scotland to obtain a factual account of the state of affairs there. A fellow Scot, John Stuart, a lay brother also at Louvain, followed him. Stuart reported back in 1614 and after further difficulties (largely financial) two Irish priests, Patrick Brady and Edmund McCann, set out with Stuart in the guise of soldiers to Montana Scotia in 1619 (Giblin, 1964: ix). Brady started working in the western Highlands while McCann went to the islands. However news of their work was quickly brought to the attention of the Kirk.[8] McCann was imprisoned and later banished.

During his imprisonment a major change was made in the Catholic Church's organisation of missionary work. In 1622 Pope Urban VIII established the Congregation of Propaganda Fide with the responsibility for co-ordinating the missionary work of the Church on a world-wide basis. The Scottish mission was a low priority for the authorities in Rome. Greater opportunities for evangelisation existed in the New World and the Far East. However, the provision of additional Irish priests for the Scottish mission was promoted, and funds for another Franciscan missionary venture from Louvain were provided. On this occasion it was decided to send four priests. As well as Father McCann who decided to return despite his banishment, Paul O'Neill, Patrick Hegarty and Cornelius Ward set out for Scotland in 1624. They travelled from Antrim to Kintyre and with their landing increased the Franciscan

---

[6] Thomas Abernethy was attached to the household of the Marquis of Huntly at Strathbogie in 1636. Gilbert Blackhall (a secular priest) stayed in the households of a number of north-eastern gentry including Alexander Hervey of Grandhome, Laird of Shivas and Patrick Conn of Cotrachy from 1637. He also became chaplain to Lady Aboyne and served her household until her death in 1641. See Gordon: 514, 523.
[7] Clan Chisholm Society, 1999. "Fr Aeneas Mackenzie's Memoirs", *Clan Chisholm Journal*, vol. 42. 65-6.
[8] *Register of the Privy Council of Scotland* xii, 47 "Against Ex-communicate Trafficking Papists".

presence in the Highlands and Islands to five – Fr Brady was still working on the Scottish mainland but John Stuart had been arrested and exiled (Giblin, 1964: x).

The difficulties faced by the missionaries were considerable. To have any chance of success they required help from the local population. The inter-clan warfare which plagued the region made this difficult. James VI had capitalised on clan enmity to use the Campbells and Mackenzies as agents to implement his policies for the Highlands and Islands. A number of clans were hostile to the central authorities and it was to these clans that the missionaries looked for a favourable reception (Roberts: 33-40). Prior to their leaving Louvain there had been contact with Scottish Catholics such as Sir James McDonald – at the time an exile in Spain – Col Ciotach McDonald of Colonsay and Roderick Macleod of Harris; agreement had been made to meet with the latter two lords on the missionaries' arrival in Scotland. An initial meeting was pre-arranged with Hector McNeill of Carskey in Kintyre on the first day of their arrival.[9] McNeill was one of the most prominent men in Kintyre and helped the Franciscans at the start of their mission. providing them with guides and introductions. This help was much needed since the instructions laid down by Propaganda Fide make it clear that they were poorly informed about the prevailing conditions in Montana Scotia. The Roman authorities had stipulated that the missionaries should meet every third night to discuss progress and agree plans.[10] The utter impracticability of this and other requirements had to be explained to Propaganda Fide and became a continuing theme in the missionaries' reports.

Over the next two years the missionaries, working primarily as individuals, travelled through and evangelised in large areas of the Highlands and Islands. Most frequently they worked in Kintyre, Western Inverness-shire, the Ross of Mull and Bute. Father Ward worked particularly in the Outer Hebrides, making many converts in North and South Uist, Barra and the surrounding islands. In the Inner Hebrides they covered Islay, Oronsay, Jura, Colonsay, Gigha and Arran. Among the smaller islands they visited were Canna, Rum, Eigg and Muck. Father O'Neill spent most of his two years on the mission working on Skye before he had to retire to Ireland due to ill health. Father Brady, who had been working on the mission for five years when the others arrived, continued working in Caithness and Sutherland (Giblin, 1964: xi-xii). Following a visit to see Father Brady in northern Scotland Father Ward reported to Propaganda Fide that conversions were not so easily obtained there. The people were afraid of openly professing Catholicism because of the legal penalties. The likelihood of penalties being exacted was high due to the greater number of officers of the State and the level of activity of Kirk ministers in that region.[11]

Life on the Scottish Mission was not easy. The missionaries' problems came in a number of different forms. Physical attack was threatened as well as imprisonment and banishment. In 1627 Fr. Brady reported being set upon by fourteen ministers of the Kirk, thrown from his horse, robbed and left severely injured (Bellsheim, 4: 68). In 1629 Clanranald was ordered by his overlord, Seaforth, to arrest Fr. Ward who had recently returned to Uist. However, thirty of Clanranald's tenants accompanied by his uncle intervened and prevented the arrest.[12] Despite his escape on this occasion, Fr. Ward and each of the other Franciscan missionaries were imprisoned on at least one occasion (Bellsheim, 4: 66-72).

The living conditions presented other hardships for the priests. Shelter and food were not easy to come by and when obtained were often of very poor quality. In a report to Propaganda Fide on 7 April 1625 they said that had to sleep in the open for several nights at a time and on

[9] Archivum de Sacra Congregatione De Propaganda Fide, *Scritt. Rif. Nelle cong. Gen.*vol. 312 ff. 15v-16v.
[10] Archivum de Sacra Congregatione De Propaganda Fide *Instruziioni diversi f.* 69r.
[11] Archivum de Sacra Congregatione De Propaganda Fide, *Scritt. Rif. Nelle Cong. Gen.* vol. 312 ff. 25r.-27r. *"ministellorum fequentia et audacia [....]legum in hisce partibus severitas et rigorosa in catholicos animadversion".*
[12] *Register of the Privy Council of Scotland*, 2nd series IV. 391.

occasions had only shellfish to eat which they had collected themselves from the seashore. Of the inhabitants of the western highlands they said that they "have a greater taste for military exploits than for food and are content with fare which would be scarcely sufficient for other people when fasting".[13] The greatest difficulties which the missionaries had to face, however, were presented by dealings with Propaganda Fide itself. Financial support was often slow in coming. But the description by the missionaries of such primitive conditions was felt by the officials of Propaganda Fide to be exaggerated and this belief may have been reinforced by Scottish priests in Rome expressing doubts about the accuracy of the Irish priests' reports (Giblin, 1964: xii-xiii). The requests for special faculties to cater for their unusual situation, such as the need to allow the priests to say mass without a server or without candles, were not understood in Rome. Even when given, approval was often hedged with conditions that rendered it unhelpful. Requirements included seeking dispensations from strict adherence to rules from a bishop; the nearest bishop being located in Ireland.

Despite their difficulties and the constant shortage of financial support, their work was successful. Their reports to Propaganda Fide state that they had converted over 6600 people and baptized a further 3000.[14] These figures are probably best viewed as reconciliations to the faith rather than conversions from Protestantism. In Rome the response to their claims was somewhat guarded. Cardinal Rospigliosi could still write in1669: "The natives of the islands adjacent to Scotland can, as a general rule, be properly called neither Catholics nor heretics .... They go wrong in matters of faith through ignorance, caused by want of priests to instruct them".[15] The Kirk, however, was concerned about their success. Alexander Knox, Bishop of the Isles, an appointee of James VI, heard of the Franciscan missionaries and wrote to the king in London asking him to take measures to stop them. The king's response was to laugh and say that there was no need to be angry with those who were converting people so wild as the natives of Kintyre to Christianity, even if that Christianity came from Rome. However, he declared that such missionaries deserved to be thanked.[16] The king in London, nearing the end of his life, with his queen having converted to Catholicism, might take that enlightened view but the Protestant clerics in Scotland continued their opposition.

The eventual withdrawal of the Franciscan missionaries was due to a number of factors but the principal one was the failure of Propaganda Fide to understand the true needs of the missionaries. Their reports to Propaganda frequently pleaded for greater freedom from rules in order to minister to the spiritual needs of their congregations. They needed regular and reliable financial support, as the country could not support them. The people were too poor to spare food, and items such as wheaten bread and wine for use in the Mass were unobtainable. Trips to Ireland or the Lowlands of Scotland were necessary to replenish their supplies (Giblin, 1952: 89-98).

Propaganda Fide's reaction to requests for help was influenced by its belief, in its world-wide role, that the missions should be able to support themselves from the contributions of their congregations. It was difficult for the Franciscans to convince them that this was impossible in the Highlands of Scotland. The lack of relevant knowledge on the part of the officials in Rome almost certainly contributed to their tardiness in providing financial support. Communication with Rome became more difficult as the civil wars progressed and physically and financially exhausted the missionaries withdrew to Ireland – O'Neill in 1626, Brady in 1630, Hegarty in 1631 and Ward in 1637. The date of McCann's final withdrawal from the Scottish mission is unknown, but he preceded Ward (Giblin, 1952: xv).

---

[13] Archivum de Sacra Congregatione De Propaganda Fide, *Scritt. rif. Nelle cong. gen.* vol. 312, ff. 24rv, 25r-27r, 15v-16v.

[14] Archivum de Sacra Congregatione De Propaganda Fide, *Scritt. Rif. Nelle Cong. Gen.* vol. 312 ff. 228v-229v.

[15] Archivum de Sacra Congregatione De Propaganda Fide, *Act f.* 462.

[16] Archivum de Sacra Congregatione De Propaganda Fide, *Scritt. Fir. Nelle Cong. Gen.* vol. 312 f. 3rv.

## The Dominicans

The Scottish Province of the Dominican Order was defunct by the early part of the seventeenth century, and the General Chapter meeting of 1629 committed the care of Scotland to the Irish province. Appeals for priests for missionary work in Scotland were made to the Dominican Order just as they had been to the Franciscans. Their response, however, was much slower in coming. In 1632 the papal nuncio in Paris was petitioned by the Irish Dominicans for permission to go to Scotland.[17] Father Dominic Burke and three companions were appointed and promised financial support from Propaganda Fide to work in the Highlands, in areas where there were no Franciscans operating.

This mission, however, never took place. The records of the Irish Chapter meeting in Youghal list a series of problems preventing implementation (Fenning, 1969: 299-303). These included an unwillingness to engage in a very arduous mission. The records noted that Irish Dominicans studying abroad were often reluctant to return to Ireland at the end of their theological studies. In light of this, inducing those who had agreed to return to take up the more arduous work in Scotland would be very difficult and was also disadvantageous to their mission in Ireland. Nevertheless, it was agreed that any Scot who wished to join the order in Ireland would be allowed to carry out missionary work in Scotland (ibid).

For these reasons the Dominicans attempted no missionary work in Scotland at this time. Both they and Propaganda Fide saw more rewarding areas for their efforts elsewhere in the world. The opportunities for missionary work in the Far East, the Americas and elsewhere were greater and were seen to represent easier returns (Fenning, 1971). In 1647 a further attempt to send a Dominican mission to Scotland was made. The Master-General granted permission to Fr John Baptist Fitzgerald to lead a group of four other friars to Scotland. However Propaganda Fide refused permission on the grounds that four Franciscans were already working in the Highlands and Islands.[18]

Shortly after this disappointment, Thomas Primrose, a Scot who was a member of the Irish province started to associate with fellow Scots in Paris and Rome with the intention of working on the Scottish mission. He discussed this with two secular priests, William Bannatyne – later to become the first Prefect of the Scottish Mission – and John Walker. He also began recruiting a number of young Scots into the Dominican Order. Of these, two were Gaelic speaking, William Lumsden and Vincentius Marianus Scotus. Primrose started to set up his mission in Scotland in the mid 1650's. Lumsden is believed to have worked in the North until 1664 when he returned to Paris. Vincentius Marianus was working in Morar in 1658 and believed to have continued in the Western Highlands until 1677.[19] In 1663 an Irish Dominican friar, Fr George Fanning, joined them, working in Barra. Fr Fanning died in Arisaig in 1678, having worked for fifteen years on the mission.

Thomas Primrose died in 1671 and with him ended any co-ordinated effort by the Dominican Order to provide support to the Scottish mission. There are no detailed records of the work done or the successes achieved by these Gaelic speaking Dominicans although Francis MacDonnell, who met Fr Fanning on Barra in 1671, wrote to Propaganda that "he has laboured much and with great fruit" (Campbell: 15-16).

---

[17] Archivum de Sacra Congregatione De Propaganda Fide, *Acta* 1623-1670 as reported in *Innes Review* vol. 5. 50
[18] Archivum Generale Ordinis Praedicatorum IV, 85, 132. Priory of Santa Sabina, Rome.
[19] Archivum de Sacra Congregatione De Propaganda Fide, *SOCG* f. 297, 329r.

## The Second Franciscan Mission

When Patrick Hegarty returned to Ireland from Scotland in 1631 he stayed at Bonamargy friary on the Antrim coast, ministering to Scottish Catholics who made the journey from the Highlands and Islands to visit. In 1641 he was imprisoned, being incarcerated until 1646. During this time Propaganda Fide sanctioned a renewed Franciscan mission to Montana Scotia. Four missionaries were chosen to go – Edmund McCann, Patrick Brady, Paul O'Neill, who had been in Scotland before, and Daniel MacNeill (Giblin, 1952: xiv). There is no direct evidence that this mission was ever sent. Propaganda's statement to the Dominicans in 1647 that their request to send missionaries to Scotland was being denied because there were four Franciscans already there is at best indirect evidence. It may have been no more than a statement of intent rather than fact.

## Vincent de Paul

Other indirect evidence makes it unlikely that the second Franciscan mission took place. In 1651 Clanranald sent a message from South Uist to Ireland begging for more priests. The request was forwarded via Propaganda Fide to Vincent de Paul, the founder of the Lazarists. Fathers Francis White and Dermot Duggan, both natives of Limerick, were sent in the company of "Young Glengarry"[20] who escorted them safely to Glengarry Castle. Father White remained there to work in the Western Highlands, mainly in Glengarry. Father Duggan moved on to the islands moving between the Uists and Barra. Vincent de Paul sent a third priest, Fr Lumsden, a Scot, to Orkney, Ross and Caithness (Bellsheim, 3: 84-85). The work of these Irish missionaries continued until their deaths – Fr Duggan in 1657 and Fr White in 1679. In their reports to Propaganda Fide they describe their ministries as pastoral care of the Catholic communities rather than large scale conversions to the faith.

A primary role of the Lazarist Order was in the provision of education. However, the practical problems associated with the Highland mission were such that it took until 1664 before they managed to open their first school in Glengarry. The letters of Fr Duggan to Vincent de Paul describe the difficulties and hardships faced by them as they travelled, and the poverty of the provisions available to them. The school was only possible through a stipend of fifty crowns per year to pay a schoolmaster being provided by Propaganda Fide (Campbell: 11).

## The Archbishop of Armagh and the See of the Hebrides

In 1669 Propaganda Fide decided to re-create the See of the Hebrides and place it under the authority of the Archbishop of Armagh, Oliver Plunkett (Bellsheim, 4: 86). The archbishop was making plans to visit the islands in 1671 when he was dissuaded by Fr Francis MacDonnell. Fr MacDonnell was an Irish Franciscan from Louvain who had been working in the Hebrides for a number of years, initially with his brother Mark. Father MacDonnell's argument was that the Highlands and Islands were full of rumours of landings by the French. A visit by the archbishop would be interpreted as politically motivated to assist the French, and therefore treasonable. Father MacDonnell also wrote to Propaganda declaring that the continued use of Irish priests in Scotland was politically dangerous. It was imperative, in his opinion, that Scottish priests be appointed to positions of authority. The Irish missionaries could then be their auxiliaries. Only by this means would they be able to counter the

---

[20] Angus Macdonnell, 1st Lord Macdonnell and Aros. At this time he was effectively head of the Macdonnells of Glengarry and known as "Young Glengarry" to distinguish him from his grandfather, "Old Glengarry", who was over ninety years of age at the time. Stevenson: 277-78.

arguments of the Kirk authorities that the actions of the Catholic Church were seditious. Archbishop Plunkett endorsed this view and added that schools in the islands were essential to provide for the education of potential candidates for the priesthood.[21] Propaganda responded by providing a further stipend to open a school in Barra, which was achieved in 1675. Archbishop Plunkett never visited his See of the Hebrides. With his execution at Tyburn in 1681 the See came to an end and authority for this mission passed to the Prefect of the Scottish Mission. Irish missionary involvement in Scotland did not end at this point, but Scottish responsibility for the whole of the country was established and, as far as it was possible, acted upon.

## Conclusion

### Leslie's Report

In 1677 Propaganda Fide was deliberating on a number of issues concerning the Scottish mission. There had been representations for the re-establishment of the hierarchy and the appointment of a bishop. In Rome, King Charles II was seen as being personally sympathetic to Catholicism in his kingdoms and his brother James, Duke of York, a Catholic, was heir presumptive. These factors led many to believe that opportunities for missionary work might be greatly improved and therefore would justify greater investment in effort and money. Propaganda Fide, however, felt that they had insufficient knowledge of the true conditions in Scotland on which to base sound judgements. They decided to send a visitor (i.e. a senior churchmen appointed as an inspector) to conduct a thorough survey of the Scottish mission (Bellsheim, 2: 128).

The man selected for the job was Alexander "Hard boots" Leslie. Leslie travelled throughout the greater part of the country including the Highlands and Islands (Bellsheim, 4: 126).[22] Father Leslie submitted his report to Rome in1681.[23] The report showed that there were 14,000 communicants at that time. This figure has since been extrapolated to 40,000 Catholics to take account of children and other non-communicant Catholics. They, therefore, represented about 4% of the population of Scotland at the time (Darrock: 49-59).

Of 14,000 communicants, Leslie reported that 12,000 lived in the Highlands and islands. Whole districts were largely or entirely Catholic. The areas supported by the Irish missionaries since 1624 were the main centres of Catholic population. In the Lowlands, by comparison, there were very few; Glasgow and the surrounding district had only 50 communicants recorded. In the North East, however, there was a significant population of Catholics, with 1500 in Banff and Aberdeenshire.

### The Kirk's Census

The Presbyterian Kirk continued to be concerned about Catholicism and in 1704 a report into the numbers of declared Catholics in Scotland was commissioned by the Kirk. The report, entitled "List of Popish Parents and their Children in Various Parts of Scotland",[24] states that

---

[21] Archivum de Sacra Congregatione De Propaganda Fide, *Scritt. Rif. Nelle Cong. Gen.* vol. 1 as reported in Campbell: 15-16.

[22] To help him in this region he was accompanied by Robert Munro, the first native Gaelic speaking Scottish secular priest in Scotland since the Reformation. Munro was a native of Strathglass who had been educated at the Scots Colleges in Rome and Paris and represented the type of priest that the Scottish mission felt it most needed. Munro went on to work on the mission for over twenty years before dying while imprisoned in Glengarry Castle in 1704.

[23] Archivio Segreto Vaticano. *Cod. Vatic. Ottobon* 3182 f. 23 as reported in Bellesheim: 356-364.

[24] Maitland Club. 1843. *Miscellany of the Maitland Club*. vol. iii pt. 2. 387-441.

significant numbers of Catholics remained in the western Highlands in Ardnamurchan, Lochaber, Kilmonivaig, Knoydart, Morar and Arisaig. In the Hebrides the islands of South Uist, Barra, Canna, Rum, Muck, Eigg, Coll and Tiree were almost entirely Catholic. Of the areas ministered to by the Irish missionaries in the previous century, only the southern islands of Islay, Jura and Colonsay with the Ross of Mull and Kintyre had very few Catholics remaining there. The Kirk's report stated that elsewhere in the Gaidhealtachd, a few glens in the Eastern Highlands had significant concentrations of Catholics. The northeast of Scotland had a large number of professed Catholics but all other parts of Lowland Scotland had very few. This survey largely supported the findings of that of "Hardboots" Leslie conducted a quarter of a century earlier.

## The Legacy

The Irish missionaries were helped by the remoteness of the areas in which they worked. They had less to fear from the attentions of the central authorities which affected missionaries in the other parts of Scotland. This does not, however, detract from the enormous efforts which they made in combating extremely arduous physical conditions, occasional attacks by officers of the Kirk and State, and most significantly in persevering with inadequate and unreliable support from the Roman authorities. Their work ensured that significant parts of the population in the western Highlands and Islands remained Catholic throughout the seventeenth century. This had a political as well as a confessional significance.

During the civil wars and the Jacobite risings, loyalism did not equate to Catholicism but Catholic clans were invariably supportive of the royalist and later Jacobite objectives. This support was disproportionaty large given the small number of Scottish Catholics as reported by Alexander Leslie. There were, however, large numbers of Catholics in exile with the Stewarts in France and Italy.[25] The Catholics of the western Highlands and Islands were actively engaged in the attempts of James VII to regain his throne and also those of his son and grandson (Halloran: 80-98). When Charles Edward Stewart launched his attempt to regain the throne in 1745, he chose the Western Isles as his first landing place before moving onto the mainland at Moidart. The choice was undoubtedly influenced by the strength of Jacobite support among the mainly Catholic population. If the Irish missionaries of the seventeenth century had not succeeded in their work it is possible that the course of Jacobite history would have been different.

The confessional legacy of the missionaries has endured for longer. When Pope Leo XIII restored the Hierarchy of Scotland in 1878 one of the six dioceses created was that of Argyll and the Isles (Anson: 57). This diocese was made up of parishes in the area originally ministered to by the Irish missionaries. These communities had remained distinctively Catholic despite adversities such as the Clearances. It is therefore little exaggeration to claim that the missionaries' work in the seventeenth century has been the foundation for the survival of Catholicism in the western Highlands and Islands of Scotland.

## References

Anson, Peter F. 1970 *Underground Catholicism in Scotland* Montrose: Standard Press
Bellesheim A. 1890 *History of the Catholic Church in Scotland*. Volumes 3 & 4
        Campbell, Ed. 1936. *Book of Barra*. London

---

[25] Halloran: 81-90. The staff and students of the Scots college in Paris were close to the activities of the Court at St Germain –the college principal, Louis Innes, became one of James VII's closest advisers. Students and alumni engaged in work as couriers, fund raisers, bankers, diplomats and soldiers.

Clan Chisholm Society. 1999. *Clan Chisholm Journal*. Vol 42. London

Darroch James. 1953. "Catholic Population of Scotland since 1680". *Innes Review*. 4. Edinburgh

Fenning, Hugh O.P. 1969. "Archivum Fratrum Praedicatorum XXXIX". *Registers of the Dominican Order*

Fenning, Hugh O.P. 1971. "Archivum Fratrum Praedicatorum XLI". *Registers of the Dominican Order*

Giblin, Cathaldus OFM. 1952 "The Irish Mission to Scotland in the Seventeenth Century". *Franciscan College Annual*. Multyfarnham

Giblin, Cathaldus OFM. Ed. 1964. "Irish Franciscan Mission to Scotland 1619-1646". *Documents from Roman Archives*. Dublin

Gordon, JFS. 1869 *Catholic Church in Scotland 1603-1869*. Glasgow: John Tweed

Halloran, Brian M. 2003. *The Scots College Paris, 1603-1792*. Edinburgh: John Donald

Macdonald, Roderick. 1978. "The Catholic Gaidhealtachd". *Innes Review*. 29: 56-72

Maitland Club. 1843. *Miscellany of the Maitland Club*. Edinburgh

New Spalding Club. 1906. *Records of the Scots Colleges*. vol. 1. Aberdeen: Aberdeen University Press

O'Connell, Patricia. 2001. "The Early-modern Irish College Network in Iberia, 1590-1800". In *The Irish in Europe 1580 – 1815*. Ed. Thomas O'Connor. Dublin: Four Courts Press

O'Scea, Ciaran. 2001. "The Irish Catholic exile in early-modern Galicia, 1598-1666". In *The Irish in Europe 1580 – 1815*. Ed. Thomas O'Connor. Dublin: Four Courts Press

Roberts, A. 1988. *Bonamargy and the Scottish Mission*. The Glynns

Stevenson, David. 1980. *Highland Warrior Alistair MacColla and the Civil Wars*. Edinburgh: The Saltire Society

# Vampires, Cannibals, Half-Breeds, and Jews: Encounters with the Other in Maturin's *Melmoth the Wanderer*

*Christina Morin*

Charles Robert Maturin's gothic novel *Melmoth the Wanderer*, published in 1820, appeared in the immediate aftermath of the passing of the infamous Six Acts[1] which broadened the definition of treason, increased the severity of the punishment for such acts, and thereby recommended caution to the politically motivated writer. In this context of renewed suppression and censorship, *Melmoth* functions on the level of political allegory. Thus, while the novel's many interconnected narratives ostensibly concern Civil War England, Inquisitorial Spain, and life on an unchartered Indian island, they also reflect on Ireland, a near-contemporary version of which serves as the setting for the novel's framing narrative. By deliberately choosing such an unconventional setting in terms of the gothic, Maturin highlights his maternal country and suggests that it will play a substantial role in the remainder of the novel. And yet, the country remains curiously marginalised. After a few pages, Ireland becomes mere background material as Maturin pursues his investigation of issues of nationalism, specifically Irish national identity, by displacing those issues onto other countries. Tying the major scenes of his novel together through a shared emphasis on colonisation and domination, Maturin implies that he perceives a similar scenario within his own country. Enmeshed in the Union with England, he argues, Ireland risks becoming a victim of England's colonising impulses.

The central process of colonisation that Maturin underscores evinces itself most clearly in the related ideas of vampirism and cannibalism which recur throughout the novel. Both vampire and cannibal serve as projections of nameless uncertainties; in the discourse of colonialism they represent many of the subconscious fears felt by European colonisers during their colonising endeavours. Indeed, Bram Stoker's *Dracula* (1897) and other such vampire narratives have been read as illustrations of the fear of "reverse colonisation" – the fear of the invasion of the colonised other (Malchow, 1996: 149). The terror that the vampire arouses as a general metaphoric symbol lies in his ability to cross conventional geographical and temporal boundaries, in his shape-shifting, and in his mesmerising influence over individuals. Since his threat is all-encompassing and all-inclusive, no one and no place is safe. The threat the vampire represented, at least in the heyday of Western European expansionism, resulted in the metaphorical equation of the vampire with "the generalized fear of strangers, outsiders, and the dark "Other"" (ibid.: 162). Unhindered by normal territorial and spatial boundaries, the vampire located himself not only on the peripheries but also at the heart of European culture, undermining the careful demarcations of Self and Other that underpinned the colonial project.

Similarly, the cannibal seemed able to cross boundaries, to inspire fear of the outsider while also implicating the insider in its savagery. During the colonial period, cannibalism was perhaps "the most notorious process of colonial 'othering'" (Kitson, 2001: 204). It was used as

---

[1] Passed in 1819 after a prolonged period of rioting and discontent, the Six Acts declared that every meeting for "radical reform" was "an overt act of treasonable conspiracy against the king and his government". They were meant to lessen the dangers presented by dissenters and radicals, and they consisted of the Training Prevention Act, the Seizure of Arms Act, and Seditious Meetings Act, the Blasphemous and Seditious Libels Act, the Misdemeanours Act, and the Newspaper and stamp Duties Act. See Marjie Bloy. "The Six Acts 1819". *The Victorian Web*. www.victorianweb.org/history/riots/sixacts.

a process by which imperial Europe could distinguish itself from the subjects of its colonial expansion while, at the same time, justifying that expansion. Accusations of ritual cannibalism allowed Western colonisers to identify certain cultures as barbaric and in need of Western civilising forces. And yet, such accusations represent at least in part an attempt to displace onto the Other the fear of internal transgressions, for the threat of cannibalism lay not only without but also within Western culture. In fact, the threat of cannibalism was a very real one for eighteenth and even nineteenth-century European cultures which were, especially in times of warfare, subject to periods of famine and the ensuing resort to survival cannibalism.[2] At the same time, certain social customs and institutions fell prey to accusations of cannibalism, thus locating the practice firmly within Europe.

The domestic, if metaphoric, cannibalism pervading European civilisation during the early nineteenth century was nowhere more evident than in the practice of scientific dissection and research. As H.L. Malchow has argued, a combination of the increasing professionalisation of medical training and a new vogue for comparative anatomy sponsored an objectification of the dead body and encouraged a popular understanding of the surgeon and medical student as "bizarrely inhumane" (111). In their scientific dissection and consumption of cadavers, medical professionals were seen to participate in an inherently cannibalistic endeavour (ibid. 110-1).

Medicine and science, however, were not the only realms of British and European society in which elements of cannibalism emerged. Many local British traditions suggesting cannibal superstition and ritual survived well into the nineteenth century and even longer. For instance, various folk remedies revolved around the actual consumption of human body parts – human blood was promoted as a remedy for epilepsy, the fat of executed criminals as a cure for scrofula and rheumatism, and dessicated corpse, otherwise known as "mummy", as a general cure-all (Malchow, 1996: 56). In addition to such traditional medical remedies, certain local traditions, specifically those related to death and dead bodies, held wide sway. The Welsh, for example, practised an ancient custom of hiring a "sin-eater", or an individual who received money to eat food placed on the chest of a corpse, a tradition closely associated with the "corpse cake", or funeral food that was placed on or near the dead body (ibid.: 55).

Such customs, which may have derived from ancient, pre-Christian practice, eventually became connected to the implied cannibalism of the Eucharist. In both Catholicism and Protestantism the sacrament of the Eucharist exists as a cornerstone of faith in which believers consume bread and wine believed to symbolise (in Protestantism) or actually be (in Catholicism) the body and blood of Jesus Christ. Understandably, outsiders as well as insiders came to understand this sacrament, in Protestantism and especially in Catholicism, as condoning and supporting cannibalism (Kitson, 2001: 214). Moreover, a connection with the related notion of vampirism could also be made since believers drink wine supposed to be the blood of Christ. The modern critic Victor Sage (1998: 50) highlights this link but attributes the charges of vampirism and cannibalism laid against Catholicism to the Protestant "reductio ad absurdum" of the Catholic doctrine of transubstantiation. Despite the ridicule with which Sage seems to view the idea of vampirism in Catholic communion, early church leaders were keen to discourage the actual drinking of blood. They wanted to emphasise the essential link between blood and life in the Eucharist. At the same time, however, they acknowledged the necessity of discouraging men from killing for blood, and they called for support on the many

---

[2] Kitson (219) uses the term "survival cannibalism" or "white cannibalism" to refer to the practice of humans eating human flesh out of necessity, as in times of famine. He cites the example of sailors at sea who have run out of food and have no immediate prospect of reaching land to restock. The element of need separates "survival cannibalism" from the ritualistic cannibalism allegedly engaged in by colonised cultures.

Bible verses that warn against drinking blood.[3] The perceived need to dissuade men from enacting the Eucharist meal in everyday life suggests an awareness of the intrinsically cannibalistic/vampiric nature of transubstantiation, but it also indicates a consciousness of man's potential animalistic urges even when supposedly civilised. It is exactly this fear, an anxiety over man's inner barbarity breaking free from the tenuous confines of society and culture, that seems to underpin eighteenth- and nineteenth-century British condemnations of cannibalism and vampirism. For with the supposed cannibalism and vampirism of the Catholic Church, as well as with the very real threat of famine, burgeoning medical and scientific methods, existing folk tradition, and the sacrament of the Eucharist, cannibalism and vampirism proved dishearteningly grounded within European culture, a culture that eagerly displaced that atrocity onto the savage Other.

The strong presence of vampirism and cannibalism within Maturin's novel is reinforced by the seemingly unrelated reference to the legend of the Wandering Jew. In his wandering of the world searching for a victim, unable to die, Melmoth certainly recalls the figure of The Wandering Jew, and Maturin was at least partially inspired by the legend when writing *Melmoth*. This Christian legend first appeared in the early thirteenth century telling of a Jewish man named Cartaphilus, later christened Joseph, who was condemned to await the Last Judgment for taunting Jesus shortly before his crucifixion (Briggs, 1981: 137). A slightly altered version next appeared in Europe in the sixteenth century and told of a Jewish cobbler named Ahasverus who had similarly mocked Jesus and consequently had been doomed to wander the earth until the Judgment Day (ibid.: 137-8). For centuries after its initial appearances the legend continued to hold sway over the popular imagination. For instance, the tale had wide currency during the seventeenth century, an era that often credited the Wanderer with healing power. The eighteenth century witnessed "imposters" claiming to be the Wandering Jew and madmen who really believed they were, and in the nineteenth century the Wandering Jew became one of Romanticism's well-loved symbols.[4]

The popularity of the Wandering Jew in Britain during the eighteenth and nineteenth centuries stems partially from longstanding anxiety about the Jew's position in British society. The Jew's ability to assimilate into that society inspired a great deal of anti-Semitic feeling, and important issues of national identity inevitably arose with the threat of a lack of differentiation between Jew and Brit (Malchow, 1996: 163). At times, however, attempts were made to better incorporate Jewish people into British society. For instance, the 1753 Naturalisation Bill sought to ease the difficulties Jews faced in attaining naturalisation, classified as they were as aliens even when born in Britain. Since naturalisation would allow the Jewish citizen a more equal status in society by permitting him to own land and engage in trade, the bill arguably made steps towards integration. Despite vocal opposition from city merchants and High Church leaders, it passed easily through both houses of Parliament, but tangible gains for British Jews were very few (Hoad, 2002: 125-6). Thus, while the intent of the Bill was in essence good-willed, exhibiting as it did a certain benevolence and tolerance, the actual outcome suggests a latent desire to continue Jewish marginalisation. At the very least the disparity between intent and outcome points to the ambivalence felt toward the Jew in Britain, where both positive and negative stereotypes existed side by side. For instance, Jewish intelligence and emotionalism often figured as positive "Jewish traits", but those same traits could also feed into the image of the Jew as "excessive, dangerous, and suspect" (Garb, 1995: 26).

---

[3] See Twitchell, 1981: 14. These verses include Deuteronomy 12:16, Genesis 9:4, and Leviticus 17:11. Significantly, these warnings occur in the Old Testament, thus linking the Jew, rather than the Catholic, to a predilection for human blood and suggesting an anti-Semitic prejudice underlying the anti-Catholic/anti-transubstantiation arguments proposed by Protestants.

[4] David Punter (1996: 100) observes that the figure of the Wanderer, a variation of the Wandering Jew, served as a principal symbol of terror for the Romantics and can be found in works by such Romantic greats as Coleridge, Shelley, Byron, and Blake.

Fittingly, given the ambivalence so often directed toward the Jew, the Wandering Jew's curse of immortality was not always interpreted negatively. Indeed, the original Wandering Jew was a "convinced penitent" rather than a "demonic figure", and the theme of noble repentance appears consistent in all versions of the legend up to modern times (Briggs, 1981: 137). David Punter further notes that the Wanderer as a literary and cultural figure from ancient legends to the nineteenth century has done the proper or fitting penance for his crime, whatever it may be. Nevertheless, his punishment continues, enforced by a God jealous of human aspiration. The Wanderer thus becomes a figure of persecution, the ultimate victim: "He is the exemplary sacrifice to repression." (1996: 101). Despite the dignity conferred upon the Wandering Jew by his atonement, however, the figure remained open to hostility as when, in the Romantic period, it became associated with the Old Clothes Man, a figure that sold contaminated clothing to unsuspecting individuals.

The Jew's connection to the Old Clothes Man highlighted his outsider position in British society and negatively located him within "larger anxieties of contamination of nationhood, class, and domesticity" (Sicher, 2002: 139).[5] Much like colonised peoples, Jews came to represent the Other in nineteenth-century Britain. In this context, the Jewish race was not only identified as the ancient foe of Christ but also as a degenerate Oriental race (ibid.: 141). On a racial scale, where whites were the "apogee of civilization" and blacks/Negroes represented the bottom of the evolutionary scale, Jews were ambivalently placed "between the extreme antimonies of blackness and whiteness, always tainted with the one, never quite embraced within the other" (Garb 1995: 22). Indeed, as the realm of European conquest spread in the eighteenth and nineteenth centuries, the idea that Jews possessed an "African character" and were a "mongrel" race with Negro blood became prevalent (Malchow, 1996: 150) The association between the black and the Jew based itself on an assumption of mutuality between the two groups and their supposed practice of blood sacrifice, self-mutilation, and cannibalism. Proponents of the link between the black, or perhaps more specifically, the black cannibal of the Pacific Islands, and the Jew, cited the Old Testament tale found in the second Book of Kings (2 Kings, 6:29) which told of a group of starving women eating their own children. Moreover, the connection received support from the widely held belief that a wandering "lost tribe" of Israel had mingled with the Pacific Islanders on its way through Asia and into the Pacific, contributing genetically to the Islanders' racial inheritance (ibid.). Thus, the Jew became ineluctably linked to cannibalism, and a belief in the Jew's desire for human flesh became so widespread that by the end of the century liberal utilitarian and social evolutionist Herbert Spencer hypothesised that Jewish circumcision was a surviving remnant of a historical stage when primitive cannibalism had given way to symbolic mutilation (ibid.).

Not only did the Jew fall prey to accusations of cannibalism, but he also became inevitably linked to the vampire. The Jew's traditional image as usurer or bloodsucker laid him open to charges of vampirism, as did the belief in the Jewish practice of occult rituals dependent on the blood of Christian children (Malchow, 1996: 152). Even when it presents the Jew favourably, the legend of the Wandering Jew falls victim to the vampire association, particularly in the curse of immortality shared by both figures. As Malchow observes, in the rhetorical idea of

---

[5] See also Bewell (1999) who traces the links between contamination, disease, and colonial geography, arguing that displacing disease onto colonial cultures allowed Western civilisation to differentiate itself and place itself on a higher social, cultural, and political level. Colonial regions were deemed "sick" and thus in need of European intervention. According to the dominant model of disease transmission from the late seventeenth century until the emergence of modern germ theory in the 1870s, their sicknesses were caused by contamination (30). By linking the Jew living in Britain with contamination, and labeling him a "contaminant" British society acknowledged the threat of colonial disease crossing borders, locating itself at the heart of European civilization, and thus effectively erasing the fragile demarcation between "self" and "other," "us" and "them".

"the eternal Jew", immortality characterised the entire Jewish race, which was seen as "condemned to eternal diaspora, unevolving, an enduring primitive presence in Western society" (161). As such, the Jew, like the vampire, represented a threat within.

Significantly, colonial discourse's preoccupation with the threat of the vampire, the cannibal, and the Jew suggests a concurrent concern with national identity. The need to distinguish between the self and the other, the civilised and the savage, the foreign and the native, represents a fundamental issue of national identity formation and maintenance as understood by critics such as Homi Bhabha, Ernest Gellner, and Benedict Anderson. When a living human, bitten by a vampire, becomes a member of the "undead", the vampire destroys the victim's identity by replacing it with a version of his own; his threat is therefore a subversive one. He undermines identity and forces new identities onto people and places. Similarly, the cannibal threatens to erase borders in his consumption of others; his incorporation of others into himself represents the breakdown of order, structure, and hierarchy. Likewise, the assimilated Jew represents a blurring of boundaries, an imposition of Jewishness on unsuspecting British subjects. All three figures thus embody the threat of self-erasure, of the substitution of one identity for another. Their prominence within the novel therefore suggests Maturin's interest in issues of national identity formation.

I would argue that Melmoth, as a character, takes on vampire-like qualities. For example, his eyes exhibit a lustre typically associated with the vampire, he simultaneously disgusts and enthrals his victims, and his lifespan is preternaturally long. I would further argue, however, that blood-sucking and flesh-eating, both literal and metaphorical, recur regularly throughout the novel. For instance, Maturin's criticism of Catholicism largely bases itself on the practice of displaced penance in which one person's sins are forgiven because of another person's sacrifice. The Catholic Monçada bemoans the falseness of a religion that makes of "aggravating the sufferings of others" an individual's mediator with God (Maturin, 1998: 147). Monçada's own mother falls victim to these beliefs, sacrificing her son to the Church in exchange for her perceived sin. Similarly, the parricide who leads Monçada out of the monastery only to betray him firmly believes in his ability to excuse himself to God by betraying, denouncing, and punishing his fellow sinners (224). According to these teachings, a person ultimately attains salvation through the sacrifices of others, much as a vampire or a cannibal gains renewed existence through the sacrifice of others.

The Church itself partakes of these vampiric and cannibalistic qualities in its quest to maintain power through the sacrifice of its believers, a program most obviously seen in the Inquisition, which figures as a mechanism for corrupt Church officials to guarantee the retention of their supreme power. The threat of imprisonment within the Inquisition appears time and time again as an effective check on apparent questioning of that authority. For instance, Father Jose employs the threat in a conversation with Don Fernan over Immalee's fate. Don Fernan, eager to wed his sister to nobility, bridles at the priest's suggestion that the girl is fit only for the cloister. His objection is met with Fr. Jose's dramatic comment: "I forgive your illiberal reflections on me, – but let me remind you, that the same immunity will not be extended to the insult you offer to the Catholic faith" (337). The threat produces the intended effect – Don Fernan immediately professes terrified contrition. And yet his crime/sin was not in questioning Catholicism but in questioning Father Jose and his motives, highlighting Maturin's condemnation of the Inquisition as a system based more on upholding the authority of the Catholic hierarchy than in administering the faith.

Maturin further attacks the Catholic Church in the story of the two young lovers told by the parricide to Monçada. The two lovers accept the parricide's offer of help when the convent superiors discover their secret love, but instead of leading them to safety as promised, the parricide imprisons them in a small underground chamber, condemning them to death by starvation. Hunger turns them from devoted lovers to confirmed enemies, and cannibalism becomes a perceived necessity. The parricide graphically describes hearing on the fourth night "the shriek of the wretched female" as her lover, "in the agony of hunger", "fastened his teeth in her shoulder" (212-13). Maturin's suggestion with such incidents is clear: the Catholic Church, in its readiness to sacrifice believers in a ruthless quest to maintain power and authority, has reduced itself to nothing more than savage cannibalism. Further, Maturin's emphasis on the Inquisition highlights the ritual nature of the Church's cannibalism, contrasting it with the survival cannibalism of the young lovers, and thus places the Church on a level with barbaric colonial cultures.

Significantly, Maturin's attack on the Catholic Church via the Inquisition also implicates the extant political structures in Britain. As Mark Canuel (1995: 509-11) argues, from the Reformation onward, religious uniformity served as a key component of British national identity. Britain's Protestantism was understood to separate it from the continent and therefore served as an essential marker of Britishness. The importance invested in religious uniformity and unity necessarily affected political institutions, which demanded religious conformity as a prerequisite for participation in the political and civic life of Britain. In his *Church of Englandism and its Catechism Examined* (1818), Jeremy Bentham argued against the pervasiveness of religious uniformity and against the oaths and tests required in the nation's university system, which he believed were reminiscent of the Inquisition. He further contended that the government's insistence on religious uniformity served to illogically eliminate non-conformists from political and civic identity as well as to produce the very insincerity religious uniformity was intended to avoid in its quest to guarantee the moral integrity of the nation. The oaths and tests demanded of people made lying inevitable, "a necessary byproduct of the structure of established religion" (ibid.). Thus, while Maturin specifically attacks the Catholic Church and its hypocrisy in his criticism of the Inquisition, we can also read there a condemnation of the hypocrisy of a government that would impose homogeneity and conformity on its citizens for the sake of "Britishness".[6]

In terms of colonial discourse, perhaps the most significant element of Maturin's depiction of the Catholic Church, and by extension, the British government, is his location of the colonial situation within Europe. This points to a trend in the novel, that colonisation repeatedly occurs within the West rather than in a foreign land invaded by the West. Time and time again, Melmoth serves as a symbol of colonisation. He freely crosses national boundaries attempting to overpower his intended victims, to colonise them and to make them his own. Meaningfully, however, he confines his colonial efforts to Western Europe. Except for a brief excursion to Immalee's Indian island, Melmoth works within the traditional boundaries of Western civilisation, seemingly giving voice to the anxieties over colonialism that animated colonial European culture. We see this in Melmoth's metaphoric cannibalism and vampirism, and in his affinity to the Wandering Jew, but also, significantly, in his fathering of a child, an act that itself projects a cannibalistic nature. The narrator implies that Melmoth's happiness over Immalee's pregnancy stems from his desire to raise and foster his replacement: his own child becomes "fatally fitted for his purpose" (511). In brief, Melmoth would cannibalise his own offspring.

Melmoth's child deserves notice as she too highlights the unsettling possibility of the blurring of the lines between coloniser and colonised. Theoretically, she is the fusion of the

---

[6] Maturin was a well-known eccentric and, while also a cleric in the Church of Ireland, often voiced concerns in his works over the role of religion, specifically institutionalised religion, and the state in personal identity formation and maintenance. Dale Kramer argues that Maturin actually tied *Melmoth the Wanderer* together with his depiction of oppressive religious, social, and political institutions and their clash with the individual will and inclination. According to Kramer, Maturin believed in man's innate desire to do good, but also that this desire was often thwarted by repressive and hypocritical religious and political institutions, thus inhibiting man from achieving his full potential and realising his true identity (Kramer 1973: 102).

West and the Orient, the product of an immensely problematic relationship. While the West projected an idealised version of the courtship plot, in which England and the Orient were happily joined, the end goal was not synthesis as such (Lew, 1994: 18). Rather, Europeans turned a blind eye to Englishmen impregnating colonised women but rejected the idea of their offspring entering England, citing issues of racial corruption, degeneration, and the "sullying the pure white of the English complexion" (ibid.). The threat of such a movement led to the branding of relationships between coloniser and colonised as socially taboo. Thus, by the early nineteenth century racial intermarriage in much of the British Empire had ended. Native women became mistresses and/or prostitutes. Their children, as half-breeds, assumed the added social stigma of "prostitute's bastard" (Malchow, 1996: 177).

Immalee's baby, as a product of coloniser and colonised, good and evil, white and dark, signals the actual location of the feared product of such mergers within Europe itself. She becomes the half-breed within Western society, threatening Europeans with their own fallibility. As the product of an act of passion, in the Victorian mind the half-breed signified not rationality, but the loss of white self-control (ibid.), and thus symbolised the white man's transgressions, his own straying from Western culture. Hence, the half-breed trope rests firmly not on the fear of the Other but on the fear that the European could somehow become Other himself. In this way, the image of the half-breed bypasses the savage black mistress/prostitute to implicate the white man who had "gone native" and become "a half-caste, a monstrous self-transformation, a Crusoe mastered by Friday" (ibid.: 189).

Like the white man who fathers a child with a "savage" woman, Melmoth is a social transgressor. In his pursuit of forbidden knowledge, he rejects his own kind and flees from civilized community, becoming himself a strange half-breed. Likewise, Immalee represents a sort of social half-caste. Technically a pure-blooded, old-Christian Spaniard, her existence on a deserted Indian island, coupled with her lack of "proper" education, Orientalises her (Lew, 1994: 18). Her former existence taints her and assimilation into Spanish society proves impossible. Instead, she hovers between the two worlds and identities she has known. Like the colonised, she is both part of European society but also inherently separate from it. Her union with Melmoth, as the representative of European civilisation, represents the ambiguous merger between colonised and coloniser. And yet, Maturin problematises this union, introducing elements that complicate the position of Immalee's child.

Notably, the midnight marriage ceremony in which Melmoth and Immalee are united remains highly questionable, as does its validity. The child produced from this ambiguous relationship is neither exactly a bastard nor legitimate. English and Spanish civil law would have considered the couple's dubious marriage invalid, but Ecclesiastical Law, applicable in Spain and retained in England after the Reformation, held that as long as one party believed the marriage ceremony valid, any offspring were legitimate (Lew, 1994: 18). Immalee's child is thus a half-breed in more than one sense. She remains perpetually suspended between Western and Oriental, coloniser and colonised, legitimate and illegitimate. Neither fully "us" nor fully "them", the child, rather than symbolising a synthesis between differing identities, represents a battleground between opposing forces, clearly embodying colonialism's central struggle.

Maturin further complicates this struggle by identifying Melmoth as an Irishman and thus undermining his ability to represent European civilisation. Being Irish, Melmouth partakes in the ambiguous identity of colonised, just as much as Immalee does. While he figures as a colonising force, his nationality compromises that position. Nineteenth-century Ireland was very much at the margins of British society, which often pictured the country as equally savage and barbaric as Africa or India. The Act of Union (1800) and the ensuing political amalgamation of Ireland with Britain ostensibly erased the borders between the British and the Irish, but, in reality, the Union only seemed to increase British anxiety over the infiltration of the savage other, in this case the Irish, into mainstream British society. Such concern exposes itself quite clearly in the literature of the day. For instance, in essays written in 1809, 1812, and 1828, Southey argued against the granting of full rights to Irish Catholics, speaking of Catholicism in terms of disease, contagion, and infection, and thus explicitly establishing Ireland as a savage colonial territory according to Bewell's ideas of colonial geography.[7] Southey only enforced this image of Ireland by comparing the Irish people to African kings renowned for their barbarity and equating Catholic processions with Hindu customs: "Ireland became Africanized and Indianized in his account, as he sought to portray the military government he thought necessary to prevent Irish infections as a civilizing paternalism that, as in the newer colonies, would save heathens from themselves" (Fulford, 1998: 38). Other British authors similarly compared Ireland to more traditional colonial territories such as India and Africa, confirming and reinforcing the British social and political opinion of Ireland as a colonial territory and the Irish as a colonial Other. That Melmoth should represent a colonising force in the novel signifies a reversal of roles, the same reversal the Western world so feared. Rather than being a representation of European civilisation, I would argue Melmoth purposely embodies the threatening Other. His movements, like those of Dracula, suggest the infiltration of the other within British society itself. His child hints at an eventual colonisation of the coloniser by the original colonised, the overpowering of England by Ireland. Her death, however, suggests the unfeasibility of such an agenda. Independence from England, the overthrow of the coloniser, seems not to figure, at least in Maturin's mind, as the solution to Ireland's problems.

And yet England's presence in Ireland hardly manifests itself as desirable in the novel. Maturin clarifies this partially through his depiction of Melmoth. Chris Baldick (Maturin, 1998: xvi) suggests that Melmoth, in his simultaneous centrality and marginality, approximates Irish landlords of the day. He is an "absentee villain": his direct presence is not actually necessary to the "dissolution of stable identities" that animates the novel. The image of Melmoth as an absentee landlord is a compelling one, his nationality notwithstanding. If we accept the characteristics of colonisation in Melmoth's character and also accept the picture of him as an absentee villain, we begin to see what may be Maturin's most coherent condemnation of England's presence in Ireland. Like Melmoth, England crosses boundaries with the intent of feeding off its victims, in this case Ireland. It is neither noticeable all the time, nor is it the cause of all of Ireland's problems, but it exasperates the national situation, making the forging of national identity an extremely difficult and arduous process.

## References

Bewell, A. 1999. *Romanticism and Colonial Disease*. Baltimore: Johns Hopkins University Press

Briggs, K.M. 1981. "The Legends of Lilith and of the Wandering Jew in Nineteenth-Century Literature". *Folklore* 92.2: 132-140

Canuel, M. 1995. "'Holy Hypocrisy' and the Government of Belief: Religion and Nationalism in the Gothic". *Studies in Romantism* 34.4: 507-30

Fulford, T. 1998. "Romanticism and Colonialism: Races, Places, Peoples, 1800-1830". In *Romanticism and Colonialism* (35-47). Eds.T. Fulford and P.J. Kitson. Cambridge: Cambridge University Press

Garb, T. 1995. "Modernity, Identity, Textuality". In *The Jew in the Text*. Eds. L. Nochlin and T. Garb. London: Thames and Hudson. 20-30

---

[7] Fulford (1998) discusses Southey's views of Ireland and Irish Catholicism, as well as those of several other British Romantic writers, including Coleridge, Shelley, and Byron. See also Southey, 1971.

Hoad, N. 2002. "Maria Edgeworth's *Harrington*: The Price of Sympathetic Representation". In *British Romanticism and the Jews*. Ed. S.A. Spector. New York: Palgrave. 121-137

Kitson, P.J. 2001. "Romantic Displacements: Representing Cannibalism". In *Placing and Displacing Romanticism*. Ed. P.J. Kitson. Aldershot: Ashgate. 204-225

Kramer, D. 1973. *Charles Robert Maturin*. New York: Twayne Publishers

Lew, J.W. 1994. "'Unprepared for Sudden Transformations': Identity and Politics in *Melmoth the Wanderer*". *Studies in the Novel* 26.2: 173-95

Malchow, H.L. 1996. *Gothic Images of Race in Nineteenth-Century Britain*. Stanford: Stanford University Press

Maturin, C.R. 1998. *Melmoth the Wanderer*. Oxford: Oxford University Press. [First published 1820]

Punter, D. 1996. *The Literature of Terror*. Vol. 1. 2nd edn. London: Longman

Sage, V. 1988. *Horror Fiction in the Protestant Tradition*. Basingstoke: Macmillan

Sicher, E. 2002. "Imagining 'the Jew': Dickens' Romantic Heritage". In *British Romanticism and the Jews*. Ed. S.A. Spector. New York: Palgrave. 139-153

Southey, R. 1971. *Essays, Moral and Political*. Shannon: Irish University Press. [First published 1832]

Twitchell, J.B. 1981. *The Living Dead: A Study of the Vampire in Romantic Literature*. Durham: Duke University Press

# Soutar, Scots and Sectarianism[1]

*Niall O'Gallagher*

> Scots steel tempered wi' Irish fire
> Is the weapon that I desire.[2]

1927 was an important year in the history of Scottish writing. In the five years since adopting his *nom de guerre*, Hugh MacDiarmid (C.M. Grieve) had published three of his most celebrated collections of Scots poetry, *Sangschaw* (1925), *Penny Wheep* (1926) and the book-length poem *A Drunk Man Looks at the Thistle* (1926). By 1927 MacDiarmid had already written most of his major Scots-language work. He was followed by a number of younger poets, many of whom would write in Scots throughout their careers. Despite his own move away from Scots-language poetry, MacDiarmid became the catalyst for a literary and linguistic movement that would influence the development of Scottish poetry for large parts of the twentieth century.

In 1923 the General Assembly of the Church of Scotland published a now infamous pamphlet on the subject of Irish immigration into Scotland, which had reached its modern peak in the years since the Famine (General Assembly of the Church of Scotland 1923). Entitled 'The Menace of the Irish Race to our Scottish Nationality', and written more than half a century after modern Irish immigration to Scotland had reached its high water mark, this pamphlet offers us a glimpse of one of the different kinds of nationalism at work in Scotland in the 1920s, the moment of Scotland's modern literary renaissance and the beginning of the modern Scots language movement.[3]

In 1927 George Malcolm Thomson published *Caledonia: or the Future of the Scots*. Thomson's *Caledonia* is a state of the nation address, a prophetic text in which its author attacks, with considerable verve, the complacency of the Scottish nation over such subjects as religion, education and the arts, the relationship of Scotland to its neighbours and its place within the British Empire. Ideologically, in his condemnations of early twentieth-century Scottish cultural complacency, much of Thomson's *Caledonia* would sit quite comfortably alongside the polemics of MacDiarmid or Lewis Grassic Gibbon, often thought of today as the leaders of the Renaissance movement in poetry and prose respectively. Like MacDiarmid, Gibbon and others, Thomson perceived a malaise at the heart of Scottish life. For Thomson, this could be related directly to "the great racial problem" diagnosed by the Kirk's Church and Nation Committee (MacDiarmid 1927: 29).

The relationship of a people to its language was one of the central concerns of writers associated with the Scottish Renaissance of the inter-war years. In 1934 MacDiarmid and Gibbon published *Scottish Scene or the Intelligent Man's Guide to Albyn*. In "Literary Lights", an essay which Gibbon contributed to the volume, the Scots language is described as "the tongue adopted by the basic Pictish strain in Scotland as its chief literary tool" (Gibbon and MacDiarmid 1934: 196). While Gibbon does not seem concerned to link the language with the racial provenance of the Lowland Scots people, the idea of Scots as a Pictish language was nothing new. In John Jamieson's 1808 *Etymological Dictionary of the Scottish Language* he includes a "Dissertation on the Origin of the Scottish Language" in which he attempts to prove that the Picts, from whom he believes the Lowland Scots to be descended, were descended

[1] The author would like to thank the Caledonian Research Foundation, which has funded the research presented in this paper.
[2] Hugh MacDiarmid, "The Weapon" (Riach and Grieve 1994: 134).
[3] The term 'Scottish Renaissance' was first coined by Denis Saurat in 'Le Groupe de "la Renaissance Écossaise"', *Revue Anglo-Americaine*, April 1924: 1-13 (See McCulloch 2004: 53-54).

from the Goths and that the Scots language is a direct descendent of the Gothic speech they brought with them to the island of Britain from the north European mainland.[4] Throughout this lengthy preface Jamieson goes out of his way to de-Celticise the Picts and, in so doing, to distance the Lowland Scots from the Highland Scots and the Irish.

For Thomson, the Scots language was one of the distinctive traditions of the Scottish race that was under threat from what MacDiarmid called the "Irish invasion" (MacDiarmid 1927: 1). His attack on Scottish cultural complacency addresses a national community that he defines racially. In the final section of *Caledonia* Thomson imagines a conversation between a Scotsman and a New Zealander visiting Scotland in the year 2027 in which the Scotsman explains the history of his country during the century since Thomson's book was published. In the final paragraph the Scots language is seen as a defining characteristic of the Scots people who, by 2027, have all but died out. Despite his insistence that the life of the Scottish nation was not dependent "on a sense of racial unity" (Thomson 1927: 93), it seems that for Thomson the Scots language cannot meaningfully exist after the "Scottish race" has lost its distinctive character.

I want to suggest that Thomson's views about the relationship between the Scots people and the Scots language may have been just as typical as Gibbon's and as such offer another way of understanding elements within the Scots language revival movement of the period. "The Makar" (a Scots word for poet) is one of William Soutar's most famous poems. It reads:

Nae man wha loves the lawland tongue
But warsles wi' the thocht –
There are mair sangs that bide unsung
Nor a' that hae been wrocht.

Ablow the wastrey o' the years,
The thorter o' himsel',
Deep buried in his bluid he hears
A music that is leal.

And wi' this lealness gangs his ain;
And there's nae ither gait
Though a' his feres were fremmit men
Wha cry: *Owre late, owre late*.[5]

Soutar's poem establishes a direct link between language and race. It begins with the premise that Scots has underachieved as a literary language, leaving a great lack of poems that any revivalist movement must address. In the second verse the rhetoric changes. It is the poet's self that has declined. The lines "Deep buried in his bluid he hears / A music that is leal" tell us that for Soutar, language is something that runs in the blood. In *Caledonia* Thomson writes, "Half Scotland is slum-poisoned. The taint of the slum is in the nation's blood; its taint in their minds has given birth to a new race of barbarians" (Thomson 1929: 21). Soutar shares Thomson's rhetoric of blood. Like many of the poets associated with the Scottish Renaissance movement, he went to dictionaries to broaden his linguistic resources. "Leal" has a number of different meanings listed in the *Concise Scots Dictionary* (Robinson 1999). It can mean "loyal, faithful to one's allegiance or duties", "faithful in religion; Christian", "genuine" or "sound" of doctrine and, in the ballad tradition with which Soutar was familiar, "chaste" or "pure".

---

[4] I am grateful to Professor Richard Finlay of the University of Strathclyde for alerting me to this.
[5] William Soutar, "The Makar" (MacDougall and Gifford 2000: 39).

Perhaps the most intriguing meaning of "leal" is the first given in the *Concise Scots Dictionary*, "legally valid" or "just". The legal connotations of this word suggest that blood and language are linked to legal notions of inheritance in Soutar's poem. The inheritance of future generations of Scots is in doubt unless the blood is kept pure and allowed to speak through a new body of poems in Scots. In the last two lines it is "fremmit" or "foreign" friends who cry *"Owre late, owre late"*. Owre late for what? Perhaps the anxiety expressed by Soutar's speaker is not over the dilution of the Scots language but the dilution of Scottish blood upon which that language depends.

In Soutar's poetry, as in Thomson's *Caledonia*, Irish immigration is partly responsible for the cultural atrophy perceived by both writers in early twentieth-century Scotland. Anti-Irish sentiment informs Soutar's poetry and indeed his use of Scots as the language of that poetry. In "The Auld Tree", a longer poem dedicated to Hugh MacDiarmid but which the older poet left out of his edition of Soutar's *Collected Poems* (MacDiarmid 1948), the speaker has a vision of a tree being suffocated by a two-headed snake. William Wallace is on hand and after some encouragement from the speaker dispatches the snake with a large axe. The two resulting snakes, which have been suffocating the Scottish nation, then go home, one to England, the other to Ireland:

> The ane haud'n southard to his hame,
> The ither wast owre Irish faem.[6]

Perhaps the reason that MacDiarmid left "The Auld Tree" out when he edited Soutar's *Collected Poems* was not that he felt threatened by the younger poet, as MacDougall and Gifford suggest in their recent edition of Soutar's poems (MacDougall and Gifford 2000), but because he did not want to be associated with Soutar's racial politics.

This kind of ethnic nationalism can be linked to tendencies within Scots-language writing of the period, which sought to define the Scots language as that which is not English, to emphasise the distinctiveness of Scots by avoiding any vocabulary shared with English. This approach is illustrated by the poet and translator Douglas Young:

> If Lallans fails, coin something from Latin or Greek if you like, as King's English does; if all else fails admit a Hottentotism rather than another Anglicism. This should be our intransigent policy for the next five hundred years or so.[7]

The problem with this kind of "radical nationalism", as diagnosed in an Irish context by Gerry Smyth (1998), is that it means that the Scots language becomes a kind of photonegative of English, dependent for its definition on the very language whose influence it seeks to avoid. Against this tendency, which insists on strict border controls between languages, there is another tendency visible in Scots language writing of the period, which uses the position of Scots as an unstandardised language to break down the barriers between languages, bringing together elements from different registers, historical periods, and geographical areas. This second tendency can be associated with MacDiarmid's poetic project, from the early Scots lyrics to his later experiments with the languages of science and philosophy.

The context which informed the excluding tendency within early twentieth century Scots language writing is alluded to by Tom Leonard in 'Ghostie Men':

---

[6] William Soutar. "The Auld Tree" (MacDougall and Gifford 2000: 89).
[7] Douglas Young: 1946: 23

right inuff
ma language is disgraceful
ma maw tellt mi
ma teacher tellt mi
thi doacter tellt mi
thi priest tellt mi

ma boss tellt mi
ma landlady in carrington street tellt mi
thi lassie ah tried tay get aff wi in 1969 tellt mi
sum wee smout thit thoat ah hudny read chomsky tellt mi
a calvinistic communist thit thoat ah wuz revisionist tellt mi

po-faced literati grimly kerryin the burden a thi past tellt mi
po-faced literati grimly kerryin the burden a thi future tellt mi
ma wainz came hame fray school an tellt mi
jist aboot ivry book ah oapnd tellt mi
even thi introduction tay thi Scottish National Dictionary tellt mi

ach well
all livin language is sacred
fuck thi lohta thim[8]

Leonard refers here to the *Scottish National Dictionary*, a major academic project cataloguing those element of Scots vocabulary not shared with English from 1700 onwards. As Leonard points out in his introduction to *Radical Renfrew* (1990), the introduction to the *Scottish National Dictionary* states that "Owing to the influx of Irish and foreign immigrants in the industrial area near Glasgow the dialect has become hopelessly corrupt" (Grant 1931: xxvii).

So, Glasgow's language is not Scots because its people are no longer sufficiently Scottish. Leonard's essay points towards an element in the history of twentieth-century Scottish writing which is often ignored. For many, fears about the future of the Scots language were part of a wider fear for the future of the Scots race. Irish immigration was seen as a threat to both and as such lent momentum to the Scots-language revival and influenced the future directions that movement would later assume.

## References

Corbett, J. 1997. *Language and Scottish Literature*. Edinburgh: Edinburgh University Press
The General Assembly of the Church of Scotland. 1923. "The Menace of the Irish Race to our Scottish Nationality". Edinburgh: The Church of Scotland
Gibbon, L. G. and MacDiarmid, H. 1934. *Scottish Scene or the Intelligent Man's Guide to Albyn*. London: Hutchison & Co.
Grant, W. 1931. ed. *The Scottish National Dictionary*. Vol 1. Edinburgh: The Scottish National Dictionary Association
Jamieson, J. 1808. *An Etymological Dictionary of the Scottish Language*. Edinburgh: University Press
Leonard, T. 1984. *Intimate Voices*. Newcastle: Galloping Dog Press

---

[8] Tom Leonard. 'Ghostie Men' (1984: 120).

Leonard, T. 1990. "Literature, Dialogue, Democracy". In 1995. *Reports from the Present: Selected Work 1982-94*. London: Jonathan Cape, 45-62

MacDiarmid, H. 1927. *Albyn: or Scotland and the Future*. In ed. Alan Riach. 1996. *Hugh MacDiarmid: Albyn: Shorter Books and Monographs*. Manchester: Carcanet

MacDiarmid, H. 1948. ed. *William Soutar: Collected Poems*. London: Andrew Dakers Limited

MacDougall, C. and Gifford, D. eds. 2000. *Into a Room: Selected Poems of William Soutar*. Glendaruel: Argyll

McCulloch, M. P. 2004. *Modernism and Nationalism: Literature and Society in Scotland 1918-1939*. Glasgow: Association for Scottish Literary Studies

Riach, A and Grieve, M. eds. 1994. *Hugh MacDiarmid: Selected Poems*. London: Penguin

Robinson, M et al. eds. 1999. *The Concise Scots Dictionary*. Edinburgh: Polygon

Thomson, G. M. 1927. *Caledonia: or The Future of the Scots*. London: Kegan Paul, Trench, Trubner & Co

Young, D. 1946. *'Plastic Scots' and the Scottish Literary Tradition*. Glasgow: William MacLellan

# Incarnation and Impotence: Joyce and a Rhetoric of Genesis

*Michael O'Sullivan*

The recent "turn to theology"[1] in literary criticism, and specifically in that variety of literary criticism having its roots in French phenomenology, has called for a rigorous investigation of the religious figure so as to rejuvenate literary analysis and interpretation in general. Aldo Gargani (Derrida & Vattimo 1998: 114) calls for a "recovery of the signs and of the annunciations immanent within the history of a religious tradition" so that they become "figures for an interpretative perspective on life". James Joyce's work parodies both the themes and linguistic styles and practises of the training he received in theology and exegesis as a student in Dublin; he incorporates rhetorical styles of scripture and theological training into his own devotional work on the aesthetics of narrative fiction. In 'Oxen of the Sun' there are many examples of this interdisciplinary transmission between the linguistic styles of religious language and Joyce's narrative. On one occasion Joyce employs the question and answer style of primary school catechism to reveal the reasons behind Stephen Daedalus's (and we might also read Joyce's autobiographical response in these words) reluctance to join the priesthood:

> To be short this passage was scarce by when Master Dixon of Mary in Eccles, goodly grinning, asked young Stephen what was the reason why he had not cided to take friar's vows and he answered him obedience in the womb, chastity in the tomb but involuntary poverty all his days. (512)

Later in the same episode we have a more direct parody of a well-known religious maxim: "Greater love than this, he said, no man hath that a man lay down his wife for his friend. Go thou and do likewise" (513). Joyce turns *from* the theological in parodying and interrogating its linguistic structures, playfully pre-figuring recent tendencies in French phenomenology and literary criticism. I wish to suggest here that Joyce interrogates any perceived potential liturgical language may possess for fashioning *"figures for an interpretative perspective on life"*. Joyce's parody of religious conceptions of transformation and transubstantiation, through his employment of the aesthetic motifs of epiphany and *epiclesis*,[2] recovers for literature a sense of the sacred that was reserved for the religious discourses of his day, a sense that is now regarded as beneficial for theory and criticism.

Joyce may be read as pre-figuring the work of an important strand of French phenomenology, one that offers an empowering alternative to deconstruction's predominance as a theory of signification. The work of Michel Henry, and specifically his final work *Incarnation* (2000), calls for the *"le renversement de la phénomenologie"* or the reversal of phenomenology. Michel Henry initiates a thinking of the body as *la chair*, or the flesh. The

---

[1] I refer here to what has been termed a "theological turn" in French theory, literary theory, and phenomenologically motivated cultural theory. In Phenomenology and the "Theological Turn" (2000), I am also referring here to the large body of work, which has emerged in recent years, and which investigates the potential within religious interpretive styles and tropes for philosophical and critical discourses. A selection of such works includes: Hent de Vries, *Religion and Violence: Philosophical Perspectives from Kant to Derrida* (2002), Jacques Derrida *Acts of Religion* (2002); Jacques Derrida and Gianni Vattimo, *Religion* (1998); Gianni Vattimo, *After Christianity* (2002).

[2] In a letter dated from July 1904, which Joyce wrote to Constantine Curran from Paris, he refers to his motivations for *Dubliners* in relation to the notion of epiclesis: "I am writing a series of epicleti —10 – for a paper. I have written one. I call the series *Dubliners*, to betray the soul of that hemiplegia or paralysis which many consider a city" (Ellman 1982: 169).

death of Michel Henry in 2002 marks the passing of a distinct style of phenomenological thought, one that has enriched debates in the phenomenology of religion, theology, and philosophy. Henry's seminal work *The Essence of Manifestation* (1963) revitalised phenomenology's interrogation of immanence. Even though Henry's work employs an elaborate Christological and onto-theological rhetoric, it can, nevertheless, be employed to temper the prevailing deconstructive strain within phenomenology and cultural theory, one that delimits phenomenology's potential. Dominique Janicaud's *Phenomenology and the "Theological Turn"* is a work that offers a last glimpse of Henry in conversation with the other 'masters' of a phenomenology of religion: Jean-Luc Marion, Jean-Louis Chrétien, Dominique Janicaud, and Paul Ricoeur. The collection brings together, in translation, the proceedings of the seminar conducted at the 'Centre de recherches phénoménologiques et herméneutiques-Archives Husserl de Paris' during the two academic years 1990-1991 and 1991-1992. Henry's essay in this collection, "Speech and Religion: The Word of God", prefigures his final complete work *Incarnation* for which we still await an English translation. *Incarnation* offers readers a source of inspiration for moving beyond the academy's delimiting of phenomenological investigation by apodictically designating its transcendental (Husserl), existential (Heidegger), and textual messianic (Derrida) varieties. Henry intimates here, and it is something that he returns to in *Incarnation*, that any positing of primordial difference denies life the opportunity of experiencing the auto-revelation of its flesh within itself, it denies the experience of *"le sens ek-statique"*, of the body, now conceived as flesh, experiencing auto-revelation through its *"passivité radicale"* (242). Henry has spoken of the necessity to "return to life" through the "denunciation of phenomenology", *"le retour à la vie impose la dénonciation de la phenomenology"*. He states that "it is not enough to recall the duality of the modes of givenness of the real, it is necessary, once again, to understand the possibilities and the modalities of the passage from one to the other" (Le Lannou 2003: 984). Henry's work urges an inspection of any separation or *déliaison* that deconstruction might advocate between thought and an "inner voice". Henry urges us to move beyond the "vacuity of finitude" phenomenology has brought us to. His project of *dé-finitisation* speaking of the means of moving beyond phenomenology does not have an English equivalent. It speaks for both our abstraction from a phenomenology of finitude, and a rigorous defining of our terms, processes that must occur simultaneously. The project of *dé-finitisation* rather seeks to conjoin the separation involved in phenomenology's ontological duality with what such a separation must consistently remove itself from, what Henry terms *l'ekstatique* (ibid.: 984).

Joyce may also be regarded as extracting some aesthetic potential from liturgical "mystery", and from the ambitious interpretive designs of religious discourses that seek to represent and enact such conceptual difficulties as incarnation. Joyce seeks to incorporate such discourses' metaphysical potential into the art of fiction. The Irish fiction "industry" would not have been allowed to make such blasphemous claims at the time Joyce was writing; it could not have been seen to be representing anything as sacred as the mystery of incarnation. Mary Kenny informs us in *Goodbye to Catholic Ireland* that 1916, the year Joyce had *A Portrait* published and a year during which *Ulysses* was well under way, marked the "beginning of the most energetic period of Ireland's modern phase of evangelization" (124). Joyce, however, is not unwilling to inspect the nature of the transfer of meaning such an ambitious interpretive schema entails. His writings can be regarded as referencing a phenomenology of religion that necessitates a conception of the body tied to notions of incarnation. His writing works against the grain of Jacques Derrida's "messianic eschatology," a phenomenology of religion that does not accept Husserl's an account of "presence", identity, or objectivity. This reading is solely based on what Derrida (1973: 16) refers to as "the intentional animation that transforms the body of the word into flesh" in his seminal work *Speech and Phenomena*. My discussion here inspects two tropes within Joyce's work that can be regarded as explicitly referencing both the language of religious discourses and the philosophy of the body rejuvenated by Michel Henry. The tropes of incarnation and impotence, each receiving extensive critical commentary in recent works by writers such as Giorgio Agamben, Luce Irigaray, and Michel Henry, explicitly relate language to the body and corporeity in a manner that Joyce prefigures in his writing. He does not only thematically reference these tropes as themes in his work but also employs them as motivations for his understanding of the aesthetic and signification.

Joyce consistently draws our attention to the transformative, material, and theological aspects of language. In a letter to Frank Budgen in 1918 he writes of *Ulysses* as "Among other things [...] the epic of the human body [...] In my book the body lives in and moves through space and is the home of a full human personality" (Budgen 1960: 21). Colin MacCabe is also aware of this material quality in Ulysses: he writes (1979: 2) that Joyce emphasises the "possibilities of transformation" inherent in language. The consistency with which such aspects of language are presented in Joyce, works to emphasise notions of unity and auto-affection, concepts that, once again, challenge deconstruction's embrace of "radical alterity" and difference. Jean-Michel Rabaté finds in Joyce's fondness for elaborating the materiality and corporeity of human existence a respect for the exegetical roots of linguistic investigation; he writes that "[p]erhaps more than any writer of this century, Joyce has forced criticism to acknowledge its theological nature" (1). One might therefore suggest that, rather like Henry, Joyce employs a rhetoric of the sacred that has discarded any residual dogmatism. Joyce displays a particular fondness for the mutability of language, a fondness that his characters' monologues, in turn, assign to their own bodies. Genetic and archival criticism of Joyce, perhaps the most vibrant strand of Joycean criticism (indeed it must be asked whether Joyce's preserved manuscripts may have influenced the methodologies of genetic criticism), stresses that the "processes by which he wrote the book cannot be separated from other aspects of its meaning" (Groden 1977: 203). Since genetic criticism is chiefly concerned with the processes of artistic endeavour, with the methods of annotation and redrafting that contribute to the artwork, it is perhaps somewhat ironic that the moments of pain and strife Joyce suffered in order to complete *Ulysses* and *Finnegans Wake* are now treated as a kind work in progress themselves. The collation, preservation, and arrangement of the Joycean archive has not only served to extend the metaphor of Joyce's work as a body which evolves, but has also begun to reincarnate or enact a kind of textual metempsychosis of Joyce's unprecedented methods of writing which brought *Ulysses* to us in the first place.

Joyce's characters and language are works in progress, characters over-burdened by the nature of meaning and by endless semantic mind games, yet "subsisting peasemeal upon variables" through "life's high carnage of semperidentity", as Joyce suggests in *Finnegans Wake* (582). They subsist in unfriendly social environments only through their persistent and sensitive deliberations on language and its capability to embody sensual and material experiences life has denied them. They are driven by the belief that their individual struggle to discover some personal meaning in language will present them with the possibility for further self-discovery. Their individuality is consistently haunted by images of that to which they are united through some process of creation, be it dead fathers, mothers or children. Their selfhood is unravelled through a rigorous evaluation of the further possibilities that "life's high carnage" can throw at them. Bloom return at the end of *Ulysses* to lie beside Molly, their only conversation or "intercourse" of the day being on re-incarnation, or metempsychosis. Molly's interior monologue reiterates the reason for their union through the epiphanic harkening, or "harking" back to that moment on the hills around Dublin when she "gave him [Bloom] all the pleasure I could leading him on till he asked me to say yes" (932). Hélène Cixous's *The Exile of James Joyce* (1976) reads Joyce's employment of the symbols of communion, reconciliation, and incarnation as seeking to "invert the relationship between interior and surface, and to recover from holy objects their privileged profundity" (608). Cixous regards the epiphany as a "revitalising devotion to the ordinary real. Joyce designed the plan of his works as a challenge to the enemy, reproducing in a structure composed of one single metaphor the unbearable situation which his writing was intended to destroy: the separation of soul and body caused by the national guilt-complex of Catholic Ireland" (635).

In *Ulysses*, Joyce's "epic of the body", the "body lives in and moves through space and is the home of a full human personality" (Budgen 1960: 21) as he wrote of it to Frank Budgen. Many deconstructive readings of Joyce, including Derrida's own reading of the 'Penelope' chapter, employ a rhetoric of difference and *déliaison*, or seek to read into Joyce what Derrida (2002: 60) refers to as "the always-safe, always-to-be-saved possibility of this *secret of disassociation*" (my italics). Such discourses are, therefore, often incapable of disentangling the corporeal message of the Joycean text where "[t]he untireties of livesliving being the one substance of a streamsbecoming" (Joyce 1999: 597) connote a phenomenological sense of language and signification closer to Henry's "radical passivity" and ecstatic auto-affection; they limit the workings of the Joycean text which instead enacts the "incarnate significance", transubstantiation, or process of metempsychosis operative between language and consciousness. And perhaps we should leave the last word on Derrida's commentary with Molly herself:

> I tried to draw a picture of it before I tore it up like a sausage or something I wonder theyre not afraid going about of getting a kick or a bang or something there and that word met something with hoses in it and he came out with some jawbreakers about the incarnation he never can explain a thing simply the way a body can understand. (893)

Molly's words are removed of the corset-like constraints of the rules of punctuation; each reading can place its own stresses and allocate emphases according to the natural rhythms of each. Molly informs us here in her "monologue" that the "body can understand", and that it understands "simply". Molly intimates that she is aware of how the body understands in a manner very different to the manner in which Bloom employed to explain to her the meaning of the word metempsychosis in the 'Calypso' chapter. Many deconstructive theories do not inspect the specific nature of the "understanding" Molly references here. The above lines from Molly can also be regarded as humorously phrasing the incarnation as "and that word met something with hoses in it and he came out". It might be read as a parody of "and the Word was made flesh" from John the Evangelist. In reading Molly's words as monologue we are not in any way constricting the performativity or dialogic nature of the writing, but are rather allowing Joyce to burrow deep with fiction's formal experimentation, allowing him to express as never before the individual body as flesh in writing. The reader takes up the role of communicant in this text, only discovering and enacting a readerly "auto-revelation" through what she realises is the verbal expression of a singular voice speaking to itself. The attentive, affective presentation of monologue only enables the reader to vicariously experience "auto-revelation" through the intensity of the self-revelation he feels he is reading in Molly's words.

It is interesting to investigate another term, namely impotence, that voices the writing/genesis parallel important to recent critical theory. The leading men of *Ulysses* do not deal in intercourse. These characters voice residually the Joycean paralysis the reader might have considered left behind with Gabriel Conroy in the bedroom scene ending "The Dead". Julia Kristeva has suggested that Joyce's *Finnegans Wake* challenges paternal authority "not only ideologically, but in the workings of language itself, by a return to [pre Oedipal] semiotic rhythms connotatively maternal" (Henke 1990: 7). Motivated by such language, I would like to consider how Joyce challenges, figuratively counters, and offers readings for, an alternative representation of "paternal authority". In a sense it is a sublimated "paternal *authority*" (my italics), delayed in its encounter, and frustrated in its realisation, through the representation of a physical impotence Joyce's aesthetic theories can be regarded as bringing to fruition. There is a complex linguistic architectonics at work here, one which seeks to reinsert Joyce's unrelenting paternity, into the evaluation of his sexual politic of care, a sexual politic heretofore only achieving the rubber-stamp, either due to its capabilities for an anti-logocentric discourse, or due to its careful phrasing of a disrupted paternalistic discourse. His analysis of figures, his epiphanic detailing of moments of perception leading to artistic inspiration, and his attention to the word, both colour Joyce's own early critical works, and the aesthetic theories fostering his artworks, and in doing so, suggest a particular handling of desire. A theme of physical and paternal impotency haunts Joyce's characters' meticulously described conscious forethoughts, suggesting to the reader how a writer's devotion to the word might serve as a sublimation for physical inadequacy.

The construction of the Joycean artwork was to consume the life of its progenitor. Joyce may in fact have been guilty of what David Ellison, alluding to Kant, has suggested was a "mode of acting deviously". Kant speaks on the role of conscience in moral behaviour, and for Ellison, believes that "[t]o act according to one's advantage is, finally, to *aestheticize life*, to live it as if it were a work of art, which is to say, a fictional universe of symbols in which meaning itself is veiled in impenetrable obscurity" (2001: 18). The flesh is indeed made word for Joyce, and yet it is a slow and carefully detailed eroticisation of the word and its textual promiscuity. It is possible to give a reading of Joyce's use of the figure which might be suggestive, not solely of what David Tracy (1991: 408) describes as "a language of ordered relationships articulating similarity in difference", of a forgetting of the dialectical sense within the analogy producing "deadening univocity" (413), but of a truncated move towards encounter that ends only in the *representation* of inspiration and epiphany. Joyce thus invests in a distinct sense of symbolism, a sense evolving throughout his work to elaborate the vast potential placed within the flesh made word, the embodied text, for self-reflexivity, or resigned representative onanism. Just as Luce Irigaray (1985: 186) suggests that classical metaphysics is "captive to the lure of a (male) Same", so does Joyce frequently negate such pre-emptive sameness, not solely through a careful allowance for the female *double syntax*, but by way of a careful recounting of a truncated rumination on what an encounter with the other should reveal. The careful evisceration of a sameness that Irigaray rightly instigates so as to speak for a *double syntax*, presupposes an acute understanding of the two entities initially formative of the couple, or syntactic *differance*, we are to invest with liberatory potential. Joyce's artwork grounded on a scrupulous regard for the moment of apprehension, for that moment of recollection towards one's own perception of phenomena, should have awakened the reader to the future progress of the Joycean artwork. If Joyce is to provide us with a sexual politic of care it is one more caught in a repetitive preparation of the move towards an encounter allowing for a qualified sameness, than in an assured displacing of a problematised metaphysical yearning for equipollence. Even though Irigaray (1999) might argue that the "received symbolic order has been based upon the male *imaginary* within which the feminine is but a foil for the development of masculine subjectivity", Joyce is never so assured of the nature of this foil, and of the characteristics that instil change in the perceiver. Irigaray claims that such an *imaginary* remains caught within the lure of imaginary identifications, because the parties are directed towards a consumption of one another, thereby co-opting the symbolic. The symbolic is, therefore, not working in tandem with these "imaginary identifications" but rather already set up against them as despoiler to their imaginative profligacy. One must therefore read the Joycean elaboration of symbol, not solely as a recapitulation of equanimity for a double sexual voice, but rather as an elaboration of repetitive straining and tentative regret for an encounter growing ever more elusive. And ironically the encounter only appears elusive through an apprehensive faculty transferring the impotency back onto its own powers of perception, ultimately stymieing the understanding of other.

In the 'Potentiality and Law' chapter of *Homo Sacer: Sovereign Power and Bare Life* (1998) Giorgio Agamben gives new readings of potentiality and im-potentiality. Agamben writes: "Potentiality (in its double appearance as potentiality to and as potentiality not to) is that through which Being founds itself *sovereignly*, which is to say, without anything preceding or determining it (*superiorem non recognoscens*) other than its own ability not to be" (46). Agamben reads potentiality as that which only founds itself *sovereignly* through its "ability not to be" or through its "im-potentiality, so as to return to man the ability to claim his own life". He informs us that an act is sovereign "when it realizes itself by simply taking away its own potentiality not to be, letting itself be, *giving itself to itself* " (46, my italics). This is reminiscent of Henry's understanding of incarnation. It is suggestive of a move to regain for man an ability to admit to the loss of all presupposed relations to Being conceived as realised potential. From this realisation man is allowed to experience his untainted origins and to regain potential for himself by *giving itself to itself*. Joyce also inspects the full ramifications of this other aspect of the body, namely, its impotence. Leopold Bloom may be regarded as an introvert, prone to sublimation, impelled in impotency to direct his sexual instinctual forces onto a plethora of new objects and aims. Freud's notes on impotence inform us that an instinct is "the physical representation of an endosomatic, continuously flowing source of stimulation" (1991: 310). When the course of action presumed necessary by the subject possessive of such a physical representation is frustrated due to impotence, there is a tendency "to linger over the preparatory activities" (299) for the sexual aims. One might regard the stream of consciousness narration, its interior monologue, as representative of a "preparatory activity" in the character towards engaged living or communicative action. Bloom appears most content in the 'Calypso' chapter of *Ulysses*, in preparation for the day to come, administering to Molly and the cat, preparing their breakfast. The word that guides the chapter is the polyvalent *metempsychosis*, inculcating a semantic flow in the chapter whereby objects, concepts, and characters' words segue into one another. Molly's "sleepy soft grunt", her "Mn" (67) merges with the cat's "Mrkrgnao!" (66), and Milly, the daughter, merges with Molly; "Milly too. Young Kisses: the first, Far away now past. Mrs Marion" (81). The device enables the reader to invest the words of Bloom's interior monologue with a protean and restless semantic agency. Bloom, the father of a daughter and a deceased son, does indeed linger over the "preparatory activities" which will ultimately lead to his wife's sexual fulfilment, yet Bloom merely administers the "fore-pleasure" while the sexual fulfilment or "end-pleasure" will come with Blazes Boylan. Bloom's latent feelings of inadequacy due to an implied lack of sexual prowess, surface spasmodically in the aporias of his monologue; a woman he follows from Dlugacz's sausage shop turns off to the right, slipping from view as we are informed, "The sting of disregard glowed to weak pleasure within his breast. For another: a constable off duty cuddled her in Eccles Lane. They like them sizeable. Prime sausage. O please, Mr. Policeman, I'm lost in the wood" (71). Bloom is informing us that he is not large, not of prime sausage, lost in a policed and regulated sexual space of imagined representations of virility.

A few moments later Bloom reads of a planter's company seeking to buy vast tracts of land from the Turkish government for cultivation. He falls into a reverie on his ancestor's homeland bordering the Dead Sea, a thought-association leaving a sensation of "[g]rey horror sear[ing] his flesh" (73). Why does he have such an adverse reaction to the depiction of his people's fatherland? A close reading offers some clues. Bloom muses: "The oldest people. Wandered far away over all the earth, captivity to captivity, multiplying, dying, being born everywhere. It lay there now. Now it could bear no more. Dead: an old woman's: the grey sunken cunt of the world" (73). Bloom gives an almost biblical narrative of genesis, describing the generative work of his ancestors. The juxtaposition of this trail of fertility is spawned from the interiorisation of the image and resonance of the 'Dead Sea', a lifeless, motionless sea of salt that "lay there now". However, if a reading of this section is mindful of the protean tendency of the chapter's guiding noun, its 'metempsychosis', and is also mindful of the semantic multi-layering of the Joycean sentence, then the passage also works on another level. "It lay there now" comes to speak of Bloom's resigned manhood, of the latent tenor of inadequacy driving his word association, of the motif of "dead meat" running through the chapter. Bloom can "bear no more", he is a metaphor for the barren land of a nomadic people. His member is "[d]ead: an old woman's". Not only is he de-sexed but he is one with the guiding theme of the chapter, its metempsychosis, his dormant sexuality assigned to the personification of his fatherland as a "grey sunken cunt of the world". Joyce's dexterous formal play comes to reference for the reader the life of the artist. The metempsychosis unravels its workings in a momentary ensnaring of meanings and disciplines, enabling the reader to invoke all kinds of parallels at this narrative juncture. The barren motif works here to reference the author himself who we have read had stopped reading literature at this time, suffering from chronic eye problems and an implied impotency of his own. This barren motif will re-surface at the end of the next chapter where Bloom in his bath will refer to his penis as a "limp father of thousands, a languid floating flower" (107). These passages work to evoke a central current of anxiety and sexual inadequacy. The formal arrangement of the narrative, the aesthetic belief and model it works through and from, can also be taken to map the figurative representation of im-potentiality described by Agamben; a subject must return to an admission of their unconnectedness and remoteness so as to discover an empowering means for self-discovery. Joyce's language of the body prefigures many of the concerns and tropes of recent critical theory, enabling the reader to think language in relation to a body that exists as a "unity in diversity".

## References

Agamben, Giorgio. 1998. *Homo Sacer: Sovereign Power and Bare Life*. Stanford: Stanford University Press

Budgen, Frank. 1960. *James Joyce and the Making of Ulysses*. Bloomington: Indiana University Press

Cixous, Hélène. 1976. *The Exile of James Joyce*. Trans. Sally Purcell. London: John Calder

Derrida, Jacques. 2002. *Acts of Religion*. Ed. Gil Anidjar. London: Routledge

Derrida, Jacques. 1973. *Speech and Phenomena: And Other Essays on Husserl's Theory of Signs*. Trans. David B. Allison. Evanston: Northwestern University Press

Ellison, David. 2001. *Ethics and Aesthetics in European Modernist Literature: From the Sublime to the Uncanny*. London: Cambridge University Press

Ellmann, Richard. 1982. *James Joyce*. New York: Oxford University Press

Ellmann, Richard ed. 1975. *The Selected Letters of James Joyce*. New York: Viking Press

Freud, Sigmund. 1991. *The Essentials of Psycho-Analysis: The Definitive Collection of Sigmund's Freud's Essays*. Ed. and Intro. Anna Freud. Trans. James Strachey. London: Penguin

Groden, Michael. 1977. *Ulysses in Progress*. Princeton: Princeton University Press

Henke, Suzette A. 1990. *James Joyce and the Politics of Desire*. Routledge, London

Henry, Michel. 2000. *Incarnation: Une philosophie de la chair*. Paris: Seuil

Irigaray, Luce. 1991. *Marine Lover of Friedrich Nietzsche*. New York: Columbia

Irigaray, Luce. 1985. "Cosi Fan Tutti". In *This Sex Which Is Not One*. Trans. Catherine Porte and Carolyn Bourke. Ithaca, N.Y.: Cornell University Press

Irigaray, Luce. 1999. "Luce Irigaray and the Advent of the Divine: from the metaphysical to the symbolic to the eschatological". *Pacifica* 12.1: 27–54. Accessed <http://dlibrary.acu.edu.au/staffhome/dacasey/Luce%20Irigaray>

Joyce, James. 1986. *Ulysses. The Corrected Text*. Eds. Hans Walter Gabler with Wolfhand Steppe and Claus Melchior. New York: Random House

Joyce, James. 1999. *Finnegans Wake*. New York: Penguin

Kenny, Mary. 1997. *Goodbye to Catholic Ireland*. London: Sinclair-Stevenson, Random House

Kristeva. Julia. 1980. *Desire in Language: A Semiotic Approach to Language and Art*. London: Basil Blackwell

Le Lannou, Jean-Michel. 2003. "Le 'renversement de la phénoménologie' selon Michel Henry". *Critique* 58.667: 968-985

Tracy, David. 1991. *The Analogical Imagination: Christian Theology and the Culture of Pluralism*. New York: Crossroad

# "Benevolent or Malign?": Performing Mythology in Representations of St Kilda's Lost Community

*Margitta Rouse*

## Introduction

St Kilda, the remote and now depopulated Scottish archipelago west of the Outer Hebrides, has achieved substantial cultural, even symbolic significance for contemporary Scotland. The Scottish Parliament has drawn inspiration from it, as have environmental campaigners and a number of artists. "The island", writes Fraser MacDonald (2000: 17) in an article commemorating the 70th anniversary of the evacuation, has become "a prized metaphor for the hoary old battle between tradition and modernity, with a dash of heroic defeat thrown in for good measure." The popular narrative attributed to the island allowing it to achieve such importance is quickly told; the cover of a popular history of St Kilda by Charles Maclean (1996) has it thus:

> For more than 2,000 years the people of St Kilda remained remote from the world. Its society was viable, even Utopian; but in the nineteenth century the island was discovered by missionaries, do-gooders and tourists, who brought money, disease and despotism. St Kildan culture gradually disintegrated and in 1930 the few remaining islanders asked to be evacuated.

"The story badly needs retelling" asserts MacDonald (2000: 17), for obvious reasons: it is now commonly argued that such a romanticist view of Scottish history is simplistic and regressive as it depicts the islanders as passive victims of modernity rather than wilful agents of their own lives. Numerous versions of the St Kildan story could serve to illustrate the apparent dichotomy between people of the economically dominant core culture and those of the Celtic periphery, and they belong – in a wider context – to the post-colonial debate initiated by Edward Said's *Orientalism* (1978).

Rather than retelling the St Kildan story, I would like to examine a completely different outlook on the island's legacy, one that is neither constraining, nor debilitating, but has just as much symbolic potential: Douglas Dunn's well-known poem 'St Kilda's Parliament' of 1981 (Dunn 1981: 13–15). Dunn uses the popular history and mythology of the island to comment on the representational process as such, and therefore does not only add to the cultural significance of the island, but also comments critically on the representational strategies in operation where rural Scotland is concerned.

In my reading of the poem, I will concentrate on two central aspects which have not been investigated so far, either in the scholarship concerned with Dunn's poetry, or in investigations of representations of St Kildan society. I shall examine Dunn's treatment of St Kildan mythologised history, and subsequently I shall discuss the functions of the representational strategies employed in the poem. The sophistication of Dunn's 'St Kilda's Parliament' calls for a wider range of responses than a single theoretical or thematic approach can cover and, because of this, I shall follow a number of different paths. I will highlight representational strategies surrounding the island against the background of Dunn's poem, and will take a closer look at the functions of spatial representation with regard to mythology.

## Spatial Representation

First of all, it is crucial to notice that the 300-year-old fascination with St Kilda, since it was first portrayed in detail by Martin Martin's *A Late Voyage to St Kilda* in the late seventeenth century, is rooted in its liminality. As a liminal space, St Kilda only exists in relation to the 'cultural centre': we mostly have external representations of St Kildan life, as the St Kildans themselves were illiterate for the largest part of their history. It is clear, then, that portrayals of St Kilda have to be interpreted in relation to other sites, to sites that are contrasted, mirrored, questioned or contradicted by St Kildan culture. Not in-between. External representations of the island, therefore, simultaneously represent the cultural frame in which they exist.

Foucault's concept of 'Heterotopia' (cf. Foucault 1984), 'the other space', is ideally suited to describe St Kilda, especially with regard to Dunn's poem. Heterotopias, in Foucault's sense, are fundamentally real places, places like gardens, theatres or cemeteries. As opposed to Utopias these places exist in reality, but like Utopias they are counter-sites reflecting on the society in which they occur. Even though they are real places, their existence depends on the society that surrounds them. Reflection, then, is the key function of a Heterotopia.

Foucault uses the metaphor of looking into a mirror to illustrate his concept: looking into a mirror, we see ourselves in a virtual space that does not exist. Our reflections are real and unreal at the same time, because for a reflection to be perceived by a real self in a real place it has to pass through a virtual place that does not exist – but it is made possible by the mirror that *does* exist. The reflection, distortion of reality, is not real, but is not necessarily interpreted as a representation, as it takes place in a real place. I suggest that Heterotopias are, therefore, ideal spaces for myth-making in the Barthesian sense (cf. Barthes 1973). Barthes' concept of myth is concerned with the perpetuation of the ideologies of the 'ruling class'; their myths are integrated into the social structure to make them appear 'natural'. Let me develop this argument further by considering briefly the way representations of the island and its mythology have changed.

## Myth-Making

Research carried out independently by Fraser MacDonald (2001) and Ian Spring (2000) suggests that two major strands of representations of St Kildan life existed alongside each other before the evacuation in 1930 and later blended into one. There was, to begin with, the notion of St Kilda as an isolated Garden of Eden, inspired largely by Martin Martin, and of the St Kildans as benevolent primitives. In the nineteenth century, travellers in search of the Ossianic sublime portrayed the islanders as primitive and kindly on the one hand, but also as lazy, dirty and malevolent on the other. Many of the nineteenth-century visitors objected to the islanders' Calvinism, as it clashed horribly with a more romantic image of the Celtic periphery. By the end of the nineteenth century it was a common view that the island had been spoilt by missionaries, even though the islanders' faith hardly differed from that in the west of Scotland.

Both strands together – utopian St Kilda and corrupted St Kilda – informed today's popular perception that evolved after the evacuation: St Kilda as the island utopia brought down chiefly by education, religion and tourism. This narrative, argues Macdonald (2001: 152), "ascribes an Edenic character to the St Kildans but implicitly blames them for having material aspirations". This view is inspired largely by the best-selling histories of the island, Tom Steel's *The Life and Death of St Kilda* (1975) and Charles MacLean's *St Kilda. Island on the Edge of the World* (1996). Both relate various anecdotes blending mythology into reality to portray the island's society as endearingly primitive and genuinely utopian, a society "amazed by such things as windows, looking-glasses and tapestries (which they considered vain and unnecessary)" (MacLean 1996: 76).

The myth of the society without mirrors is a poignant one, cited again and again in various accounts of the islanders' lives, as it epitomises their assumed progression from idyllic Arcadia to a society that lost its innocence. The first mirror on St Kilda is supposed to have been a gift from a sea captain to a St Kildan man, Norman MacQueen, in 1903. This is how the story goes in a recent article in the *Observer* (Griffiths 1998: 14): "MacQueen kept it [the mirror] in his pocket and looked at it secretly. Legend has it that MacQueen's wife once saw him leave it under his pillow, suspected it was a picture of another woman, and took a look. When she'd inspected it, her comment was: 'Och, she's not a beauty anyway'." The patronizing conclusions drawn in the same article are rather disturbing: "[Y]ou could say that the St Kildans looked at themselves for the first time, saw themselves as others saw them and weren't taken with the sight. The distorting mirrors told them they were neither beautiful nor rich nor happy, when they had thought they were all three" (ibid.). At the same time the mirror myth served to illustrate the islanders' evil slyness, allegedly used to exploit the tourists: visitors described men cowering in terror before a mirror and then attempting to look behind it, even though it was obvious that they had shaved that very morning in front of a mirror.[1]

The most popular myth about St Kilda is the so-called *St Kilda Parliament*, which refers to the islanders' way of discussing daily affairs. Nobody has ever had any doubt that the St Kildans did have such an assembly, but it differed little from meetings on other islands where collective labour was essential. Questions arise as to whether the term 'Parliament' is an adequate one, as it places a strong emphasis on a modern notion of democracy, even though the islanders did not vote, and had no representative in Westminster (cf. MacDonald 2001, Smith 2000). George Clayton Atkinson (1838) was the first to employ the idea of 'Parliament' for St Kilda in 1831, but the most influential representation that was to shape all future perceptions of the island was a photograph of the *St Kilda Parliament* from George Washington Wilson's Edinburgh studio taken in the late 1880s. This picture, frequently reprinted on postcards, hand-coloured prints and lantern slides, was taken to be an unmistakable proof of the unique island democracy.

Figure 1: George WashingtonWilson's Photograph of St Kilda's Parliament

[1] See Maev Kennedy's (2000) recent article in *The Guardian*, using this myth to argue that "there was also evidence that the islanders were not only taking tourists in their stride but learning to exploit them".

## Mythology revisited

It is this photograph, in itself a representational act, that inspired Douglas Dunn's poem 'St Kilda's Parliament: 1879-1979' with the significant subtitle, 'The photographer revisits his picture' (Dunn 1981: 13), ensuring that we identify the double-mode of representation while reading the first lines of the poem. The title also suggests that the fictional photograph, the poetic replica of its real model, is supposed to have been taken in 1879, but that its contemplation takes place a hundred years later. The photographer, therefore, is depicted as a fictional, hypothetic voice from a future self that cannot literally revisit its creation of the past.

Not only does the poem cut across various temporal spheres, it also calls together various modes of perception. It begins with the photographer's description of the assembly captured by the photograph, noting details that can also be found in Wilson's image: the two neat rows of bearded men wearing waistcoats and Tam-O-Shanters, the dogs and the old woman in the background, and the old man sitting on a bench leaning against a house, staring into the distance – but far from describing the image objectively, the speaker sets out to explain the islanders' facial expressions: the way their faces *look*. "Looking", appearing eleven times throughout the poem in various syntactic and semantic variants (cf. Crawford 1992: 112), marks the central idea of the poem: a contemplation of the way we create perception while we perceive, how looking (perceiving) depends on looks (appearances) and vice versa, and how using our eyes relates to our search for truth in what we create.

The photographer interprets what he sees against the background of what he knows, i.e. popular history and mythology, and ends with a contemplation of photography itself. "Benevolent, or malign?" the poem asks without giving a definite answer – thus transferring the two common representational modes that have been employed to portray the islanders, to the act of representation itself, and making the poem a reflection of representational strategies in art. The poem, though it uses popular mythology, challenges the efficacy of the island as a utopian ideal now lost forever.

To begin with, Dunn uses quaint utopian elements of popular history rather uncritically as it seems: the photographer, having described the assembly briefly, explains the islanders' smiles with:

> their ignorance of what a pig, a bee, a rat,
> Or rabbit *look* like, although they remember
> The three apples brought here by a traveller
> Five years ago, and have discussed them since.
> [...]
> You also *see* how each is individual,
> Proud of his shyness and of his small life
> On this outcast of the Hebrides
> [...]
> Clear, too, is manhood, and how each man *looks*
> Secure in the love of a woman. (13, my emphasis)

Lines like these have prompted critics to dismiss Dunn's poem as "fatally compromised by middle-class liberal patronage and sentimentality" (Williams 1988: 9). Such an analysis, encouraged originally by John Ash's 1983 review of Dunn's poetry, and often repeated since, falls short of the poem's finer implications.

As for "liberal patronage", a close reading of the poem soon reveals that Dunn adapts and contorts St Kildan myths, rather than using them uncritically. While the photographer's patronising information on the islanders' conversations is undoubtedly based directly on the popular histories,[2] Dunn makes clear from the outset that everything is seen through the photographer's lens and might therefore be a distortion. The doubtful myth of the society without mirrors thus finds its equivalent in the more complex image of photography. The multifaceted interplay between photographer, photograph, viewer and photographed object become a central topic of investigation within the poem.

After the initial contemplation of his photograph, the speaker addresses his audience, which can be – given the complex temporal-spatial makeup of the poem – thought of as his fictional nineteenth-century contemporaries, as well as the present and future readers of the poem and the imagined viewers of the imagined photograph:

> Traveller, tourist with your mind set on
> Romantic Staffas and materials for
> Winter conversations, if you should go there,
> Landing at sunrise on its difficult shores,
> On St Kilda you will surely hear Gaelic
> Spoken softly like a poetry of ghosts.
> [...]
> You need only *look* at the faces of these men
> Standing there like everybody's ancestors.
> This flick of time I shuttered on a face. (14, my emphasis)

No matter if we visit the depopulated island or travel back in time, as long as our mind is set on what we want to see, we will see it, and it is the representations of the island through the visual arts, that will influence how we will see. Therefore, the patronising view has little to do with reality, but is generated in the spectator's eye, who is looking at a mere reflection, consciously engineered by the artist. The unusual use of "shutter" as an active verb makes the islanders' faces the recipients of the photographer's interpretation at the moment of the creative act, which, subsequently, sets the mind of the person looking at it. All it takes to see what my mind wants me to see is to look at the faces in the photograph.

Interestingly, the artist's immediate influence on our perception of reality is echoed in the poetic technique. To an informed reader, the reference to "Romantic Staffas" calls to mind William Turner's painting *Staffa* of 1832, also called Fingal's *Cave*, and the controversial poems of Ossian and the Romantic obsession with Highland mythology of the photographer's nineteenth-century travelling contemporaries. Without being too explicit, this multi-layered evocation of romanticised rural Scotland is achieved by a simple plural: "Staffas".

The Heterotopia of the photograph, and that of the poem itself, the creation, brings mythology to life. The faces of the islanders, pre-conceived by the photographer and translated into the photograph, recalled by the poem, become the 'other space' through which we perceive ourselves, as the men are "standing there like everybody's ancestors". Within a complex system of representational modes, the representation of the photograph within the poem is the paradoxical real space that does not exist, allowing not just the photographer, but also the reader to come back to a "slice in time" – to an image which opens up, within its virtual existence, a space to reflect on the real grounds we are in now.

---

[2] For example: "The members [of the St Kilda Parliament] sat around in all weathers on top of dykes, wind-breaks or on the ground to discuss a wide range of topics [...] Stories, myths, sagas, tales of bravery on the cliffs, famous fowling incidents also found their way on the agenda, though by the nineteenth century they had been replaced by long and detailed accounts of visits to the mainland or discussions about the last steamer load of tourists" (Maclean 1996: 36-7). "But it was nonetheless remarkable that as late as 1851, the time of the Great exhibition when the paraphernalia of progress was being displayed to the world, there should have been living in Britain a community of people who had never seen rabbits, rats, pigs, nor bees let alone iron-works and railways" (Maclean 1996: 78).

Dunn not only uses the quaint, romanticising elements of popular history, but also incorporates the negative ones, the image of the islanders covertly making fun of the tourists:

Look at their sly, assuring mockery.
They are aware of what we are up to
With our internal explorations, our
Designs of affluence and education. (14)

Having read the islanders' smiles as those of simpletons at first, the photographer now ascribes a level of thought to the islanders that matches his own – and again, this is only to be seen in the representation. By inverting the mirror myth and the myth of the calculating islanders, Dunn asserts the islanders' active role in the creative act – they are willing to pose and to perform what the artist wants us to see. If they were the naïve primitives who had no view of themselves in the popular narratives, the islanders in the photograph represent their conscious willingness to pose forever, just as much as the photographer, re-viewing his picture, is reminded of his part in engineering their performance:

You can *see* they have already prophesied
A day when survivors look across the stern
Of a departing vessel for the last time
At their gannet-shrouded cliffs, and the farewells
Of the St Kilda mouse and St Kilda wren
As they fall into the texts of specialists,
Ornithological visitors at the prow
Of a sullenly managed boat from the future.
They pose for ever outside their parliament,
Looking at me, as if they have grown from
Affection scattered across my own eyes. (15, my emphasis)

This passage makes clear beyond doubt that for the photographer as an observer of his own image, the islanders may be creations in the moment of perception. Just as the photographer himself is – within his fictional frame – a fiction from his future, but our past, the St Kildans in the photograph, in the representation, embody their past as well as their future, and the future of representations concerning their culture. These lines also echo to some extent Maclean's (1996: 9) ironic observation that the St Kildans' story "is chiefly told by outsiders, who, however unwittingly, contributed to the destruction of the island society by breaking its isolation. But without them there would have been no story to tell". The photographer is aware that his fondness for the islanders helped in creating their past, present and future, but – unlike Maclean – he does not go into detail about the cause of the island's evacuation. There is no mention of material aspirations on the part of the islanders anywhere in the poem; their move to the mainland is explained as a joint decision out of human necessity, as a means to "ease them from their dying babies" (13). However, even though the islanders in the photograph could exist only through the photographer's affection for them, it was also he who defined their future failure within the moment of creation, as the "flick of time", expressed in the islanders' faces, includes the prophecy of the future backwards glance on their past history. This awareness of the destructive power of representation is the reason for the photographer's renewed consideration of his 100 year old image:

And it is because of this that I, who took
This photograph in a year of many events?
The Zulu massacres, Tchaikovsky's opera?
Return to tell you this, and that after
My many photographs of distressed cities,
My portraits of successive elegants,
Of the emaciated dead, the lost empires,
Exploded fleets, and of the writhing flesh
Of dead civilians and commercial copulations,
That after so much of that larger franchise
It is to this island that I return. (15)

As Robert Crawford (1992: 110) reminds us, 'St Kilda's Parliament 1879-1979' "invites thoughts of a wider Scottish political context. For if 1879 is the year the photograph of the remote parliament described in the poem was taken, then 1979 is the year of the Scottish Devolution Referendum". That year, Scotland was offered, but failed to achieve, the electoral result necessary to implement a devolved parliament after a decade of vigorous political and cultural action. The majority of voters had opted for a Scottish parliament, but due to an insufficient number of votes, the Devolution Referendum had been fruitless. The photographer's return to his image could thus be read as a complex metaphor for the uncovering of a political rhetoric that anticipated the contemporary defeat within its positive predictions: just as "it was easy, even then, to imagine St Kilda return to its naked self, / Its archaeology of hazelraw" (14), the idea of a devolved Scottish Parliament, as such an analysis would suggest, was predestined to fail. The fact that Dunn places the photograph in 1879, even though the original that inspired the poem was taken later in the 1880s, the precise gap of 100 years in the title, and the allusion to parliamentary democracy in the text ("It is a remote democracy, where men […] outstare a sea") would all support a Scottish reading of the poem. But far from being patronising (towards the St Kildans) or sentimental (about the Scottish cause), the poem comprises a general analysis of how representation might be responsible for the shortcomings of our age. The "emaciated dead", the "dead civilians", "exploded fleets", the "Zulu massacres", the "lost empires", the "writhing flesh" and even the allusion to Tchaikovsky's opera *Eugen Onegin* all strongly point towards a global context of destruction, beyond the parochial as well as the national. The photographer pictures himself as a chronicler of his century – the note of gloom, failure, death and obliteration surrounding St Kilda is thus given a universal dimension.

The St Kildans, however 'Scottish' they might have been, are the 'other within'; their lives are documented for 'us' by 'specialists' from the mainland, strangers to their culture like us. Britain's colonial past is mirrored in the story of the small island archipelago, seeing that the poem undoubtedly draws attention to the effects of colonisation (the Zulu massacres of 1879), as are cultural divisions within Scotland (the speaker can be assumed to have a Scottish persona, as G.W. Wilson's studio was based in Edinburgh). To reduce the political significance of the poem to the question of a devolved Scottish parliament would not do it justice. Its actual theme goes beyond the scope of nations and, in an age of increasingly globalised political action, is more relevant today than it has ever been: the moral implications of representation itself and its contribution to myth-making. The photographer contemplates just that: the "flick of time" on the islanders' faces in the Heterotopia, the 'other space' of the photograph, enables him to see himself and the islanders passing through a virtual place – his camera – that *is not* but once *was*, and it allows him to call his own art into question:

Here I whittle time, like a dry stick
  [...]
Outside a parliament, looking at them.
As they, too, must always look at me,
Looking through my apparatus at them
Looking. Benevolent, or malign? But who,
At this late stage, could tell, or think it worth it?
For I was there, and am, and I forget. (15)

The poem, then, allows the photographer to step out of the photograph to reconsider his image, in which he had been invisibly present for a hundred years, as it was he who had staged the islanders' performance. Benevolent, or malign? – the question, referring to the islanders as well as photography – remains unanswered while the poem invites us to revisit our own image of the St Kildans and our view of how we perceive. By linking St Kilda to a global context of destruction Dunn scrutinises the role of representation, that of representational art and that of political representation, in our conscious creation of world history.

## Conclusion

If St Kilda has the doubtful potential to be a "bewitching symbol" of contemporary Scotland because of its popular history, signifying independent democracy, indigenous tradition and warnings of a modern age, Dunn's poem opens up an alternative reading of St Kildan mythology and history with the makings of similar symbolic value. 'St Kilda's Parliament 1879-1979' contemplates the representational process itself, thus making St Kilda a dire warning of the representational strategies in operation not only where rural Scotland is concerned but also in a universal context. If representations of Scottish culture are drawn to ubiquitous images and debilitating conclusions, it is crucial to expose the representational strategies engineering them, and it is just as necessary to discover and uncover alternative concepts. But there is danger in reducing Scottish authors to supporters simply of the Scottish cause, and if St Kilda has been made a metaphor for the battle between tradition and modernity, Dunn's poem has been made a metaphor for Scotland's struggle for parliamentary independence. As regards ideas of the nation and national identity, there has been a definite tendency for recent criticism coming from Scotland to fuse critical objectives with patriotic feelings. W.N. Herbert (1992: 122) has gone as far as calling Dunn "Scotland's poetic ambassador to the South". He writes that, "In many ways we are reliant on Dunn to 'explain' Scotland to the South in terms it can comprehend (briefly, Ireland without the urgency of the Armalite). So it is that two Dunns emerge across the canon, subtly different from each other and both, one suspects, divorced from his ideal persona. One is the poet who speaks for us (the Scots), the other is the poet who speaks to them (the English)."

In this reading of Dunn's 'St Kilda's Parliament: 1879-1979' I have tried to show that the poem is more than a "monumental elegy to a remote democracy" (Walker 1996: 301) and that there is indeed more to the text than can be explained in a purely Scottish context. There is also the Dunn who speaks to an international audience, and there is much to be gained from perceiving Dunn's Scottish poems as reaching far beyond the scope of place, space and nation.

## References

Ash, J. 1983. "Pleasures of invention, rigours of responsibility. Some notes on the poetry of Douglas Dunn". *Poetry Nation Review* 34: 43–6

Atkinson, G.C. 1838. "An Account of an Expedition to St Kilda in 1831". *Transactions of the Natural History Society of Northumberland*. Durham and Newcastle 2: 215–25

Barthes, R. 1973. *Mythologies*. Translated by Annette Lavers. London: Paladin. First Published 1957

Crawford, R. 1992. "Secret Villager". In *Reading Douglas Dunn*. Eds. R. Crawford and D. Kinloch. Edinburgh: Edinburgh University Press. 108-21

Dunn, D. 1981. *St Kilda's Parliament*. London: Faber

Foucault, M. 1984. "Des espaces autres". (Conférence au Cercle d'études architecturales, March 14, 1967). *Architecture, Mouvement, Continuité* 5: 46-9

Griffiths, J. 1998. "Movement of the People". *The Observer*. November 22: 14–17

Herbert, W.N. 1992. "Dunn and Dundee". In *Reading Douglas Dunn*. Eds. R. Crawford and D. Kinloch. Edinburgh: Edinburgh University Press. 122-137

Kennedy, M. 2000. "Islanders' Canny Plea of Poverty". *Guardian Unlimited Archive*. December 29. www.guardian.co.uk/Archive/ (accessed 12 February 2004)

MacDonald, F. 2001. "St Kilda and the Sublime". *Ecumene* 8.2: 151–74

MacDonald, F. 2000. "The World They Left Behind". *The Herald (Glasgow)*. August 28: 17

MacLean, C. 1996. *St Kilda. Island on the Edge of the World*. Reprinted with new afterword by Margaret Buchanan. Edinburgh: Canongate. [First published 1972]

Martin, M. ed. 1999. *A Description of the Western Islands of Scotland ca 1695 and A Late Voyage to St Kilda*. Edinburgh: Birlinn. [First published 1698]

Said, E. 1978. *Orientalism: Western Conceptions of the Orient*. London: Routledge & Kegan Paul

Smith, I. 2000. "Britain's Lost Republic". http://apocalypse.luton.ac.uk/imperium/ (accessed 12 February 2004)

Steel, T. 1975. *The Life and Death of St Kilda*. London: Fontana

Walker, M. 1996. *Scottish Literature since 1707*. London: Longman

Williams, D. 1988. "'They Will Not Leave Me, the Lives of Other People'. The Poetry of Douglas Dunn". *Studies in Scottish Literature* 23: 1–24

# Double Nots and Beckettian Loopholes in James Kelman's *Not Not While the Giro*

*Paul Shanks*[1]

Samuel Beckett's name has frequently (if sometimes spuriously) been invoked in criticism of James Kelman's fiction.[2] Indeed, key motifs and phrases from Beckett's post-war fiction often appear to make uncanny reappearances through the mouths, as it were, of Kelman's protagonists. To choose but one example, in Kelman's Booker Prize winning novel, *How Late It Was How Late*, Beckett's most famous note of fortitude within adversity – "you must go on, I can't go on, I'll go on" (Beckett 1979: 381) – is translated into the main character, Sammy's, idiom as, "ach it was hopeless [...] ye just plough on, ye plough on" (Kelman 1995: 37). Intrigued as to whether this might be a conscious decision on Kelman's part, I asked (in a private interview conducted during the 2003 Word Festival at Aberdeen) whether he considered Beckett to be an influence on his writing. His reply was in the negative:

> I didn't read Beckett, at least until my mid-twenties, maybe my late twenties ... and I haven't been a reader of Beckett in the sense that I would say I was a reader of Kafka ... I don't think he's influenced me really, I don't feel that. He may have done occasionally [...] I can't even remember how much I read at certain periods of Beckett ... I remember Tom Leonard kept saying, Jim, look, you should really read Beckett and I'd glance and say you should really read Kafka. At that time Tom had a bit of a blind spot with Kafka, maybe like I had with Beckett ... (I didn't meet Tom till I was about twenty six) ... and I remember a guy at the buses, a guy from Dublin ... and he was always on at me to read Beckett ... so I'd be about twenty two and he'd be about twenty two and he is *carrying* Beckett in his pocket all the time. (Kelman, 2003, cited with Kelman's permission)

Despite this disavowal, there appears to be some correspondence between Kelman's reading of Beckett (mid to late twenties) and the initial publication of the stories in which a specifically Beckettian tone first becomes apparent (1976 to 1979, respectively).[3] However, the similarities may be considered fortuitous rather than intrinsic to the writing: in the same interview, Kelman argues that it is between the ages of sixteen and twenty-five that a writer is most likely to be influenced by other writers (whether this is true or not of creative fiction in general is another matter). Nevertheless, although Kelman does not consider Beckett to have been a major "influence" on his work, his writings could have been tempered, however indirectly, by the fact that his contemporaries in the late sixties and early seventies were reading Beckett. The exchange between Kelman and Leonard may, therefore, bear more than anecdotal significance. Moreover, Kelman, in relation to my question, reiterated a point frequently made in other interviews and essays in which he sees his writing as emerging from a specific tradition (or set of traditions):

---

[1] I would like to acknowledge the support of the Arts and Humanities Research Council.
[2] C.f. Ellen-Raissa Jackson and Willy Maley's introduction to the sequence of essays in *Kelman and Commitment:* "often compared with a whole host of major European literary figures—Beckett, Joyce, Kafka, Zola—he also belongs firmly within a radical Scottish tradition, and is keenly aware of, and arguably part of new literatures in English" (2001: 23).
[3] I have discussed these stories in an earlier paper, "The Unnamed Itinerant in Beckett's Novellas and Kelman's 'Lean Tales' " which was delivered at the New Voices Conference 2004 in Derry.

> When you read about a writer that people may link you to … you can see how there's
> certain goals, or you feel as if there's certain similarities … but you find out again that
> these writers are also very much influenced, or rather they're very keen on the writers
> you are also interested in, so that … you're kind of like in a similar tradition. (Kelman
> 2003)

To be part of this tradition may indicate a similar set of formal concerns or a similar set of
"goals". In his essay on Chomsky, Kelman identifies some of these: "the technical problems to
be resolved by the artist concern space and time. These have been the preoccupations of –
among other artists – Cézanne, Claude Monet, Gertrude Stein, James Joyce, Franz Kafka,
Carlos Williams and also W. S. Graham and Samuel Beckett" (2002: 181). He further argues
that that which distinguishes this form of art is a concern with "present-time consciousness"
and a formal tendency towards "recursiveness" (2002: 180–1). Kelman applies the latter term
to James Hogg's *Confessions of a Justified Sinner*, arguing that the various narrative layers create
multiple perspectives, none of which hold ultimate authority. The word "recursive" is here
used in a similar sense to that employed by Gödel in his "recursive function theory" which
concerns the discrepancy between systems of knowledge and the inability of one system to
validate another. (Kelman 2002: 182–3)[4]

In what follows, I will examine some of the ways in which Beckett and Kelman employ
hypothesis and uncertainty as a narrative technique. Firstly, I will offer a brief analysis of the
recursive language games employed in Beckett's novel *Watt* (first published in 1953) and the
transference of these formal structures in the works of R.D. Laing and Tom Leonard. This
will preface discussion of Kelman's early short story, 'Not not while the giro' (first published
in 1983), in which the central protagonist and narrator (an unemployed and disaffected
Glaswegian) is entrapped within an interminable dialectic of negative creation. The theoretical
terminology to be used for this part of the discussion will be Bakhtinian, with particular
reference to Bakhtin's concept of the "word with a loophole". I will then look at the fuller
implications of this linguistic *"perpetuum mobile"* (Bakhtin 1984: 230) when applied to
Beckett's *The Unnameable* (*L'Innomable*, first published in French in 1952 and subsequently
published in English in 1959).

Beckett's *Watt* might be described as a novel that operates through the puns, "Watt/what"
and "Knott/not" (c.f. Beckett 1988: 165): these refer to both the names of the characters (Watt
and Mr Knott) and the ways in which the novel textually enacts its enquiry into the nature of
language and the objective world. This enquiry frequently involves "an exercise in rationalistic
circumlocution" (Mooney 1990: 165) involving numerous passages which are extended to
repetitious and sometimes baffling lengths. For instance, Watt's hypotheses while in Mr
Knott's house as to the feeding of leftovers (Knott's meal) to its recipient (a suitably "famished"
dog) expands into an enormous yarn, one told by "a little voice" which Watt overhears (Beckett
1988: 88). This voice proceeds to open up an immense vista of narrative contrivance, involving
a vast family of congenitally deformed dogowners (the Lynch family) and a seemingly endless
supply of "famished" dogs. The tale, to use a well-worn cliché, grows arms and legs.
Throughout this narrative, the reader is in much the same position as Watt himself: "Watt
never knew quite what to make of this particular little voice, whether it was joking, or
whether it was serious" (Beckett 1988: 88). What is unnerving in the passage is the way in
which it appears to eat away at the containing narrative ('Watt had not been four months with
Mr Knott when Liz the wife of Sam lay down and expelled a child' [Beckett 1988: 102]) before
fading away as insidiously as it first appeared (the story is never referred to again in the novel).

---

[4] Beckett perhaps refers to an emerging sense of recursiveness in art when, in his essay 'Recent Irish
Poetry', he speaks of "the breakdown of the object" and what he perceives as a "rupture of the lines of
communication" (Beckett, 1983: 70).

This reflects upon the dual trajectory of Watt's inquiries which tend to resolve themselves through "the mischievous machinery of grammatical relations" (Davies 1994: 46) before vanishing "into the dark" (Beckett 1988: 115). Knowledge has, in this sense, the potential to cancel itself out, leaving nothing or, at least, as little as what was begun with. The sense of recursivity is reflected in the text itself where each phrase is qualified and, to a certain extent, cancelled out by the use of negatives (or "nots") as in the following example which opens the second section of the novel: "Watt had no direct dealings with Mr Knott, at this period. Not that Watt was ever to have any direct dealings with Mr Knott, for he was not. But he thought, at this period, that the time would come when he would have dealings with Mr Knott, on the first-floor" (Beckett 1988: 64).[5] The construction which begins with "not" and concludes, "for he was not", repeats itself throughout the text like a musical refrain. A further meaning is therefore added to the term "recursiveness", one which may be derived from the older usage of the word where it was used to denote a process (such as a musical phrase) which is "periodically or continually recurring".[6] Complementing these syntactical patterns are the numerous instances of repetition and displacement in *Watt* where a number of grammatical constituents are reconjugated interminably. The type of motion this involves is exemplified in Erskine's speech where it is stated that "this in my opinion is the type of all information whatsoever, be it voluntary or solicited. If you want a stone, ask a turnover. If you want a turnover, ask plum pudding" (Beckett 1988: 44). The trajectory of the novel may also be summed up in reference to the picture that Watt discovers in Erskine's room: "Watt wondered what the artist had intended to represent (Watt knew nothing about painting), a circle and its centre in search of each other, or a circle and its centre in search of a centre and a circle respectively" (Beckett 1988: 127).

With *Watt*, Beckett homes in on some of the concerns of epistemology. It is in consideration of the semantic and syntactical knots involved in such an enquiry that I wish to refer to R.D. Laing's *Knots* insofar as it conjoins Beckett's experimentation both during and after World War II with the social and literary context of Glasgow in the late 1960s and early 70s. In this work, Laing attempts to illustrate familial and personal neuroses as a series of lexical "knots". One of these syntactic cul-de-sacs appears to exemplify and re-enact the psychological procedure of Laing's own "false self system":[7]

> if it's not me, it's not me
> it's not me if it's not me
> if it's me, it's me
> if it's me, it's me
> I am it
> if it is not me
> if it is not me, I am it, if I am not it, I
> am it, if I am it, I am not it. (Laing, 1970: 47)

These diagrams are useful up to a point (although at times they make for even more vexatious reading than *Watt*) in that they illustrate the expansion of belief systems upon the foundation of one or two arbitrary premises. Nevertheless, these constructions through their very abstraction undermine their potential application, removing, in the process, considerations of

---

[5] Anthony Cronin notes Beckett's "superb use of the comma" in extracts such as these (Cronin, 1997: 337).
[6] http://dictionary.oed.com/cgi/entry/00199823?single=1&query_type=word&queryword=recursive&edition=2e&first=1&max_to_show=10.
[7] Laing used the term, "false self system" to describe the ways in which the schizoid individual interacts with the external world: "instead of the individual meeting the world with an integral selfhood, he disavows part of his own being along with his disavowal of immediate attachment to things and people in the world" (Laing, 1965: 82).

locality and class difference (this critique is effaced if we consider *Knots* as poetic autobiography). It might be argued that some of these issues are redressed in Tom Leonard's poem, 'breathe deep, and regular with it' (Leonard 1984: 139): while Leonard appears to be imitating the structure of *Knots*, he also represents the speaker's voice in working-class Glaswegian, thereby situating his poem within a societally specific context. The poem begins with the phrases, "if yiv nuthin ti say lets/not talk about not/sayin it" (l.1-3), and proceeds to take these to their logical extreme through the use of double negatives, or "nots". What is created is a kind of verbal web in which it is hard to tell whether the speaker is making an assertion in the positive or in the negative. But Leonard's poem does not merely reiterate the premises of Laing's psychological diagrams but would appear to be referring to a certain Scottish/Glaswegian mode of articulation (as in the Scottish phrase, "it's no a bad day") in order to make a statement about language which is of great philosophical import; the idea that it is impossible to recede into total non-sense; the idea, as expressed in the companion poem 'hangup', that an existence outside language is inconceivable ("a stull think yi huvty say sumhm", Leonard 1984: 138). It is perhaps the way in which Leonard is able to make Glaswegian function in this way that inspired Kelman in his early years and perhaps initiated similar formal strategies in his prose works. Indeed, Tom Leonard's "breathe deeply" is used as an epigraph in the story, 'Not not while the giro', and the poem may have contributed, at least in part, to the recursive strategies which Kelman chose to give voice to his protagonist.

In this story, the central character, Hamish Smith – a self-confessed "neer do-well" with a "death wish" (Kelman 1989: 188, 192) – is trapped within a cycle of thoughts which mirror his own limited economic circumstances. His consciousness is conveyed formally in the text by paragraphs which are separated into blocks, thereby creating the sense of both retentive thought patterns and of a fragmented consciousness: these narrative blocks are also used to suggest a dialogic series of thought processes. At various stages in the text, these thought utterances interrupt, or negate, one another: an incomplete or abandoned train of thought is represented as an incomplete or interrupted paragraph to be resumed in the next by a dissenting voice whose typical exclamation might be, "to hell with that for a game" (192).[8] The voice, or voices within the text are in continual conflict with one another: for instance when Hamish contemplates suicide there is another voice which reins him in: "Well throw yourself out the fucking window then. Throw myself out fuck all window – do what you like but here I am" (200).[9]

The voice of the narrator is also distinguished by the regular use of negations through which he attempts to apprehend his circumstances: "my coat is in the fashion of yesteryear but I am wearing it. How comes this coat to be with me yet. Not a question although it bears reflecting upon at some later date. Women may have something to do with it. Probably not, that cannot be correct. Anyway, it has nothing to do with anything" (182). Each assertion is dismissed or cancelled out and, as with Beckett's texts and Leonard's "breathe deeply", the "truth" of each statement is held in suspense to the extent that it becomes hard to define exactly what is being said (or 'unsaid'). Another integral feature of voice in the story is the way in which certain speech genres are relativised through their incorporation into the narrator's discourse. The effect is predominantly satiric: liturgical, literary or legal language is employed to almost Swiftian effect, as in the following example where Hamish describes an attempt to pawn his coat:

---

[8] Ben Knights has noted a similar pattern in Kelman's novels: "the voice that recurs in his novels is that of a kind of interior monologue, or, more accurately, an interior dialogue, the conversation in the character's head" (1999: 186).
[9] C.f *Malone Dies* (Beckett, 1979: 201): "What tedium. And I thought I had it all thought out. If I had the use of my body I would throw it out of the window. But perhaps it is the knowledge of my impotence that emboldens me to that thought. All hangs together, I am in chains".

Imitation crombies are unbecoming these days, particularly the kind with narrow lapels. This shrewd man I occasionally have dealings with refused said coat on the grounds of said lapels rendering the coat an undesired object by those who frequent said man's premises. Yet I would have reckoned most purchasers of 2nd hand clothing to be wholly unaware of fashions current or olden. (183)

Here, a desperate bid for cash is represented in pompous and archaic language. Such usage is ironic; it reveals the gap between Hamish's circumstances and the kind of social mobility assumed by these discourses.[10] This tendency to highlight the discrepancy between discourse and reality is further illustrated in Hamish's frequent daydreams. In looking at *Watt*, I noted the way in which the text illustrated the expansive yet recursive nature of speculative reason: this is also an important feature of Kelman's narrative. At one point, Hamish invents the background story of his neighbour, a certain Mrs Soinson "who appears unaware of [his] existence" (185) and of whom Hamish knows nothing. His hypotheses about this woman draw upon familiar stories of spinsters and spurned lovers. As the story begins to grow arms and legs, however, it becomes increasingly contrived:

Ever since that day Mrs Soinson has remained a spinster, virginal, the dutiful but pathetic aunt – a role she hates but accepts for her parents' memory. Or she could have looked after the aged father till it was too late and for some reason, on the day he died, vowed to stay a single lassie since nobody could take the place of the departed dad and took on the title of Mistress to ward off would-be suitors although of course you do find men more willing to entertain a single Mrs as opposed to a single miss which is why I agree with Women's Lib. Ms should be the title of both married and single women.
        In the name of god. (195-6)

There is a sense of bafflement, even amazement, conveyed in that last phrase at the absurd flights of fantasy to which the mind seems prone. There is also, however, a satiric emphasis to these imaginings: this becomes especially marked when Hamish envisages a series of deliberately clichéd dialogues amongst the "Captain(s) of Industry" to refer to an unforeseeable return to "paid employment".

Where is that godforsaken factory. Let me at it. A trier. I would say so your Magnateship. And was Never say Die the type of adage one could apply to the wretch. I believe so Your Industrialness.
        Fuck Off. (196)

The narrator imagines being spoken for by the languages of authority but undermines these from within by stretching them to ridicule, by coining forms of mock address such as "Your Industrialness". However, there is a paradox in the fact that the character's material powers over the locus of these languages (in Kelman's case this locus is economic and political) are limited: he can only parody the voice of these languages, he cannot attain mastery over them. So, in a certain sense, the languages resist the narrator and maintain their institutional power: this might explain Hamish's frustrated rejoinder.
        There is awareness in the narrative of a potentially hostile audience: in this sense, Kelman's story invites comparison with Dostoevsky's "Notes From Underground", particularly Bakhtin's discussion of the novelistic techniques used in the latter novella *(Problems of Dostoevsky's Poetics)*. In this study, Bakhtin formulates a term for the specific mode of

---

[10] Liam McIlvanney has written cogently on this extract in his review of Kelman's most recent novel, *You have to be careful in the land of the free* (McIlvanney: 2004).

dialogism employed which he describes as the "word with a sidewards glance" or "loophole": in defining the former term, he argues that "this 'sideward glance' manifests itself above all in two traits characteristic of the style: a certain halting quality to the speech, and its interruption by reservations" (1984: 205). The "loophole", he argues, is "judging by its meaning, an ultimate word about oneself, a final definition of oneself, but in fact it is forever taking into account internally the responsive, contrary evaluation of oneself made by another" (1984: 233). As Bakhtin notes, this cyclical discourse stems partially from the desire to attain "the final word" (1984: 229) but the problem is that, when language works in interdependence to an imagined response, such a desire is unachievable:

> Thanks to this attitude toward the other's consciousness, a peculiar *perpetuum mobile* is achieved, made up of his internal polemic with another and with himself, an endless dialogue where one reply begets another, which begets a third, and so on to infinity, and all of this without any forward motion. (1984: 230)

In Kelman's narrative, a similar trajectory is hinted at in that the interiorised voices are involved in a constant stream of modifications and qualifications: the title of the story is itself a kind of loophole or semantic knot; a double negation. In both Dostoevsky's novella and Kelman's short story this mode of thinking feeds into the "death wish": "cynical of self, this is the problem. Each time I make a firm resolution I end up scoffing. Yes. I sneer. Well well well, what a shite" (Kelman 1989: 201). The consequence of such double-edged and self-negating thought patterns is the wish to put a spanner in the works of every serious endeavour, to cackle from the sidelines. It is a potentially destructive mode of discourse: as a self-perpetuating and enclosed circle there is no hope of any linear progression. Nevertheless, the point must be reiterated, that this voice also has a protective function: as argued in relation to the Leonard poem, it offers a culturally distinctive means of apprehending reality.

The latter connotation becomes clear if we turn again to Beckett, for it is in Beckett's *The Unnameable* that these speech acts are taken to their logical extreme. Unlike *Watt*, where the use of these negations is relatively stylised and contained, in this novel there is a frenetic edge to the discourse:

> I say I. Unbelieving. [...] what am I to do, what shall I do, what should I do, in my situation, how proceed? By aporia pure and simple? Or by affirmations and negations invalidated as uttered, or sooner, or later? Generally speaking. There must be other shifts. Otherwise it would be quite hopeless. But it is quite hopeless. (Beckett 1979: 267)

Increasingly in this text, a staccato series of enquiries, "invalidated as uttered", convey an accumulating sense of uncertainty and growing panic: "these things I say, and shall say, if I can, are no longer, or are not yet, or never were, or never will be, or if they were, if they are, if they will be, were not here, are not here, will not be here, but elsewhere" (1979: 276). The discursive basis of these utterances is hinted at in the text: frequently, the unnamed narrator (like a disaffected Caliban) speaks of his instruction by several interlocutors who have enforced upon his understanding what might be described as "humanist" notions of "God"; "Love"; and "intelligence". One of these instructors, Basil, later renamed Mahood, appears to encroach upon the narrator's utterances: "though he plagues me no more his voice is there, in mine, but less, less. And being no longer renewed it will disappear one day, I hope, from mine, completely" (1979: 283). This seems an apt illustration of brainwashing, or rather, the way in which the mind becomes interpellated *in* the "other". The narrator fears that this voice may reappear when he is "off-guard", so to speak: "now I'll tell one of Mahood's stories, I need a rest [...] but now, is it I now, I on me? Sometimes I think it is. And then I realize it is not"

(1979: 284). In Kelman's texts there is, at times, a similar awareness of the invasive potential of another's discourse: as I argued earlier, Hamish Smith's parodic treatment of the discourses of mobility belies the fact that he can have no "real" power over them. He is also unable to resist reiterating their precepts (albeit in a cynical manner) as his frequent lapses into daydream seem to illustrate. His sudden awareness of this fact, at one point in the story, leads to the cryptic exclamation: "black and white consumer and producer parasite thief come on shake hands you lot" (Kelman 1989: 200).

A persistently mocking and audience-aware voice can also be detected in the narrative discourse of *The Unnameable* (and throughout the *Trilogy*) which is similar to the intonationally marked passages that were identified in 'Not not while the giro': "here's your file, no convictions, I assure you, come now, make an effort, at your age, to have no identity, it's a scandal […] here's the record, insults to policemen, indecent exposure […] I beg your pardon, does he work, good God no, out of the question, look, here's the medical report" (1979: 347). Indeed, both texts are marked by a "legalistic streak": as Paul Davies has noted, in Beckett's *Trilogy* it is as if the "mode of writing in these novels has been conditioned or determined by a panel of interrogators, "they", "Basil and his gang". However, Davies also notes that "the net effect of reading the prose is as much one of being bombarded with evasive devices as of scrupulousness" (Davies 1994: 68). In *The Unnameable* though, the narrator castigates himself for having evaded the true nature of his task for so long: "between me and the right to silence, the living rest, stretches the same old lesson, the one I once knew by heart but would not say, I don't know why, perhaps for fear of silence, or thinking any old thing would do, and so for preference lies, in order to remain hidden" (Beckett, 1979: 280).

In Kelman's story, the narrator frequently rails against himself for lying with such frequency: "this is all bastarn lies. Why in the name of fuck do I continue. What is it with me at all" (1989: 194). There are also moments when the reader is left uncertain as to the truth or falsity of Hamish's stories or when the fictionality of a certain recollection only becomes apparent on closer reading. At one point, Hamish tells of a former time when he lived "on a tiny islet not far from Toay" where he came to experience "the inner recesses. Self knowledge and acceptance of the awareness" (204). But when Hamish claims that "food requires no mention" the reader may infer a certain irony while the description of "nicotine wool" at the edges of rocks brings the reader back to Hamish's present circumstances where nicotine, one of the many crutches used to physically counteract boredom, has run out. However, near the conclusion to his narrative, Hamish appears to have reached some formulation of the exact source of his problems – that he is happy when unhappy – that his giro is the axle to the wheel insofar as it perpetuates the recurring cycle of his present circumstances. The decision to go for perfect misery culminates in his final plan, which becomes his final fantasy; he will be "The Land's End to John O'Groats Man" (205), then, after some modification, "The Scottish Coastroad Walker": "being a circular route no such thing as a return would exist ie. I would be travelling on an arc" (206). Like the passages cited previously, however, this narrative becomes increasingly unbelievable as it progresses. There is a subtle mixture of attitudes; while on the one level the voice is deliberately parodic, there is another sense in which the narrator becomes carried away by his own invention:

> Dont give him money Your Lordship you'll just hurt his feelings. Just a bit of your cheese piece and a saucer of milk for the whelp. Group photographs with me peering suspiciously at the camera from behind shoulders at the back or in the immediate foreground perhaps, It is rumoured the man was a Captain of Industry Your Grace, been right round the Scottish Coastroad 28 times and known from Galloway to Berwick as a friend to Everyone. Yes, just a pinch of your snuff and a packet of cigarette-papers for chewing purposes only. No sextants or compasses or any of that kind of shite but (207)

The concluding sentence illustrates a particularly halting sense of the "word with a loophole", a growing awareness of the whole venture's impracticality. Taken as a whole, the passage has poignancy in that it becomes a diagrammatic outline of the cycle in which Hamish finds himself entrapped.

There are some striking correspondences between Hamish's Coast Road journey and the account of Mahood's one-legged homeward journey in *The Unnameable*. The latter narrative commences in mock-epic style with its inflated time scheme and geographic sweep (there is an undertone, perhaps, of Odysseus's return voyage):

> At the particular moment I am referring to, I mean when I took myself for Mahood, I must have been coming to the end of a world tour, perhaps not more than two or three centuries to go. My state of decay lends colour to this view, perhaps I had left my leg behind in the pacific, yes, no perhaps about it, I had, somewhere off the coast of Java and its jungles red with rafflesia stinking of carrion, no, that's the Indian ocean, what a gazetteer I am, no matter somewhere round there. In a word I was returning to the fold. (Beckett 1979: 291)

From the beginning, the reader (or listener) is encouraged to regard the whole account as an "untruth", a yarn: the Indian ocean becomes synonymous with the pacific ocean because what is transpiring is just talk; words contrived in order to pass (or to evade) the time. The final stage of Mahood's journey takes place in a "yard" which is "surrounded by high walls": "at the centre of this enclosure stood a small rotunda, windowless, but well furnished with loopholes" (Beckett 1979: 291). Mahood makes painfully slow progress on his crutches, his pains allayed by a regular supply of narcotics. As he nears his home, the family are overheard discussing his slow progress and the length of time it might take him to complete his journey: "since my arrival they had a subject of conversation [...] Time hung less heavy on their hands. What about throwing him a few scraps? No, no, it might upset him [...] What about throwing him a sponge? No, no, it might confuse him" (Beckett 1979: 292). The sensitivity towards the traveller's feelings in such circumstances is farcical and recalls that attitude towards monetary reward which Hamish imagines in his 'Coastroad Walker' daydream. However, the comic dimension to such stereotypes is undercut by the unsettling appearance of the enclosure itself: with its central rotunda from which Mahood is watched perpetually (at night time by "searchlight"). This space is like an inverted theatre or Panopticon and marks the repetition throughout the narrative of confining circular spaces.

Mahood's telling of this inverted epic is also dischronological and confused: the family's death (of "sausage poisoning") before Mahood's arrival is referred to, then it hasn't happened, then it is about to happen. At times, the narrator takes on the personality of Mahood then, at others, appears to be telling the story of another (as told by Mahood). The narrator tires of the story when it becomes foreign to him, when he becomes aware of it as mythology rather than personal recollection: as he ceases to believe in his story, the details gradually change: the "world tour" is refuted when the narrator claims that the journey in fact took place on an "island", the one which he "never left" (Beckett 1979: 300) and the spiral or arc described in the preceding account is exchanged for random and irregular movement. As with Hamish Smith's fantasy, the illusion breaks down and the narrator returns to the indefinable and irresolvable immediacies of his "pensum".

It is, perhaps, an awareness of the coercive potential of language which makes Beckett's work so readily translatable for other writers, especially those who see their work as emerging

---

[11] "There is a literary tradition to which I hope my own work belongs, I see it as part of a much wider process – or movement – toward decolonization and self determination [...] it is a tradition premised on a rejection of the cultural values of imperial or colonial authority, offering a defence against cultural assimilation, in particular imposed assimilation" (Kelman 1994: 2).

from a context of linguistic and institutionalised colonisation.[11] It might further be argued that the ontological and discursive dilemmas found in Beckett's works gain new potency and political weight when placed within the context of Scottish working-class consciousness. Nevertheless, Kelman's protagonists, unlike Beckett's, are far more directly grounded in the situational (the "local") and the "concrete" (Nicoll 2000: 81). Where Beckett's texts tap into a reservoir or matrix where the living ends of consciousness are postulated in imaginative form, Kelman's texts rarely depart from the sphere of the "actual" according to the laws of "present time consciousness". Nevertheless, I would argue that what links Kelman and Beckett's texts is a mutual preoccupation with the dual nature of modern interior thought which can be both a source of liberation and a form of entrapment.

## References

Bakhtin, Mikhail. 1984. *Problems of Dostoevsky's Poetics*. Trans. Caryl Emerson. London and Minneapolis: University of Minnesota Press

Beckett, Samuel. 1979. *The Beckett Trilogy (Molloy, Malone Dies, The Unnameable)*. London: Picador

Beckett, Samuel. 1983. *Disjecta*. London: John Calder

Beckett, Samuel. 1988. *Watt*. London: Picador

Cronin, Anthony. 1997. *Samuel Beckett: The Last Modernist*. London: Flamingo

Davies, Paul. 1994. *The Ideal Real: Beckett's Fiction and Imagination*. London and Toronto: Associated University Presses

Jackson, Ellen-Raissa and Willy Maley eds. 2001. *Kelman and Commitment*. *Edinburgh Review*, 108: 21–122

Jacoby, Russell, 1975. *Social Amnesia: A Critique of Conformist Psychology from Adler to Laing*. Hassocks: Harvester Press

Kelman, James. 1989. *Not Not While the Giro*. London: Minerva

Kelman, James. 1992. "Artists and Value". *Some Recent Attacks: Essays Cultural and Political*. Stirling: AK Press. 5–15. huigh

Kelman, James. 16 Oct 1994. 'Elitist Slurs Are Racism By Another Name'. *Scotland On Sunday:* Spectrum Supplement: 2

Kelman, James. 1995. *How Late It Was How Late*. London: Minerva

Kelman, James. 2002. *'And The Judges Said …'*. London: Secker and Warburg

Kelman, James. 16 May 2003. Personal Interview with David Borthwick, Scott Hames and Paul Shanks. Taylor Building, University of Aberdeen

Knights, Ben, 1999. *Writing Masculinity: Male Narratives in Twentieth-Century Fiction*. London: Macmillan

Laing, R.D. 1965. *The Divided Self*. Harmondsworth: Pelican

Laing, R.D. 1970. *Knots*. London: Tavistock

Leonard, Tom. 1984. *Intimate Voices*. Newcastle: Galloping Dog Press

McIlvanney, Liam. 2004. 'Give or Take a Dead Scotsman'. *London Review of Books* 26.14: 15–16

McNeill, Kirsty. 1989. "Interview with James Kelman" *Chapman*, 57: 1–9

Mooney, Michael E. 1990. *'Watt:* Samuel Beckett's Sceptical Fiction'. In *Rethinking Beckett: A Collection of Critical Essays*. Eds. Lance St John Butler and Robin J. Davies. London: Macmillan Press. 160-8

Nicoll, Lawrence. 2000. "'This is Not a Nationalist Position': James Kelman's Existential Voice". *Edinburgh Review* 103: 79–84

# "Self-parodic Operations": Atmosphere and Texture in Eoin McNamee's *The Ultras*

*Daniel Smith*

Eoin McNamee's *The Ultras* is an account of one of Northern Ireland's most famous British military casualties, Captain Robert Nairac. The intriguing gaps in the narrative of Nairac's life and death make him the ideal subject for speculative fiction. As in his previous novels, *Resurrection Man* and *The Blue Tango*, McNamee has taken historical events and characters and transformed them into a fictionalised account, inventing and changing characters and events as he finds necessary. Yet this technique raises obvious (and not so obvious) questions about how far a novelist might be permitted to go:

> Slippery though they may be, we do operate with intuitions about what is accepted historical "fact" and how far any fictional version deviates from that "fact." Another way to formulate this constraint would be to say that freedom to improvise actions and properties of historical figures is limited to the "dark areas" of history, that is, to those aspects about which the "official" record has nothing to report. (McHale, 87)

McHale is here talking about those devices of postmodernist fiction that overtly challenge our sense of historical realism, such anachronistic outrages as a televised report of Abraham Lincoln's assassination,[1] compared to the more modest liberties taken by Walter Scott with historical events and personages. His statement suggests that we have some inbuilt sense of history that allows us to detect when an author deviates too far from accepted reality. Yet that sense of history which allows us to detect such blatant anachronisms as a telephone in Lincoln's Whitehouse is not intuition; the historical knowledge required to identify something as ahistorical here is basic, but is still acquired knowledge. This distinction becomes crucial when looking at *The Ultras'* relationship with real historical events, since it is not immediately obvious what liberties have been taken, and why. Whereas it requires only a little historical knowledge to spot blatant anachronisms, the more subtle rewriting of history undertaken by McNamee is more difficult to identify.

Yet McNamee is dealing with a period and set of events that one might legitimately claim to be entirely "dark" – not just about which the "official" record has nothing to report, but rather where the 'official' record is suspect and it is the very suspect nature of that record that is one of the subjects being explored. This is one of the features that Linda Hutcheon identifies as belonging to "historiographic metafiction":

> historiographic metafiction, […] plays upon the truth and lies of the historical record. In novels like *Foe, Burning Water*, or *Famous Last Words*, certain known historical details are deliberately falsified in order to foreground the possible mnemonic failures of recorded history and the constant potential for both deliberate and inadvertent error. (1996: 483)

However, this is not all McNamee is doing, as an examination of his use of known "facts" about Nairac's last few hours in the first chapter of *The Ultras* shows:

---

[1] McHale's example is Ishamael Reed's *Flight to Canada*.

All accounts place Robert in the bar. He sang Danny Boy. It was a favourite. He was attracted to the bogus émigré charm of it, the attempt at swamping melancholia. He had been there for several hours. He told the other drinkers that he was a PIRA operative called Danny McErlean from Belfast. They knew that he was lying. Robert went in without backup. That was the way he did it. He drove the red Dolomite from Bessbrook Mill to the Three Steps Inn. (1)

Several things stand out about this passage once some external journalistic accounts of Nairac's final hours are brought into the picture. McNamee chooses to give Robert's alias as Danny McErlean. In *The Dirty War*, Martin Dillon also names this as the pseudonym Nairac was using that night, although he makes much of the fact that it was remembered by drinkers in the bar as "Danny McElean", suggesting to Dillon that Nairac had not quite mastered the Irish accent of which he was so proud (Dillon, 170). This comic ineptitude also features heavily in *The Ultras*, as Nairac's handlers listen with horrified disbelief – and fascination – to his misplaced conviction in his ability to mimic the locals:

> David wanted to hear the accent. He wanted to hear the Guardsman do a Belfast accent, work his way into the consonantal squawks, the post-industrial falsetto, the semi-hysteric tailing off. But Nairac didn't do it. (45)

John Parker, in *Death of a Hero*, gives Nairac's alias as Danny McAlevey – a name that would be hard to mishear as McElean or McErlean, no matter how mangled the accent.[2] Where McNamee chooses one version of the known facts over another, he could be justifiably said to be drawing attention to "failures of recorded history and the constant potential for both deliberate and inadvertent error", but other aspects of his technique are not so easy to explain. Why, for example, is the car a red Triumph Dolomite, when both accounts already mentioned (accounts McNamee has obviously consulted) clearly state it was a Triumph Toledo? The change signals that McNamee does not feel himself constrained by the same rules as a biographer or journalist, or even the looser conventions of the postmodern fiction writer as outlined by McHale. Whereas the biographer or journalist can speculate around the known facts and even challenge their veracity, he cannot wilfully alter them to fit a preconceived notion of character. McNamee is likewise prepared to alter known "facts" that are more crucial to the story. Nairac's secret identity was actually that of a "sticky" – a member of the Official IRA, not the Provisionals, as McNamee states. Here the change is genuinely baffling: adopting an Official IRA cover would have been far more overtly risky than a PIRA one, which would have fitted the image McNamee paints of Nairac as a foolhardy risk-taker convinced of his own invulnerability. There seems no textual reason for the change, as if McNamee is simply being wilfully perverse. Yet the change is also too slight to simply be McNamee's way of muddying the waters, distancing his account from the actual events of Nairac's last days; this change would only be picked up by the reader prepared to study *The Ultras* alongside other more conventional texts about the case.

Not only are the historical facts changed, the change itself is not immediately obvious. This means that McNamee is not, here, deploying the misinformation in order to highlight the novel as an artificial construct, nor to make the reader aware of the slipperiness of history, because if either of these now-standard postmodern techniques were to be effective they would require the reader to have an awareness of the actual historical events that borders on the encyclopaedic. This then leaves the question of what exactly McNamee is doing.

---

[2] Parker (1999: 201) states: "In the pubs of Crossmaglen, Nairac had started to call himself Danny McAlevey, from Ardoyne, and apparently had a fake driving license with that name on it."

Once you start writing fiction that is close to real events, even if you're blurring the known facts with invention, then it becomes coy and bookish not to use the real names. (McNamee, 2001b: n.p.)

So writes McNamee in a review of David Peace's book about the last great miner's strike, *GB84*. In *Resurrection Man*, McNamee renames the infamous Lenny Murphy, leader of the Shankill Butchers, as Victor Kelly in his fictional retelling of those murders. In *The Ultras*, the real names are insisted upon – at least for the most part. Indeed, the 'Billy McClure' of *Resurrection Man* becomes William McGrath, thus making more explicit the textual importance of the associations that name possesses. Perhaps the McNamee of ten years ago was more coy and bookish than today, but a more likely explanation of the change of names is actually to heighten this "blurring the known facts with invention", and to place some distance between the fictional account and the historical one. Blurring this line between "fact" and "invention" is always controversial and never more so than with fresh, violent events; it invites charges firstly of disrespect to those involved in such events, but more subtly, of failing to pay respect to the sanctity of the historical record. However, McNamee deliberately chooses for his subjects historical events about which the facts are especially disputed. Moreover, they are events where the inability to move beyond supposition and conjecture to these supposed "known facts" is part of the atmosphere which he tries to evoke. From the same review, he continues:

And then there are the cases where it becomes something akin to an artistic imperative to drag people into the light. People whose lives are masterpieces of obfuscation and evasion, of whispered conspiracies and cold-hearted myth-making. People like Robert Nairac, people like Robin Jackson. The kind of light that I have tried to shed in *The Ultras*. (2004b: n.p.)

To "drag people into the light" is an odd phrase to use in association with McNamee's treatment of Captain Robert Nairac in *The Ultras*. From this statement, one would expect a work of the highest journalistic integrity, separating the murky world of myth and conspiracy theory from the "known facts". Yet McNamee sometimes provides ostensibly 'correct' historical details, and sometimes purposefully twists and misstates the facts. Some of these techniques are familiar to the world of the drama-documentary: the use of composite characters for example, or the telescoping of events separated by time or distance into one place and period. If these techniques were overt, or if we could assume our reader was near-omniscient of the stories of the historical Nairac, then we could read this as a now-standard technique of the postmodern novel. By presenting an obvious dissonance, such a work asks its reader to treat all information as suspect, all facts to be potentially fiction. Because *The Ultras* does not distinguish between well-sourced facts, conjecture, conspiracy theory, lack of information and simple error, this cannot be the effect. Here, the reader is in danger of falling into the same paranoiac state as the characters: he or she "knows" that this is a fictionalised account of actual historical events and that some details must, therefore, be "false". But to start searching for a grand narrative, the evidence of a conspiracy in these altered details is to miss the point. McNamee is attempting to create the impression of a factual narrative, not a fiction based on fact. Were he to use the known facts consistently, deviating only when matters were obscure or contested, his novel would be a (carefully coded) directed argument, establishing the facts of the case as he regards them. By wilfully altering minor details as well as major ones, he refuses to allow *The Ultras* to be considered as a historical corrective, replacing the official version of events with an alternative, more "correct" narrative.

In this sense, *The Ultras* might be said to be fulfilling Hutcheon's definition:

> Postmodern fiction suggests that to re-write or to re-present the past in fiction and in history is, in both cases, to open it up to the present, to prevent it from being conclusive and teleological. (1996: 479)

Except that the very conclusive nature of the past is precisely what McNamee is interested in. The way events play out as if all the participants have one eye on their representation, the way murderers plot the course of their own demise – or have it plotted for them. Moreover, he is specifically interested in the textual quality of this self-awareness. Speaking of *Blue Tango*, McNamee says:

> The more I read about the murder, and the investigation, the more noir-ish the world seemed … It was almost as if some of the protagonists, most notably the investigating officers, were acting in a stylised way learned from fiction and film. They knew what was required of them, the part they were to play in a script that had nothing to do with justice and everything to do with getting a conviction. A kind of old order had to be maintained, and individuals were sacrificed in order to maintain it. That's a motif that comes up time and time again in the post-war world of British crime. (McNamee in O'Hagan, n.p.)

McNamee's historical characters are, in many ways, less 'real' than entirely invented ones might be. He feels no responsibility to give them individual voices because he approaches them as already textualised, already elements in a fictive world. In studying Don DeLillo's mammoth work, *Underworld*, James Wood expertly identifies how DeLillo's theme infects the book's form:

> What is striking is how many paranoid people there are in Underworld, and how this multitude drives so many perforations of unreality into the book's form that its truths come to seem ragged and uncertain, while its untruths have an airy consistency. (199)

McNamee's characters are given a similar sort of consistency. Writing about his earlier work, *Resurrection Man*, Glenn Paterson has stated that McNamee's characters speak in: "an idiom which the reader has to strain to believe as belonging to any of the characters" (23). McNamee's characters seem complicit in his task of describing the world as a bleak, predestined Baudrillardian dystopia:

> Darkie was haunted by the idea that the photograph was always of the same man taken from different angles. He brought Heather a sheaf of photos clipped from different books. Look, he said, the same shabby grey suit, the ill-matched socks and pale shins revealed by trouser legs which weren't long enough. The same uneven pavement. The same sensation that the man had been working all his life to achieve this position, this carefully-contrived attitude of death something he had aspired to since birth. (McNamee, 1994: 92)

The gap between narrator and character here is practically non-existent. By the time we reach *The Ultras*, however, this attitude has extended even to the textualisation of this fatalism, and the relationship between author, narrator and character is more complex:

Knox said nothing. He was beginning to sense a structure to the things Agnew was telling him. There was a thematic progression which was stark, modernist... Agnew knew that Knox owned him, but felt an obligation to mark the moment with some hard bluster, feeling that it was expected of him at this point in the conversation. The point of hard talk usually preceded the point of weary ironies.
"Inform Jackson that he is an asset. At the minute. Inform him that assets can turn into liabilities very quickly."
Agnew could tell that Knox was pleased with the phrasing of that. Assets and liabilities. There was a menacing equilibrium to the sentence. However, he doubted that it would mean a fiddler's fuck to the likes of Jackson, whose life was posited on different orders of equilibrium, on the fundamentals of carnage. (37-8)

Here we can see the characters involved in a weary game of macho posturing, well aware of the rules of that game and the order of play. Yet Knox and Agnew are here almost comically aware of the overt textualisation of their conversation. The language of literary criticism is applied as if coming directly from the thoughts of these men, but it jostles for supremacy with the more earthy analysis of character and situation provided by "hard bluster" and "fiddler's fuck". The question remains as to how much McNamee wants his reader to believe that his characters actually think the way he is writing them. By shifting registers here so blatantly, it is tempting to suggest that he wants to alert his readers to the false thoughts he is planting in the minds of his characters, and that "fiddler's fuck" emerges as a powerful signal of their real thoughts. Yet Wood's insight about the effect of a multitude of paranoiac characters in *Underworld* applies equally well to *The Ultras*. Such moments of lexical inconsistency are common, but they are buried under the sheer weight of paranoiac prose in the idiom of an overbearing interlocutor. McNamee's characters are not all uniform in their suspicions, but those suspicions all begin to sound the same. The end result is that the reader is left without a variety of viewpoints: one character's conspiracy theory, because it is couched in the same terms, slots very neatly into another's, without an external voice of rationality.

One of the functions of the novelist is to uncover or suggest connections that are not immediately apparent. Those connections may be thematic parallels between insanity and war, as in Joseph Heller's *Catch-22*, or they may be scraps of common humanity amidst cultural alienation, as in E.M. Forster's *A Passage to India*. As an artistic imperative, this act can create a novel greater than the sum of its plot and characters, suggesting a much wider significance to the work. Carried too far, however, the act of finding connections goes beyond an artistic duty and becomes an obsession, and an obsessive devotion to discovering hidden connections is the mark of the paranoiac and the conspiracy theorist. It is this connection between the novelist – specifically, the novelist dealing with historical actuality – and the paranoiac that McNamee explores in *The Ultras*, both through his theme of the shadowy "dirty war" in Northern Ireland and the characters involved with it, but also through the form of his book and the identification he shows as an author and unreliable narrator of events with those characters.

The narrative makes explicit the working methods behind the production of McNamee's brand of historical fiction based on fact. Through the example of his characters' obsessive collection of information, McNamee addresses the difficulties and absurdities of the novelist's own compromises and accommodations that he finds necessary when writing fiction about actual events and people.

The novel imagines his slow undoing, the execution and disposal of his remains. And, by conjecture, it links his presence to another mythic event – the bombing in 1975 of the Miami Showband, an infamous borderland atrocity. The blending of fact and fiction is stealthily managed. The world of security agents and terrorists sticks to the page like dirty goods. The verisimilitude of acronyms stipples the prose: MI5, 14th Int, MRU, IntCom, PsyOps and MI6. (Adair, n.p.)

In fact, it is unclear as to whether the "blending" or even 'blurring' of fact and fiction is entirely McNamee's goal in *The Ultras*. Certainly, it is unclear from a reading of *The Ultras* alone which details of the novel are factual and which are fictional, but this indicates more than that these details are murky, difficult to decipher. The characters in *The Ultras* attach great importance to physical evidence: photos, documents, film. Yet as the novel progresses, it becomes clear how inadequate such means are of grasping a truth. McNamee is also concerned with the potential for deliberate misuse of data whether or not the facts are accurate. A hidden camera used to blackmail the clients of a brothel is turned against its operators by being used to film a brutal murder, the film left in the reel as a warning. There is also the cover-up that McNamee describes surrounding Nairac himself, the conspiracy that Blair Agnew, himself surrounded by thousands of documents that are slowly rotting beyond use, attempts to pierce.

Blair Agnew is one of the principal characters of *The Ultras*, both a participant in and a researcher of Nairac's activities. A policeman who never quite seems sure whether or not he is working undercover, he is present at the botched loyalist operation that leads to the murder of several members of the Miami Showband and the deaths of two of the paramilitaries when the bomb they are planting in the band's van explodes prematurely. One of the moments of violence around which the book is structured is also handled unusually as McNamee's writing is almost blasé in its description of the explosion and of the deaths of Loyalists Boyle and Somerville. McNamee quite deliberately places the explosion in the middle of a sentence itself in the middle of a dense paragraph, the effect being to surprise the reader, especially since there has been no direct foreshadowing of what is to come as one might expect. For example Agnew, our focus for this paper, is more interested in Jackson's interrogation of the band members and the possibility of Nairac's presence on a distant hill than with the details of the operation. There is considerable irony in this; Agnew has constantly attempted to elicit information from the Ultras about the exact nature of the operation, despite their heightening suspicion of him, but never quite gets an answer. Afterwards, he becomes obsessed with the tiniest details, not just of the explosion and gunning down of the Miami Show Band, but also of the career of Nairac. As readers, the explosion may take us by surprise, but we have the luxury of returning to it and re-reading the incident as it was narrated. Agnew, who was there, has no such short-cut to represent the event in his memory. McNamee's technique here, and our reaction to it as readers, parallels Agnew's own lack of attention, and the way this incident took him, too, by surprise. It may also reflect the teleological distorting effect of Agnew's later obsession with Nairac as he runs over the events in his past.

The novel is shaped by several violent, ambiguously-presented acts besides the Showband massacre. It opens with the disappearance and presumed murder of Nairac, and closes with the suicide of Agnew's daughter, Lorna. The twin timelines of the novel are structured so as to provide the irony of Agnew's obsessive collection of vast quantities of historical data on Nairac with his inability (or unwillingness) to find the single slim volume of Lorna's diary that might provide a clue to arresting her self-destructive slide. "Knowledge" is presented again and again as being compromised by the character's inability to approach it without distorting it. Partly this is due to the way the weight of that data and the analysis of it begins to warp over time. Describing an infamous Polaroid photograph of John Francis Green, an alleged IRA commander killed just over the Armagh border, the narration claims:

Later in his life he would say that something in him anticipated the shadowy trajectory that the photograph would take, its provenance becoming uncertain, its very existence being questioned, its meaning transmuting. It gathered authority to itself. Its jurisdiction was unwavering. (175)

The Polaroid is crucial, since it provides one of only two pieces of material evidence that links Nairac with the Green shooting and hence, tenuously, with the Miami Show Band massacre, due to the fact that the same Star pistol was used in both. The formulation 'Later in his life he would say' foregrounds the teleological nature of all history, whether it is a journalistic investigation or a personal recollection, and the way in which knowledge of outcomes distorts the reporting of past events. Time and again in *The Ultras*, we are made aware of the constructed nature of the "facts" and the futility of Agnew's obsession with collecting them all.

When Agnew begins bringing home stolen photographs belonging to the families awoken in pre-dawn raids, he explains them to his lover, Janet, as pictures of his own family. The absurdity of this deception is highlighted by Janet's erroneous identification of one young boy as Agnew himself:

She sat down beside him, picking out photographs, dwelling on the mothers, the children. He gave them histories, devised small, poignant events occurring in childhood. He ascribed elements of quiet heroism to the women, cited examples of selflessness. He found that he couldn't stop adding incident to their lives. Janet picked up a photograph of a small boy wearing shorts.

'That's you, isn't it?' she said.
'That's me,' he said. 'I was in the scouts. Five years old.' (65)

Agnew himself can't resist the irony of describing himself as a boy scout even as his lies get more and more outrageous. His self-destructive compulsion to fabricate stories can perhaps be seen as mirroring McNamee's own efforts in "adding incident" to his own characters' lives. A central motif in McNamee's *The Blue Tango* was a single newspaper picture of a murdered teenage girl, the dark spaces of which come to represent the lacunae McNamee attempts to fill in with invented narrative. *The Ultras*' use of the motif of evidence is more complex: from Agnew's rotting files to Nairac's collection of illicit crime-scene photos to the clandestine camera in the Gemini club, the means of collecting information in *The Ultras* are all flawed, all compromised, and some are even turned on their supposed masters. Yet, as suggested, McNamee is not merely saying that all information is suspect, that there is no such thing as fact. Throughout the novel, Agnew is exhorted by his ex-wife to search for their daughter Lorna's secret diary, in the belief that it may help them arrest her slide into anorexia and depression. Lorna commits suicide at the end of *The Ultras*, and Agnew finally finds the diary, something he could realistically have managed at any time. As he finds it, once again we are plunged into the murky world of conspiracies, secrets and the occult: "The binding had come loose, and the cover was foxed and stained. It had the feel of a document that had lain unopened in an archive for decades" (253). Yet the last chapter of the novel is given over to the last entry in this diary, written in a notably different style and without overt authorial intervention. We are aware here that, perhaps, this apparently unmediated document could have saved Lorna's life, had it been found earlier. Lorna's thoughts are scattered and confused, but there is no deliberate deception. What there is, is a desperate desire to hide, to be secret:

I can't help thinking about Robert I look at his photograph I look into his eyes. I can't see anything there. Maybe that is the meaning of the word ultra. That you are ultra secret and do not give away anything no matter what. That they look and look and look and cannot find you. When I was small I hid in the dark and they called but I did not come out. Each to his own Robert had to learn his own secrets I had to learn mine but I think his secrets were about killing lots of people and mine are just sad secrets a bit pathetic really that you learn to stop them getting near you to stop them feeding you when you don't want. That to wear big clothes to hide you. That to drink water then more water to fill you and clean you as clean as a whistle on the inside. To hang your hair over your face to hide you. That to hide you that to hide you. (255-6)

Agnew's method of collection is quite different from Lorna's. While Agnew displays a desire to collect and collate every single piece of documentary evidence available on Nairac, Lorna is content to raid her father's files and randomly select documents to read. She also periodically raids the files that her mother keeps on Agnew, all while her mother is desperately attempting to gain access to her daughter's diary. This farcical scenario is, on the one hand, an expression of the seductive power of documentary sources, the promise they hold of original evidence, eyewitness statements and contemporary photographs. The members of this broken family are unable to talk to each other, but are still fascinated with each other to the extent of searching for hidden answers. But some sources of evidence derive their power from their very secrecy or contested nature. For the conspiracy theorist, nothing is more alluring than the idea of the concealed document, the doctored photograph, the missing frames of film. Hence Lorna's destructive fascination with the power of the ultra-secret, and with finding a connection – however pathetic – with the paranoiac world of Nairac. Ultimately, however, *The Ultras* is an account of McNamee's fascination with Nairac:

> Peter Wild: Many biographers claim to fall out of love (or at the very least cease to be fascinated) by the object of their attention as the work proceeds. Was that the case with you and Captain Nairac?
>
> Eoin McNamee: In terms of the way biographers approach their subject ... I suppose there is an imperative to like your subject, which I didn't really feel. One interesting thing here is that you would expect to acquire some intimacy with your subject, but Nairac resisted enquiry and intimacy. At the end of the book I adapted Nietzsche's dictum that when you look long into the abyss, the abyss also looks into you. Substitute void for abyss and you have the way I felt about Robert Nairac. (Wild, n.p.)

We have already seen that McNamee does not feel himself constrained by the same conventions as biographers in terms of working with the known facts. Another implicit convention, that a biography is an attempt to explain someone's entire life (as the etymology of the term would suggest) is also being rejected by McNamee here. Evidently a conventional biography would not, McNamee implies, adequately express the 'void', the ineffable quality which he detects in Nairac.

Ultimately, the form of *The Ultras* is paranoiac: the reader is made aware on two levels of the importance of fact. The characters themselves in the plot are continuously searching for reliable information about both the present and the past, and the vagaries of this process are continually foregrounded. Yet on a formal level, we are made aware, if we did not already know from an extra-textual source, that *The Ultras* is based on actual historical events, by reference to other sources, documents, accounts. We are, as a result, constantly, numbingly suspicious of the authority of the text. It is impossible to simply ignore the possibility that McNamee may be presenting us with "false" information, because the characters receive it all the time, usually with disastrous consequences. This fictionalised account cannot be read merely on the level of a 'purely' fictional novel. Yet to go through *The Ultras* obsessively checking facts and hunting for meaning in each deviation or apparently arbitrary clarification is itself the behaviour of an obsessive paranoiac. Stylistically, this effect is reliant on the overarching idiom of a narrator himself obsessed with the predetermined nature of things, one who presents his characters' paranoia through the prism of his own language, thus preventing the reader from gaining any sense that this overarching paranoiac vision is not reality as the characters see it.

## References

Adair, Tom. 2004. "Provisional Realities: Interview with Eoin McNamee." *Scotsman*.http://news.scotsma.com/features.cfm?id=459502004. Consulted 5 May 2005.

Dillon, Martin. 1991. *The Dirty War*. London: Arrow

Hutcheon, Linda. 1996. "'The Pastime of Past Time: Fiction, History, Historiographical Metafiction." *Essentials of the Theory of Fiction*. Eds. Michael J. Hoffman and Patrick D. Murphy. 2nd Edition. London: Leicester University Press

McHale, Brian. 1987. *Postmodernist Fiction*. London: Routledge

McNamee, Eoin. 1994. *Resurrection Man*. London: Faber, 1994

McNamee, Eoin. 2004a. *The Ultras*. London: Faber

McNamee, Eoin. 2004b. "Hand-held Narrative." *Guardian* 30 April: n.p.

O'Hagan, Sean. 2001. "Dreaming Blue Murder." *Observer*. 8 July: n.p.

Parker, John. 1999. *Death of a Hero: Captain Robert Nairac G.C., and the Undercover War in Northern Ireland*. London: Metro

Patterson, Glenn. "Reclaiming the Writing from the Walls." *Independent*. 9 September: Arts, 23

Wild, Peter. Interview with Eoin McNamee. *Bookmunch*. 24 June 2004 http://www.bookmunch.co.uk/view.php?id=1378. Consulted 5 May 2005

Wood, James. 1999. *The Broken Estate*. London: Cape

# Tobias Smollett, Gentleman and Novelist: A Contradiction in Terms?

*Carol Stewart*

When Tobias Smollett published his first novel, *Roderick Random*, in 1748, it must have seemed that prose fiction, now given a degree of legitimacy by Samuel Richardson and Henry Fielding, offered a largely unexplored, and potentially respectable, literary arena. Richardson's novel *Pamela* was published in November 1740 and it received unprecedented attention and acclaim. The Rev Benjamin Slocock recommended *Pamela* from the pulpit of St. Saviour's Church in Southwark in December of that year, and by January 1741 the *Gentleman's Magazine* judged that it was "as great a Sign of Want of Curiosity not to have read *Pamela* as not to have seen the French and Italian dancers". Plays based on the novel, spurious sequels to it, and Richardson's own continuation of the work in *Pamela in Her Exalted Condition* (1741) soon followed. Fielding's *Joseph Andrews* (1742), purporting to be the story of Pamela's brother, but actually a 'comic epic' in its own right, was one of many works to trade on Richardson's success. A new market for fiction as a morally respectable medium was being created. The final volumes of Richardson's *Clarissa* came out in 1748 and Fielding's *Tom Jones* followed in 1749. Both of these were works of epic length and huge ambition. Smollett's endeavours in the 1740s in the realm of drama, on the other hand, had met with little success. He had experienced many frustrations and humiliations while trying, and ultimately failing, to get his play, *The Regicide*, staged in London. This was a disappointment which he felt very acutely. The story of the eight years which elapsed between 1739 and 1747 as he approached theatre managers John Rich and James Lacy, and other patrons, was rehearsed in fictionalised form in Melopoyn's tale in *Roderick Random*, elaborated in the preface to the printed version of the play, finally published in 1749, and alluded to again, at least twice, in *Peregrine Pickle*, Smollett's novel of 1751. Howard Buck (1925: 54) goes so far as to say that all Smollett's many literary quarrels may be traced back to the matter of *The Regicide*. A novel, though, stood in less need of patronage or an entrée into London's literary cliques. It might provide a focus for Smollett's considerable energies and ambitions. It could, in fact, make him independent of patronage when those in a position to offer it were, as Smollett represents the matter, either corrupt, or simply devoid of true taste.

For Smollett, independence had personal, political and perhaps even national dimensions. Independence deriving from the ownership of land was one sure sign of a gentleman, but Smollett himself was not in that fortunate position. He was the younger son of a younger son, whose father had married, without parental consent, a woman without money. Though he described himself, defiantly, as a "gentleman by birth, profession and education" in a letter of 1753 (Knapp, 1970: 23), he lacked more solid credentials, as the rather defensive formulation might itself suggest. It was with this issue in mind, presumably, that he used some lines from Horace's Satires as the epigraph to *Roderick Random*, his semi-autobiographical novel: "And yet birth and worth without substance, are more paltry than seaweed" (Smollett, 1979: 437n).

Independence of patronage was also a political issue. In Opposition writing of the previous thirty years – that is to say, the writing of Swift, Gay and especially Pope – the independence of the landed country gentleman had been represented as safeguarding British liberty at a time when Walpole and the Whigs had surrendered it to monied interests (cf. Ross, 1982). The financial independence of the country gentleman was the best guarantee of his integrity, and disinterested love of country. For eighteenth-century Scottish writers like Smollett and Henry Mackenzie, the issue of independence had another dimension. "In 1707", argues John Robertson (1983: 137), "Scotland effectively faced a choice: either the nation preserved its existing political institutions at the cost of severely restricting its economic opportunities, or it yielded up its institutional independence and accepted union with England in return for free trade across the border and access to the English commercial empire." The Act of Union, then, gave the priority to commerce and wealth. So, in terms of the tradition which J.G.A. Pocock (1975) has termed "civic humanist", this meant that Scotland, by virtue of the Act of Union, had lost the basis for independent, and therefore uncorrupted, virtuous activity on the part of those citizens who would have formed the élite. Given the inescapability of the market in the eighteenth century, and particularly in the later eighteenth century, this predicament might not only present itself in Scotland, but English writers seem fairly untroubled by it. Smollett and Mackenzie, though, plainly are troubled by the potential conflict between independence and involvement in the market, and the lack of a truly independent and effectual protagonist anywhere in Mackenzie's fiction is telling.

The country gentleman figures in all but one of Smollett's novels: as desired end-point in *Roderick Random*, as endangered ideal in *Peregrine Pickle*, as possible anachronism in *Sir Launcelot Greaves* (1760-61), and as one rather more privileged voice, among others, in the epistolary *Humphry Clinker* (1771). But as this brief summary might indicate, the ideal of the country gentleman was waning, and it was not a role which Smollett himself could ever hope to fulfil. Perhaps, though, the role of country gentleman as moral conscience of the nation could be taken up by the professionally independent gentleman.

In *Roderick Random*, the hero's brief career as naval surgeon offers one conception of the professional man as guardian – albeit beleaguered guardian – of British liberty. (Smollett himself was a naval surgeon for eighteen months.) Roderick is pressed aboard the *Thunder*, and gains a position from which lack of money had previously debarred him. Even after passing examination by the Surgeon's Hall, he would have to have paid a bribe to the secretary at the Navy-Office and to the naval commissioners. As soon as the *Thunder* sets sail, the tyrannical Captain Oakhum orders the sick to be brought on deck. Here they are made to work, and all but a few die. When a sailor's leg is broken in a storm, Mackshane, the chief surgeon, is too terrified to come on deck to treat him. Mackshane recommends an unnecessary amputation, a course only avoided thanks to the intervention of Morgan, another surgeon, and Roderick. In revenge, Mackshane has Roderick tied down to the deck, from where he witnesses what seems to be a largely unnecessary engagement with a French man of war. The head of a marine is shot off and lands on Roderick's face. A drummer is disembowelled by another shot and lands on his chest.

Preventing a total descent into chaos and corruption, however, is the society of professional men, drawn from all quarters of Britain: Morgan the Welshman, Thomson the Englishman and Roderick the Scot. The ship of state is only kept afloat, as it were, by these professional men. They bond together against the common enemies, for, as we discover, Oakhum and Mackshane are both Irish Roman Catholics. The professional man here is the upholder of justice and the law. Morgan is tied down to the deck on suspicion of mutiny, but the captain is soon ready to release him again, quite arbitrarily. As a Protestant, of course, Morgan prefers justice and the law to arbitrary rule, and Oakhum is forced, by him, to go through the motions of a trial. The professional man might also be the guardian of culture. Roderick is accused of conspiring to kill the captain, partly on the basis of a journal found in his chest which appears to be written in code. As Roderick tells his accusers, it is actually a diary of the voyage written in classical Greek. Morgan, Roderick's fellow surgeon and gentleman-in-distress, can read and understand it. Mackshane reads it as Irish – or, "some gibberish" (175), as Roderick puts it. Two of the crew who had travelled in the Levant are called in to verify Roderick's writing as Greek, but they are illiterate and Roderick cannot understand the "barbarous corrupted language"(176) – the Greek vernacular – that they speak. Roderick's education, and his facility with language, is of no immediate use to him here, but perhaps this is precisely the point. One definition of gentlemanly knowledge might be that it is practically useless, as the true gentleman did not need to work. The diary in Greek offers an image of the material of chaos – the voyage – over-written, as it were, by another language of ancient pedigree in the possession of a select group.

Smollett used *Roderick Random* to comment on matters of national importance: the disastrous British siege of Carthagena, in particular, and more broadly, the moral degradation of almost every public office. There is little record of actual commentary on the novel, but it was the work with which he was most consistently associated. Some verses written at the time of his death speak of "Death's *Random* darts" (Kelly 1987: 216). *Roderick Random* helped to establish Smollett as a public figure. Three years later, with a successful novel behind him, Smollett published *Peregrine Pickle*, in which the situation of the eponymous hero is also much more secure. Peregrine is the eldest son of the owner of the family estate. Half-way through the novel, he inherits £30,000 and property from his uncle. Peregrine here attains a situation of independence which Roderick Random only achieves at the conclusion of the earlier novel. However, Peregrine's claim to the rank of gentleman is actually based on unstable foundations. The opening of the novel makes clear how fragile are the Pickle family's claims to gentility. Their lineage was not, as Smollett (3) writes, "to be traced two generations back, by all the power of heraldry or tradition". Peregrine's father, Gamaliel, is the son of a merchant who has acquired his money by trade. Gamaliel has retired to an estate in the country not because of some Horatian ideal, but because he is ineffectual, and incapable of amassing more money: after fifteen years in trade he has lost five thousand pounds of his father's bequest.

It is important, then, that as in effect a first-generation gentleman – that is to say, a man whose rank is only one generation removed from trade – Peregrine should live up to his responsibilities. His early attributes are promising. He has an instinct for the "right" kind of authority: at school, another arbitrary master, Keypstick, incurs his "contempt and displeasure" (57). As soon as the assistant teacher, Jennings (who practises Lockean methods of education and control) leaves the boarding school at which he has been placed, Peregrine asks to be removed from it. Yet he is also inordinately proud. As soon as he excels at school, he becomes even more ambitious, and subjects all his fellow pupils by force. At Winchester, he leads a rebellion, rather than submit to public punishment. In due course, he fears that his passion for Emilia, who has no fortune, may detract from his own dignity. The prospect of travelling in Europe flatters his vanity and ambition. Once abroad he engages in a series of ill-advised sexual liaisons.

Back in England, Peregrine courts the favour of noblemen, and makes an appearance in the fashionable world, determined to live up to the reports of his great fortune. He believes that he will be able to marry an heiress, or a rich widow, before his funds are exhausted. Later, he is under the protection of a nobleman, at whose instigation he decides to contest an election for Member of Parliament; and within a few chapters, with his fortune nearly exhausted, he is styled "Minister's Dependent" (618).

Smollett still insists on Peregrine's exercise of gentlemanly prerogatives in unlikely or incongruous situations, indicating his sense that the responsibilities of the gentleman could be transferred to less traditional spheres of activity. In the same chapter in which the hero begins to be initiated into the London *beau monde*, he also undertakes the supervision of his sister's marriage. Peregrine's unappealing behaviour with Emilia, whom he tries to rape at one point, contrasts with his care of his uncle during the commodore's illness, and his insistence that he should not be the only beneficiary of his uncle's will. At the same time that he is "panting with the desire" (365) to distinguish himself in Bath, he interests himself on behalf of Godfrey, Emilia's brother, and gains him a commssion. Moreover, if the Pickle family's claims to gentility are fragile, and Peregrine's own conduct endangers his independence, he has an alternative, and apparently entirely stable career as moral censor and critic. The account of the "practical satire" with which he exposes, and punishes, libertines, homosexuals, social climbers, card-sharpers, pedants, republican or High Church sympathisers, and pretenders to taste, is practically a separate narrative, apparently unimplicated in the story of Peregrine's own moral decline.

Peregrine Pickle can be read as articulating the fear that the position of the gentry would be undermined by dependency. Given that the novel ends with Peregrine morally reformed and inheriting his father's estate, we can see it as arguing for a continuation of the old order. It can be read, though, as an account of the transference of the responsibility for upholding what was conceived of as the character of the nation from the landed gentleman, to the writer and critic: a person of uncertain social status. Towards the end of the novel, Peregrine himself becomes a writer and critic. In the same chapter that Peregrine discovers that he will never be able to recover the £10,000 he lent to a now-deceased nobleman, he recommences as author, and is invited to join what might be construed as a professional society, in the form of the "college of authors" (638). As member of the college, two chapters later, he is able to carry out the duties of a gentleman, and earn the respect to which a gentleman would be entitled. He uses his influence with the creditor of an imprisoned writer to facilitate the writer's release. On the other hand, *Peregrine Pickle* can also be read as a metaphor for Smollett's deep ambivalence about involvement in the market. As a gentleman, Peregrine is only at one remove from trade. His own ambition and love of reputation, not to mention his need of money on a practical level, has the potential to push him into a state of dependency. The novel offers us a character almost split into two halves: a morally compromised gentleman by birth, and a seemingly rootless but morally impeccable writer and critic.

The schematic tendency is even more marked in Smollett's third novel, *Ferdinand Count Fathom*. Fathom is the arch-villain, and bastard son of an unknown father and an English camp follower, born in a wagon travelling between Holland and Flanders. He is the binary opposite of the faultless Renaldo Melvile, son of a count, with whom he is brought up as a brother. In contrast with Smollett's other heroes of mixed moral character, Fathom is completely heartless. But apart from cheating at cards, plagiarising essays, stealing, and seducing virgins, his career is not dissimilar to theirs, or Smollett's. He is engaged in the pursuit of reputation and money. Like Smollett in relation to his characters, Fathom is master of various languages and dialects. In Paris, Fathom is believed to be, variously, from provincial France, Tuscany, Germany, Holland and England, and is supposed to be "a personage of great consequence" (90). He endlessly reconstructs himself for public approval. With an Italian he discourses on music, with a French abbé, he talks of taste and genius, of industry with the Dutchman, and endears himself to the Englishman by not talking to him at all. Settled in England, he gains the approval of the nobility by expounding on mathematics, politics, military strategy, painting and music: there is a parallel here with Smollett's career as editor of and chief contributor to the *Critical Review*, founded in 1756. Like Smollett in his career as critic, he cultivates the taste by which he himself might be appreciated. Once established in society, Fathom is able to sell diamonds of uncertain value at three times their cost. He counterfeits Cremona violins. "[H]e himself" writes Smollett, "was astonished at the infatuation he had produced. Nothing was so wretched among the productions of art, that he could not impose upon the world as a capital performance" (151). When Fathom appears in the novel, very briefly, as an author, he has lost the appearance of a gentleman: "his watch [...] began, about this time, to be very much out of order, and was committed to the care of a mender, who was in no hurry to restore it. His tye-wig degenerated [...] he sometimes appeared without a sword, and was even observed in public with a second day's shirt: at last, his cloaths became rusty" (269).

Why does Smollett's third novel present such a striking image of lost personal integrity? The answer may lie in the critical reception of *Peregrine Pickle*, and Smollett's response to it.

Reaction to *Peregrine Pickle* had been mixed. Reviews in the *Monthly* and *The Royal Magazine* were not unfavourable, with John Cleland in the former offering a measured defence of Smollett's use of "low" material. However, Cleland (Kelly 1987: 54), commented, urbanely, that "to pronounce with an air of decision, that [Smollett] has every where preserved propriety and nature, would sound more towards interested commendation than genuine criticism". Cleland extracted episodes involving Peregrine's satirical verses on the low birth of his tutor Jumble, and the perforation of Mrs. Trunnion's chamberpot, to allow readers to form their own judgement. The reviewer in the *Royal Magazine* (Kelly 1987: 60) wrote: "Our author fills several pages with a minute account of the many pranks play'd by Peregrine, till he arrived at the age of twelve years, the narration whereof can be no ways entertaining to those, who are older than Peregrine is said to have been." Some of Peregrine's subsequent "outrages, irregularities and indiscretions" might have been better omitted. Smollett railed against the restrictions which critics would impose on him in a lengthy diatribe early in *Ferdinand Count Fathom*. It begins: "Have a little patience, gentle, delicate, sublime, critic; you, I doubt not, are one of those consummate connoisseurs, who in their purifications, let humour evaporate, while they endeavour to preserve decorum, and polish wit, until the edge of it is quite wore off" (7-8). These hypocritical readers might "explore the jakes of Rabelais, for amusement, and even extract humour from the dean's description of a lady's dressing-room" – but would stop their nose at the bare mention of a china chamber-pot. What is at issue here, really, is Smollett's awareness that he would have to take account of the shift in the direction of "feminised" standards of taste. For gentle and delicate, in the description of the reader, we might read "female". Whatever, Smollett's protestations, and posture of independence – he dedicates the novel to *himself* – *Ferdinand Count Fathom* itself actually makes many concessions to feminised standards of taste. Only three chapters (the scenes in prison) contain any swearing. There are no perforated chamber-pots, no urine in beds. There are plots of persecuted female virtue more characteristic of Richardson. Fathom's own feminisation figures as a facility in music. Richard Leppert (1988: 24) has noted that conduct book writers of the period generally agreed that music was improper for a gentleman because it was unmanly. Repeated reference is made to Fathom's ability, however. At one point he makes use of this facility to court the approval of his female audience and then refuses to gratify it. Some women admirers ask him to play the violin, but, we read, "it was his interest to inflame their impatience, rather than to gratify their expectation: and therefore he tantalized them for some hours, by tuning his violin, and playing some flourishes, which, however, produced nothing to fulfil their wishes" (249). Smollett courting female taste for his own interests but refusing to become completely de-masculinised, perhaps?

However, if Fathom's machinations are generally successful, he is also prone, throughout the novel, to fall foul of the power and influence of women, at the very same time that he is trying to court them. Pursuing a simultaneous intrigue with the Wilhemina, the jeweller's daughter, and her step-mother, he twice finds himself trapped in a cupboard in Wilhemina's room. In England, he conducts an affair with Mrs. Trapwell, only to find himself the victim of a plot by the husband to extort money from him. He is subsequently involved in a lawsuit and imprisoned; "deprived" as Smollett puts it, "of his reputation, rank, liberty and friends; and his fortune reduced from two thousand pounds, to something less than two hundred" (181). Other women in the novel place him in situations of fear or degradation. Travelling through German woods at night in the middle of a storm, he takes refuge in a lonely cottage, the sole occupant of which is a seemingly hospitable old woman. When he retires to his room, he finds himself locked in with a corpse. The woman and her family conspire, it seems, to kill and rob passing travellers.

Seven years elapsed before Smollett published another novel, though a revised edition of *Peregrine Pickle* did appear in 1758. From 1760 to 1761, Smollett published *Sir Launcelot*

*Greaves* in serial form in the *British Magazine*, a journal which Smollett himself founded. Its method of publication, as well as its content, suggests that Smollett's sense of himself as, on the one hand, a gentleman who fulfilled his role by upholding moral standards, and, on the other, as a professional gentleman who worked for a living, were beginning to cohere. The decision to publish the novel in serial form made sound commercial sense. Smollett had written *Roderick Random* in eight months in 1747-48 by devoting himself exclusively to that task, but by 1759-60, his numerous other commitments made it impossible to take such a single-minded approach to the composition of a novel. By serialising the work, he could realise an income from *Sir Launcelot Greaves* as he wrote it. He could gauge the public's response before committing himself to a protracted piece of writing. Less text was required, and Smollett was even able to send his instalments by post whilst on a journey to Scotland. Publication in a magazine meant access to a wider readership, and initial printing costs were avoided. It is telling, then, that the narrative itself is shared by Sir Launcelot, a quixotic baronet who is on a quest to right wrongs and expose corruption, and a group of professional men: Mr. Fillet, a surgeon and midwife, Captain Crowe, a naval officer, and Thomas Clarke, an attorney.

In the second instalment, Launcelot describes his aims: "I do purpose [...] to act as a coadjutor to the law, and even to remedy evils which the law cannot reach; to detect fraud and treason, abase insolence, mortify pride, discourage slander, disgrace immodesty, and stigmatize ingratitude" (14). As it turns out, though, he is far from self-sufficient, or completely effectual; he needs professional assistance, and it is actually the group of professional gentlemen who appear first, in the first instalment. By 1761, the dream of independence, status and a social role that is Sir Launcelot Greaves, had less to do with the by now anachronistic ideal of the country gentleman, than it had with a conception of the role of the writer. The fact that Smollett used *Don Quixote* as his model for the novel suggests that he himself recognised the anachronism. It is the professional gentlemen, rather, who cohere around the ethic Greaves proposes. Moreover, Sir Launcelot himself is a feminised man, very much in the Grandisonian mode. His morals are exemplary: there is no question of intrigues or sexual misadventures. Although he wears armour, and carries a lance, he seldom engages in physical combat. He is more likely to serve his opponents with a writ. Typically, he wreaks a change in reprobates by the power of words alone.

Did the novel offer Smollett the independence that he dreamt of? Not in any absolute sense. Novels catered to the market, and there ended any possibility of pristine autonomy. Whatever the unwelcome compromises, though, Smollett's career as an author of fiction, and the concerns of national moment which his novels took on, indicated that the professional novelist need not be a mere hack, nor an obscure and anonymous figure. He might, after all, approximate to what was traditionally conceived of as the character of a gentleman.

## References

Buck, Howard. 1925. *A Study in Smollett*. New Haven: Yale University Press

Kelly, Lionel, ed. 1987. *Tobias Smollett: The Critical Heritage*. London: Routledge and Kegan Paul

Knapp, Lewis, ed. 1970. *The Letters of Tobias Smollett*. Oxford: Clarendon Press

Pocock, J.G.A. 1975. *The Machiavellian Moment: Florentine Political Thought and the Atlantic Republican Tradition*. Princeton: Princeton University Press

Robertson, John. 1983. "The Scottish Enlightenment at the Limits of the Civic Tradition". In *Wealth and Virtue: The Shaping of the Political Economy in the Scottish Enlightenment*. Eds. Istvan Hont and Michael Ignatieff. Cambridge: Cambridge University Press

Ross, Ian Campbell. 1982. "'With Dignity and Importance': Peregrine Pickle as Country Gentleman". In *Smollett: Author of the First Distinction*. Ed. Alan Bold. London: Vision and Barnes and Noble. 148-169

Smollett, Tobias. 1964. *The Adventures of Peregrine Pickle*. Ed. James L. Clifford. London: Oxford University Press

Smollett, Tobias. 1971. *The Adventures of Ferdinand Count Fathom*. Ed. Damien Grant. London: Oxford University Press

Smollett, Tobias. 1973. *The Life and Adventures of Sir Launcelot Greaves*. Ed. David Evans. London: Oxford University Press

Smollett, Tobias. 1979. *The Adventures of Roderick Random*. Ed. Paul-Gabriel Boucé. Oxford: Oxford University Press

# Goths and Celts: Interlocking Myths of Ethnic Identity

*Brendan Sweeney*

During the last two centuries, the Celtic heritage of the British Isles has provided a foundation myth for the construction of national identities in Ireland, Scotland and Wales. But the literature created by this revival also had a huge influence on the rest of Europe – and especially on Sweden which is my own field of study. Narrative templates from Scotland and Ireland were employed by Northern Europeans to reinterpret their own past, and in Sweden many of the attributes of the ancient Celts were successfully reformulated within the context of their own Gothic heritage. In this paper I will explore the influence of the Celtic revival on constructions of national identity in Sweden, and show how literature inspired by Celtic mythology allowed the Swedish elite to reinterpret their own foundation myths.

## Defining Myth

More than anyone else, Anthony D Smith, the leading proponent of the ethno-symbolist theory of nationalism, has argued for the significance of mythmaking to the development of modern national and ethnic identities. In *Myths and Memories of the Nation*, he states:

> Since the late eighteenth century, spokesmen for every ethnic community have made frequent appeals to their alleged ancestry and histories, in their struggle for recognition, rights and independence. In the course of these struggles, ethnic spokesmen have drawn on, or in some cases invented, a 'myth of origins and descent' which then inspired writers and artists to recreate for their publics the events, atmosphere, and heroic examples of remote archaic eras found in the epics and sagas of Homer and Aeschylus, Dante, Ossian and the Edda. (Smith, 1999: 60)

By the mid-nineteenth century, most of Western and Eastern Europe was caught up in the romantic quest for origins, and during the following century the search for ethnic roots spread to Asia and Africa (ibid).

Smith identifies many different categories of ethnic and national myth, and focuses particularly on myths of origins and chosenness, but he does not specify exactly what a myth is. For that I would like to refer to the work of Bruce Lincoln, a specialist in Indo-European and Middle Eastern religions. Like Smith, Lincoln regards myths as powerful narratives which consolidate and maintain ethnic and national identity, but, in addition, he categorises them along with other forms of narrative according to the *credibility, truth-claims* and the *authority* invoked by their authors. Under Lincoln's system of classification, myth can be directly compared with history, legend and fable as narrative forms, and may be regarded as a more powerful narrative even than history since it is frequently backed up by the authority of the state (Lincoln, 1989: 24 ff).

Lincoln also makes what I consider to be an important point regarding the formation of myth, namely that myth thrives where history has least to say. One could take this a step further and argue that where identity cannot be firmly rooted in a deep, historically attested past, then myth may be employed by elites to fill in this epistemological vacuum (1999: 211). Lincoln's insight that myth can be used to fill in the empty pages in national narratives leads us directly to the subject of the Goths and their place in the Swedish myth of origins.

## The Gothic Myth of Origins

The modern Swedish state was founded by Gustav Vasa in the sixteenth century after a short war of independence with Denmark. By the early seventeenth century, this upstart nation had become a major player in European history, winning wars for the Lutheran cause in Germany, Poland and Russia, and developing colonies all along the Baltic coast. However, because of the country's peripheral location and late conversion to Christianity, Sweden lacked the written records that could bestow a sense of legitimacy and a glorious myth of descent. There was simply no Swedish equivalent of Saxo Grammaticus' monumental early 13th century history of Denmark (*Saxonis Grammatici Historia Danica*), which provided the Danes with an ancient foundation myth and became an early best seller when it was printed in Danish translation in 1575.

The Swedish elite got around this embarrassing absence of historical records by inventing an ancient past and a myth of origins. Thanks to a statement in Jordanes' 6th century work *Getica*, and a number of place names such as Gotland and Vestergötland, it was decided that the Swedes were descendants of the Goths, a heathen people who swept over the boundaries of the Roman Empire in the 4th century.

The movement to define the country's ethnic origins was called Gothicism (in Swedish *götticism*) and during its first manifestation culminated in Johannes Magnus's *Historia de omnibus Gothurum Sveonumque regibus*, a massive work of scholarship published in 1554, which aimed to fill in the gaps in the Swedish national chronicles. Magnus's opus was part of a European trend; all the major nations were at the time producing great patriotic histories in Latin. But it had one major flaw: it had been written in exile by the last Roman Catholic archbishop in Sweden. Over a hundred years later, another Swede, with an impeccable Lutheran background, set out to improve on Magnus' work. This was the polymath, Olof Rudbeck, who published an encyclopaedic work, *Atlantica*, in four volumes between 1672 and 1679. *Atlantica* took on board all of the mythical origins concocted by Johannes Magnus, and earlier historians, and with wonderful hubris added a new layer of myth. Sweden now became not only the original home of the Goths[1] but the site of the lost civilization of Atlantis. Through a system of etymological calculations, Rudbeck revealed that Swedish place names were actually the original forms of ancient Greek localities. Thus, Thebes was a transposition of Swedish Täby, Hercules found himself performing his labours beside the Öresund, and Odysseus as well as the Argonauts bravely sailed the chilly Baltic instead of the Mediterranean or Black Sea.

According to Rudbeck, the Goths were a chosen people, who had invented the art of writing and timekeeping, and had populated the rest of Europe with their progeny. Thanks to the chilly Northern climate, Swedish men were hardier and more masculine than their southern counterparts and Swedish women more fertile than Southern European women. Not only that, all the other major languages, Greek as well as Hebrew, were based upon an ancient form of Swedish, i.e. Gothic.

In terms of Anthony Smith's theory of nationalism, Rudbeck had created a perfect myth of origins to promote the sense of Sweden's chosenness and world destiny. *Atlantica* also offers an example of the malleability of myth and its usefulness as propaganda: by focusing on the Goths and 'proving' that the Swedes were their descendants, Rudbeck turned the preconceptions of classical culture on their head. Instead of Sweden being an upstart nation with no historical tradition, he revealed that Sweden was the fountainhead of European culture. Scandinavia moved from the absolute periphery of Western civilization to its centre, and was redefined as a Nordic version of Greece.

---

[1] The Goths, Visigoths, Ostrogoths, Vandals and Burgundians et al, who contributed to the demise of the Roman Empire consisted of motley bands of warriors and cannot be attributed to any specific region or ethnic grouping (Moore, 2002: 4-5).

With support from the monarchy and the University of Uppsala, where Rudbeck carried
out his research, the Gothic myth gained a dominant position in Swedish culture during the
seventeenth and early eighteenth centuries. As a narrative, it fits in with Lincoln's description
of myth, i.e. a powerful narrative claiming credibility and authority, since it was officially
incontestable during Rudbeck's lifetime (Hall, 1998: 150). And it also achieved a certain
influence in other parts of Europe. When Voltaire published his *History of Charles XII, King of
Sweden*², in 1731 one of the most popular history books of the century he repeated the myth,
i.e.:

> It is said that the Goths [which] flocked Europe and liberated it from a Roman Empire
> that for five hundred years had been its invader, tyrant and lawmaker, came primarily
> from Sweden. (quoted in Hallberg 2001: 30; Hall's translation)

## Goths and Celts

Ever since antiquity, the ethnic origins of the Germanic Goths have been intertwined with
those of the Celts. To some extent, this confusion was understandable, since the very first time
that the Germans were mentioned in a classical text they were fighting in a Gaulish army
against the Romans (Römer 1989: 85 ff). Rudbeck had also stated that the Celts were a Gothic
tribe, but then again Rudbeck insisted that the Greeks too were a subcategory of Goths.

In fact, one could say that the most clear-cut similarity between the Goths and the Celts
was that they lived in the North of Europe, were not Latins, and that they fought the ancient
Romans. By the eighteenth century, when the Enlightenment was creating a new, more radical
philosophy of human society, both of these shadowy early peoples were regarded as possessing
the sort of 'primitive nobility' which was lauded by writers such as Paul-Henri Mallet and
Jean-Jacques Rousseau. While Rousseau inaugurated a change in European attitudes to nature
and the primitive, Mallet was one of the pioneers of the Nordic and Celtic Renaissances,
restating the Rudbeckian myth that the Scandinavians had played a major role in world
history. Not only that, Nordic society was, *pace* Mallet, characterized by an insatiable desire for
freedom and an unbending sense of honour. In contrast to Rudbeck, however, the Swiss
historian regarded the Germans and Scandinavians as branches of the great Celtic family of
nations. After he published his six-volume *Introduction to the History of Denmark* (1755-56)
which promoted the myths of the Icelandic *Eddas* as being of fundamental importance to
European culture (Lincoln, 1999: 50), Mallet wrote a supplementary volume entitled:
*Monuments of the Mythology and the Poetry of the Celts, and especially the ancient Scandinavians*
(Schmidt, 2003: 437).

Mallet's work achieved considerable popularity in Europe and his writings were well
received in Sweden and the rest of Scandinavia. However, to understand the most far-reaching
connections between the Gothic myth of origins and the Celtic Renaissance, one has to travel
to Britain, where the theoretical and historical approach to the Celts and Scandinavians was
adapted to meet new tastes in literature.

The first writer to spin gold from Celtic narratives was the English poet, Thomas Gray,
who created a stir about 1755 with a poem entitled *The Bard*. Based on a Welsh legend, the
eponymous Bard denounces the army of Edward I after the subjugation of Wales in 1283. He
laments the slaughter of his own bardic companions by the English and then commits suicide
to show his defiance (Lonsdale, 1977: 52). Apart from taking an interest in Welsh and Scottish
mythology, Gray also made translations of Icelandic sagas as did his contemporary, Thomas
Percy (Mack, 2000). Their work was, however, quickly overshadowed by the translations of a
Scotsman – James Macpherson – who became a sensation not only in the British Isles but also
across the whole of Europe.

---

² There were at least 60 French editions (Hallberg, 2001: 30).

Unfortunately, it is not possible here to give more than a few sketchy details of the implications of Macpherson's writings on European literature but it is no exaggeration to say that his bogus translations of the poetry of Ossian and the work of his admirers, especially his fellow Scot, Hugh Blair, paved the way for the Romantic Movement in Europe. Much of the appeal of Macpherson's translations was based on their presumed authenticity. In the preface to his first publication *Fragments of Ancient Poetry, Collected in the Highlands of Scotland*, Hugh Blair makes the claim that dogged Macpherson's career thereafter, i.e. that the poems were translations of original poetry from the 3rd or 4th century. The writings were actually composed by Macpherson himself.

This is not to say that the translations of Celtic and Icelandic poetry by Thomas Gray and the reproduction of old Scottish and English ballads by Thomas Percy, were always much more authentic but, unlike Macpherson, these two English writers were not meeting any deep-felt desire to mythologize their own ethnic origins. In short, Macpherson's writings have to be regarded within the context of Scottish national identity and as a reaction to the destruction and repression of the Highland clan system in the aftermath of 1745. Macpherson's patriotic intentions are obvious and in many ways prefigure the misuse of national identity in the nineteenth century. He promoted, for instance, the idea of a Caledonian myth of ethnic origins and descent unsullied by foreign influence: both culturally and linguistically Macpherson considered the Irish to be inferior to their cousins on the east coast of Scotland, and he insisted that the Irish had falsely claimed to be the originators of Scottish themes and mythical characters (Macpherson, [1792] 1996: 338). Despite an enthusiastic reception in England, contemporary southern commentators were not so easily taken in by Macpherson's claims to authenticity. Dr Johnson, for instance, was never in doubt about the bogus nature of the poems, and stated after his trip to the Western Isles, that the Scots have good reason:

> …for their easy reception of an improbable fiction: they are seduced by their fondness for their supposed ancestors. A Scotchman must be a very sturdy moralist who does not love Scotland better than truth…. (Johnson cited in Wordsworth, 1996: vii)

But there was also an intriguingly pan-nationalistic side to this obsession with glorious ancestors. Macpherson's work could be used as a template for other ethnic groups who wished to evoke a noble ancient past. The plasticity of ethnic mythmaking and the absence of firm historical sources encouraged this tendency, and Macpherson actively facilitated the process by fudging the issue of the origins of the ancient Caledonians. In a dissertation on the antiquity of Ossian's poems, he mentions that Tacitus was of the opinion that the Caledonians were of German extraction although he himself considered them to have originated in Gaul. As a sort of compromise, Macpherson suggested that the Caledonians might have been a colony of Celtic Germans (Macpherson, [1762] 2004: iii).

I mentioned previously Mallet's conflation of the Scandinavians with the Celts. This appears rather odd to us today, but it was not a particularly eccentric point of view in the eighteenth century. Although some works pronounced that the Germanic and Celtic languages were quite separate as far back as 1610, there were numerous studies by German scholars during the seventeenth and eighteenth centuries which attempted to prove that these two language groups belonged together (Schmidt, 2003: 450 ff). In 1700, for instance, Daniel Morhof, published a book on the Germanic languages and argued that Celtic, German and Greek shared a common origin. Even Leibniz regarded Celtic as closely related to German (Schmidt, 2003: 451), and thanks to the enormous success of Macpherson's translations in Germany, this tendency to equate the Germans with the Celts intensified during the second half of the eighteenth century. According to the German historian, Klaus von See, Celtic gods, druids and bards were used to fill in the gaps in German prehistory, and this process of cultural borrowing continued until the end of the nineteenth century: "Without this influence, the spread of Ossianism in Germany and the German bardic poetry would not have been possible" (von See, 1994: 64). In a monograph on Macpherson's translation, Herder compared Ossian directly to Homer, and the bard was frequently referred to as 'the Homer of the North' in Germany and England.

The impact of the Celtic revival was felt all over Europe, but this process of cultural repackaging was particularly intense in Sweden. Although Macpherson's writings were based on Gaelic themes, they included numerous references to Vikings and Scandinavia, which made them amenable to reinterpretation by Nordic authors. Abraham Niklas Clewberg-Edelcranz (1754-1821), the first Swede to use Nordic mythology to write a modern national poem, (*Ode to the Swedish People*), was heavily indebted to Macpherson and, like his Scottish predecessor, he combined the effect of stirring landscape descriptions – cliffs and moody seascapes are endemic in Macpherson's writings – with mythical Scandinavian themes (Blanck, 1911: 324-32).

But the influence of Macpherson's vision of the past was not confined to the eighteenth century: by the early 1800s, it took on a new importance as the necessity of updating the previous myth of Swedish origins had become acute. Sweden's status as a great Baltic power had collapsed and Rudbeck's theory of the Gothic origins of the nation had fallen into disrepute. After the humiliating loss of Finland in 1809, the Swedish elite desperately required a new patriotic narrative to inspire the population.

Swedish poets copied the style and content of both Gray and Macpherson's poetry and began to adapt it to the Gothic myth created by Rudbeck. The most successful of these writers were Erik Gustaf Geijer and Esaias Tegnér who were both co-founders of the Gothic Society, a patriotic fellowship of young writers and poets established in 1811 with the express goal of reviving ancient Nordic culture and ideals. Geijer produced the first major poem that helped define the Gothic revival, namely *The Last Scald* from 1811, and the influence of both Gray and Macpherson is unmistakable when the Swedish poet describes the Gothic bard:

His size was giantlike, but bowed down by the years,
With slow steps he strode across the heath;
From his crown, the white hair flowed,
On each side, his beard hung to the girdle down[5]. (Geijer, 1926: 11)

Here is how Gray described his Welsh poet fifty years earlier:

Robed in the sable garb of woe,
With haggard eyes the Poet stood;
Loose his beard, and hoary hair
Stream'd, like a meteor, to the troubled air. (Gray in Lonsdale, 1977: 53)

And it is also worth comparing Geijer's scald to Macpherson's Ossian:

By the side of the rock on the hill, beneath the aged trees, old Ossian sat on the moss; the last of the race of Fingal. Sightless are his aged eyes; his beard is waving in the wind. (Macpherson, [1760] 1966: 37)

Just as in Gray's eighteenth century work, Geijer's bard criticises the king and dies at the end of the poem. But the thematic parallels with Macpherson's Ossian are even more marked. Geijer's scald – who like Ossian was also a warrior – is the last of his kind and facing death remembers the bards whom he once knew:

[5] Unless otherwise stated, all translations are by the author of this article.

Methinks I see them
The grey shadows
in stilly earnest
loftily stand
among the noisy guests.
I come, I come!
Not in vain do they wave,
I long to be with you,
With you the noble heroes! (Geijer 1926: 15)

Compare this to Ossian's melodramatic farewell to life, where the ghosts of his past also beckon him to the otherworld:

The voice of Ossian has been heard. The harp has been strung in Selma. 'Come, Ossian, come away,' he says, 'come fly with thy fathers on clouds.' I come, I come, thou king of men! The life of Ossian fails. (Blanck, 1918: 192)

There is no evidence that Geijer read Gray's poetry, but he acknowledged his debt to Macpherson and he was also an avid reader of Walter Scott, whose writings were inspired by both Gray and Macpherson. The borrowing of stylistic and thematic effects was made easier because Geijer and his contemporaries accepted the Ossianic poems as historical documents, and because the Swedes regarded many of Macpherson's characters – especially Fingal, the father of Ossian – as being of Scandinavian descent (Blanck 1918: 385). As Anton Blanck, the chief expert on Geijer's literature put it: "All of Geijer's scaldic poetry is permeated with a grey Ossianic mist… The nuances between Gray and Macpherson are almost imperceptible."

In 1811, the same year *The Last Scald* was printed, Geijer's friend, Tegnér published an overtly patriotic poem called *Svea*, and he also makes allusions to Macpherson's literary universe. In *Svea* – the title invokes the ancient name of Sweden – the Goths fill the same sort of mythical space as the heroic Caledonians, and Tegnér directly compares the heir to the Swedish throne, Oscar I, with his namesake, the brother of Ossian and the son of Fingal:

and Victory stands close, admired by the world,
and Oscar grows tall to take up Fingal's sword. (Michanek, 2003: 249)

It is difficult for modern people to imagine poetry as an influential mass media, but the work of Geijer and Tegnér became an integral part of national culture in Sweden. Not only did they spellbind their contemporaries, these two poets also influenced generations of Swedes until well into the twentieth century. In fact, the literature produced during the Gothic revival in Sweden fits in much more neatly with Lincoln's definition of myth than Macpherson's work, which never enjoyed official support, and whose authenticity was constantly challenged.

Unlike the Ossianic 'translations', Geijer's poetry and historical works were backed up by the authority of the Swedish state. Apart from being a popular poet, lecturer and historian, Geijer was also a leading member of the committee which designed the curriculum for the first national school system in 1826. His poetry and his patriotic view of the past became incorporated into the Swedish national and secondary school syllabus, and it was only in the 1950s, when modernity began to replace the past as the basis of Swedish identity, that this cultivation of the Gothic heritage was seriously challenged (cf Tingsten, 1969). The debt that Geijer and Tegnér owed to Macpherson probably explains why Swedish secondary school children were still reading not only *their* poetry but also extracts from the songs of Ossian until well into the 1960s.

But there was a downside to this hyperbolic praise of the ancient Scandinavians. When national character began to be expressed in racial terms at the end of the nineteenth century, some Swedish archaeologists and scientists enthusiastically attempted to prove that the Swedish people were the purest and most racially valuable element in the Germanic family of peoples. Sweden became the original homeland of the Nordic race rather than that of the ancient Goths. And, in contrast to the provenance of the Goths, these mythical roots could be proven 'scientifically' by measuring skulls, height and hair colour.

This pseudo-scientific view of ethnic origins reached a peak during the 1920s when the Swedish parliament approved the establishment of the world's first National Institute for Race-Biology at Uppsala. Its first director, Herman Lundborg, carried out large-scale biometric surveys of the Swedish population and conjectured:

> [T]here are compelling reasons to believe that the people who developed the original [Indo-Germanic] tongue were of the Nordic race. Through wide-scale migration and colonisation they have transferred their language to people of non-Nordic race…Even linguistic factors indicate that the original home of the Indo-Germans was situated on the Baltic. (Lundborg, [1927] 1995: 440)

It is interesting to note the similarities between Rudbeck's Gothic myth of Swedish origins during the seventeenth century, and Lundborg's racist theory of origins in the 1920s. Just as Rudbeck had concluded that all European culture could be traced back to Sweden, which he maintained was the original homeland of the Goths, Lundborg insisted that all the Indo-European languages originated in the Baltic. Not surprisingly, Lundborg became an enthusiastic supporter of the National Socialists in Germany and his theories were quietly shelved once it was clear that the Germans would lose the war. However, his research and that of many of his colleagues in archaeology and physical anthropology, cast a pall over the whole subject of Swedish origins in the post-war period.

## The Return of the Goths and Celts

At both the official and popular level, history suffered a decline in Sweden after the Second World War and Swedes began to regard their identity as essentially modern and progressive. However, in the wake of the country's accession to the EU in 1995 and the perceived decline of the welfare state, Swedish interest in history and the deep past has enjoyed a renaissance. Unfortunately, this trend has also reactivated old tensions about racism and ethnic exclusivity, especially when the Gothic tradition tries to make a comeback. In the summer of 2001, a museum in Värnamö, in Southern Sweden, organised an exhibition about the Vandals. The catalogue accompanying the exhibition put forward evidence that the origins of these near-relatives of the Goths could be traced to Småland and that after their defeat in North Africa the survivors made their way back to Sweden, as evidenced by place names such as *Vendel* and *Vendsyssel*.

Dick Harrison, a well-known medievalist from the University of Lund, roundly attacked these speculations in the leading daily newspaper, *Svenska Dagbladet:*

> Why am I upset? Why am I criticising one of our country's most respected museum personalities in modern times? The answer is that I see a spectre wandering through the book, and that spectre is Olof Rudbeck, the ghost of Ancient Swedish Gothicism, a howling guest from the past which has once again put on its blood-red sheet and rusty chains. The "true story" about the origins of the Vandals seems to have sprung out of the Swedish rural romantic past which I had fooled myself into believing we had left behind us long ago. (7 October 2001)

Another historian, who is an expert of Old Norse, commented on the debate started by Harrison:

> Dick Harrison thought that the Rudbeck's had played out his role but that is unfortunately not the case. There are many notions in circulation about the Goths and Vikings, originating in Rudbeck's haunted castle, and not just in Neo-Nazi circles but also in more respectable environments, which we are not really aware of, both inside and outside the university. (Johansson, 2001)

Interestingly enough, the Celts still have a role to play in this discourse of origins. Their usefulness was highlighted by a two-part series on ethnic origins, presented and written by the award-winning historian, Maja Hagerman, and shown repeatedly on Swedish public service television in 2001 and 2002. Predictably, Hagerman concentrated on just two ancient peoples, the Celts and the ancient Germans.

While the first programme *Germans, The Art of Inventing One's Ancestors* takes viewers back to the golden age of Germanic culture in Sweden, and focuses initially on the struggle between the ancient Germans and Romans, the second programme *The Celtic Riddle* promotes the view that the Celtic heritage can be understood as a generalized European identity rather than being specifically connected to any particular ethnicity. As the British archaeologist, J D Hill, one of the experts interviewed in the programme expresses it: "I suspect that all a Celt is … is actually a person who lived in Western Europe."

Hagerman traces the development of Germanic identity all the way from Tacitus to Rudbeck, from Geijer and Herder to Wagner, until it reaches its final dissolution in racism and Nazi terror in the twentieth century. The Celtic heritage, meanwhile, flows relatively harmlessly from Iron Age art and Celtic mythology into New Age religions and fantasy fiction. In terms of its importance as a basis of national identity, the programmes inform us that Celtic roots lead to the politically correct 'good' nationalism that brought Irish independence in the 1920s, while the Gothic heritage is indelibly linked to the extremism of German militarism and genocide. Scotland is never mentioned in *The Celtic Riddle*, but as the camera dwells on the bleak windswept cliffs of Ireland's Atlantic coast or Hagerman interviews modern-day druids, one can sense the influence of Macpherson's Ossianic universe.

In these programmes, the strange interweaving narrative of the Celts and the Goths seems to have come full circle. Once again, just as in the eighteenth and nineteenth centuries, the Celtic past seems to be functioning as an acceptable stand-in for the Gothic, providing attractive narratives that are independent of the cultures of Latin and Mediterranean Europe. Unlike the Goths, the Celts never became seriously tainted by the theories of extreme nationalists or racists. The Celtic heritage can therefore be promoted as a sort of catch-all myth of origins for Western Europe, thus assisting Swedish efforts to construct a new, less constricted sense of national identity.

## References

Blanck, Anton. 1911. *Den nordiska renässansen i sjuttonhundratalets litteratur: En undersökning av den "götiska" poesiens allmänna och inhemska förutsättningar. Stockholm:* Albert Bonniers Förlag

Blanck, Anton. 1918. *Geijers götiska diktnin.* Stockholm: Albert Bonniers Förlag

Eriksson, Gunnar. 2002. *Rudbeck 1630-1702: Liv, lärdom, dröm i barockens Sverige.* Stockholm: Atlantis

Hallberg, Peter. 2001. "Mirrors of the Nation, The Construction of National Character and Difference in the Historical Writings of E. G. Geijer". *Scandinavian Journal of History*. 26.1

Geijer, Erik Gustaf. 1926 *Dikte. Andra upplagan*. Stockholm: P. A. Norstedt & Söners Förlag

Hall, Patrik. 1998. *The Social Construction of Nationalism: Sweden as an Example*. Lund: Lund University Press

Johansson, Karl. 2001. "Varför forska om fornisländska i 2000-talets Sverige?" *Humanetten*, no. 9, Autumn. Institution of the Humanities, University of Växjö

Lincoln, Bruce. 1989. *Discourse and the Construction of Society: Comparative Studies of Myth, Ritual, and Classification*. Oxford: Oxford University Press

Lincoln, Bruce. 1999. *Theorizing Myth, Narrative, Ideology and Scholarship*. Chicago: The University of Chicago Press

Lonsdale, Roger, ed. 1977. *Thomas Gray and William Collin: Poetical Works*. Oxford: Oxford University Press

Lundborg, Herman. 1927. "Svensk raskunskap". *Svenska kruskbär, En historiebok om Sverige och svenskar*. Eds. Björn Linnell & Mikael Löfgren. 1995. Stockholm: Bonnier Alba

Mack, Robert L. 2000. *Thomas Gray: A Life*. New Haven: Yale University Press

Macpherson, James. 1760. *Fragments of Ancient Poetry*. 1966. The Augustan Reprint Society, 1966. Los Angeles: University of California

Macpherson, James. 1762. "Fingal an Ancient Epic Poem in Six Books," in: *Ossian and Ossianism*. Ed. Dafydd Moore. Volume II. 2004. London: Routledge

Macpherson, James. 1792. *The Poems of Ossian the Son of Fingal*. Ed. Jonathan Wordsworth. 1996. New York: Woodstock Books

Michanek, Germund, ed. 2003. *Vår klassiska lyrik: Från ballader till Karlfeldt*. Avesta: Wahlström & Widstrand

Moore, R. I. 2002. "A Toxic Waste Dump? Inventing Goths and Other Ancestors". *Times Literary Supplement*. 15 March

Römer, Ruth. 1989. *Sprachwissenschaft und Rassenideologie in Deutschland*. Munich: Wilhelm Fink Verlag

Schmidt, Wolf Gerhard. 2003. *Homer des Nordens und Mutter der Romantik: James Macphersons Ossian und seine Rezeption in der deutschsprachigen Literatur*. Band I. Berlin: Walter de Gruyter

Smith, Anthony D. 1999. *Myths and Memories of the Nation*. Oxford: Oxford University Press

Tingsten, Herbert. 1969. *Gud och fosterlandet: Studier i hundra års skolpropaganda*. Stockholm: P. A. Norstedt & Söners Förlag

Von See, Klaus. 1994. *Barbar, Germane, Arier: Die Suche nach der Identität der Deutschen*. Heidelberg: Universitätsverlag C. Winter

# Ideological Architecture And Regional Identities: Workhouses in Ireland

*Liz Thomas*

During the nineteenth century the distribution of poverty relief throughout the British Isles was completely revised. England, Wales, Ireland and Scotland endeavoured to curb and contain the forces that were increasing poverty in the newly industrialized society. The workhouse was central to these new poor laws. Three different poor laws, although very similar, were introduced into the four countries throughout the nineteenth century. Ireland was unique as unlike the other countries Ireland had no record of previous poor laws. Even so, in Ireland the most conservative measures were made in undertaking the new poor law. This paper will look at how workhouses were introduced into the British Isles, especially focussing on Ireland and ultimately how the architecture and standard plan of the workhouses in Ireland, England and Scotland reflect the ideologies of the period, in particular the ideologies that influenced the poor law policies.

The nineteenth century was a radical period in poor law reform. The 1834 Poor Law (Amended) Act, that was quickly assembled and put through parliament, revolutionised poor relief. Society was changing. Between 1821 and 1831 the population of many British urban towns had expanded by forty percent (Rose: 2). Scotland underwent its fastest rate of population increase in its history, doubling its population to 2,620,184 by 1841 (Cage: 1). Conversely, although Ireland had a massive population, the population growth had begun to slow down in the 1820s and 1830s (Kennedy: 26). It is believed that as England made the shift from an agrarian to industrial society, there was great uneasiness as "both the poor rates and the discontent of labourers had risen alarmingly, threatening the existence of the political, economic and social order" (Brundage: 8). There was fear of "social disintegration" (Driver: 26). It seems that the new 1834 act was a panicked reaction to this changing society. This new act was fundamentally influenced by the key ideologues of the nineteenth century which were in turn moulded by the writings of Adam Smith and David Hume. Being both stoics and materialist philosophers, Smith and Hume influenced nineteenth century political ideologies, by rejecting religious superstitions and re-introducing the concepts of order, regularity of form between the personal and political state, and the idea that God's Providence provided for the well-being of society as a whole, and not every individual (Fitzgibbons: 25-33). Hence, fundamentally the same law, despite objections, was conferred on Ireland; since 1801, the country was an integral part of the British Empire. Scotland was distinct from England and did not introduce such a poor law until 1845. In Scotland the rapid increase in population, the newly industrialised country, and most importantly, the depressions in 1819, 1825-6, 1829, 1837 and 1840-3 caused great poverty. This poverty, however, was not equated with economic forces but rather blamed on the "personal behaviour", ultimately, the "moral degradation" of the people (Cage: i).

The new Poor Laws were instrumental in establishing utilitarian control, harnessing a hold on political power, social insurrection and poverty relief. In 1838 a Poor Law Act was conferred on Ireland. The acts in England, Wales, Ireland and Scotland were almost uniform; however, there existed a fundamental difference between the act in England, Wales and Scotland and the one in Ireland. Outdoor relief was forbidden under the Irish poor law act. In Ireland there was also one basic difference in the implementation of the Poor Law, as reflected in the workhouse designs. In England, although model plans existed, there was considerable diversity in the forms of the workhouses. In contrast, rigid uniformity was imposed from on high in Ireland through the appointment of a single architect. Furthermore, this single architect chose to use essentially the same plan throughout the country although he had previously authored a diversity of plans for use in England. The main objective of the Irish Poor Law was to introduce a centralised power. Although it was argued that the new Poor Law would introduce self-government by using a centralised power "Local self-government [...] has not been destroyed [...] by centralizing and combining the best elements existing in a large district, in lieu of the scattered, desultory, and imperfect old parochial administrations" (Nicholls: 33). Essentially, centralisation was the institutionalisation of poverty relief in Ireland and England. The utilitarian elements of control were seen at microcosmic level in the workhouse design, where there was also centralised control.

**Principle Ideologies and Policies of the new Poor Laws**

The poor law ideologies were dominated by Jeremy Bentham and Reverend T.R. Malthus, whose ideologies in turn had been strongly influenced by Adams and Hume. Essentially, the view was that society sheltered the "deserving" and "undeserving" poor and surplus population caused shortages in employment and food. Bentham claimed that "[the] *Poor Laws* proper object is to make provision for the relief not of poverty, but of indigence" (Quinn: 3). His belief was that to "banish poverty would have no effect or a bad one" and "Indigence may be provided for: Mendicity may be extirpated: but to extirpate poverty would be to extirpate man" (Quinn: 5). The abolition of poverty was not amongst Bentham's chief concerns. His most influential ideologies were centralisation of poverty relief and the classification of paupers. He recommended the establishment of the "central office", along with the creation of the following offices within the workhouse, "spiritual", "medical", "chaplain", and "surgeon" (Quinn: 67-68).

Malthus was one of the most renowned and most brutal critics of the old Poor Law. He believed that the law had encouraged early marriages, surplus population and poverty. According to Malthus, the old Poor Law was a "direct constant and systematical encouragement to marriage by removing from each individual that heavy responsibility which he would incur by the laws of nature for bringing human beings into the world which he could not support" (Huzel: 430). Malthus adopted the position of extreme *laissez-faire* as he denied the existence of any right to subsistence. He claimed that it was the moral responsibility of the individual to prevent poverty. The only form of relief condoned was private charity to only the most deserving poor. In concurrence with Malthus' opinion, it was commonly held that the old Poor Law had nurtured the indolent nature of the undeserving poor. Outdoor relief was refused to able-bodied paupers. It was both morally and economically wrong to offer charity to the able-bodied poor. The same problem existed in Ireland according to Nicholls, who toured the country in 1836. He commented that "mendicancy and indiscriminate alms-giving seem to have produced the same results in Ireland that indiscriminate relief produced in England" (Nicholls: 11). Private charity was perverting the social order. Bentham believed that in a civilised political community, no one "for the want of [...] necessaries of life, be left to perish outright" (Quinn: 10).

The Poor Laws were, in essence, a system of laws that were designed based on the key ideologies of the nineteenth century. The policies of the new Poor Laws are particularly reflective of Bentham's thoughts on centralisation and this centralisation institutionalised poverty relief in Britain. The new laws addressed several of the problems identified by the key thinkers of the century. Firstly, the law classed the poor as either deserving or undeserving and provided for the deserving poor, while it simultaneously prevented indigence. Another function was to restore the proper social order by "the restoration of the pauper to a position below that of the independent labourer" (Morrison: 43). An important aim of the new law was to inspire self-discipline, developing an awareness of prudence amongst the pauper population. These policies rectified the defects caused by the old Poor Law, as it had, according to Bentham, distorted the system and natural balance of society. The workhouse was one of the tools of the new act through which these policies were executed. However, critics of the workhouse argued that poverty was still being treated as a crime (Driver: 61). In response to these attacks and in line with the ideologues, the Poor Law Commissioners explained that no physical punishment played any part in the workhouse policy, rather the workhouse regime was dictated by the need for order rather than punishment (Driver: 64).

## Workhouse Policy

The principal policy was to have a well-regulated workhouse where the paupers were exposed to a harsh regime. Nicholls stated that the governing principle of the workhouse was "that the support which is afforded at the public charge in the workhouse, shall be, on the whole, less desirable than the support to be obtained by independent exertion" (Nicholls: 23). It was believed that the "workhouse test" would restore the natural social order, by deterring those seeking relief and inviting only the utterly desperate into the workhouse. The concept of the Workhouse Test dates back to 1723 when Knatchbull's Act (The Workhouse Test Act) was passed. This act enabled parishes to set up workhouses, offering relief only from within. Scotland's earliest workhouse dates back to 1720 with the opening of the Edinburgh Correction House. The workhouse was a punitive system since by entering the workhouse the paupers lost their freedom. The inmate's time, space, relationships, clothing and diet were strictly regulated. It was envisaged that the Workhouse Test would eliminate the indolent disposition of the pauper. One Poor Law authority stated that "the able-bodied subjected to such courses of labour and discipline as will repel the indolent and vicious" (Morrison: 44).

The Poor Law authorities in England realised that Irish paupers were already subjected to harsh living conditions. However, Nicholls still recommended the workhouse system as the ideal instrument to eradicate indigence. The punishment for the Irish pauper, therefore, would not be the squalid conditions of the workhouse. Rather, the loss of freedom would repel the Irish pauper from entering the workhouse. Nicholls stated that "Confinement of any kind is more irksome to an Irishman than it is even to an Englishman […he will] never enter the workhouse, unless driven thither for refuge by actual necessity; and he will not then remain there one moment longer than that necessity exists" (Nicholls: 24). Workhouses had the physical capability to enforce the principle policies of the new Poor Laws: centralisation, classification, discipline and deterrence. However, the archetypal workhouse was not developed for some time.

## Development of Workhouse Plan

Over two thousand Poor Law Unions were formed in England and Wales when the English Poor Law (Amended) Act was passed in August 1834. The Poor Law Commission desired that each union established a workhouse. Between 1834 and 1839, over three hundred and fifty new workhouses were constructed in England (O'Dwyer: 13). Naturally a different pattern occurred in Scotland. By the time the Scottish Poor Law Act was passed the workhouse system was becoming more and more controversial. Additionally, workhouses were not a compulsory part of the Scottish Act. In spite of the controversy of the workhouse system, the late introduction of the act and the non compulsory element, workhouses were a popular option in Scotland where seventy workhouses were erected. In England, Wales and Scotland old parish workhouses were modified to suit the criteria of the union workhouse. Hence, workhouses with a diversity of architectural plans and styles were the legacy of over five hundred years of English Poor Law reform. By the end of the 1830s the Poor Law Commission realised that the newly constructed and converted workhouses did not satisfy the stipulations of the new Poor Law. The Commissioners held that the variety of workhouses was not indicative of the principle policy of the new law, namely, the centralisation of poverty relief. The Poor Law Report of 1834 stated little regarding the desired physical form of the union workhouses, although the classification of paupers was ardently imposed. The classification scheme comprised the following classes: 1. males above the age of 15 years; 2. boys between 2 years and 15 years; 3. females above the age of 15 years; 4. girls between 2 years and 15 years, 5. children under 2 years of age, 6. male idiots, 7. female idiots.

Many unions used different buildings to house the different classes of paupers. In other cases, especially with converted parish workhouses, the structures were not designed to segregate the different categories of inmates (Morrison: 65). The new workhouse was intended to be a powerful symbol of the new approach to poverty relief. Therefore, the Poor Law Commission recommended the "mixed workhouse" (Morrison: 44). This edifice would accommodate all classes of paupers under the one roof. This system was more efficient with financial, moral and administrative advantages being derived. Since the paupers were safely segregated it was easier to admit and expel paupers and their families. Although important, it was of secondary benefit to the authorities that it cost less to erect and manage one building that housed all classes of paupers rather than several separate blocks.

The Poor Law Commission endeavoured to regulate the construction of workhouses in England and Wales by publishing plans of model workhouses. In Scotland in 1847, the Board of Supervision produced plans that were suitable for Combination Poorhouses. They were very similar to the plans recommended in England. Sampson Kempthorne's model workhouses were published in the Annual Poor Law Reports of 1835 and 1836. He produced two radial designs known as the square and the hexagon. His model elevations were minimal in style and cost. His designs were emulated throughout the country. The *Architectural Magazine* praised his work in 1835:

> "[they] appear to us, from a cursory inspection, excellently arranged; and it is most gratifying to see the attention that has been paid by the architect to the principles of separation and classification, to cleanliness, to ventilation, and to general convenience." (Morrison: 46)

Due to the publication of Kempthorne's model plans English workhouses shared a commonality of design. However, his plans and later adaptations did not escape criticism. In some cases, they were condemned as being prison-like in form, whilst others were accused of appearing like paupers' palaces. In addition, Kempthorne's designs lacked all the desired criteria. Although they enabled the Master to view all the yards, he could not view the internal sections of the building. Hence, the plans did not accommodate central control. Perhaps Kempthorne's designs were rebuked simply because he owed his position as architect to the Poor Law Commission to his father's friend, the prominent Nicholls (Morrison: 65). Apparently, the government was dogged with cases of nepotism which was another cause for antagonism and local resistance to the new Poor Law (McCord: 98).

## Workhouses in Ireland

In 1838 the Poor Law Act was conferred on Ireland. As already mentioned the Poor Law Commissioners were more rigid with the implementation of the new law. Cases of antagonistic guardians had emerged previously in England and Wales. In 1838, thirty-eight unions, mostly in Wales, had not provided workhouses as recommended by the Poor Law Commissioners. The guardians in these unions objected to the directions from the Poor Law Commission. Evidently, the Commissioners did not have the power to compel them to follow their instructions (Morrison: 44). Perhaps this is the reason why the Commissioners were particularly severe, fearing insurgency from the Irish landlords. It is also possible that only one architect was employed for economic reasons alone. Nonetheless, in Ireland, the Poor Law Commission executed their policies of poverty relief in an unwavering manner. This is identified at first hand with the contract for workhouses. Consultant architects in Ireland did not compete for workhouse contracts as they did in England. Instead, three architects were invited to Ireland to submit their plans. These architects were Sampson Kempthorne, George Wilkinson and an anonymous architect. The Irish architects were outraged; accusations of nepotism and sectarianism were made. Eventually, Wilkinson was employed directly by the Irish Poor Law Commissioners. Irish architects were especially angered that the one hundred and thirty union workhouses had been entrusted to a twenty five year-old Oxford man. Nevertheless, Wilkinson enjoyed an excellent professional reputation. He had already designed nineteen workhouses in England where his selection of plans included square, double courtyard and St Andrew's cross models. Although he had a diversity of plans at his disposal, his most famous 'square' plan was erected exclusively throughout Ireland. His scheme showed greater precision than Kempthorne's, expressing the idea of classification and principle of uniformity. Wilkinson's square plan was commended by the Poor Law Commissioners in 1839 when they stated that he "had given the greatest satisfaction as regards arrangement and economy" (Morrison: 65).

**Figure 1: Workhouse plan taken from the First Annual Report of the Poor Law Commissioners, 1848**

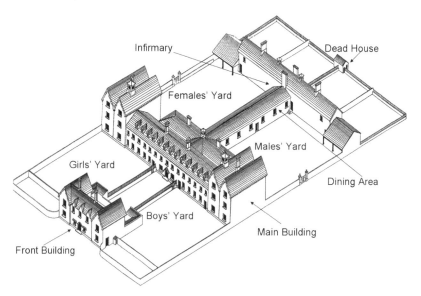

For the first time in British history, workhouses were built with a distinct architectural identity. In Ireland, a total of one hundred and thirty workhouses were erected between 1838 and 1843.

**Figure 2: Map of Workhouses in Ireland**

Wilkinson's specifications for the construction of all of these workhouses were extremely unyielding. He was suitably pedantic as an employee of the Poor Law Commission. As outdoor relief was totally forbidden, the workhouses in Ireland were substantially larger than those in England. Despite the extra size, Wilkinson achieved savings of one third of the cost per capita. Expenditure was reduced by lowering the standard of accommodation compared to that in English workhouses. For example, earthen floors, instead of timber, were considered suitable for the Irish paupers. Wilkinson also introduced his own innovations: the dormitories were equipped with sleeping platforms instead of bedsteads; internal walls were not plastered, just white-washed; and the workhouses in Ireland had no ceilings, simply bare rafters. The buildings built before 1850 adhered strictly to the same plan which consisted of three main parts, the Front, Main and Infirmary Buildings. After 1850 his plans were comprised of the same buildings but with a different layout. Nevertheless, the same principles of uniformity and classification applied. Having only one assistant, Wilkinson made lithographed standard elevations and details, which were combined with hand-drawn plans and site maps. This is further evidence of the stringent economy employed. The only workhouses not built to the standard plan were those in Ballycastle, Downptrick, Carlow and Killarney. In 1855, when the funds from the Poor Law Commission were exhausted Wilkinson was pensioned off (O'Dwyer: 13, 15-6).

Administratively and physically the workhouse system encapsulated the ideologies driving the new Poor Laws. The standard plan of Wilkinson's buildings enabled the practical implementation of the governing ideologies; centralisation, classification, deterrence and discipline. Wilkinson had these policies firmly in mind when designing the layout of the standard plan. Through the use of uniformity, spatial segregation, ceremony and symbolism, the workhouse plan provided the physical manifestation of the ideological thinking of the Poor Laws.

## Centralisation and Uniformity

Jeremy Bentham's key proposal with respect to the new Poor Law was centralisation, effectively institutionalising poverty relief (Quinn: 62). Following his insistence on centralised inspection, the Poor Law Commission, comprising of Commissioners and their assistants was established. The process of centralisation involved the election of a Board of Guardians for each union. Though the Guardians directed the purchasing of the workhouse site, construction and the management of the inmates, they did not make the ultimate decision on any of these issues. The final authority was vested in the Poor Law Commission. Similarly, the Master of the workhouse exercised absolute control within each individual workhouse. Though having minor prestige in Victorian society as a whole, nonetheless, within the workhouse, the Master was the government's representative. The positioning of the Master's room was deliberately central, serving both functional and symbolic ends. His room overlooked every section of the workhouse. The inmates were his subjects, the workhouse his dominion. Like the government he too continuously observed those under his watchful eye. Symbolically, he represented the centrality of disciplinary order (Driver: 61).

Centralised control was more evident in Ireland than in England, Wales and Scotland, due to the appointment of a single architect with a single plan, implemented under stricter supervision of the Poor Law Commissioners. This increased emphasis on centralisation facilitated the construction of uniform workhouses. The desire for uniformity was motivated by a fear of social disintegration and a need to maintain discipline. Additionally, Bentham claimed that a uniform system of workhouses throughout the country increased economic benefits (Quinn: 63). Ireland was viewed as prone to insurrection. The uniformity of design undoubtedly served a political purpose. Both widespread and virtually identical, the workhouses underlined the reach and authority of the British political system through the Poor Law Commission. With very few exceptions the workhouses erected in Ireland shared the same lithographed plans; deviation from the standard plan was almost impossible. The Victorian concern to impose order extended beyond the external homogeneity as even the internal structures within the workhouse complex were symmetrical. Each side was a mirror image of the other.

**Figure 3: Workhouse taken from plans of George Wilkinson**

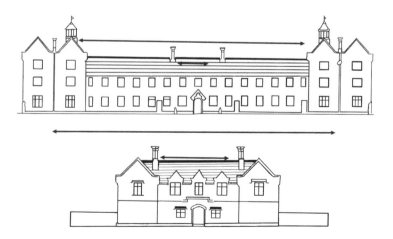

The entrance, main building, work areas, dining hall and the infirmary maintain perfect symmetry in height and size. Smaller features such as wells, privies, washrooms and turf or straw stores are mirrored on either side of the workhouse. Windows, doors, chimneys and ventilation shafts also show symmetry in design and layout. Even the yards and walls were standardised under the Wilkinson plan. This standard plan permitted neither irregularity nor non-conformity within the workhouse.

## Classification and Spatial Segregation

The poor law policy of the classification of paupers was given physical manifestation through spatial segregation throughout the workhouse. Bentham, both proposed and later endorsed classification. Classification was the division of inmates into definitive groups for administrative purposes. The Commissioners required, at the very least, that men and women were separated. In practice, the classification in the plan mirrored the distinctions made in contemporary Victorian England between the able bodied and those unable to work. Men, women, boys, girls, elderly men, elderly women, male 'idiots', female 'idiots', and the sick were separated by the layout of the workhouse. In Scotland the classification was very precise, being, "old men of good character", "desolate old men", "doubtful old men", "boys" and "bastards". Wilkinson's standard workhouse plan paralleled Bentham's idea of the "pauper-land" (Driver: 64). The seven different classes of paupers labelled in the 1838 Poor Law Report are listed above and the Poor Law Commissioners envisioned further subdivision of the categorisation of paupers. Ideally, paupers were to be further divided within the categories of age, illness and mental disposition. Even in burial it was anticipated that these subdivisions would be retained, with each class being buried in separate plots. In reality, this objective was unfeasible. Instead, paupers were assigned a mass burial plot away from the town's cemetery.

**Figure 4: Extract taken from O.S. map 1910**

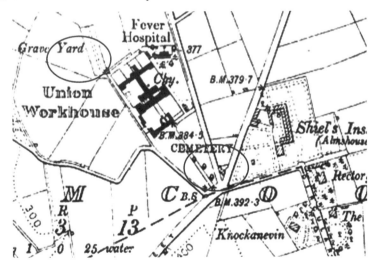

However, future excavations of workhouse burial plots could cast more light on this matter. The Commissioners believed that this further subdivision could only be achieved through the erection of separate buildings, harking back to the pre-new Poor Law days. From 1847, this new classification was initiated in Ireland with the erection of Fever Hospitals. Later, special wards for lying-in women, vagrants and the insane were erected (Driver: 65).

Initially, the commissioners viewed the mixed workhouse as an efficient and economical way to accommodate and manage all classes of pauper. In reality, spatial segregation served three purposes: as a medium for suitable management, as a punitive measure and as an obstacle to prevent both moral and physical contagion (Driver: 65). The separation of couples and families functioned as the biggest deterrent. The Poor Law Commission expected that this type of separation would discourage most from entering the workhouse. Additionally, the separation of men from women prevented procreation, targeting the problem of surplus populations. The final purpose of spatial segregation was to maintain the moral geometry of the workhouse (Driver: 65). Pauperism was treated like a disease. The orphan child was considered the most vulnerable to moral contagion while the prostitute was the most corrupt. It was totally forbidden for one class of pauper to have contact or communication with another class. Otherwise, the prostitute would taint all, the man defile the woman, the adult pauper tarnish the innocent child and the idiot torment the sane.

The geometry of the paupers' quarters is significant, reflecting the ideas of moral gradation. The arrangement of the wards portrays the governing power, discipline and paternal government. Additionally, they reflect a scale ranging from supreme morality to base morality. The plan shows that the Guardians are at the very top of this scale. The Front Building facing onto the town, in essence, has contact with the town dwellers. Their quarters are exclusive, isolated from corruption from within the workhouse. The children's wards are nestled around the Master. As pauper inmates, children are morally closest to the Master. However, his position is to ensure that the children are safe from contamination. The Master is almost like a father, protecting the young from the evils of the world; in this case, from the ills of pauper land. The pauper adults, being worse in nature, are placed in the extreme wings of the workhouse. It appears that the Master is holding them at arms length. The 'idiots' are banished to the extreme end of the workhouse. They cannot judge right from wrong and thus potentially present the greatest moral threat.

## Architectural Style and Decoration

The Poor Law Commissioners recommended the style and decoration suitable for workhouse architecture. Wilkinson produced plain elevations and designs for decorative features, such as the barge boards, gates and ventilation towers. An exact design was not imposed because the Guardians were given liberty to choose their own style. Ideally, the architecture was to be discreet and fitting to the manner for which the workhouse was built. The pauper's regime and the architectural style of the workhouse were akin, that is, frugal in nature. Aesthetics of beauty was not the objective. Instead, austere aesthetics were desired. The uniformity of architectural style reinforced the presence of authority and the policies of classification and prudence.

In Ireland, the architectural style made a significant impression on the residents of the unions, both those destined and not destined for the workhouse. The workhouse was not designed exclusively for the pauper. According to one commissioner, the architecture sent a potent message to all:

> The very sight of a well-built efficient establishment would give confidence to the Board of Guardians; the sight and weekly assemblage of all servants of their Union would make them proud of their office: the appointment of a chaplain would give dignity to the whole arrangement, while the pauper would feel it was utterly impossible to contend against it. (Morrison: 45)

The impact of such immense buildings on the Irish rural and urban landscape is unquestionable. The need for salubrity decreed that the workhouses commanded domineering views of the towns. Additionally, the foreign architectural style contrasted with the native. Conspicuous on the Irish landscape, these structures symbolised an expression of power from the government.

Workhouse architecture has generally been described as cheap and unimaginative. Conversely, it is argued that the different Boards of Guardians commissioned further expense on style and decorative features, making a statement through the medium of architecture. The styles chosen by the Boards of Guardians signalled different ideological expressions, as evidenced by the workhouses in Ulster. For example, the Ballymena construction has a prison-like appearance, with its projecting wings and dark stone. While the workhouse of Lisnaskea is the antithesis to Ballymena; Dutch stepped gables, wood and stone barge boards and an elegantly decorative porch adorn the Front Building of the this site.

**Figure 5: Workhouse in Ballymena**

**Figure 6: Worhouse at Newtown-Limavady**

The workhouse at Newtown-Limavady smacks of the style of the traditional alms-houses. A combination of designed quoins, barge-boards, gable moulds, decorated windows and the burnt-red brickwork, accompanied by the low stature of the buildings, create this benevolent effect. Other buildings have no decorative features, just a simple plain elevation such as Banbridge and Ballymoney. After the Great Famine various Guardians took it upon themselves to decorate the previous plain structures, such as was done at Banbridge. Therefore, even with the initial erection of workhouses, the policy of uniformity was never completely adhered to.

Additionally, evidence suggests that centralisation was not completely implemented. The decoration on many of the workhouses in Ulster indicated local intervention and preference. For example, the buildings at Ballymena and Lisnaskea display an unusual feature, inverted relieving arches. These arches have no functional purpose and are purely decorative. Other workhouses, such as those in Armagh, Lisnaskea and Newtown-Limavady, display barge-boards made from stone or wood.

**Figure 7: Workhouse at Lisnaskea, copyright Derek Gardiner, 2002**

Most of the buildings in Ulster are fabricated with rusticated walls and decorated corner stones In addition, the regularity of orientation and location was not consistent, although the only requisites for the construction of the workhouse given by the Poor Law Commission were as follows; 1. be near the town forming the centre of the union; 2. be in a salubrious situation; 3. possess the certainty of an abundant supply of water; 4. have a perfect system of drainage for the building; 5. be obtained at a reasonable cost.

However, the location of the building was generally on a hill commanding a domineering view of the town. Most of the workhouses look onto the towns, acting as potent symbols against indolence. Nonetheless, Guardians of some unions apparently chose not to display their workhouses prominently. In Clogher, Lisnaskea and Enniskillen, the workhouses face away from the towns. Clogher is the most surprising case, as this workhouse is situated in a valley with its back to the town. Perhaps this site was chosen because the land was purchased at a low cost, adhering to the requisite of the Poor Law Commission. The standard plan and the cost of land had no influence on the orientation of the building. However, it is possible that the Guardians were signalling their own ideologies of poverty relief, as the Poor Law Commissioners did through decoration and architectural style. This deviance also raises an important question: were the ideologies of poverty relief changing as the new Poor Law was introduced into Ireland or was the deviance simply a reaction against government infiltration?

## Ceremony

At an administrative and practical level the general plan of the workhouse hints at the ceremony of the mechanics of poverty relief. The acceptance of a pauper into the workhouse was based on several conditions: the pauper had to prove he was destitute and then sacrifice his lands. Upon entering the workhouse his clothes and worldly chattels were taken away from him, his family divided into their appropriate classes and delivered to the Main Building into their designated quarters. The new Poor Laws did not condemn poverty as a crime. Nevertheless, the layout of the buildings and rooms within the workhouse complex express the ritual of punishment. Most strikingly, every workhouse was enclosed by a ten-foot wall or fence. Some, such as, Newtown-Limavady, even had a surrounding ditch. Foucault has pointed out, in reference to crime and the judicial system, that by the end of the eighteenth century punishment was the most hidden part of the new processes of reform (Focault: 116-129). The body was no longer the object of the torture. The same happened with the reformation of the Poor Laws, the ceremonial aspects of punishment declined but survived in the administrative practice.

Additionally, the arrangement of these structures enforced a ritual style of entry into the workhouse. The upper storey of the Front Building served as the Board of Guardians Meeting Room. However, on the ground floor the pauper underwent the ritual of de-clothing and cleansing. The ritual continues from exiting the Front Building along the passage through to the workhouse, where access to non-designated areas, is denied to inmates. Along the axis of the plan is a clear and direct entry into the workhouse, although there is no opposing exit. The building, in this respect is almost prison-like. The government had the power to punish as is displayed not only by the central positioning of the Master's room but also by the Front Building. This Front Building is the most decorative of all the buildings within the complex. The Board of Guardians sat here and administered the poor relief policies. An inmate would never be permitted into such a building.

## Social Stigma

One of the conditions of the Poor Law in Ireland was that no church members could sit on the Board of Guardians, thus reducing any religious influence. It was also decided that no church would be erected on the site of the workhouse grounds. Apparently, in Ireland there existed too much religious contention. The efficient management of workhouses was threatened when religion played a dominant factor (Nicholls: 30). This policy deprived the paupers of another social freedom, a permanent and official place of worship. Religious practice was a very important aspect in Victorian society. In Ireland, Catholicism was the religion of the vast majority of paupers. The church building was often an object of pride or refuge for people within communities. Numerous towns and villages boast fine churches of architectural significance, for example, Armagh, Banbridge, Belfast and Newtown-Limavady. Bentham wanted paupers to be put in their rightful position in society. As paupers did not pay tax they were not entitled to a private church. Inmates of the workhouse could not always attend the local church. The standard plan of the workhouse was arranged so that there was no area exclusively set-aside for worship. Instead, when necessary, the Dining area was partitioned for this purpose. Likewise, there is no specific schoolroom in the workhouse plan. Pauperism was considered a hereditary disease. Bentham concluded that education would eradicate this disease, but only through an education that befitted them as pauper children. The children were trained according to their rank in society. Boys were taught how to mend shoes and girls were taught domestic duties. Instead, their work areas, on the ground floor, were converted into schoolrooms for three hours during the day. The children were socially stigmatised by being prevented from attending a regular school and studying regular subjects. What education they did receive insured that they as adults would remain in the lowly ranks as paupers. Therefore, the standard plan again expresses another ideology of that period, not to banish poverty but to extirpate indigence and maintain the pauper population for labour.

## Conclusion

The standard workhouse plan, indeed, reflected the ideologies that drove the new Poor Law. Its form essentially, was a physical manifestation of the policies of centralisation, classification, deterrence, discipline, prudence and uniformity. Trial and error, with the development of the workhouse plan in England, resulted in the perfect archetypal workhouse in Ireland, where the policies of the new Poor Law were conducted at a practical, administrative and ideological level. The implementation of such a rigid standard plan was a potent effort to restore the natural social order and introduce political control in Ireland. A similar plan was introduced into Scotland, although it was not rigidly imposed. Evidently, the standard plan and workhouse test conformed to Adam Smith's stoicism. The government insisted that only those in the worse possible state of poverty were entitled to relief, otherwise any deviation from this ideal would lead to the indiscriminate distribution of public money which would result in the "rapid spread of the contagion of pauperism" (Rose: 10). Another question to be answered is how coherently the standard plan reflect the ideologies of society. In 1847 this type of plan was still compliant with current public thinking as it was introduced into Scotland. However, the workhouse system was under severe criticism. The development of charitable institutions, hospitals and schools, from the middle of the nineteenth century, contradict Smith's golden mean to moral insight and Hecquet's philosophical declaration, "The poor of a State [...] are like the shadows in a painting: they provide the necessary contrast" (Cunningham & Innes: 3). We have seen that the standard plan of the workhouse reflected the ideologies of the new Poor Laws. Finally we must consider at what crucial point in the nineteenth century the standard plan and its reflected ideologies became obsolete.

## References

Brundage, Anthony. 1978. *The Making of the New Poor Law; The Politics of Inquiry, Enactment and Implementation*, 1833-39. London: Hutchinson
Cage, R.A. 1981. *The Scottish Poor Law 1745-1845*. Edinburgh: Scottish Academic Press
Coats, A.W. 1983. "Economic Thought and Poor Law Policy in the Eighteenth Century". In *Social Policy And Social Welfare*. Ed. M. Loney. Milton Keynes: Open University Press
Cunningham, Hugh and Joanna Innes, Eds. 1998. *Charity, Philanthropy and Reform: from 1690s to 1850*. Basingstoke: MacMillan
Driver, Felix. 1993. *Power And Pauperism; The Workhouse System, 1834-84*. Cambridge: Cambridge University Press
Fitzgibbons, Athol. 1995. *Adam Smith's System of Liberty, Wealth and Virtue; The Moral and Political Foundations of the Wealth of Nations*. London: Oxford Clarendon Press
Focault, Michel. 1977. *Discipline and Punish; The Birth of the Prison*. Middlesex: Penguin
Fraser, Derek, ed. 1976. *The New Poor Law in The Nineteenth Century*. London and Basingstoke: MacMillan

Huzel, J.P. 1983. "Malthus, the Poor Law, and Population in Early Nineteenth Century England". In *Social Policy and Social Welfare*. Ed. M. Loney, Milton Keynes: Open University Press

Kennedy, L., et al. 1999. *Mapping The Great Irish Famine*. Dublin: Four Courts

McCord, Norman. 1976. *Photocopies from the Architectural Archives*. Dublin

Morrison, Kathryn. 1999. *The Workhouse: A Study of Poor Law Buildings in England*. Swindon: Royal Commission

Nicholls, George. 1838. *Three Reports by George Nicholls, Esq., To Her Majesty's Principal Secretary of State for the Home Department*. London: W. Clowes and Sons for H.M.S.O.

O'Dwyer, Frederick. 1997. *Hospital Architecture*. Dublin: Department of Health and Children

Quinn, M. ed. 2001. *The Collected Works of Jeremy Bentham: Writings on the Poor Laws*. Vol. 1. Oxford: Clarendon

Rose, M.E. ed. 1985. *The Poor and the City: The English Poor Law In Its Urban Context, 1834-1914*. Leicester: Leicester University Press

# Irish Immigrants and Local Politics in the Monklands: A Path to Integration?

*Geraldine Vaughan*[1]

Immigrants are often, and accurately so, perceived as a rootless people – they are men and women of transience (as opposed to settlers),[2] of often no real fixed abode, who struggle to build bridges between their origins and their host society. Of migrants in general, Irish emigrants have been described as a "peculiar tramping people", and the study of their arrival and installation in all parts of the world has flourished in the past 25 years (McCready: 37-50). The case of the sons of Erin in the West of Scotland has provided scope for research, and an area that has been little examined so far will be considered here – namely, the Monklands. Situated a few miles east of Scotland's industrial capital, Glasgow, the Monklands, and in particular the towns of Airdrie and Coatbridge, were a destination favoured by Irish migrants, mainly because of the industrial jobs available in iron foundries and mines. From the years following the Great Famine to the beginning of the last century, the Irish and their descendants represented at one stage a third of the total Monklands population.[3]

Throughout a fifty year period, from the mid 1850s into the first years of the last century, one can argue that the Irish migrants in the Monklands developed both a certain sense of *belonging* – as opposed to the supposed permanent transients they always were – as well as a degree, in the eyes of their hosts, of respectability (for some) and tolerability (for others). This can be grasped through the study of Irish participation in *local politics*, both in the towns of Coatbridge and Airdrie.[4] In that sense, evaluating the degree and the reality of Irish involvement in various local government matters provides a means to grasp the extent of the migrants' integration into the Monklands' society. Local politics as a research tool is thus both revealing of Irish assimilation and of the desire of Irish migrants to integrate into Scottish society.

"Local politics", or the "government of a particular place" by "its inhabitants, whether by means of a general meeting [...], or by elected representatives, or through appointment of certain persons among the inhabitants" (Atkinson: 7-10) on matters such as "police, public health, poor law, education, roads" (Atkinson: 12) included a wide range of bodies, i.e. parochial and parish boards, town councils[5] and the school boards established by the 1872 Education (Scotland) Act.[6] Focusing on the Irish interest in local matters goes against the famous Irish adage "Our politics from Home" – that is, the Irish were known to always put

---

[1] I would like to thank Aileen and Patrick Vaughan and Anthony McIlwham for their patient reading and correcting.

[2] See Fitzpatrick: 1992.

[3] In 1861, the Irish-born represented 18.45 per cent of the Airdrie population and 14 per cent in 1871 ; in 1851 an estimation made for Coatbridge showed a total of 21.44 per cent; in 1869 the Catholic population represented 35 per cent of the total Coatbridge population, in 1901 the Irish-born amounted to 15 per cent of the Burgh population (see various *Census Reports*).

[4] The etymology of the noun "local" is the late Latin word *localis* which means "to belong to a place". Although the French word 'local' has the same Latin roots, there is no equivalent in French of the expression "local politics", which can be at best very poorly translated as *"politique municipale"* (or "municipal politics") – that has the inconvenience of designing urban areas only, whereas the British expression has a much wider and fuller meaning. It is also a sign of the importance of local government in the United Kingdom, a notion almost unknown to the French centralised and Jacobine tradition.

[5] Coatbridge Town Council started existing from 1885, when the town was elevated to burgh status.

[6] The town and parish councils were elected by the parliamentary electors residing within the area, together with women and peers who would be disqualified but for their rank or sex. The school boards were elected by all persons of lawful age entered in the valuation roll as an owner or occupant of lands of £4 annual value or upwards.

forward national (Irish) matters before local issues (whether it be Scottish issues in general, or municipal issues in particular). If, in national political issues (such as parliamentary elections) the Irish Catholic community was prepared to follow the Nationalist guidelines, what happened in local political contests was a very different matter. Hence a close study of Irish implication in local issues reveals a most interesting aspect of the immigrant community: the perspective is turned upside down – the new question being rather how far were the Irish prepared to forget national unity and give up Irish issues when it came to municipal elections? Firstly, an overall account of Irish participation in local politics in the Monklands will be given; secondly, religious issues at stake shall be examined, and thirdly, local politics a means of integration to the host society will be assessed.

The primary element to consider in this examination of the Irish contribution in local matters is the motive for such an involvement. Here, the group under study will mainly be Irish Catholics, as information is very seldom available for Irish Protestants. The first incentive was certainly of a financial nature: as it was sometimes levelled at them, the Catholic ratepayers' interests came first, and the aim was to keep the rates as low as possible, or to prevent them from increasing too much.[7] This was especially true in educational matters – where the Catholics were not getting anything back from their rates. Furthermore, it almost became a stereotype, as the Catholics were viewed as obsessive misers: an example of this can be found in a letter written to the local newspaper, *The Airdrie Advertiser*, in 1900: "Here we have four Roman Catholic elected whose prime object [...] is to keep down taxation".[8] Yet this money saving attitude was regarded as a great quality by Catholics, as the (Catholic) Glasgow Observer boasted in 1888: there weren't, stated the newspaper: "more careful and economising than the Catholic members".[9] Economic interests could also mean the protection of trade – mainly the wine and spirit trade,[10] especially as, during the second half of the nineteenth century, out of the ten most prominent Monkland Irish Catholic gentlemen, eight were spirit merchants.[11] Indeed, the Irishmen that engaged in the spirit commerce were often very active in local politics – firstly as a means for them to keep an eye on the granting of licences,[12] and secondly in order to oppose any attempts at passing overly severe temperance bye-laws.

Next to keeping the ratepayers' burden lighter, came the religious interest – that of the protection of Roman Catholics who were under the jurisdiction of local councils and boards. This was true of Parochial Boards, which then became Parish Councils (1894). These councils dealt with the administration of the poor: i.e. the churching of Roman Catholic inmates, the boarding out of Catholic children into Protestant families, the paying of school rates for Catholic children attending Catholic schools, the internment of Catholic paupers – these were the most familiar issues Catholic members on such boards were keen to deal with. The religious question was also the focus in the elected school boards, created by the 1872 Education (Scotland) Act – where the delegates of the voluntary schools were eager to protect their interests – as will be fully examined later on.

Although the two first types of motivation for entering local politics were to be a regular feature during the second half of the nineteenth century, some spurs appeared later on in that period. Municipal socialism and the labour question became important factors in Irish involvement in Monkland politics in the 1890s. For instance, at an Airdrie town council

---

[7] *The Airdrie and Coatbridge Advertiser* (AC), 3/11/1860.
[8] *AC*, 14/4/1900.
[9] *The Glasgow Observer* (GO), 7/4/1888.
[10] *AC*, 5/4/1902 : Two Irish Catholic prominent local gentlemen, ex-Bailie McKillop and Daniel Carlin (Parish Councillor) acted as croupiers of the Airdrie and district Licensed Trade Defence Association.
[11] The list is thus composed: John Benson, Daniel Carlin, John Lavell, James McAuley, Alexander McKillop, Arthur Malone, George Mulvey, John Mulvey, and Charles O'Neill.
[12] Even though the Magistrates of the Licensing Court were not to be engaged in the spirits trade.

monthly meeting in 1894, the Roman Catholic councillor Alexander McKillop proposed that in contracts for the burgh, working men should be paid the standard wages as agreed by trade unions, because, as he declared: "the rights of labour should be looked after".[13] In time, the Irish Catholics promoted their own labour representatives, such as James Donaldson, a miners' agent, elected in the 1894 elections for the Old Monkland Parochial School Board,[14] or John Cooper, a Coatbridge craneman, defeated in 1900.[15] In the early 1900s, Patrick Agnew, an Irishman active in trade unionism, once the chairman of the first ward electors in Airdrie, was to be found regularly questioning candidates on their views on labour issues.[16] If Irish Catholics' reasons for entering local politics have been briefly examined, what can be said regarding Irish Protestants? Apart from religious matters, which will be detailed later, one of the sole testimonies on municipal matters is that of an Irish Orangeman, the minister of the Coatbridge Episcopal Church appointed in 1895, the Reverend William Harris Winter. It should be emphasised that, even if almost unique, his exposed thoughts are of great value, as he was very influential amongst the Irish Orangemen in Coatbridge, as the *Coatbridge Express* put it: "He has taken considerable interest in public affairs".[17] At a meeting of the Coatbridge Literary Society in 1903, the native of County Sligo pastor detailed "The needs of Coatbridge":

> as far as 1898 he [Mr Harris] wrote [...] advocating that a public library and Nursing Association were needed for Coatbridge [...] It would be a good thing if the Corporation would build working mens' houses out in the country, where men could get a piece of ground to till [...] The reverend gentleman advocated public baths, an additional sanitary inspector, a proper inspection of public houses, a better administration of the licensing laws [...].[18]

Without venturing too far, a deduction made from a few references in various sources suggests the possibility of the existence of a strong link between Orangemen and the 'Temperance Party' or temperance interests in local politics – for instance, Reverend Harris was himself in 1898 the President of the Coatbridge Ministers' Temperance Association.[19] Also, in 1895, Coatbridge Orangemen supported two candidates in the Parish Council Elections, of which Stewart J. Bell, a miner, who pledged the teetotallers votes.[20]

After reviewing the major local preoccupations of the Irish in the Monklands, consideration should be given to the category of Irishmen who actually became very involved in local politics. From the 1850s to the 1900s, around a dozen Catholic laymen natives of Erin (or of Irish origin) became prominent local figures in both Coatbridge and Airdrie. From available biographical details, a few common characteristics emerge: the great majority were first-generation Irish from Ulster, they almost all belonged to the merchant class (most of them being spirits dealers), they were practising Catholics and very active in the Church, and once they had secured a municipal position, they usually remained in place for an extensive period of time.

The first example of a prominent Irishman's progression to local honours was the exceptional career that James McAuley pursued in Airdrie. Born in 1813 in county Donegal, he trained as a teacher and then left for Scotland in September 1836. From 1836, he was a teacher (and then head teacher) in Saint Margaret's school, Airdrie, for 24 years. He retired from teaching in 1860 to enter the spirits trade, as this left him more time to attend to his local functions. In the late 1850s, he became a member of the New Monkland Parochial Board, and

---

[13] *AC*, 7/4/1894.
[14] *Glasgow City Archives (GCA), COI 5/1/8/7: Workhouses in Ireland*5), p. 198.
[15] See *AC*, 12/9/1900.
[16] *AC*, 21/10/1905.

[17] *Coatbridge Express (CE)*, 6/12/1899.
[18] *AC*, 7/11/1903.
[19] *CE*, 6/12/1899.
[20] *CE*, 6/2/1895.

at the first School Board elections in 1873, he was returned for Old Monkland and Airdrie. Even the Scottish Protestant local newspaper acknowledged his great talent for politics: "The Almighty had endowed him with the material necessary to constitute a leader. He was well-educated, a fluent and ready speaker, a man of sound common sense".[21] In Coatbridge were found equally brilliant Irish men such as Hugh O'Hear, Arthur Malone or Charles O'Neill – who left Glenravel, County Antrim, when he was 15 years old, and arrived in the 'Iron Burgh' in 1865. Originally a spirits dealer, which he remained throughout his life, he took a degree in medicine and botany at Glasgow University in 1892 (he retired from medical practise in 1898, but remained Assistant Professor of Botany in St Mungo's College). He was a well-travelled man, as his continuous fervour for the national cause (he was a member of the Fenian Brotherhood when a young man in Glasgow) led him to visit America twice, and numerous capitals of Europe.[22] Five years after arriving in the Monklands, he was elected member of the Board of Guardians (1870), and in 1887 became a member of the Old Monkland School Board. He acceded to municipal honours in 1893 by being returned as a town councillor, and was appointed Bailie in 1898.[23]

If these Catholic Irishmen managed to secure seats on local boards, it was mainly through the support of Catholic voters. The historian's main difficulty here is finding a way of evaluating the numerical force of the Catholic vote. The Collectors' books (when they have survived) and bound lists of parliamentary and municipal electors give no indication as to the nationality or the religion of the voters. John McAffrey, in an article published in 1970, proceeded to evaluate the number of Irish voters in an area of Glasgow by identifying Irish-sounding names (McCaffrey: 30-36). This way of proceeding can give approximate results as to the numbers of Irish Catholic voters, but to identify the Irish Protestant electors is a much more difficult task, as one must accept that there is no exact method in that case. It is nonetheless possible to evaluate the strength of the Catholic vote by relying on newspaper articles and various other sources. The first distinction, however, to be made is of the gap between myth and reality, or the Catholic claims of voting power and the numbers actually on the electoral roll. Early evidence shows the confidence Irish Catholics had as an electoral force to be reckoned with, and that led them to declare in 1862: "we [Irish Catholics] by our united action have often put in our friends and expelled our enemies [...] and enables us to get at the different Civic Boards of the town [Airdrie] and parish every manner of justice and fair play".[24] In 1889, Hugh O'Hear, a prominent local Irishman, declared to the Old Monkland School Board, while discussing the Bill against cumulative voting, that the Catholic body in Coatbridge had never abused its voting powers: "we could have returned three members", he stated, but they voluntarily only secured one seat.[25]

What was the reality of such proclaimed electoral power? The first point is that, in fact, Irish Catholics managed to secure at least one member on every (Parochial and School) board and council throughout the period under examination. The sources only give scattered evidence of the number of Catholic voters: in 1868, the local paper mentioned 300 Catholic electors from a total of 1670 (17.9 per cent, not far from a fifth of the total electorate) for Airdrie[26]; in 1895, the *Coatbridge Express* stated that in Airdrie's third ward 100 of the 741 electors were Catholics. As the list of voters for Airdrie in 1894-5 has survived, it gives us an opportunity to put the Irish-sounding name method to the test. Only 59 Irish-sounding Catholic surnames (combined with first names) were counted, which is 40 per cent under the real total.[27] This proportion of less than one in five for Airdrie was small compared to the

[21] *AC*, 10/9/1881.
[22] *Glasgow Examiner* (GE), 22/8/1903 and 23/12/1905.
[23] *AC*, 5/11/1898.

[24] *AC*, 4/10/1862.
[25] *AC*, 4/5/1889.
[26] *AC*, 21/11/1868.

Coatbridge figures, where in 1897, in the fourth ward, 322 Catholic electors were to be found amongst a total of 996 (32.32 per cent, or nearly a third of the electorate). The cumulative vote system for School Boards did favour 'minorities', and as such, Catholics, as often their candidates were returned with very decent scores (James McAuley was returned third of the poll in the first Old Monkland School Board Elections in 1873; and so was Hugh O'Neill in 1891). The cumulative vote system was a frequent subject of dispute on school boards, as a 'One candidate, one vote' correspondent put it in a 1900 letter: "Minorities [Catholics] should scramble on to School Boards by ordinary means same as they do on other boards".[28] However, other local elections (Parish Boards and Town Councils) did not use the cumulative vote system, thus whether the Catholic vote represented 20 per cent or 30 per cent of the electorate at the best in both towns, it meant that, as Charles O'Neill very frankly put it in a letter written to Archbishop Eyre in 1897: "in no ward in the Burgh can a Catholic candidate hope to be returned either to the Town Council or the Parish council, without a very large amount of support from the Protestant electorate".[29]

Yet if Catholics had a potentially great electoral force, the first need for local Irish politicians was to ensure that they registered as voters. Thus, Hugh O'Hear's unsuccessful re-election bid to the Old Monkland Parochial Board in 1888 was partly attributed to the fact that "a lot of his supporters weren't on the rolls".[30] Canvassing and electoral meetings played a central part in the local elections, and Catholic papers insisted on this fundamental necessity, as for instance did the *Glasgow Observer*: "Pay your rates. Get your qualification. Look to your votes and those of your neighbours. Be dynamic".[31] This call for enthusiasm was met in the numerous electoral meetings held throughout the 1851-1901 period in both towns. Thus the practical aspects of elections such as canvassing and campaigning were often directed by local nationalist organisations: even if the latter were more preoccupied with national and purely Irish matters, getting the Irish Catholic on the voters' rolls for municipal elections (as well as parliamentary) and for the defence of Catholic interests in school boards was one of their essential aims (see, for example, the role of Nationalists acting as defenders of Irish Catholics in the Voters' registration Court).[32] Once the Irish voter was on the roll, the electoral committees' next priority was to make sure that Catholic electors would go to the polling stations on voting day. Some committees were so efficient, that for example, for the 1891 Old Monkland School Board election, one of its members, to avoid the loss of a voter "took his place at one in the iron furnaces while the voter went off to the polling station, which was quite far away".[33] This energy spent in canvassing was acknowledged by Protestant citizens, as is shown in a 1900 newspaper commenting on the Catholics candidates' high scores in the Old Monkland School Board election: "the spoils of the election are to those who canvass hardest".[34] Yet, concerning Irish Protestant local political participation and campaigning, little evidence is available: nevertheless, a press report in 1890 stated that at a meeting of the Coatbridge District Loyal Orange Lodge (no.22), a resolution was adopted: "a committee be appointed to draw up a scheme or organisation […] give expression to our views in any contest, whether Municipal

---

[27] *North Lanarkshire Archives* [NLA], UA 1/13/05: "List of persons entitled to vote in the Parliamentary and Municipal elections in Airdrie, Year 1894-1895".

[28] *AC*, 4/4/1900.

[29] *Glasgow Archdiocese Archives* [GAA], GC 29/95: letter from Dr O'Neill, Coatbridge, 15th December 1897.

[30] *GO*, 7/1/1888.

[31] *GO*, 13/4/1889.

[32] *AC*, 1/10/1892: At the Coatbridge Voters Registration Court, Charles O'Neill, acting on the behalf of Irish Nationalists, succeeded in 12 of the 13 claims he defended.

[34] *GO*, 18/4/1891. See also *GAA*, GC 29/95: during the 1897 Coatbridge municipal election, of 138 Roman Catholic fourth ward electors living in Whifflet parish, only two failed to record their votes.

or Parliamentary".[35] In 1895, the same lodge decided to propose two candidates in the Old Monkland Parish Elections,[36] one of whom, John Stewart Bell, was a 25 year old Irish-born coal miner.[37]

While assessing Irish involvement in local issues, we have made references to religious issues. Mixing political and religious matters was a characteristic of the Irish Catholic community, and as W. M. Walker wrote in an 1872 article: "Irish Catholic parochial life was a way of life, and one in which religious, political, economic, educational and recreational elements were so fused as to form a culture from which total withdrawal was unlikely and partial withdrawal appeared as inconsistency".[38] In that perspective, (although W. M. Walker's use of the word 'inconsistency' is undoubtedly excessive), Catholic priests were to play a key role in every form of politics – whether local or national. One particular institution received the clergy's full attention, from 1872 onwards: it was that of the school boards, on which many local clergymen were to be found very active. Since the passing of the Education (Scotland) Act in 1872 and the formation of elected School Boards, the Catholics, in order to safeguard their interests as ratepayers, took an active part in the functioning of these boards (Handley: 298-320). The *Glasgow Observer* explained in an 1888 leader: "We can return our representatives to the Boards where they will act usefully in many ways. In most cases the Catholic representative is the Reverend manager of the schools in the district".[39] In fact, the Monklands might have figured as an exception to this rule, at least in the first (1873) School Board elections. Interestingly, the question of clerical participation on School Boards – whether it be Protestant or Catholic, was a matter of debate in the Monklands. The main local newspaper, in a leader on the matter in February 1873, stated it would be best not to have any clergymen appointed on the boards because of the numerous different religious denominations: in that way, sectarianism would be avoided.[40] To this, the local priests reacted differently: in Airdrie, Father James McIntosh, the senior priest of Saint Margaret's Church, agreed to stand down in favour of a Catholic layman for election (to the discontentment of some of his parishioners);[41] whereas in Coatbridge, Father Michael O'Keeffe, of Saint Patrick's Church,[42] stood in the election with two other Catholic laymen, only to be defeated.[43] When James McAuley died in 1881, Father O'Keeffe sent the Old Monkland School Board a letter stating that a meeting of the Catholic parishioners had agreed on the nomination of Father Thomas Reilly to replace the late member: the board unanimously agreed to it.[44] In the 1873-1903 period (during which eleven

[34] *AC*, 7/4/1900. The four Roman Catholic candidates arrived in the 3rd, 5th, 7th and 9th position (respectively, Father Hughes with 4672 votes; Hugh O'Hear with 4334 votes; Charles O'Neill with 4245 votes and Father Kirke with 4080 votes).

[35] *AC*, 15/11/1890.

[36] *CE*, 6/2/1895. We are assuming here that the Orangemen in Coatbridge were mostly Protestant Irishmen. Links between Irishmen and Orangemen are only referred to once in a newspaper report (*CE*, 25/10/1899) as Reverend Duncan addressed a meeting of the Airdrie L.O.L. no. 125: "A great many of those present had a connection with Ireland [...] There was an impression in this country that Orangeism was an Irish Order".

[37] *Local History Department*, Airdrie Library: 1891 Census Old Monkland, 652/2, enumeration district 35.

[38] See Walker, W. M. 1972. "Irish Immigrants in Scotland: Their Priests, Politics and Parochial Life", The Historical Journal XV: 657.

[39] *GO*, 3/3/1888.

[40] *AC*, 15/2/1873.

[41] *AC*, 15/3/1873: at the meeting of ratepayers, Father McIntosh declined to be nominated, by stating that "It had been said that the ministers should not go upon the Board: and he made up his mind to decline doing so (hear, and some slight hisses)".

[42] See Catholic Directory, 1848. 116: Michael O'Keeffe, born in County Limerick in 1818, ordained in 1845, was appointed to the Coatbridge Mission in 1848. He remained there until his death in 1893.

[43] *GCA*, COI 5/1/8/1: *Minute Book of Old Monkland School Board (1873-79)*, 4-5.

triennial elections were held), while the Airdrie school board remained the Catholic laymen's realm, on the Old and New Monkland Boards local priests sat at regular intervals.[45] This clerical involvement in local school board management implied active participation in electoral meetings, canvassing etc. Thus, often, the church's hall and schoolroom provided a convenient meeting place for Catholic electors – for instance, in 1891, Father O'Keeffe, in view of the forthcoming School Board elections, gave use of his schoolroom to the electoral committee preparing the election and nightly attended the meetings during the month of April.[46] However, it seems that the influence exercised by Catholic clergymen, in all aspects of Irish Catholic life (in spiritual as well as political matters), cannot be described as of a "dictatorial nature"[47] – on numerous occasions, Irish parishioners expressed different views and held opposite political positions from their parish priest.[48]

Before closing the subject of clerical participation in local politics, a few remarks may be made as regards the attitude of Irish Protestant ministers in the Monklands. The Episcopal Irish Reverend, William Winter, as was seen earlier, held specific views on municipal matters. He was an active Orangeman too, and manifested his opinions on local boards. In 1900, he headed a delegation sent to the Old Monkland School Board, objecting to a Roman Catholic being nominated in place of a dead Catholic member. The deputation brought to the board a memorial signed by 1150 electors,[49] but it failed in its request, as Arthur Malone, a familiar figure of Irish Catholic politics was elected in place of the late Father Hughes. On this state of affairs, the infamous Reverend Jacob Primmer, in a conventicler held in Coatbridge in 1901, addressing Irish Protestants, stated that it was scandalous that "in Coatbridge there should be four Papists looking after the education of their Protestant children", and despised what he described as the Catholic way of canvassing (and obtaining votes from Protestants): "Catholics went, say to a grocer, and told him that if he did not vote for the Catholic candidate the Catholics wouldn't buy his sugar".[50]

Other than clerical participation, the second aspect to consider here is the religious issues that arose in local politics, and the Irish Catholic response to them. The Catholics were anxious to secure seats on Parochial, and later on Parish Boards, as it was essential that the interests of the Irish Catholic Poor should be looked after – to that effect, Father McIntosh, of Airdrie, wrote in a letter addressed to the Archbishop: "The absence of Catholic members for the operations of the Parochial Board would be a serious evil. In Airdrie it would be simply disastrous".[51] The Catholics' first concern was probably for children boarded in the poorhouse or boarded out in Protestant families: it was feared what might become of them if they were brought up in a "Protestant atmosphere".[52] Thus, various concerns could arise from Catholic

[44] *GCA*, COI 5/1/8/2: *Minute Book of Old Monkland School Board (1880-84)*. 108 (31/10/1881).

[45] For Old Monkland School Board : Father Thomas O'Reilly (a native of County Meath, appointed to Coatbridge in 1879) was elected in 1882; Father Daniel Thomas Browne (assistant priest in Coatbridge from 1884) sat on the board from 1885 to 1891; and Father John Hughes was elected (appointed to Langloan in 1892) in 1900. On the New Monkland School Board, Father John Nyhan (appointed to Longriggend in 1890) sat as representative of Catholic ratepayers from 1900 to 1903, when he was then replaced by Father Muller.

[46] *GO*, 18/4/1891.

[47] See Walker, W. M., op. cit., 659: "Nevertheless, Catholic Social Organisation was inimical to free expression and suspicious of spontaneity". He compares the role of priests with this of Communist Party secretaries in the USSR, as far as parochial organizations were concerned.

[48] See for example a 'Meeting of Roman Catholics' described in the *AC* (30/10/1869), chaired by Fr MacIntosh in the Saint Margaret Schoolroom in Airdrie. For the coming municipal elections, the priest recommended "Mr Deedes [a Conservative] as a fit and proper person to represent them", but his motion "fell to the ground".

[49] *CE*, 26/9/1900.

[50] *AC*, 10/7/1901.

[51] *GAA*, GC/11/1/1: letter from James McIntosh to Archbishop Eyre, 24/4/1879.

inmates (children and adults) boarded at poorhouses. Irish Catholic members were careful to ensure that the inmates could go to Mass freely and be taught the Catholic catechism. For example, at a meeting of the Poorhouse Committee of the New Monkland Parochial Board, in April 1865, James McAuley, the Irish Roman Catholic member, mentioned the case of Thomas Barrett, who had been sent to the Poorhouse as a Test case by the Inspector, and suggested that he might now be allowed to go out to the Catholic chapel on Sundays.[53] Yet the commission decided he be kept in for another three months, as he had already fled for a period of three days on a previous occasion. A range of different religious matters were discussed; it could be the providing of Roman Catholic Prayer Books,[54] or the burial of Catholic paupers in the Catholic cemetery.[55] Concerning education, the Parochial board, on examining parents' application, could pay the school fees: in 1878, for example, Father James McIntosh replied to the New Monkland Parochial Board which had requested a reduction in fees of the Catholic school for children taken in charge by the Board, that the fees couldn't be reduced, and there were only 13 pauper children attending the school.[56]

On school boards, a wide range of material problems connected with religion arose. At first, the presence of Roman Catholic members on certain committees wasn't easily accepted: for example, in 1882, members on the Old Monkland School Board objected to the presence of a Catholic priest on the committee of a Protestant school.[57] Catholic members aimed to protect Catholic children frequenting Board schools: in 1873, McAuley asked that if the Shorter (Presbyterian) Catechism was to be taught in Board schools, Roman Catholic children should be able to leave the class while this religious instruction was taking place.[58] Furthermore, the interest of fee-paying and rate-paying Catholics were defended by Catholic board members – e.g. the issue of double-fees paid by Irish Catholic working men was tackled by the boards. In March 1878, James McAuley presented the Parochial Board with a list of 62 children whose parents had to pay double fees (the employers of the Summerlee Colliery for instance deducted one penny a week to maintain a works Protestant school which Catholic children didn't attend).[59] The School Board members resolved unanimously to "intimate all the public works that this practise [*sic*] ought to be discontinued henceforth".[60] Keeping the rates low was an electoral motto for Catholics, on whom fell the burden of paying both rates for board schools and fees for the maintenance of their own denominational schools: thus, Irish Catholic members often supported motions against increase of teachers and headmasters' salaries,[61] or the erection of a new school that didn't seem desperately needed, etc. The welfare of Catholic teachers was promoted by Catholic representatives: although this motion was not carried forward, Hugh O'Hear and Charles O'Neill in 1903 voted that the retirement allowances of Catholic teachers be paid by the School Boards.[62]

---

[52] *CE*, 10/7/1901.
[53] *GCA*, CO1/50/12 : *New Monkland Parochial Board Poorhouse (Committee) Minute Book (1863-1878)*.
[54] *GCA*, CO1/50/12, *New Monkland Parochial Board Poorhouse (Committee) Minute Book (1863-1878)*.
[55] *GCA*, CO1/50/1: *New Monkland Parochial Board Minute Book (1878-1881)*. 415: at a meeting (29/4/1880) John Mulvey, the superintendent of Saint Margaret R.C. cemetery made a request that the Board should pay the same fees for the internment of paupers in the Catholic Cemetery as they paid for burial in the New Monkland (Protestant) Cemetery.
[56] *GCA*, CO1/50/1: *New Monkland Parochial Board Minute Book (1878-1881)*. 33-4, meeting of 2/4/1878.
[57] *AC*, 22/4/1882.
[58] *AC*, 1/11/1873.
[59] *AC*, 30/3/1878; GCA, CO1/5/1/8/1, *Minute book of Old Monkland School Board 1873-1879*.
[60] ibid.
[61] See for example CE, 1/6/1904: Arthur Malone voted an amendment against the increase of headmasters' salaries, supported by Charles O'Neill and Hugh O'Hear, in the meeting of the Old Monkland School Board, (31/5/1903).
[62] *AC*, 21/5/1903.

Was participation in local politics a means of social ascension? In 1903, the *Glasgow Examiner* boasted the new comfortable social position acquired by Irish immigrants in the West of Scotland: "Socially, also our people have progressed by leaps and bounds [...] in the Town Boards we have representatives; a large number of gentlemen have been placed on the Justices of the Peace roll".[63] In this statement, the new local political posts acquired by Irish migrants were cited as a sign of *respectability*, a notion dear to Victorian mentalities. It must be stressed here that the decorum that went along with municipal positions contributed to this newly acquired uprightness. Thus, Irish Catholic municipal leaders became respectable and important figures of local life: e.g. regular sketches of their career were reported in the local Protestant press, in a laudatory tone. For example, Alexander McKillop, the first Roman Catholic councillor to be nominated in Airdrie (1887), elected Bailie in 1891, and nominated Justice of the Peace in 1898, was thus described in the *Advertiser*: "Mr McKillop was for some years the Irish leader (Co. Mayo) in the Parliamentary Debating Association and possesses a fluent speech and florid oratory; he has frequently lectured with marked appreciation [...] Mr McKillop is a keen politician [...] He is president of the local branch of the National League, vice-president of the Airdrie Liberal Association, and is now president of the Airdrie Burns Club".[64] The Burns Club gave annual suppers, where Irish local leaders, such as Alexander McKillop or Charles O'Neill took a prominent part, along with the most respected Scottish personalities of the town. The Irish members who took part in club gatherings or town council dinners didn't object to toasting the Royal Family repeatedly,[65] whilst on various boards, their reluctance to celebrate with the British crown was shown on numerous occasions.[66]

Was the Irish Catholic community united in local action? Although Irish Catholics did tend to vote according to nationalist instructions in parliamentary elections, local elections were a different matter altogether. Voting orders in municipal elections were seldom given by nationalist organisations, probably owing to the diversity of situations to be found in each particular town. Nevertheless, a general guideline was handed out by the organiser of the Irish National League, D. J. Sheehan, in 1891, on municipal elections: he stated that when these were "contested on political principles", the branches should "support those candidates only who are supporters of Mr Gladstone's Irish policy".[67] Thus, the main nationalist recommendation throughout the period examined was to favour, as in national politics, the Liberal party. However, as D. J. Sheehan put it, this was true *when* local elections were disputed on political principles, which was not always the case. Hence, political division amongst Irish Catholic voters in local elections can be identified as early as 1859: a controversy in the *Airdrie Advertiser* revealed that some 'renegade' Catholics had supported Tory candidates in the late municipal elections.[68] In 1860, an electoral meeting called by an Irishman, John Devlin, and chaired by James McAuley, was organised in support of two conservative candidates, Mr Brown and Mr Fleming.[69] Surviving Airdrie municipal poll books (1861-1867) give us an interesting insight into the political behaviour of different local Irishmen.

[63] *GE*, 3/1/1903. The Irish Catholics who became Justices of the Peace in the Monklands before the First World War were: Alexander McKillop (1898); Thomas Lavell, Hugh O'Hear and Dr Charles O'Neill in 1910.

[64] *AC*, 28/1/1893.

[65] See, for example, the annual supper of the Coatbridge Burns Club, 29/1/1898, where Bailie Lavell and Councillor O'Neill were present.

[66] See, for instance, the Irish Catholic local politicians' reaction towards the Coronation celebrations: in 1902, at the Old Monkland School Board monthly meeting (March), where none of the Irish members made any proposals in connection with Coronation day, Father Kirke "jocularly remarked that he was not a loyalist" (*CE*, 26/3/1902).

[67] *GO*, 21/11/1891.

[68] See *AC*, 29/10/1859, 12/11/1859 and 19/11/1859.

[69] *AC*, 3/11/1860.

Throughout this six-year period, the choices of at least five local prominent Irishmen (out of the claimed 25 voters)[70] that could be identified were examined.[71] Scottish candidates in competition for municipal honours rarely claimed a party allegiance: but an attentive reading of the local Liberal paper *The Airdrie and Coatbridge Advertiser*, is useful in deciphering the political preferences of the contestants. Besides, the key to Irish voting was given in an 1862 leader, where a correspondent of a Catholic paper in Airdrie was quoted: "our mode of action in Airdrie [...] we, some fifteen years ago, adopted the two following resolutions", that were firstly, always to hold a Catholic meeting where each candidate would be examined and "the best men selected"; and secondly, be unanimous on three candidates and "leaving each other the power of voting for whom we please for the fourth".[72] The analysis of the poll books reveals that such a pattern was usually followed: the Irish went together to the polling station, at the same time of the day, and their choices, if different, varied in the choice of one or two men at the most. The Irishmen voted both for Conservative and Liberal candidates,[73] but their choices might differ: two Irishmen generally represented opposite tendencies, namely James McAuley (Liberal) and John Lavell of Airdrie (Conservative). Nevertheless, voting patterns changed from one election to another: for example, in 1861, all Irishmen but John Lavell voted for three Liberal candidates and another who was "the publicans' candidate" (Mr Black)[74] whereas John Lavell voted for two Conservative and one Liberal nominees.[75] In 1865, all Irishmen selected two Tory and two Liberal contestants.

Furthermore, the Irish Catholic community could also split on matters other than purely political ones: as mentioned earlier, the temperance question could be a serious source of division. The implication of most prominent Irish local men in the spirit trade was a steadfast feature of that period, and as Dr O'Neill, himself a spirit merchant, explained in 1897: "Some of us have been in the district for over a quarter of a century, and all the time have identified ourselves with the spirit trade [...] only business which we [the Irish Catholics] can practise with any hope of earning a livelihood".[76] In that sense, temperance advocates were bound to oppose Irish publicans, who formed the majority of Irish Catholic candidates. In 1893, an Airdrie Catholic Temperance writer and worker, Mary Grass, addressed a letter to the third ward Catholic electors asking them not to vote for Bailie McKillop, who although not a spirit dealer, had acquaintances with the trade, but to support Peter Horn, a Scottish Temperance worker.

Some Scottish (Protestant) citizens did not always appreciate the will of Irish Catholics to participate in local elections and administration. In 1868, a correspondent of the local newspaper, criticised the Tories for having introduced the 'No Popery' cry in the Airdrie Municipal Elections: however, this seemed to be a rare occurrence, as it was alleged to be "the first time that religion has been imported into municipal matters".[77] Discrimination against Irish Catholics was sometimes shown on boards: thus, in 1860, a correspondent reported the insulting words used by the Chairman of the New Monkland board regarding an application of some Irish female pauper whose husband had just died: "Ay, my; you Irish as soon as you have a claim on the Parish, you die", to which Mr McAuley replied, with humour: "I have been upwards of twenty years in the Parish and I have never died yet – (laughter) – and the last

[70] *AC*, 4/10/1862.
[71] NLA, UA/1/11/2/3: *Airdrie poll register detailing elections of councillors (1861-1867)*. The Irishmen identified were : James McAuley; Daniel Carlin; Michael McKillop, pawnbroker (father of Alexander McKillop); John Lavell, pawnbroker; Charles M'Geechan, grocer; Francis M'Kearney, spirit dealer.
[72] *AC*, 4/10/1862.
[73] *ibid*.: "the political parties are so equally balanced with us".
[74] *AC*, 25/10/1862.
[75] *ibid*. Airdrie Municipal election, 5/11/1861.
[76] *GAA*, GC 29/95; Letter from Charles O'Neill to Archbishop Eyre, 12/12/1897.
[77] *AC*, 21/11/1868.

thing that either a Scotchman or an Irishman does in this world is to die"; Mr Collins, another Irish member, retorted to a further offending remark made by the chairman that the expression "was insulting, not only to the Irish applying for relief, but to the Irish members of the Board".[78] In 1870, at a New Monkland Parochial Board meeting, James McAuley accused the chairman, JC Waddel, of excluding Roman Catholics from the House Committee.[79] The presence of Orangemen on School Boards didn't help soften sectarianism: in 1901, John Carter, master of a Coatbridge Loyal Orange Lodge and member of the Old Monkland Board, complained of the presence of Roman Catholics on the board, by denouncing the "impudence of Romanist meddling" with Protestant affairs.[80]

Yet, on the whole, these incidents were quite rare, and the Scottish response to Irish participation in the towns affairs was one of acceptance and furthermore in some cases, of gratitude. The keen interest and active participation of Catholic Irish councillors on local boards was recognised by their Scottish counterparts: for instance, James McAuley's devotion to parochial affairs was described at his death in 1881 by his colleagues as follows: "For nearly half a century Mr McAuley had laboured earnestly in the interest of the Board and proved himself an able counsellor in all matters of difficulty and of great assistance in managing its affairs. He had served on all its committees [New Monkland Parochial Board], and was intimately acquainted with its business in all its details so that his loss will now be keenly felt".[81]

To conclude, one could argue that, on the whole, involvement in local politics was one of the Irishmen's paths to integration in Scottish society, as it was both a means of integration (acquiring political experience, working on the boards with their Scottish counterparts) and a sign of the desire (although more often unconscious) the Irish had to integrate. Truly enough, this newly acquired respectability for some prominent local Irishmen did not entirely change the global image of Irish Catholic migrants. As late as 1909, Bailie David, a Scottish magistrate who sat in the Coatbridge council with other Irish councillors, made this remark at a Police Court: "A lot of you Irishmen think you have a right to come here and disgrace the town. You will get the town a bad character".[82] But the global acceptance of Irish Catholic involvement in local matters was certainly a sign of a change that was slowly taking place (although this slow change did not follow a linear progression in time, as the Irish Catholics were to encounter great obstacles to integration in the inter-war period).[83]

There are two topics that need to be further explored. The first matter is the relationship between local Irish Catholic politicians and the Nationalist movement – as in the Monklands, some of the prominent local Irishmen were also great figures in the Irish Nationalist party in Scotland. Could the local political experience acquired on local councils and boards be wisely used in national politics? The second subject which needs further exploration is the involvement of Irish Protestants in local matters: this is a most delicate matter for the historian, as these migrants are difficult to identify in sources. If it could be ascertained that a great majority of Orangemen in the Monklands were Ulstermen – then what would simply be required, is a close study of Orange participation in local politics. However, one should be careful not to postulate an *Irish Protestant* political strategy in local matters. Finally, what political lessons could the Irishmen learn from their participation in local affairs? The *Glasgow Examiner* gives one possible answer, in a sketch of Dr O'Neill's career in 1905: "His [local]

[78] *AC*, 8/12/1860.
[79] *AC*, 5/2/1870.
[80] *CE*, 6/11/1901.
[81] *GCA*, CO1/50/1; *New Monkland Parochial Board Minute Book (1878-1881)*, 663-4.
[82] *The Coatbridge Leader*, 3/4/1909.
[83] This theme was developed by T.M. Devine at a conference in March 2003, "Racism and Anti-Catholicism in Scotland from the Irish Famine to World War Two".
[84] *GE*, 23/12/1905.

career shows that is no bar to public advancement for a man to be consistent in his [radical and nationalist] political views and fearless in expressing them, even though such views be not shared by the majority of his [Scottish] townsmen".[84]

### References

*Airdrie and Coatbridge Advertiser*

Atkinson, M. 1904. *Local Government in Scotland*. Edinburgh

*Coatbridge Express*

*Coatbridge Leader*

Fitzpatrick, D. 1992. "The Irish in Britain: Settlers or Transients?" *Labour History Review*. 57.3

*Glasgow Examiner*

*Glasgow Observer*

Handley, J. E. 1964. *The Irish in Modern Scotland*. Cork: Cork University Press

McCaffrey, J. 1970. "The Irish Vote in Glasgow in the Later Nineteenth Century: A Preliminary Survey". *The Innes Review (Scottish Catholic Historical Studies)*. XXI: 30-36

McCready, R. B. 2000. "Revisiting the Irish in Scotland: the Irish in Nineteenth and Early Twentieth-Century Scotland". In *The Irish Diaspora*. Ed. A. Bielenberg. Edinburgh: Pearson Education. 37-50

# "The Wiser and Better View?": J.G. Lockhart at the Limits of Romantic Biography

*Dan Wall*

John Gibson Lockhart's *Life of Robert Burns*, published in 1828, has, perhaps, been eclipsed by his far more impressive *Life of Scott*, which appeared a decade later. Nevertheless, it remains a fascinating insight into its author's cultural preoccupations, and suggests an ambitious, if not wholly convincing attempt to articulate them. Lockhart's Burns appeared when the extended literary biography was still in its infancy, having only been preceded by approximately a dozen works. Among these was Johnson's 1775 *Life of Savage*, an example of a shorter literary biography. Boswell's 1791 *Life of Johnson* was considerably longer, and Walter Scott's 1808, *Life of Dryden*, annotated by Lockhart in 1834, was the first single volume literary biography.[1] The purpose of this paper is to analyse J.G. Lockhart's biographical approach, and to consider the effect of this upon the image of Burns that he creates.

Both David Ellis and Francis Russell Hart place Lockhart's *Life of Burns* in the context of the Romantic biography, a genre of literary biography originating in the Romantic period and defined, crucially, by its preoccupation with the creative mind and imagination of the subject. It is from this perspective that Lockhart approaches Burns, a choice that accounts for the absence of many of the material details relating to Burns's life. The emphasis upon Burns's creative impulses is perhaps the catalyst for much of the criticism heaped upon Lockhart's *Life of Burns*, most notably from D.H. Lawrence who labelled Lockhart "lily arsed" for his apparent avoidance of Burns's radicalism and sociability (Lawrence in Trilling, 267). Similarly, the Burns scholar Franklyn Bliss Snyder was driven to label Lockhart's biography as "deliberately mendacious", adding that "it should not be trusted in any respect or detail" (488).

It is only by re-reading Lockhart's *Life of Burns* as a Romantic biography that we can understand previous criticisms of their inaccuracy, and recognise the tensions that arise between Burns's life, and Lockhart's conception of him (Carruthers, 97). A key example of this is his analysis of "Holy Willie's Prayer", a poem stripped, as Hart notes (90), of its potency by Lockhart's assertion that Burns's attack on the impiety and hypocrisy of the *Auld Licht* divines was motivated out of little more than the thoughtless flights of fancy of a "reckless young satirist" (1907: 44). Furthermore, Lockhart continues:

> Had Burns received, at this time, from his clerical friends and patrons, such advice as was tendered, when rather too late, by a layman who was as far from religious bigotry on religious subjects as any man in the world, this great genius might have made his first approaches to the public notice in a very different character. (1907: 47)

Lockhart appears to recoil in genuine horror at what he judges to be the blasphemous content of the poem, while simultaneously seeming to absolve Burns of any such intent. Moreover, the tables are completely turned on the *New Licht* clergy who he claims led the young poet astray, and who, to Lockhart's incredulity, enthusiastically greeted the poem upon its publication, a reaction he ascribes to the "heightened state of party feeling" (1907: 44) in Ayrshire at the time (Carruthers, 96). Throughout his apparent condemnation of the Kirk Satires Lockhart consistently qualifies his irritation at the religious and political import of Burns's attacks (Carruthers, 96), perhaps most notably where his own satirical instincts lead him to concede that:

---

[1] For an illuminating theoretical contextualisation of biographical genre see Batchelor (1-11).

The prominent antagonists of these men (Magill and Dalrymple, both ministers of Ayr) and chosen champions of the *Auld Light*, in Ayrshire, it must now be admitted on all hands, presented, in many particulars of personal conduct and demeanour, as broad a mark as ever tempted the shafts of a satirist (1907: 41).

Lockhart follows with a denunciation of the *Auld Licht* of considerable severity, depicting them as:

Bigoted monks ... austere and ungracious of aspect, coarse and repulsive of address and manners – very Pharisees as to the lesser matters of the law, and many of them, to all outward appearance at least, overflowing with pharisaical self-conceit, as well as monastic bile (1907: 41).

Thereafter, Lockhart delicately claims that Burns had "grossly overcharged his portraits" of the *Auld Licht*, before instructing the reader (not altogether convincingly) that underneath all that "monastic bile", "pharisaical self-conceit" and those "repulsive manners" there also lay some "admirable qualities" (1907: 41). Lockhart's strategy as biographer becomes particularly interesting during these sections as he struggles to override Burns's radical impulses in order to promote him as an example of Scottish literary genius. Lockhart's Romantic conception of Burns, taking as its focus Burns's creativity, therefore requires Lockhart to confront aspects of his subject's life that Lockhart is required to reconcile with his own political views. Where such hurdles exist, Lockhart intervenes personally in the circumstances of Burns's life, damning those who supposedly set him upon a more radical poetic path, whilst simultaneously conceding the legitimacy of his satirical targets.

As part of this strategy, Lockhart conveniently styles his subject as having been prone to distraction and "flights of fancy", as in his treatment of "Holy Willie's Prayer". Therefore, traits that Lockhart finds unpalatable can be excised from the *Life*. The effect of this editorial intervention is to de-politicise Burns's poetry so that Lockhart's Romantic agenda can be superimposed upon it. This recurs in Lockhart's treatment of "The Holy Fair". Here he contends that, despite having been encouraged by "the roar of applause" (1907: 46) with which the Kirk Satires were met in certain circles, Burns has managed to produce a work in which "satire keeps its own place, and is subservient to the poetry of Burns" (1907: 46). Thus, as Gerard Carruthers acknowledges, Lockhart attempts to re-style it as a poem that confirms Burns's status as a "national poet".[2] Yet Lockhart's methodology is compromised by his failure to convincingly account for the evidence of Burns's radicalism that he encounters.

Elsewhere in the *Life* the imposition of Lockhart's cultural and political agenda is equally apparent, and extends beyond literary criticism and into the poet's life. Burns's supposed involvement in the capture of a suspect brig (the Rosamonde) on the Solway Firth on 27 February, 1792, is one such example. The revelation of Burns's subsequent gift of four carronades, seized on board "by way of trophy" (1907: 164), to the French Asssembly seems to be irreconcilable with Lockhart's attempts to de-politicise Burns. Indeed it is, for Lockhart goes on to castigate his subject for his "most absurd and presumptuous breach of decorum" (1907: 165) after arguing that "nobody" (meaning not even Lockhart) "can pretend that Burns was not guilty". Lockhart then attempts to limit the impact of the story by first vividly describing how the dragoons, led by Burns, bravely stormed the brig, though encountering practically no opposition. Lockhart insinuates that jealousy over his role in the capture of the Rosamonde amongst his fellow excisemen led to the carronade affair, though still very serious in Lockhart's eyes, being blown out of all proportion. Added to this is a great deal of reflection

---

[2] Carruthers does concede that Lockhart recognises Burns's innovation and subversion of critical and moral imperatives in poetry (101).

by Lockhart concerning the ruin that faced Burns as a result of the incident, communicated through the inclusion of the letter to Mrs Dunlop of 2 January 1793 (1907: 166). Its incorporation into the biography enables Lockhart to focus upon the apparent contrition felt by Burns in the during the excise board's enquiry for having dabbled in politics at all. As a result, the ruin subsequently suffered by Burns corresponds to Lockhart's impression of him, promulgated throughout the *Life*, as a flawed, fanciful genius. Again, such insight into the human side of the poet occurs safely within the confines of Lockhart's manipulation of his life; a somewhat erroneous reference to William Pitt's admiration of Burns's is quoted (1907: 171), in order to nullify the implications of the Rosamonde episode. Prior to this, Burns's refusal to drink a toast to Pitt, preferring instead to raise a glass in honour of George Washington, is explained away in the following, rather unsatisfactory, manner:

> I suppose the warmest admirer of Mr Pitt's talents and politics would hardly venture to dissent substantially from Burn's estimate of the comparative merits of these two great men. The name of Washington, when contemporary passions have finally sunk into the peace of the grave, will undoubtedly have its place in the first rank of heroic virtue…. (1907: 160)

For Snyder, the Rosamonde affair is also a key example of how Lockhart mendaciously attempts to utilise the concept of the Romantic biography in order to emphasise Burns's Romanticism. Snyder's claim, as Hart suggests, fell foul of manuscript evidence that later emerged, apparently vindicating Lockhart's account (83). Yet problems do emerge as Lockhart attempts to discredit evidence which clearly hint at Burns's radicalism. These sections of the biography are undoubtedly the most awkward that Lockhart wrote, rather than deliberately mendacious. In short, these instances in the *Life* suggest that Burns's biographical details are not sufficiently malleable to carry the weight of Lockhart's view of him as a politically "reliable" "national poet".

Elsewhere in the *Life* Lockhart argues rather more effectively for his conception of Burns. The initial chapters stress the importance of Burns's reading in informing his creativity, in spite of some rather self-conscious attempts to simultaneously assert the wholesome nature of Burns's upbringing. Implicit here is Lockhart's connection between Burns's rural roots and his literary genius, a connection that culminates in the following extract:

> The four years during which Burns resided on this cold and ungrateful farm of Mossgiel were the most important of his life. It was then that his genius developed its highest energies; on the works produced in these years his fame was first established, and must continue to rest: it was then also that his personal character came out in all its brightest lights, and in all but its darkest shadows; and indeed from the commencement of this period, the history of the man may be traced, step by step in his own immortal writings. (1907: 35)

This is perhaps Lockhart's most explicit statement of intent regarding his analysis of Burns. For Lockhart, Romantic biography entails a synthesis of the life of the poet and his works – the two eventually becoming one. Consequently, Lockhart alights upon "The Cottar's Saturday Night" as one of the best examples of this symbiotic relationship. He commends the poem for its "easy", "gentle", "placid" and "undulating" motion (1907: 52), before praising it for capturing the "artless beauty and solemnity of the feelings and thoughts that ennoble the life of the Scottish peasant" in a "vein of unmixed merriment" (1907: 53). However, Lockhart's appreciation extends beyond a celebration of the poem purely on the grounds of its artistry; crucially for Lockhart, the poem is also an embodiment of rural piety, expressed vividly and compellingly. In this respect, Lockhart attempts to cite the poem as evidence of Burns's own religious devotion, in order to counter the supposedly "blasphemous" connotations of "The Holy Fair" (1907: 54). In attempting to reconcile the two poems with each other, Lockhart's view of Burns as a "national poet" is truly unveiled:

> A scene of family worship, on the other hand, I can easily imagine to have come from his hand as pregnant with the ludicrous as that Holy Fair itself. The family prayers of the Saturday's night ... are part of the same system – the same system that has made the people of Scotland what they are – and what, it is hoped, they will continue to be. (1907: 54)

"The Cotter's Saturday Night" thus becomes crucial to Lockhart in establishing Burns as a cultural icon, perfectly attuned to the traditions and feelings of rural Scottish life.

Another major criticism levelled by Snyder at Lockhart was an overwhelming tendency to "moralise" the circumstances of Burns's life, through his portrayal of him as a gifted peasant-poet, living, apart from the occasional impulsive lapse, a life of virtue and piety (Snyder, 354). Lockhart's squeamishness concerning the realities of Burns's private life does, as Hart acknowledges, warrant condemnation by modern biographical standards. Yet elsewhere in the *Life* we find Romantic biography operating under pressures which suggest that, both commercially and personally, Burns's biography in 1828 was especially difficult terrain for Lockhart. However, Lockhart's intentions here are important; he faced the difficult, task of having to complete his biography without offending the sensibilities of Burns's widow Jean. In this respect Lockhart's emphasis upon Burns's poetic imagination was, in this case, rather convenient.

Ultimately, the issue is one of emphasis.[3] Lockhart does not actively deny the "reality" of Burns, but neither is it presented in any great detail, since Lockhart was only preoccupied with the nature of Burns's poetic creativity. Burns's affairs, like his more "dangerous" politics, are similarly swept aside through references to "fits of passion" over which Burns had no control. Such fits of passion, Lockhart implies, were nothing more than that, and so do not feature prominently in the biography. In Lockhart's hands such details do nothing more than enhance Burns's Romantic sensibility. This partially explains Lockhart's positioning of Burns as a victim of the sexual desires of others:[4]

> Though, when he was young, he was bashful and awkward in his intercourse with women, yet when he approached manhood, his attachment to their society became very strong, and he was constantly the victim of some fair enslaver. (1907: 16)

The other reason has to be Lockhart's consideration of the sensibilities of Jean. Among Burns's so-called "fair enslavers" was Mary Campbell (the enigmatic "Highland Mary"), whom Burns juggled with Jean, who eventually became Burns's wife. In the *Life* Lockhart distances the two women in time (1907: 55), placing Campbell before Jean, and thus avoiding any suggestion of "improper" conduct on Burns's part. A similar approach is taken towards Agnes McLehose, with whom Burns enjoyed a highly charged correspondence. Meanwhile, Mary Paton, who gave birth to Burns's first child, (subsequently raised by Jean), and Anna Park, with whom Burns often met in the Globe tavern in Dumfries during 1790, scarcely warrant attention at

---

[3] Carruthers acknowledges that Lockhart does not flatly deny the evidence of Burns's extra-marital adventures, (with the exception of Anna Park), nor does he completely airbrush out evidence of Burns's drinking habits (101).

[4] One finds in this quotation more than a hint of Lockhart's own personality, again reinforcing the view that Lockhart's Burns is in some sense a projection of himself.

all. Such scant regard of these details is entirely in keeping with Lockhart's conception of Romantic biography, allowing him capture a sense of the poet without getting too entangled in political and personal details which he would rather avoid. Indeed, in his preface to the *Life of Burns* Lockhart criticises the interest in Burns's personal life that characterised earlier studies of Burns. These details, he suggests, were best kept out of the public eye. In this respect, a critical consensus emerges between Lockhart, and one of his critical adversaries at the *Edinburgh Review*. Francis Jeffrey in his 1809 *Edinburgh Review* essay on Cromek's Reliques made a similar point (Jeffrey in Morgan, 33), as did Walter Scott in his letter to Lockhart of June 1828 in praise of the *Life*, when he praised Lockhart's approach as the "the wiser and better view" (Scott in Lochhead, 154).

Lockhart's omission of much of the material relating to Burns's private life was doubly convenient; Lockhart had a great deal personally invested in his *Life of Burns*. His attributions of political and religious radicalism to Burns's own youthful recklessness as a satirist strongly echo the controversies that enveloped him during the early years of his own literary career, in particular the controversies surrounding the "Chaldee Manuscript" (Lockhart, 1817: 89), and the "Cockney School"[5] articles. Lockhart's second novel, *Adam Blair* (1822), had caused uproar upon publication due to its portrayal of a steamy affair between the eponymous minister and a widowed parishioner, Charlotte Campbell (Ian Campbell in Lockhart, 1996: x). Consideration of these incidents suggests an image of Lockhart radically different from the supposedly buttoned-up biographer of Burns. The extent to which such controversies appear to resurface in the *Life* suggest that Lockhart, rather than pursuing a pristine moral agenda in relation to Burns, was actually more eager to avoid further acrimony in his own literary career. By 1828 the stakes were higher than ever for Lockhart: John Murray had appointed him editor of the *Quarterly Review* in 1825, and the deal to publish the life with Constable was prestigious (although it was curtailed by the financial crash of 1826). In such a mass-market biography the recklessness of Lockhart's early career at *Blackwood's* had to be avoided. The controversy that Lockhart attracted had not always been welcomed by either William Blackwood or John Murray (a major shareholder in *Blackwood's*). In a letter to Murray of 23 October 1821 Lockhart reveals the pressure that he had been under to refrain form scurrilous character assassination, as well as his willingness to comply for the sake of his career:

> Blackwood has just been here who has pleased me much by repeating your approbation of this number of the Magazine. Depend upon it – the succeeding ones will have <u>more</u> of what you like and <u>less</u> of what you dislike in it. Personalities we all agree must stop – they have stopped.[6]

The presence of these autobiographical elements in the *Life of Burns* indicates a remarkable proximity between biographer and subject, and to some extent accounts for Lockhart's incredibly sympathetic treatment of him. The *Life of Burns*, therefore, reflects an attempt by him to garner literary respectability and credibility; the resulting image of Burns is therefore strongly dictated by circumstances in Lockhart's own life.

Lockhart's biography, despite appearing to "bowdlerise" Burns's life, simultaneously enabled Lockhart reconfigure him as an icon of Scottish literary inspiration, and also write a "respectable" *Life*. Yet Lockhart, in imposing his own demands so heavily upon Burns's poetry is forced to awkwardly intervene in the role of editor when "problematic" material is encountered. Consequently, Burns's radical tendencies, and ultimately the circumstances of his life, are completely sidelined in order to mould him to Lockhart's Romantic conception of the gifted "national poet". The result is a fundamental tension throughout the *Life of Burns*

---

[5] See *Blackwood's*, October 1817 – December 1822.
[6] Lockhart to John Murray, 23 October 1821: Blackwood Archive, NLS Edinburgh, MS. 4003, f.131

between Lockhart's biographical intentions and his partly autobiographical approach, a tension that stretches Romantic biography to its very limits.

## References

Batchelor, John, ed. 1993. *The Art of Literary Biography*. Oxford: Clarendon
Carlyle, Thomas. 1987. *Selected Writings*. Ed. Alan Shelston. London: Penguin
Carruthers, Gerard. 2002. "Remaking Romantic Scotland". In *The Art of Romantic Biography*. Ed. Arthur Bradley and Alan Rawes. Aldershot: Ashgate. 93–108
Ellis, David. 2000. *Literary Lives: Biography and the Search for Understanding*. London: Routledge
Hart, Francis Russell. 1971. *Lockhart as Romantic Biographer*. Edinburgh: Edinburgh University Press
Lang, Andrew. 1897. *The Life and Letters of John Gibson Lockhart*. London: John C. Nimmo
Lawrence, D.H. 1958. *Selected Letters of D.H. Lawrence*. Ed. Diana Trilling. New York:
Lochhead, Marion. 1954. *John Gibson Lockhart*. London: John Murray.
Lockhart, John Gibson. 1996. *Adam Blair*. Ed. Ian Campbell. Edinburgh: Mercat Press
Lockhart, John Gibson. 1907. *The Life of Robert Burns*. Ed. Ernest Rhys. London: Dent
Lockhart, John Gibson. 1977. *Peter's Letters to His Kinsfolk*. Ed. William Ruddick. Edinburgh: Scottish Academic Press
Lockhart, John Gibson, with James Hogg and John Wilson. 1817. "The Chaldee Manuscript". *Blackwood's Edinburgh Magazine*. October. II: 89
Lockhart to John Murray, 23 October 1821: Blackwood Archive, NLS Edinburgh, MS. 4003, f.131
Morgan, Peter F., Ed. 1983. *Jeffrey's Criticism*. Edinburgh: Scottish Academic Press
Scott, Sir Walter. 1963. *The Life of John Dryden*. Ed. Bernard Kreissman. Lincoln: University of Nebraska Press
Snyder, Franklyn Bliss. 1968. *The Life of Robert Burns*. New York: Archon Press
Trilling, Diana, Ed. 1958. *Selected Letters of D.H. Lawrence*. New York: Farrar Straus and Cudahy

324

# The Differing Motivations for Preventing Transatlantic Emigration: A Case Study From West Ulster, 1718-1729

*Patrick Walsh*

In May 1729, a Co. Londonderry land agent wrote to his landlord pressing for legislation to prevent the departure of tenants to America. The agent was Robert McCausland and he was the agent for the vast Conolly estates in Counties Londonderry and Donegal. His master was William Conolly, Ireland's wealthiest commoner, Speaker of the Irish House of Commons and one of the Lord Justices of Ireland. McCausland was echoing the fears of many Ulstermen who were becoming alarmed at the increased levels of emigration to America in the late 1720s. At the same time that he was writing to Conolly about his local concerns, the Irish administration were getting worried about the levels of transatlantic migration particularly from Ulster. In November 1728 Lord Carteret, the lord lieutenant of Ireland, had written to the Lord Justices, including Conolly, voicing his concerns about the level of emigration to the North American colonies, and seeking proposals to address this problem. The level of emigration to America which had reached its highest level yet in the years 1727-29 and showed no signs of abatement was a concern both for those at the top of the socio-political scale like Carteret and those lower down like McCausland. Of concern to each was the economic effects of emigration but also the diminution of the Protestant interest in Ireland. Conolly himself straddled these groups, as a lord justice he was concerned about the macro effects on the national economy, both moral and material, while as a landlord he was concerned about the micro effects on his own rental income and estate interest. In his reply to McCausland, he wrote, "as to what you mention about Government preventing passengers going to America two weeks before they go, this cannot be done without an act of parliament which I hope will be taken care of next session,"[1] suggesting that he agreed with McCausland's concerns and was determined to address them at the national rather than the local level. This paper examines the effects of the depressed national economy on the Conolly estates in Ulster and Conolly's responses both on a local and national level to the increased numbers emigrating from Ulster in the late 1720s.

Emigration to North America from Ulster was a relatively new phenomenon. The first major wave had only begun in 1718, although there had been sporadic movements previous to this. In the beginning there were few objections either at local or national level. Indeed, Robert McCausland had written to Conolly in 1718 about the departure of tenants going to America complaining only that they were not paying their debts before departure: "But all I would have done if it were possible to oblige these rogues who goes to pay their just debts before they go."[2] The scale of migration in 1718 was different, however, and there was no difficulty in replacing the departing tenants. In 1718 nine tenants from the Grocers proportion in Co. Londonderry which was leased by Conolly left for England and according to McCausland, "many more were just on termes of selling their lands."[3] Each of these tenants was replaced straight away either by the agent or in two cases following a private sale. Economic factors played their part in this first wave of Ulster emigration and it has been suggested that many of the emigrants in these years were originally Scots who came to the north of Ireland in the 1690s to escape famine and to take advantage of cheap Ulster land which lay desolate following the war of 1689/90. Recent estimates suggest that 41,000 Scots arrived in Ulster in the 1690s (Fitzgerald,

[1] William Conolly to Robert McCausland 27 May 1729, (Irish Architectural Archive (IAA) Castletown Papers Ref: 97/84 C/27/1-92
[2] R. McCausland to W. Conolly 18 November 1718, IAA Ref: 97/84 C/27/1-92.
[3] A list of persons in the Manor of Grocers that are gone or going to New England and how they disposed of their lands, IAA Ref: 97/84 C/11/1-21

79). Many of the leases granted in the 1690s to these settlers climaxed in the late 1710s and most landlords took the chance to increase rents. Those who departed the Conolly estates were not necessarily the poorest tenants either. Amongst those who left the Grocers proportion were four freeholders, James Cochran, John Cochran, Jonathan Colman and Alexander Mackey. It is possible to infer that many of these tenants were Scotsmen, who had come to Ireland when conditions were favourable and were now moving onwards across the Atlantic as conditions deteriorated. Ireland had been a convenient stepping stone on the path to America.[4]

Economic conditions were hard in 1718 in the county and Robert McCausland writing in November commented that "trade is fallen very much in this county and particularly the yarn and if I am not mistaken it will not appear soon. However I do not fear for your estates in this county for some time."[5] The falling trade in yarn suggests a general economic recession prompted by a deficient harvest as the effects of a poor season were not simply those of a reduction of subsistence, they were also accompanied by a slump in prices for linen, yarn and other elements of output on struggling to pay their rents and the prospect of new horizons in America no doubt seemed attractive. This collapse of trade in 1718-19 has been regarded by some historians as the first Irish instance of a domestic economic crisis serving as an impetus for emigration.[6] This "homeland disaster" theory has been highlighted by Marianne Wokeck in her comparative study of Irish and German migrants to America in this period (1991: xvii). The combination of evidence of the numbers leaving and the economic conditions (including the failure of debtors to clear their accounts) in Co. Londonderry provided by Robert McCausland suggest that economic motivations were the primary cause of emigration to North America from this region.

The alternative viewpoint that Ulster emigration was motivated by religious grievances has been posited by Patrick Griffin in his study of Ulster Presbyterian migration to North America. He has seen the large scale transatlantic migration of the late 1720s as being motivated primarily by religious factors. The effects of the failure to achieve a repeal of the Test Act in 1719 – something he terms the "badge of slavery" – and the non-subscription controversy of the 1720s he believes contributed to the migration of so many Ulster Presbyterians. Their migration, he argues, was motivated by their position on the cultural margins of the greater British polity. Their "religious difficulties illustrated just how far and to whom Britishness extended" (Griffin, 35). This thesis, while in many ways attractive, does not do justice to the economic factors which were so important in motivating large scale emigration in the late 1720s. It is hardly coincidental that the greatest waves of emigrants departed in times of economic crisis and then died down until the next crisis. Large numbers of Presbyterians emigrated because large numbers of Presbyterians lived in the areas worst affected by economic disasters. As Kirkham and Dickson pointed out, "the fact that most northern emigrants were dissenters does not necessarily prove that they departed because of religious reasons" (Kirkham, 85). The Conolly estates had a substantial Presbyterian community: there was a meetinghouse on Conolly's estate in Limavady in Co. Londonderry[7] and in 1724 he had asked the Synod of Ulster to nominate a minister to preach to his tenants (Kirkham, 87). Conolly both in the national and local spheres was a supporter of the Presbyterian interest. This did not prevent his tenants emigrating to America; rather, the economic conditions of the late 1720s gave them little choice.

The economic climate of the late 1720s when famine almost struck Ulster is clear from Conolly's estate correspondence from his agents in Donegal, Fermanagh and Londonderry. In July 1728 Thomas Dickson (Conolly's brother in law) wrote from Ballyshannon Co. Donegal:

---

[4] On Irish and Scottish migration in this period, see the chapters by Cullen and Smout, Devine and Landsman in Canny (1994).
[5] R McCausland to W Conolly 18 November 1718, IAA Ref: 97/84 C/27/1-92
[6] ibid, p xvii.
[7] See Rent Roll for Manor of Limavady 1728 in IAA Ref: 97/84 C/11/1-21

there is a ship in Killybegs that is taking passengers for New England, several tradesmen and young men, some about this town is going with him but none of the tenants although there is several of them that intends going there the next time. I know there are many families already gone there this year out of Laggan.[8]

The departure of tradesmen and young men suggests a general economic recession affecting not just crops but also other aspects of the local economy dependent on profits and other outputs from the land. The situation in Ballyshannon had been deteriorating since 1727 when Dickson had written to Conolly warning him that it was "likely to be a hard year for the poor", and that the price of "bread grain is extravagant" suggesting a harvest failure. Conolly's Ballyshannon estate was not his only estate affected by harvest failure in these years. The Manor of Newporton in neighbouring Co. Fermanagh suffered even more than Ballyshannon. In 1728 the Newporton tenants dispatched a petition to Conolly outlining their plight, "the common calamity of Ulster has been grievously felt by your petitioners."[9] They made reference to the "excessive prices they took their leases when that price was at its highest", a common complaint across the province at this time. This, however, is not the principle cause of their trouble, that honour is reserved for a higher cause: "God in his anger has for these three years past after the seasons blasted their labours and withheld the ground from issuing its usual increase".[10] These religious undertones indicate the sense of despair that the petitioners felt, and are continued in their appeal to Conolly: "we want your excellency to share misfortune that no human prayer can remedy."[11] Reference is also made to those who have fled to new world, "but they will not seek your compassion."[12] This implies that emigration was still a last resort for some, their preference was to stay on the estate but this was only going to be possible if certain allowances were made.

Conolly, however, was reluctant to share his tenants' misfortune and he wrote to his agent James Crawford outlining his opinions on the matter: "I am sorry for the misfortune of the country by the bad harvest, but the ready way to ruining tenants is to suffer them to be so much in arrears- which pray by all means you will prevent."[13] Conolly thus advocated the collection of rent despite the poor conditions the tenants laboured under rather than allowing the tenants go further into debt. In Ballyshannon, however, at the same time Robert McCausland was allowing the poorest tenants to default on their May rent, he "ordered the very poorest tenants of the manor of Ballyshannon to be dropped for the then May rent",[14] suggesting that Conolly was willing to make some allowances for his poorest tenants. The conditions in Fermanagh in Autumn 1728 are clearly illustrated in Crawford's reply:

> There was a fair at Maguire-bridge the 21st of July which is the most material and leading fair in these parts and also one at Ballyshannon about a fortnight past. And the markets were verlow which has put a great damp on grazers which together with the low price of linen cloth and the bad harvest occasioned by a great wind that shifted a great part of the grain that, has put this county in a very bad condition. I have not driven a beast yet for May rent, but I will next Monday begin and force payment of last May rent without lots of fines and will remit it to you as soon as any manner of opportunity arises.[15]

[8] Thomas Dickson to W Conolly 16 July 1728, IAA Ref: 97/84 C28/1-25.
[9] Petition sent by James Crawford (Agent) and tenants of Newporton 1728, IAA Ref: 97/84 C/20/1-17.
[10] ibid.
[11] ibid.
[12] ibid.
[13] W Conolly to James Crawford 21 September 1728, IAA Ref: 97/84 C/20.
[14] R McCausland to W Conolly 2 May 1728, IAA Ref: 97/84 C/27
[15] J Crawford to W Conolly 24 September 1728, IAA Ref: 97/84 C/20.

The bad harvests had hit the Conolly lands in the county as the above extract demonstrates. The wider effects of the harvest failure on the local economy are clear, and it is no wonder that tradesmen and others were departing from Ballyshannon in the same period for the new world. Conolly's reaction to this bulletin from Crawford was to request the collection of the rent but also to express his sorrow at the "bad account … of the country",[16] suggesting he was not fully aware of the situation in Fermanagh. The Newporton estate was the poorest of Conolly's northern estates with an annual rental of only £528.4s.11d for a total acreage for 4212 acres,[17] but the wealthier estates and tenants were not immune to the economic difficulties in these years. In June 1728 Robert McCausland wrote to Mrs Conolly outlining the difficulties facing Captain Ash of Muff one of Conolly's freeholders in the Vintners proportion in Co. Londonderry and asking her to "procure my lord Conolly's interest to get any better post in the West Indies."[18] It seems that Conolly interceded on Ash's behalf as McCausland in a later letter thanks Conolly for obliging Captain Ash, who it seems remained in Ireland.[19] This case demonstrates the economic difficulties facing even the more prosperous tenants and the measures needed to prevent them from emigrating. All of the above evidence points to the economic causes of emigration from Ulster in these years and certainly suggest that at least on the Conolly estates, the effects of the bad harvests in 1727-29 were the pre-eminent causes. It is now necessary to turn away from specific instances and examine the reaction of the Irish Administration, of which William Conolly as the leading native representative was a key figure.

The levels of emigration from Ulster to North America in the late 1720s as noted earlier was a cause for concern amongst the highest levels of the Irish administration. From 1727 onwards there are a number of references in the State Papers to the issue of emigration. In contrast, no official concern was apparent in 1718/19 when the first large scale wave of emigration started. In 1727 the Protestant Dissenters of Dublin and the South of Ireland submitted an address to the King outlining their grievances especially regarding the Sacramental Test Act of 1704, which prohibited their full participation in public life. The writers of this address noted that the grievances that many Dissenters laboured under meant that:

> they had in great numbers transported themselves the American plantations for the sake of the liberty and ease they are denied in their native country, and we have too much reason to fear that many more will follow their example, if this occasion of their grievances should not be timely removed, greatly to the weakness of the Protestant interest in general and the prejudice of the linen manufacture, which is the principal support of this nation.[20]

While the purpose of the writers of this address was to obtain a relaxation of the penalties that the Dissenters suffered under, the use of the prospect of emigration and the ensuing security and economic repercussions showed they were aware of the perception of emigration in official circles. Another government correspondent, this time a Belfast ships captain informed the Dublin Castle administration in 1728 "that 40,000 people out of Ulster and the low part of

---

[16] W Conolly to J Crawford 5 October 1728, IAA Ref: 97/84 C/20.
[17] See James Crawford's accounts with Conolly for 1727/28 in IAA Ref: 97/84 C/20.
[18] R McCausland to Katherine Conolly 20 June 1728, in IAA Ref: 97/84 C/26. The use of term West Indies is not particularly significant as contemporaries often used it to describe all the North American Colonies. See Dickson, 221.
[19] R McCausland to W Conolly 1729 (n.d.), in IAA Ref: 97/84 C/26.
[20] Address of the Protestant Dissenting ministers of Dublin and the south of Ireland to the King 1727 (Public Record Office Northern Ireland (PRONI) T659 Transcripts of State Papers Ireland (T.S.P.I) 20-3).

Connaught had gone to the colonies these past eight years."[21] He suggested that rising rents were the crux of the problem and that many landlords had a great rent roll "and don't receive half the money."

It was not just the Irish administration who were concerned about rising levels of emigration. In December 1728 the Duke of Newcastle wrote to the Archbishop of Armagh referring to the "infatuation that has of late prevailed amongst the common people in the North of Ireland of removing from whence to the Plantations."[22] It is clear that officialdom on both sides of the Irish Sea were concerned. Newcastle's attitude that it was nothing more than an "infatuation" was echoed by Irish Lord Justice Thomas Wyndham who remarked in a letter to a member of the British cabinet that "nothing remarkable has happened here since my last, except the spreading of a humour among the tenants of Ulster, of quitting their lands here and transporting themselves to America." In the same letter he referred to the harvest failures in Ulster but saw no link; instead, he ascribed the rising emigration levels to rising rents. His concern about the situation is evident but he believed that it seemed "to be an affair of too private and particular nature for the Government to interpose in: at least no scheme of that sort has yet being offered, which had the appearance of a proper adequate remedy."[23] This demonstrates that the Irish government were considering bringing in a bill to prevent emigration. Putting a legal bar on emigration would have been difficult, previous laws in Scotland in 1698 and Britain in 1719 had been widely ignored. Furthermore, the British Attorney General Philip Yorke was unsure whether such a bill could be introduced. In a letter to the Duke of Newcastle he referred to "methods which have been thought necessary to be used to prevent their going to *our own colonies*" (emphasis added).[24] In essence, it was difficult to prevent movement of peoples within the greater Empire.

The Irish Lord Justices, including Conolly, were still unhappy with the situation and they conducted their own investigation into the reasons for emigration in early 1729. In March of that year they wrote to the Lord Lieutenant, Lord Carteret, describing their investigation into the reasons for the high level of emigration. The Presbyterian character of the emigrants was stressed and the Lord Justices seem to have relied on the testimony of dissenting ministers to support their conclusions. The reason stated for halting emigration was that it was of "fatal consequences to the Protestant interest and of Ireland in particular."[25] Presbyterian ministers, they suggested, could admonish their congregations and attempt to persuade them not to depart for America, "such admonitions would very much contribute to put a stop to it."[26] This belief that the Presbyterian clergy could help prevent emigration suggests that religious grievances were not the primary motivation for emigration. This is confirmed in a report drawn up for the Lord Justices by two Presbyterian ministers, Francis Iredell and Robert Cragdell, which outlined the reasons why so many Ulster Protestants were departing for America. High rents, the inequities of the tithe system and bad harvests were all cited as well as the effects of the sacramental test. Economic factors – or what they termed the "poverty to which that part of the country is reduced"[27] – were seen as the primary reasons for emigration. The conclusions reached by Iredell and Craghead were backed up by two reports drawn up by members of the Irish Judiciary who drew up reports based on their travels in the North of

[21] Thomas Whitney to _____ 27 July 1728, (PRONI T659 T.S.P.I., 52-3)

[22] Duke of Newcastle to Archbishop Hugh Boulter 5 December 1728, (PRONI T659 T.S.P.I., 59.)

[23] Thomas Wyndham to Lord _____ 11 January 1728/29, (PRONI T659 T.S.P.I., 64-6).

[24] See Phillip Yorke to Newcastle 14 April 1729, (PRONI T659 T.S.P.I., 70.)

[25] Lord Justices (Boulter, Conolly & Wyndham) to Lord Carteret 8 March 1729, printed in Latimer, 388.

[26] ibid.

[27] Memorial by Francis Iredell and Robert Craghead to their Excellencies, the Lord Justices and General Governors of Ireland 1729 (n.d.), printed in Latimer, 389. See also Abp Boulter to Duke of Newcastle 13 March 1728/29 in Boulter, Vol. 1, 321-36.

Ireland on the legal circuits in the Spring of 1729. Their reports stressed economic grievances related to the bad harvests of the previous two years as well as rising rents. The religious grievances were also acknowledged but they pointed out that "in the counties they passed through they did here of any prosecutions under the Test Act or any other penal laws." This reflects the difference between the letter of the law and the real practice of penal legislation in eighteenth century Ireland. Both Judges reports also stressed the attractions of the colonies and the influence of former emigrants and shipping agents on prospective migrants.[28]

Dispatching these reports to Carteret in June 1729 the Lord Justices wrote that,

> We hope if the approaching harvest proves good, it may contribute very much to abate this humour in the people, but if it shall continue, we are humbly of the opinion that an adequate remedy cannot be had from the laws now in being to put a stop to this evil.

The link between the bad harvests was recognised by the Lord Justices but they were also sufficiently worried to propose the drafting of legislation to prevent emigration. The concerns of the Irish administration, and in particular Conolly and his fellow Lord Justice Archbishop Boulter, can be seen in their charitable contributions for the benefit of the Ulster poor. In January 1729 Boulter set up a subscription to raise money to buy corn to be sent to the "northern part of the country" and both he and "Judge Connolly" (sic) donated £500 each to the fund to encourage further donations. The purpose of this concentration on the northern province, as one astute Vatican correspondent identified, "pointed to the necessity of stopping the defection from the province of Ulster of so many protestant families … to America" (Giblin, 11-2). Conolly's generosity in this instance was motivated by more than just charitable instincts; instead, it reflects the "alarmist response" to the significantly greater outflow in 1728/29, which, while the exact figures are unknown, was substantially greater than what had gone before (Kelly, 83).

Charity was not enough, however, and official concern about emigration led to the drafting of a bill in 1729 to prevent transatlantic migration. This bill was entitled *An act to prevent persons from clandestinely transporting themselves to America in order to defraud their creditors* but it's intended scope was much wider than the title suggests (Dickson, 90). The adequacy of such a bill as a solution to the problem was a matter of debate. From Conolly's response to McCausland's request for such a bill we can assume he was a supporter of the measure. Primate Boulter, on the other hand, was less enthusiastic and in a letter to the Duke of Newcastle in November 1728 expressed his doubts: "But whatever can be done by law, I fear it may be dangerous forcibly to hinder a number of needy people from quitting us."[29] Boulter, however, unlike Conolly, was not personally affected by the increased levels of migration and therefore could afford to be more altruistic. He also was less keen to maintain a Presbyterian interest in Ulster, unlike Conolly who was a longstanding supporter of the Presbyterian interest.[30] The bill, however, was not enacted because of the improved harvests following 1729 and the ensuing decline in emigration. The willingness to draw up legislation to restrict emigration shows the scale of the perceived problem The urgency of the situation that had prompted Robert McCausland to write to William Conolly in May 1729 had passed with the bad harvests. Emigration levels fell back to more manageable levels until the outbreak of the next economic crisis in 1740/41 and official concerns abated.

---

[28] See report of Judges of the Northern Circuits in Lord Carteret to Newcastle 26 June 1729, (PRONI T659 T.S.P.I, 74-9.
[29] Boulter to Newcastle 23 November 1728 in Boulter, vol. 1, 211.
[30] Writing to the Lord Lieutenant in 1715, Conolly praised the Presbyterian's "zeal and steadiness to the Hanoverians" (Dickson, 5). See also Hayton (1997).

In conclusion, this paper has shown how Ulster emigration to the American Colonies was viewed both at local and national levels and how pressure was coming both from above and below to prevent the continuance of "this evil". The agents on the ground stressed the economic consequences of increased migration while those in Government were more inclined to think of the effect on the Protestant Interest.

## References

Boulter, H. 1770. *Letters to Several Ministers of State in England*. 2 vols. Dublin.

Canny, N.P., ed. 1994. *Europeans on the Move: Studies on European Migration, 1500-1800*. Oxford: Clarendon Press

Dickson, R.J. 1988. Ulster *Emigration to Colonial America 1718-1775*. Belfast: Ulster Historical Foundation

Fitzgerald, Patrick. 2004. "'Black '97': Reconsidering Scottish migration to Ireland in the Seventeenth Century and the Scotch Irish in America". In *Ulster and Scotland 1600-2000: History, Language and Identity*. Eds. William Kelly and John Young. Dublin: Four Courts Press. 71-84

Giblin, Cathuldus. 1966. "Catalogue of Material of Irish Interest in the Collection  Nuziatura di Fiandra Vatican Archives Part 5 vols 123-132". *Collecteana Hibernica*. 9: 7-70

Graham, I.C.C. 1956. *Colonists from Scotland: Emigration to North America 1707-1783*. Oxford: Oxford University Press

Griffin, Patrick. 2001. *The People with No Name: Ireland's Ulster Scots, America's Scots Irish and the Creation of the British Atlantic World 1689-1764*. Princeton: Princeton University Press

Hayton, D.W. 1997. "Exclusion, Conformity, and Parliamentary Representation: The Impact of the Sacramental Test on Irish Dissenting Politics". In *The Politics of Irish Dissent, 1650-1800*. Ed. Kevin Herlihy. Dublin: Four Courts Press

Kelly, James. 1992. "Harvests and Hardship: Famine and Scarcity in Ireland in the Late 1720s". *Studia Hibernica*. 26: 65-106

Kirkham, Graeme, "Ulster Emigration to North America 1680-1720". In *Ulster and North America: Transatlantic Perspectives on the Scotch Irish*. Eds. H.T. Blethen and C.W. Wood. 76-97. Tuscaloosa, Alabama: University Of Alabama Press. 76-97

Latimer, W.T. 1902. "Ulster Emigration to North America". *Journal of the Royal Society of Antiquaries of Ireland*. 32: 385-92

Wokeck, M.S. 1999. *Trade in Strangers: The Beginning of Mass Migration to North America*. Pennsylvania: Penn State University Press

# Eoin Mcnamee's *Resurrection Man*: A Critique of the Troubles Thriller and the Historical Text

*Jacquilyn Weeks*

Because "Troubles trash" thrillers (Patten, 128-9) are of such poor literary quality, and because historical works are generally perceived to be outwith the provenance of literary criticism, few critics have primarily addressed the implications of the thriller and historical genres' formal and linguistic conventions, or the ways in which those fixed forms of representation actually affect the readers' moral and rational perceptions of the Troubles. Having written his own "Troubles trash" under the pseudonym of John Creed, Eoin McNamee is in a unique position to both understand and explore the shortcomings of the genre. McNamee's novel *Resurrection Man* is also loosely based on a popular historical text by Martin Dillon, *The Shankill Butchers: A Case Study of Mass Murder*. Through parodic imitation as well as direct critique, McNamee overtly draws attention to the formal limitations and structural dangers of the thriller and historical genres. He employs a number of simultaneously detailed and heavy-handed linguistic nuances which have, so far, been largely undervalued. Nearly every McNamee critic has picked up on the image of the severed tongue and the literal/metaphorical failure of language (McNamee, 16), but few have seriously explored the fact that this image is an almost excessive expression of the deliberate linguistic failures which resonate from sentence to sentence and page to page. This paper deals not primarily with what is said but with methods of saying, and the ways in which literary and linguistic structures affect (and effect) our ability to read and understand the Troubles.

### John Creed, *The Sirius Crossing: A Jack Valentine Thriller*

First, it must be stated that *The Sirius Crossing* is "Troubles trash" in the fullest sense of the term. As enthusiast Ali Karim noted: "*The Sirius Crossing* is a seriously good thriller from a writer who *despite at times bordering on the literary* certainly cooks up a real contemporary espionage brew …" [emphasis mine]. That animated summary of Creed's sequel thriller *Day of the Dead* also applies to *The Sirius Crossing*: "Sniper rifles, grenades, bombs, poison drugs, torture, machine guns, helicopters, car chases – sheesh this book has them all!" McNamee (as Creed) certainly lives up to that promise. Improbable car chases, corny lines, massive gun battles, a beautiful woman, and a high mortality rate for American and English soldiers do, in fact, punctuate the novel like the repeated shuddering machine gun fire.

*Sirius Crossing* is narrated by Jack Valentine in the standard thriller-convention of first person, past tense. The immediate implications of this choice seem fairly straightforward: because it is a retrospective narrative, the reader knows that the adventures, however hair-raising, will not include the death of its hero, Jack Valentine. This is reinforced by the fact that Valentine refers to the narrative as an isolated, conclusive event:

> … there would be one more campaign. A good one it may not have been, for both of us were to pay a dear price, but perhaps it was good, if the erasing of one small part of the evil of your own time is a good thing. (Creed, 29)

---

[1] Anyone who is not easily contained by this exclusively sealed adult (primarily masculine) classification is marginalized and ignored. Crucially, there are no third parties and no non-Protestant/Catholics (Muslims, etc.), much less peace activists or conflict mediators. International intervention (for good or ill) is also ignored.

However, the narrative's implicit resolution also requires a linear moral development from good to better (or, more cynically, evil to less evil). The clarity of form allows for an improbable lucidity of ethical vision and judgment. Valentine's statement, although jaded, is rhetorical. Of course the elimination of evil, if possible, is a positive thing. The thriller novel, although it may transcend sectarian lines, is clearly divided into "good guys" and "bad guys" with a neatly impossible moral fluency; but in the world of the thriller: "Sometimes a man puts on a uniform and it ennobles him. More often he puts it on and it turns him into a slobbering repository of evil and hatred" (24). Clearly, there is no middle ground.

The absolute moral dichotomy is reinforced by the genre and structure of the novel. McNamee draws on convention by locating the text within a tradition of morally polarized genres: Liam's history is compared to a bad Anglo-Irish romance novel (30); desert helicopters are described as "monstrous science-fiction insects" (39), and one of the many numerous gunfights "felt like something out of a World War Two drama" (49). The narrative is also told from a single point of view and in an unvarying authorial register: there is no contradiction; the narrative voice is absolute. Given enough time, Jack Valentine, covert operative, will provide the readers with all the information necessary to understand and ethically judge the events which are taking place. Genre conventions preclude the possibility that one of the other characters might intervene in the last two pages and disagree with or reinterpret Jack's narrative. Projected thoughts, feelings, and motives are unquestionable because they cannot be challenged, and the moral is practically and symbolically unassailable.

What is being presented is a thinly veiled liberal humanism through which, as Elmer Kennedy-Andrews suggests: "Progress is achieved through moral education rather than political revolution" (14). Again, the idea of didactic moral training is explicitly reinforced by the narrative structure. Valentine's narrative is punctuated with flashbacks which summarize the formation of his own moral code: "I was a young operative, a bit wet behind the ears, and labouring under the delusion that I was working in the cause of justice, liberty and democracy. I had a lot to learn" (37). The reader is taken through the process of Jack's global and bloody education, and the unquestioning reader accepts Jack's lionization of loyalty (26); his reliance on intuitive knowledge (53); belief in uncanny telepathy (31); and dependence on instant and accurate intuitive assessment (49). The pre-set code of the genre dictates that the hero has empirical and ethical intuition; consequently, the reader is being implicitly and repeatedly asked to blindly trust Jack's moral and practical interpretation of events (Harper, 4-6).

The structure and conventions of the thriller novel allow terror to go on, but only in a strictly controlled sequence where there is an identifiable ultimate good which will eventually prevail. It renders the conflict inevitable, justifiable, and unambiguous. Evil people will crop up, and good guys must fight them. Such a simplistic and logical assertion proclaims the efficacy of justice and reason at the (very slight) expense of anything resembling actual human conflict:

> There were two situations that had to be impelled to a conclusion. The first was Liam and his supposed treachery. The second was Sirius. Both matters needed a conclusion forced upon them. In many ways, both were dangerous abstractions…My idea was to bring everybody face to face. Not just the footsoldiers, but the principals.…To have them kill or to be killed if that was what they wanted. To have them make deals if that was what was required. (207)

The structure and form of the thriller is the only thing that necessarily impels this narrative to a settled resolution. The idea of being able to orchestrate an absolute conclusion to terror and to bring complete understanding (or at least resolution via death) to all sides of a conflict is a highly stylized and dubious assertion. In this genre, loose ends are "dangerous" and any "abstractions" must be brought back under the provenance of concrete moral justice. The thriller is fundamentally preoccupied with finding a solution, a moral conclusion, a "truth" that explains (and through that explanation cauterizes and somehow justifies) the horror of everything that leads up to the conclusion (Denning, 14). Indeed, it is reiterated in the novel that finding truth is somehow not only possible but cathartically necessary: "There's a few old women around here – all they really want to know is what happened to the men they loved. Sometimes we have a duty by the dead" (80). In this context, finding closure through "truth" finalizes the hermetic seal on the strictly controlled text.

**Martin Dillon,** *The Shankill Butchers: A Case Study of Mass Murder*

Dillon's work focuses on the serial murders in the 1970s associated with the UVF gang known as the Shankill Butchers. Although the historical text is a much more prestigious genre than the thriller, there are many striking parallels, structurally and semantically, between Creed's "Troubles trash" fiction and Dillon's historical documentation. As in the *Sirius Crossing*, the narrative is retrospective and the narrator locates himself in the text, not as a principal actor, but as an investigator explicitly uncovering and reinterpreting the primary events. Although well-researched and evidentially supported, Dillon's historical text imbues distinctly characteristic overtones of the fictional detective genre as the narrator uncovers the plot piece by piece. In fact, by including poetic metatext and allusive chapter headings such as "Murder Most Foul" – *Hamlet* I, v, 27 – Dillon explicitly locates his text within a fictional context; even the opening "This story begins …" has the fictional resonance of "Once upon a time …".

Unlike the thriller, however, the narrative is also framed by an introduction and conclusion which provide a gloss on the historical text and prepare the reader's mind to accept the narrative as Dillon presents it. Yet, like the thriller, the author is working towards morally unambiguous, firmly settled conclusion, this time even more explicitly didactic. The preface author, Dr. Conor Cruise O'Brien, suggests that the "objective" factual accounts presented by Dillon will allow the readers to "demythologize" and move away from the militant rhetoric of both Protestants and Catholics. However, in the process of removing one myth (callous demonization of either Catholics or Protestants), Dillon merely substitutes another (egalitarian demonization of both Catholics and Protestants). In Dillon's credo, each "side", whether passive or active, is assigned equal culpability:

> When I began to write this book I was determined not to apportion blame to either of the two communities in the Northern Ireland conflict, because both Catholics and Protestants must share equally in the guilt for what has happened over the past twenty years. (Dillon, xii)

There are a few problems with the logic of this argument. First, he divides the community absolutely and without exception into two political camps – conveniently excluding anyone who does not fit into the neatly polarized socio-religious dichotomy.[1] Secondly, any claim to objectivity will bias the author because he will necessarily be skeptical of extreme reports and will be tempted to seek parallels where there may be none. Finally, he seems to believe that guilt can (and somehow should) be quantified, assigned, and accepted. Can it possibly be more just to blindly apportion blame to two groups rather than to one?

As in the thriller, there is a foregrounded sense of polarity. The authoritative narrative voice confidently discerns truth from falsity and, as the title portentously suggests, exposes the "real" facts and truths behind the murders. Although the reader may question these assumptions, the commanding authorial tone does not encourage such questioning. Although the formats are very different, the historical text achieves the same omniscient authorial voice associated with the thriller.

Structurally, Dillon's presentation of facts, formulas, and photographs add weight to his domineering tone:

> It is interesting to note the coding formula used by medics to establish the time of death …
> $$\frac{99F - 95F}{1.5} = 2.6$$
> Close examination of the body revealed the terrible beating Shaw had received, though Moore was later to attribute the injuries to a "kicking". The injuries were in fact substantial.

> Scalp: 4 serious lacerations.
> Face: lacerations and considerable bruising
> Neck: bruising
> Trunk: patchy bruising
> Right and left upper limbs, right and left lower limbs: considerable bruising and abrasions. (85)

Although the inquisitive mathematical interest in numbers and the clinical listing of injuries seem to objectively distance the narrator from his subject, the subtle placement of a judgmental adjective like "terrible" signifies the author's subjective opinion. No doubt the beating was terrible, both morally and physically; yet, while one cannot and should not deny the horror of murder, it is important to point out that the self-proclaimed "objective" author makes a crucial elision between absolute "fact" and moral assessment. In fact, the book is riddled with ethically judgmental and emotionally charged descriptions. Dillon introduces Lenny Murphy, the leader of the Shankill Butchers, as a man "who would express a power and an evil hitherto unrivalled in the UVF" (xxvii). Again, without necessarily disagreeing with Dillon's assessment, one must be aware that he is making a polarized moral classification that is inconsistent with a strictly factual account. Even if these assessments are relatively justified, Dillon's belief that "truth" (morally or practically) is something which can be identified and contained, mastered and communicated leads him towards increasingly interventionist commentary:

> [Moore] worshipped and feared Murphy, possessed a good knowledge of the sectarian geography of the city and had been well tutored by Lenny in the art of killing. Some people have suggested that Moore was easily led by Murphy and there is some truth in that assertion … (140)

Note that this passage purports to have insight into William Moore's mind – so much so that Dillon rejects first-hand testimony in favour of his own intuitive assessment. Any recreation of a dead man's thoughts, however thoroughly his life might be researched, must be fictional. This is an important parallel to the thriller conventions because the narrator claims omniscient insight and takes on the godlike responsibility of discerning truth from lie. However, because the circumstances are presented as non-fiction, the subtle shifts from fact to judgment, and belief to fact, are surely questionable failures to acknowledge the differences between fact, belief, and truth.

The Shankill Butcher story continues to take on new moral dimensions as the "historical" text progresses.

> … people in a war situation adapt and become anesthetized. They are aware of danger but come to accept it as part of life, and thus, through lack of prudence they offer themselves as victims. (110)

Dillon indeed blames all Protestants and Catholics equally and goes so far as to incriminate the victims of the conflict. Setting aside the grotesque implications of such an inferral, it is crucial to recognize how such judgments hermetically seal the conflict in a Protestant/Catholic, 1970s Belfast. This isolating representation of the city does not encourage the reader's studied thought or empathy; rather, it invites readers to self-righteously distance themselves from the conflict, to see "*their* war" and its "adaptations" as somehow inevitable. The comment is a direct invitation for readers to shake their heads grimly and join in the sage condemnation of murderers and victims alike. and the only wisdom imparted by this kind of "knowing" is a self-congratulatory justification of the reader's non-involvement. The claim to absolute truth does not re-create the past, it insistently contains it as a finished, unfortunate incident. As in the thriller, the events are represented as contained, morally absolute, and somehow inevitable.

These representations are highly problematic and it is easy to guess why McNamee chose to address them; however, his choice of medium is crucial. McNamee elected not to tackle the issues head-on via a literary critique, but exposes the fictionality of historical texts by usurping historical conventions in a fictional context. *Resurrection Man* is a loose retelling of the Shankill Butcher story, but the names are rewritten and extensive liberties are taken with names, details and chronologies. The central figure Lenny Murphy is reinvented as Victor Kelly, but McNamee does more than fictionalize the account; he uses a style that echoes thriller and historical conventions with such exaggerated hyperbole and self-conscious repetition that language itself must come into question.

## Eoin McNamee, *Resurrection Man*

It is really difficult to tell whether or not McNamee locates himself, as the author, within *Resurrection Man*. Brief poetically abstract passages are narrated in present tense – "The Harland and Wolff cranes are visible from everywhere in the city. Scaffolding abandoned from the beginnings of the world" (231) – but they seem to be outwith the scope of the "story" as such. Certainly, any kind of omniscient authorial narrative quickly breaks down. Although the majority of the novel is told in a consistent third-person, segments of the book are told from different narrative perspectives, and different blocs of text (which generally signify a temporal, spatial or narrator shift) are visually set apart by double spacing of the paragraphs. However, even within these structurally helpful blocs, consistent narratives are undermined:

> James was a dock labourer…He protected himself by effacement. He was a quiet accomplice to the years of his fatherhood and left no detectable trace.
> Sometimes if Dorcas insisted he would take his own son to Linfield matches at Windsor Park. He could get excited and shout at the team …Victor would look at him then but he would have put the shout away … (4)

It is very plausible that James consciously "protected himself by effacement", but the grammatically awkward idea that he would "take his own son", sounds like a transcription of Dorcas' nagging "… [won't even] take [your] own son …". Similarly, the observation that he "put the shout away" seems to be influenced by Victor's burgeoning perception of his father. The lack of commas or internal punctuation adds to the confusion because the narratives in this text do not complement each other; they compete. McNamee acknowledges and challenges the single imperious authorial voice by offering a baffling multiplicity of contending stories and deliberately withholds (or defies) a key for discerning which narrative is "right".

With a complete post-structural disregard for binary categories, McNamee also fails to identify and universally condemn the "bad guys" while universally applauding the "good guys". Instead, he further develops the idea that narratives (and therefore identities) elide:

> After a job Victor would meet with the others in the Pot Luck to watch the evening news. It was an early ambition of his to have a job as first item on the news but then he became distrustful of the narrative devices employed. The newsreaders' neutral haircuts and accents, the careful placing of stresses to indicate condemnation or approval, the measured tones of reassurance. The suggestive, shifting vernacular used left Big Ivan more confused than anyone. (39)

The initial shift from Victor to "him" would imply that the ambition was Victor's, but the fluid transition from "him" to Big Ivan relocates the ambition with Big Ivan. It is possible that both men had the same dream and disillusionment, but the pronominal ambivalence underscores the impossible nature of narrative synthesis. While Glenn Patterson dismisses this as "an idiom which the reader has to strain to credit as belonging to any credible character" (cited in Haslam, 207), it is, rather, a crucial commentary on the nature of dialogue. McNamee is undermining previous narratives, represented by the newscasters, which are so careful and neutral that they become meaningless. It is important that the newscasters never actually say anything, but that the method of their non-saying speaks volumes. Again, the fragmented sentences and unhelpful punctuation add to the reader's confusion, but the act of struggling with the defamiliarized text compels the attentive reader to reconsider the ways in which traumatic events have been represented. "Suggestive" and "shifting" employment of "narrative devices" indeed.

In what seems like a desperate grasp at coherence, McNamee then borrows languages wholesale. However, instead of actually using the language conventions, he refers the reader to the convention and assumes that the reader can supply the details: "A language of denial was being employed" (22); "an invented language of sex" (23); "Words of haunting blame and violence" (147). The effect, of course, is to inform the reading audience that they do have and frequently employ such coded language systems and that they *can* supply the details. This may sound like an intimate and intuitive form of communication, but the explicit choice of a pre-coded language does not allow for more accurate communication:

> …newspapers and television were developing a familiar and comforting vocabulary to deal with violence. Sentences which could be read easily off the page. It involved repetition of key phrases. Atrocity reports began to achieve the pure level of a chant. It was no longer about conveying information, it was about focusing the mind inwards, attending to the durable rhythms of violence. (58)

On the contrary, its familiar rhythms lull the reader into focusing on the act of reading; the predictable words prevent the reader from re-absorbing the ideas embedded in the words. McNamee imitates to demonstrate the faith of known language patterns. He co-opts the style and then informs the reader of the style's absolute inadequacy.

In *Resurrection Man*, language continually falls short of representation: "…somehow words had been denied…it occurred to her that speech itself is a cruel deceiver or kind of hoax which could not be relied upon" (56). This self-conscious preoccupation with the forms of language resonates not only from page to page, but from paragraph to paragraph. Through the constant bombardment of language systems, McNamee in some sense recreates the experience of living through a linguistically numbing decade of Terror rhetoric. The constant reiteration of phrases, ideas, and basic themes is a kind of groping after sufficient language, but the chronic repetition itself is a kind of stuttering linguistic failure. Events and emotions "are like", "seem to be", or "feel as if"; they so infrequently "are" absolutely that even those few unqualified statements seem out of place and pretentious. In the end, only a selective approximation can be accepted: "She would pass over many of the things that came out of their mouths as words were not adequate" (55). And yet, as with the thrillerl, there are "expected" and "necessary" forms to be gone through. The act of speaking about violence becomes a voyeuristic spectator-driven event in which the entire city colludes:

> The murders were reported in the papers but the detail was still suppressed. People examined street maps to trace possible routes used by the killers. The victim's last movements were discussed exhaustively as if this might reveal what marked you out for this kind of death. Their final moments seemed to contain something that the city needed. There might have been concealed passages of grace and people wished to secure accounts of them. (145)

It is the coding and suppression of language which prompts the people to minutely speculate about the detail. The act of speaking is tied to a wistful hope that language (and through language, understanding) can insulate the potential victims from the crime. Victims look for a "passage of grace" but, although the words ambivalently refer to both a literal escape route and to a liberating literary passage, in McNamee's literary map of Belfast, the slippery language never provides a safe way out. The literary nature is reemphasized by the quest for a "secure account" whose absolute structure makes sense of the violence. However, again, the search is flawed because the people's assumptions are wrong; the city does not *need* violence. The reader might assume that the thought is voiced through the perception of one of the mass murderers, but the elusiveness of narrative assignation allows the author to implicate more than the killers. Only a "true crime" narrative, or a genre of violence *needs* violence to exist, but by so closely associating violence and the literature of violence, McNamee queries the *reader's* voyeuristic need to see and absorb the violent act. This breakdown of language at the formal level echoes much larger breakdowns of communication and empathy.

However, if in some respects the text is overly fragmented, other aspects are hyperbolically structural. The novel is a form which lends itself to structure; each chapter heading is written out "one", "two", and the use of numbers through the novel takes on the ritualistic form of an incantation:

> Later Victor would see that these events had a formal structure. The men settled down after the first round of drinks. They took their jackets off and precision became important ... The third stage came around 3 a.m. No one spoke. The men's breathing was laboured. It was 3 a.m. hour of mile-deep disappointments. Futility and exhaustion began to set in.
> At 4 a.m. Victor took McGinn into the toilets where he cut his throat. (29)

The plot and the formal conventions are suddenly intertwined and, in a sentiment echoed by the thriller novel, Victor sensed that "There were lulls, setbacks, small triumphs, but they always seemed to be moving towards a particular and timely conclusion" (109). Of course, this is a novel, and the progressive chapter headings gradually move the novel towards the inevitable historical conclusion: Victor's death. But although the murders can be timed to the minute – "At eight o'clock that morning" (138), "By 12 a.m." (138), "At 9.36 p.m." (139), "At 11.40" (141) – at Victor's death the action returns to the symbolic hour:

> She looked at the alarm and saw it was 4 a.m. It seemed a fictional hour, derived from films she had seen, with wet streets, the sound of men's boots and pounding at the door. An hour packed with menace and grainy, dreamed happenings. (205)

This preoccupation with numbers and formal security perhaps questions the idea of inevitability. The numbers do not have a logical form, they are both arbitrary and improbable, but the self-consciousness of this artifice implore the sensitive reader to consider the wider textual constructions of violence. Again, the emphasis on "seemed".

In comparing genres, it seems appropriate to define the genre which McNamee uses to critique other established genres, but as Nuala Johnson clearly points out, *Resurrection Man* employs and then discards many genres as insufficient (724). To assign any such definition is to miss the point of what McNamee is arguing. Neat pre-coded and definitive forms of language and genre are inadequate modes of expression when dealing with incomprehensible murder and horror. Although *Resurrection Man* can be eloquently serious, it contains scathing elements of farce and of parody, particularly in the ways in which it directly utilizes and then mocks the "standard" languages of violence and of the Troubles. Unlike the thriller or historical genres, McNamee's "new language" makes it nearly impossible for the engaged reader to quietly accept a received moral code and condemn or label the Troubles from an "objective" emotional distance.

His own metafictional acknowledgement of narrative sleight-of-hand further calls the readers' attention to their inability to trust the narrative of *Resurrection Man*, but also calls into question the larger use of narrative technique. The shifting moral standards and competing narratives defy any kind of moral coherence or binary definition while the obvious blurring of history and fiction further queries the historian's ability to distinguish between the two. If McNamee's failure to construct literary truths results in "formal desolation" (*RM*, 42), how can other narratives so confidently construct anything but a "subtly changed counterfeit" (*RM*, 135)? Ultimately, the elusive and writerly nature of *Resurrection Man* implicates the reader, and by switching the focus back to the reader, McNamee implicitly critiques readerly texts whose neat solutions are didactically imparted to a quietly receptive audience. Each narrative quirk is an insistent demand that the reader struggle with and respond to the text, to the Troubles, and to any absolute representation of the Troubles.

## References

Creed, John. 2002. *The Sirius Crossing*. London: Faber

Dillon, Martin. 1989. *The Shankill Butchers: A Case Study of Mass Murder*. London: Hutchinson

Haslam, Richard. 2000. "'The Pose Arranged and Lingered Over': Visualizing the 'Troubles'". In *Contemporary Irish Fiction: Themes Tropes, Theories*. Eds. Liam Harte and Michael Parker. London: Macmillan Press. 193-212

Johnson, Nuala C. 1996. 'The Cartographies of Violence: Belfast's *Resurrection Man*'. *Environment and Planning: Society and Space*. 17.6: 723-36

Karim, Ali. 2002. "A John Creed Double Shot". *Shots: The Crime and Mystery Magazine*. March. <http://www.shotsmag.co.uk/SHOTS%2018/creed.htm>

Kennedy-Andrews, Elmer. 2003. *Fiction and the Northern Ireland Troubles since 1969: (De-)constructing the North*. Dublin: Four Courts Press

McNamee, Eoin. 1994. *Resurrection Man*. London: Picador

Patten, Eve. 1995. "Fiction in Conflict: Northern Ireland's Prodigal Novelists." In *Peripheral Visions: Images of Nationhood in Contemporary British Fiction*. Ed. Ian A. Bell. Cardiff: University of Wales Press. 128-45

# "The Affectionate Punch": Constructions of Identity, Masculinity, Race and Gender in Contemporary Scottish Fiction

*Andy Wood*

> We knew our country was smalltime dump
> where nothing ever happened and
> there was nothing to do.
> And nobody had a name like Jelly Roll Morton. (Williams, 1972)

> *Where do you come from?*
> 'Here', I said, 'Here. These parts'. (Kay, 1993)

Within contemporary Scottish culture, and equally within debates about contemporary Scottish literature and culture, there have been a great many attempts to define or redefine what exactly is meant by the phrase 'Scottish identity'. Much of the debate seems to involve deconstructing or renegotiating many of the myths surrounding prevalent concepts of Scottishness. One of the most successful forms of novel in recent years has been that of the 'working-class' or 'under-class' novel with writers such as Irvine Welsh, James Kelman, Jeff Torrington, Laura Hird and Gordon Legge seeking to give voice to a group within society which the dominant discourses of the nation have either marginalised, ignored or identified simply as a problem. Novels such as Torrington's *Swing Hammer Swing!* (1992), with its portrayal of the death knell of the working-class communities of the Gorbals of the late 1960s, or Welsh's *Trainspotting* (1993), which depicts the fragmented lives of an emerging under-class in 1980s Edinburgh, successfully brought new, and largely unheard, voices into contemporary literature. However, while such novels helped challenge long-established and prevailing views of Scottishness, and the myths that surround such views, in order to dismiss the dominant outlook of a homogeneous Scottish culture, they often left in the place of old orthodoxies a vision of Scottish cultural identity that was less than heterogeneous.

At the same time, in much of the critical debate of the 1980s and 1990s a number of commentators and writers have attempted to portray Scottish culture as a post-colonial culture. For example, this is the position taken by Craig Beveridge and Ronald Turnbull in *The Eclipse of Scottish Culture* (1989). This seems a strange assumption to make but it is a view which resurfaces in fiction in Irvine Welsh's first two novels, *Trainspotting* and *Marabou Stork Nightmares* (1995). Both narratives offer the premise that Scotland itself is a colony under the rule of England, a trope that is consistently invoked by a number of cultural commentators. Mark Renton in *Trainspotting* declares that Scotland is "a country ay failures. It's nae good blamin it oan the English fir colonising us [...] Ah hate the Scots" (78). This outburst resonates with the central thesis of Beveridge and Turnbull's work on several levels. In *The Eclipse of Scottish Culture* they unequivocally argue that Scotland was, in the aftermath of the Union of Parliaments in 1707, a colony, and that it remains colonised by England. Drawing heavily upon Frantz Fanon's seminal work on the effects of colonisation, *The Wretched of the Earth* (1965), they suggest that Scots have more in common with Algerians during and in the immediate aftermath of a ferocious war of independence with France, or with African-Americans. These two examples are deployed in order to support their central thesis of how the Scots have been colonised and oppressed at the hands of a prejudiced English middleclass. Beveridge and Turnbull base their arguments, in part, on Fanon's concept of inferiorisation as "this seems to us to yield valuable insights and perspectives on the Scottish predicament" (1). Fanon (2002: 190) describes inferiorisation as being a form of external control where "every effort is made to bring the colonized person to admit the inferiority of his culture [...] to recognise the unreality of his 'nation'".

While *The Eclipse of Scottish Culture* is an interesting and provocative work, it seems arrogant and untenable to make comparisons between Scotland and the brutal independence struggles undertaken by groups seeking national liberation. As Fanon states in the opening paragraph of *The Wretched of the Earth*, "Decolonisation is always a violent phenomenon" (27). Beveridge and Turnbull may point to the despairing cry of "Ah hate the Scots" as being emblematic of a national inferiority complex, but it would be erroneous to maintain the argument that Scotland is a colony. Nor does it exist within the paradigm of post-coloniality. In *The Origins of Scottish Nationhood* (2000), the historian Neil Davison points out that Beveridge and Turnbull are "not alone in seeking parallels to the Scottish situation among the African liberation movements" (96). Ireland took part in the imperial project as well – was it a colony – the argument here needs to be more rigorous.

Davison's work represents a valuable resource in tackling the prevalent myths surrounding the construction of a Scots identity built upon the dual foundations of victim-hood and repression. Along with other historians, including Tom Devine, Davison has helped to highlight the centrality of Scots to the Imperial project and the establishment of a unitary British identity from the cusp of the eighteenth century onwards. Yet, as I have previously suggested, such myths have a long shelf-life in Scottish culture. The arguments contained in works such as *The Eclipse of Scottish Culture*, in making spurious alliances and perpetuating historical myths, have failed to explore the real meanings of Imperialism and colonialism which thoroughly undermine any attempts to provide a clearer definition of contemporary Scottish cultural identity.

Equally, such writings fail to take into account the cultural identifications and works of marginalized groups within Scottish society. In an attempt to portray the negative effects of a dominant outside culture imposing itself upon Scottish culture, these writings give the impression that Scotland is a homogenous and relatively stable society with no differences in ethnicity and culture. Debates about difference are reduced to arguments concerning largely imagined English and Scottish cultures which gloss over or simply ignore the vast schisms within both cultures. Robert Crawford (1992:1) suggests that:

> There were also areas of difference which almost all of the consciously theorized writing of the period, as well as the more traditionally orientated criticism, obscured or ignored in a gesture which, deliberate or not, curiously reproduced distortions perpetuated by traditional literary criticism or historiography.

For many writers and critics, it does seem that there is a certain mileage to be obtained from such strategies of myth-sustaining and obfuscation. This is reflected in the invisibility of black Scots both in contemporary culture and in the wider society. One central myth surrounding Scottish identity is that the Scots, unlike their neighbour, the 'other' against whom such an identity is defined, are an egalitarian and welcoming people unlike the 'colonists' South of the border. The rationale involved in promoting such a viewpoint necessitates the denial of the integral role of Scotland and the Scots in both the creation of a British identity and in the Imperial project, and, further, suggests that racism is neither an issue nor a problem in Scotland. Angus Calder (1996) points out that the myth of Scottish identity and the concept of Scotland as an English colony are both fairly recent phenomena, appearing intermittently in the period since the First World War.

The issue of colonialism resurfaces in Welsh's second novel, *Marabou Stork Nightmares*. After migrating for a short period to apartheid South Africa, the narrator, Roy Strang, discovers that his family are to return to Scotland. Having relocated from a marginalised, impoverished existence in a peripheral housing scheme in the Scottish capital, to a position of relative privilege where skin colour rather than class defines status, elevating the Strangs, Roy reflects upon his family's encroaching return to Scotland:

> I was gloomy in my resignation, only a sick anxiety brought on by the dread of leaving occasionally alleviating my depression. Edinburgh to me represented serfdom. I realised that it was exactly the same situation as Johannesburg; the only difference was that the Kaffirs were white and called schemes or draftpacks. Back in Edinburgh, we would be Kaffirs; condemned to live out our lives in townships like Muirhouse or So-Wester-Hailes-To or Niddrie, self contained camps with fuck all in them, miles fae the toon. Brought in tae dae the crap jobs that nae cunt else wanted tae dae, then hassled by the polis if we hung around at night in groups. Edinburgh had the same politics as Johannesburg; it had the same politics as any city. Only we were on the other side. (80)

Although it is vaguely possible to read this passage as an attempt to link issues of race and class and the struggles which groups who organise themselves around such identifications undertake, it seems a somewhat clumsy parallel. Equally, the arguments in works such as *The Eclipse of Scottish Culture* fail entirely to discuss issues of Scottish involvement in the British project and Empire. Nor do they take into account the cultural identifications and works of marginalised groups within Scottish society. In such writings, the quest for identity seems to be founded on an often spurious attempt to portray Scots as victims, their culture one where class is the only (vaguely) defining difference. Other differences are glossed over or ignored, as are aspects of history which appear troublesome.

Two recent novels, the poet Jackie Kay's *Trumpet* and musician Luke Sutherland's *Jelly Roll*, both debut novels published in 1998, offer us new ways to look at questions of race, gender, sexuality and identity that move beyond attempts – conscious or unconscious? to portray or condemn non-white Scots as a marginal or invisible minority. Both novels explore gender and race and view them as being intrinsically entwined, integral parts of identity that cannot be ignored, conveniently dismissed or compartmentalised. Both novels also offer new voices previously absent from Scottish literature, giving perspectives rarely heard before which question received wisdom on problematic notions and concepts of what it means to be Scottish in an increasingly multicultural and multiracial society.

*Trumpet* tells the story of Joss Moody, a famous jazz musician, who, after his death, is found to have been a woman called Josephine Moore. The story is related to us in a series of different voices: Moody's wife Millie, the only person to have known the 'truth'; their adopted son, Colman; Sophie Stones, a tabloid journalist who is writing a book on Joss Moody with the help of Colman; Edith Moore, Joss Moody's mother; a number of minor voices including former school friends, band members and employees. Sophie Stones hopes her book will make her a bigger celebrity than Joss Moody, though she lacks any discernible talent. However, she thinks "they should have no problem selling this book. People are interested in weirdos, sex changes, all that stuff" (125). Sophie Stones does not dare to think about what lies under the surface, what drove a black Scottish girl of mixed race parentage to become Joss Moody, a male jazz trumpeter more than holding his/her own in a predominantly male environment. She does briefly consider this issue much later in the novel in the wake of a number of articles supportive of Moore/Moody taking such a radical step, but she dismisses such theories speculating instead that dressing up as a man simply "turned her on" (263). Although Stones does come to accept it must have been a long, thought-out conversion, one which would give her power in her chosen field, she still cannot help using tags like perversion. Millie feels that her life with Joss was perfectly normal, while Colman feels betrayed and distraught that no one told him the truth. The public furore and interest in Joss Moody's gender and private life affect Millie and Colman in different ways, and in very different ways they try to come to terms with life after Joss without their own identities being further eroded by the public and private revelations. Throughout *Trumpet* we only ever hear Joss Moody's own voice once, in a form that is not mediated by another character's memory. We are given a portrait of Joss and Josie through recollections, memories, photographs and quotes but s/he looms larger than life throughout the novel even post-mortem. The voices in *Trumpet* work in a similar way to those in Kay's poetry, particularly in *The Adoption Papers* (1991) with its array of distinctive narrative voices deployed to give a wide range of perspectives on a single story.

Colman is devastated by the revelation that his adoptive parents could hide such a secret from him. In comparison with them, Colman's identity and sense of self are much more fragmented and insecure. Although born in Scotland to Scottish parents he feels that he is not really Scottish, nor is he English despite having resided in London for a quarter of a century. Nor does he feel much identification or sympathy with other young black men he meets in London, particularly those who choose to identify with the belief that Africa is their spiritual and cultural home. Colman describes Scotland as his "father's country" (181) and recalls his father telling him, "The minute I hit Carlisle, I know I'm in my own country. My heart starts beating the minute I cross the border" (184). When Colman asks him why he does not live there any more, Joss blames the lack of work. Colman also recalls that while his father was proud of his Scots heritage he spent a lot of time talking about his role models and heroes, all African Americans such as Martin Luther King Jnr, Louis Armstrong, Fats Waller, Miles Davis and Duke Ellington, people whom Colman derisively refers to as "Black Yanks" (192) without pausing to think of what alternative role models were available to him. Kay has discussed and written about this issue on a number of occasions, particularly the ways that "people can't contain both things, being Black and being Scottish", treating it as an "anomaly", and that growing up in Scotland she "never had any sense of Black culture at all, until I went about finding and creating that for my self" (Wilson and Somerville-Arjat 1993: 121–22). This would seem an odd situation for a nation and culture that prides itself on giving a voice to the marginalised or dissident, a nation that, in Maud Sulter's words, prides itself on having "such a radical, rebellious nature" (ibid. 29), that there are so few sites and opportunities through which to dispel false notions of Scotland as a homogenous country and culture. And this in a period when cultural identity is widely seen as "a 'production' which is never complete, always in process, and always constituted within, not outside representation" (Hall 1994: 392).

While the characters' attention is mostly focused on Joss Moody's gender and sexual orientation, the issues of race, racism, cultural identity and belonging are strong themes within *Trumpet*. Although Sophie Stones's crude attempts at 'biography' gloss over the issues of race and cultural identity in favour of those of swapping sex and sexual behaviour, *Trumpet* makes it clear that these areas cannot be truly separated. Cheris Kramarae (1996: 20) makes the point that:

> Talking about race, class, and gender together is not easy, and not even always desirable. These systems have important historical and contemporary differences as well as connections [...] They are not discrete systems however and we too seldom consider the ways they interweave. For example, when we focus on the tags homosexual and gay, we may forget that there are many gays who are women and people of colour and working class and poor and disabled and old.

Kay (2000: 10) says herself that *Trumpet* is "about a person who crosses over the border between male and female and I'm really interested in that, these borders between England and Scotland, black and white, gay and straight [...] how that affects people, when they feel they belong and don't belong, when they fit in and don't fit in".

Colman realises from finally reading his father's last letter to him that, as a child growing up as the only black girl in Greenock, Josephine became her father, the only other black person she had ever known, a man who died when she was eleven. Colman now becomes the father looking after his real memory and legacy. Having been evasive and elusive about his roots in life, in death Joss now tells Colman about his past and his family, especially his father, a man he had never really discussed before:

> You wanted the story of my father, remember? I told you his story could be the story of any black man who came from Africa to Scotland. His story, I told you, was the diaspora. Every story runs into the same river and the same river runs into the sea. But I've changed my mind [...] We were both changed for ever by the death of John Moore. There was no-one to look at me like he did, with shining, adoring eyes, no-one to clap in rhythm when I danced and sang. My mother's love was sensible, but different. Not like him. I missed holding his black hand in the street. Looking at it, comparing it to my own. I was on my own then. Looking at my own hand, trying to remember my father's lines. They were darker than mine, his lifeline, his heart. Maybe you will understand, maybe you won't [...] It is quite simple: all of this is my past, this is the sum of my parts; you are my future. I will be your son now in a strange way. You will be my father telling or not telling my story. (275-7)

Kay does not hint at which story (if any) Colman will choose to tell, but her belief in the idea that all the interesting things happen "in the margins between things [...] the in-between land" (2000: 10) leads one to believe that Colman will tell the whole story, of Joss Moody, the man, and Josephine Moore, the girl, rather than leave her further diminished, languishing voiceless and invisible, doubly marginalized as a black female. Such a scenario is described by Heidi Safia Mirza (1997: 1) as:

> [speaking] of the separate narrative constructions of race, gender and class: in a racial discourse, where the subject is male; in a gendered discourse, where the subject is white; and a class discourse, where race has no place. It is because of these ideological blind spots that black women occupy a most critical place? a location whose very nature resists telling. In this critical space we can imagine questions that could not have been imagined before; we can ask questions that might not have been asked before.

It is into this critical space that *Trumpet* seems to fall. Unlike the voices of the people who see only the man Joss or the girl Josephine, through Colman's position we begin to see the person, their whole life, emerge from the compartments that are used to conveniently label and contain identity.

If Josephine Moore as Joss Moody is able to transcend genders to 'make it' in a male environment, where his/her memory is protected by former band members who remember him as a person, as a talented musician and always as a friend, Luke Sutherland's novel paints a far less positive picture of racism and gender roles in contemporary Scotland. While Kay in *Trumpet* never lets us forget completely that racism can and does exist in Scotland, it never spills into violence like it so often does in *Jelly Roll*. Here racist abuse and violence are ever present, often as an implied threat but also as a very real event. As with *Trumpet, Jelly Roll* is concerned with jazz musicians and follows the story of an all white Glaswegian jazz band, The Sunny Sunday Sextet, who recruit Liam, a black Scots-Irish saxophonist, when their barely competent but highly volatile and deranged former sax player Malc quits the band. They tour the north of Scotland taking in some strange musical backwaters with largely disastrous results, but the worst of the violence occurs in metropolitan Glasgow.

For Roddy the white narrator, Liam is exotic, 'other'. When Paddy tells Roddy that Liam is black, Roddy feigns nonchalance, asking why he is pointing this out and why it should make a difference. Paddy replies that for some people it does make a difference, to which Roddy retorts, "I'm not some people." He goes on to tell Paddy, "I don't care if he's black, white or sky-blue pink. The point is he might be the man for the job and if he wants it we should give him a chance. From what you've told me already, as far as I'm concerned, he's in, so who gives a fuck what anyone thinks?" (33).

Roddy seems almost to be in love with Liam, or at least his idea of him, building up a myth around Liam before he really knows him. He tells the rest of the Sunny Sundays that Liam looks the part and is the essential thing for their image as a jazz band. He drops this into the conversation as a hint, a suggestion, but does not elaborate or tell the rest of the group that Liam is black, only Irish. It is almost as though Roddy is willing a scene to occur, consciously or otherwise, so that he can prove his own liberal credentials are not to be found wanting in comparison with the rest of his colleagues. Several of the remaining members of the band do not disappoint him. After a productive but tense rehearsal Liam takes his leave, having spent the session being referred to as Leroy and continually questioned as to where it is he is really from. Roddy accuses Duckie of being a racist, a yokel and a hypocrite, to which Duckie replies that Roddy is the real hypocrite for lying to them: "You told us he was Irish":

> He came close to shouting again, – Whit the fuck d'ye think Malc'd dae if this Leroy joined the band? He'd go mental.
> – This isn't about Malc, it's about you! You not wanting a talented guy to join the band just because of the colour of his skin. I mean for fucksake, do you know where jazz comes from?
> He stood up, pitted red, tilting at me. – Get off yir fucking high horse you!
> I turned facing him full on. – What fuckin high horse?
> He came closer scowling, both hands stabbing with the cigarette wafting around my face, – Yir such a fuckin hypocrite man!
> – How?
> – It's the way your mind works. Yir such a fuckin poser wi yir wee copy ay Nietzsche stickin out yir pocket and yir foreign film club. Yir a joke. Ye want the guy in the band because he is black. Like ye says in the kitchen on Sunday, he suits the image better than any ay us. Ye'd love this guy tae get intae the band cos it'd be the ultimate pose fir you ya shallow cunt. He'd be like the ultimate fashion accessory fir ye, every cunt thinkin yir some deep cosmopolitan bastart when yir just a doss cunt like the rest ay us. (102-3)

Roddy is incapable of seeing difference at all, whether in a positive or negative way; it is almost as though he is saying race doesn't matter. Meanwhile Duckie, Mouse, Malc and a number of other characters reduce difference to purely physical ones, such as skin colour (they continually call Liam 'Leroy' or 'Bob' [Marley]), or hair (Liam is constantly referred to as Dreidlock [Dreadlock]); or racial stereotypes. Mouse particularly is obsessed with Liam's alleged sexuality and virility as a black man, despite the fact that Liam is happily married to Paddy's sister with whom he has a small daughter. At one of the dates on their tour Mouse makes a rather obvious move on the female singer of one of the other bands and she rebuffs him. Later Mouse sees Liam speaking to the same woman and tries to assert his largely fictional status as the band's ladies man, resorting to a stock of racial clichés and abuse:

> – Ah dunno whit they fuckin teach yous cunts in the jungle, but here, wan ay the first rules ay the game is, ye dinni cut away wi a guy's fuckin bird. OK?
> Liam frowned. – What?
> – Ah mean this morning at the work, that wis cool y'know and that's the way it should be. But the night? Fuckin hell man, the night ah wis set up an you ruined it wi yir fuckin dark and mysterious act.

– Ruined what?

– Dinni you fuckin back chat me, ye wee Monkey.

Liam looked away and I jolted down beside them. – Is that the fucking best you can do Mouse? Monkeys in the jungle? It's fucking shite. After all the crap you've heard in the last few months surely to Christ you can say what you've got to say without having to fall back on these stupid wee racist jibes.

He turned his head, spitting, – I thought this cunt woulday learned his lesson by now.

– Ah get lost. Liam pushed away from the wall.

There was no getting out of it.

Mouse called after him, – ah dunno whit they taught ye in the fuckin jungle, but this is *Scotland, we do things differently here*. (181-2, my emphasis)

The last sentence is particularly important. Mouse and his 'friends' address the concept of Scottishness that is, in his mind, fixed and essential. It is a Scotland of machismo and brutality where violence is the best, if not the only answer to everything. Mouse sees Liam as a fair target for the abuse he receives, not only from Mouse but from the others, not just because he is a different colour, but because he does not fight back or respond with violence. It is Mouse who, with his rants about loyalty, gangs and sticking together, betrays Liam to Malc and tries to create further bad feeling towards Liam by stealing money and property belonging to individual members of the band and pointing the finger discretely at the black man. Mouse constantly tries to invoke a sense of belonging, of identity among the members of the Sunny Sunday Sextet, but fails to do so. Based upon exclusion rather than inclusion, Mouse's idea of a sense of cultural identity is outdated and doomed to failure, constructed upon a notion of a racial belonging built "upon a hegemonic white ethnicity" that never really identifies itself or "speaks its presence" (Mirza 1997: 5). Nor does it feel that it has to.

Finally, although the racist language and the behaviour of many of the characters in *Jelly Roll* would not be out of place in a number of other recent novels, the perspective and the closeness of the narrator and Liam within the novel means that such behaviour does not go unchallenged. Liam's position is a central rather than a marginal one, and Sutherland's portrayal of a young black male is thoughtful and realistic. He does not make Liam a stereotype or simply a signifier of a positive representation of a black man acting as a counterpoint to his racist white contemporaries. As in *Trumpet* there are radically different roles here in terms of race and gender, well beyond the flat caricatures that barely inhabit other novels. We can read and examine these novels as texts which subvert dominant discourses of Scottishness as white, male, working class, physically strong, violent. In this context the narrative constructions of both *Trumpet* and *Jelly Roll* offer a much needed vantage point from where we can question dominant discourses, ideologies and myths surrounding concepts of national identity, cultural heritage and history, race and gender.

Despite attempts to state Scotland's case for consideration as a colonial/post-colonial nation, the presence of diverse groups of non-white Scots with roots in former colonies makes this myth unsustainable. That Scotland may no longer be able to deny its important role in the construction and expansion of the British Empire is a fact that continues to be resisted by many, although the edifice of this fiction is beginning to be chipped away now. Within literary criticism such interventions have also been rare, with a few notable exceptions. In an essay entitled "'The Challenge of 'Black British'", Gail Low (2002: 20) draws attention to this absence:

The questions posed by an exploration of 'Black British' have been directed mostly at an Englishness that has occupied centre stage in the consideration of British identity. In the rush towards the consolidation of the discipline, what has been missing from the fray in the era of devolution is any discussion of how 'Black British' intersects with the production of Scottish identities. There has been an equally long and 'illustrious' historical link between Scotland and British Empire (particularly India); yet there has been very little attempt to think through the legacy of these links or to explore some of its artistic consequences (20).

These novels are an important and integral part of re-imaging and reinventing Scottish cultural identity, and therefore they should be seen as such and perhaps become catalysts for an emerging cultural move away from the hegemonies of the recent and the distant past.

## References

Beveridge, Craig & Ronald Turnbull. 1989. *The Eclipse of Scottish Culture*. Edinburgh: Polygon

Calder, Angus. 1996. "By The Water Of Leith I Sat Down And Wept: Reflections On Scottish Identity". In *New Scottish Writing VII*. Ed. Harry Ritchie. London: Bloomsbury. 218-238

Crawford, Robert. 1992. *Devolving English Literature*. Oxford: Clarendon Press

Davidson, Neil. 2000. *The Origins of Scottish Nationhood*. London: Pluto Press

Devine, T. M. 1999. *The Scottish Nation 1700 – 2000*. London: Penguin

Fanon, Frantz. 2001. *The Wretched of the Earth*. London: Penguin. [First published in English 1965]

Gilroy, Paul. 2002. *There Ain't No Black In The Union Jack* London: Routledge. [First published 1987]

Hall, Stuart. 1994. "Cultural Identity and Diaspora". In *Colonial Discourse and Post-Colonial Theory: A Reader*. Eds. L. Chrisman and P. Williams.London: Harvester WheatSheaf. 392-403

Kay, Jackie. 1991. *The Adoption Papers*. Newcastle: Bloodaxe

Kay, Jackie. 1993. *Other Lovers*. Newcastle: Bloodaxe

Kay, Jackie. 1997. *Bessie Smith*. Bath: Absolute Press

Kay, Jackie. 1998. *Trumpet*. London: Picador

Kay, Jackie. 2000. *Herald*. 2 April: 10

Kramarae, Cheris. 1996. "Classified Information: Race, Class and (always) Gender". In *Gendered Relationships*. Ed. J. Wood. California: Mayfield. 20-38

Low, Gail. 2002. "The Challenge of 'Black British'". *European English Messenger* XI.2: 17-21

Lumsden, Alison. 2000. "Jackie Kay's Poetry and Prose: Constructing Identity". In *Contemporary Scottish Women Writers*. Eds. Aileen Christianson and AlisonLumsden. Edinburgh: Edinburgh University Press. 79-91

Mirza, Heidi Safia. 1997. *Black British Feminism:* A Reader. London: Routledge

Saadi, Suhayl. 2000. "Infinite Diversity in New Scottish Writing". Paper given at *Association for Scottish Literary Studies Conference*. Full text available at http://saredm.members.beeb.net/index/speeches/infinite/infinite.htm

Sutherland, Luke. 1998. *Jelly Roll*. London: Anchor

Torrington, Jeff. 1992. *Swing Hammer Swing!* London: Secker & Warburg

Welsh, Irvine. 1992. *Trainspotting*. London: Minerva

Welsh, Irvine. 1995. *Marabou Stork Nightmares*. London: Jonathan Cape

Wilson, Rebecca and Gillean Somerville-Arjat, eds. 1993. *Sleeping With Monsters: Conversations with Scottish and Irish Women Poets*. Edinburgh: Polygon

# History, Hunger Strike and Republican Collective Memory

*Jonathan Wright*

In recent years memory has emerged as a leading concept in both the social sciences and the humanities (Radstone, 1). While sufficiently nebulous to facilitate application to disciplines as diverse as philosophy and architecture, the concept has, in particular, transformed the study of history (Radstone, 1). Indeed, the American historian Kerwin Lee Klein has claimed that the prevalence of the concept has led to a "remaking [of] historical imagination", with memory "replacing old favourites – *nature, culture, language* – as the word most commonly paired with history" (128). Klein attributed this development to the "postmodern reckoning of history as the marching black boot and of historical consciousness as an oppressive fiction", and argued that "our sudden fascination with memory" offered "an alternative to historical discourse" in an age of "historiographical crisis" (Klein, 145).

While recent years have seen an exponential growth in "memory studies" – which may well reflect a postmodern unease with historical narratives – those who have sought to understand the "Irish psyche" have long appreciated the importance of memory. Indeed, the supposed Irish – and in particular Northern Irish – preoccupation with history has led one of our more combative literary critics to suggest that we build a monument to amnesia and forget where we put it (Longley, 230–231). Some, however, would argue as to whether or not it is possible for the Irish to forget the past. In his 1977 book *The Narrow Ground*, the influential Ulster historian A.T.Q. Stewart, in an analysis that many modern "memory" theorists would be proud of, claimed that the "form and course" of "the Troubles" had been "determined by patterns concealed in the past, rather than by those visible in the present" (183). For Stewart, the Northern Ireland from which "the Troubles" erupted "was a frightening revelation, a nightmarish illustration of the folk-memory of Jungian psychology. [In which] Men and women who had grown to maturity in a Northern Ireland at peace… saw for the first time the monsters which inhabited the depths of the community's unconscious mind" (16).

However, while memory has proved to be a popular concept, an analysis of the 1981 hunger strikes will show that eye-catching arguments such as Stewart's can lead to deterministic and simplistic readings of the past, which, despite their emphasis on memory, offer few insights into the working of republican collective memory.[1]

On 5th May 1981, Bobby Sands, the republican prisoner and Member of Parliament for Fermanagh/South Tyrone, died while on hunger strike in the Maze prison: he had refused food for sixty-six days. Two weeks after his fast had begun on the 1 March 1981, a fellow republican prisoner, Francis Hughes, had joined Sands on hunger strike and thereafter republican prisoners joined the protest at weekly intervals. Hughes died on 12th May 1981, 59 days into his hunger strike, and by the time the protest was ended on 3rd October 1981, a further eight republican hunger strikers – Patsy O'Hara, Raymond McCreesh, Joe McDonnell, Martin Hurson, Keven Lynch, Kieran Doherty, Thomas McElwee and Michael Devine – had died.

In his psychoanalytical monograph *Protest and Hunger Strike in H-Block, the Disavowal of Passivity*, Paddy Maynes described the hunger strike as "an unbearable and incomprehensible period of Irish history" (1). Yet, as unbearable and incomprehensible as the period was, it was also a pivotal one and, as such, has received much attention from investigative journalists,

---

[1] In this paper, "memory" is defined loosely as "historical consciousness".
[2] See: English (2003) for an historical approach; Beresford (1997) for investigative journalism; Maynes (2000) for a psychoanalytical approach; Ellmann (1993) and Kearney (1997) for literary criticism.

historians, psychoanalysts and literary theorists.[2] Almost all of the literature on "the Troubles", not all of which is of equal merit, contains an obligatory chapter on the hunger strike, many of which emphasise the "historical" nature of republican hunger strike. Indeed, one commentator has gone so far as to describe hunger strike as "the ultimate weapon in the republican armoury" (Ryder, 196).

There is some evidence to support this claim. In his 1993 article "Irish Hunger Strike and the Cult of Self-Sacrifice", George Sweeney argued that hunger strike, though not unique to Ireland, was "an integral part of Irish history and mythology" (421). The first written records of the practice are found in the *Senchus Mor* (the civil law code of pre-Norman Ireland), where guidelines for the use of *Troscad* (fasting against a person) and *Cealachan* (achieving justice by starvation) are recorded (Beresford, 14). While the practice seems to have declined during the early modern period – a development Sweeney attributed to the growing influence of Christianity – it was dramatically revived by republicans in the early twentieth century (Sweeney, 422).

W.B. Yeats, whose 1904 play *The King's Threshold* told the story of a poet's hunger strike against his king, claimed some responsibility for this, but the revival can be more convincingly attributed to the changing cultural climate of early twentieth century Ireland (Beresford, 16). As Sweeney explained:

> At the dawn of the twentieth century … a revival of Gaelic tradition and culture and a devotional revolution within Catholicism was to metamorphose Ireland from a society engulfed by self-doubt to one which nurtured a cult of self sacrifice. (Sweeney, 422)

Statistics seem to support Sweeney here. Between 1913 and 1922, approximately 1,000 republican prisoners took part in hunger strikes (Sweeney, 424). The majority of these fasts ended without fatality, but a handful of the protestors did die. The death of Terence MacSwiney, in particular, was to have a lasting significance for republicans.

MacSwiney, the then Lord Mayor of Cork, died while on hunger strike in 1920. Having been arrested at an IRA meeting and sentenced to two years imprisonment, MacSwiney launched a fast, protesting "that the British had no jurisdiction in Ireland" (Beresford, 17). Ultimately his death was the logical outcome of a philosophy of suffering and endurance, which he had expounded during his first speech as Lord Mayor of Cork:

> … the contest on our side is not one of rivalry and vengeance but of endurance. It is not those who can inflict the most but those that can suffer the most who will conquer…It is conceivable that the army of occupation could stop us [the IRA] functioning for a time. Then it becomes simply a question of endurance. Those whose faith is strong will endure to the end in triumph. (Coogan, 15)

Republican prisoners continued to use hunger strike sporadically throughout the twentieth century, against both the British and Irish governments, but it is the hunger strikes of the 1916–1923 period that are held to have had the most influence upon the 1981 hunger strikers.

An overemphasis on the similarities and continuities between 1918 and 1981 has, however, led to simplistic and deterministic readings of the 1981 hunger strikes. This is seen in Padraig O'Malley's claim that the actions of the hunger strikers "were not the actions of autonomous individuals but rather a reflexive embrace of the way in which prisoners throughout Irish history were presumed to have behaved", and in Maynes's argument that the prisoners deaths illustrate a Freudian "compulsion to repeat" (McBride, 14; Maynes, 24).

While any comprehensive examination of the 1981 hunger strike must take the tradition of republican hunger strike into account, the 1981 protest must also, as Ian McBride has contended, be placed within the context of a dispute over the withdrawal of special category status (14–15). While this dispute (referred to by republicans as "the H-Block Struggle"), boiled over with the hunger strike in 1981, it had in fact been simmering since 14 September 1976, the date on which Ciaran Nugent entered the H-Blocks of the newly built Maze prison.[3]

As the first republican convicted since the withdrawal of "special category" status in March 1976, Nugent was classified not as a political prisoner, but as a common criminal. In protest, he refused to wear a prison uniform and embarked upon the blanket protest. During his time in the Maze, Nugent wore a prison uniform on only one occasion, in order to receive a visit from his mother. He is reputed to have told her "[y]ou will not be seeing me for three years because to have a visit I will have to wear uniform. If they want me to wear a uniform they will have to nail it to my back" (Bishop and Mallie, 250). The "reaction of the authorities", as the journalist Vincent Browne noted in his 1981 article "H-Block Crisis: Courage, Lies and Confusion", "was extreme":

> Nugent was denied all privileges (visits, letters, parcels, newspapers, books etc.) He was kept in solitary confinement, denied exercise and for every day of his protest he lost a day's remission, which in the circumstances meant that his sentence was doubled. (Browne, 8)

The severity of the authorities' reaction notwithstanding, the protest escalated. With approximately nine out of every ten republicans who entered the Maze joining Nugent, there were some 500 prisoners 'on the blanket' by the protests end in 1981 (Bishop and Mallie, 355; Purbrick, 104).

The 1981 hunger strike was the culmination of this protest but it was also, in fact, the second hunger strike in less than six months. A previous hunger strike had been abandoned, without fatality, on 18 December 1980, when it appeared as though the government was willing to compromise on the issue of political status.[4] When the expected compromise did not materialise, a second hunger strike was planned for March 1981. Viewed in this context the hunger strike appears, as Richard English has recently argued, "not [as] some obsessive death-fast but [as] an attempt, albeit a drastic and dangerous one, practically to achieve what republicans considered to be their due treatment in the jails" (English, 193–4). While not denying that there were "unavoidable echoes" between the "Icon generating, quasi-religious martyrdom… [and] republican reaping of benefits from technical defeat" of 1981 and 1916, English contends that the deaths should be viewed, first and foremost, within the context of the dispute over political status (English, 211).

If the hunger strikers were motivated by politics, however, it remains the case that, like earlier republican prisoners, they were prepared to die. When challenged by the prison chaplain Father Denis Faul to end his fast, Bobby Sands replied with a quote from the bible: "Greater love than this hath no man, that he lay down his life for a friend" (Beresford, 77). Such willingness to accept death was far from unique to Sands. Before joining the hunger strike Laurence McKeown received a comm regarding his participation in the hunger strike.[5] It read:

---

[3] Between 1976 and 1980, the "the H-Block Struggle" went through a number of distinct phases. The "blanket protest" (prisoners dressed only in blankets), "no-wash protest" (prisoners refused to leave their cells to wash), "dirty protest" (prisoners refusing to slop out smeared excrement on the walls of their cells), and "hunger-strike". See Beresford, 27–8.

[4] For the prisoners' definition of "political status" and details of their five demands, see Purbrick 105.

[5] Comms were small letters written on cigarette paper covered with cling film and discreetly circulated among prisoners.

> Comrade you have put your name forward to embark upon the hunger strike. Do you realise the full implications? What it means, comrade, is that in a short time you will be dead. Rethink your decision. (Taylor, 285)

For McKeown, who was preparing to join the hunger strike, this must have been chilling. Yet, fully aware of the implications of his choice, he joined the strike. Fortunately for him, the protest was ended before he died.

While the hunger strikers were prepared to die, it does not necessarily follow that they wanted to. In Brian Campbell, Laurence McKeown and Felim O'Hagan's *Nor Meekly Serve My Time*, a history of the 'H-Block Struggle' compiled from the accounts of former participants, Joe McDonnell, the fifth hunger striker to die, is recalled by his cell mate, Jaz McCann:

> In a rare show of humility he [McDonnell] confessed that… he was not made of the quality that makes a martyr and a patriot. He laughed at the idea that anyone could ever hold him in high esteem and he ridiculed himself for having the audacity to try to gatecrash membership to that gallant band of Plunkett, Pearse and Tone, etc. He had no desire to be a martyr; he enjoyed life and wanted to live it to the full. (McCann cited in Campbell, McKeown and O'Hagan, 212).

Similarly, another friend of McDonnell's, Tommy Gorman, commented that there "was nobody loved life as much as Joe McDonnell, and lived life to the full as Joe McDonnell… If somebody had put a thousand people in front of me, Joe was the last one I'd pick to go on hunger strike" (English, 201).

Moreover, on the hunger strike, the prisoners conducted themselves with quiet, composed dignity. In September 1981, James Prior the then Secretary of State (for Northern Ireland) visited the prison and met with some of the hunger strikers. Recalling his meeting with James McCloskey – another of the hunger strikers who did not die – Prior explained: "It had a profound effect on me, I expected to find someone who was very up tight and struggling and very uncomfortable. But this man seemed to be serenely quiet and content with himself" (Taylor, 293). The prisoners may have been prepared to die but, as English has written, they "were not people destined [to die] through long-term inclination for martyrdom" (English, 201). Rather, the logic of a hunger strike dictated that, while not necessarily wanting to, the participants had to be prepared to "go the distance"; the point of a hunger strike being, as Patrick Bishop and Eamonn Mallie have bluntly put it, "that you got your way or died" (Bishop and Mallie, 244).

Given this, it seems reasonable to suggest that interpretations of the hunger strike that stress the prisoners' desire, conscious or otherwise, to follow in the footsteps of MacSwiney, are misleading. But that is not to say that "memory" played no role in the protest. On the contrary, there is much evidence to suggest that the prisoners were in possession of a profound sense of historical consciousness.

During the initial stages of his hunger strike, Bobby Sands kept a diary. His final entry reads:

> They won't break me because the desire for freedom, and the freedom of the Irish people, is in my heart. The day will dawn when all the people of Ireland will have the desire for freedom to show. It is then we'll see the rising of the moon. (Sands cited in Beresford, 98–9)

The "rising of the moon", as David Beresford notes, is a reference to a poem written in celebration of the 1798 rebellion by the Fenian poet John Casey who, in 1879, died of ill health caused, allegedly, by harsh treatment received while incarcerated by the British (Beresford, 99). It can be argued that Sands, a songwriter who was – in the words of one friend – "mad about poetry", was atypical of republican prisoners (English, 197). However, his historical consciousness, as the statements released by republican prisoners during the hunger strikes illustrate, was far from unique.

On 21 October 1980, six days before the 1980 hunger-strike began, Brendan Hughes, the IRA OC for the H-Blocks, issued a statement in which he clearly placed the H-Block struggle within a tradition of prison protests that had "been a focal point through successive liberation struggles of the past three centuries" (English, 192). This was soon followed by a statement in which the prisoners, announcing the start of the 1980 hunger strike, described themselves as "captured combatants in the continuing struggle for national liberation and self determination" (Campbell, McKeown and O'Hagan, 114). Among republicans it was understood that the "continuing struggle" was one that stretched back for hundreds of years. This theme was repeated in subsequent statements, such as that released to mark the end of the second hunger strike. The "age-old struggle for Irish self-determination and freedom", it declared, "had been immeasurably advanced" by the hunger strike (Campbell, McKeown and O'Hagan, 264).

The historical consciousness of the protesters is further revealed in the very structure of the hunger strikes. As Beresford has noted, the decision to commence the 1980 hunger strike with seven men was loaded with symbolic significance for republicans, seven being the number of men who had signed the "Proclamation of a Republic" with which the 1916 rising was launched (Beresford, 41). Similarly, it was no accident that the second hunger strike began on 1 March 1981, the fifth anniversary of the withdrawal of special category status (Bishop and Mallie, 325).

This "memory" or "historical consciousness", however, is not found only during the period of the hunger strike. On the contrary, republican prisoners had always perceived the "H-Block Struggle" as part of the ongoing fight against British rule, a perspective neatly articulated in Francis Brolly's *H-Block Song*. The song was written in 1976 and its chorus – "So I'll wear no convicts uniform/Nor meekly serve my time/That Britain might brand Ireland's fight/Eight hundred years of crime" (Campbell, McKeown and O'Hagan, xi) – offered a clear and concise explanation of the rationale behind the blanket protest. To wear a uniform was to accept criminal status. For republicans, who believed in the historical integrity of their struggle, to accept criminal status was, by implication, to accept that Irelands "eight hundred year struggle" had been a criminal one.

By July 1978, the blanket protest had developed into the "dirty protest". Conditions were foul. Following a visit to the Maze in 1978, Cardinal Tomas O'Fiaich, Primate of all Ireland, released a statement expressing his shock at the conditions in which the prisoners were living:

Having spent the whole of Sunday in the prison I was shocked by the inhuman conditions prevailing in H-Block 3, 4 and 5, where over 300 prisoners are incarcerated. One would hardly allow an animal to remain in such conditions, let alone a human being. The nearest approach to it that I have seen was the spectacle of hundreds of homeless people living in sewer pipes in the slums of Calcutta. The stench and filth in some of the cells, with the remains of rotten food and human excreta scattered around the walls, was almost unbearable. In two of them I was unable to speak for fear of vomiting. (O'Fiaich cited in Beresford, 184)

History provided the prisoners with a logic with which to justify and rationalise the conditions in which they lived. As Pedar Wilson, a prisoner at the time, has explained:

"I saw putting shit on the wall as an aspect of the struggle I was part of. At the time words and ideas about pride, dignity and principles were a large part of our vocabulary and thinking. I believe we were influenced by the images of past Republican heroes but as our struggle was going on in different circumstances, we had to use what methods we had. Putting shit on the walls was one such method and we had to come to terms with it in that light." (Wilson, cited in Campbell, McKeown and O'Hagan, 41)

There are clear echoes here of MacSwiney's philosophy of suffering and endurance. By contextualising their protest in this way, the prisoners were able to rationalise and legitimise their hardships, hardships which, it must be remembered, they could have ended at any time by putting on a prison uniform.

In a description that can just as easily be applied to the historical consciousness (or "memory") of republican prisoners, Eugene O'Brien has written that "Nationalist [historical] narratives very often read as coherent and teleological, leading cohesively from past to future" (O'Brien, 151). For republican prisoners, the H-Block struggle was part of a narrative of British oppression and republican struggle that linked 1981 to 1916 and 1916 to 1798. However, rather than seeking to recreate the past, they were using it to interpret and rationalise their present; that they were able to do so points to the existence of republican collective memory.

The classic sociological exposition of collective memory is found in the work of Maurice Halbwachs's groundbreaking study *On Collective Memory*, first published during the 1920s. For Halbwachs, memory was determined by a "social framework" (Halbwachs, 6). McBride has summarised his argument thus:

When we recall the past... we do so as members of groups – a family, a local community, a workforce, a political movement, a church or trade union. What we remember or forget therefore has as much to do with external constraints, imposed by our social and cultural surroundings, as with what happens in the frontal lobes of our brain. (McBride, 6)

For republican prisoners prison itself, as Louise Purbrick has shown, offered a framework in which collective memory could develop:

By sharing memories, especially of speaking and studying the Irish language, republican prisoners created a collective culture of resistance. It is clear from prisoners accounts of being on the blanket that being part of a collective helped them withstand both physical deprivation and constant confrontation. (Purbrick, 105)

A recurring theme in the accounts of republicans who participated in the "H-Block Struggle" is that of the strong camaraderie that developed among them. Indeed, one former blanketman interviewed by Tim Pat Coogan for his 1980 book *On the Blanket*, went so far as to say that some of the memories he had from his time in prison were "fantastic" (Coogan, 4).

Yet, while the prison experience doubtless acted as a catalyst for the development of collective memory among the prisoners, it was by no means unique to them. On the contrary, historical consciousness is a defining characteristic of republicanism, which, as Fearghal McGarry has noted, is "an introspective tradition with a marked preoccupation with the past and its own place within it" (McGarry, 1). While this assessment is applicable to all branches of the tangled family tree of Irish republicanism, it is of particular relevance to the Provisional IRA.

Formed in 1969, following a split from the Official IRA, the Provisional IRA, or "Provos" as they are otherwise known, are obsessed with their historical legitimacy. This much is clear from their training manual – the "Green Book" – which contains the claim that as the "direct representatives of the Dail Eireann parliament established in 1919" they are the "legal and lawful government of the Irish republic" (McGarry, 1). In order to validate this claim, shortly after their breakaway from the Official IRA, members of the Provisional IRA's "Army Council" visited the home of Tom Maguire, the last surviving republican member of the 1922 Dail, who, by agreeing that the Provisional IRA "retained the deeds of the republican tradition", conferred upon the movement the legitimacy it required to justify the armed struggle (Bishop and Mallie, 138). Further, the "Green Book" places the IRA's struggle in historical context, stating categorically that the IRA's war is "that self same war which was fought by all previous generations of Irish people" (McGarry, 1). During the 1970s this historical obsession was realised in the form of Irish language and history classes which were run to ensure that new recruits were adequately educated in the historical integrity of the struggle (Coogan, 102–103).

Many recruits, however, were steeped in republican history and tradition long before they joined the movement. Significantly, Halbwachs identified the family as the fundamental unit in the development of collective memory (Halbwachs, 54–83). Given this, it is hardly surprising that Chris Ryder has identified several of the hunger strikers as having come from staunch republican families (Ryder, 299–206). An insight into the way in which families influenced the development of collective identity can be derived from the autobiographies of those brought up in nationalist/republican communities. Gerry Adams, for example, writes that his mother's family (the Hannaways) "were always republicans, and members of each generation found themselves crossing the tracks of the preceding one as the struggle against injustice continued" (Adams, 27). Somewhat incongruously, however, Adams claims, despite his family background, not to have been politically aware until the later years of his adolescence. A claim which, as Roy Foster notes:

> … seems rather unlikely for someone who attended a Christian Brother school and
> inhabited a home where traditions of nationalist struggle were imbibed with every cup
> of strong tea. (Foster, 177)

While Adams was somewhat circumspect about admitting the political influence of his family, the veteran civil rights campaigner Eamonn McCann provided a much more open-handed account of the development of political awareness and collective memory in his 1974 book *War in an Irish Town*. Writing that "[o]ne learned, quite literally at one's mothers knee that Christ died for the human race and Patrick Pearse for the Irish section of it", McCann made it quite clear that political ideas were developed from an early age (McCann, 9). Further, he identified Roman Catholicism as playing a crucial role in the development of politics and historical consciousness among the nationalist/republican community in post war Derry. So much so that "the fear that it was possibly sinful to vote against the Nationalist Party was quite real" and religion and politics "bound up together, were regarded… as being in many ways the same thing" (McCann, 12–13). This strong sense of identity and collective memory was vital in enabling the republican community to 'place' itself in history.

Writing in the introduction to *On Collective Memory*, an anthology of Halbwach's most significant work on the subject of collective memory, Louis A. Cozer argued that "the present generation may re-write history but it does not write it on a blank page" (Halbwachs, 34). During the early 1980s, republicans viewed themselves as writing the most recent chapter in a narrative of struggle against the British that could be traced back for eight hundred years. The page on which they wrote was far from blank. When the prisoners embarked upon their hunger strikes in 1980 and 1981, they were following a course of action imbued with deep symbolic meaning for the republican community, which, unsurprisingly, interpreted their actions in light of the past. As Sweeney has shown, a vital part of nationalist and republican narrative is the sacrificial tradition of the early twentieth century. It is therefore understandable that the republican community chose to interpret the hunger strikers deaths as sacrificial martyrdoms.

This interpretation is clear in contemporary republican posters and murals, many of which drew explicit comparisons between the hunger strikers and the ultimate example of sacrifice: Christ. Richard Kearney has observed that:

> The Blanket-men and hunger strikers were depicted in popular posters wrapped in loin-cloths. While wall-drawings showed battered and emaciated prisoners in Christ-like posture, the wire of Long Kesh transformed into crowns of thorns. (Kearney, 112)

Such murals illustrate the way in which the republican community used a religious framework to contextualise, and invest with meaning, the hunger strikers' deaths; an impulse that is easy to understand given that the protest ended without the government officially granting political status. This does not, however, show that the prisoners themselves were in the grip of a suicidal mania or consciously sought to emulate the actions of republican martyrs from the past.

During this period hunger strike would seem to have fulfilled all the criteria that Pierre Nora requires of *lieux de memoire* (sites of memory). For Nora, "any significant entity, whether material or nonmaterial in nature, which by dint of human will or work of time has become a symbolic element of the memorial heritage of any community" could be a *lieu de mémoire* (Nora, 1996a: xvii). Hunger strike and the concept of sacrificial martyrdom was clearly a central part of the republican community's memorial heritage (its historical narrative). Nora, however, argues that a community can only have *lieux de memoire* once they have left behind the *milieux de memoire* (settings in which memory is a real part of everyday experience) (Nora, 1996b: 1). In 1981 the republican community clearly lived in a *milieux de memoire*. Hunger strike was not just a symbolic site of memory, but a course of action that republican prisoners were still choosing to take. While it is understandable, given the historical baggage associated with hunger strike, that some have seen the hunger strikers as mere "quotations of their forbears" (Ellmann, 14) such an interpretation misunderstands the nature of republican collective memory. The hunger strikers were not prisoners of their history, destined to follow in the footsteps of earlier generations. Far from being pieces of driftwood swept away by the atavistic and sacrificial currents of Irish republican history, the hunger strikers were active participants, "driven by politics but inspired by myth" as Kearney would have it (Kearney, 110), adding another chapter to the republican narrative of struggle.

## References

Adams, Gerry. 1996. *Before the Dawn: An Autobiography*. London: Heinemann
Beresford, David. 1997. *Ten Men Dead*. London: Grafton
Bishop, Patrick and Eamonn Mallie. 1987. *The Provisional IRA*. London: Corgi
Browne, Vincent. 1981. "H-Block Crisis: Courage Lies and Confusion". *Magill*. August: 6, 8-15 and 56-60
Campbell, Brian, Laurence McKeown, and Felim O'Hagan, eds. 1998. *Nor Meekly Serve My Time: The H-Block Struggle 1976-1981*. Belfast: Beyond the Pale
Coogan, Tim Pat. 1980. *On the Blanket: The H-Block Story*. Dublin: Ward River Press

Ellmann, Maud. 1993. *The Hunger Artists: Starving Writing and Imprisonment*. London: Virago Press

English, Richard. 2003. *Armed Struggle: The History of the IRA* London: Macmillan

Foster, R.F. 2001. *The Irish Story*. London: Allen Lane

Halbwachs, Maurice. 1992. *On Collective Memory*. Ed. and Trans. Lewis A. Cozer, Chicago: University of Chicago Press

Kearney, Richard. 1997. *Postnationalist Ireland: Politics, Culture, Philosophy*. London: Routledge

Klein, Kerwin Lee. 2000. "On the Emergence of *Memory* in Historical Discourse". *Representations*. 69: 127-50

Longley, Edna. 2001. "Northern Ireland: Commemoration, Elegy, Forgetting". In *History and Memory in Modern Ireland*. Ed. Ian McBride. Cambridge: Cambridge University Press. 223–53

Maynes, Paddy. 2000. *Protest and Hunger strike in H-Block the Disavowal of Passivity*. London: University of East London

McBride, Ian. 2001. "Memory and National Identity in Modern Ireland". In *History and Memory in Modern Ireland*. Ed. Ian McBride. Cambridge: Cambridge University Press. 1–42

McCann, Eamonn. 1974. *War in an Irish Town*. London: Penguin

McGarry, Fearghal. 2003. "Introduction". In *Republicanism in Modern Ireland*. Ed. Fearghal McGarry. Dublin: University College Dublin Press. 1–7

Nora, Pierre. 1996a. "From *Lieux de Memoire* to *Realms of Memory*". In *Realms of Memory: The Construction of the French Past*, Vol. 1: *Conflicts and Divisions*. Ed. Pierre Nora. New York: Columbia University Press. xv–xxiii

Nora, Pierre. 1996b. "Between Memory and History." *Realms of Memory: The Construction of the French Past*, Vol. 1: *Conflicts and Divisions*. Ed. Pierre Nora. New York: Columbia University Press. 1–20

O'Brien, Eugene. 2003. "A Nation Once Again: Towards an Epistemology of the Republican 'Imageinaire'". In *Republicanism in Modern Ireland*. Ed. Fearghal McGarry. Dublin: University College Dublin Press. 145–166

Purbrick, Louise. 2004. "The Architecture of Containment". In Donovan Wylie, *The Maze*. London: Granta Books. 91–110

Radstone, Susannah. 2000. "Working with Memory: An Introduction". In *Memory and Methodology*. Ed. Susannah Radstone. Oxford: Oxford University Press. 1–22

Ryder, Chris. 2000. *Inside The Maze: The Untold Story of the Northern Ireland Prison Service*. London: Methuen

Stewart, A.T.Q. 1977. *The Narrow Ground: Aspects of Ulster, 1609-1969*. London: Faber

Sweeney, George. 1993. "Irish Hunger Strike and the Cult of Self-Sacrifice". *Journal of Contemporary History*. 28.3: 421–37

Taylor, Peter. 1999. *Behind the Mask: The IRA and Sinn Fein*. New York: TV Books